R. SEDGEWICK

DISCRETE MATHEMATICS IN COMPUTER SCIENCE

DONALD F. STANAT

Department of Computer Science
University of North Carolina

DAVID F. McALLISTER

Department of Computer Science
North Carolina State University

PRENTICE-HALL, INC.

Englewood Cliffs, N. J. 07632

Library of Congress Cataloging in Publication Data

STANAT, DONALD F (date)
  Discrete mathematics in computer science.

  Bibliography: p.
  Includes index.
    1. Mathematics—1961–   2. Electronic
data processing. I. McAllister, David F.
(date)   joint author. II. Title.
QA39.2.S688   512′.1   76-48915
ISBN 0-13-216150-8

© 1977 by Prentice-Hall, Inc., Englewood Cliffs, N.J.

10 9 8 7 6 5 4 3 2 1

Printed in the United States of America

PRENTICE-HALL INTERNATIONAL, INC., *London*
PRENTICE-HALL OF AUSTRALIA PTY. LIMITED, *Sydney*
PRENTICE-HALL OF CANADA, LTD., *Toronto*
PRENTICE-HALL OF INDIA PRIVATE LIMITED, *New Delhi*
PRENTICE-HALL OF JAPAN, INC., *Tokyo*
PRENTICE-HALL OF SOUTH-EAST ASIA PTE. LTD., *Singapore*
WHITEHALL BOOKS LIMITED, *Wellington, New Zealand*

To Sylvia and Beth

CONTENTS

‡Denotes optional section

3   BINARY RELATIONS   120

4   FUNCTIONS   193

5   COUNTING AND ALGORITHM ANALYSIS   218

PREFACE

This text is intended for use in a first course in discrete mathematics in an undergraduate computer science curriculum. The level is appropriate for a sophomore or junior course. The student is assumed to have experience with a high-level programming language. No specific mathematics is prerequisite, but some previous exposure to college-level mathematics is desirable.

The mathematics taught to students of computer science has changed radically since the early days of this academic discipline. Initially, nearly all topics were drawn from electrical engineering and numerical analysis. Over the years, however, the mathematics of computer science has developed a distinct character, incorporating and melding aspects from such areas as logic, universal algebra and combinatorics as well as analysis. Moreover, as the field has evolved, its use of mathematics has become more sophisticated. It is our view that a computer scientist must have substantial training in mathematics if he is to understand his tools and use them well. The purpose of this text is to provide a foundation for the discrete mathematics used in the theory and application of computer science.

The major part of this book treats classical mathematical topics, including sets, relations, functions, cardinality, and algebra. The approach, however, is not classical; we have emphasized the topics of importance to computer science and provided examples to illustrate why the material is of interest.

The first two topics of the text are usually not treated explicitly in a course of this type. Chapter 0 is a brief description of the nature and purpose of mathematical models. Chapter 1 treats mathematical reasoning, including the representation of assertions, how inferences are made, and how assertions are proved. The final section of the chapter is a description of how programs can be proved correct. The material of Chapter 1 is difficult for some students, especially those who have not had some previous experience in proving theorems in a college-level mathematics course. For this reason, many of the proofs in succeeding chapters are presented in considerable detail with explicit references to the concepts and techniques of Chapter 1. The symbol ▮ is used throughout the text to indicate the end of a proof.

Chapter 2 begins with the usual topics of an introductory treatment of set theory, and then proceeds to inductive definitions of sets, proofs by induction, and recursive programs. The final section of the chapter treats languages, or sets of symbol strings over a finite alphabet. These sets play an important role in computer science, but they are usually not considered in an introduction to set theory.

Chapter 3 treats relations, using digraphs as a visual representation of binary relations on sets. Trees, equivalence relations and order relations are covered, as well as operations on relations, including composition and transitive closure.

Chapter 4 treats functions as a special class of relations. Several important classes of functions are defined and their properties investigated.

Chapter 5 is a treatment of counting techniques and their application to algorithm analysis. The first section introduces basic concepts, including permutations and combinations. The second section develops the concept of the asymptotic behavior of a function and how it can be used to measure algorithm complexity. Recurrence equations and their use in the analysis of algorithms are treated in the next section. The final section of the chapter uses the tools developed in the first three sections to investigate the optimality of several algorithms.

Chapter 6 treats infinite sets and cardinalities, emphasizing enumeration and diagonalization. A cardinality argument is used to show the existence of a real number which is not computable.

Chapter 7 is an introduction to the concepts of universal algebra, including homomorphisms, congruence relations, and quotient and direct product algebras. Semigroups, monoids, groups and Boolean algebras are described.

Through Chapter 4, the material of the text should be covered in the order in which it is presented, although sections and subsections which are marked with a double daggers (‡) can be omitted. The material of Chapter 1 is often ignored or treated in a cursory fashion, but we feel that these fundamental concepts of mathematics are better understood if studied explicitly. Many of the topics of Chapters 1 through 4 may have been studied previously by some students; these topics can be covered as rapidly as is appropriate.

Chapters 5, 6 and 7 assume a knowledge of Chapters 1 through 4 but not each other; any subset of these three chapters can be presented. It is our opinion that Chapter 5 is the most important.

The examples which occur throughout the text range from very simple ones, included only as illustrations of the definitions, through ones which are both difficult and substantive. (The halting problem is treated in an example of Chapter 1, hashing functions are described in an example in Chapter 4, and the existence of a non-computable real number is established in an example of Chapter 6.) In a few of the examples which relate the subject matter to applications, the reader may not be familiar with terminology used (e.g., PERT charts); these examples are included for the benefit of those who can easily understand them and should not cause concern to those who can not. A number sign (#) is used to denote the end of a collection of examples.

Exercises are given at the end of each section in the approximate order in which the topics are presented in the text; within topics, they are ordered according to increasing difficulty. A problem marked ‡ treats material from an optional sub-section. The programming problems given at the end of some sections will usually require additional specification before they can be worked by novice programmers. For example, in a set theory problem, one might want to consider only sets with no more than 100 elements.

This text has evolved over a period of several years. Preliminary versions have been used extensively at the University of North Carolina at Chapel Hill and North Carolina State University. It would be impossible to list all those who have contributed to the final product. Jon Bentley, Don Johnson and Neil Jones deserve particular mention; they provided comments and suggestions on the entire manuscript. Others who made substantial contributions include Peter Calingaert, James W. Hanson, Yale N. Patt, Stephen M. Pizer, James Thatcher, Victor L. Wallace and Stephen F. Weiss. Anne Presnell and David Tolle assisted in the preparation of problem solutions. Finally, we wish to thank the many students who studied from the manuscript and contributed to its final form.

Our secretarial help has come from many quarters, but three individuals deserve special mention. Nina Eaker worked on endless drafts and revisions in the early stages of the manuscript, Gloria Edwards carried the work forward, and Anne Edwards brought the manuscript to its final form. We thank them for their help and support.

DONALD F. STANAT
DAVID F. MCALLISTER

NOTATION

Logic

$\neg P$	not P
$P \vee Q$	P or Q
$P \wedge Q$	P and Q
$P \Rightarrow Q$	P implies Q
$P \Leftrightarrow Q$	P if and only if Q
$\forall$	Universal quantifier: for all . . .
$\exists$	Existential quantifier: there exists . . .
$\exists!$	There exists a unique . . .

Numbers

$\lceil x \rceil$	the integer n such that $x \leq n \leq x + 1$
$\lfloor x \rfloor$	the integer n such that $x \geq n \geq x - 1$
$\mathbf{N}$	the set of natural numbers, or nonnegative integers: $0, 1, 2, \ldots$
$\mathbf{I}$	the set of all integers: $\ldots, -2, -1, 0, 1, 2, \ldots$
$\mathbf{I}+$	the set of positive integers: $1, 2, 3, \ldots$
$\mathbf{Q}$	the set of rational numbers.
$\mathbf{Q}+$	the set of positive rational numbers.
$\mathbf{R}$	the set of real numbers.
$\mathbf{R}+$	the set of positive real numbers.
(a, b)	the open interval in $\mathbf{R}$ from a to b: $(a, b) = \{x \mid x \in \mathbf{R} \wedge a < x < b\}$.
$[a, b]$	the closed interval in $\mathbf{R}$ from a to b: $[a, b] = \{x \mid x \in \mathbf{R} \wedge a \leq x \leq b\}$.
$(a, b]$	the half-open interval in $\mathbf{R}$ from a to b: $(a, b] = \{x \mid a < x \leq b\}$.
$[a, b)$	the half-open interval in $\mathbf{R}$ from a to b: $[a, b) = \{x \mid a \leq x < b\}$.
(a, ∞)	$\{x \mid x \in \mathbf{R} \wedge x > a\}$.
$[a, \infty)$	$\{x \mid x \in \mathbf{R} \wedge x \geq a\}$.
$\mathbf{N}_k$	the set of integers $\{0, 1, 2, \ldots, k - 1\}$.

Sets

$a \in A$	a is an element of the set A.
$a \notin A$	a is not an element of the set A.
$A \subset B$	the set A is contained in the set B.
$A \not\subset B$	the set A is not contained in the set B.
ϕ	the empty, or void set.
$A \cup B$	the union of the sets A and B.
$A \cap B$	the intersection of the sets A and B.
$A - B$	the relative complement of B with respect to A.

$\bar{A}$	the absolute complement of A.
$\mathcal{P}(A)$	the power set of A.
$\bigcup_{i \in S} A_i$	$\{x \mid \exists i[i \in S \wedge x \in A_i]\}$.
$\bigcap_{i \in S} A_i$	$\{x \mid \forall i[i \in S \Rightarrow x \in A_i]\}$
$A \times B$	the cartesian product of A with B.
$\overset{n}{\underset{i=1}{\mathsf{X}}} A_i$	the cartesian product of the sets A_i, $1 \leq i \leq n$.

Sets of character strings

Σ	a finite alphabet.
Λ	the empty string.
$\|x\|$	the length of a string x.
Σ^+	the set of all strings of finite nonzero length over the alphabet Σ.
Σ^*	the set of all strings of finite length over the alphabet Σ, including Λ.
AB	$\{xy \mid x \in A \wedge y \in B\}$.
A^n	$\{x_1 x_2 x_3 \ldots x_n \mid x_i \in A\}$.
A^+	$\bigcup_{i \in I^+} A^i$.
A^*	$\bigcup_{i \in \mathbf{N}} A^i$.

Relations and partitions

$\langle a_1, \ldots, a_n \rangle$	the n-tuple whose ith component is a_i.
aRb	a is related to b under the relation R.
$a\cancel{R}b$	a is not related to b under the relation R.
$\langle A, R \rangle$	the digraph with node set A and relation R.
$R_1 R_2$	the composite relation of R_1 with R_2.
R^n	the nth power of the relation R; the composition of R with itself n times.
$r(R)$	the reflexive closure of R.
$s(R)$	the symmetric closure of R.
$t(R)$	the transitive closure of R.
R^c	the converse of R: $\{\langle x, y \rangle \mid \langle y, x \rangle \in R\}$.
R^+	$t(R)$
R^*	$rt(R)$
$\leq$	a partial order.
$a \equiv b \pmod{k}$	a is equivalent to b modulo k.
$[a]_R$	the equivalence class of a with respect to R.
π	a partition.
A/R	the partition of A induced by the equivalence relation R.
$\pi_1 + \pi_2$	the sum of the partitions π_1 and π_2.
$\pi_1 \cdot \pi_2$	the product of the partitions π_1 and π_2.

Functions

$f(a)$	the value of the function f for the argument a.
$f: A \longrightarrow B$	f is a function with domain A and codomain B.
$f(A)$	the image of the set A under the function f.
$f \circ g$, or fg	the composite function of f with g.
A^B	the set of functions from B to A.
$\mathbf{1}_A$	the identity function on the set A.
f^{-1}	the inverse of f.
$f^{-1}(A)$	the inverse image of A under f.
$f\mid_A$	the function f restricted to A.
χ_A	the characteristic function of A.

Cardinality and order notation

$\mid A \mid$	the cardinality of A.
$P(n, r)$	the number of permutations of n objects taken r at a time.
$\binom{n}{r}$	the number of combinations of n objects taken r at a time.
$O(f)$	the set of functions asymptotically dominated by f.
$\aleph_0$	Aleph null, the cardinality of $\mathbf{N}$.
$\mathbf{c}$	the cardinality of $[0, 1]$.

Algebras

$\langle S, \circ, k \rangle$	an algebra with carrier S, operation $\circ$, and constant k.
$+_k$	addition modulo k
$A \times A'$	the product algebra of A with A'.
$A/\sim$	the quotient algebra of A' with respect to the congruence relation $\sim$.

0

MATHEMATICAL MODELS

0.0 INTRODUCTION

The goal of this text is the development of mathematical concepts and techniques which are fundamental to the field of computer science. We define computer science broadly, as the discipline concerned with the representation and processing of information. We consider computer science to lie somewhere between mathematics and technology, close enough to each to be profoundly affected by developments in either of these fields but dominated by neither. The mathematical topics we will develop are classical ones which predate computer science, but which are generally recognized as necessary and fundamental tools for the investigation of many problems in the field. Our aim is to present these mathematical tools and illustrate their use in characterizing the phenomena of computer science. In this chapter we describe the ways in which mathematics can be used to represent objects of study.

0.1 PRINCIPLES AND MODELS

Observation is the ultimate basis of our understanding of the world around us. But observation only provides information about the specific events which we observe; alone, it provides little help for dealing with new situations. Useful knowledge results from our ability to recognize similarities in different events, isolate the important factors, and generalize from our experience. Generalization enables us to operate effectively in new environments by using inferences drawn from past experience.

Knowledge varies in sophistication from simple classification to understanding based on a system of principles. A *principle* is a generalization, or an abstract assertion. Principles are expressed in a variety of ways ranging from "old saws" to equations which express relationships between physical properties. The following assertions are examples of principles.

"Virtue is its own reward."

"All matter is composed of earth, air, fire, and water."

"Ontogeny recapitulates phylogeny."

"$F = ma$."

Principles vary in their validity as well as their precision. They also vary in their importance and the degree to which they affect the way we think and act.

The concept of "model" is even more vague than that of "principle." Roughly speaking, a *model* is an analogy for some object or phenomenon of interest. As we will use the term, models are used to "explain" a process or to predict an event. For example, a wind tunnel, used with a miniature replica of an aircraft, makes it possible to predict some characteristics of the aircraft's performance, since the behavior of the full-sized craft is strongly related to that of the model. Similarly, a world globe allows us to estimate distance between locations on the earth, and an orrery provides a visual model of the movement of the planets about the sun. Genetic models for the transfer of traits provide a basis for predicting the frequencies with which inherited characteristics will appear in successive generations.

Models can also be misleading. A medieval model of human reproduction proposed that babies develop from homunculi contained *ab initio* in a woman's body. Of course, female homunculi also contained other homunculi nested within. Since it was felt that this nesting could not go on without limit, this model had the uncomfortable implication that the race would become extinct, since reproduction would cease after the innermost homunculi were born. A model of our universe which was commonly accepted in the fifteenth century predicted that Columbus would not return from his voyage to the west. This model of a flat earth of finite extent was clearly an important one, partly because of its influence on exploration, but it seems wrong to call it a valuable model. The value of a model might best be defined as the degree to which it enables us to answer questions and make predictions correctly.

Mathematics, because of its rigor and lack of ambiguity, has always provided a good language for the expression of principles. Models based on mathematically stated principles are called *mathematical models*. The purpose of this text is to develop mathematics for expressing principles and constructing models in computer science. While the mathematical topics we treat cannot be nicely categorized, our emphasis will be on what is often referred to as discrete mathematics.

0.2 MATHEMATICAL MODELS

A *mathematical model* is a mathematical characterization of a phenomenon or process. Such a definition is necessarily imprecise, but some illustrations should establish the notion. A mathematical model has three essential parts: a process or phenomenon which is to be modeled, a mathematical structure capable of expressing the important properties of the object to be modeled, and an explicit correspon-

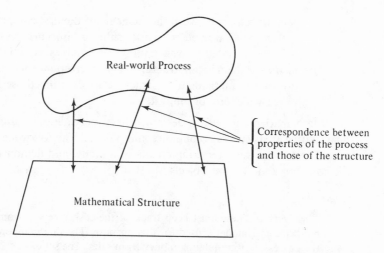

Real-world Process

Correspondence between
properties of the process
and those of the structure

Mathematical Structure

Fig. 0.2.1 Components of mathematical model

dence between the two. Such a model is represented by Fig. 0.2.1. Some comments
will help to clarify the concept.

(a) The first component of a model is a *phenomenon* or *process* which we
    wish to characterize mathematically. Examples include physical processes,
    such as planetary motion, fluid flow, or the pattern of weather change,
    as well as such things as economic processes, learning patterns, and so
    on. Examples in computer science include the execution of a program,
    the allocation of resources of a computation center, and the flow of
    information in a computer network. Although the phenomena of interest
    need not be taken from the "real world," they usually are, and in our
    discussion, the phrase "real world" will denote this component of a
    mathematical model. The real world component is described quantita-
    tively by such things as parameter values and times at which events occur.

(b) The second component of a model is an abstract *mathematical structure*.
    The set of integers with the operations of addition and multiplication
    provides one example of such a structure. In itself, this structure is abstract
    and has no intrinsic relation to the real world. However, because of its
    abstractness, the structure can be used to model many different phenom-
    ena. Every mathematical structure has an associated language for
    making assertions. In our familiar system of algebra, the assertions

$$5 + 6 \leq 10, \text{ and } 7x + y = 18$$

    can both be made, although one is incorrect. If a mathematical model
    is successful, the language of its mathematical structure can be used to
    make assertions about the object being modeled.

(c) The third component of a model is a specification of the way in which
    the real world is represented by the mathematical structure, that is, a

correspondence between the elements of the first component and those of the second. Parameters, relationships, and occurrences in the real world will be associated with such things as variables, equations, and operations in the mathematical structure. This correspondence makes possible the use of the mathematical structure to describe those facets of the real world which are of interest.

Mathematical models, as described here, pervade our culture, particularly in quantitative areas such as economics and physics. The following example provides an illustration of the three components of a model and demonstrates that models are common and familiar objects.

Example

Every business must keep track of the cash received from sales each day. A mathematical model is used for this purpose. The first component of the model is the process of accumulating money from sales. The set of integers (denoting cents), together with the operation of addition, provides a simple but appropriate mathematical structure. Receiving cash from a sale corresponds to adding the amount of the sale to the current receipts. The principal parameter of the model represents cash received. This parameter takes on integer values; at the beginning of the day its value is 0, and at any time during the day the value of the parameter is the current amount received from sales. The occurrence of a cash sale is represented in the structure by the operation of addition; selling an item worth k cents is represented by adding k to the current value of the parameter. At the end of the business day, the store owner can determine the total cash receipts by noting the value of the parameter.   #

The above example illustrates all the crucial points of our description of a mathematical model. It also illustrates that mathematical models ignore certain aspects of the real world process. For example, the model described above does not keep track of how many one dollar bills or how many pennies have been received. This failure is not considered to be a defect of the model, since the store owner is willing to assume that the actual form of currency received will not cause him any particular inconvenience. If, however, all of his income for one day happened to be in pennies, he might find himself with a serious transportation problem when it came time to take the day's receipts to the bank. Other factors which are ignored by the model may be more important. The model does not try to answer such questions as how the storeowner can maximize his profits. It is legitimate to use a mathematical model to deal with this kind of question, but the question is beyond the scope of a model designed simply to keep track of the store's daily receipts. Thus, the suitability of a mathematical model depends strongly on the problem at hand. Ideally, we want a model to represent everything that is important about the process and ignore everything else. It is difficult to realize this ideal, because we are often not sure what aspects of the real world are important. In fact, the process of deciding which aspects are important can be one of the most difficult and rewarding steps in specifying a mathematical model.

Without going into detail, we can give examples of more elaborate mathematical models and describe how they are used.

Examples

(a) A set of simultaneous partial differential equations is useful as a mathematical structure to describe planetary motion. Newton first proposed such a model based on observations of the planets and his work on gravitational attraction.

(b) Differential equations are used to determine the flow of current in electrical circuits by establishing a correspondence between the parts of an electrical circuit and the terms of mathematical equations. The same equations can be used to describe mechanical systems involving objects with mass, springs, and damping devices called dashpots. Thus, the same mathematical structure can be used in models of entirely different phenomena. These examples also show that not all models need be mathematical: a mechanical system consisting of springs, masses, and dashpots can be used as a mechanical model of an electrical circuit, and vice versa. Analog computers exploit this fact and use electrical models to solve problems which are expressed mathematically.

(c) Mathematical models are the basis for all computer simulations. Consider the problem of simulating the operation of a computer center. We can view a computer center as a system which accepts programs and program data as inputs and produces outputs in a variety of forms, including program listings and program output. At any time, the state of the system is described by parameter values which specify what programs are being executed, which disk and tape drives are busy, the length of the input queue, etc. Other parameters, such as average turnaround time and the total number of programs processed, can be used to measure the performance of the system. A mathematical model for simulation of the system in discrete time steps will incorporate these parameters into a set of mathematical equations which describe how the values of the parameters and the system input at any time t can be used to determine the values of the parameters at time $t + 1$. Different machine configurations and different operation policies will be represented by different sets of equations. The system is simulated by hypothesizing initial parameter values for time $t = 0$ and then successively solving the equations for times $t = 1, 2, 3, \ldots, n$. If the simulation is successful, then the system parameters at time $t = n$ will accurately forecast the behavior of the system. Such simulation models can be used as a basis for choosing among various alternatives, e.g., the performance of a model can be used to predict the result of a proposed change in either a hardware configuration or in operations policy. #

The rapid progress of computer science is largely due to the development of appropriate mathematical tools. Mathematical models have been applied successfully to a broad range of problem areas, including

design of computers and computer systems,
allocation of resources of computer systems, such as paging algorithms for storage management,
analysis of the cost of algorithm execution,

measurement of the intrinsic "difficulty" of certain classes of problems, development of programming languages and language processors, and methods of proving program correctness.

We will mention some of these problems explicitly when the appropriate mathematical tools are developed. But more importantly, we will develop a basis for the treatment of all these topics. Thus, although it is not feasible to present even superficial treatments of all these problems, a contemporary approach to any of them would be based on the mathematical topics which we treat here.

0.3 PURPOSES OF MODELS

The purposes of models fall into three categories. In the most straightforward applications, models are used to present information in an easily assimilated form. For example, graphs may be used to present genealogies and family trees. It is much easier to decide if cousin Joseph is a descendant of great-grandfather John's sister Martha when we have a drawing of the family tree before us instead of a written record of marriages and offspring. In the same way, a roadmap provides a descriptive model of a highway network. Planning a trip would not be so easy if, instead of a roadmap, we had a list of distances between adjacent cities.

A second use of models is to provide a convenient method for performing certain computations. Familiar examples include optimization methods and Fourier analysis. The choice of a model for the purpose of computation is often directly affected by the set of available mathematical techniques. For example, a system known to have nonlinear components may be modeled approximately with a set of linear equations so that linear programming can be used to estimate a solution.

Thirdly, models are used for investigation and prediction. Simulation, both with physical models and with computers, is an excellent example. The Wright brothers invented the wind tunnel so they could use physical models to compare the lifts of different airfoils. Analogous experiments in water tanks use models of ship hulls to determine which shapes produce the least turbulence and drag. Models are frequently used to predict parameter values of events which have not yet occurred, such as the time of tomorrow's sunrise or the implications for the national economy of a change in the tax laws. The equations used for calculating the time of tomorrow's sunrise are well established and thoroughly tested; consequently, we have a great deal of faith in these predictions. The same is not true for current models of the national economy, and our prediction in this case is not likely to be so accurate. In many cases, the predictive ability of a model determines its worth. The value of Newton's model of planetary motion was established beyond any doubt when deviations from the model's predictions led to the discovery of the planet Neptune. The location of Neptune was estimated by determining what could be the source of observed deviations from the predicted orbit of Uranus.

A mathematical model is an abstraction which associates parameters and processes of the real world with expressions and operations in a mathematical structure. This abstraction allows us to ignore those aspects of the real world which are not of interest and provides a framework for studying those which are. If the model is successful, the properties of the mathematical structure are strongly related to the phenomena being studied.

Much of this text will be devoted to the development of mathematical structures for models which are important to computer science. Our goal is to provide a basis for a reasonable and fruitful correspondence between the computational process and the mathematical structures which we use to represent it.

Suggestions for Further Reading

The first chapter of Maki and Thompson [1973] gives an excellent description of how models are built and refined. Their discussion treats the roles of axioms and theorems in models and provides a basis for some of the topics of our next chapter. Chapter 2 of their book is a collection of case studies from a variety of areas. The first chapter of Roberts [1976] is also a good description of model types and the modeling process.

1

MATHEMATICAL REASONING

1.0 INTRODUCTION

Mathematics is the study of the properties of mathematical structures. In this chapter we will study mathematical reasoning, which is the process used to verify these properties.

A mathematical structure is defined by a set of *axioms*. By definition, an axiom is a true statement about the properties of the structure. Other true assertions which can be inferred from the truth of the axioms are called *theorems*. A *proof* of a theorem is an argument which establishes that the theorem is true for a specified mathematical structure. A proof is often presented as a sequence of assertions such that each assertion is either an axiom of the mathematical structure, a previous theorem, or a logical inference from previous steps of the proof. Therefore, in order to prove theorems, we must be able to make assertions about mathematical structures and to determine when one assertion follows from others. To establish that one assertion follows from another, we must use only principles of reasoning which we accept as valid; these principles are called *rules of inference*.

In this chapter we will study how to make careful assertions about mathematical structures as well as how to combine these assertions and draw conclusions from them. Because of the importance of these topics to any development of the theory of computer science, we will treat them carefully. The concepts and tools we develop in this chapter are directly relevant to certain important areas, such as proving programs correct. Our primary concern, however, is with the more general topic of mathematical reasoning, and our goal is to develop the student's ability to discern and construct sound mathematical arguments.

The material in this chapter is a mathematical model of the reasoning process, or careful argument. It also serves as a brief introduction to some of the concepts and notations of mathematical logic.

1.1 PROPOSITIONS

An *assertion* is a statement. A *proposition* is an assertion which is either true or false, but not both.† If a proposition is true, we say it has a "truth value" of *true*; if a proposition is false, its truth value is *false*.

Examples

The following are all propositions:

(a) The moon is made of green cheese.

(b) 4 is a prime number.

(c) $3 + 3 = 6$.

(d) 2 is an even integer and 3 is not.

(e) It snowed on the island that is now called Manhattan on the day the King of England signed the Magna Carta.

(f) My most recently written computer program always halts if allowed to run for a sufficiently long time.

Of the above propositions, (a) and (b) are false, (c) and (d) are true, and (e) may or may not be true; we have no way of ascertaining its truth value. Nevertheless, we assume the assertion is either true or false and therefore classify it as a proposition. The truth of proposition (f) may be difficult to determine; establishing the truth of such assertions is the subject of some profound mathematical results in the theory of computation.

The following are not propositions:

(g) $x + y > 4$.

(h) $x = 3$.

(i) Are you leaving?

(j) Buy four of them.

The first example is an assertion but not a proposition because its truth value depends on the values of x and y. Similarly, the truth value of the second assertion depends on the value of x. Examples (i) and (j) are not assertions and are therefore not propositions.   #

A *propositional variable* denotes an arbitrary proposition with an unspecified truth value. We will use the letters $P, Q, R, \ldots$ for propositional variables. Propositions as well as propositional variables can be combined to form new assertions

---

†A system in which propositions must be either true or false is said to use a *two-valued logic*. The characteristic that "a proposition which is not true is false, and vice-versa" is known as the *law of the excluded middle*. Some mathematicians do not consider the law of the excluded middle to be an accurate reflection of our reasoning. To understand some of the reasons for rejecting the law of the excluded middle and for a description of logical systems with more than two truth values, the reader is referred to Rescher [1969].

using words such as "and," "or," and "not." For example, from the propositions "John is six feet tall" and "There are four cows in the barn," we can form

"John is six feet tall and there are four cows in the barn."
"John is six feet tall or there are four cows in the barn."
"John is not six feet tall."

In the same way,

"P and Q"
"P or Q"
"not P"

are assertions which can be formed from the propositional variables P and Q. In expressions such as the above, the variables P and Q are called *operands*, and the words "and," "or," and "not" are called *logical operators*, or *logical connectives*. Logical connectives denote operations on propositions in the same way that "plus" and "times" denote operations on numbers. This terminology is common throughout mathematics; for example, in algebra the expression "$4 + x$" has 4 and x as operands and $+$ as an operator.

An assertion which contains at least one propositional variable is called a *propositional form*. When propositions are substituted for the variables of a propositional form, a proposition results. Thus, if P represents "John is six feet tall" and Q represents "Two is a prime number," the propositional form "P and Q" represents the proposition "John is six feet tall and two is a prime number," and "not P" represents "It is false that John is six feet tall." *When no confusion will result, we will often refer to propositional forms as propositions.* The principal distinction between propositions and propositional forms is that every proposition has a truth value whereas a propositional form is an expression whose truth value may not be determined until propositions are substituted for its propositional variables.

When a logical operator is used to construct a new proposition from old ones, the truth value of the new proposition depends on both the logical operator and the truth values of the original propositions. We will now discuss how the logical operators "and," "or," and "not" affect the truth value of propositions. We will see that the meaning of the logical operators does not always coincide precisely with English usage.

The logical operator "not," or *negation*, is denoted by the symbol $\neg$. Let P denote a proposition; then "P is not true" is a proposition which we represent by "$\neg P$" and refer to as "not P," or the *negation of P*. It follows from the law of the excluded middle that $\neg P$ is true if P is false, and vice versa. The relationship between the truth value of $\neg P$ and that of P is defined by a *truth table* for the logical operator $\neg$. The truth table of a logical operator specifies how the truth value of a proposition using that operator is determined by the truth values of the operands. A truth table lists all possible combinations of truth values of the operands in the leftmost columns and the truth value of the resulting proposition in the rightmost column. The truth table for $\neg$ is the following:

P	$\neg P$
false	*true*
true	*false*

In order to make truth tables easier to read, we will generally use the symbol 1 to denote *true* and 0 to denote *false*. Using this convention, the truth table for $\neg$ is given as

P	$\neg P$
0	1
1	0

While negation changes one proposition into another, other logical operators combine two propositions to form a third. An example is the logical operator "and," which we will denote by the symbol $\wedge$. If P and Q are propositions, then "P and Q" is a proposition which we represent by "$P \wedge Q$" and refer to as the *conjunction* of P and Q. The following truth table defines the logical operator $\wedge$.

P	Q	$P \wedge Q$
0	0	0
0	1	0
1	0	0
1	1	1

The truth table defines $P \wedge Q$ to be true if and only if both P and Q are true.

Like "and," the logical operator "or," denoted by the symbol $\vee$, combines two propositions to form a third. If P and Q are propositions, then the proposition "P or Q" is called the *disjunction* of P and Q and is denoted by "$P \vee Q$." The following truth table defines the logical operator $\vee$.

P	Q	$P \vee Q$
0	0	0
0	1	1
1	0	1
1	1	1

It follows from the truth table that $P \vee Q$ is true if at least one of P or Q is true. This operator is known as "logical or" or "inclusive or." One can also define an "exclusive or," denoted by $\oplus$, by the following truth table:

P	Q	$P \oplus Q$
0	0	0
0	1	1
1	0	1
1	1	0

The English language uses the word "or" to denote both the "inclusive or" and the "exclusive or." For example, an "inclusive or" is intended in the sentence

"It will rain or snow today"

since the speaker would presumably not be branded a liar if it both rained and snowed. On the other hand,

"You have to wash the dishes or you must clean the garage"

is not likely to be considered a true statement if, in fact, you are required to wash the dishes and to clean the garage as well. In mathematics, we use different symbols for the "inclusive or" and the "exclusive or" to preclude any ambiguity.

The logical operator "implies" is denoted by the symbol $\Rightarrow$; the proposition "P implies Q" is represented by "$P \Rightarrow Q$" and is called an *implication*. The operand P is called the *premise*, *hypothesis*, or *antecedent*, and Q is called the *conclusion* or *consequence*. The truth table for the operator $\Rightarrow$ is the following:

P	Q	$P \Rightarrow Q$
0	0	1
0	1	1
1	0	0
1	1	1

The proposition $P \Rightarrow Q$ is false only when P is true and Q is false. Implications may be stated in a number of ways; the assertion $P \Rightarrow Q$ may be expressed as

"If P, then Q"
"P only if Q"
"P is a sufficient condition for Q"
"Q is a necessary condition for P"
"Q if P"
"Q follows from P"
"Q provided P"
"Q is a logical consequence of P"
"Q whenever P."

The *converse* of $P \Rightarrow Q$ is the proposition $Q \Rightarrow P$, and the *contrapositive* of $P \Rightarrow Q$ is the proposition $\neg Q \Rightarrow \neg P$. If $P \Rightarrow Q$ is true, then P is said to be a *stronger* assertion than Q; thus "x is a positive integer" is a stronger assertion than "x is an integer."

The English language uses implication to assert a causal or inherent relationship between a premise and a conclusion. Thus, "If I fall in the lake, then I will get wet" relates a cause to its effect, and "If I am a man, I am mortal" characterizes a property of men. However, in the language of propositions, the premise of an implication need not be related to the conclusion in any substantive way. This can be disturbing, as illustrated by the following example.

Example

> If P represents "oranges are purple" and Q represents "the earth is not flat," then $P \Rightarrow Q$ represents "If oranges are purple, then the earth is not flat." Although no causal or inherent relationship holds between the color of oranges and the shape of the earth, the implication $P \Rightarrow Q$ is true since the premise is false and the conclusion is true.   #

If P and Q have the same truth values, then they are said to be *logically equivalent* propositions. A logical operator called "equivalence" and denoted by $\Leftrightarrow$ produces a true proposition if the operand propositions are logically equivalent. The truth table which defines the operator "equivalence" is the following:

P	Q	$P \Leftrightarrow Q$
0	0	1
0	1	0
1	0	0
1	1	1

Comparison of the truth tables for implication and equivalence shows that if $P \Leftrightarrow Q$ is true, then $P \Rightarrow Q$ and $Q \Rightarrow P$ are both true. Conversely, if both $P \Rightarrow Q$ and $Q \Rightarrow P$ are true, then $P \Leftrightarrow Q$ is true. For these reasons, the terminologies for equivalence and implication are closely related. The proposition $P \Leftrightarrow Q$ is read "P is equivalent to Q," "P is a necessary and sufficient condition for Q," or "P if and only if Q." The abbreviation "iff" is often used to represent the phrase "if and only if."

Other logical operators can be defined and are of interest for a variety of reasons; some of them will be described in the exercises of this section.

Truth tables for individual operators can be used to construct truth tables for arbitrarily complex propositional forms. The truth table for a propositional form specifies its truth value for every possible combination of truth values of its propositional variables. Each propositional variable can assume either of two values, *true* or *false*. Therefore, if k variables occur in a proposition, the associated truth table must describe 2^k cases. Each case occurs as a separate line in the truth table.

Examples

(a) Construct a truth table for the proposition $(Q \wedge \neg P) \Rightarrow P$.

P	Q	$\neg P$	$(Q \wedge \neg P)$	$(Q \wedge \neg P) \Rightarrow P$
0	0	1	0	1
0	1	1	1	0
1	0	0	0	1
1	1	0	0	1

(b) Construct a truth table for the proposition $[(P \wedge Q) \vee \neg R] \Leftrightarrow P$.

P	Q	R	$P \wedge Q$	$\neg R$	$(P \wedge Q) \vee \neg R$	$[(P \wedge Q) \vee \neg R] \Leftrightarrow P$
0	0	0	0	1	1	0
0	0	1	0	0	0	1
0	1	0	0	1	1	0
0	1	1	0	0	0	1
1	0	0	0	1	1	1
1	0	1	0	0	0	0
1	1	0	1	1	1	1
1	1	1	1	0	1	1

#

In the above truth tables, we have used two conventions which aid readability:

(i)   All propositional variables occur in the leftmost columns.
(ii) Truth values are assigned to the propositional variables by "counting in binary" from 0 to $2^k - 1$, where k is the number of propositional variables.

A *tautology* is a propositional form whose truth value is *true* for all possible values of its propositional variables, e.g., $P \vee \neg P$. A *contradiction* or *absurdity* is a propositional form which is always *false*, such as $P \wedge \neg P$. A propositional form which is neither a tautology nor a contradiction is called a *contingency*.

Properties of a propositional form can sometimes be determined by constructing an "abbreviated" truth table. For example, if we wish to show that a propositional form is a contingency, it suffices to exhibit two lines of the truth table, one of which makes the proposition true and another that makes it false. To determine if a propositional form is a tautology, it is only necessary to check those lines of the truth table for which the proposition could be false.

Example

Consider the problem of determining whether $(P \wedge Q) \Rightarrow P$ is a tautology. We will use an abbreviated truth table. If an implication $A \Rightarrow B$ is false, then A must be true and B must be false. The truth table for $(P \wedge Q) \Rightarrow P$ has only one line where the value of the premise $P \wedge Q$ is *true*. Since this is the only instance where $(P \wedge Q) \Rightarrow P$ could be false, it suffices to consider this line.

P	Q	$P \wedge Q$	$(P \wedge Q) \Rightarrow P$
1	1	1	1

Since the value of the propositional form for this line is *true*, it follows that the proposition is a tautology.   #

It is often convenient to replace one propositional form by another which is logically equivalent. If two propositional forms are logically equivalent, one can be substituted for the other in any proposition in which they occur; thus, since P is logically equivalent to $P \vee P$, it follows that $P \vee Q$ is logically equivalent to $(P \vee P) \vee Q$. Table 1.1.1 is a list of important equivalences, often called *identities*. The symbols P, Q, and R represent arbitrary propositional forms. The symbol "1" is used to denote either a tautology or a true proposition. Likewise, the symbol "0" represents a false proposition or a contradiction. The names which appear to the right of the identities refer to properties and "rules of inference" which will be discussed later.

Certain of the identities are particularly important. Identity 18 permits the replacement of implications by disjunctions. Identities 7 and 8 permit the replacement of disjunctions by conjunctions and vice versa. Most of the identities in

Table 1.1.1 LOGICAL IDENTITIES

1.	$P \Leftrightarrow (P \vee P)$	idempotence of $\vee$
2.	$P \Leftrightarrow (P \wedge P)$	idempotence of $\wedge$
3.	$(P \vee Q) \Leftrightarrow (Q \vee P)$	commutativity of $\vee$
4.	$(P \wedge Q) \Leftrightarrow (Q \wedge P)$	commutativity of $\wedge$
5.	$[(P \vee Q) \vee R] \Leftrightarrow [P \vee (Q \vee R)]$	associativity of $\vee$
6.	$[(P \wedge Q) \wedge R] \Leftrightarrow [P \wedge (Q \wedge R)]$	associativity of $\wedge$
7.	$\neg(P \vee Q) \Leftrightarrow (\neg P \wedge \neg Q)$	DeMorgan's Laws
8.	$\neg(P \wedge Q) \Leftrightarrow (\neg P \vee \neg Q)$	
9.	$[P \wedge (Q \vee R)] \Leftrightarrow [(P \wedge Q) \vee (P \wedge R)]$	distributivity of $\wedge$ over $\vee$
10.	$[P \vee (Q \wedge R)] \Leftrightarrow [(P \vee Q) \wedge (P \vee R)]$	distributivity of $\vee$ over $\wedge$
11.	$(P \vee 1) \Leftrightarrow 1$	
12.	$(P \wedge 1) \Leftrightarrow P$	
13.	$(P \vee 0) \Leftrightarrow P$	
14.	$(P \wedge 0) \Leftrightarrow 0$	
15.	$(P \vee \neg P) \Leftrightarrow 1$	
16.	$(P \wedge \neg P) \Leftrightarrow 0$	
17.	$P \Leftrightarrow \neg(\neg P)$	double negation
18.	$(P \Rightarrow Q) \Leftrightarrow (\neg P \vee Q)$	implication
19.	$(P \Leftrightarrow Q) \Leftrightarrow [(P \Rightarrow Q) \wedge (Q \Rightarrow P)]$	equivalence
20.	$[(P \wedge Q) \Rightarrow R] \Leftrightarrow [P \Rightarrow (Q \Rightarrow R)]$	exportation
21.	$[(P \Rightarrow Q) \wedge (P \Rightarrow \neg Q)] \Leftrightarrow \neg P$	absurdity
22.	$(P \Rightarrow Q) \Leftrightarrow (\neg Q \Rightarrow \neg P)$	contrapositive

Table 1.1.1 have straightforward intuitive interpretations; all of them can be established by constructing truth tables.

If propositional forms are not carefully written, ambiguities in their interpretation can arise. For example, the expression $P \Rightarrow Q \Rightarrow R$ could be interpreted as $(P \Rightarrow Q) \Rightarrow R$ or $P \Rightarrow (Q \Rightarrow R)$. Since these two expressions are not logically equivalent, the ambiguity is not acceptable and parentheses must be used to specify which expression is intended. However, $(P \wedge Q) \wedge R$ and $P \wedge (Q \wedge R)$ are logically equivalent (by identity 6), and consequently the use of $P \wedge Q \wedge R$ does not result in an ambiguous truth value. Parentheses are often deleted if all interpretations are equivalent propositional forms. For example, we commonly write $P \wedge Q \wedge R$, $P \vee Q \vee R$, and $P \Leftrightarrow Q \Leftrightarrow R$. We will adopt one further convention for reducing the number of parentheses in an expression: the negation sign will apply to the smallest possible subexpression consistent with the parentheses. Thus, $\neg P \vee Q$ will denote $(\neg P) \vee Q$ rather than $\neg(P \vee Q)$.

Identities such as those in Table 1.1.1 can be used to show relationships between propositional forms and to find logically equivalent expressions.

Example

Simplify the following propositional form:

$$[(A \Rightarrow B) \vee (A \Rightarrow D)] \Rightarrow (B \vee D).$$

The numbers at the right indicate which identities are applied at each step.

$[(\neg A \vee B) \vee (\neg A \vee D)] \Rightarrow (B \vee D)$	(18)
$[\neg A \vee (B \vee D)] \Rightarrow (B \vee D)$	(5, 3, 1)
$\neg[\neg A \vee (B \vee D)] \vee (B \vee D)$	(18)
$[A \wedge \neg(B \vee D)] \vee (B \vee D)$	(7, 17)
$(A \vee B \vee D) \wedge [\neg(B \vee D) \vee (B \vee D)]$	(3, 10)
$(A \vee B \vee D) \wedge 1$	(15)
$A \vee B \vee D$	(12)

#

Table 1.1.2 is a list of useful tautologies which are implications. The names associated with some of the implications correspond to "rules of inference"; these will be discussed in Section 1.4.

Table 1.1.2 LOGICAL IMPLICATIONS

1.	$P \Rightarrow (P \vee Q)$	addition
2.	$(P \wedge Q) \Rightarrow P$	simplification
3.	$[P \wedge (P \Rightarrow Q)] \Rightarrow Q$	*modus ponens*
4.	$[(P \Rightarrow Q) \wedge \neg Q] \Rightarrow \neg P$	*modus tollens*
5.	$[\neg P \wedge (P \vee Q)] \Rightarrow Q$	disjunctive syllogism
6.	$[(P \Rightarrow Q) \wedge (Q \Rightarrow R)] \Rightarrow (P \Rightarrow R)$	hypothetical syllogism
7.	$(P \Rightarrow Q) \Rightarrow [(Q \Rightarrow R) \Rightarrow (P \Rightarrow R)]$	
8.	$[(P \Rightarrow Q) \wedge (R \Rightarrow S)] \Rightarrow [(P \wedge R) \Rightarrow (Q \wedge S)]$	
9.	$[(P \Leftrightarrow Q) \wedge (Q \Leftrightarrow R)] \Rightarrow (P \Leftrightarrow R)$	

The following example illustrates how a facility with propositions can be useful in dealing with some vexing problems of everyday life.

Example

A man who was captured by savages was promised his freedom if he could determine with a single "yes or no" question the color of the tribe's idol. He knew the idol was either white or black. Unfortunately, the tribe contained two kinds of individuals: liars, who invariably gave the wrong answer to any question they were asked, and truth-tellers, who invariably gave the right answer. Fortunately, the victim was well-educated. He knew he must ask a question which would be answered according to the following table:

	Color of Idol	
	White	Black
Liars	Yes	No
Truth-tellers	Yes	No

However, since a liar always gave the wrong answer, he realized he must ask a question whose correct answers could be tabulated as follows:

	Color of Idol	
	White	Black
Liars	No	Yes
Truth-tellers	Yes	No

Whereupon he asked his nearest captor "Is it true that either you tell the truth and the idol is white or that you lie and the idol is black?"† This question enabled him to determine the color correctly, since an answer of *yes* meant the idol was white and *no* meant it was black. Unfortunately, the savages thought it was just a lucky guess and reneged on their promise. That's why you never heard this story before.   #

In this section we have introduced the notions of proposition and logical operations. We then illustrated the use of truth tables to establish whether a propositional form is a tautology, contingency or absurdity. These concepts and tools will form the basis for the remainder of our discussions of mathematical reasoning.

Problems: Section 1.1

1. Using truth tables, show that if $P \Leftrightarrow Q$ is true, then $P \Rightarrow Q$ and $Q \Rightarrow P$ are both true. Conversely, show that if $P \Rightarrow Q$ and $Q \Rightarrow P$ are both true, then $P \Leftrightarrow Q$ is true.

2. Show that $P \Rightarrow Q$ has the same truth value as $\neg P \vee Q$ for all truth values of P and Q, i.e., show that $(P \Rightarrow Q) \Leftrightarrow (\neg P \vee Q)$ is a tautology.

†Simpler questions of equivalent power can be formulated, e.g., "Would the other kind of person say *yes* if I asked him if the idol is black?"

3. Establish whether the following propositions are tautologies, contingencies, or contradictions:
   (a) $P \lor \neg P$
   (b) $P \land \neg P$
   (c) $P \Rightarrow \neg(\neg P)$
   (d) $\neg(P \land Q) \Leftrightarrow (\neg P \lor \neg Q)$
   (e) $\neg(P \lor Q) \Leftrightarrow (\neg P \land \neg Q)$
   (f) $(P \Rightarrow Q) \Leftrightarrow (\neg Q \Rightarrow \neg P)$
   (g) $(P \Rightarrow Q) \land (Q \Rightarrow P)$
   (h) $[P \land (Q \lor R)] \Rightarrow [(P \land Q) \lor (P \land R)]$
   (i) $(P \land \neg P) \Rightarrow Q$
   (j) $(P \lor \neg Q) \Rightarrow Q$
   (k) $P \Rightarrow (P \lor Q)$
   (l) $(P \land Q) \Rightarrow P$
   (m) $[(P \land Q) \Leftrightarrow P] \Leftrightarrow [P \Leftrightarrow Q]$
   (n) $[(P \Rightarrow Q) \lor (R \Rightarrow S)] \Rightarrow [(P \lor R) \Rightarrow (Q \lor S)]$

4. Let P be the proposition "It is snowing."
   Let Q be the proposition "I will go to town."
   Let R be the proposition "I have time."
   (a)   Using logical connectives, write a proposition which symbolizes each of the following:
         (i)   If it is not snowing and I have time, then I will go to town.
         (ii) I will go to town only if I have time.
         (iii) It isn't snowing.
         (iv) It is snowing, and I will not go to town.
   (b)   Write a sentence in English corresponding to each of the following propositions:
         (i) $Q \Leftrightarrow (R \land \neg P)$
         (ii) $R \land Q$
         (iii) $(Q \Rightarrow R) \land (R \Rightarrow Q)$
         (iv) $\neg(R \lor Q)$

5. State the converse and contrapositive of each of the following:
   (a)   If it rains, I'm not going.
   (b)   I will stay only if you go.
   (c)   If you get 4 pounds, you can bake the cake.
   (d)   I can't complete the task if I don't get more help.

6. For each of the following expressions, use identities to find equivalent expressions which use only $\land$ and $\neg$ and are as simple as possible.
   (a) $P \lor Q \lor \neg R$
   (b) $P \lor [(\neg Q \land R) \Rightarrow P]$
   (c) $P \Rightarrow (Q \Rightarrow P)$
   For each of the following expressions, use identities to find equivalent expressions which use only $\lor$ and $\neg$ and are as simple as possible.
   (d) $(P \land Q) \land \neg P$
   (e) $[P \Rightarrow (Q \lor \neg R)] \land \neg P \land Q$
   (f) $\neg P \land \neg Q \land (\neg R \Rightarrow P)$

7. Establish the following tautologies by simplifying the left side to the form of the right side:

(a) $[(P \wedge Q) \Rightarrow P) \Leftrightarrow 1$

(b) $\neg(\neg(P \vee Q) \Rightarrow \neg P) \Leftrightarrow 0$

(c) $[(Q \Rightarrow P) \wedge (\neg P \Rightarrow Q) \wedge (Q \Rightarrow Q)] \Leftrightarrow P$

(d) $[(P \Rightarrow \neg P) \wedge (\neg P \Rightarrow P)] \Leftrightarrow 0$

8. Relate the following assertion to the logical operator $\Rightarrow$: "If you start with a false assumption, you can prove anything you like." HINT: Consider the truth table of $\Rightarrow$.

9. An operation with two operands is said to be *commutative* if the order of the operands does not affect the result. Thus, addition is commutative since $x + y = y + x$ for all values of x and y, but subtraction is not commutative since $4 - 2 \neq 2 - 4$. A logical operator with two operands is commutative if reversing the order of the operands produces a logically equivalent proposition.

(a) Determine which of the following logical operators are commutative: $\wedge$, $\vee$, $\Rightarrow$, $\oplus$.

(b) Prove your assertions by using truth tables.

10. Let "$\square$" denote a logical operator with two operands; the expression $x \square y$ denotes the result of applying $\square$ to the operands x and y. The operator $\square$ is said to be *associative* if $x \square (y \square z)$ and $(x \square y) \square z$ are logically equivalent for all operands x, y, and z.

(a) Determine which of the logical operations $\wedge$, $\vee$, $\Rightarrow$, $\Leftrightarrow$, and $\oplus$ are associative.

(b) Prove your assertions using truth tables.

11. The operation of multiplication is said to *distribute* over addition because $x \cdot (y + z) = x \cdot y + x \cdot z$. On the other hand, addition does not distribute over multiplication, since $x + (y \cdot z) \neq (x + y) \cdot (x + z)$ for all values of x, y and z. If $\square$ and $\circ$ are logical operators with two operands then $\square$ is said to distribute over $\circ$ if $P \square (Q \circ R)$ and $(P \square Q) \circ (P \square R)$ are logically equivalent.

(a) Using truth tables and the identities of this section, show that $\wedge$ and $\vee$ distribute over each other, and each of $\wedge$, $\vee$, and $\Rightarrow$ distributes over itself.

(b) Does either addition or multiplication distribute over itself?

12. (a) We have seen that $\Rightarrow$ can be expressed in terms of $\vee$ and $\neg$ since $P \Rightarrow Q$ and $\neg P \vee Q$ are logically equivalent. Find a way of expressing $\oplus$ using only $\wedge$, $\vee$, and $\neg$.

(b) Show that all the logical operators described in this section can be expressed using only $\wedge$ and $\neg$.

13. (a) The *Sheffer stroke*, or *nand* operator, is defined by the following truth table:

P	Q	$P \mid Q$
0	0	1
0	1	1
1	0	1
1	1	0

Nand is an acronym for *not-and*; $P \mid Q$ is logically equivalent to $\neg(P \wedge Q)$. Show that

(i) $P \mid P \Leftrightarrow \neg P$

(ii) $(P \mid P) \mid (Q \mid Q) \Leftrightarrow P \vee Q$

(iii) $(P \mid Q) \mid (P \mid Q) \Leftrightarrow P \wedge Q$

(b) The *Peirce arrow*, or *nor* operator, is defined by the following truth table:

P	Q	$P \downarrow Q$
0	0	1
0	1	0
1	0	0
1	1	0

For each of the following, find equivalent expressions which use only the *nor* operator.

(i) $\neg P$

(ii) $P \vee Q$

(iii) $P \wedge Q$

Programming Problem

Write a program to construct truth tables of propositions. Assume the proposition will have no more than three variables (P, Q, and R) and calculate the truth value of the proposition for each possible set of truth values for P, Q, and R.

1.2 PREDICATES AND QUANTIFIERS

The language of propositions is not sufficiently powerful to make all the assertions needed in mathmatics. We also need to make assertions such as "$x = 3$," "$x \geq y$," and "$x + y = z$." Such assertions are not propositions, since they are not necessarily either true or false. However, if values are assigned to the variables, each of these assertions becomes a proposition. Similar assertions occur in English where pronouns and improper nouns are often used as variables; e.g.,

"He is tall and blonde," ("x is tall and blonde").

"She lives in the city," ("x lives in y").

These assertions are formed using variables in a "template" which expresses a property of an object or a relationship between objects. These templates are called *predicates*. Assertions made with predicates and variables become true or false when the variables are replaced by specific values. In the assertion "x is tall and blonde," x is a variable and "is tall and blonde" is a predicate; in the assertion "x lives in y," x and y are variables and "lives in" is a predicate. For ease of discussion, we will often refer to an assertion containing a predicate simply as a "predicate."

Example

Predicates are commonly used in control statements in high-level programming languages. For example, a statement of the form

$$\textbf{if } x > 3 \textbf{ then } y \leftarrow z$$

includes the predicate "$x > 3$." When the statement is executed, the truth value of the assertion "$x > 3$" is determined using the current value of the variable x; the assertion is assigned either the value 1 (representing *true*) or 0 (representing *false*). The coding of truth values as integers is sometimes exploited in strange ways in programming languages. For example, in PL/I,

$$A = X > 3;$$

is a legitimate assignment statement; execution of this statement causes the numeric variable A to be assigned the value of 1 if $X > 3$ is true and 0 if $X \leq 3$.   #

Some predicates are sufficiently important to warrant special notation. Examples include the use of "$=$" in assertions of the form "x is equal to y" and "$>$" to assert "x is greater than y." We will use these and other special notations wherever convenient and denote other predicates by capital letters, e.g.,

"x is a female" can be denoted by $F(x)$,
"x is married to y" can be denoted by $M(x, y)$, and
"$x + y = z$" can be represented by $S(x, y, z)$.

When a symbol, such as F, M, or S above or the symbol "$=$" in the assertion "$x = y$," denotes a specific predicate, it is called a *predicate constant*. (We will use the term "predicate" to refer to either a predicate constant or a predicate variable when the context makes the intended meaning clear.) A variable which appears in the parenthesized list after a predicate or is used with a predicate constant such as "$=$" is called an *individual variable*. In the expression $P(x_1, x_2, \ldots, x_n)$, P is a predicate constant or variable, each x_i is an individual variable, and P is said to have *n arguments* or be an *n-place predicate*.

Values of the individual variables must be drawn from a set called the *universe of discourse*, or simply the *universe*. For example, in discussing the predicate "$x < 3$," we would presumably choose a set of numbers as our universe of discourse, thus avoiding the possibility of assertions such as "green < 3." To be precise it is necessary to establish explicitly the universe of discourse; in practice, the universe is frequently left implicit. We require that the universe of discourse contain at least one element.

Any predicate has *n* arguments, where *n* is some natural number, i.e., *n* is a nonnegative integer. If P is an *n*-place predicate constant and values $c_1, c_2, \ldots, c_n$ are assigned to each of the individual variables, the result is a proposition. Suppose the universe of discourse is U. If the value of $P(c_1, c_2, \ldots, c_n)$ is *true* for every choice of arguments $c_1, c_2, \ldots, c_n$ selected from U, then P is said to be *valid in the universe U*. If the value of $P(c_1, c_2, \ldots, c_n)$ is *true* for some (but not necessarily all) choices of arguments selected from U, then P is said to be *satisfiable in the universe U*, and the values $c_1, c_2, \ldots, c_n$ which make $P(c_1, c_2, \ldots, c_n)$ true are said to *satisfy* P. If P is not satisfiable in the universe U, then we say P is *unsatisfiable in U*. Note that a predicate is permitted to have zero arguments. Since a predicate constant must have a value of either *true* or *false* when values are assigned to all its arguments, it follows that a predicate constant with no arguments is a proposition. Similarly, a predicate variable with zero arguments is a propositional variable.

In order to change a predicate into a proposition, each individual variable of the predicate must be *bound;* this may be done in two ways. The first way to bind an individual variable is by assigning a value to it.

Example

Consider the predicate "$x + y = 3$" which we will denote by $P(x, y)$. If the value 1 is assigned to x, and 2 to y, the predicate is changed into a proposition $P(1, 2)$ whose truth value is *true*. On the other hand, if we assign the values 2 and 6 to x and y, respectively, the resulting proposition, $P(2, 6)$, is false. #

The second method of binding individual variables is by *quantification* of the variable. The most common forms of quantification are *universal* and *existential*. If $P(x)$ is a predicate with the individual variable x as an argument, then the assertion

"For all x, $P(x)$,"

which is interpreted as

"For all values of x, the assertion $P(x)$ is true,"

is a statement in which the variable x is said to be *universally quantified*. The symbol $\forall$, called the *universal quantifier*, is used to denote the phrase "for all." Thus, "For all x, $P(x)$" is written "$\forall x P(x)$." The symbol $\forall$ may be read "for all," "for every," "for any," "for arbitrary," or "for each." If the assertion $P(x)$ is true for every possible value of x, then $\forall x P(x)$ is true; otherwise, $\forall x P(x)$ is false. Thus, if the universe of discourse is U, the assertion $\forall x P(x)$ is true if and only if the predicate P is valid in U. It follows that for any predicate P and any element c of the universe of discourse, the implication

$$\forall x P(x) \Rightarrow P(c)$$

is true.

Examples

The following propositions are formed by universal quantification:

(a) $\forall x[x < x + 1]$ (for all x, x is less than $x + 1$)

(b) $\forall x[x = 3]$ (for any x, $x = 3$)

If the universe is the set of integers **I**, the predicate $x < x + 1$ is true for all values of x, but "$x = 3$" is false when x is assigned the value of 1. Consequently, for this universe (a) is true and (b) is false.

(c) If A is an integer array with 50 entries, $A[1], A[2], \ldots, A[50]$, then we can assert that all entries are nonzero as follows:

$$\forall i\{(1 \leq i \land i \leq 50) \Rightarrow A[i] \neq 0\}.$$

The entries of the array are sorted in nondecreasing order if the following assertion holds.

$$\forall i\{(1 \leq i \land i < 50) \Rightarrow A[i] \leq A[i+1]\}.$$

We may also use more than one quantifier with predicates which have more than one variable, e.g., the assertion

(d) $\forall x \, \forall y [x + y > x]$ is read "for all x and all y, $x + y$ is greater than x." This proposition is true if the universe of discourse consists of positive integers $\mathbf{I}+$ and false if the universe is the set of all integers $\mathbf{I}$.   #

Another common form of quantification is *existential*. The individual variable x in the assertion

"For some x, $P(x)$",

or equivalently,

"There exists a value of x for which the assertion $P(x)$ is true,"

is said to be existentially quantified. The symbol $\exists$ is used to represent the phrase "there exists" and the above statement can be written "$\exists x \, P(x)$." The symbol $\exists$ may also be read "for some" or "for at least one." If the assertion $P(x)$ is true for at least one element in the universe of discourse, then the proposition $\exists x P(x)$ is true; otherwise, it is false. More succinctly, $\exists x P(x)$ is true if and only if $P(x)$ is satisfiable in the universe of discourse. It follows that for any element c of the universe, the implication

$$P(c) \Rightarrow \exists x P(x)$$

is true.

Examples

The variable x is existentially quantified in the following propositions:

(a) $\exists x [x < x + 1]$ (There exists an x such that x is less than $x + 1$).

(b) $\exists x [x = 3]$ (There exists an x such that $x = 3$.)

Both of these are true propositions if the universe of discourse is the set of integers. The proposition

(c) $\exists x [x = x + 1]$ (There exists an x such that $x = x + 1$.)

is false, since no matter what value we assign to x, the assertion "$x = x + 1$" is false.   #

A third form of quantification can be used to assert that there is one and only one element of the universe of discourse which makes a predicate true. This quantifier is denoted $\exists!$, and the sequence of symbols $\exists! x$ is read "There exists a unique x such that . . ." or "There is one and only one x such that . . ."

Examples

Let the universe of discourse be the set of natural numbers **N**. Then the following propositions are true.

(a) $\exists!x[x < 1]$

(b) $\exists!x[x = 3]$

In (a), assigning the value of 0 to x makes the assertion $x < 1$ true; no other value will do. In (b), the unique value of x is 3. For the same universe, the assertion

(c) $\exists!x[x > 1]$ is false, since the assertion "$x > 1$" is true if x is assigned any value other than 0 or 1.   #

An assertion with quantified variables can be expressed using propositions obtained by assigning values to the individual variables of the predicates which occur in the assertion. This relationship can be made explicit by considering a finite universe of discourse. Let the universe consist of the integers 1, 2, and 3. Then the proposition

$$\forall x P(x)$$

is equivalent to the conjunction

$$P(1) \wedge P(2) \wedge P(3),$$

and the proposition

$$\exists x P(x)$$

is equivalent to the disjunction

$$P(1) \vee P(2) \vee P(3).$$

The proposition

$$\exists!x P(x)$$

is equivalent to the proposition

$$[P(1) \wedge \neg P(2) \wedge \neg P(3)] \vee [P(2) \wedge \neg P(1) \wedge \neg P(3)]$$
$$\vee [P(3) \wedge \neg P(1) \wedge \neg P(2)].$$

If the universe of discourse is infinite, a quantified assertion cannot always be represented by a finite conjunction or disjunction of propositions without quantifiers. However, the concept can be extended, and it is often convenient to consider a universally quantified assertion over an infinite universe as an infinite conjunction and an existentially quantified assertion as an infinite disjunction.

Example

Consider the universe of nonnegative integers, and let $P(x)$ denote the assertion "$x > 3$." Then the proposition

$$\forall x P(x)$$

can be interpreted as the infinite conjunction

$$P(0) \wedge P(1) \wedge P(2) \wedge P(3) \wedge \cdots$$

which is false, since some of the operands, e.g., $P(0)$, are false. The proposition

$$\exists x P(x)$$

can be interpreted as the infinite disjunction

$$P(0) \lor P(1) \lor P(2) \lor P(3) \lor \cdots$$

which is true, since at least one of the operands, e.g., $P(4)$, is true.   #

All of the individual variables of a predicate must be bound in order to transform the predicate into a proposition. Recall the two ways of binding individual variables: values can be assigned to them or they can be quantified. Individual variables which are not bound are called *free*. If P is a predicate with n free variables, then binding an individual variable reduces the number of free variables by one; the resulting assertion is equivalent to a predicate with $n - 1$ variables. As we stated earlier, a predicate with no free variables is a proposition.

Examples

The predicate $P(x, y, z)$ representing "$x + y = z$," has three variables, all of which are free in the assertion

$$P(x, y, z).$$

If we assign x the value of 2, the result is the predicate P with a bound variable.

$$P(2, y, z).$$

This assertion is equivalent to a predicate with two free variables, which we can denote by $Q(y, z)$, where $Q(y, z)$ is true if $2 + y = z$. Similarly,

$$\exists y P(x, y, z)$$

is an assertion with two free variables. The truth value of this assertion is equivalent to that of a predicate with two variables which we will call $R(x, z)$; if the universe is the natural numbers, then

$$R(x, z) \Leftrightarrow \exists y P(x, y, z) \Leftrightarrow \exists y[x + y = z] \Leftrightarrow (x \leq z).   \#$$

If y does not occur as an individual variable in $P(x_1, x_2, \ldots, x_n)$, then the assertions $\forall y P(x_1, x_2, \ldots, x_n)$ and $\exists y P(x_1, x_2, \ldots, x_n)$ are both equivalent to $P(x_1, x_2, \ldots, x_n)$, since none of the individual variables of P are bound by the quantification. As a special case, if P is a proposition, then the truth value of $\exists x P$ or $\forall x P$ is equal to the truth value of P.

If more than one quantifier is applied to a predicate, the order in which the variables are bound is the same as their order in the quantifier list; for example,

$$\forall x \, \forall y P(x, y) \text{ denotes } \forall x[\forall y P(x, y)].$$

The binding order can profoundly affect the meaning of an assertion. For example, the sequence "$\forall x \, \exists y$," can be paraphrased informally as "No matter what value of x is chosen, a value of y can be found such that . . ." In this quantifier sequence, since y is chosen after x, the value of y may depend on the value of x. In contrast, the sequence "$\exists y \, \forall x$" asserts "A value of y can be chosen so that no matter what value is chosen for x . . ." In this case, since y is bound first, the value of y must be specified independently of the value of x.

Examples

Let the universe of discourse be the set of married persons. Then

(a) $\forall x \, \exists y [x$ is married to $y]$ is true. However,

(b) $\exists y \, \forall x [x$ is married to $y]$ asserts that there is some person in the universe who is married to everyone; this is false.
Now let the universe of discourse be the integers **I**. The assertion

(c) $\forall x \, \exists y [x + y = 0]$ (For all x, there exists a y such that $x + y = 0$.) is true, since for any value of x there is a value of y (i.e., y is equal to $-x$) which makes the assertion "$x + y = 0$" true. The proposition

(d) $\exists y \, \forall x [x + y = 0]$ (There exists a y such that for all $x, x + y = 0$.) asserts that the value of y can be chosen independently of the value of x. Since no y exists which yields zero when added to an arbitrary integer, this proposition is false. The proposition

(e) $\forall x \, \forall y \, \exists ! z [x + y = z]$ asserts that for every pair of integers x and y, there is a unique integer z equal to their sum; the assertion is true. If we interchange the last two quantifiers of part (e), we obtain the proposition

(f) $\forall x \, \exists ! z \, \forall y [x + y = z]$ which asserts that for every x, a unique z can be chosen such that no matter what y is added to $x, x + y = z$. This proposition is false. The proposition

(g) $\exists ! x [x \cdot 6 = 0]$ is true since equation $x \cdot 6 = 0$ is true if and only if $x = 0$. The proposition

(h) $\exists ! x \, \forall y [x \cdot y = 0]$ is true, but

(i) $\forall y \, \exists ! x [x \cdot y = 0]$ is false, since, if $y = 0$, any value of x will yield zero. Similarly,

(j) $\forall y \, \exists ! x [x + y < 0]$ is false, since for any value of y there are many values of x for which the sum of x and y is negative.   #

Although the order in which individual variables are bound cannot always be changed without affecting the meaning of an assertion, there are two notable exceptions: the sequence $\forall x \, \forall y$ can always be replaced by $\forall y \, \forall x$, and the sequence $\exists x \, \exists y$ can always be replaced by $\exists y \, \exists x$.

Example

Let the universe be the nonnegative integers. For any predicate P, the proposition

$$\forall x \, \forall y P(x, y)$$

can be expanded† to

---

†Throughout this chapter, we will frequently expand quantified statements into infinite conjunctions or disjunctions, rearrange the terms using the identities of Table 1.1.1 and derive a new quantified assertion. This technique does not always constitute a careful mathematical argument and in fact cannot be applied to some universes. We use it as an intuitive aid for understanding quantified assertions.

$$[\forall y P(0, y)] \land [\forall y P(1, y)] \land [\forall y P(2, y)] \land \cdots$$

which can be interpreted as

$$[P(0, 0) \land P(0, 1) \land P(0, 2) \land \cdots]$$
$$\land [P(1, 0) \land P(1, 1) \land P(1, 2) \land \cdots]$$
$$\land [P(2, 0) \land P(2, 1) \land P(2, 2) \land \cdots]$$
$$\land \cdots$$
$$\vdots$$

Applying the commutativity and associativity of $\land$ (identities 4 and 6 of Table 1.1.1) to rearrange the terms by collecting the propositions in each column, we obtain the infinite conjunction

$$[P(0, 0) \land P(1, 0) \land P(2, 0) \land \cdots]$$
$$\land [P(0, 1) \land P(1, 1) \land P(2, 1) \land \cdots]$$
$$\land [P(0, 2) \land P(1, 2) \land P(2, 2) \land \cdots]$$
$$\land \cdots$$
$$\vdots$$

which represents

$$[\forall x P(x, 0)] \land [\forall x P(x, 1)] \land [\forall x P(x, 2)] \land \cdots$$

This is an expansion of

$$\forall y \, \forall x P(x, y). \quad \#$$

It is common practice in mathematics to omit leading universal quantifiers from assertions. For example, it is acceptable to assert "$x + y = y + x$." According to our definition, this is a predicate rather than a proposition because the variables x and y are apparently free. However, the intended assertion is

$$\forall x \, \forall y [x + y = y + x],$$

which has no free variables. We will follow this convention of deleting universal quantifiers in later chapters, but will refrain from doing so for the present.

The notions of predicates and quantified variables described in this section provide a strong extension to the language of propositions. Most substantive mathematical arguments involve quantification, and the tools introduced in this section will be used throughout the remainder of this text.

Problems: Section 1.2

1. Let $S(x, y, z)$ denote the predicate "$x + y = z$," $P(x, y, z)$ denote "$x \cdot y = z$," and $L(x, y)$ denote "$x < y$." Let the universe of discourse be the natural numbers N. Using the above predicates, express the following assertions. The phrase "there is an x" does not imply that x has a unique value.

(a) For every x and y, there is a z such that $x + y = z$.

(b) No x is less than 0.

(c) For all x, $x + 0 = x$.

(d) For all x, $x \cdot y = y$ for all y.

(e) There is an x such that $x \cdot y = y$ for all y.

2. Show $\exists x \, \exists y P(x, y)$ and $\exists y \, \exists x P(x, y)$ are equivalent by expanding the expressions into infinite disjunctions.

3. Determine which of the following propositions are true if the universe is the set of integers $\mathbf{I}$ and $\cdot$ denotes the operation of multiplication.

(a) $\forall x \, \exists y [x \cdot y = 0]$

(b) $\forall x \, \exists ! y [x \cdot y = 1]$

(c) $\exists y \, \forall x [x \cdot y = 1]$

(d) $\exists y \, \forall x [x \cdot y = x]$

4. Let the universe be the integers. For each of the following assertions, find a predicate P which makes the implication false.

(a) $\forall x \, \exists ! y P(x, y) \Rightarrow \exists ! y \, \forall x P(x, y)$

(b) $\exists ! y \, \forall x P(x, y) \Rightarrow \forall x \, \exists ! y P(x, y)$

5. Specify a universe of discourse for which the following propositions are true. Try to choose the universe to be as large a subset of the integers as possible. Explain any difficulties.

(a) $\forall x [x > 10]$

(b) $\forall x [x = 3]$

(c) $\forall x \, \exists y [x + y = 436]$

(d) $\exists y \, \forall x [x + y < 0]$.

6. Let the universe of discourse consist of the integers 0 and 1. Find finite disjunctions and conjunctions of propositions which do not use quantifiers and which are equivalent to the following:

(a) $\forall x P(0, x)$

(b) $\forall x \, \forall y P(x, y)$

(c) $\forall x \, \exists y P(x, y)$

(d) $\exists x \, \forall y P(x, y)$

(e) $\exists y \, \exists x P(x, y)$

7. Consider the universe of integers $\mathbf{I}$.

(a) Find a predicate $P(x)$ which is false regardless of whether the variable x is bound by $\forall$ or $\exists$.

(b) Find a predicate $P(x)$ which is true regardless of whether the variable x is bound by $\forall$ or $\exists$.

(c) Is it possible for a predicate $P(x)$ to be true regardless of whether the variable is bound by $\forall$, $\exists$ or $\exists !$? Justify your answer.

8. Let P be an arbitrary predicate and let the universe of discourse be the integers 1, 2, and 3. Is the truth of the proposition $\exists ! x P(x)$ equivalent to the truth of the proposition $P(1) \oplus P(2) \oplus P(3)$?

9. Consider the universe of integers and let $P(x, y, z)$ denote $x - y = z$. Transcribe the following assertions into logical notation.

(a) For every x and y, there is some z such that $x - y = z$.

(b) For every x and y, there is some z such that $x - z = y$.
(c) There is an x such that for all y, $y - x = y$.
(d) When 0 is subtracted from any integer, the result is the original integer.
(e) 3 subtracted from 5 gives 2.

1.3 QUANTIFIERS AND LOGICAL OPERATORS

A careful transcription of mathematical statements often involves quantifiers, predicates, and logical operators. Such assertions can take a variety of forms.

Examples

Let the universe be the integers and let $N(x)$ denote "x is a nonnegative integer," $E(x)$ denote "x is even," $O(x)$ denote "x is odd," and $P(x)$ denote "x is prime." The following examples illustrate the transcription of assertions into logical notation.

(a) There exists an even integer.

$$\exists x E(x)$$

(b) Every integer is even or odd.

$$\forall x [E(x) \vee O(x)]$$

(c) All prime integers are nonnegative.

$$\forall x [P(x) \Rightarrow N(x)]$$

(d) The only even prime is two.

$$\forall x [(E(x) \wedge P(x)) \Rightarrow x = 2]$$

(e) There is one and only one even prime.

$$\exists ! x [E(x) \wedge P(x)]$$

(f) Not all integers are odd.

$$\neg \forall x O(x), \text{ or } \exists x \neg O(x)$$

(g) Not all primes are odd.

$$\neg \forall x [P(x) \Rightarrow O(x)], \text{ or } \exists x [P(x) \wedge \neg O(x)]$$

(h) If an integer is not odd, then it's even.

$$\forall x [\neg O(x) \Rightarrow E(x)]. \quad \#$$

In previous examples, the quantifiers occur at the beginning of the assertion. However, in transcribing many mathematical statements, quantifiers may naturally go elsewhere and their placement is important.

Examples

Consider the universe of integers and let $P(x, y, z)$ denote "$xy = z$". The following are examples of mathematical statements and equivalent formulations in logical notation. Note that informal statements of propositions frequently omit the universal quantification of individual variables.

(a) "If $x = 0$, then $xy = x$ for all values of y."

$$\forall x[x = 0 \Rightarrow \forall y P(x, y, x)]$$

(b) "If $xy = x$ for every y, then $x = 0$."

$$\forall x[\forall y P(x, y, x) \Rightarrow x = 0]$$

Observe that $\forall x \, \forall y[P(x, y, x) \Rightarrow x = 0]$ is not a correct transcription of assertion (b). The latter transcription represents the false assertion "for all x and y, if $xy = x$, then $x = 0$." The values of $x = 1$ and $y = 1$ provide a counterexample to this assertion, whereas the assertion (b) is true.

(c) "If $xy \neq x$ for some y, then $x \neq 0$."

$$\forall x[\exists y \neg P(x, y, x) \Rightarrow \neg(x = 0)]. \quad \#$$

The preceding examples illustrate a variety of ways in which assertions can involve predicates, quantifiers and logical operators. In constructing proofs, we frequently need to establish relationships between assertions. For example, consider the statements

$$\exists x[P(x) \Rightarrow Q(x)] \text{ and } \exists x P(x) \Rightarrow \exists y Q(y).$$

Are they equivalent, or does one imply the other, or is no statement of this kind possible? In order to resolve such questions, it is necessary to understand the ways in which logical operators, quantifiers, and predicates interact.

An assertion involving predicate variables is *valid* if it is true for every universe of discourse no matter how the predicate variables are interpreted. An assertion is *satisfiable* if there exists a universe and some interpretation of the predicate variables which makes it true. If an assertion is not true for any universe or interpretation, it is *unsatisfiable*. Valid, satisfiable and unsatisfiable assertions are the analogs of tautologies, contingencies, and contradictions in the language of propositions. In this section, we will develop some fundamental identities which can be used to determine the validity of assertions. In our discussion we will often refer to "equivalent" assertions. Two assertions A_1 and A_2 are said to be (*logically*) *equivalent* if and only if for every universe of discourse and every interpretation of the predicate variables, A_1 is true if and only if A_2 is true. In other words, A_1 and A_2 are equivalent if and only if the assertion $A_1 \Leftrightarrow A_2$ is valid.

We first consider how the negation operation affects quantified assertions. Let $P(x)$ be a predicate and consider the meaning of the proposition $\neg \forall x P(x)$. We can interpret this proposition as "the assertion '$\forall x P(x)$' is false," which is equivalent to the statement "for some x, $P(x)$ is not true," or "$\exists x \neg P(x)$." This leads to the valid assertion

$$\neg \forall x P(x) \Leftrightarrow \exists x \neg P(x).$$

Similarly, the proposition $\neg \exists x P(x)$ asserts that "it is false that there exists an x such that $P(x)$ is true." This is equivalent to the assertion that "there does not exist an x such that $P(x)$ is true" or "for all x, $P(x)$ is false." This establishes the valid assertion

$$\neg \exists x P(x) \Leftrightarrow \forall x \neg P(x).$$

These two equivalences can be used to propagate negation signs through a sequence of quantifiers, as illustrated by the following example.

Example

$$\neg \exists x \; \forall y \; \forall z P(x, y, z) \Leftrightarrow \forall x \; \neg \; \forall y \; \forall z P(x, y, z)$$
$$\Leftrightarrow \forall x \; \exists y \; \neg \; \forall z P(x, y, z)$$
$$\Leftrightarrow \forall x \; \exists y \; \exists z \; \neg \; P(x, y, z) \quad \#$$

Propagation of negations through quantifier sequences is often useful in constructing proofs and counterexamples. Consider the following assertion:

For every pair of integers x and y, there exists a z such that $x + z = y$.

This statement can be formulated as follows:

$$\forall x \; \forall y \; \exists z[x + z = y].$$

This proposition is true for the universe of integers **I**, but false for the natural numbers **N**. We establish its falsity for the universe **N** by showing that its negation is true. The negation has the form

$$\neg \forall x \; \forall y \; \exists z[x + z = y]$$

which is somewhat difficult to interpret. The equivalent form

$$\exists x \; \exists y \; \forall z \; \neg \; [x + z = y], \text{ or } \exists x \; \exists y \; \forall z[x + y \neq z]$$

is more tractable and can easily be shown to be true for the nonnegative integers by choosing $x > y$.

The *scope* of a quantifier is the part of an assertion in which variables are bound by the quantifier.

Examples

(a)   In the assertion

$$A \; \vee \; \forall x[P(x) \; \vee \; Q(x)]$$

the scope of the universal quantifier is $[P(x) \; \vee \; Q(x)]$.

(b)   In the assertion

$$[\forall x P(x)] \Rightarrow [\exists x Q(x)]$$

the scope of the universal quantifier is $P(x)$, and the scope of the existential quantifier is $Q(x)$.

(c)   In the assertion

$$\forall x[P(x) \Rightarrow (A \; \vee \; B)]$$

the scope of the universal quantifier is $[P(x) \Rightarrow (A \; \vee \; B)]$.   #

Parentheses and brackets can be used to make the scope of a quantifier explicit. We adopt the convention that the scope of a quantifier is the smallest subexpression possible, consistent with the parentheses of the expression. Consequently, the assertion

$$\forall x P(x) \; \vee \; Q(x)$$

does not denote the proposition

$$\forall x[P(x) \lor Q(x)]$$

but instead the predicate

$$[\forall x P(x)] \lor Q(x).$$

This assertion has two variables, one bound and one free, both of which are denoted by x. It is equivalent to

$$\forall y P(y) \lor Q(x)$$

which uses different symbols for the bound and free variables. Using the same symbol for different variables, although formally correct, is often confusing and should be avoided.

Example

In the expression

$$\forall x[P(x) \lor Q(y) \lor R(x, z)]$$

both occurrences of x refer to the same variable. But in the expression

$$\forall x[P(x) \lor Q(y)] \lor R(x, z),$$

the occurrence of the variable x in the predicate $P(x)$ is bound while the occurrence of x in the predicate $R(x, z)$ is free. The last expression is therefore equivalent to

$$\forall x[P(x) \lor Q(y)] \lor R(w, z). \quad \#$$

We now consider the way quantifiers affect conjunctions and disjunctions. We first note that if a proposition occurs in a disjunction or conjunction within the scope of a quantifier, it can be removed from the scope of the quantifier. Thus,

$$\forall x[A(x) \lor P] \Leftrightarrow [\forall x A(x) \lor P],$$

$$\forall x[A(x) \land P] \Leftrightarrow [\forall x A(x) \land P],$$

$$\exists x[A(x) \lor P] \Leftrightarrow [\exists x A(x) \lor P],$$

and

$$\exists x[A(x) \land P] \Leftrightarrow [\exists x A(x) \land P]$$

are all valid. Predicates whose variables are not bound by a quantifier can be treated in the same way, e.g.,

$$\forall x[P(x) \lor Q(y)] \Leftrightarrow [\forall x P(x) \lor Q(y)],$$

and

$$\forall x[\forall y P(x, y) \land Q(z)] \Leftrightarrow [\forall x \, \forall y P(x, y) \land Q(z)]$$

are also valid.

The reader may obtain a better understanding of these equivalences by expanding them into infinite conjunctions and disjunctions. Thus, for the universe of natural numbers $\mathbf{N}$, the first identity above can be treated as follows:

The assertion $\forall x[A(x) \lor P]$ is equivalent to the infinite conjunction

$$[A(0) \lor P] \land [A(1) \lor P] \land [A(2) \lor P] \land \cdots$$

which can be rearranged using the distributive laws to form

$$[A(0) \wedge A(1) \wedge A(2) \wedge \cdots] \vee P$$

which is equivalent to $\forall x A(x) \vee P$.

Now suppose the variable bound by a quantifier occurs in both predicates of a disjunction or conjunction. We will first show that the proposition $\forall x[P(x) \wedge Q(x)] \Leftrightarrow [\forall x P(x) \wedge \forall x Q(x)]$ is valid. The proposition

$$\forall x[P(x) \wedge Q(x)]$$

can be read "For all x, $P(x)$ is true and $Q(x)$ is true" or "For all x, $P(x)$ and $Q(x)$ are both true." The proposition

$$\forall x P(x) \wedge \forall x Q(x)$$

states that "For all x, $P(x)$ is true and for all x, $Q(x)$ is true." We show the equivalence of these two assertions for the universe of natural numbers **N** by first expanding $\forall x[P(x) \wedge Q(x)]$ into an infinite conjunction:

$$[P(0) \wedge Q(0)] \wedge [P(1) \wedge Q(1)] \wedge [P(2) \wedge Q(2)] \wedge \cdots$$

Appealing to the associative and commutative properties of $\wedge$, (identities 4 and 6 of Table 1.1.1), we rearrange these terms to obtain

$$[P(0) \wedge P(1) \wedge P(2) \wedge \cdots] \wedge [Q(0) \wedge Q(1) \wedge Q(2) \wedge \cdots]$$

which is equivalent to

$$\forall x P(x) \wedge \forall x Q(x),$$

or equivalently

$$\forall x P(x) \wedge \forall y Q(y).$$

Our argument has used the universe **N**, but the two assertions are equivalent for any universe of discourse. Thus the following assertion is valid:

$$\forall x[P(x) \wedge Q(x)] \Leftrightarrow [\forall x P(x) \wedge \forall x Q(x)].$$

This relationship between $\forall$ and $\wedge$ is informally characterized by the assertion that the universal quantifier $\forall$ *distributes* over the logical connective $\wedge$. However, the existential quantifier $\exists$ does not distribute over the logical connective $\wedge$. That is, $\exists x[P(x) \wedge Q(x)]$ is not equivalent to $\exists x P(x) \wedge \exists x Q(x)$, as the following argument shows. The proposition $\exists x[P(x) \wedge Q(x)]$ asserts that "There exists an x such that $P(x)$ and $Q(x)$ are both true." This assertion requires that the same value of x satisfies both P and Q. On the other hand, the assertion "There exists an x such that $P(x)$ is true and there exists an x such that $Q(x)$ is true," which can be represented by

$$\exists x P(x) \wedge \exists x Q(x)$$

permits different values of x to be chosen to satisfy P and Q.

To show the two assertions $\exists x[P(x) \wedge Q(x)]$ and $\exists x P(x) \wedge \exists x Q(x)$ are not equivalent, we can use the preceding analysis to construct a universe and predicates P and Q such that one assertion is true and the other false. Let the universe be the the integers and let $P(x)$ denote "x is an even integer" and $Q(x)$ denote "x

is an odd integer." Then $\exists x P(x) \wedge \exists x Q(x)$ is a true proposition, whereas $\exists x[P(x) \wedge Q(x)]$ is false.

Although $\exists x[P(x) \wedge Q(x)]$ and $\exists x P(x) \wedge \exists x Q(x)$ are not equivalent, the first implies the second, that is, the assertion

$$\exists x[P(x) \wedge Q(x)] \Rightarrow [\exists x P(x) \wedge \exists x Q(x)]$$

is valid. For if $\exists x[P(x) \wedge Q(x)]$ is true, then there is some element c of the universe such that the proposition $P(c) \wedge Q(c)$ is true. Therefore, $P(c)$ is true and $Q(c)$ is true. From the truth of $P(c)$, we can conclude that $\exists x P(x)$ is true. Similarly, we can conclude from $Q(c)$ that $\exists x Q(x)$ is true and therefore, the conjunction $\exists x P(x) \wedge \exists x Q(x)$ is true.

By changing predicate variable names, we can use the previous results to establish that $\exists$ distributes over $\vee$ but $\forall$ does not. Since our results were established for arbitrary predicates, we can replace P by $\neg R$ and Q by $\neg T$ in the valid assertion

$$\forall x[P(x) \wedge Q(x)] \Leftrightarrow [\forall x P(x) \wedge \forall x Q(x)].$$

Since an equivalence remains valid when both sides are negated, the following is also valid:

$$\neg \forall x[\neg R(x) \wedge \neg T(x)] \Leftrightarrow \neg[\forall(x) \neg R(x) \wedge \forall x \neg T(x)].$$

Applying identities, we obtain the following sequence of equivalences.

$$\exists x \neg[\neg R(x) \wedge \neg T(x)] \Leftrightarrow [(\neg \forall x \neg R(x)) \vee (\neg \forall x \neg T(x))]$$

$$\exists x[\neg(\neg R(x)) \vee \neg(\neg T(x))] \Leftrightarrow [(\exists x \neg(\neg R(x))) \vee (\exists x \neg(\neg T(x)))]$$

$$\exists x[R(x) \vee T(x)] \Leftrightarrow [\exists x R(x) \vee \exists x T(x)]$$

This establishes that $\exists$ distributes over $\vee$.

Using the same technique of replacing the predicate variables P and Q by $\neg P$ and $\neg Q$ in the valid assertion

$$\exists x[P(x) \wedge Q(x)] \Rightarrow [\exists x P(x) \wedge \exists x Q(x)]$$

we can establish

$$[\forall x P(x) \vee \forall x Q(x)] \Rightarrow \forall x[P(x) \vee Q(x)].$$

The converse of this implication is not valid.

Once we have established how to deal with the quantifiers for the operators $\wedge$, $\vee$ and $\neg$, we can treat the remaining connectives $\Rightarrow$ and $\Leftrightarrow$ by applying identities relating them to $\wedge$, $\vee$, and $\neg$.

Example

We show that $\exists$ does not distribute over $\Rightarrow$; that is, the assertion

$$\exists x[P(x) \Rightarrow Q(x)] \Leftrightarrow [\exists x P(x) \Rightarrow \exists x Q(x)]$$

is not valid.

Since $A \Rightarrow B$ is equivalent to $\neg A \lor B$, it follows that

$$\exists x[P(x) \Rightarrow Q(x)] \Leftrightarrow \exists x[\neg P(x) \lor Q(x)]$$
$$\Leftrightarrow [\exists x \, \neg P(x) \lor \exists x Q(x)]$$
$$\Leftrightarrow [\neg \forall x P(x) \lor \exists x Q(x)]$$
$$\Leftrightarrow [\forall x P(x) \Rightarrow \exists x Q(x)].$$

Hence, the original assertion is equivalent to the assertion

$$[\forall x P(x) \Rightarrow \exists x Q(x)] \Leftrightarrow [\exists x P(x) \Rightarrow \exists x Q(x)].$$

We can construct a truth table for the propositional form of this assertion, taking the components $\forall x P(x)$, $\exists x Q(x)$, and $\exists x P(x)$ as propositional variables. However, since $\exists x P(x)$ is true whenever $\forall x P(x)$ is true, two lines of the truth table do not apply.

$\forall x P(x)$	$\exists x P(x)$	$\exists x Q(x)$	$\forall x P(x) \Rightarrow \exists x Q(x)$	$\exists x P(x) \Rightarrow \exists x Q(x)$
0	0	0	1	1
0	0	1	1	1
0	1	0	1	0
0	1	1	1	1
1	0	0	n.a.	n.a.
1	0	1	n.a.	n.a.
1	1	0	0	0
1	1	1	1	1

Considering the last two columns of the table, we conclude that the implication holds in one direction,

$$[\exists x P(x) \Rightarrow \exists x Q(x)] \Rightarrow [\forall x P(x) \Rightarrow \exists x Q(x)].$$

However, we can show the converse is not valid by exhibiting a counterexample. From the third line of the truth table, we know that any counterexample must be an interpretation of the predicate P in which $\forall x P(x)$ is false and $\exists x P(x)$ is true, and an interpretation for Q in which $\exists x Q(x)$ is false. For the universe of the integers, let $P(x)$ denote "$x = 0$" and $Q(x)$ denote "$x \neq x$." This provides a counterexample and establishes that $\exists$ does not distribute over $\Rightarrow$.   #

Table 1.3.1 is a list of useful logical relationships between assertions involving quantifiers. Each relationship of the table also holds when additional free variables are inserted consistently in each occurrence of a predicate. Thus, from identity 4 we can infer

$$\forall x P(x, y) \Rightarrow \exists x P(x, y)$$

and from identity 6 we can infer

$$[\forall x P(x, y) \land Q(z)] \Leftrightarrow \forall x[P(x, y) \land Q(z)].$$

Table 1.3.1   A summary of logical relationships involving quantifiers

1. $\forall x P(x) \Rightarrow P(c)$, where c is an arbitrary element of the universe
2. $P(c) \Rightarrow \exists x P(x)$, where c is an arbitrary element of the universe
3. $\forall x \neg P(x) \Leftrightarrow \neg \exists x P(x)$
4. $\forall x P(x) \Rightarrow \exists x P(x)$
5. $\exists x \neg P(x) \Leftrightarrow \neg \forall x P(x)$
6. $[\forall x P(x) \wedge Q] \Leftrightarrow \forall x [P(x) \wedge Q]$
7. $[\forall x P(x) \vee Q] \Leftrightarrow \forall x [P(x) \vee Q]$
8. $[\forall x P(x) \wedge \forall x Q(x)] \Leftrightarrow \forall x [P(x) \wedge Q(x)]$
9. $[\forall x P(x) \vee \forall x Q(x)] \Rightarrow \forall x [P(x) \vee Q(x)]$
10. $[\exists x P(x) \wedge Q] \Leftrightarrow \exists x [P(x) \wedge Q]$
11. $[\exists x P(x) \vee Q] \Leftrightarrow \exists x [P(x) \vee Q]$
12. $\exists x [P(x) \wedge Q(x)] \Rightarrow [\exists x P(x) \wedge \exists x Q(x)]$
13. $[\exists x P(x) \vee \exists x Q(x)] \Leftrightarrow \exists x [P(x) \vee Q(x)]$

A compact form of logical notation is often used to express mathematical assertions. For example, the assertion

"For every x such that $x > 0$, $P(x)$ is true,"

which would be written in our current notation as

$$\forall x [(x > 0) \Rightarrow P(x)]$$

can be written more compactly as

$$\forall x_{x>0} \, P(x).$$

Similarly,

"There exists an x such that $x \neq 3$ and $Q(x)$ is true,"

which would be written

$$\exists x [(x \neq 3) \wedge Q(x)]$$

can be written

$$\exists x_{x \neq 3} \, Q(x).$$

Using these conventions, the formal statement of assertions becomes both more compact and more readable. Furthermore, the compact notation allows a negation sign to be propagated through a sequence of quantifiers in the same manner as was illustrated earlier.

Example

Consider the limit of a function defined over the real line. The definition is usually expressed as follows.

Definition: The *limit of $f(x)$ as x approaches c is k* (denoted $\lim\limits_{x \to c} f(x) = k$) if for every $\epsilon > 0$, there exists a $\delta > 0$ such that for all x, if $|x - c| < \delta$ then $|f(x) - k| < \epsilon$.

This can be transcribed in the abbreviated logical notation as follows.

Definition:

$$\lim_{x \to c} f(x) = k \Leftrightarrow \forall \epsilon_{\epsilon>0} \ \exists \delta_{\delta>0} \forall x [|x - c| < \delta \Rightarrow |f(x) - k| < \epsilon].$$

To show that $\lim_{x \to c} f(x) \neq k$, we form the negation of both sides of the above definition giving

$$\lim_{x \to c} f(x) \neq k \Leftrightarrow \exists \epsilon_{\epsilon>0} \ \forall \delta_{\delta>0} \ \exists x [|x - c| < \delta \ \wedge \ |f(x) - k| \geq \epsilon].$$

This establishes that $\lim_{x \to c} f(x) \neq k$ if and only if there exists an $\epsilon > 0$ such that for every $\delta > 0$, there is some x such that $|x - c| < \delta$ and yet $|f(x) - k| \geq \epsilon$.   #

The virtues of the compact notation will be obvious to anyone who writes out the definition of a limit using the conventional logical notation.

In this section we have described ways in which quantifiers and logical operators interact with each other. These interactions are often subtle, and dealing with them requires some care, but a facility with them is invaluable in the construction of sound mathematical arguments.

Problems: Section 1.3

1. Let $P(x, y, z)$ denote $xy = z$;
    $E(x, y)$ denote $x = y$; and
    $G(x, y)$ denote $x > y$.
   Let the universe of discourse be the integers. Transcribe the following into logical notation.
   (a) If $y = 1$, then $xy = x$ for any x.
   (b) If $xy \neq 0$, then $x \neq 0$ and $y \neq 0$.
   (c) If $xy = 0$, then $x = 0$ or $y = 0$.
   (d) $3x = 6$ if and only if $x = 2$.
   (e) There is no solution to $x^2 = y$ unless $y \geq 0$.
   (f) $x < z$ is a necessary condition for $x < y$ and $y < z$.
   (g) $x \leq y$ and $y \leq x$ is a sufficient condition for $y = x$.
   (h) If $x < y$ and $z < 0$, then $xz > yz$.
   (i) It cannot happen that $x = y$ and $x < y$.
   (j). If $x < y$ then for some z such that $z < 0$, $xz > yz$.
   (k) There is an x such that for every y and z, $xy = xz$.

2. Let the universe of discourse be the set of arithmetic assertions with predicates defined as follows:
    $P(x)$ denotes "x is provable"
    $T(x)$ denotes "x is true"
    $S(x)$ denotes "x is satisfiable"
    $D(x, y, z)$ denotes "z is the disjunction $x \vee y$"
   Translate the following assertions into English statements. Make your transcriptions as natural as possible, e.g.,

$$\forall w \ \forall x \ \forall y \ \forall z [[D(w, x, y) \ \wedge \ D(x, w, z) \ \wedge \ P(y)] \Rightarrow P(z)]$$

becomes "If y is the assertion $w \lor x$, z is the assertion $x \lor w$ and y is provable, then z is provable."

   (a) $\forall x[P(x) \Rightarrow T(x)]$

   (b) $\forall x[T(x) \lor \neg S(x)]$

   (c) $\exists x[T(x) \land \neg P(x)]$

   (d) $\forall x \, \forall y \, \forall z\{[D(x, y, z) \land P(z)] \Rightarrow [P(x) \lor P(y)]\}$

   (e) $\forall x\{T(x) \Rightarrow \forall y \, \forall z[D(x, y, z) \Rightarrow T(z)]\}$

3. Put the following into logical notation. Choose predicates so that each assertion requires at least one quantifier.

   (a) There is one and only one even prime.

   (b) No odd numbers are even.

   (c) Every train is faster than some cars.

   (d) Some cars are slower than all trains but at least one train is faster than every car.

   (e) If it rains tomorrow, then somebody will get wet.

4. Find an assertion which is logically equivalent to $\forall x P(x)$ but uses only the quantifier $\exists$ and the logical operator $\neg$. Similarly, express $\exists x P(x)$ in terms of $\forall$ and $\neg$.

5. Find an assertion which is logically equivalent to $\exists ! x P(x)$ but which uses only the quantifiers $\forall$ and $\exists$ together with the predicate for equality and logical operators.

6. Show that the following propositions are valid.

   (a) $[\forall x P(x) \Rightarrow Q] \Leftrightarrow [\exists x[P(x) \Rightarrow Q]]$

   (b) $\forall x[P \Rightarrow Q(x)] \Leftrightarrow [P \Rightarrow \forall x Q(x)]$

7. For the following assertions, establish those which are true and find interpretations for P and Q which provide counterexamples for those which are false.

   (a) $\forall x[P(x) \Rightarrow Q(x)] \Rightarrow [\forall x P(x) \Rightarrow \forall x Q(x)]$

   (b) $[\forall x P(x) \Rightarrow \forall x Q(x)] \Rightarrow \forall x[P(x) \Rightarrow Q(x)]$

   (c) $[\exists x P(x) \Rightarrow \forall x Q(x)] \Rightarrow \forall x[P(x) \Rightarrow Q(x)]$

   (d) $\forall x[P(x) \Rightarrow Q(x)] \Rightarrow [\exists x P(x) \Rightarrow \forall x Q(x)]$

8. (a) For a universe containing only the elements 0 and 1, expand

$$\exists x[P(x) \land Q(x)] \text{ and } [\exists x P(x) \land \exists x Q(x)]$$

into propositions involving $P(0)$, $P(1)$, ... etc., and without quantifiers. Rearrange the terms of this expansion to show

$$\exists x[P(x) \land Q(x)] \Rightarrow [\exists x P(x) \land \exists x Q(x)].$$

   (b) Show that the converse of the implication of part (a) is not valid.

   (c) For the same universe, show

$$\forall x[P(x) \Leftrightarrow Q(x)] \Rightarrow [\forall x P(x) \Leftrightarrow \forall x Q(x)].$$

   (d) Show that the converse of the implication of part (c) is not valid.

9. Show that the following are valid for the universe of natural numbers **N** either by expanding the statement or by applying identities.

   (a) $\forall x \, \forall y[P(x) \lor Q(y)] \Leftrightarrow [\forall x P(x) \lor \forall y Q(y)]$

   (b) $\exists x \, \exists y[P(x) \land Q(y)] \Rightarrow \exists x P(x)$

   (c) $\forall x \, \forall y[P(x) \land Q(y)] \Leftrightarrow [\forall x P(x) \land \forall y Q(y)]$

   (d) $\exists x \, \exists y[P(x) \Rightarrow P(y)] \Leftrightarrow [\forall x P(x) \Rightarrow \exists y P(y)]$

   (e) $\forall x \, \forall y[P(x) \Rightarrow Q(y)] \Leftrightarrow [\exists x P(x) \Rightarrow \forall y Q(y)]$

10. (a) Write out the definition of $\lim_{x \to c} f(x) = k$ in the usual logical notation rather than the compact notation used in the last example of this section.

    (b) Find the condition for $\lim_{x \to c} f(x) \neq k$ by forming the negation of both sides of the definition.

11. Let A be a two-dimensional integer array with 20 rows (indexed from 1 to 20) and 30 columns (indexed from 1 to 30). Using compact logical notation, make the following assertions. Assume the universe of discourse is the set of integers $\mathbf{I}$.

    (a) All entries of A are nonnegative.

    (b) All entries of the 4th and 15th rows are positive.

    (c) Some entries of A are zero.

    (d) The entries of A are sorted in row-major order (the entries are in order within rows, and every entry of the ith row is less than or equal to every entry of the $(i + 1)$st row).

1.4 LOGICAL INFERENCE

A *theorem* is a mathematical assertion which can be shown to be true. A *proof* is an argument which establishes the truth of a theorem. A mathematician will not usually accept an assertion as true unless he is convinced that a proof of the assertion can be constructed.

Mathematicians have long been concerned with the question of what constitutes a proof. Their work has resulted in the concept of a *formal mathematical system* in which the notions of axiom, theorem, and proof are precisely defined. Ideally, these systems would provide a formal basis for describing all rigorous mathematics. In fact, the systems are not powerful enough to describe either all mathematical systems or all the modes of argument which mathematicians use. Nevertheless, work in formal systems has increased our understanding of mathematical reasoning, and we will use the terminology of formal systems to describe the concepts of theorem and proof.

In the remaining sections of this chapter, we address the problem of formulating and constructing proofs. The novice in mathematics is often puzzled by the question of what constitutes a proof. When is an argument convincing? The question is not easily answered. In fact, mathematicians sometimes disagree among themselves as to whether an argument is sound. Their disagreement may be over whether to allow a particular proof technique, such as the use of the law of the excluded middle; such differences are essentially philosophical and, in some sense, unresolvable. Even when mathematicians can agree on the acceptablilty of a proof technique, disagreement sometimes occurs when a purported proof is thought to contain some error of commission or omission. The existence of such disagreements indicates the difficulty of constructing and evaluating proofs.

There are no general algorithms for deciding whether an assertion is true or false; if there were, mathematicians would use them. The construction of proofs is a craft, and while we can offer a modicum of advice, the skill can only be learned by means of examples and practice. The proofs which occur throughout this text are intended to serve both as convincing arguments and as models of proof techniques. The exercises are intended to provide practice in the construction of proofs.

A proof of an assertion is a sequence of statements which represents an argument that the theorem is true. Some of the assertions which occur in a proof may be known to be true *a priori*; these include axioms or previously proved theorems. Other assertions may be hypotheses of the theorem, assumed to be true in the argument. Finally, some assertions may be inferred from other assertions which occurred earlier in the proof. Thus, to construct proofs, we need a means of drawing conclusions or deriving new assertions from old ones. This is done using *rules of inference*. Rules of inference specify conclusions which can be drawn from assertions known or assumed to be true.

Perhaps the most fundamental rules of inference are those which permit substitutions. Thus, we are generally allowed to replace any expression in an assertion by another expression which is equivalent to it; we consider the new assertion to be true if and only if the original assertion was true. We learn this rule of inference at an early age; it is sometimes expressed as "equals can be substituted for equals." Other rules governing substitution are commonly used in mathematics, and we will apply them freely without explicitly stating them. For example, if S is a tautology in which propositional variables occur, substitution of propositions for the propositional variables in the usual way results in a new tautology.

Another rule of inference can be stated as follows: If it is known that a statement P is true, and also that the statement $P \Rightarrow Q$ is true, then we can conclude that the statement Q is true.

Example

> Suppose we know "Samson is strong" and "If Samson is strong, then it will take a woman to do him in." We can conclude "It will take a woman to do Samson in."

$$\#$$

This rule of inference is called *modus ponens*; it is often presented in the form of an *argument* as follows:

$$P$$
$$\underline{P \Rightarrow Q}$$
$$\therefore Q$$

In such a tabular presentation of an argument, the assertions above the horizontal line are called *hypotheses* or *premises*; the assertion below the line is the *conclusion*. The symbol $\therefore$ is read "therefore" or "it follows that," or "hence." An argument is said to be *valid* if, whenever all the premises are true, the conclusion is true. A rule of inference is an argument form which is taken to be valid in the same sense that an axiom is taken to be true.

The rule of inference known as *modus ponens* is related to the tautology $[P \wedge (P \Rightarrow Q)] \Rightarrow Q$ in the language of propositions. Other rules of inference have similar interpretations; we have listed some of the most important rules of inference in Table 1.4.1.

Table 1.4.1 RULES OF INFERENCE RELATED TO THE LANGUAGE OF PROPOSITIONS

Rule of Inference	Tautological Form	Name
$\dfrac{P}{\therefore P \vee Q}$	$P \Rightarrow (P \vee Q)$	addition
$\dfrac{P \wedge Q}{\therefore P}$	$(P \wedge Q) \Rightarrow P$	simplification
$\dfrac{\begin{array}{c}P\\P \Rightarrow Q\end{array}}{\therefore Q}$	$[P \wedge (P \Rightarrow Q)] \Rightarrow Q$	*modus ponens*
$\dfrac{\begin{array}{c}\neg Q\\P \Rightarrow Q\end{array}}{\therefore \neg P}$	$[\neg Q \wedge (P \Rightarrow Q)] \Rightarrow \neg P$	*modus tollens*
$\dfrac{\begin{array}{c}P \vee Q\\\neg P\end{array}}{\therefore Q}$	$[(P \vee Q) \wedge \neg P] \Rightarrow Q$	disjunctive syllogism
$\dfrac{\begin{array}{c}P \Rightarrow Q\\Q \Rightarrow R\end{array}}{\therefore P \Rightarrow R}$	$[(P \Rightarrow Q) \wedge (Q \Rightarrow R)] \Rightarrow [P \Rightarrow R]$	hypothetical syllogism
$\dfrac{\begin{array}{c}P\\Q\end{array}}{\therefore P \wedge Q}$		conjunction
$\dfrac{\begin{array}{c}(P \Rightarrow Q) \wedge (R \Rightarrow S)\\P \vee R\end{array}}{\therefore Q \vee S}$	$[(P \Rightarrow Q) \wedge (R \Rightarrow S) \wedge (P \vee R)] \Rightarrow [Q \vee S]$	constructive dilemma
$\dfrac{\begin{array}{c}(P \Rightarrow Q) \wedge (R \Rightarrow S)\\\neg Q \vee \neg S\end{array}}{\therefore \neg P \vee \neg R}$	$[(P \Rightarrow Q) \wedge (R \Rightarrow S) \wedge (\neg Q \vee \neg S)] \Rightarrow [\neg P \vee \neg R]$	destructive dilemma

Examples

Fallacious arguments are often the result of incorrect inferences. Here we present some examples of common fallacies.

(a) *The Fallacy of Affirming the Consequent*
Consider the following argument:

> If the butler did it, he will be nervous when he is interrogated.
> The butler was very nervous when he was interrogated.
> Therefore, the butler did it.

Presented in the form of our rules of inference, this argument can be presented as follows:

$$\frac{\begin{array}{c}P \Rightarrow Q\\Q\end{array}}{\therefore P}$$

The argument is not correct because the conclusion P can be false even though the hypotheses $P \Rightarrow Q$ and Q are true; i.e., the assertion $[(P \Rightarrow Q) \wedge Q] \Rightarrow P$ is not a tautology: the source of the butler's discomfort may not have been guilt but rather the behavior of the stock market on the day that he was questioned.

(b) *The Fallacy of Denying the Antecedent*
This form of fallacious argument can be represented as

$$P \Rightarrow Q$$
$$\neg P$$
$$\therefore \neg Q$$

The following example illustrates the fallacy:

If the butler's hands are covered with blood, then he did it.
The butler is impeccably groomed.
Therefore, the butler is innocent.

The argument ignores the compulsive cleanliness of the butler, who always washes his hands immediately after committing a crime. From $P \Rightarrow Q$ and $\neg P$, one can conclude neither Q nor $\neg Q$. #

The following example illustrates the correct application of some of the rules of inference given in Table 1.4.1.

Example

Consider the following argument:

If horses fly or cows eat artichokes, then the mosquito is the national bird. If the mosquito is the national bird, then peanut butter tastes good on hot dogs. But peanut butter tastes terrible on hot dogs. Therefore, cows don't eat artichokes.

The first three assertions are the hypotheses of the argument; the last assertion is the conclusion. We are asked to determine whether the truth of the conclusion is implied by the truth of the hypotheses. We begin by representing the component propositions as follows:

F denotes the proposition "horses fly";
A denotes the proposition "cows eat artichokes";
M denotes the proposition "the mosquito is the national bird";
P denotes the proposition "peanut butter tastes good on hot dogs."

The argument can be represented as follows:

1. $(F \vee A) \Rightarrow M$

2. $M \Rightarrow P$

3. $\neg P$

$\therefore$ $\quad \neg A$

Assertions 1, 2, and 3 are the hypotheses, and 4 is the conclusion. One way to test whether the conclusion is implied by the hypotheses is to construct a truth table for the implication which has the conjunction of the hypotheses as its antecedent and the conclusion as its consequent; in the present case this is the implication

$$\{[(F \lor A) \Rightarrow M] \land (M \Rightarrow P) \land \neg P\} \Rightarrow (\neg A).$$

If the implication is a tautology, then we say the conclusion follows logically from the hypotheses and hence the argument is valid. If the implication is a contingency or contradiction, then the conclusion $\neg A$ may be false even though all the hypotheses are true. (An assignment of truth values for the propositional variables which makes the implication false is called a "disproof by counterexample"; we will discuss this in more detail in the following section.)

When several hypotheses and propositional variables are involved, construction of a truth table can become unwieldy. An alternative way to show an argument is valid is to construct a proof using the hypotheses, logical identities, and rules of inference. A proof is an expansion of the argument in which the hypotheses are augmented by additional assertions such as axioms, previously proved theorems, or assertions obtained by applying rules of inference. The conclusion of the argument must be shown to follow from these assertions by a rule of inference. The following is a proof of the argument given above.

Proof:

Assertion	Reasons
1. $(F \lor A) \Rightarrow M$	Hypothesis 1
2. $M \Rightarrow P$	Hypothesis 2
3. $(F \lor A) \Rightarrow P$	Steps 1 and 2 and hypothetical syllogism
4. $\neg P$	Hypothesis 3
5. $\neg(F \lor A)$	Steps 3 and 4 and *modus tollens*
6. $\neg F \land \neg A$	Step 5 and DeMorgan's law (identity 7, Table 1.1.1)
7. $\neg A \land \neg F$	Step 6 and commutativity of $\land$ (identity 4, Table 1.1.1)
8. $\neg A$	Step 7 and simplification

Each assertion of the proof is considered true, either because it is a hypothesis, or because it is known to be logically equivalent to a preceding assertion of the proof, or because it is obtained by applying a rule of inference to preceding assertions of the proof. Since the last assertion of the proof is the conclusion, it follows that if the hypotheses are true, then the conclusion is true.   #

Additional rules of inference are necessary to prove assertions involving predicates and quantifiers. A careful treatment of these rules is beyond our scope, but we will illustrate some of the techniques. The following four rules describe when the universal and existential quantifiers can be added to or deleted from an assertion.

The first rule is known as *universal instantiation*; it may be represented as follows:

$$\frac{\forall x P(x)}{\therefore \quad P(c)}$$

where P is a predicate and c is some arbitrary element of the universe of discourse. As an example of the use of this rule, let the universe be the set of all humans, and let $P(x)$ denote "x is mortal." If we can establish $\forall x P(x)$, that is, "all men are mortal," then the rule of universal instantiation permits us to conclude, "Socrates is mortal."

A second rule of inference, known as *universal generalization*, permits the universal quantification of assertions. If we can show that the assertion $P(c)$ holds for every element c of the universe of discourse, then universal generalization allows us to conclude that the universally quantified assertion $\forall x P(x)$ holds. Thus, the rule of inference

$$\frac{P(x)}{\therefore \forall x P(x)}$$

can be applied if we can show that the hypothesis $P(x)$ is true for every possible value of x.

The third rule of inference is known as *existential instantiation*. It takes the form

$$\frac{\exists x P(x)}{\therefore P(c)}$$

where c is some element of the universe of discourse. However, the element c is not arbitrary (as it was in the case of universal instantiation), but must be one for which $P(c)$ is true. It follows from the truth of $\exists x P(x)$ that at least one such element must exist, but nothing more is guaranteed. This places constraints on the proper use of this rule of inference. For example, if we know that $\exists x P(x)$ and $\exists x Q(x)$ are true, we can conclude that the statement $P(c) \land Q(d)$ is true for some choice of c and d, but we cannot conclude that $P(c) \land Q(c)$ is true. For suppose $P(x)$ represents "x is even" and $Q(x)$ represents "x is odd" in the universe of integers. Then $\exists x P(x)$ and $\exists x Q(x)$ are true, but $P(c) \land Q(c)$ is false for every c.

The last rule of inference we will describe is known as *existential generalization*. It is represented as

$$\frac{P(c)}{\therefore \exists x P(x)}$$

where c is an element of the universe. This rule asserts that if $P(c)$ is true for some element c, then the assertion $\exists x P(x)$ is true.

When quantifiers are involved, construction of proofs is more involved because of the care required in the application of the rules of inference. An exploration of the subtleties of proofs involving quantifiers is beyond the scope of this chapter, but the following simple example will illustrate the application of some of the rules of inference.

Example

Consider the following argument:
Every man has two legs. John Smith is a man.
Hence, John Smith has two legs.

Let $M(x)$ denote the assertion "x is a man,"
$L(x)$ denote the assertion "x has two legs," and
J denote John Smith.
Expressed in logical notation, the argument is
1. $\forall x[M(x) \Rightarrow L(x)]$
2. $M(J)$

$\therefore$3. $L(J)$

A formal proof is as follows:

Assertion	Reasons
1. $\forall x[M(x) \Rightarrow L(x)]$	Hypothesis 1
2. $M(J) \Rightarrow L(J)$	Step 1 and universal instantiation
3. $M(J)$	Hypothesis 2
4. $L(J)$	Steps 2 and 3 and *modus ponens* ■ #

In this section we have dealt with the problem of logical inference, i.e., inferring the truth of one statement from the known or assumed truth of others. A rule of inference is an explicit statement of when such an inference can be made. We commonly apply rules of inference in mathematical arguments without explicit reference to them; this is one reason why mathematical arguments are sometimes difficult to follow. By treating these rules explicitly, we aim to provide a basis for the understanding, construction, and description of mathematical arguments.

Problems: Section 1.4

1. For each of the following sets of premises, list the relevant conclusions which can be drawn and the rules of inference used in each case.
   (a) I'm either fat or thin. I'm certainly not thin.
   (b) If I run I get out of breath. I'm not out of breath.
   (c) If the butler did it, then his hands are dirty. The butler's hands are dirty.
   (d) Blue skies make me happy and gray skies make me sad. The sky is either blue or gray.
   (e) If my program runs, then I am happy. If I am happy, the sun shines. It's 11:00 p.m. and very dark.
   (f) All trigonometric functions are periodic functions and all periodic functions are continuous functions.
   (g) All cows are mammals. Some mammals chew their cud.
   (h) All even integers are divisible by 2. The integer 4 is even but 3 is not.
   (i) What's good for the auto industry is good for the country. What's good for the country is good for you. What's good for the auto industry is for you to buy an expensive car.

2. Show that the tautological form of the following rules of inferences given in Table 1.4.1 are tautologies:
   (a) *modus tollens*
   (b) disjunctive syllogism
   (c) constructive dilemma
   (d) destructive dilemma

3. Construct a proof for each of the following arguments, giving all necessary additional assertions. Specify the rules of inference used at each step. (The word "or" denotes the "logical or" rather than the "exclusive or.")
   (a) It is not the case that IBM or Xerox will take over the copier market. If RCA returns to the computer market, then IBM will take over the copier market. Hence, RCA will not return to the computer market.
   (b) (My program runs successfully) or (the system bombs and I blow my stack). Furthermore, (the system does not bomb) or (I don't blow my stack and my program runs successfully). Therefore, my program runs successfully.

4. Supply the missing assertions to prove the following argument. Justify the inclusion of each assertion in the proof.

$$(P \land Q) \Rightarrow (R \land S)$$
$$(T \Rightarrow Q) \land (S \Rightarrow U)$$
$$(W \Rightarrow P) \land (T \Rightarrow U)$$
$$\underline{\neg R}$$
$$\therefore W \Rightarrow \neg T$$

5. Determine which of the following arguments are valid. Construct proofs for the valid arguments. For those which are not valid, show why the conclusion does not follow from the hypotheses.

(a) $A \land B$
   $\underline{A \Rightarrow C}$
   $\therefore C \land B$

(b) $A \lor B$
   $\underline{A \Rightarrow C}$
   $\therefore C \lor B$

(c) $A \Rightarrow B$
   $\underline{A \Rightarrow C}$
   $\therefore C \Rightarrow B$

(d) $A \Rightarrow (B \lor C)$
   $D \Rightarrow \neg C$
   $B \Rightarrow \neg A$
   A
   $\underline{D}$
   $\therefore B \land \neg B$

6. Determine which of the following are valid arguments. Construct proofs for those that are valid and describe the fallacies of those that are not.
   (a) If today is Tuesday, then I have a test in Computer Science or a test in Econ. If my Econ professor is sick, then I will not have a test in Econ. Today is Tuesday and my Econ professor is sick. Therefore, I have a test in Computer Science.
   (b) I am happy if my program runs. My happiness is a necessary condition for me to enjoy life. Hence, if my program runs, then, if I enjoy life, then I am happy.
   (c) It is not the case that some trigonometric functions are not periodic. Some periodic functions are continuous. Therefore, it is not true that all trigonometric functions are not continuous.
   (d) Some trigonometric functions are periodic. Some periodic functions are continuous. Therefore, some trigonometric functions are continuous.

7. Consider the implication

$$\forall x[P(x) \lor Q(x)] \Rightarrow [\forall x P(x) \lor \forall x Q x].$$

(a) Show that this implication is not valid.

(b) The following is an argument which purports to prove the above implication. Find and explain the flaw.

$$\forall x[P(x) \lor Q(x)] \Leftrightarrow \neg \exists x \neg [P(x) \lor Q(x)]$$

$$\Leftrightarrow \neg \exists x[\neg P(x) \land \neg Q(x)]$$

$$\Rightarrow \neg[\exists x \neg P(x) \land \exists x \neg Q(x)]$$

$$\Leftrightarrow [\neg \exists x \neg P(x) \lor \neg \exists x \neg Q(x)]$$

$$\Leftrightarrow \forall x P(x) \lor \forall x Q(x)$$

8. One must exercise care in the application of rules of inference to avoid fallacious conclusions. In the following argument, locate and explain all misapplications of rules of inference.

Let the universe of discourse be the set of integers **I**. The assertion that there is no smallest integer can be put into logical notation as follows:

$$\forall x \, \exists y[x > y].$$

It follows universal instantiation that for arbitrary d,

$$\exists y[d > y].$$

Now applying existential instantiation we conclude that for some element c

$$d > c.$$

Since d was arbitrary it follows by universal generalization that

$$\forall x[x > c].$$

By universal instantiation, we can conclude

$$c > c,$$

and by universal generalization,

$$\forall x[x > x].$$

1.5 METHODS OF PROOF

In the preceding section, we described the use of rules of inference to infer the truth of one assertion from others. Rules of inference are characterizations of the syntactic constraints which a proof must obey; in a formal mathematical system, where the structure of proofs is precisely specified, the rules of inference enable us to determine if an argument is a proof. In this section, we are concerned with the structure of proofs as well as strategies for their construction. Although it is not possible to consider all proof techniques, we will describe some of the most common ones, give examples of their use, and relate them to the rules of inference described in the previous section.

The most elementary form of theorem is the tautology. A tautology is a theorem because of its sentential structure rather than its content; its truth is actually independent of the interpretation or meaning of any of the propositions involved. For this reason, tautologies are easily proved: one need only construct a truth table.

Example

Consider the universe of integers. Denote by $E(x)$ the assertion "x is even" and by $O(x)$ the assertion "x is not even"; i.e., $O(x) \Leftrightarrow \neg E(x)$. If we read $O(x)$ as "x is odd," then we can prove the theorem

The integer 3 is either even or odd.

The theorem is stated as

$$E(3) \lor O(3),$$

or alternatively

$$E(3) \lor \neg E(3),$$

which, if we use the letter P to denote $E(3)$, can be written

$$P \lor \neg P.$$

From the truth table of the proposition $P \lor \neg P$, we know it is a tautology, and the theorem is established.   #

A theorem is often expressed as a propositional form which is not a tautology. The truth of such an assertion is dependent on both the logical structure of the assertion and the meaning of the component propositions. Because the component propositions cannot assume all possible truth values, certain lines of the truth table cannot occur; the theorem is proved by showing that all the lines which can occur result in a value of *true*. We will treat such theorems by considering the most important of the logical operators.

Let T be an assertion of the form $\neg P$, where P is a proposition. In order to prove T, we must establish that P is false. Similarly, if T is of the form $P \land Q$, then we must show that both P and Q are true. An assertion of the form $P \lor Q$ is often established by proving the logically equivalent proposition $\neg P \Rightarrow Q$ (or, by symmetry, $\neg Q \Rightarrow P$). A truth table can be used to show the logical equivalence of $P \lor Q$ and $\neg P \Rightarrow Q$.

A variety of proof techniques are used for proving implications, and because these techniques are so common, they are frequently referred to by name. Recall that the truth table for $P \Rightarrow Q$ has the following form:

P	Q	$P \Rightarrow Q$
0	0	1
0	1	1
1	0	0
1	1	1

The four most common techniques for proving implications are the following:

1. *Vacuous Proof of $P \Rightarrow Q$*
    The truth value of $P \Rightarrow Q$ is *true* if that of P is *false*. Consequently, if we can establish that P is false, only the first two lines of the above truth

table can possibly apply, and it follows that the assertion $P \Rightarrow Q$ is true. A *vacuous proof* of $P \Rightarrow Q$ is constructed by establishing that the truth value of P is *false*.

While vacuous proofs appear to be of little value, they are often important in establishing limiting or special cases. We will point out many examples of vacuous proofs in the next chapter.

2. *Trivial Proof of $P \Rightarrow Q$*

If it is possible to establish that Q is true, only the second and fourth lines of the truth table for implication can apply, and it follows that the theorem $P \Rightarrow Q$ is true. Construction of a *trivial proof* of $P \Rightarrow Q$ requires showing that the truth value of Q is *true*.

Like the vacuous proof, the trivial proof has limited applicability and yet is extremely important. It is frequently used to establish special cases of assertions.

3. *Direct Proof of $P \Rightarrow Q$*

A *direct proof* of $P \Rightarrow Q$ shows that the truth of Q follows logically from the truth of P, i.e., the third line of the truth table for implication cannot hold. Such a proof begins by assuming P is true. Then, using whatever information is available, such as previously proved theorems, it is shown that Q must be true. Since all the lines of the truth table except the third have the value *true* assigned to $P \Rightarrow Q$, the assertion is established.

The following examples illustrate the use of direct proofs.

Examples

(a)   **Theorem:** If $6x + 9y = 101$, then either x or y is not an integer.

   Proof: Assume $6x + 9y = 101$. This can be rewritten as $3(2x + 3y) = 101$. But $101/3$ is not an integer; therefore, $2x + 3y$ is not an integer and hence either x or y is not an integer. ∎

(b)   **Theorem:** Let S be a set of one- and two-digit integers such that each of the digits 0 through 9 occurs exactly once in the set S. Then the sum of the elements of S is divisible by 9.

   Proof: Assume that the hypothesis of the theorem is true. The digits 0 through 9 sum to 45. In any set S, some of the digits will occur in the 10's position and the remainder will occur in the 1's position. Let T denote the sum of digits which occur in the 10's position. Then the sum of the elements of S can be expressed as $10T + 45 - T$, which can be put in the form $9T + 45$. Since both terms of this sum are divisible by 9, the sum is also divisible by 9, regardless of the value of T. ∎   #

4. *Indirect Proof of $P \Rightarrow Q$* (Proof of the contrapositive)

The implication $P \Rightarrow Q$ is logically equivalent to the implication $\neg Q \Rightarrow \neg P$. Consequently, we can establish the truth of $P \Rightarrow Q$ by establishing that $\neg Q \Rightarrow \neg P$. The latter implication is usually shown by means of a direct proof, i.e., by showing that if Q is false, then P is necessarily false. Hence, the third line of the truth table for $P \Rightarrow Q$ cannot occur.

Example

A *perfect number* is an integer which is equal to the sum of all its divisors except the number itself. Thus, 6 is a perfect number, since $6 = 1 + 2 + 3$, and so is 28. We will prove the following theorem by establishing the contrapositive.

Theorem: A perfect number is not a prime.

Proof: The contrapositive is the following: A prime number is not a perfect number. Suppose p is a prime number. Then $p \geq 2$ and p has exactly two divisors: 1 and p. The sum of all its divisors less than p is therefore 1, and it follows that p is not perfect.   ∎   #

In summary, to establish $P \Rightarrow Q$ by a proof of the contrapositive,

1. Assume that Q is false;
2. Show on the basis of that assumption and other available information that P is false.

If the premise is a conjunction and we wish to show

$$(P_1 \wedge P_2 \wedge \cdots \wedge P_n) \Rightarrow Q,$$

the contrapositive of the assertion is

$$\neg Q \Rightarrow (\neg P_1 \vee \neg P_2 \vee \cdots \vee \neg P_n).$$

To establish this assertion, it suffices to show that $\neg Q$ implies $\neg P_i$ for at least one value of i.

We frequently wish to establish implications of the form

$$(P_1 \vee P_2 \vee \cdots \vee P_n) \Rightarrow Q.$$

These implications are usually handled using a technique called *proof by cases*, a method justified by the following tautology:

$$[(P_1 \vee P_2 \vee \cdots \vee P_n) \Rightarrow Q] \Leftrightarrow [(P_1 \Rightarrow Q) \wedge (P_2 \Rightarrow Q) \wedge \cdots \wedge (P_n \Rightarrow Q)]$$

A proof by cases requires proving each "case," $P_i \Rightarrow Q$, for each i from 1 to n. Often proofs by cases are not presented in full; if several of the implications, $P_i \Rightarrow Q$, have similar proofs, then usually only one case is treated explicitly.

Example

Let "$\sqcup$" denote the operation "max" on the set of integers $\mathbf{I}$; if $a \geq b$ then $a \sqcup b = b \sqcup a = a$. For example, $4 \sqcup 2 = 4$ and $1 \sqcup 3 = 3$.

Theorem: The binary operation "max" is associative; that is, for any integers a, b, and c, $(a \sqcup b) \sqcup c = a \sqcup (b \sqcup c)$.

Proof: For any three integers a, b and c, one of the following six cases must hold: $a \geq b \geq c, a \geq c \geq b, b \geq a \geq c, b \geq c \geq a, c \geq a \geq b$ or $c \geq b \geq a$.

Case 1:   Assume $a \geq b \geq c$. Then $(a \sqcup b) \sqcup c = a \sqcup c = a$ and
$a \sqcup (b \sqcup c) = a \sqcup b = a$.

Case 2:   Assume $a \geq c \geq b$. Then $(a \sqcup b) \sqcup c = a \sqcup c = a$ and
$a \sqcup (b \sqcup c) = a \sqcup c = a$.

There are four other cases; the proofs are all similar.   ∎   #

The last logical operator we will consider is logical equivalence. Theorems of the form $P \Leftrightarrow Q$ are usually handled in one of two ways. Most commonly, the separate implications $P \Rightarrow Q$ and $Q \Rightarrow P$ are proven and the assertion $P \Leftrightarrow Q$ is inferred. Sometimes a more economical proof is possible, beginning with a true assertion of the form $R \Leftrightarrow S$ and proceeding through a sequence of "if and only if" statements such that each statement is logically equivalent to the one preceding. If the last statement in the sequence is $P \Leftrightarrow Q$, the theorem is established. This technique will be used frequently in the next chapter.

Other proof techniques can be used to establish the truth of a proposition P. A *proof by contradiction*, or *reductio ad absurdum*, assumes that P is false and derives a contradiction, such as the proposition $Q \wedge \neg Q$; this establishes $\neg P \Rightarrow (Q \wedge \neg Q)$. Taking the contrapositive of this implication and applying one of DeMorgan's laws, we obtain $(\neg Q \vee Q) \Rightarrow P$. Since the premise of this implication is true and we have shown the implication to be true, we conclude that P is true.

Examples

(a) **Theorem:** There is no largest prime number.

The proof is by contradiction; we begin by assuming that a largest prime number exists, and then show how to construct another which is larger.

Proof: Assume a largest prime exists; call it p. Because all primes are greater than 1 and none are greater than p, there must be a finite number of them. Form the product of all these primes and call it r; $r = 2 \cdot 3 \cdot 5 \cdot 7 \cdot \ldots \cdot p$. We now assert that $r + 1$ is a prime. For if we divide $r + 1$ by any prime between 2 and p, the remainder is 1, which means that $r + 1$ cannot be expressed as a product of any two integers other than $r + 1$ and 1. Since $r > p$, $r + 1$ is a prime number greater than p. This contradicts the assumption that p is the largest prime number, and the theorem is proved. ∎

The logical structure of the preceding proof can be described as follows. Let P denote "there is no largest prime number," and Q denote "p is the largest prime number." The proof proceeds by assuming the theorem is false:

(i) $\neg P$

It follows that (for some particular integer p),

(ii) $\neg P \Rightarrow Q$

We then show how to construct a prime greater than p, i.e., we show

(iii) $Q \Rightarrow \neg Q$

From (ii) and (iii), applying the rule of hypothetical syllogism, we conclude

(iv) $\neg P \Rightarrow \neg Q$

From (i) and (ii) and *modus ponens*, it follows that

(v) Q

and from (i) and (iv) and *modus ponens*,

(vi) $\neg Q$

Then from the rule of conjunction applied to (v) and (vi), we conclude

(vii) $Q \wedge \neg Q$

This is a contradiction. We conclude that the hypothesis (i) is false and the theorem is proved.

(b)   Consider the problem of determining whether a program P will terminate normally, i.e., not as the result of such things as exceeding its allotted execution time or register overflow. It is conceivable that a computer program could be written which would decide, for any program P, whether P will halt; such a program would be a "decision procedure" to solve what is known as the *halting problem*. We can show by means of a proof by contradiction that no procedure exists which will solve the halting problem.

For ease of exposition, we restrict our discussion to procedures which do not read any input, although they may call other procedures. This corresponds to a subproblem of the original problem; if we cannot devise a decision procedure for the input-free procedures, then we clearly cannot devise one for arbitrary procedures. Let P be an input-free procedure. We assume (as a hypothesis to be proved false) that there exists a decision procedure HALT such that the value of HALT(P) is "yes" if the procedure P halts and otherwise the value of HALT(P) is "no." Then the following procedure could be executed†:

```
procedure ABSURD:
if HALT(ABSURD) = "yes" then
    while true do print "ha"
```

Now consider the behavior of the procedure ABSURD.

Suppose ABSURD halts. Then HALT(ABSURD) will return "yes" causing execution of the *while* loop. The *while* loop prints "ha" as long as *true* has the truth value *true*; thus, execution of the *while* loop results in (unending) gales of laughter. We conclude that if ABSURD halts, then ABSURD does not halt.

Now suppose ABSURD does not halt. Then HALT will return "no," causing the test of the *if-then* statement to fail, and ABSURD will halt. Thus, if ABSURD does not halt, then ABSURD will halt.

The assumption that HALT can decide whether an arbitrary program P terminates has led to an absurdity, and we conclude that no procedure has the behavior assumed for HALT. Note that we do not infer that it would be very difficult to write HALT, or that we don't know how to write it; we conclude the much stronger statement that no procedure exists which has the behavior ascribed to HALT.   #

The proof methods described so far are often inadequate for proving quantified assertions. We now describe some additional proof techniques based on the rules of inference for quantified statements. We will discuss techniques for proving assertions in each of the following forms:

$$\neg \exists x P(x), \ \exists x P(x), \ \neg \forall x P(x), \text{ and } \forall x P(x).$$

An assertion of the form $\neg \exists x P(x)$ is most often proved by contradiction: to show something does not exist, we assume it does and arrive at a contradiction.

---

†This program and those in the remainder of the book will be written in an informal ALGOL-like language described in the Appendix.

This technique was used in our earlier proof that there is no largest prime number; we assumed there was a largest prime and derived a contradiction of the form $Q \wedge \neg Q$. We also note that $\neg \exists x P(x)$ is equivalent to $\forall x \neg P(x)$. Hence, our later remarks on proving universally quantified statements will sometimes apply.

Proofs of assertions of the form $\exists x P(x)$ are referred to as *existence* proofs. Existence proofs are classified as either *constructive* or *nonconstructive*. A constructive existence proof establishes the assertion by exhibiting a value c such that $P(c)$ is true. By applying the rule of existential generalization, we conclude that $\exists x P(x)$ is true. Sometimes, rather than exhibiting a specific value of c, a constructive existence proof specifies an algorithm for obtaining such a value.

A nonconstructive existence proof establishes the assertion $\exists x P(x)$ without indicating how to find a value c such that $P(c)$ is true. Such a proof most commonly involves a proof by contradiction; it shows that $\neg \exists x P(x)$ implies an absurdity or the negation of some previous result.

A constructive existence proof specifies an element precisely, while a nonconstructive proof may not provide any information other than an assertion of existence. Some results in mathematics fall between these two extremes. For example, the mean value theorem of differential calculus asserts the existence of a parameter value with a special property. Although the proof places bounds on the parameter value (and thus provides useful information), the exact value of the parameter is not specified. Theorems of this character are common in numerical analysis.

Assertions of the form $\neg \forall x P(x)$ are often most naturally proved by proving the equivalent assertion $\exists x \neg P(x)$. Both constructive and nonconstructive existence proofs can then be used. A constructive existence proof involves finding an element c of the universe of discourse such that $P(c)$ is false; such an element is called a *counterexample* to the assertion $\forall x P(x)$. The element c forms the basis of a *proof by counterexample* of the assertion $\neg \forall x P(x)$.

Counterexamples can also be used to show that assertions involving predicate variables are not valid. Construction of such a counterexample requires that we exhibit a universe of discourse and an interpretation of the predicate variables which makes the assertion false.

Example

Construct a counterexample to show the following assertion is not valid:

$$\exists x[P(x) \Rightarrow Q(x)] \Rightarrow [\exists x P(x) \Rightarrow \exists x Q(x)].$$

A disproof requires that we exhibit a universe and predicates P and Q such that the assertion is false; to disprove the above assertion we must find a universe and interpretations for predicates P and Q such that

(a) $\exists x[P(x) \Rightarrow Q(x)]$ is true and

(b) $\exists x P(x) \Rightarrow \exists x Q(x)$ is false.

From (b) it must happen that

(c) $\exists x P(x)$ is true and

(d) $\exists x Q(x)$ is false.

Let the universe consist of the integers 1 and 2, and let $P(x)$ denote "$x = 1$" and $Q(x)$ denote "$x \neq 1 \ \wedge \ x \neq 2$." With these predicates, the conditions of (a) through (d) are satisfied; consequently, these choices of universe and interpretations for P and Q constitute a counterexample to the assertion. #

A universally quantified assertion, $\forall x P(x)$, is generally proved by applying the rule of universal generalization described in the previous section. We first show that $P(x)$ is true for an arbitrary element x of the universe. Once this has been established, the rule of universal generalization can be applied to conclude $\forall x P(x)$.

Example

Theorem: For all integers x, x is even if and only if x^2 is even.

Proof: Using logical notation, the theorem can be expressed as

$$\forall x[x \text{ is even} \Leftrightarrow x^2 \text{ is even}].$$

We prove the theorem by first establishing

$$x \text{ is even} \Leftrightarrow x^2 \text{ is even}$$

for an arbitrary element x of the universe of discourse.

(a) First, we show the implication from left to right (the "only if" part, or "necessity") by a direct proof. If x is even, then $x = 2k$ for some integer k. Then $x^2 = (2k)^2 = 4k^2 = 2(2k^2)$, which is an even number.

(b) We next show the implication from right to left (the "if" part, or "sufficiency") by showing the contrapositive: x is not even $\Rightarrow x^2$ is not even. If x is not even, then $x = 2k + 1$ for some integer k, and $x^2 = (2k + 1)^2 = 4k^2 + 4k + 1$. Since the first two summands are even, the sum is odd and the contrapositive is established.

This completes the proof of

$$x \text{ is even} \Leftrightarrow x^2 \text{ is even}.$$

Since the proof was for arbitrary x, we can apply universal generalization to conclude that

$$\forall x(x \text{ is even} \Leftrightarrow x^2 \text{ is even}). \quad \blacksquare \quad \#$$

The forms of mathematical argument we have considered are common and widely accepted, but by no means exhaustive; indeed new proof techniques are still being devised. In future chapters we will develop additional proof techniques and apply them.

Our discussion of proof techniques has been "informal" in the sense that we have not worked within a formal system in which all axioms and rules of inference have been explicitly stated. The advantage of a formal system is that a characterization of the axioms and rules of inference implicitly defines the set of theorems: it is the set of all statements which can be obtained from the axioms by applying the rules of inference in all possible ways. In such a system it becomes possible to distinguish between assertions which are true and those which are provable. An assertion is *provable* if it is a theorem, i.e., if a proof of the assertion exists. (Note that the definition does not require that we be able to construct the proof.) The truth of an assertion may depend on the choice of universe of discourse and the interpretation of the predicates; we have seen examples of assertions which are true in some universes and not in others. Thus we can ask two things of a formal system:

(a) That it be powerful enough to prove all valid assertions, that is, all those assertions which are true regardless of the universe of discourse and the interpretation of the predicate symbols.

(b) That it be powerful enough to prove all assertions which are true of some particular universe with a specified interpretation of certain predicate symbols. An example would be the universe of natural numbers with predicates corresponding to equality and identities of arithmetic.

Without going into detail, we can say that mathematics has been rather successful with (a), but not with (b). It has been established that, to a considerable extent, our lack of success in (b) is inherent in our mathematical methods. For example, a result due to Gödel asserts that if a formal system is powerful enough to express assertions about integer arithmetic but permits only true assertions about arithmetic to be proved, then there are other assertions which are true of arithmetic but cannot be proved in the system.

The development of an understanding of the distinction between assertions which are true and those which are formally provable was a magnificent accomplishment of mathematics; the work has profound implications for both philosophy and mathematics. To explore further in this area, the student should consult the excellent book of DeLong [1970].

When an argument is presented within a formal system, whether it is a proof can be decided algorithmically, but formal systems do not encompass all of mathematics. When an argument is presented outside a formal system, as most proofs are, its validity must be determined by mathematicians; they must decide whether the argument is convincing. Thus, the question is usually decided by consensus; an argument is accepted as a proof if no one can perceive any flaws in its structure. Agreement in such matters is very good, but the mechanism is not foolproof. Although mathematical proofs are intended to be the quintessence of careful argument, perceiving the flaws of an alleged proof can be a profoundly difficult task. Examples exist of arguments which were widely accepted as proofs for many years but were then shown to be fallacious by someone who discovered a possibility which had been overlooked in the original argument. Sometimes such a discovery results in a new argument being devised, which is then accepted as a proof of the original assertion. But it is not uncommon for the overlooked possibility to provide a basis for a counterexample to the original assertion, thus disproving it. In summary, while a purported proof which is generally accepted is rarely shown to be fallacious, examples of such occurrences do exist, and we must conclude that "proof" is not a label which can never be removed.

Problems: Section 1.5

1. Prove or disprove each of the following assertions. Indicate the proof technique employed. Consider the universe to be the set of integers **I**. Put each assertion into logical notation. You may assume the following five definitions and properties of integers.

    (i)   An integer n is *even* if and only if $n = 2k$ for some integer k.
    (ii) An integer n is *odd* if and only if $n = 2k + 1$ for some integer k.
    (iii) The product of two nonzero integers is positive if and only if the integers have the same sign.
    (iv) For every pair of integers x and y, exactly one of the following holds: $x > y$, $x = y$, or $x < y$.
    (v)   If $x > y$, then $x - y$ is positive; if $x = y$, then $x - y = 0$; if $x < y$, then $x - y$ is negative.

    (a)   An integer is odd if its square is odd.
    (b)   The sum of two even integers is an even integer.
    (c)   The sum of an even integer and an odd integer is an odd integer.
    (d)   There are two odd integers whose sum is odd.
    (e)   The square of any integer is negative.
    (f)   There is some prime number whose square is even.
    (g)   There does not exist an integer x such that $x^2 + 1$ is negative.
    (h)   For any two integers x and y, either $x - y$ or $y - x$ is nonnegative.
    (i)   If $1 = 3$, then the square of any integer is negative.
    (j)   If $1 = 3$, then the square of any integer is positive.
    (k)   The sum of any two primes is a prime number.
    (l)   There exist two primes whose sum is prime.
    (m)   If the square of any integer is negative, then $1 = 1$.

2. Prove that the square root of 2 is irrational, that is, $\sqrt{2}$ cannot be expressed as a ratio of two integers. (Hint: Use the fact that x is even if x^2 is even to construct a proof by contradiction.)

3. Suppose we wish to show $(H_1 \land H_2 \land \cdots \land H_n) \Rightarrow Q$.
    A common proof method is to assume $\neg Q$ as an additional hypothesis and deduce a contradiction, i.e.,

    $$(H_1 \land H_2 \land \cdots \land H_n \land \neg Q) \Rightarrow C$$

    where C is a contradiction.

    Example

    > **Theorem:** Show that if P and $P \Rightarrow Q$ are true, then Q is true.
    >
    > *Proof:*

Assertion	Reasons
1. P	Premise 1
2. $P \Rightarrow Q$	Premise 2
3. $\neg Q$	Assumption (negation of conclusion)
4. $\neg P \lor Q$	2, implication
5. $\neg P$	3, 4, disjunctive syllogism
6. $P \land \neg P$	1, 5, conjunction

But $P \wedge \neg P$ is a contradiction. Therefore, Q follows logically from the hypotheses.

∎   #

(a)   Justify the above technique using truth tables (assume only two hypotheses H_1 and H_2).
(b)   Explain how this proof technique relates to proof by contradiction.

1.6 PROGRAM CORRECTNESS

Writing good computer programs is not a well-defined process, and criteria for the evaluation of programs are often vague and ill-formed. There are, however, three questions that are commonly used to assess the quality of a program:

(a)   Is the program "well written"?
(b)   Is the program efficient?
(c)   Does the program do what it is supposed to do?

The first question addresses the matters of style, clarity, and ease of modification; evaluation of these properties will probably always be difficult and, to some degree, subjective. The second question concerns the cost of program execution, usually measured in terms of storage requirements and program execution time; the study of program efficiency, often called *algorithm analysis*, will be treated in Chapter 5. To answer the third question, we must first specify precisely what task is to be performed. Then we must prove that the program is *correct* in the sense that it performs the specified task. Establishing that a program is correct, also known as *program verification*, is generally more difficult than writing the program, but the costs which result from an incorrect program can easily exceed the cost of verification. As a consequence, techniques for establishing program correctness are of singular importance to the computer scientist.

Most program errors can be classified as either syntactic or logical. A syntactic error is one which violates the definition of a well-formed program in the given programming language. Syntactic errors are generally detected by the language translator program (i.e., the compiler or interpreter) and can usually be corrected easily. After all syntactic errors have been eliminated, a program is usually tested for errors in logic by executing the program on a selected set of input data. But correct performance of a program on test data does not guarantee that the program is correct unless the program is tested with every possible input. Because it is usually impractical to test all possible inputs, logical errors may remain even if the program produces the correct results for the test data. As a consequence, program verification usually requires the use of proof methods similar to those described earlier in this chapter.

In this section we will describe a method for program verification based on assertions about the program variables before, during, and after program execution; we will call such assertions *program assertions*. For simplicity we will restrict our examples to integer arithmetic, that is, the universe of discourse for numerical variables is taken to be the integers. Furthermore, as is customary in treatments of this topic, we will ignore such potential problems as storage limitations and register overflow.

Program assertions characterize properties of program variables and relationships between them at various stages of program execution. These assertions can utilize whatever predicates are appropriate, such as

"x is nonnegative"
"$x = y$"
"$x \leq y$"
"$x + y < z$"
"The entries of the vector V are sorted in nondecreasing order."

We will use program assertions to describe the state of the computation at each step of program execution, that is, before the program begins execution and after each program statement has been executed. The individual variables which appear in program assertions need not be program variables. For example, if V is a vector and i is not a program variable, then the assertion

$$\exists i(V[i] = x)$$

establishes that the value of the variable x is an entry in the vector V. Because a program assertion must be a proposition at the appropriate point in program execution, all variables which occur in a program assertion must be bound when the assertion applies. Any program variable used in such an assertion will have an assigned value and is therefore bound by assignment. A variable other than a program variable may be bound either by quantification or by assignment.

In order to establish that a program is correct, we must first have a precise specification of what the program is intended to do. This is given by means of two program assertions called the *initial assertion* and the *final assertion*. The initial assertion characterizes what is known or to be assumed about the program variables before program execution begins. If no assumption is made, the initial assertion is the tautology *true*. The final assertion of the program specifies what is to be true of the program variables if the program terminates normally (i.e., not as the result of something like arithmetic overflow or exceeding its allotted time). Together, the initial and final program assertions specify the task to be performed by the program. The question of whether a program is correct can only be addressed if a pair of initial and final assertions has been accepted as a correct characterization of the task to be performed; that is, program correctness must be judged relative to a specified task. The following definition applies both to programs and to finite sequences of program statements known as *program segments*.

Definition 1.6.1: A program or program segment $\mathcal{P}$ is *correct with respect to an initial assertion I and a final assertion F* if,† whenever I is true of the program

---

†Here and throughout the book we follow mathematical convention for definitions and use "if" where in fact "if and only if" is intended. For example, when we assert "An integer is prime if it is greater than 1 and has no positive divisors other than 1 and itself," the intention is "An integer is prime if and only if it is greater than 1 and has no positive divisors other than 1 and itself." This convention is used only in stating definitions.

variables prior to execution of $\mathcal{P}$, and $\mathcal{P}$ terminates, then F will be true of the program variables after execution of $\mathcal{P}$ is complete.

We now describe some notation which will be useful in treating program correctness. Let Ai and Aj be program assertions, and let S be a program segment. We will use the notation

$$Ai \{S\} Aj$$

to denote "if Ai is true prior to the execution of S, and S is executed and terminates, then Aj will be true immediately following the termination of S." Using this notation we can restate Definition 1.6.1 by saying a program $\mathcal{P}$ is correct with respect to an initial assertion I and a final assertion F if and only if $I \{\mathcal{P}\} F$. When S consists of a number of program statements it will sometimes be more convenient to state that "The program segment

$$Ai$$
$$S$$
$$Aj$$

is correct" rather than using the notation $Ai \{S\} Aj$.

Example†

The program segment

$A1: true$
$x \leftarrow 1;$
$y \leftarrow 2$
$A2: x = 1 \wedge y = 2$

is correct. Equivalently, we can state

$$true \{x \leftarrow 1; y \leftarrow 2\} x = 1 \wedge y = 2. \quad \#$$

In order to prove that a program is correct, we need a way to characterize the effect on the program variables of executing the program. This implies that we need such a characterization for each kind of executable statement of the programming language, as well as a way of combining these characterizations into a description of the effect of executing the entire program. We begin by describing some fundamental rules of inference. As with the rules of inference described in Section 1.4, these rules are not meant to be surprising or profound; in fact they should be as simple and transparent as possible. But they must be powerful enough to enable us to prove programs correct, and they must characterize precisely and correctly the effect of executing programs and program segments.

The first rule of inference establishes that we can break a proof of correctness of a program into a series of proofs of correctness for successive parts of the program. Let S_1 and S_2 denote program segments, and denote by $S_1; S_2$ the program segment obtained by placing a semicolon after S_1 and then concatenating S_2 with the result. Thus $S_1; S_2$ denotes a program segment whose execution has the same

---

†The early examples of this section will rely on the reader's understanding of the effect of executing an assignment statement. A careful treatment of this topic will be given later in this section.

effect as first executing S_1 and then executing S_2. The first rule of inference, called the *rule of composition*, states that if both $Q_1\{S_1\}Q_2$ and $Q_2\{S_2\}Q_3$, then it follows that $Q_1\{S_1;S_2\}Q_3$; that is, if the program assertion Q_1 is initially true of the program variables and $S_1;S_2$ is executed, then after termination of the segment $S_1;S_2$, the assertion Q_3 will be true. Presented in the tabular form of our previous rules of inference, this is stated as follows:

$$\frac{\begin{array}{c} Q_1\{S_1\}Q_2 \\ Q_2\{S_2\}Q_3 \end{array}}{\therefore Q_1\{S_1;S_2\}Q_3} \qquad \textit{Rule of Composition}$$

We can interpret the rule of composition in terms of both flowcharts and programs by adding the program assertions to the flowchart or the program text. Note that program assertions are associated with states of the computation rather than actions. For this reason, program assertions are associated with the edges of flowcharts, and they either precede or follow the statements of a program. Whenever an edge of a flowchart is traversed, the associated program assertion is true. Immediately before a program statement is executed, the program assertion which precedes it is true.

The rule of composition can be interpreted with flowchart diagrams as follows:

"If

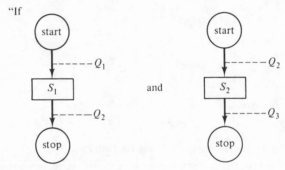

and

are both correct, then

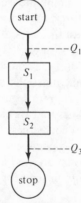

is correct."

Using program segments, the rule of composition can be stated as:

"If $A1:Q1$　　　　　　　　　　$A1:Q2$
　　$S1$　　　　　and　　　　$S2$
　　$A2:Q2$　　　　　　　　　$A2:Q3$
are both correct, then
　　$A1:Q1$
　　$S1;$
　　$S2$
　　$A2:Q3$
is correct."

Example

　　　　If we can establish that

$A1:true$　　　　　　　　　　$A2:x = 1$
$x \leftarrow 1$　　　　　and　　　　$y \leftarrow x + z$
$A2:x = 1$　　　　　　　　　　$A3:y = z + 1$

are both correct, then we can conclude from an application of the rule of composition that

$A1:true$
$x \leftarrow 1;$
$y \leftarrow x + z$
$A3:y = z + 1$

is correct.　#

The rule of composition makes it possible to infer the correctness of a program from the correctness of its program segments. Thus, if we wish to show $I\{\mathcal{P}\}\ F$ for some program $\mathcal{P}$, we can break $\mathcal{P}$ into program segments $S_1, S_2, \ldots, S_n$ such that $\mathcal{P} = S_1; S_2; \ldots; S_n$ and then devise "intermediate assertions" $Q_1, Q_2, \ldots, Q_{n-1}$. If we are able to prove the n lemmas

$$I\ \{S_1\}\ Q_1,\ Q_1\ \{S_2\}\ Q_2, \ldots, Q_{n-2}\{S_{n-1}\}\ Q_{n-1}, \text{ and } Q_{n-1}\ \{S_n\}\ F,$$

it will follow from repeated applications of the rule of composition that $I\ \{\mathcal{P}\}\ F$.

　　The next rules of inference, called *rules of consequence*, state that a program assertion which precedes a program segment can be replaced by a stronger one, and an assertion which follows a program segment can be replaced by a weaker one without affecting the correctness of the segment. (Recall that P is stronger than Q if $P \Rightarrow Q$.) The rules are given as follows:

$$
\begin{array}{ll}
Q_1 \Rightarrow Q_2 & Q_1\ \{S\}\ Q_2 \\
\underline{Q_2\ \{S\}\ Q_3} & \underline{Q_2 \Rightarrow Q_3} \\
\therefore Q_1\ \{S\}\ Q_3 & \therefore Q_1\ \{S\}\ Q_3 \qquad \textit{Rules of Consequence}
\end{array}
$$

The two rules of consequence allow us to ignore information about the program variables if it is not important for the proof of correctness. For example, the value of an index variable might play an important role in the program assertions which hold during execution of a loop, but when execution proceeds past the loop, the value of this variable may not be significant.

In the rule of consequence the variables Q_1, Q_2, and Q_3 denote program assertions. The implications $Q_1 \Rightarrow Q_2$ and $Q_2 \Rightarrow Q_3$ which appear as hypotheses in the rules are propositions which relate two program assertions. These implications are proved using the techniques of the previous sections of this chapter; this is done independently of any consideration of the program.

Example

If the program segment

$A1$:*true*
$x \leftarrow 1;$
$z \leftarrow y + x$
$A2$:$z = y + 1$

is shown to be correct, then since $z = y + 1 \Rightarrow z > y$, we can conclude that

$A1$:*true*
$x \leftarrow 1;$
$z \leftarrow y + x$
$A2'$:$z > y$

is correct.   #

We next treat the rules of inference which are concerned with some of the control statements of our programming language. The control statements include conditional branches and loops; they can cause program statements to be executed in an order different from that in which they appear in the program text. We will treat three fundamental types; "**if** *condition* **then** S," "**if** *condition* **then** S_1 **else** S_2," and "**while** *condition* **do** S." In each statement type, *condition* is an assertion (but not a program assertion) about the values of the program variables; whenever *condition* is evaluated, it is either true or false. For each statement type, the portion of the program to be executed next is determined by the truth value of *condition*. The precise effect of executing each statement type is characterized by a rule of inference.

When the statement "**if** *condition* **then** S" is executed, the program statement S is executed if and only if *condition* is true. (Note that S can be a single statement or a sequence of statements enclosed in a **begin** . . . **end** pair.) A rule of inference for this statement type must involve preceding and following program assertions which will be true whether or not the statement S is executed. The rule, called the *if-then* rule, is the following:

$$\frac{(Q_1 \wedge condition)\, \{S\}\, Q_2}{(Q_1 \wedge \neg condition) \Rightarrow Q_2}$$
$$\therefore Q_1\, \{\textbf{if } condition \textbf{ then } S\}\, Q_2 \qquad \textit{The if-then Rule}$$

Note that the implication $(Q_1 \wedge \neg condition) \Rightarrow Q_2$ is a proposition which must be proved without reference to the program. The *if-then* rule can be interpreted using flowcharts in the following way. (Note that when edges of a flowchart converge, the point of convergence is treated as a node and different assertions can appear on the edges which enter and leave it.)

"If we can show that

$$(Q_1 \wedge \neg condition) \Rightarrow Q_2$$

and

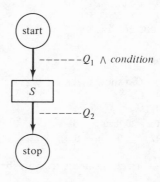

is known to be correct, then we can infer that

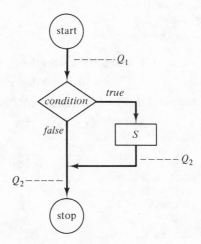

is correct."

In terms of programs, the *if-then* rule can be stated as follows:
    "If the implication

$$(Q_1 \wedge \neg condition) \Rightarrow Q_2$$

is true and

$A1: Q_1 \wedge$ *condition*
S
$A2: Q2$

is correct, then

$A1: Q_1$
if *condition* **then** S
$A2: Q2$

is correct."

Example

To show that

$A1: true$
if $x < 0$ **then** $y \leftarrow 0$
$A2: x \geq 0 \vee y = 0$

is correct, it suffices to show that the implication

$$[true \wedge \neg(x < 0)] \Rightarrow [x \geq 0 \vee y = 0]$$

is true and that

$A1': true \wedge x < 0$
$y \leftarrow 0$
$A2: x \geq 0 \vee y = 0$

is correct. It then follows from the *if-then* rule that

$$true \{ \textbf{if } x < 0 \textbf{ then } y \leftarrow 0 \} x \geq 0 \vee y = 0.$$

The proof that the implication holds uses the identities in Table 1.1.1:

$$[true \wedge \neg(x < 0)] \Rightarrow \neg(x < 0) \qquad \text{simplification}$$
$$\neg(x < 0) \Leftrightarrow x \geq 0 \qquad \text{definition of} \geq$$
$$x \geq 0 \Rightarrow [x \geq 0 \vee y = 0] \qquad \text{addition}$$

To prove that

$A1': true \wedge x < 0$
$y \leftarrow 0$
$A2: x \geq 0 \vee y = 0$

is correct, we first observe that, since y is assigned the value 0 and the value of x is not changed,

$A1': true \wedge x < 0$
$y \leftarrow 0$
$A2': true \wedge x < 0 \wedge y = 0$

is correct. Since $A2' \Rightarrow A2$, it follows from a rule of consequence that

$A1': true \wedge x < 0$
$y \leftarrow 0$
$A2: x \geq 0 \vee y = 0$

is correct.   #

When the statement "**if** *condition* **then** S_1 **else** S_2" is executed, if *condition* is true, then S_1 is executed; otherwise S_2 is executed. The *if-then-else* rule of inference is the following:

$$\frac{(Q_1 \wedge condition) \{S_1\} \, Q_2}{(Q_1 \wedge \neg condition) \{S_2\} \, Q_2}$$
$$\therefore Q_1 \, \{\textbf{if } condition \textbf{ then } S_1 \textbf{ else } S_2\} \, Q_2 \qquad \textit{The if-then-else Rule}$$

We leave the flowchart and program formulations of the *if-then-else* rule as exercises.

Example

In order to establish that

$A1: true$
if $x < 0$ **then** $y \leftarrow -1$ **else** $y \leftarrow 1$
$A2: (x < 0 \wedge y = -1) \vee (x \geq 0 \wedge y = 1)$

is correct, it suffices to show that both

$A1': true \wedge x < 0$
$y \leftarrow -1$
$A2: (x < 0 \wedge y = -1) \vee (x \geq 0 \wedge y = 1)$

and

$A1'': true \wedge \neg(x < 0)$
$y \leftarrow 1$
$A2: (x < 0 \wedge y = -1) \vee (x \geq 0 \wedge y = 1)$

are correct.   #

When a "**while** *condition* **do** S" statement is executed, if *condition* is false, then execution proceeds to the next statement of the program. Otherwise, the statement S is executed repeatedly until *condition* becomes false; *condition* is evaluated after each execution of S. Note that unless *condition* becomes false, execution of the **while** statement (and therefore of the program) will not terminate.

The rule of inference for the **while** statement, called the *rule of iteration*, requires a program assertion which is true before the statement is executed and remains true after each execution of the statement S. This assertion is known by such names as the *loop invariant relation* or *loop invariant condition*; it describes a relationship which holds among the program variables each time *condition* is evaluated and consequently after every execution of *S*. Formulation of the proper loop invariant relation is often a difficult step in proving a program correct. The rule of iteration is the following (where the program assertion Q is the loop invariant relation):

$$\frac{Q \wedge \text{condition} \{S\}\ Q}{\therefore Q\ \{\textbf{while}\ \text{condition}\ \textbf{do}\ S\}\ (\neg\text{condition} \wedge Q)} \qquad Rule\ of\ Iteration$$

The rule of iteration can be characterized using flowcharts as follows:

"If

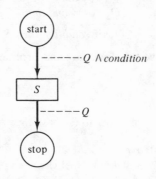

is correct, then

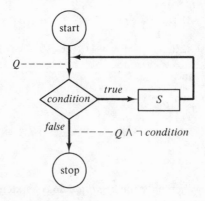

is correct."

In terms of programs, the rule of iteration states
    "If

    $A1: Q \wedge \text{condition}$
    S
    $A2: Q$

is correct, then

$A1:Q$
while *condition* **do** *S*
$A2:Q \land \neg condition$

is correct."

Example

The procedure PRODUCT given in Figure 1.6.1 sets y equal to the product of a and b, where a is a nonnegative integer. The procedure multiplies a and b by repeated addition, that is, y is initialized to 0 and then b is added to y a times.

procedure PRODUCT:
comment: set $y = ab$, where $a \geq 0$.
$A1:a \geq 0$
begin
    $i \leftarrow 0;$
    $A2:a \geq 0 \land i = 0$
    $y \leftarrow 0;$
    $A3:a \geq 0 \land i = 0 \land y = 0$
    $A4:y = ib \land i \leq a$
    while $i < a$ **do**
        $A5:y = ib \land i < a$
        begin
            $y \leftarrow y + b;$
            $A6:y = (i + 1)b \land i < a$
            $i \leftarrow i + 1$
            $A4:y = ib \land i \leq a$
        end
    $A7:y = ab$
end

Fig. 1.6.1 A procedure for multiplication by repeated addition

The procedure has been annotated with program assertions, one of which holds after each step of the computation; $A1$ is the initial assertion and $A7$ is the final assertion. We will now describe how to prove PRODUCT is correct with respect to $A1$ and $A7$.

The proof of correctness can be divided into two parts by proving the following two lemmas.†

Lemma 1: $A1 \{i \leftarrow 0; y \leftarrow 0\} A4$.

Lemma 2: $A4 \{$**while** $i < a$ **do begin** $y \leftarrow y + b; i \leftarrow i + 1$ **end**$\} A7$.

Proof of Lemma 1:   We first use the intermediate assertion $A2$ and observe that $A1 \{i \leftarrow 0\} A2$, that is,

$$a \geq 0 \{i \leftarrow 0\} a \geq 0 \land i = 0,$$

†We continue to rely on the reader's understanding of the effect of an assignment statement.

since the assignment statement does not affect the value of a and it sets the value of i to 0. Similarly, $A2 \{y \leftarrow 0\} A3$, that is,

$$a \geq 0 \wedge i = 0 \{y \leftarrow 0\} a \geq 0 \wedge i = 0 \wedge y = 0.$$

By the rule of composition, we conclude

$$A1 \{i \leftarrow 0; y \leftarrow 0\} A3.$$

From the rules of arithmetic and the properties of $\leq$ it is clear that $A3 \Rightarrow A4$. Therefore we can apply a rule of consequence to conclude that

$$A1 \{i \leftarrow 0; y \leftarrow 0\} A4.$$

This completes the proof of Lemma 1.

Proof of Lemma 2:   To prove the *while* loop is correct with respect to the initial assertion $A4$ and the final assertion $A7$, we must first establish that the hypothesis of the rule of iteration holds, that is,

$$A4 \wedge i < a \{y \leftarrow y + b; i \leftarrow i + 1\} A4.$$

Observe that $(A4 \wedge i < a) \Leftrightarrow A5$, so it suffices to show

$$A5 \{y \leftarrow y + b; i \leftarrow i + 1\} A4.$$

We use the intermediate assertion $A6$ and first show

$$A5 \{y \leftarrow y + b\} A6.$$

Since the value of y is changed by the assignment statement, let y' denote the value of y before the assignment statement is executed. Then $A5$ is the assertion

$$y' = ib \wedge i < a.$$

The assignment statement sets y equal to $y' + b$. The conjunction of the propositions $y' = ib \wedge i < a$ and $y = y' + b$ implies $A6$, so we conclude that $A5 \{y \leftarrow y + b\} A6$. Similarly, letting i' denote the value of i before the statement $i \leftarrow i + 1$ is executed,

$$(y = (i' + 1)b \wedge i' < a \wedge i = i' + 1) \Rightarrow (y = ib \wedge i \leq a),$$

so we conclude that $A6 \{i \leftarrow i + 1\} A4$. By the rule of composition, we infer that $A5 \{y \leftarrow y + b; i \leftarrow i + 1\} A4$ and therefore the hypothesis of the rule of iteration holds.

Applying the rule of iteration, we conclude

$$A4 \{\textbf{while } i < a \textbf{ do begin } y \leftarrow y + b; i \leftarrow i + 1 \textbf{ end}\} A4 \wedge i \geq a.$$

We then show that $(A4 \wedge i \geq a) \Rightarrow A7$ and apply a rule of consequence to complete the proof of Lemma 2.

It follows from Lemma 1 and Lemma 2 and the rule of composition that PRODUCT is correct with respect to $A1$ and $A7$.   ∎   #

The program verification method we have described requires the following steps:

1. Formulate initial and final assertions which characterize the task to be accomplished by the program.
2. Segment the program into sections which accomplish subtasks, and for-

mulate initial and final assertions for each subtask. In every case in which a program segment S_1 may be executed immediately prior to a segment S_2, the final assertion of S_1 should imply the initial assertion of S_2.

3. Prove that each program segment is correct with respect to its initial and final assertions.

4. Conclude that the program is correct with respect to its initial and final assertions.

Note that if intermediate assertions have been chosen correctly for a program and the initial assertion was true prior to program execution, then each program assertion is true at the appropriate point of the computation. It follows as a special case that if execution reaches the end of the program (that is, if the program terminates) then the final assertion will be true when execution is complete.

Formally, a program is correct so long as it has performed the correct task whenever it halts. In fact, according to Definition 1.6.1, a program that never halts is correct for every pair of initial and final assertions; it follows that proving program termination is just as important as proving correctness. It is common to refer to what we have called "correctness" as "partial correctness," and to call a program "correct" if it is both "partially correct" and always halts if the initial assertion is true prior to execution. We will treat one technique for proving program termination in Section 3.6.

Axioms of Assignment

The preceding discussion of the formal rules of program verification has only treated rules of inference. Rules of inference are always of the form "if we know one thing is true, then we can conclude something else is true." Unless we have a characterization of some true statements, we cannot apply the rules of inference; thus we need some axioms for our system in order to complete the specification of our proof mechanism. The axioms for program verification describe the effect of executing an assignment statement.

Consider a program with variables $x_1, x_2, \ldots, x_n$. An assignment statement has the form

$$x_i \leftarrow \mathcal{E}(x_1, x_2, \ldots, x_n),$$

where $\mathcal{E}(x_1, x_2, \ldots, x_n)$ is an expression involving (some of) the variables $x_1, x_2, \ldots, x_n$. If the program assertion $A(x_1, x_2, \ldots, x_n)$ holds prior to the execution of the assignment statement, then the following assertion will hold after the assignment statement:

$$\exists y[A(x_1, x_2, \ldots, x_{i-1}, y, x_{i+1}, \ldots, x_n) \land$$
$$x_i = \mathcal{E}(x_1, x_2, \ldots, x_{i-1}, y, x_{i+1}, \ldots, x_n)]$$

This program assertion states that there exists some value for y (namely the former value of x_i) which makes the assertion

$$A(x_1, x_2, \ldots, x_{i-1}, y, x_{i+1}, \ldots, x_n)$$

true, and if this value of y is substituted for x_i in the expression $\mathcal{E}$ together with the current values of the other variables x_j, where $j \neq i$, the result will be the current value of x_i. Not only is the above assertion correct, but it is the strongest correct assertion which can be made based only on the knowledge that $A(x_1, x_2, \ldots, x_n)$ holds prior to the statement execution. Because this way of constructing program assertions generates them in the same order as program execution, it can be used for the "forward" construction of program assertions for assignment statements. The forward construction of the strongest possible program assertion is characterized by the following axiom concerning the effect of the assignment statement.

$$A(x_1, x_2, \ldots, x_n) \{x_i \leftarrow \mathcal{E}(x_1, x_2, \ldots, x_n)\} \exists y[A(x_1, x_2, \ldots, x_{i-1}, y,$$

$$x_{i+1}, \ldots, x_n) \wedge x_i = \mathcal{E}(x_1, x_2, \ldots, x_{i-1}, y, x_{i+1}, \ldots, x_n)]$$

Axiom of Assignment.

The effect of an assignment statement can also be described in a "backward" direction. Suppose $A(x_1, x_2, \ldots, x_n)$ is an assertion which follows the assignment statement

$$x_i \leftarrow \mathcal{E}(x_1, x_2, \ldots, x_n).$$

Then the assertion which precedes the assignment statement must imply the assertion

$$A(x_1, x_2, \ldots, x_{i-1}, \mathcal{E}(x_1, x_2, \ldots, x_i, \ldots, x_n), x_{i+1}, \ldots, x_n).$$

This assertion is obtained by replacing every occurrence of x_i in $A(x_1, x_2, \ldots, x_n)$ by the expression on the right side of the assignment statement; it is the weakest statement which will assure that $A(x_1, x_2, \ldots, x_n)$ will hold after execution of the assignment statement. The backward construction of assertions is formalized by the following axiom of assignment, which can be used in place of the one given previously.

$$A(x_1, x_2, \ldots, x_{i-1}, \mathcal{E}(x_1, x_2, \ldots, x_i, \ldots, x_n), x_{i+1}, \ldots, x_n)$$

$$\{x_i \leftarrow \mathcal{E}(x_1, x_2, \ldots, x_n)\} A(x_1, x_2, \ldots, x_n). \qquad \textit{Alternate Axiom of Assignment.}$$

This axiom is commonly used to construct a program assertion to precede an assignment statement based on the assertion which follows the statement. The backward construction of assertions for assignment statements is usually easier than constructing them in the forward direction. The two axioms of assignment are redundant in that only one is required for program verification.

Examples

    (a)   Consider the program segment

        $A1$
        $x \leftarrow x + y + z$
        $A2$

        If $A1$ is the assertion

$$A1 : x + y + z = 9$$

then the strongest assertion that can be made for $A2$ is

$$A2\!: \exists x'[x' + y + z = 9 \wedge x = x' + y + z].$$

It is easy to show that this statement implies

$$A2'\!: x = 9$$

Using backward construction, if we suppose $A2$ is the assertion

$$A2\!: x = 9$$

then $A1$ is obtained by substituting $x + y + z$ for x in $A2$, giving

$$A1'\!: x + y + z = 9.$$

(b) Consider the following program segment to interchange the values of x and y.

$A1\!: x = x' \wedge y = y'$
$temp \leftarrow x;$
$x \leftarrow y;$
$y \leftarrow temp$
$A4\!: x = y' \wedge y = x'$

The assertions $A1$ and $A4$ involve variables x' and y' which are not program variables. They are auxiliary variables bound by assigning them the original values of x and y respectively.

To prove the program segment is correct with respect to $A1$ and $A4$, we use the backward construction of assertions. From $A4$ we construct $A3$ by substitution of $temp$ for y in $A4$; thus $A3$ is

$$A3\!: x = y' \wedge temp = x'$$

Using backward construction from $A3$, we obtain

$$A2\!: y = y' \wedge temp = x'$$

Applying backward construction to $A2$ yields $A1$. By the rule of composition, it follows that the program segment is correct with respect to $A1$ and $A4$.   #

Program verification using the techniques we have described in this section is a difficult task; only relatively simple programs can be verified in this way. Programs will not be verified to the level of precision and detail we have described in this section unless more powerful tools are developed or the major part of the verification can be done using a computer. Because program verification is a young subject, there is no doubt that more powerful mathematical tools will be developed. Some success has already been achieved with computer-aided verification of programs, and there is no doubt that these tools will also be improved. Nevertheless, it seems likely that many programs will never be subjected to the rigors of careful verification. It does not follow that the concepts of program verification will have no impact on programming practice. An understanding of techniques for proving programs correct affects the way a programmer approaches his work. Through an appreciation of the characteristics that make a program difficult to verify, he will learn to write programs which can be verified if the need arises. The result is likely to be a good program: easy to read, modify, and understand.

Problems: Section 1.6

1. (a)   Give a flowchart interpretation of the *if-then-else* rule of inference.
    (b)   Give an informal statement of the *if-then-else* rule of inference using program segments.

2.   Write a program segment which is correct with respect to the initial assertion *true* and the final assertion *false*. (Hint: Study Definition 1.6.1.)

3.   Prove the following program segments are correct. Use both forward and backward construction of assertions.

   (a) AI:*true*
         $x \leftarrow 1;$
         $y \leftarrow 2$
         AF:$x = 1 \wedge y = 2$

   (b) AI:$x > 0$
         $y \leftarrow z + x$
         AF:$y > z$

   (c)   **comment**:   Set $y = ax^2 + bx + c$
         AI:*true*
         $y \leftarrow a * x;$
         $y \leftarrow (y + b) * x;$
         $y \leftarrow y + c$
         AF:$y = ax^2 + bx + c$

4.   Prove the following program segments are correct. State which rules of inference are used.
   (a)   In the following, x' is an auxilliary variable.

         comment: Set x to the absolute value of x.
         AI:$x = x'$
         if $x < 0$ **then** $x \leftarrow -x$
         AF:$(x' < 0 \Rightarrow x = -x') \wedge (x' \geq 0 \Rightarrow x = x')$

   (b) AI:*true*
         if $x \geq y$ **then** $max \leftarrow x$ **else** $max \leftarrow y$
         AF:$(x \geq y \wedge max = x) \vee (x < y \wedge max = y)$

5.   Consider the following program segment which sets d equal to $max\,(a, b, c)$.

      AI: *true*
      $d \leftarrow a;$
      if $b > d$ **then** $d \leftarrow b;$
      if $c > d$ **then** $d \leftarrow c$
      AF:$(d = a \vee d = b \vee d = c) \wedge d \geq a \wedge d \geq b \wedge d \geq c$

   (a)   Construct the intermediate assertions.
   (b)   Prove the program segment is correct.

6.   Provide intermediate assertions and show that the procedure ZERO given in Fig. 1.6.2 is correct with respect to the initial assertion

$$AI:n > 0$$

and the final assertion

$$AF: \forall j[1 \leq j \leq n \Rightarrow V[j] = 0].$$

Use the following loop invariant relation

$$i \leq n + 1 \wedge \forall j[1 \leq j < i \Rightarrow V[j] = 0].$$

procedure ZERO:
comment: Set all entries of $V[1:n]$ to zero.
begin
    $i \leftarrow 1$;
    while $i \leq n$ **do**
        begin
            $V[i] \leftarrow 0$;
            $i \leftarrow i + 1$
        end

end

Fig. 1.6.2 A procedure to zero the vector $V[1:n]$

7. The procedure PRODUCT which was proved correct in this section is not the only procedure which is correct with respect to the given initial and final assertions. Consider the following procedure.

procedure SNEAKY:
$AI:a \geq 0$
begin
    $b \leftarrow 0$;
    $y \leftarrow 0$
    $AF:y = ab$
end

How could the initial and final assertion be changed so that SNEAKY would not be correct with respect to AI and AF? Address the general question of how to rule out unintended solutions.

procedure SUM:
comment: Set *sum* equal to sum of entries of $V[1:n]$.
$AI: n > 0$
begin
    $sum \leftarrow 0$;
    $i \leftarrow 1$;
    while $i \leq n$ **do**
        begin
            $sum \leftarrow sum + V[i]$;
            $i \leftarrow i + 1$
        end
    $AF: sum = \sum_{i=1}^{n} V[i]$
end

Fig. 1.6.3 Procedure to sum the elements of a vector

8. (a) Construct intermediate assertions for the procedure SUM given in Fig. 1.6.3. Identify the loop invariant relation.

   (b) Prove SUM is correct with respect to AI and AF.

9. (a) Construct intermediate assertions for the procedure SEARCH given in Fig. 1.6.4. Identify the loop invariant relation.

   (b) Prove SEARCH is correct with respect to AI and AF.

```
procedure SEARCH(arg):
comment:  Set index to smallest value such that V[index] = arg in V[1:n].
          Assume arg is an entry in V and the while loop terminates.
AI: n ≥ 1 ∧ ∃i[V[i] = arg]
begin
    index ← 1;
    while V[index] ≠ arg do index ← index + 1
    AF: V[index] = arg ∧ ∀i[1 ≤ i < index ⇒ V[i] ≠ arg]
end
```

Fig 1.6.4   Linear search procedure

Suggestions for Further Reading

The concepts and terminology of this chapter come principally from the field of mathematical logic. Wilder [1965] gives a very readable treatment of many of the basic issues in this area; his book is relevant to later chapters as well as this one. Shoenfield [1967] gives an excellent introduction to mathematical logic, including treatments of formal systems and the mathematical theory of models. DeLong [1970] describes the historical development of mathematical logic, the nature of its results, and its philosophical implications. The halting problem and related questions are treated nicely in Minsky [1967].

The original papers by Floyd [1967] and Hoare [1969] provide an excellent introduction to the topic of program verification. The survey by Elspas, *et al.*, [1972] treats several topics associated with proving program correctness; their article is broader in scope and more difficult reading than those by Floyd and Hoare. The text by Manna [1974] treats program verification for both flowchart programs and programs in an ALGOL-like language.

2

SETS

2.0 INTRODUCTION

The concept of a set is of fundamental importance in modern mathematics. Most mathematicians believe it is possible to express all of mathematics in the language of set theory. Our interest in sets is due both to their role in modern mathematics and their usefulness in modelling and investigating problems in computer science.

Sets were first studied formally by G. Cantor (1845–1918). After set theory had become a well-established area of mathematics, contradictions, or *paradoxes*, were found in the theory. Eventually, more sophisticated approaches than Cantor's were developed in order to eliminate these paradoxes. Introductory treatments of set theory usually describe a "naive" set theory, which is quite similar to Cantor's original work, rather than developing the axiomatic framework necessary to avoid the paradoxes. We will take this simpler approach and develop a set theory in which it is possible to derive contradictions. It may seem strange to pursue such a course deliberately, but the naive theory does not lead to contradictions if the universe of discourse is suitably defined, as it always will be in our investigations. Furthermore, the existence of the paradoxes in the naive theory will not affect the validity of our results because the theorems we will present can also be developed in alternative systems in which the paradoxes cannot occur.

In Section 2.2 we will describe some of the paradoxes of naive set theory and discuss how a more sophisticated theory can circumvent them.

2.1 THE PRIMITIVES OF SET THEORY

A *set* is any collection of objects which can be treated as an entity, and an object in the collection is said to be an *element*, or *member*, of the set. Given any object x and set S, if x is an element of the set S, we will write $x \in S$; if x is not an element of S, we will write $\neg(x \in S)$ or $x \notin S$. The terms *set*, *collection*, and *class* will be used as synonyms, as will the terms *element* and *member*.

Note that we have not given either a formal definition of a set, or a basis for deciding when an object is a member of a set. Any mathematical theory must ultimately rest on some *primitive*, or undefined notions (e.g., the notions of "point" and "line" in geometry); the notion of "set" and the relation "is an element of" are the primitive concepts of set theory. As a consequence of not having definitions for these concepts, we have no formal test to determine whether something is a set or whether a given object is an element of a specified set. Because there is no test, we must rely on a common understanding of the meaning of the terms.

Examples

Almost anything which would be called a set in ordinary conversation is an acceptable set in the mathematical sense. The following examples will illustrate this point.

(a) *The set of nonnegative integers less than 4.* This is a finite set with four members: 0, 1, 2, and 3.

(b) *The set of books in the New York Public Library at the present time.* This is also a finite set. It would be difficult to list the members of this set because of the constant flux in the Library's collection, but the difficulties are practical ones rather than theoretical.

(c) *The set consisting of the names of the people who spoke to Charlemagne on May 10, 810 A.D.* This set is finite and probably contains at least one element. It has the disturbing characteristic that there may not be a way to determine the members of the set. Most mathematicians, however, would not regard this as detracting from its acceptability as a mathematical set.

(d) *The set of live dinosaurs in the basement of the British Museum.* Assuming there have been no sinister experiments in the basement of the British Museum, this set has the property of not having any members, and is called a *null*, or *empty*, set.

(e) *The set of integers greater than 3.* Even though this set is infinite, there is no difficulty in determining whether a specified integer is a member.

(f) *The set of all programs in the ALGOL language which can be punched on no more than 500 cards.* This set is very large, but finite, and a correctly operating compiler can determine whether or not a program is an element of this set.

(g) *The set of all programs in the ALGOL language which would halt if run for a sufficiently long time on a computer with unbounded storage.* This set is not finite because no matter how large a program we write, it is possible to write a larger one by inserting another statement. (The statement need not perform any useful task.) Although there is a maximum size of ALGOL programs which can be run on any given computer, there is nothing about the ALGOL language itself which limits the size of a program. Computability theory has established that no algorithm exists to determine whether an arbitrary program is an element of this set; such a set is called *undecidable*.

(h) *The set of true assertions about the integers.* This is an infinite set, as we can easily demonstrate by considering assertions of the form

$$3 + 1 = 4.$$

The assertion

For every natural number n, $\sum_{i=0}^{n} i = n(n + 1)/2$

is considerably less obvious, but can be proven. There are still other statements which are conjectured to be true, but have never been proved. The following assertion, known as "Fermat's Last Theorem," is an example.

Fermat's Last Theorem: If x, y, z, and n are positive integers and $x^n + y^n = z^n$, then $n \leq 2$.

This assertion has been a source of frustration to mathematicians for centuries. In spite of much effort, neither a proof nor a counterexample is known.

(i) *The set with two members, one of which is the set of even integers and the other the set of odd integers.* This example illustrates that sets can have other sets as members. Denote the set of even integers by A and the set of odd integers by B, and let C be the set with elements A and B. Then C has only two elements, each of which is a set: $A \in C$ and $B \in C$. Note that $2 \in A, 2 \notin B$ and $2 \notin C$.

#

Since a set is characterized by its members, a set can be specified by stating when an object is in the set. A finite set can be specified explicitly by listing its elements. The elements of the list are separated by commas, and the list enclosed in braces.

Examples

The following are explicit specifications of finite sets.

(a) The set which contains the elements A, B, and C is denoted by $\{A, B, C\}$.

(b) The set which contains all the even, nonnegative integers less than 10 is specified by $\{0, 2, 4, 6, 8\}$.   #

The elements of an infinite set cannot be explicitly listed; consequently, we need a way to describe these sets implicitly. Implicit specification is most often done by means of a predicate with a free variable. The set is defined to be those elements of the universe of discourse which make the predicate true. Hence, if $P(x)$ is a predicate with one free variable, the set $\{x \mid P(x)\}$ denotes the set S such that $c \in S$ if and only if $P(c)$ is true.

Examples

The following are implicit specifications of sets. The first two examples are infinite sets; the third is finite.

(a) The set of integers greater than 10 is specified by

$$\{x \mid x \in \mathbf{I} \wedge x > 10\}.$$

(b) The set of even integers can be specified as

$$\{x \mid \exists y [y \in \mathbf{I} \wedge x = 2y]\}.$$

(c)   The set $\{1, 2, 3, 4, 5\}$ can be specified as

$$\{x \mid x \in \mathbf{I} \wedge 1 \leq x \leq 5\}. \quad \#$$

Less formal means are often used to describe sets. One technique is to partly specify the predicate by the entry to the left of the vertical bar.

Examples

(a)   The set of integer multiples of 3 can be specified by $\{3x \mid x \in \mathbf{I}\}$ rather than $\{x \mid \exists y [y \in \mathbf{I} \wedge x = 3y]\}$.

(b)   The set of rational numbers can be specified by $\{x/y \mid x, y \in \mathbf{I} \wedge y \neq 0\}$. $\#$

If a set is finite but too large to list easily, or if a set is infinite, ellipses can be used to specify the set implicitly.

Examples

The following specifications use ellipses to characterize a list of the elements of a set.

(a)   The set of integers from 1 to 50 is specified by $\{1, 2, 3, \ldots, 50\}$.

(b)   The set of nonnegative even integers is specified by $\{0, 2, 4, 6, \ldots\}$. $\#$

All of these informal techniques of set specification are convenient, and we will use them freely.

In more formal developments of set theory, the following axiom is used to establish that sets are completely specified by their elements. The axiom serves as a definition of equality of sets.

Axiom of Extension: Two sets A and B are *equal*, $A = B$, if and only if they have the same members (i.e., every element of A is an element of B and every element of B is an element of A).

The axiom of extension can be expressed in logical notation in two ways:

(a) $A = B \Leftrightarrow \forall x [x \in A \Leftrightarrow x \in B]$

(b) $A = B \Leftrightarrow \{\forall x [x \in A \Rightarrow x \in B] \wedge \forall x [x \in B \Rightarrow x \in A]\}$

The axiom of extension asserts that if two sets have the same members, then regardless of how the sets are specified, they are equal. It follows that if a set is specified explicitly with a list, the order of the listing is immaterial; the set denoted by $\{A, B, C\}$ is the same as (equal to) the sets denoted by $\{C, B, A\}$ and $\{B, A, C\}$. Furthermore, it is of no consequence if an element appears in such a list more than once; $\{A, B, A\}$, $\{A, B\}$, and $\{A, A, A, B, B\}$ are different specifications of the same set. A finite set can be characterized either explicitly or implicitly, as with the specifications $\{1, 2, 3, 4, 5\}$ and $\{x \mid x \in \mathbf{I} \wedge 1 \leq x \leq 5\}$. Moreover, the same set can be specified implicitly with different predicates, e.g., the sets $\{x \mid x = 0\}$ and $\{x \mid x \in \mathbf{I} \wedge -1 < x < 1\}$ are equal.

Problems: Section 2.1

1. Specify the following sets explicitly:
   (a) The set of nonnegative integers less than 5.
   (b) The set of letters in your first name.
   (c) The set whose only element is the first president of the United States.
   (d) The set of prime numbers between 10 and 20.
   (e) The set of positive multiples of 12 which are less than 65.

2. For each of the following, choose an appropriate universe of discourse and a predicate to define the set. Do not use ellipses.
   (a) The set of integers between 0 and 100.
   (b) The set of odd integers.
   (c) The set of integer multiples of 10.
   (d) The set of human fathers.
   (e) The set of tautologies.

3. List the members of the following sets:
   (a) $\{x \mid x \in I \wedge 3 < x < 12\}$
   (b) $\{x \mid x$ is a decimal digit$\}$
   (c) $\{x \mid x = 2 \vee x = 5\}$

4. Determine which of the following sets are equal. The universe of discourse is I.
   $A = \{x \mid x$ is even and x^2 is odd$\}$
   $B = \{x \mid \exists y[y \in I \wedge x = 2y]\}$
   $C = \{1, 2, 3\}$
   $D = \{0, 2, -2, 3, -3, 4, -4, \ldots\}$
   $E = \{2x \mid x \in I\}$
   $F = \{3, 3, 2, 1, 2\}$
   $G = \{x \mid x^3 - 6x^2 - 7x - 6 = 0\}$

‡2.2 THE PARADOXES OF SET THEORY

As we indicated in the introduction to this chapter, the naive set theory which we have described was ultimately found to lead to logical inconsistencies known as *paradoxes*. Although set theory had its bitter opponents, by the time the paradoxes were discovered around the turn of the century, the theory was widely accepted and work was under way to establish it as the foundation of logic and mathematics. Discovery of the paradoxes seemed to threaten this fundamental role of set theory. But the paradoxes were not generally viewed as a basis for abandoning set theory and starting over again; instead, mathematicians felt that the theory had to be patched in some way which would eliminate the paradoxes but not affect the usefulness of the theory. In this section, we will describe the best known paradox and briefly indicate some of the means of modifying the theory to avoid such paradoxes. These modifications can be imposed by axiomatizing set theory in such a way that the paradoxes cannot occur.

‡Denotes optional section.

A paradox similar to the one which will concern us is the "liar paradox." Consider a man who asserts

"I am lying."

Is he lying or is he speaking the truth?

If he is lying, then what he asserts is false; since he claims he is lying, he must actually be telling the truth. We conclude that if he is lying, then he is telling the truth.

On the other hand, if he speaks the truth, then what he says is true, namely that he is lying. We conclude that if he is telling the truth, then he is lying.

From the above analysis, we conclude he must be neither lying nor telling the truth. Thus, the assertion "I am lying," which appears to be a proposition, cannot in fact be assigned a truth value.

The liar paradox has been known since antiquity and has no obvious relation to set theory. Yet it resembles the first widely known paradox, commonly known as *Russell's paradox*, which was discovered by Bertrand Russell in 1901 and independently by E. Zermelo. This paradox exploits the absence of restrictions in naive set theory on the ways in which sets can be characterized. In order to present the paradox, we consider the possibility of a set being a member of itself. Most sets which occur to us are not elements of themselves; e.g., $\{1\} \notin \{1\}$. However, the set of concepts is itself a concept, and hence this set is apparently a member of itself. The assertions $x \in x$ and $x \notin x$ are therefore predicates which can be used to define sets.

Russell proposed the following paradox. Let the universe of discourse be the set of all sets, and define S to be the following set:

$$S = \{x \mid x \notin x\}$$

Thus, S is the set of all sets which are not members of themselves. We now ask "Is S a member of itself?"

Suppose S is not a member of itself. Then S satisfies the predicate $x \notin x$ which defines the set S and therefore $S \in S$. On the other hand, if $S \in S$, then S must satisfy the predicate which defines S and therefore $S \notin S$.

Thus, we are led to a contradiction analogous to that of the liar paradox: neither $S \in S$ nor $S \notin S$ can be true. A "set," such as S, which leads to a contradiction is said to be not *well-defined*.

The Russell paradox established that set theory, as originally conceived, led to inconsistencies. Mathematicians were faced with the necessity of abandoning the theory or modifying it in some way which would eliminate the paradoxes. The difficulty was felt to originate in the unrestricted way in which sets could be defined; in particular, the concept of a set being a member of itself was considered suspect. A number of approaches were developed, each of which used axioms to restrict the way in which sets can be specified.

Russell and Whitehead, in the *Principia Mathematica*, developed what they called the "theory of types." This is a set theory in which sets exist in a hierarchy. The lowest level of the hierarchy contains "individuals." All other levels of the hierarchy contain sets whose members must be elements of the next lower level of the hierarchy. Each level of the hierarchy is called a *type*. Since x can be a member of y only if y is a level higher in the hierarchy than x, a set cannot be a member of another set of the same type. Thus, in the theory of types, expressions such as $x \in x$ are not meaningful and we are spared the problem of dealing with them.

Other formulations of set theory have been created which also avoid the Russell paradox. In each of these formulations, there are restrictions on the ways in which sets can be related, and these restrictions imply that no set is permitted to be a member of itself. The axiomatic formulations of these theories are too complex to present here, and we will forego a description of them even though they are currently more popular than the theory of types created by Russell and White-head.

Having axiomatized set theory in a way which avoids the Russell paradox, it is natural to ask if we can be sure that no other paradoxes are lurking in the formal structure we have created. Using the mathematical techniques which are currently available, there is no way to show that new paradoxes will not arise. A logical theory which does not lead to paradoxes is called a consistent theory; more formally, a logical theory is *consistent* if it is impossible to prove both an assertion P and its negation $\neg P$. Since we only want to prove assertions which are true and no assertion is admitted to be both true and false, we naturally want to use logical systems which are consistent. However, consistency by itself is not enough, since a theory which does not permit any theorems to be proved is consistent but worthless. A system in which it is possible to prove all the theorems that are true is called *complete*. A trivial example of a complete system is one in which every assertion can be proved, but such a system is obviously not consistent. What we really want is a logical system which is both complete and consistent; in this case, we can prove everything that is true and nothing that isn't. It has been proved that no axiomatic formulation of set theory can be both complete and consistent. Furthermore, in order to prove the consistency of one of these formulations, we must construct the proof in a more powerful system. But to be sure that such a proof is acceptable, the more powerful system must itself be proved consistent, which requires a still more powerful system, and so on. It follows that there does not exist any way to establish that new paradoxes will not arise in set theory.

Problems: Section 2.2

1. (The Barber Paradox) The only barber of a small town vowed that he would only shave those citizens who did not shave themselves. If only a barber is permitted to shave someone other than himself, how did the barber get shaved?

2. Show that the assertion

    This statement is false.

    is not a proposition.

3. Define an adjective to be *homological* if it applies to itself and *heterological* if it does not. The words "ugly," "English," "erudite" and "eroneous" are homological, because

"ugly" is an unattractive word, "English" is an English word, "erudite" is a learned word and "eroneous" is erroneous. The words "German," "big" and "Lilliputian" are heterological because "German" is not a German word, "big" is a small word, and "Lilliputian" is large.

(a)   Show that the assertion

"Heterological" is heterological.

is not a proposition.

(b)   Is "heterological" homological?

2.3 RELATIONS BETWEEN SETS

There are two fundamental relations that can hold between two sets: equality and containment. The relation of set equality has already been defined by the Axiom of Extension. The set containment relation is defined as follows:

Definition 2.3.1:   Let A and B be sets. Then A *is a subset of* B, denoted $A \subset B$, if each element of A is an element of B (ie., $A \subset B \Leftrightarrow \forall x[x \in A \Rightarrow x \in B]$).

If $A \subset B$, we also write $B \supset A$ and say A is *contained* in B, or B *contains* A, or B is a *superset* of A. We write $A \not\subset B$ if A is not a subset of B. If $A \subset B$ and $A \neq B$, we say A is a *proper subset* of B.

Examples

(a)   The set of even integers is a proper subset of the integers.

(b)   The set of men is a subset (and also a proper subset) of the set of humans.

(c)   The set $\{1, 2, 3, 4, 5\}$ is a subset (but not a proper subset) of the set $\{x \mid x \in \mathbf{I} \wedge 0 < x < 6\}$.   #

In all our discussions, we assume a universe of discourse U which may or may not be explicitly specified. Every variable which denotes an element of a set can only take on values from this universe. The following theorem is a consequence.

Theorem 2.3.1:   Let U be the universe of discourse and A a set. Then $A \subset U$.

Proof: The proof is an example of a trivial proof based on the fact that $x \in U$ for every element x. The set A is a subset of U if and only if the implication

$$x \in A \Rightarrow x \in U$$

is true. But $x \in U$ is always true; hence the implication is true. Since x was arbitrary, it follows by universal generalization that

$$\forall x[x \in A \Rightarrow x \in U]$$

and therefore $A \subset U$.   ∎

The next theorem establishes the relationship between set equality and set containment.

Theorem 2.3.2: Let A and B be sets. Then $A = B$ if and only if $A \subset B$ and $B \subset A$.

Proof: The theorem is established in two parts using direct proofs.

(a) (the "only if" part): $A = B \Rightarrow [A \subset B \wedge B \subset A]$.

Suppose $A = B$. Then by the Axiom of Extension, every member of A is a member of B. Therefore, by Definition 2.3.1, $A \subset B$. This establishes that if $A = B$ then $A \subset B$. By the same argument, but interchanging the role of A and B, if $A = B$ then $B \subset A$. Hence,

$$[A = B \Rightarrow A \subset B] \wedge [A = B \Rightarrow B \subset A]$$

which is equivalent to

$$(A = B) \Rightarrow [(A \subset B) \wedge (B \subset A)].$$

(b) (the "if" part): $[A \subset B \wedge B \subset A] \Rightarrow A = B$.

Suppose $A \subset B$ and $B \subset A$. By Definition 2.3.1,

$$A \subset B \Rightarrow \forall x[x \in A \Rightarrow x \in B] \quad \text{and} \quad B \subset A \Rightarrow \forall x[x \in B \Rightarrow x \in A].$$

Hence,

$$(A \subset B \wedge B \subset A) \Rightarrow [\forall x[x \in A \Rightarrow X \in B] \wedge \forall x[x \in B \Rightarrow x \in A]].$$

Thus,

$$[A \subset B \wedge B \subset A] \Rightarrow (A = B). \quad \blacksquare$$

The preceding theorem will be used in many of our proofs of set equality; rather than showing directly that $A = B$, we will show $A \subset B$ and $B \subset A$, and then conclude that they are equal.

The following corollary is a consequence of the preceding theorem. The proof is left as an exercise.

Corollary 2.3.2: For any set A, $A \subset A$.

Theorem 2.3.3: Let A, B and C be sets. If $A \subset B$ and $B \subset C$, then $A \subset C$.

Proof: Let x be an arbitrary element of the universe of discourse.
Since $A \subset B$ it follows that

$$x \in A \Rightarrow x \in B.$$

Since $B \subset C$ it follows that

$$x \in B \Rightarrow x \in C.$$

Therefore

$$x \in A \Rightarrow x \in C.$$

Since x was arbitrary, it follows that $\forall x[x \in A \Rightarrow x \in C]$ and therefore $A \subset C$. $\blacksquare$

Definition 2.3.2:   A set with no members is called an *empty, null,* or *void* set. A set with one member is called a *singleton* set.

Theorem 2.3.4:   Let ϕ be an empty set, and A an arbitrary set. Then $\phi \subset A$.

Proof: Let x be an arbitrary element of the universe of discourse. Because ϕ has no members, the implication

$$x \in \phi \Rightarrow x \in A$$

is vacuously true. Since x was chosen arbitrarily, the assertion can be universally quantified, giving

$$\forall x[x \in \phi \Rightarrow x \in A],$$

which establishes that $\phi \subset A$.   ∎

The next theorem establishes that there exists one and only one empty set; this is often stated as "the empty set is unique."

Theorem 2.3.5:   Let ϕ and ϕ' be sets which are both empty. Then $\phi = \phi'$.

Proof (Direct):   Since ϕ is empty, it follows from Theorem 2.3.4 that $\phi \subset \phi'$. Similarly, $\phi' \subset \phi$. Therefore, by Theorem 2.3.2, $\phi = \phi'$.   ∎

Traditionally, the symbol ϕ is reserved to denote the empty set. Note that the set ϕ is distinct from the set $\{\phi\}$; the latter has one element, namely the empty set. The empty set can be used to construct an infinite sequence of distinct sets. In the sequence

$$\phi, \{\phi\}, \{\{\phi\}\}, \{\{\{\phi\}\}\}, \ldots$$

each set except the first has exactly one element, namely the preceding set in the sequence. In contrast, the ith element of the sequence

$$\phi, \{\phi\}, \{\phi, \{\phi\}\}, \{\phi, \{\phi\}, \{\phi, \{\phi\}\}\}, \ldots$$

has i elements, if we start counting at 0. Each set of this sequence has as its elements all the sets which precede it in the sequence.

Examples

(a)   The set $\{a, b\}$ has four distinct subsets: $\{a, b\}, \{a\}, \{b\}$ and ϕ. Note that $\{a\} \subset \{a, b\}$ and $a \in \{a, b\}$, but $\{a\} \notin \{a, b\}$ and $a \not\subset \{a, b\}$. Furthermore, $\phi \subset \{a, b\}$ but $\phi \notin \{a, b\}$.

(b)   The set $\{\{a\}\}$ is a singleton set; its sole member is (the set) $\{a\}$. Every singleton set has exactly two subsets; the subsets of $\{\{a\}\}$ are $\{\{a\}\}$ and ϕ.   #

In general, a set with n elements has 2^n distinct subsets. We will prove this in a later section.

Problems: Section 2.3

1.   List all subsets of the following sets:
   (a) $\{1, 2, 3\}$

    (b) $\{1, \{2, 3\}\}$
    (c) $\{\{1, \{2, 3\}\}\}$
    (d) $\{\phi\}$
    (e) $\{\phi, \{\phi\}\}$
    (f) $\{\{1, 2\}, \{2, 1, 1\}, \{2, 1, 1, 2\}\}$
    (g) $\{\{\phi, 2\}, \{2\}\}$

2. Prove Corollary 2.3.2.

3. Let A, B, and C be sets. If $A \in B$ and $B \in C$, is it possible that $A \in C$? Is it *always* true that $A \in C$? Give examples to support your assertions.

4. Let A, B, and C be sets. Prove or disprove the following assertions:
    (a) $[A \notin B \wedge B \notin C] \Rightarrow A \notin C$
    (b) $[A \in B \wedge B \notin C] \Rightarrow A \notin C$
    (c) $[A \subset B \wedge B \notin C] \Rightarrow A \notin C$

5. Briefly describe the difference between the sets $\{2\}$ and $\{\{2\}\}$. List the elements and all the subsets of each set.

6. Briefly describe the difference between the sets ϕ, $\{\phi\}$, and $\{\phi, \{\phi\}\}$. List the elements and all the subsets of each of these sets.

7. Is it possible that $A \subset B$ and $A \in B$? Prove your assertion.

Programming Problem

Write a program which decides if two input sets are equal or if one is contained in the other. Assume all sets are finite subsets of the set of natural numbers **N**.

2.4 OPERATIONS ON SETS

An *operation* on sets uses given sets (called the *operands*) to specify a new set (called the *resultant*). We will first treat *binary* operations; a binary operation combines two operands to produce a resultant.

As in the previous sections, we assume that all sets are constructed from some implicitly specified universe of discourse U.

Definition 2.4.1: Let A and B be sets.
    (a) The *union of A and B*, denoted $A \cup B$, is the set

$$A \cup B = \{x \,|\, x \in A \vee x \in B\}.$$

    (b) The *intersection of A and B*, denoted $A \cap B$, is the set

$$A \cap B = \{x \,|\, x \in A \wedge x \in B\}.$$

    (c) The *difference of A and B*, or *relative complement of B with respect to A*, denoted $A - B$, is the set

$$A - B = \{x \,|\, x \in A \wedge x \notin B\}.$$

Examples

Let $A = \{0, 1, 2\}$ and $B = \{1, 2, 3\}$. Then

(a) $A \cup B = \{0, 1, 2, 3\}$

(b) $A \cap B = \{1, 2\}$

(c) $A - B = \{0\}$

(d) $B - A = \{3\}$ #

Definition 2.4.2: If A and B are sets and $A \cap B = \phi$, then A and B are *disjoint*. If C is a collection of sets such that any two distinct elements of C are disjoint, then C is a *collection of (pairwise) disjoint sets*.

Example

If $C = \{\{0\}, \{1\}, \{2\}, \ldots\} = \{\{i\} \mid i \in \mathbf{N}\}$, then C is a collection of disjoint sets.
#

We next define some important classes of binary operations. Note that the following definition is not restricted to operations on sets.

Definition 2.4.3: Let $\square$ denote a binary operation, and let $x \square y$ denote the resultant obtained by applying the operation $\square$ to the operands x and y. Then
(a) The operation $\square$ is *commutative* if $x \square y = y \square x$.
(b) The operation $\square$ is *associative* if $(x \square y) \square z = x \square (y \square z)$.

Examples

For the integers, the binary operation of addition is commutative and associative since for all integers x, y and z,

$$x + y = y + x$$
$$(x + y) + z = x + (y + z)$$

However, the operation of subtraction is neither commutative nor associative, e.g.,

$$6 - 4 \neq 4 - 6$$
$$(6 - 4) - 2 \neq 6 - (4 - 2) \quad \#$$

Theorem 2.4.1: The set operations of union and intersection are commutative and associative, i.e., for arbitrary sets A, B, and C,
(a) $A \cup B = B \cup A$
(b) $A \cap B = B \cap A$
(c) $(A \cup B) \cup C = A \cup (B \cup C)$
(d) $(A \cap B) \cap C = A \cap (B \cap C)$

The proofs of assertions (a)–(d) use the commutativity and associativity of the logical operators $\vee$ and $\wedge$. We will illustrate by proving assertions (a) and (c).

Proof:

(a) Let x be an arbitrary element of the universe U. Then

$$x \in A \cup B \Leftrightarrow x \in A \lor x \in B \qquad \text{Definition of } \cup$$
$$\Leftrightarrow x \in B \lor x \in A \qquad \text{Commutativity of } \lor$$
$$\Leftrightarrow x \in B \cup A \qquad \text{Definition of } \cup$$

Since x was arbitrary, it follows that

$$\forall x[x \in A \cup B \Leftrightarrow x \in B \cup A].$$

Hence, $A \cup B = B \cup A$.

(c) Let x be an arbitrary element. Then

$$x \in A \cup (B \cup C) \Leftrightarrow x \in A \lor x \in (B \cup C) \qquad \text{Definition of } \cup$$
$$\Leftrightarrow x \in A \lor (x \in B \lor x \in C) \qquad \text{Definition of } \cup$$
$$\Leftrightarrow (x \in A \lor x \in B) \lor x \in C \qquad \text{Associativity of } \lor$$
$$\Leftrightarrow x \in (A \cup B) \lor x \in C \qquad \text{Definition of } \cup$$
$$\Leftrightarrow x \in (A \cup B) \cup C \qquad \text{Definition of } \cup$$

Since x was arbitrary, it follows that

$$\forall x[x \in A \cup (B \cup C) \Leftrightarrow x \in (A \cup B) \cup C].$$

Hence, $A \cup (B \cup C) = (A \cup B) \cup C$. ∎

The following definition is not restricted to operations on sets.

Definition 2.4.4: Let $\triangle$ and $\square$ be binary operations. Then $\triangle$ *distributes over* $\square$ if the following hold:

$$x \triangle (y \square z) = (x \triangle y) \square (x \triangle z)$$
$$(y \square z) \triangle x = (y \triangle x) \square (z \triangle x)$$

(Note that if $\triangle$ is a commutative operation, then each of these "distributive laws" implies the other.)

Examples

For the set of integers, multiplication distributes over addition:

$$x \cdot (y + z) = x \cdot y + x \cdot z$$

Addition does not distribute over multiplication, e.g.,

$$4 + (6 \cdot 2) \neq (4 + 6) \cdot (4 + 2) \quad \#$$

Theorem 2.4.2: The set operations of union and intersection distribute over each other, i.e., for arbitrary sets A, B and C.

(a) $A \cup (B \cap C) = (A \cup B) \cap (A \cup C)$

(b) $A \cap (B \cup C) = (A \cap B) \cup (A \cap C)$

Proof: (a) Let x be an arbitrary element. Then

$x \in A \cup (B \cap C) \Leftrightarrow x \in A \vee x \in (B \cap C)$	Definition of $\cup$
$\Leftrightarrow x \in A \vee (x \in B \wedge x \in C)$	Definition of $\cap$
$\Leftrightarrow (x \in A \vee x \in B) \wedge (x \in A \vee x \in C)$	Distributivity of $\vee$ over $\wedge$
$\Leftrightarrow (x \in A \cup B) \wedge (x \in A \cup C)$	Definition of $\cup$
$\Leftrightarrow x \in (A \cup B) \cap (A \cup C)$	Definition of $\cap$

Hence, $A \cup (B \cap C) = (A \cup B) \cap (A \cup C)$.

The proof of part (b) is left as an exercise. ∎

Theorem 2.4.3: Let A, B, C and D be arbitrary subsets of a universe U. Then the following assertions are true.

(a) $A \cup A = A$

(b) $A \cap A = A$

(c) $A \cup \phi = A$

(d) $A \cap \phi = \phi$

(e) $A - B \subset A$

(f) If $A \subset B$ and $C \subset D$, then $(A \cup C) \subset (B \cup D)$

(g) If $A \subset B$ and $C \subset D$, then $(A \cap C) \subset (B \cap D)$

(h) $A \subset A \cup B$

(i) $A \cap B \subset A$

(j) If $A \subset B$, then $A \cup B = B$

(k) If $A \subset B$, then $A \cap B = A$

(l) $A - \phi = A$

(m) $A \cap (B - A) = \phi$

(n) $A \cup (B - A) = A \cup B$

(o) $A - (B \cup C) = (A - B) \cap (A - C)$

(p) $A - (B \cap C) = (A - B) \cup (A - C)$

Proof:

(a) ($A \cup A = A$.) By Definition 2.4.1(a), for any $x \in U$,

$$x \in A \cup A \Leftrightarrow x \in A \vee x \in A$$

$$\Leftrightarrow x \in A$$

Hence, $A \cup A = A$.

(c) ($A \cup \phi = A$.) By Definition 2.4.1(a), $x \in A \cup \phi \Leftrightarrow x \in A \vee x \in \phi$. But since $x \in \phi$ is always false, it follows that $x \in A \vee x \in \phi \Leftrightarrow x \in A$. Hence, $x \in A \cup \phi \Leftrightarrow x \in A$, and therefore $A \cup \phi = A$.

(e) $(A - B \subset A.)$ By Definition 2.4.1(c), $x \in A - B \Leftrightarrow x \in A \wedge x \notin B$. Hence, $x \in A - B \Rightarrow x \in A$, and it follows that $A - B \subset A$.

(f) (If $A \subset B$ and $C \subset D$, then $(A \cup C) \subset (B \cup D)$.) Assume $A \subset B$ and $C \subset D$. Suppose x is an arbitrary element of $A \cup C$; then $x \in A \vee x \in C$. We now construct a proof by cases.

Case 1: Suppose $x \in A$. Since $A \subset B$ it follows that $x \in B$. Therefore $x \in B \vee x \in D$ and hence $x \in B \cup D$.

Case 2: Suppose $x \in C$. By an argument analogous to Case 1 it follows that $x \in B \cup D$.

Hence, if $x \in A \cup C$, then $x \in B \cup D$, and therefore $A \cup C \subset B \cup D$.

(j) (If $A \subset B$, then $A \cup B = B$.) We use a direct proof and assume $A \subset B$. Since $B \subset B$, it follows from part (f) that $A \cup B \subset B \cup B$ and from part (a), $B \cup B = B$. Hence, $A \cup B \subset B$, which establishes containment in one direction. From part (h), $B \subset A \cup B$, establishing containment in the other direction. Therefore, $A \cup B = B$.

(l) $(A - \phi = A.)$ $A - \phi = \{x \mid x \in A \wedge x \notin \phi\}$. But $x \notin \phi$ is always true. Hence, $x \in A \wedge x \notin \phi \Leftrightarrow x \in A$. Therefore, $A - \phi = \{x \mid x \in A\} = A$.

(o) $(A - (B \cup C) = (A - B) \cap (A - C).)$

$$x \in A - (B \cup C) \Leftrightarrow x \in A \wedge x \notin (B \cup C)$$
$$\Leftrightarrow x \in A \wedge \neg(x \in (B \cup C))$$
$$\Leftrightarrow x \in A \wedge \neg(x \in B \vee x \in C)$$
$$\Leftrightarrow x \in A \wedge [\neg(x \in B) \wedge \neg(x \in C)]$$
$$\Leftrightarrow (x \in A \wedge x \notin B) \wedge (x \in A \wedge x \notin C)$$
$$\Leftrightarrow x \in A - B \wedge x \in A - C$$
$$\Leftrightarrow x \in (A - B) \cap (A - C)$$

We leave the proofs of the remaining parts as exercises. ∎

From parts (j) and (k) of Theorem 2.4.3, it follows that for any subset A of a universe U, $A \cup U = U$ and $A \cap U = A$. When the universe of discourse is understood, a unary operation of complementation is defined.

Definition 2.4.5: Let U be a universe and A be a subset of U. The (absolute) complement of A, denoted $\bar{A}$, is the set $\bar{A} = U - A = \{x \mid x \notin A\}$.

Examples

(a) If $U = \{1, 2, 3, 4\}$ and $A = \{1, 2\}$, then $\bar{A} = \{3, 4\}$.

(b) If $U = \mathbf{N}$ and $A = \{x \mid x > 0\}$, then $\bar{A} = \{0\}$.

(c) If $U = \mathbf{I}$ and $A = \{x \mid x > 0\}$, then $\bar{A} = \{x \mid x \leq 0\}$. #

Theorem 2.4.4: Let A be an arbitrary subset of some universe U. Then

(a) $A \cup \bar{A} = U$
(b) $A \cap \bar{A} = \phi$

The proofs follow directly from the previous theorem and are left as exercises.

The following theorem states another useful relationship between a set and its complement.

Theorem 2.4.5 (Uniqueness of complement): Let A and B be subsets of a universe U. Then $B = \bar{A}$ if and only if $A \cup B = U$ and $A \cap B = \phi$.

Proof: The "only if" part follows directly from Theorem 2.4.4. To show the "if" part we assume $A \cap B = \phi$ and $A \cup B = U$. Then

$$\begin{aligned}
B &= U \cap B \\
&= (A \cup \bar{A}) \cap B \\
&= (A \cap B) \cup (\bar{A} \cap B) \\
&= \phi \cup (\bar{A} \cap B) \\
&= (\bar{A} \cap A) \cup (\bar{A} \cap B) \\
&= \bar{A} \cap (A \cup B) \\
&= \bar{A} \cap U \\
&= \bar{A}. \quad \blacksquare
\end{aligned}$$

Using the preceding result, we have the following.

Theorem 2.4.6: Let A be an arbitrary subset of U. Then $\bar{\bar{A}} = A$, i.e., the complement of the complement of A is A.

Proof: By Theorem 2.4.4, $\bar{A} \cup A = U$ and $\bar{A} \cap A = \phi$. By Theorem 2.4.5, this establishes that A is the complement of $\bar{A}$, that is $\bar{\bar{A}} = A$. $\quad \blacksquare$

Theorem 2.4.7 (DeMorgan's laws): Let A and B be arbitrary subsets of U. Then

(a) $\overline{A \cup B} = \bar{A} \cap \bar{B}$
(b) $\overline{A \cap B} = \bar{A} \cup \bar{B}$

Proof: The proofs are direct consequences of the definition of absolute complement and identities (o) and (p) of Theorem 2.4.3. $\quad \blacksquare$

When the number of sets is small, the result of many set operations can be represented pictorially using *Venn diagrams*. Examples of these diagrams are given in Fig. 2.4.1. In each case, the rectangle represents the universe and the circles

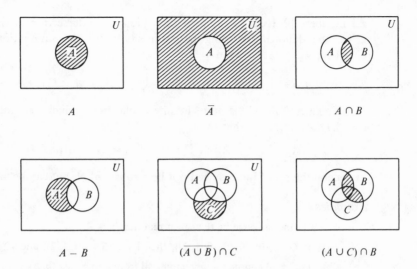

Fig. 2.4.1   Venn diagrams

represent arbitrary sets A, B and C. The shaded portion of each diagram represents the expression which appears below.

The binary operations of union and intersection can be considered as special cases of operations which form unions and intersections of any number of sets. These more general operations are defined over collections of sets.

Definition 2.4.6:   Let C be a collection of subsets of some universe U.

(a)   The *union of the members of C*, denoted $\bigcup_{S \in C} S$, is the set
$$\bigcup_{S \in C} S = \{x \mid \exists S[S \in C \wedge x \in S]\}.$$

(b)   If $C \neq \phi$, the intersection of the members of C, denoted $\bigcap_{S \in C} S$, is the set $\bigcap_{S \in C} S = \{x \mid \forall S[S \in C \Rightarrow x \in S]\}$.

These operations are natural generalizations of the union and intersection operations defined previously; if $x \in \bigcup_{S \in C} S$, then x is an element of at least one subset $S \in C$, and if $x \in \bigcap_{S \in C} S$, then x is a member of every subset $S \in C$. Note that C is required to be nonempty for $\bigcap_{S \in C} S$ to be defined. This requirement is necessary because if $C = \phi$, then the implication $S \in C \Rightarrow x \in S$ would be vacuously true for every S, and therefore, the predicate $\forall S[S \in C \Rightarrow x \in S]$ would be true for every x. Hence, the set defined would be the universal set U. By requiring that $C \neq \phi$, this possibility is eliminated.

If D is a set and a set A_d has been defined for each $d \in D$, then d is called the *index* of A_d, the collection $C = \{A_d \mid d \in D\}$ is called an *indexed collection of sets*, and D is called the *index set* of the collection. When D is the index set of a collection C, the notation $\bigcup_{d \in D} A_d$ denotes $\bigcup_{S \in C} S$, and $\bigcap_{d \in D} A_d$ denotes $\bigcap_{S \in C} S$.

If C is a finite indexed collection of sets and the index set is a set of natural numbers $\{0, 1, 2, \ldots, n\}$ then the union and intersection of the members of C can be denoted by using notation similar to the summation notion. Let $C = \{A_0, A_1, \ldots, A_n\}$; then

$$\bigcup_{S \in C} S = \bigcup_{i=0}^{n} A_i = \bigcup_{0 \leq i \leq n} A_i = \bigcup_{i \in \{0, 1, \ldots, n\}} A_i = A_0 \cup A_1 \cup \cdots \cup A_n.$$

Similarly, if C is an infinite collection which is indexed by $\mathbf{N}$, $C = \{A_0, A_1, A_2, \ldots\}$, then

$$\bigcup_{S \in C} S = \bigcup_{i=0}^{\infty} A_i = \bigcup_{0 \leq i} A_i = \bigcup_{i \in \mathbf{N}} A_i = A_0 \cup A_1 \cup A_2 \cup \cdots$$

In general the set of indices need not be a subset of $\mathbf{N}$, but can be an arbitrary set.

Examples

Let the universe be the set of real numbers $\mathbf{R}$.

(a) If $C = \{\{0\}, \{0, 1\}, \{0, 1, 2\}\}$, then $\bigcup_{S \in C} S = \{0, 1, 2\}$, and $\bigcap_{S \in C} S = \{0\}$.

(b) Let (a, b) denote the open interval from a to b, i.e., $(a, b) = \{x \mid a < x < b\}$. If $C = \{(-n, n) \mid n \in \mathbf{I} \wedge n > 0\}$, then $\bigcup_{S \in C} S = (-\infty, \infty) = \mathbf{R}$, and $\bigcap_{S \in C} S = (-1, 1)$.

(c) Let $C = \{A_i \mid i \in \{a, b, c\}\}$, where $A_a = \{0, 1, 2\}$, $A_b = \{4, 5, 6\}$ and $A_c = \{2\}$. Then $\bigcup_{i \in \{a, b, c\}} A_i = \{0, 1, 2, 4, 5, 6\}$ and $\bigcap_{i \in \{a, b, c\}} A_i = \phi$. #

We will often refer to the set of subsets of a set. Since the set of subsets of a given set A is unique, we can define a unary operation on sets whose value is the set of subsets of the operand.

Definition 2.4.7: Let A be a set. The *power set of A*, denoted $\mathcal{P}(A)$, is the set of all subsets of A.

Examples

(a) If $A = \phi$, then $\mathcal{P}(A) = \{\phi\}$.

(b) If $A = \{1\}$, then $\mathcal{P}(A) = \{\phi, \{1\}\}$.

(c) If $A = \{1, 2\}$ then $\mathcal{P}(A) = \{\phi, \{1\}, \{2\}, \{1, 2\}\}$.

(d) If A is any (finite or infinite) set of natural numbers then $A \in \mathcal{P}(\mathbf{N})$. #

If A is finite, then $\mathcal{P}(A)$ is finite; otherwise, $\mathcal{P}(A)$ is infinite.

Problems: Section 2.4

1. (a) Construct Venn diagrams for the following:
   (i) $A \cup B$
   (ii) $\bar{A} \cap \bar{B}$
   (iii) $A - (\overline{B \cup C})$
   (iv) $A \cap (\bar{B} \cup C)$

(b)   Give a formula which denotes the shaded portion of each of the following Venn diagrams.

(i)

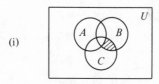

(ii)

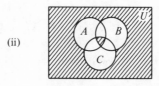

(iii)

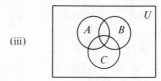

2.   Let A, B and C be arbitrary sets. Express $A \cup B \cup C$ as a union of disjoint sets.

3.   Prove parts (b) and (d) of Theorem 2.4.1.

4.   Let A, B, and C be sets
  (a)   Show that if $C \subset A$ and $C \subset B$, then $C \subset A \cap B$ (i.e., $A \cap B$ is the largest set contained in both A and B).
  (b)   Show that if $C \supset A$ and $C \supset B$, then $C \supset A \cup B$ (i.e., $A \cup B$ is the smallest set which contains both A and B).

5.   Prove part (b) of Theorem 2.4.2.

6.   Suppose $A \neq \phi$ and $A \cup B = A \cup C$. Show that it does not follow that $B = C$. Suppose in addition that $A \cap B = A \cap C$. Can you conclude that $B = C$?

7.   (a)   Show that "relative complement" is not a commutative operation; that is, there exist universes which contain sets A and B such that

$$A - B \neq B - A.$$

  (b)   Is it possible that $A - B = B - A$? Characterize all conditions under which this occurs.
  (c)   Is "relative complement" an associative operation? Prove your assertion.

8.   Prove the remaining parts of Theorem 2.4.3.

9.   Prove Theorem 2.4.4.

10.   Prove the following identities.
  (a) $A \cup (A \cap B) = A$

   (b) $A \cap (A \cup B) = A$
   (c) $A - B = A \cap \bar{B}$
   (d) $A \cup (\bar{A} \cap B) = A \cup B$
   (e) $A \cap (\bar{A} \cup B) = A \cap B$

11. In each of the following, find $\bigcup_{S \in C} S$ and $\bigcap_{S \in C} S$.
   (a) $C = \{\phi\}$
   (b) $C = \{\phi, \{\phi\}\}$
   (c) $C = \{\{a\}, \{b\}, \{a, b\}\}$
   (d) $C = \{\{i\} \mid i \in \mathbf{I}\}$

12. Let $A, B,$ and C be subsets of some universe $U,$ and let D be the following collection.

$$D = \{\bar{A} \cap \bar{B} \cap \bar{C}, \bar{A} \cap \bar{B} \cap C, \bar{A} \cap B \cap \bar{C}, \bar{A} \cap B \cap C$$
$$A \cap \bar{B} \cap \bar{C}, A \cap \bar{B} \cap C, A \cap B \cap \bar{C}, A \cap B \cap C\}$$

   (a) Construct a Venn diagram for the elements of the collection D.
   (b) Prove that $\bar{A} \cap \bar{B} \cap \bar{C}$ and $\bar{A} \cap \bar{B} \cap C$ are disjoint. Is D a disjoint collection of sets?
   (c) Prove that $\bigcup_{S \in D} S = U$.

13. Let C be a nonempty collection of subsets of some universe U. Prove the following generalization of DeMorgan's laws.
   (a) $\overline{\bigcup_{S \in C} S} = \bigcap_{S \in C} \bar{S}$
   (b) $\overline{\bigcap_{S \in C} S} = \bigcup_{S \in C} \bar{S}$

14. Specify the power set for each of the following sets.
   (a) $\{a, b, c\}$
   (b) $\{\{a, b\}, \{c\}\}$
   (c) $\{\{a, b\}, \{b, a\}, \{a, b, b\}\}$

15. Let $S_n = \{a_0, a_1, \ldots, a_n\}$ and $S_{n+1} = \{a_0, a_1, \ldots, a_n, a_{n+1}\}$. Describe how $\mathcal{P}(S_{n+1})$ is related to $\mathcal{P}(S_n)$. (Hint: $\mathcal{P}(S_{n+1})$ contains $\mathcal{P}(S_n)$.)

16. Let x and y be real numbers and define the operation $x \triangle y$ to be x^y (x raised to the power y).
   (a) Show that the operation $\triangle$ is neither commutative nor associative.
   (b) Let $\circ$ represent multiplication. Determine which of the following distributive laws hold.
      (i) $x \circ (y \triangle z) = (x \circ y) \triangle (x \circ z)$
      (ii) $(y \triangle z) \circ x = (y \circ x) \triangle (z \circ x)$
      (iii) $x \triangle (y \circ z) = (x \triangle y) \circ (x \triangle z)$
      (iv) $(y \circ z) \triangle x = (y \triangle x) \circ (z \triangle x)$

Programming Problems

1. Write a program to generate the power set of $\{0, 1, 2, \ldots, n\}$ for any natural number n given as input.

2. (a) Write a program which accepts specifications of two finite sets A and B, where $A, B \subset \mathbf{N}$, and prints a nonredundant list of the elements of $A \cup B$ and $A \cap B$.
   (b) Write a program to determine for a given set A and an arbitrary $n \in \mathbf{N}$ whether $n \in A$.

2.5 INDUCTION

Inductive Definition of Sets

Earlier in this chapter, we described how finite sets can be defined either explicitly by listing the elements of the set, or implicitly by using a predicate with free variables; we also observed that infinite sets can only be specified implicitly. But predicates do not always provide a convenient means of charactering an infinite set. For example, there is no convenient or obvious predicate to specify the set of ALGOL, PL/I, or FORTRAN programs, or even such a basic structure as the set of natural numbers **N**. Such sets are often most naturally defined using an *inductive definition*.†

An inductive definition of a set always consists of three distinct components.

1. The *basis*, or *basis clause*, of the definition establishes that certain objects are in the set. This part of the definition has the dual function of establishing that the set being defined is not empty and of characterizing the "building blocks" which will be used to construct the remainder of the set.

2. The *induction*, or *inductive clause*, of an inductive definition establishes the ways in which elements of the set can be combined to obtain new elements. The inductive clause always asserts that if objects $x, y, \ldots, z$ are elements of the set, then they can be combined in certain specified ways to create other objects which are also in the set. Thus, while the basis clause describes the building blocks of the set, the inductive clause describes the operations which can be performed on objects in order to construct new elements of the set.

3. The *extremal clause* asserts that unless an object can be shown to be a member of the set by applying the basis and inductive clauses a finite number of times, then the object is not a member of the set. The extremal clause of an inductive definition of a set S has a variety of forms, such as

    (i)   "No object is a member of S unless its being so follows from a finite number of applications of the basis and inductive clauses."

    (ii) "The set S is the smallest set which satisfies the basis and inductive clauses."

    (iii) "The set S is the set such that S satisfies the basis and inductive clauses and no proper subset of S satisfies them (i.e., if T is a subset of S such that T satisfies the basis and inductive clauses, then $T = S$)."

    (iv) "The set S is the intersection of all sets which satisfy the properties specified by the basis and inductive clauses."

In fact, all these forms of the extremal clause are equivalent in consequence though

†The term "recursive definition" is often used to denote what we call an "inductive definition."

not in form, and all serve the purpose of establishing that nothing is a member of the set being defined unless it is required to be so by the first two steps of the definition. Often the extremal clause is not stated explicitly in an inductive definition; this rarely leads to misunderstandings.

Example

If the universe of discourse is the set of integers $\mathbf{I}$, then a predicate definition of the set $\mathbf{E}$ of even nonnegative integers can be given as follows:

$$\mathbf{E} = \{x \mid x \geq 0 \land \exists y[x = 2y]\}$$

The same set can be defined inductively as follows:

1. (Basis) $0 \in \mathbf{E}$.

2. (Induction) If $n \in \mathbf{E}$, then $(n + 2) \in \mathbf{E}$.

3. (Extremal) No integer is an element of $\mathbf{E}$ unless it can be shown to be so from a finite number of applications of clauses 1 and 2.   #

We will now introduce some notation and terminology that will enable us to give some further examples of inductively defined sets. We use Σ to denote a finite and nonempty set of symbols or characters; Σ is called an *alphabet*. A string of a finite number of symbols, each of which is an element of Σ, is called a *word* or *string* (or sometimes a *sentence*) over the alphabet Σ. Let x be a word over Σ; if $x = a_1a_2a_3 \ldots a_n$, where $n \in \mathbf{N}$ and $a_i \in \Sigma$ for each $1 \leq i \leq n$, then the *length* of x is n, the number of symbols in the word x. The string of length 0, denoted Λ, is called the *empty* (or *null*) *string*. If x and y are strings of symbols over Σ, $x = a_1a_2 \ldots a_n$ and $y = b_1b_2 \ldots b_m$, where $a_i \in \Sigma$ and $b_j \in \Sigma$ for all i and j, then x *concatenated* with y, denoted xy, is the string

$$xy = a_1a_2 \ldots a_nb_1b_2 \ldots b_m;$$

if $x = \Lambda$ then $xy = y$ and if $y = \Lambda$ then $xy = x$. If $z = xy$, then x is a *prefix* of z and y is a *suffix*. If $x \neq z$, then x is a *proper prefix*; if $y \neq z$ then y is a *proper suffix*. If $w = xyz$ then y is a *substring* of w and if $y \neq w$, then y is a *proper substring*.

The following two definitions describe sets which are widely used in computer science. In later parts of this text we will develop some of the properties of these sets, and we will often refer to them in examples.

Definition 2.5.1: Let Σ be an alphabet. The set Σ^+ of all nonempty strings over Σ is defined as follows:†

1. (Basis) If $a \in \Sigma$, then $a \in \Sigma^+$.
2. (Induction) If $x \in \Sigma^+$ and $a \in \Sigma$, then $ax \in \Sigma^+$ (ax denotes the string

---

†We will not distinguish between the symbol $a \in \Sigma$ and the word over Σ which consists of the single symbol a. These two objects are not the same, but the distinction is generally not an important one for our purposes.

which consists of the symbol a juxtaposed, or concatenated, with the string x).

3. (Extremal) The set Σ^+ contains only those elements which can be constructed by a finite number of applications of clauses 1 and 2.

The set Σ^+ includes strings of length $1, 2, 3, \ldots$ and is therefore an infinite set. Note, however, that no string in Σ^+ contains an infinite number of symbols; this is ruled out by the extremal clause of the definition.

Example

$$\text{If } \Sigma = \{a, b\}, \text{ then } \Sigma^+ = \{a, b, aa, ab, ba, bb, aaa, aab, \ldots\}. \quad \#$$

The set of all finite strings of symbols from the alphabet Σ is denoted by Σ^*. The set Σ^* includes the empty string and can be defined as $\Sigma^* = \Sigma^+ \cup \{\Lambda\}$, or it can be defined inductively.

Definition 2.5.2: Let Σ be an alphabet. Then Σ^* is defined as follows:

1. (Basis) $\Lambda \in \Sigma^*$.
2. (Induction) If $x \in \Sigma^*$ and $a \in \Sigma$, then $ax \in \Sigma^*$.
3. (Extremal) Nothing is an element of the set Σ^* unless it can be constructed with a finite number of applications of clauses 1 and 2.

Examples

(a) If $\Sigma = \{a, b\}$, then $\Sigma^* = \{\Lambda, a, b, aa, ab, ba, bb, aaa, aab, \ldots\}$.

(b) If $\Sigma = \{0, 1\}$, then Σ^* is the set of all finite binary sequences, including the empty sequence. $\#$

An expression or formula which makes sense in some mathematical discourse is often referred to as a *well-formed formula,* or *wff.* Inductive definitions are used to characterize the set of well-formed formulas whenever a careful definition is required. Many examples occur in programming languages; for example, inductive definitions can be used to describe the class of algebraic expressions which may appear in an assignment statement or the class of logical expressions which may appear in a conditional statement. In some programming languages such as ALGOL, the syntax is largely described by means of inductive definitions given in BNF (Backus-Naur Form, or Backus Normal Form). A description of BNF is beyond our scope; the reader is referred to the description of ALGOL 60 given in Rosen [1967].

Examples

(a) The set of arithmetic expressions includes sequences of symbols such as "$((5 + 6)/2)$" and "$((4/2) - 13)$" but does not include sequences such as "$+ 6 +$", and "$+) ($", even though all these expressions are sequences of symbols from the same alphabet. We will illustrate how to define the set of well-formed arithmetic expressions by means of an inductive definition. For simplicity we will restrict our definition to the set of arithmetic expressions involving only integers, the unary operations of $+$ and $-$, and the binary operations of $+$, $-$, $/$ and $*$.

1. (Basis) If $D = \{0, 1, 2, 3, 4, 5, 6, 7, 8, 9\}$ and $x \in D^+$, then x is an arithmetic expression.

2. (Induction) If x and y are arithmetic expressions, then
     (i) $(+ x)$ is an arithmetic expression,
     (ii) $(- x)$ is an arithmetic expression,
     (iii) $(x + y)$ is an arithmetic expression,
     (iv) $(x - y)$ is an arithmetic expression,
     (v) (x/y) is an arithmetic expression, and
     (vi) $(x * y)$ is an arithmetic expression.

3. (Extremal) A sequence of symbols is an arithmetic expression if and only if it can be obtained by a finite number of applications of clauses 1 and 2.

The set of arithmetic expressions characterized by this definition includes $346, 0000, (-64), (3 + 7), (3*(-61))$, and $(+(-(+(6/7))))$.

(b) The set of *propositional forms* is another set which is most naturally defined inductively. Let $V = \{P, Q, R, \ldots\}$ be a set of propositional variables, where V does not contain any of the following symbols: $(,), \wedge, \vee, \Rightarrow, \Leftrightarrow, \neg, 0, 1$. Then

1. (Basis)   0 is a propositional form.
              1 is a propositional form.
              If $x \in V$, then x is a propositional form.

2. (Induction)   If E and F are propositional forms, then
              $(\neg E)$,
              $(E \vee F)$,
              $(E \wedge F)$,
              $(E \Rightarrow F)$, and
              $(E \Leftrightarrow F)$ are all propositional forms.

3. (Extremal) The set of propositional forms is the set of all expressions which can be formed by a finite number of applications of clauses 1 and 2.

Using this definition, if $V = \{P, Q, R,\}$, then $((P \wedge Q) \Rightarrow R)$ is a propositional form over V. This can be established as follows: From the basis clause, it follows that P, Q, and R are all propositional forms. Applying the induction clause to P and Q, it follows that $(P \wedge Q)$ is a propositional form, and by another application of the inductive clause, this time to $(P \wedge Q)$ and R, it follows that $((P \wedge Q) \Rightarrow R)$ is a propositional form. Thus one can show that an element is a member of an inductively defined set by exhibiting a sequence of applications of the basis and inductive steps which produces the element in question.   #

Recursive Procedures

Inductive definitions form a subclass of a more general class known as recursive definitions. As the term is commonly used in computer science, the salient characteristic of a recursive definition is "self-reference" as in the induction clause of an inductive definition. As we use the terms,† not all recursive definitions are inductive; we will give examples to illustrate the difference in a later chapter.

In programming, a recursive procedure, or recursive subroutine, is one which can call itself, either directly or indirectly. Recursive procedures are based on recursive definitions, although the definition need not be of a set. If a recursive procedure is based on an inductive definition, the segments of the procedure often correspond in a natural way to the basis and induction clauses of the definition.

It is often necessary to write procedures to determine whether an input has a specified property. If the set of elements which have the property is defined inductively, a recursive procedure is a natural and powerful mechanism for determining set membership.

Examples

(a) Consider the universe I, and let E be the set of nonnegative even integers defined inductively in the first example of this section. The recursive procedure EVEN(n) given in Fig. 2.5.1 returns "yes" if an input $n \in I$ is an element of the set E; otherwise it returns "no." The procedure has three parts. The first part causes "no" to be returned if the input is too small; this part of the procedure does not correspond to any part of the inductive definition of E. The second part of the procedure tests if $n = 0$; this corresponds to the basis clause of the definition of E. The third part corresponds to the inductive clause of the definition and causes EVEN to call itself with the parameter $n - 2$.

```
procedure EVEN(n):
comment:  If n is even and n ≥ 0, then return "yes."
          Otherwise, return "no."
if n < 0 then return "no"
else
    if n = 0 then return "yes"
    else
        return EVEN(n − 2)
```

Fig. 2.5.1 Recursive procedure EVEN to determine if n is a nonnegative even integer

(b) Consider the problem of recognizing whether a string of symbols is an arithmetic expression, where the set of arithmetic expressions is defined inductively in part (a) of the preceding example of this section. A recursive procedure ARITH(exp) based on this definition is given in Fig. 2.5.2. This procedure returns "yes" if the input expression exp is generated by the inductive definition of arithmetic expressions; otherwise, the procedure returns "no." The procedure first checks to see if exp is generated by the basis clause, that is, if exp is a

†A distinct but related meaning of the term "recursive" is used in mathematical logic and the theory of computable functions, but a discussion of the relationship between the two uses is beyond our scope. We will only use the term in the informal sense described above.

procedure ARITH(*exp*):
comment: If *exp* is an arithmetic expression, then return "yes."
               Otherwise return "no."
begin
        comment: Determine if *exp* is generated by the basis clause.
        if *exp* is a string of digits **then return** "yes"
        else begin
                comment: Determine if *exp* is generated by the inductive clause.
                if *exp* contains a substring *exp*_1 such that either exp = (+*exp*_1)
                        or *exp* = (−*exp*_1))
                        then return   ARITH(*exp*_1
                else if *exp* contains substrings *exp*_1 and *exp*_2 such that
                        exp = (*exp*_1 □ *exp*_2)
                        where □ is an operation symbol (+, −, / or ∗)
                        and ARITH(*exp*_1) = "yes"
                        and ARITH(*exp*_2) = "yes"
                        then return "yes"
            end;
        comment: *exp* is not produced by either basis or inductive clauses.
        return "no"
end

Fig. 2.5.2   Recursive procedure ARITH to determine whether a
string of symbols is an arithmetic expression

string of digits. If so, the procedure returns "yes." If *exp* is not a string of digits,
then ARITH breaks *exp* into nonoverlapping substrings to determine if *exp* is
generated from other arithmetic expressions by the induction clause. If this is
not the case, ARITH concludes that *exp* is not an arithmetic expression and
returns "no."   #

When a recursive procedure to decide if an element is in a set is based on an
inductive definition of the set, it is necessary to provide a mechanism for return-
ing a negative answer. The procedure given in Fig. 2.5.1 contains a test for a negative input. Without this test, the procedure would return "yes" if the input was
nonnegative and even, but would not terminate for other inputs. The procedure
ARITH of Fig. 2.5.2 must determine if the input can be broken into substrings of
operands and operators. All the possibilities can be considered by exhaustive test,
and if none are successful, the procedure returns "no." (In fact, there are much
faster ways of determining this information than by exhaustive testing; our examples are suitably illustrative, but they are not efficient algorithms.)

Inductive Proofs

Inductive definitions not only provide a method of defining infinite sets, but
they also form the basis of some powerful techniques for proving theorems. If
a set is finite, a statement of the form $\forall x P(x)$ can in principle be established by an

exhaustive proof by cases. But for infinite sets, some other device must be used. Proofs by induction are proofs of universally quantified assertions where the universe of discourse is an inductively defined set.

Suppose we wish to establish that all the elements of an inductively defined S have a property P; i.e., we wish to establish $\forall x P(x)$ for the universe S. A proof by induction usually consists of two parts corresponding to the basis and induction clauses of the definition of S:

1. The *basis* step establishes that $P(x)$ is true for every element of $x \in S$ specified in the basis clause of the definition of S.
2. The *induction* step establishes that each element constructed using the induction clause of the definition of S has the property P if all the elements used in its construction have the property P.

Note that there is no step in an inductive proof which corresponds to the extremal clause of the definition of S, but its role is crucial to proofs by induction. The extremal clause guarantees that all elements of S can be constructed using only the basis and induction clauses of the definition. An inductive proof establishes that every element x constructed in this way has some property P. It follows from the extremal clause that the assertion $P(x)$ holds for all elements of S, and we can therefore conclude $\forall x P(x)$.

To illustrate the technique of inductive proof, consider the set of well-formed, or *balanced* strings of parentheses. (For clarity, we will represent parentheses by square brackets.)

Definition 2.5.3:   Let Σ be the alphabet $\{[,]\}$. The set B of well-formed parenthesis strings is the subset of Σ^+ such that

1. (Basis) [ ] is an element of B.
2. (Induction) If x and y are elements of B, then
    (i) $[x]$ is an element of B, and
    (ii) xy is an element of B.
3. (Extremal) The set B consists of all symbol strings which can be constructed using a finite number of applications of clauses 1 and 2.

The set B is the set of all parenthesis sequences which can occur in algebraic formulas, such as [ ], [[ ]], [ ][ ], [[ ][ ], and [[[ ][ ]]. We now show that in any well-formed parenthesis string, the number of left parentheses is equal to the number of right parentheses.

Theorem 2.5.1:   Let x be an element of B. If $L(x)$ denotes the number of left parentheses in x and $R(x)$ denotes the number of right parentheses in x, then $L(x) = R(x)$.

Proof: The theorem asserts $\forall x[x \in B \Rightarrow L(x) = R(x)]$. The proof follows the definition of B.

Let x be an arbitrary element of B.

1. (Basis) If $x = [\ ]$, then $L(x) = R(x) = 1$.
2. (Induction) Let x and y be elements of B, and suppose they have the property that $L(x) = R(x)$ and $L(y) = R(y)$. We show that any element z which can be constructed from x and y has the property $L(z) = R(z)$.
    (i)   If $z = [x]$, then $L(z) = L(x) + 1 = R(x) + 1 = R(z)$
    (ii) If $z = xy$, then $L(z) = L(x) + L(y) = R(x) + R(y) = R(z)$.

This completes the inductive proof and establishes the theorem. ∎

Most commonly, proofs by induction deal with the natural numbers. In order to discuss these proofs, it will be useful to have the following inductive characterization of $\mathbf{N}$.

1. (Basis) $0 \in \mathbf{N}$.
2. (Induction) If $n \in \mathbf{N}$, then $(n + 1) \in \mathbf{N}$.
3. (Extremal) If $S \subset \mathbf{N}$, and S has the properties
    (i) $0 \in S$,
    (ii) For every $n \in \mathbf{N}$, if $n \in S$ then $(n + 1) \in S$,
    then $S = \mathbf{N}$.

In fact, this does not suffice to define the natural numbers because we have not carefully specified what is meant by the basis and inductive steps; we will present a proper definition of $\mathbf{N}$ in the next section. However, the above characterization will enable us to discuss inductive proofs for the universe $\mathbf{N}$. The extremal clause in the above characterization of $\mathbf{N}$ is the form customarily used in definitions of the natural numbers; it is called the *First Principle of Mathematical Induction*. This form of the extremal clause implies the procedure to be used for inductive proofs of assertions of the form $\forall x P(x)$ for the universe of natural numbers. Such a proof proceeds as follows:

1. (Basis) We first show that $P(0)$ is true, using whatever proof technique is appropriate.
2. (Induction) We next show $\forall n[P(n) \Rightarrow P(n + 1)]$.

The inductive step of the proof is usually a direct proof of the implication $P(n) \Rightarrow P(n + 1)$, where the implication is established for arbitrary $n \in \mathbf{N}$. The assertion $P(n)$ is known as the *induction hypothesis*. The induction hypothesis is often stated as "Assume $P(n)$ is true for arbitrary $n \in \mathbf{N}$". Note that this is not equivalent to assuming the truth of the theorem; $P(n)$ is assumed only for the purpose of proving the universally quantified assertion $\forall n[P(n) \Rightarrow P(n + 1)]$. Once $P(n) \Rightarrow P(n + 1)$ has been proven for arbitrary n, it follows (by the rule of inference known as Universal Generalization) that $\forall n[P(n) \Rightarrow P(n + 1)]$. Then from the First Principle of Mathematical Induction we can conclude $\forall x P(x)$. For suppose S is the subset of $\mathbf{N}$ such that $P(n)$ is true for every $n \in S$. The basis step of the proof establishes that $0 \in S$. The inductive step establishes that for every $n \in \mathbf{N}$, if $n \in S$, then $(n + 1) \in S$. By the extremal clause of the definition of $\mathbf{N}$, it follows that $S = \mathbf{N}$, i.e., $\forall x P(x)$.

To illustrate proofs by induction over $\mathbf{N}$, we will prove the following.

Theorem 2.5.2:   For all $n \in \mathbf{N}$,

$$\sum_{i=0}^{n} i = \frac{n(n+1)}{2}.$$

The theorem is of the form $\forall n P(n)$, where $P(n)$ is the assertion

$$\sum_{i=0}^{n} i = \frac{n(n+1)}{2}.$$

Proof:

1. We first establish the basis step $P(0)$:

$$\sum_{i=0}^{0} i = \frac{0(0+1)}{2}$$

The proof consists simply of evaluating each side, giving $0 = 0$.

2. The induction step establishes $\forall n[P(n) \Rightarrow P(n+1)]$. To prove this assertion, we give a direct proof of the assertion $P(n) \Rightarrow P(n+1)$ for arbitrary $n \in \mathbf{N}$. In a direct proof of $P(n) \Rightarrow P(n+1)$, the induction hypothesis, $P(n)$ is assumed to be true. $P(n)$ asserts

$$\sum_{i=0}^{n} i = \frac{n(n+1)}{2}.$$

We wish to show $P(n+1)$, i.e.,

$$\sum_{i=0}^{n+1} i = \frac{(n+1)(n+2)}{2}.$$

But,

$$\sum_{i=0}^{n+1} i = (n+1) + \sum_{i=0}^{n} i$$

$$= (n+1) + \frac{n(n+1)}{2} \qquad \text{(by the induction hypothesis)}$$

$$= \frac{2(n+1) + n(n+1)}{2}$$

$$= \frac{(n+1)(n+2)}{2}.$$

Since n was arbitrary, it follows that $\forall n[P(n) \Rightarrow P(n+1)]$. By the First Principle of Mathematical Induction we conclude that $\forall x P(x)$. ∎

The following theorem gives algebraic expressions for two more finite sums which will occur in Chapter 5 when we treat the analysis of algorithms. The proofs are by induction and are left as exercises.

Theorem 2.5.3:   Let r be a real number. Then for all $n \in \mathbf{N}$,

(a) $\displaystyle\sum_{i=0}^{n} r^i = (n+1)$ if $r = 1$,

$$= \frac{r^{n+1} - 1}{r - 1}$$ if $r \neq 1$.

(b) $\displaystyle\sum_{i=0}^{n} ir^i = \frac{n(n+1)}{2}$ if $r = 1$,

$\displaystyle\qquad\quad = \frac{nr^{n+2} - (n+1)r^{n+1} + r}{(r-1)^2}$ if $r \neq 1$.

In many proofs by induction, the assertions involve properties of the natural numbers only indirectly. The following theorem is an example; we wish to prove an assertion relating finite sets to their power sets, but the natural technique is an inductive proof.

Theorem 2.5.4:   If S is a finite set with n elements, then S has 2^n distinct subsets.

Proof: The assertion in logical notation is the following:

$$\forall n \, \forall S[S \text{ has } n \text{ elements} \Rightarrow \mathcal{P}(S) \text{ has } 2^n \text{ elements}].$$

The inductive proof has two parts.

1. (Basis) We must show $\forall S[S$ has 0 elements $\Rightarrow \mathcal{P}(S)$ has 1 element]. Let S be an arbitrary set with 0 elements. Then $S = \phi$ and it follows that $\mathcal{P}(S) = \{\phi\}$. Since $2^0 = 1$, the assertion is established for $n = 0$.

2. (Induction) We must show that if the assertion is true for sets with n elements, then it is true for sets with $(n+1)$ elements. Let $S = \{a_1, a_2, a_3, \ldots, a_n\}$, and $S' = S \cup \{a\}$ where $a \notin S$. If A is the set $\{B \cup \{a\} \,|\, B \in \mathcal{P}(S)\}$, then $\mathcal{P}(S') = \mathcal{P}(S) \cup A$, since every subset of S' is either a subset of S or is formed by adding the element a to a subset of S. By the induction hypothesis, $\mathcal{P}(S)$ has 2^n elements. Since each subset of S corresponds to exactly one element of A, it follows that A also has 2^n elements. Since $\mathcal{P}(S)$ and A are disjoint and $\mathcal{P}(S') = \mathcal{P}(S) \cup A$, it follows that $\mathcal{P}(S')$ has $2^n + 2^n = 2\cdot 2^n = 2^{n+1}$ elements.   ∎

Often sets which have been inductively defined are used as a base for other inductive definitions. Such "secondary" inductive definitions require no extremal clause because the extremal clause of the underlying set fulfills the appropriate function.

Example

The following is an inductive definition of the exponential a^n for nonnegative integer values of n. The underlying inductively defined set is **N**.

Definition 2.5.4:   Let $a \in \mathbf{R}+$ and $n \in \mathbf{N}$. The value of a^n is defined inductively as follows:

1. (Basis) $a^0 = 1$.
2. (Induction) $a^{n+1} = a^n a$.

The inductive definition can be used to establish the following:

Theorem 2.5.5: $\forall m \, \forall n[a^m a^n = a^{m+n}]$

Although the above assertion involves two universal quantifiers, it can be proved by inducton by letting m be arbitrary and proving the assertion $\forall n[a^m a^n = a^{m+n}]$ by induction on n. Since m was arbitrary, the theorem will follow by universal generalization.

Proof: Let m be arbitrary.
1.   (Basis) If $n = 0$, then

$$a^m a^n = a^m a^0 = a^m(1) = a^m = a^{m+0} = a^{m+n}.$$

2.   (Induction) Assume $a^m a^n = a^{m+n}$ for arbitrary n. Then

$$a^m a^{n+1} = a^m(a^n a) \qquad \text{Definition of } a^n$$
$$= (a^m a^n)a \qquad \text{Associativity of multiplication}$$
$$= (a^{m+n})a \qquad \text{Induction hypothesis}$$
$$= a^{(m+n)+1} \qquad \text{Definition of } a^n$$
$$= a^{m+(n+1)} \qquad \text{Associativity of addition.} \quad \blacksquare \quad \#$$

The principle of mathematical induction is, in fact, a rule of inference for the universe of the natural numbers. Using the notation of Section 1.4, the formal presentation of the rule is the following.

$$P(0)$$
$$\forall n[P(n) \Rightarrow P(n+1)]$$
$$\therefore \ \forall x P(x)$$

We often wish to prove that a predicate P holds for all $x \geq k$ for some integer k. A proof by induction is still appropriate but the basis step must be changed to prove $P(k)$. The rule of inference is then

$$P(k)$$
$$\forall n[P(n) \Rightarrow P(n+1)]$$
$$\therefore \ \forall x[(x \geq k) \Rightarrow P(x)]$$

Thus to prove that $P(x)$ holds for all integers equal to or greater than k, it suffices to show $P(k)$ is true as the basis step, and then show the inductive step $\forall n[P(n) \Rightarrow P(n+1)]$.

Another form of proof by induction over the natural numbers uses the *Second Principle of Mathematical Induction* to prove assertions of the form $\forall x P(x)$. The induction step of a proof using the Second Principle assumes $P(k)$ is true for all $k < n$ and shows that this implies $P(n)$. The formal statement of the Second Principle as a rule of inference is the following.

$$\forall n[\forall k[k < n \Rightarrow P(k)] \Rightarrow P(n)]$$
$$\therefore \ \forall x P(x)$$

The induction hypothesis for a proof using this rule of inference is

$$\forall k[k < n \Rightarrow P(k)];$$

from this hypothesis, we must establish $P(n)$. If $P(n)$ can be shown on the assumption that the induction hypothesis holds, then we can conclude $\forall x P(x)$.

Note that if $n = 0$, the assertion $k < 0$ is false for every $k \in \mathbf{N}$, and therefore the implication $k < 0 \Rightarrow P(k)$ is true. It follows that $\forall k[k < 0 \Rightarrow P(k)]$ is true and hence $\forall k[k < 0 \Rightarrow P(k)] \Rightarrow P(0)$ is equivalent to $P(0)$. Thus the basis step of the First Principle is implied by the hypothesis of the Second Principle.

An application of the Second Principle only requires that we establish a single hypothesis, but this often requires a proof by cases. This most commonly is in the form of proving the special case $P(0)$, and then proving that for any $n > 0$, if $P(k)$ holds for all $k < n$, then $P(n)$ holds. Such a proof using the Second Principle differs from one using the First Principle only in that instead of assuming an induction hypothesis of $P(n - 1)$ to prove $P(n)$, we assume that $P(k)$ is true for all $k < n$.

Proofs by induction using the Second Principle assume a stronger induction hypothesis than proofs using the First Principle. The Second Principle is a natural choice for inductive proofs in which the properties of elements generated in the $(n + 1)$th step may depend on the properties of elements generated in several previous steps.

Although the two principles of mathematical induction are different, if the universe of discourse is the natural numbers $\mathbf{N}$, their hypotheses are logically equivalent and they are therefore equally powerful. Other universes exist where the Second Principle is in fact more powerful; we will see an example when we treat order relations.

Example

   We use the Second Principle of Mathematical Induction to prove that all integers $n \geq 2$ can be written as a product of prime numbers. The induction hypothesis asserts that for arbitrary n,
   For every k such that $2 \leq k < n$, k can be written as a product of prime numbers.
On the basis of this assumption we must show that n can be written as a product of primes.
   The proof is by cases.
   Case 1:   If n is a prime, then n is such a product of one prime.
   Case 2:   If n is not a prime, then $n = ab$, where $2 \leq a, b < n$. By the induction hypothesis, both a and b can be written as products of primes and therefore their product can be written in this form.   #

Problems: Section 2.5

1. Give inductive definitions for the following sets.
    (a) The set of unsigned integers in decimal representation. The defined set should include 4, 167, 0012, etc.
    (b) The set of real numbers with terminating fractional parts in decimal representation. The defined set should include 6.1, 712., 01.2100, 0.190, etc.

(c) The set of even integers in binary representation without leading zeroes. The defined set should include 0, 110, 1010, etc.

2. Integer arithmetic operations with one nonnegative operand can often be defined inductively in terms of more "primitive" operations. Thus, the product of two integers can be defined as follows:

$$a \cdot 0 = 0,$$

$$a \cdot (b + 1) = a \cdot b + a \quad \text{for} \quad b \geq 0.$$

(a) Write a recursive procedure based on this definition which calculates the product of two integers where the second is known to be nonnegative.

(b) Give an inductive definition of a^b (exponentiation) using only multiplication and addition. Assume a and b are integers and $b \geq 0$. Write a recursive procedure to calculate a^b based on your definition.

3. Give an inductive definition of $n!$ and use it to prove the identity

$$n! = \prod_{i=1}^{n} i$$

when $n \geq 1$.

4. Prove by induction that $(1 + 2 + 3 + \cdots + n)^2 = 1^3 + 2^3 + 3^3 + \cdots + n^3$ for all $n \in \mathbf{I}+$.

5. Let a be a positive number. Prove

$$\forall m \, \forall n [(a^m)^n = a^{mn}] \quad \text{where } m, n \in \mathbf{N}.$$

6. Prove each of the following relationships for all $n \in \mathbf{N}$.

(a) $\sum_{i=0}^{n} i^2 = n(n + 1)(2n + 1)/6$

(b) $\sum_{i=0}^{n} (2i + 1) = (n + 1)^2$

(c) $\sum_{i=0}^{n} i(i!) = (n + 1)! - 1$

(d) $1 + 2n \leq 3^n$

7. Prove Theorem 2.5.3.

8. A polygon is *convex* if every line joining two points of the polygon lies within the polygon. Prove that the sum of the interior angles of a convex polygon with n sides is equal to $(n - 2) \, 180°$ for all $n \geq 3$. (Hint: If $n > 3$, the polygon can be divided into two parts by connecting nonadjacent vertices.)

9. Find predicates P and Q over the natural numbers which will establish that the basis step and the induction step of an inductive proof are independent, i.e., neither logically implies the other. Specifically, find a predicate P such that $P(0)$ is true and $\forall n[P(n) \Rightarrow P(n + 1)]$ is false and a predicate Q such that $Q(0)$ is false and $\forall n[Q(n) \Rightarrow Q(n + 1)]$ is true.

10. What is wrong with the following proof that all people are the same size? We purport to prove that for all n and for all S, if S is a set with n people, then all people in S are the same size.

1. (Basis) Let S be an empty set of people. Then for all x and y, if $x \in S$ and $y \in S$, then x is the same size as y.

2. (Induction) Assume the assertion is true for all sets containing n people. We show it is true for sets containing $n + 1$ people. Any set consisting of $n + 1$ people contains two nonequal subsets of n people which must overlap. Denote these sets by S' and S''. Then by induction hypothesis, all people in S' are the same size and all people in S'' are the same size. Since S' and S'' overlap, all people in $S = S' \cup S''$ are the same size.

11. Let $\{A_1, A_2, \ldots, A_n\}$ be a nonempty collection of sets. Prove the following generalizations of DeMorgan's Laws by induction on n.

   (a) $\overline{\bigcup_{i=1}^{n} A_i} = \bigcap_{i=1}^{n} \overline{A_i}$

   (b) $\overline{\bigcap_{i=1}^{n} A_i} = \bigcup_{i=1}^{n} \overline{A_i}$

12. A binary operation $\square$ is said to be associative if $a \square (b \square c) = (a \square b) \square c$. From this "associative law" we infer a much stronger result, namely that in any expression involving only the operation $\square$, the placement of parentheses does not affect the result, that is, only the operands and the order in which they occur in the expression are important. In order to prove this "generalized associative law," we define the "set of $\square$ expressions" as follows:
   1. (Basis) A single operand a_1 is a $\square$ expression.
   2. (Induction) Let e_1 and e_2 be $\square$ expressions. Then $(e_1 \square e_2)$ is a $\square$ expression.
   3. (Extremal) There are no $\square$ expressions other than those which can be constructed from 1 and 2 in a finite number of steps.
   The generalized associative law can now be stated as follows:

   Let e be a $\square$ expression with n operands $a_1, a_2, \ldots, a_n$ which appear in that order in the expression e. Then

   $$e = (a_1 \square (a_2 \square (a_3 \square (\ldots (a_{n-1} \square a_n) \ldots)))).$$

   Prove this generalized associative law. (Hint: Use the Second Principle of Mathematical Induction.)

‡2.6 THE NATURAL NUMBERS

In this section, we will exhibit a careful set theoretic definition of the natural numbers. In the previous section, we used the operation of addition to give an inductive characterization of **N**. Since the definition of addition of natural numbers must be based on the set **N**, the characterization we gave is circular and hence unacceptable as a formal definition of **N**. To avoid this circularity, **N** must be defined without using addition. The following is a better (but not yet successful) characterization of **N** which uses n' to denote the "successor" of a natural number n; informally, we interpret n' as $n + 1$.

   1. (Basis) $0 \in \mathbf{N}$.
   2. (Induction) If $n \in \mathbf{N}$, then $n' \in \mathbf{N}$.
   3. (Extremal) If $S \subset \mathbf{N}$ and S satisfies clauses 1 and 2, then $S = \mathbf{N}$.

The inadequacy of the above characterization stems from our not having specified exactly what is meant either by 0 in the basis step or by n' (which must be defined in terms of n) in the inductive step. As a result, models can be constructed which satisfy the inductive characterization given above, but do not have the structure of **N**. The structure we want to characterize can be diagrammed as follows:

where $a \longrightarrow b$ means b is a successor of a; in the diagram, $0'$ represents 1, $0''$ represents 2, etc. If we can find a model of the above inductive characterization of **N** which has a different structure, then we will have established the inadequacy of the characterization as a definition of **N**. The simplest "unintended" model is formed by making 0 its own successor, i.e., $0 = 0'$. In this model, the set **N** is the singleton set {0} and the structure is diagrammed as follows:

In order to rule out such a model, the set **N** must be defined so as to guarantee that *0 is not the successor of any natural number*. This change alone is not sufficient, however. Let **N** be the set of nodes of an "infinite rooted binary tree." The root denotes 0, and each natural number has a successor; in fact, it has two successors. This unintended model can be represented as follows:

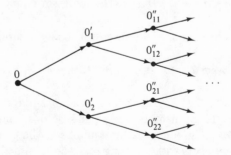

Consequently, an adequate characterization of **N** must guarantee that *the successor of a natural number is unique*. Even with this condition satisfied, however, it is still possible to construct models which do not have the intended structure. In the following diagram, 0 is not a successor of any natural number, and every natural number has an unique successor. However, two distinct natural numbers 1 and 3 have the same successor.

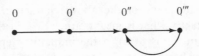

To rule out such models, the definition of **N** must guarantee that *if x' = y' then x = y*, that is, a natural number can have at most one predecessor.

A definition of **N** which satisfies all of these constraints can be constructed using set theory. Each natural number will be a set. The first natural number is defined to be ϕ, changing the basis step to

1. (Basis) ϕ is a natural number.

For each natural number n, its successor, n', is constructed as follows.

2. (Induction) If n is a natural number, then $n \cup \{n\}$ is a natural number.

The extremal step remains unchanged. The result is the following definition.

Definition 2.6.1: The set of natural numbers **N** is the set such that

1. (Basis) $\phi \in \mathbf{N}$,
2. (Induction) If $n \in \mathbf{N}$, then $n \cup \{n\} \in \mathbf{N}$,
3. (Extremal) If $S \subset \mathbf{N}$ and S satisfies clauses 1 and 2, then $S = \mathbf{N}$.

The set of natural numbers, according to this definition, has as its elements the sets $\phi, \{\phi\}, \{\phi, \{\phi\}\}, \{\phi, \{\phi\}, \{\phi, \{\phi\}\}\}, \ldots$ which we denote by the numerals 0, 1, 2, 3, ... Many of the familiar properties of the natural numbers can now be established, including the following theorems. (The proofs can be found in Chapter 1 of Cohn [1965].)

Theorem 2.6.1: 0 is not the successor of any natural number.

Theorem 2.6.2: The successor to any natural number is unique.

Theorem 2.6.3: If $n' = m'$, then $n = m$.

If these theorems are added as axioms to the inadequate inductive characterization of **N** given at the beginning of this section, we obtain the well-known *Peano Postulates* for the natural numbers. These postulates, which characterize the natural numbers without using sets, can be stated as follows:

(a) 0 is a natural number.
(b) For each natural number n, there exists exactly one natural number n', which we call the *successor* of n.
(c) 0 is not the successor of any natural number.
(d) If $n' = m'$, then $n = m$.
(e) If S is a subset of **N**, such that
    (i) $0 \in S$,

(ii) if $n \in S$, then $n' \in S$,
then $S = \mathbf{N}$.

Problems: Section 2.6

1. Construct a series of models for the axiom systems obtained from the Peano postulates by deleting each of the axioms a through e in turn. None of the models should have the structure of the natural numbers.

2. The definition we have given of the natural numbers only involves the notion of "successor." Relations such as "less than" and operations such as addition and multiplication must be defined in terms of the concept of "successor." For example, the operation of addition can be defined inductively as follows:
   1. For every integer m, $m + 0 = m$.
   2. For every pair of integers m and n, $m + n' = (m + n)'$.
      (a) Show (using the above definition) that addition is associative.
      (b) Define multiplication inductively in an analogous manner. You can use the (previously defined) operation of addition.
      (c) Define exponentiation inductively, using the operation of multiplication.
      (d) Give an inductive definition of the relation "less than."

3. Construct an alternate model of **N** using sets. The alternate model need not have the property that the set which denotes the number k has k elements.

2.7 SET OPERATIONS ON Σ*

Strings of symbols play an important role in computer science. Computer programs, texts of written documents, mathematical formulas, and theorems in a formal system are all objects which we conventionally represent as finite sequences of symbols. Thus, in order to write programs that operate on other programs, text editing programs, programs which manipulate algebraic formulas and programs which prove theorems, we must have tools for handling individual strings and sets of strings.

Throughout this text, the symbol Σ will denote a finite alphabet and Σ^* the set of all strings of finite length with symbols from Σ. The principal operation on elements of Σ^* is concatenation.

Definition 2.7.1: Let Σ be an alphabet and x and y be elements of Σ^*. If $x = a_1 a_2 \ldots a_m$ and $y = b_1 b_2 \ldots b_n$ where $a_i, b_j \in \Sigma$ and $m, n \in \mathbf{N}$ then the *concatenation of x with y*, denoted $x \cdot y$, or simply xy, is the string $xy = a_1 a_2 \ldots a_m b_1 b_2 \ldots b_n$. If $x = \Lambda$, then $xy = y$ for every y; similarly if $y = \Lambda$, then $xy = x$.

The following is a convenient notation for representing the concatenation of a string to itself n times. This inductive definition is based on a definition of **N** and therefore requires no extremal clause.

Definition 2.7.2:   Let x be an element of Σ^*. For each $n \in \mathbf{N}$, the string x^n is defined as follows:

1. $x^0 = \Lambda$,
2. $x^{n+1} = x^n \cdot x$.

Examples

(a) If $\Sigma = \{a, b\}$ and $x = ab$, then $x^0 = \Lambda$, $x^1 = ab$, $x^2 = abab$, and $x^3 = ababab$.

(b) The set $\{a^n b^n \mid n \geq 0\}$ denotes the set $\{\Lambda, ab, aabb, aaabbb, \ldots\}$.   #

We often wish to treat collections of strings rather than individual strings. For example, in programming language specification, we must characterize the entire set of programs which can be written in a language. Similarly, a compiler must be written so that it can handle all programs written in the language. Because of the importance of such sets, a considerable body of terminology and notation has been developed to deal with them.

Definition 2.7.3:   Let Σ be a finite alphabet. A *language over* Σ is a subset of Σ^*.

Examples

(a) The set $\{a, ab, abb\}$ is a language over $\Sigma = \{a, b\}$.

(b) The set of strings consisting of sequences of a's followed by sequences of b's, $\{a^n b^m \mid n, m \in \mathbf{N}\}$, is a language over $\{a, b\}$.

(c) The set of ALGOL programs is a language over the alphabet consisting of the ALGOL character set.   #

Since every language is a set, the usual collection of set operations introduced earlier in this chapter can be applied to languages. However, because they are collections of strings, other important operations on languages can be defined as well, many of which are based on the operation of concatenation. The principal goal of this section is to introduce these operations on languages and describe some of their properties. These operations are important in a variety of application areas as well as for the study of models of computation.

Definition 2.7.4:   Let A and B be languages over Σ. The *set product of A with B*, denoted $A \cdot B$, or simply AB, is the language $AB = \{xy \mid x \in A \wedge y \in B\}$.

The language AB consists of all strings which are formed by concatenating an element of A with an element of B.

Example

Let $\Sigma = \{a, b\}$, $A = \{\Lambda, a, ab\}$ and $B = \{a, bb\}$. Then

$$AB = \{a, bb, aa, abb, aba, abbb\},$$
$$BA = \{a, aa, aab, bb, bba, bbab\}.$$

Note that, in general, $AB \neq BA$; i.e., the operation of set product is not commutative. #

Theorem 2.7.1: Let A, B, C, and D be arbitrary languages over Σ. The following relations hold.

(a) $A\phi = \phi A = \phi$

(b) $A\{\Lambda\} = \{\Lambda\} A = A$

(c) $(AB)C = A(BC)$

(d) If $A \subset B$ and $C \subset D$, then $AC \subset BD$

(e) $A(B \cup C) = AB \cup AC$

(f) $(B \cup C)A = BA \cup CA$

(g) $A(B \cap C) \subset AB \cap AC$

(h) $(B \cap C)A \subset BA \cap CA$

Proof:

(a) ($A\phi = \phi A = \phi$.) By definition, $A\phi = \{xy \mid x \in A \wedge y \in \phi\}$. But for every $y \in \Sigma^*$, $y \in \phi$ is false and therefore the conjunction $x \in A \wedge y \in \phi$ is false for all x and y. Since no values of x and y satisfy the predicate, the set $A\phi$ has no members, that is, $A\phi = \phi$. A similar proof establishes the identity $\phi A = \phi$.

(d) (If $A \subset B$ and $C \subset D$, then $AC \subset BD$.) The proof is direct. Assume $A \subset B \wedge C \subset D$, and let z be an arbitrary element of AC. Then $z = xy$, where $x \in A$ and $y \in C$. Since $A \subset B$ and $C \subset D$, it follows that $x \in B$ and $y \in D$. Hence, $z = xy \in BD$. Since z was an arbitrary element of AC, it follows that $AC \subset BD$.

(e) ($A(B \cup C) = AB \cup AC$.)

    (i) $AB \cup AC \subset A(B \cup C)$: We first apply part (d) by noting that $A \subset A$, $B \subset B \cup C$ and $C \subset B \cup C$. Therefore, $AB \subset A(B \cup C)$ and $AC \subset A(B \cup C)$. Hence, $AB \cup AC \subset A(B \cup C)$.

    (ii) $A(B \cup C) \subset AB \cup AC$: If z is an element of $A(B \cup C)$, then $z = xy$ where $x \in A$ and $y \in B \cup C$. Hence, either $(x \in A \wedge y \in B)$ or $(x \in A \wedge y \in C)$. It follows that $z \in AB$ or $z \in AC$, and therefore $z \in AB \cup AC$.

We leave the remaining parts of the proof as exercises. ∎

Note that the operation of set product does not distribute over intersection. For example, if $A = \{a, aa\}$, $B = \{a\}$ and $C = \{aa\}$, then $AB \cap AC = \{aaa\}$ but $A(B \cap C) = \phi$.

Definition 2.7.5: Let A be a language over Σ. The language A^n is defined inductively as follows:

1. $A^0 = \{\Lambda\}$,

2. $A^{n+1} = A^n \cdot A$,   for $n \in \mathbf{N}$.

The language A^n is the set product of A with itself n times. Therefore, if $z \in A^n$ for $n \geq 1$, then $z = w_1 w_2 \ldots w_n$, where $w_i \in A$ for each i from 1 to n.

Example

Let $\Sigma = \{a, b\}$ and $A = \{\Lambda, a, ab\}$. Then $A^0 = \{\Lambda\}$, $A^1 = A = \{\Lambda, a, ab\}$, and

$$A^2 = A \cdot A = \{\Lambda, a, aa, aab, ab, aba, abab\}. \quad \#$$

Theorem 2.7.2: Let A and B be subsets of Σ^* and let m and n be arbitrary elements of **N**. Then

(a) $A^m A^n = A^{m+n}$

(b) $(A^m)^n = A^{mn}$

(c) $A \subset B \Rightarrow A^n \subset B^n$

Proof: The proofs of parts (a) and (b) are left as exercises. The proof of part (c) is by induction on n:

1. (Basis) Since $A^0 = \{\Lambda\}$ and $B^0 = \{\Lambda\}$, it follows that $A^n \subset B^n$ if $n = 0$.

2. (Induction) We wish to prove that for all n, if $A^n \subset B^n$, then $A^{n+1} \subset B^{n+1}$. By Theorem 2.7.1(d), if $A^n \subset B^n$ and $A \subset B$, then $A^n \cdot A \subset B^n \cdot B$, i.e., $A^{n+1} \subset B^{n+1}$. ∎

We have used the notation Σ^* to denote the set of all finite strings formed by concatenating elements of Σ. This notation can be extended in a natural way to any subset of Σ^*. We use the symbols "∗" and "+" to denote unary operations (called *closure operations*) on languages.

Definition 2.7.6: Let A be a subset of Σ^*. Then the set A^* (read "A star") is defined to be

$$A^* = \bigcup_{n \in \mathbf{N}} A^n$$

i.e., $A^* = A^0 \cup A^1 \cup A^2 \cup A^3 \cup \cdots$
$ = \{\Lambda\} \cup A \cup A^2 \cup A^3 \cup \cdots$

The set A^* is often called the *star closure*, *Kleene closure*, or simply the *closure of A*. The set A^+ (read "A plus") is defined to be

$$A^+ = \bigcup_{n=1}^{\infty} A^n$$

i.e., $A^+ = A^1 \cup A^2 \cup A^3 \cup \cdots$

The set A^+ is often called the *positive closure of A*.

Note that $x \in A^+$ if and only if $x \in A^n$ for some positive $n \in \mathbf{N}$, and $x \in A^*$ if and only if $x \in A^n$ for some arbitrary $n \in \mathbf{N}$.

Examples

(a) If $A = \{a\}$, then
$\quad A^+ = \{a\} \cup \{aa\} \cup \{aaa\} \cup \cdots$
$\quad = \{a^n \,|\, n \geq 1\};$
$\quad A^* = \{\Lambda\} \cup A^+$
$\quad = \{a^n \,|\, n \geq 0\}.$

(b) $\phi^* = \{\Lambda\} \cup \phi \cup \phi^2 \cup \phi^3 \cup \cdots$
     $= \{\Lambda\};$
  $\phi^+ = \phi.$ #

The following theorem characterizes some important properties of the language closure operations.

Theorem 2.7.3: Let A and B be languages over Σ and let $n \in \mathbf{N}$. Then the following relationships hold.
  (a) $A^* = \{\Lambda\} \cup A^+$
  (b) $A^n \subset A^*$ for $n \geq 0$
  (c) $A^n \subset A^+$ for $n \geq 1$
  (d) $A \subset AB^*$
  (e) $A \subset B^*A$
  (f) $(A \subset B) \Rightarrow (A^* \subset B^*)$
  (g) $(A \subset B) \Rightarrow (A^+ \subset B^+)$
  (h) $AA^* = A^*A = A^+$
  (i) $\Lambda \in A \Leftrightarrow A^+ = A^*$
  (j) $(A^*)^* = A^*A^* = A^*$
  (k) $(A^*)^+ = (A^+)^* = A^*$
  (l) $A^*A^+ = A^+A^* = A^+$
  (m) $(A^*B^*)^* = (A \cup B)^* = (A^* \cup B^*)^*$

Proof: Parts (a), (b), and (c) are immediate from the definition of A^n, A^+, and A^*.
  (d) $(A \subset AB^*.)$ By part (a), $B^* = \{\Lambda\} \cup B^+$. Therefore, $AB^* = A(\{\Lambda\} \cup B^+)$ $= A \cup AB^+$ which contains A. A similar proof establishes (e).
  (f) $(A \subset B \Rightarrow A^* \subset B^*.)$ If $x \in A^*$, then $x \in A^n$ for some $n \geq 0$. But $A \subset B$ so by Theorem 2.7.2, $A^n \subset B^n$. Therefore, $x \in B^n$ and from part (b) it follows that $x \in B^*$. A similar argument holds for part (g).
  (h) We show only $A^*A = A^+$. An intuitively appealing argument can be constructed by noting $A^* = A^0 \cup A^1 \cup A^2 \cup A^3 \cup \cdots$ and therefore

$$A^*A = (A^0 \cup A^1 \cup A^2 \cup A^3 \cup \cdots)A$$
$$= A^0A \cup A^1A \cup A^2A \cup \cdots$$
$$= A^1 \cup A^2 \cup A^3 \cup \cdots$$
$$= A^+.$$

The preceding argument, while valid, uses the fact that set product distributes over infinite unions, which we have not proved. The following alternative argument does not use this fact.

$$x \in A^*A \Leftrightarrow x = yz \text{ for some } y \in A^* \text{ and } z \in A$$
$$\Leftrightarrow x = yz \text{ for some } y \in A^n \text{ and } z \in A \text{ and } n \in \mathbf{N}.$$

$$\Leftrightarrow x \in A^nA \text{ for some } n \in \mathbf{N}$$

$$\Leftrightarrow x \in A^{n+1} \text{ for some } n \in \mathbf{N}$$

$$\Leftrightarrow x \in A^m \text{ for } m \in \mathbf{I}+, \text{ where } m = n + 1$$

$$\Leftrightarrow x \in A^+$$

(m) We show only $(A^*B^*)^* = (A \cup B)^*$.

    (i) $(A^*B^*)^* \subset (A \cup B)^*$:

        $A \subset A \cup B$ and therefore $A^* \subset (A \cup B)^*$; similarly, $B^* \subset (A \cup B)^*$. It follows that $A^*B^* \subset (A \cup B)^*(A \cup B)^*$. From part (j), it follows that $A^*B^* \subset (A \cup B)^*$ and so (again applying part (j)), $(A^*B^*)^* \subset ((A \cup B)^*)^* = (A \cup B)^*$.

    (ii) $(A \cup B)^* \subset (A^*B^*)^*$: From part (b), $A \subset A^*$, and from (d), $A^* \subset A^*B^*$; hence $A \subset A^*B^*$. Similarly $B \subset A^*B^*$. Therefore, $A \cup B \subset A^*B^*$, and by part (f), $(A \cup B)^* \subset (A^*B^*)^*$.

The remaining parts of the proof are left as exercises. ∎

The following theorem, due to Dean Arden, has many important applications in the study of finite automata and formal languages.

Theorem 2.7.4: Let A and B be arbitrary subsets of Σ^* such that $\Lambda \notin A$. Then the equation $X = AX \cup B$ has the unique solution $X = A^*B$.

Although the theorem may initially appear difficult to interpret, careful consideration of the assertion can make the result quite intuitive. We are given a language X such that $X \supset B$ and $X \supset AX$. What can X consist of? Since $X \supset B$, we can substitute B for X in the right side of $X \supset AX$ and conclude that $X \supset AB$. Repeating the substitution, we can conclude $X \supset AAB$, $X \supset AAAB$, etc., and in general $X \supset A^nB$. Thus $X \supset A^*B$. Now consider a string $x \in X$. Since $X = AX \cup B$, and all strings in A are nonempty, it follows that either $x \in B$, or else x has a nonempty prefix such that the prefix is in A and removal of the prefix yields another (shorter) string in X. By the same reasoning, this shorter string has the same property; either it is in B or we can remove another nonempty prefix and obtain another string in X. Since the original string was of finite length, after stripping off a sufficient number of nonempty prefixes we will eventually obtain a string in B. It follows that the original string must have consisted of a (possibly empty) sequence of prefixes, each of which is in A, followed by a suffix which is in B. Thus the original string must have been a member of A^*B. The following proof of the theorem is a formalization of these arguments.

Proof: Let X denote an arbitrary solution to the equation. We will show $X = A^*B$.

    (a) We show $X \supset A^*B$ by establishing that if X is a solution, then $X \supset A^nB$ for all $n \in \mathbf{N}$.

        1. (Basis) For $n = 0$, $A^n = \{\Lambda\}$, and $A^0B = B$. Since $X \supset B$, it follows that $X \supset A^0B$.

2.　(Induction) Assume $X \supset A^n B$. Since $X \supset AX$, it follows that $X \supset A(A^n B) = A^{n+1} B$.

This completes the inductive proof that $X \supset A^n B$ for all $n \in \mathbf{N}$. It is left as an exercise to show that $A^* B = \bigcup_{i=0}^{\infty} A^i B$. Hence, $X \supset A^* B$.

(b)　We show $X \subset A^* B$ using the Second Principle of Mathematical Induction on the length of strings in Σ^*. We wish to show that if $x \in X$, then $x \in A^* B$. The induction hypothesis asserts that every string shorter than x has this property. Let $\|x\|$ denote the length of $x \in \Sigma^*$. Then the induction hypothesis is the following quantified implication.

$$\forall w\{\|w\| < \|x\| \Rightarrow [w \in X \Rightarrow w \in A^* B]\}$$

We use this hypothesis in a direct proof that if $x \in X$ then $x \in A^* B$. Since $X = AX \cup B$, if $x \in X$ then either $x \in AX$ or $x \in B$.

Case 1: If $x \in B$, then $x \in A^* B$.

Case 2: Suppose $x \in AX$. Then $x = yz$ where $y \in A$ and $z \in X$. But $\Lambda \notin A$ so $y \neq \Lambda$ and hence $\|z\| < \|x\|$. By the induction hypothesis, it follows that $z \in A^* B$. Thus $x = yz \in AA^* B \subset A^* B$.

This completes the inductive proof that if $x \in X$ then $x \in A^* B$, and establishes that $X \subset A^* B$.

Parts (a) and (b) of the proof establish that if X is any solution to $X = AX \cup B$, then $X = A^* B$. However, the proof of the theorem is not yet complete, since we have not shown that a solution always exists. We leave it to the reader to show that $X = A^* B$ is a solution to the equation $X = AX \cup B$. ∎

Examples

(a)　If $A = \{a\}$ and $B = \phi$, then the equation $X = AX \cup B$ has the unique solution $X = A^* B = \phi$.

(b)　If $A = \{a, ab\}$ and $B = \{cc\}$, then the equation $X = AX \cup B$ has the solution $X = \{a, ab\}^* \{cc\}$.　#

Problems: Section 2.7

1.　Let $A = \{\Lambda, a\}$, $B = \{ab\}$. List the elements of the following sets.
   (a)　A^2
   (b)　B^3
   (c)　AB
   (d)　A^+
   (e)　B^*

2.　Let A, B, and C be languages over Σ. Prove the following relationships.
   (a)　$A(BC) = (AB)C$
   (b)　$A^m A^n = A^{m+n}$ for all $m, n \geq 0$. (This implies that $\{\Lambda\}A = A\{\Lambda\} = A$.)
   (c)　$(A^m)^n = A^{mn}$ for all $m, n \geq 0$

3.　Let A and B be languages such that $A^2 = B^2$. Does it follow that $A = B$? Prove your assertion.

4. While $A^* = A^+ \cup \{\Lambda\}$, it is not generally true that $A^+ = A^* - \{\Lambda\}$. For $\Sigma = \{a\}$, find the smallest set A such that $A^+ \neq A^* - \{\Lambda\}$.

5. (a) Prove that the operation of set product distributes over infinite union, i.e., show that

$$A(\bigcup_{i \in \mathbf{N}} B_i) = \bigcup_{i \in \mathbf{N}} (AB_i).$$

A similar proof can be used to show the other distributive law,

$$(\bigcup_{i \in \mathbf{N}} B_i)A = \bigcup_{i \in \mathbf{N}} (B_i A).$$

   (b) Prove that

$$A^*B = \bigcup_{i=0}^{\infty} A^i B.$$

6. Let A and B be arbitrary languages over Σ. Prove the following.
   (a) $(A^*)^* = A^*$
   (b) $\Lambda \in A \Leftrightarrow A^+ = A^*$
   (c) $(A^*)^+ = A^*$
   (d) $A^*A^+ = A^+$
   (e) $(A^*B^*)^* = (A^* \cup B^*)^*$

7. Show that if $A \neq \phi$ and $A^2 = A$, then $A^* = A$.

8. Let A, B, and C be languages over Σ. Determine which of the following assertions are true and give counterexamples for those that are false.
   (a) $(A^*)^n = (A^n)^*$ for any $n \in \mathbf{N}$
   (b) $(AB)^* = (BA)^*$
   (c) $(A - B)C = AC - BC$
   (d) $A^* \subset B^* \Rightarrow A \subset B$
   (e) $(A^*B^*)^* = (B^*A^*)^*$
   (f) $A \cup B \cup C \subset A^*B^*C^*$
   (g) $(A^+)^+ = A^+$
   (h) $(\bar{A})^* = (\overline{A^*})$, where $\bar{B} = \Sigma^* - B$
   (i) $(AB)^*A = A(BA)^*$
   (j) $(A^*B)^*A^* = (A^* \cup B^*)^*$
   (k) $A^+ = A^+A^+$

9. Let $E_1, E_2, \ldots, E_n$ be subsets of Σ^*. Is it always true that

$$(E_1 \cup E_2 \cup \cdots \cup E_n)^* = (E_1^*E_2^* \ldots E_n^*)^*?$$

   Prove your assertion.

10. Complete the proof of Theorem 2.7.4 by showing that $X = A^*B$ is a solution to the equation $X = AX \cup B$.

11. Assume the same hypotheses on A and B as in Theorem 2.7.4. Find the solutions to the equation $X = XA \cup B$. Prove your assertion.

12. Suppose $X = AX \cup B$ and $\Lambda \in A$. Show that if $C \supset B$ then $X = A^*C$ is a solution.

13. Let $A = \{a\}$, $B = \{b\}$. Using Theorem 2.7.4, find subsets X_1, X_2 of $\{a, b\}^*$ which solve the following set of simultaneous set equations. (Hint: Solve for one variable in terms of the remaining variables and then substitute.)
   (a) $X_1 = AX_1 \cup BX_2$
   $X_2 = (A \cup B)X_1 \cup BX_2 \cup \{\Lambda\}$

(b) $X_1 = AX_1$
$X_2 = AB(X_1 \cup \{\Lambda\})$

14. Use finite sets and set operations to characterize the following languages over $\Sigma = \{a, b\}$. For example, the set of string of even length is $\{aa, ab, ba, bb\}^*$.
   (a) The set of strings of odd length.
   (b) The set of strings which contain exactly one occurrence of a.
   (c) The set of strings which either begin with an a or end with 2 b's or both.
   (d) The set of strings which contain at least 3 consecutive a's.
   (e) The set of strings which contain the substring "*bbab*."

Suggestions for Further Reading

The book by Halmos [1960] is an excellent introduction to set theory as well as many of the mathematical topics we treat in Chapters 3, 4, and 6. Axiomatic treatments of set theory can be found in Suppes [1960] and Monk [1969]. Wilder [1965] discusses the set theory paradoxes and their role in the development of axiomatic set theory.

The classical development of the natural numbers from the Peano axioms, followed by a development of the rational, real, and complex numbers, is given by Landau [1951]; it is an excellent introduction to formal mathematics. The work by Knuth [1974] follows two young lovers on an uninhabited shore of the Indian Ocean as they consider some of the same foundational questions as Landau. Knuth's book is readable and it conveys the spirit of how one goes about doing mathematics; the reader also learns something about the natural numbers.

The first use of Backus-Naur Form for describing the syntax of a programming language occurs in the *Revised Report on the Algorithmic Language—ALGOL 60*, which is reprinted in Rosen [1967]. This notation is often used in presenting context-free grammars; the reader is referred to Aho and Ullman [1972].

3

BINARY RELATIONS

3.0 INTRODUCTION

Relations characterize structure. In the last chapter we studied sets and their elements. In this section we will study some basic forms of structure which can be represented by relationships between elements of sets. Relations are of fundamental importance to both the theory and applications areas of computer science. A composite data structure, such as an array, list, or tree, is generally used to represent a set of data objects together with a relation which holds between members of the set. Relations which are a part of a mathematical model are often implicitly represented by relations within a data structure. Numerical applications, information retrieval, and network problems are examples of application areas where relations occur as a part of the problem description, and manipulation of the relations is important in solution procedures. Relations also play an important role in the theory of computation, including program structure and analysis of algorithms. In this chapter we will develop some of the fundamental tools and concepts associated with relations.

3.1 BINARY RELATIONS AND DIGRAPHS

The mathematical concept of relation is based on the common notion of relationships among objects. Some relations describe comparisons between elements of a set: one box is heavier than another, one man is richer than another, one event occurred prior to another, etc. Other relations involve elements of different sets, such as "x lives in y" where x is a human and y is a city, "x is owned by y" where x is a building and y is a corporation, or "x was born in the country y in the year z."

The examples we have given are all relationships between either two or three objects, but in principle we can describe relationships which hold for n objects, where n is any positive integer. When making an assertion that a relationship holds among n objects, it is often necessary to specify not only the objects themselves but also an ordering of the objects; for example, only the relative positions of 6 and 4 differ in the two assertions "$6 < 4$" and "$4 < 6$", yet one assertion is false and the other is true. We will use "ordered n-tuples of elements" to specify a finite sequence of not necessarily distinct objects; the relative positions of the objects in the sequence will provide the necessary ordering of the objects.

Definition 3.1.1: For $n > 0$, an *ordered n-tuple* (or simply *n-tuple*) *with ith component* a_i is a sequence of n objects denoted by $\langle a_1, a_2, a_3, \ldots, a_n \rangle$. Two ordered n-tuples are *equal* if and only if their ith components are equal for all i, $1 \leq i \leq n$. If $n = 2$ or $n = 3$, an ordered n-tuple is called an *ordered pair* or an *ordered triple* respectively.

We often wish to treat collections of n-tuples where the ith component of each n-tuple is an element of some set A_i. The set of all such n-tuples is defined as follows:

Definition 3.1.2: Let $\{A_1, A_2, A_3, \ldots, A_n\}$ be an indexed collection of sets with indices from 1 to n, where $n > 0$. The *cartesian product*, or *cross product of the sets A_1 through A_n*, denoted by $A_1 \times A_2 \times \cdots \times A_n$, or $\mathsf{X}_{i=1}^n A_i$, is the set of n-tuples $\{\langle a_1, a_2, \ldots, a_n \rangle \,|\, a_i \in A_i\}$.† When $A_i = A$ for all i, then $\mathsf{X}_{i=1}^n A_i$ will be denoted by A^n.

Examples

Let $A = \{1, 2\}$, $B = \{m, n\}$, $C = \{0\}$ and $D = \phi$. Then

(a) $A \times B = \{\langle 1, m \rangle, \langle 1, n \rangle, \langle 2, m \rangle, \langle 2, n \rangle\}$,

(b) $A \times C = \{\langle 1, 0 \rangle, \langle 2, 0 \rangle\}$,

(c) $A \times D = \phi$.

When A and B are sets of real numbers, then $A \times B$ can be represented as a set of points in the cartesian plane. For example, let $A = \{x \,|\, 1 \leq x \leq 2\}$ and $B = \{y \,|\, 0 \leq y \leq 1\}$. Then

(d) $A \times B = \{\langle x, y \rangle \,|\, 1 \leq x \leq 2 \wedge 0 \leq y \leq 1\}$, and

(e) $B \times A = \{\langle y, x \rangle \,|\, 1 \leq x \leq 2 \wedge 0 \leq y \leq 1\}$.

†Associativity is sometimes an annoying problem when treating cartesian products. Definition 3.1.2 distinguishes between the sets $A_1 \times A_2 \times A_3$, $(A_1 \times A_2) \times A_3$, and $A_1 \times (A_2 \times A_3)$ because the elements of these sets are of the forms $\langle a_1, a_2, a_3 \rangle$, $\langle \langle a_1, a_2 \rangle, a_3 \rangle$, and $\langle a_1, \langle a_2, a_3 \rangle \rangle$ respectively. These distinctions are sometimes important, but we will usually wish to use the set $A_1 \times A_2 \times A_3$. We will therefore treat the binary operation of cartesian product as though it were associative, unless specific mention is made to the contrary.

These relations are represented by the shaded areas in the following diagrams.

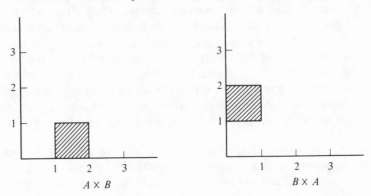

$A \times B$ $B \times A$

Let $A_1 = \{1, 2\}$, $A_2 = \{a, b\}$ and $A_3 = \{x, y\}$.

(f) $X_{i=1}^{3} A_i = \{\langle 1, a, x\rangle, \langle 1, a, y\rangle, \langle 1, b, x\rangle,$
$\langle 1, b, y\rangle, \langle 2, a, x\rangle, \langle 2, a, y\rangle, \langle 2, b, x\rangle, \langle 2, b, y\rangle\}$.

(g) $A_3^2 = A_3 \times A_3 = \{\langle x, x\rangle, \langle x, y\rangle, \langle y, x\rangle, \langle y, y\rangle\}$.   #

The preceding examples show that the operation of binary cartesian product is not commutative, i.e., it is generally not true that $A \times B = B \times A$. The following theorem establishes that the operation of binary cartesian product distributes over union and intersection.

Theorem 3.1.1:   If A, B and C are sets, then
(a) $A \times (B \cup C) = (A \times B) \cup (A \times C)$,
(b) $A \times (B \cap C) = (A \times B) \cap (A \times C)$,
(c) $(A \cup B) \times C = (A \times C) \cup (B \times C)$,
(d) $(A \cap B) \times C = (A \times C) \cap (B \times C)$.

Proof:
(a).   The proof uses the distributivity of $\wedge$ over $\vee$. Let $\langle x, y\rangle$ be an arbitrary element of $A \times (B \cup C)$. Then

$$\langle x, y\rangle \in A \times (B \cup C) \Leftrightarrow x \in A \wedge y \in (B \cup C)$$
$$\Leftrightarrow x \in A \wedge (y \in B \vee y \in C)$$
$$\Leftrightarrow (x \in A \wedge y \in B) \vee (x \in A \wedge y \in C)$$
$$\Leftrightarrow \langle x, y\rangle \in A \times B \vee \langle x, y\rangle \in A \times C$$
$$\Leftrightarrow \langle x, y\rangle \in (A \times B) \cup (A \times C).$$

The proofs of parts (b)-(d) are left as exercises. ∎

Definition 3.1.3:   Let $A_1, A_2, \ldots, A_n$ be sets. An *n-ary relation* R on $X_{i=1}^{n} A_i$ is a subset of $X_{i=1}^{n} A_i$. If $R = \varnothing$, then R is called the *empty* or *void* relation. If $R = X_{i=1}^{n} A_i$, then R is called the *universal* relation. If $A_i = A$ for all i, then R is called an *n-ary relation on A*. If $n = 1$, 2, or 3, then R is called a *unary, binary,* or *ternary* relation, respectively.

In defining the concept of equality for relations, we require not only that the sets of n-tuples be the same but also that the cross product supersets be the same.

Definition 3.1.4: Let R_1 be an n-ary relation on $\mathsf{X}_{i=1}^{n} A_i$ and R_2 be an m-ary relation on $\mathsf{X}_{i=1}^{m} B_i$. Then $R_1 = R_2$ if and only if $n = m$, and $A_i = B_i$ for all i, $1 \le i \le n$, and R_1 and R_2 are equal sets of ordered n-tuples.

In practice, the indexed collection of sets $\{A_1, A_2, \ldots, A_n\}$ is often left implicit and an n-ary relation is informally referred to as a set of n-tuples.

If each set A_i is finite, then there are a finite number of n-ary relations on $\mathsf{X}_{i=1}^{n} A_i$. Recall that if S is a finite set with k elements, then $\mathcal{P}(S)$ has 2^k elements. Since every subset of $\mathsf{X}_{i=1}^{n} A_i$ is an n-ary relation on $\mathsf{X}_{i=1}^{n} A_i$, if the cartesian product of A_1 through A_n has k elements, then there are 2^k n-ary relations on the set $\mathsf{X}_{i=1}^{n} A_i$. But if A_i has r_i elements, then $\mathsf{X}_{i=1}^{n} A_i$ has $\prod_{i=1}^{n} r_i$ elements and hence there are $2^{r_1 \cdot r_2 \cdots \cdot r_n}$ n-ary relations on $\mathsf{X}_{i=1}^{n} A_i$.

Every n-ary relation R on a set A corresponds to an n-ary predicate with A as the universe of discourse. If the relation R is given, a corresponding predicate P can be defined as follows:

$$P(a_1, a_2, \ldots, a_n) \text{ is true} \Leftrightarrow \langle a_1, a_2, \ldots, a_n \rangle \in R.$$

Conversely, a predicate P can be used to define a relation R as follows:

$$R = \{\langle a_1, a_2, \ldots, a_n \rangle \,|\, P(a_1, a_2, \ldots, a_n) \text{ is true}\}.$$

A unary relation consists of a set of 1-tuples and can be associated with a predicate with a single variable or a property of some elements of A; a unary relation on a set A is simply a subset of A.

Examples

(a) Let the universe of discourse be the set $A = \{1, 2, 3\}$. The three variable predicate "$x + y = z$" on the universe A corresponds to the relation $R = \{\langle x, y, z \rangle \,|\, x + y = z\}$ on A.

(b) Consider the universe $\mathbf{N}$. The property "x is an even integer" can be characterized by a unary predicate

$$P(x) \Leftrightarrow x \text{ is even},$$

or a unary relation

$$\{\langle x \rangle \,|\, x \text{ is even}\},$$

or a subset

$$\{x \,|\, x \text{ is even}\}. \quad \#$$

Binary Relations

The most important class of relations is the set of binary relations. Because binary relations are referred to more frequently than others, the unqualified term "relation" usually denotes a binary relation; where no confusion will result, we will adopt this convention. Relations which are not binary will be specified by such terms as "ternary" or "*n*-ary."

The following definition presents some additional terminology and notation associated with binary relations.

Definition 3.1.5:   Let R be a binary relation over $A \times B$. The set A is the *domain* of R; B is the *codomain*. We denote $\langle a, b \rangle \in R$ by the infix notation aRb and $\langle a, b \rangle \notin R$ is denoted by $a\bar{R}b$.

Examples

(a)   Let L be the relation on the integers $\mathbf{I}$ of "less than." Then we write $4 < 6$ to denote $\langle 4, 6 \rangle \in L$ and $6 \not< 4$ to denote $\langle 6, 4 \rangle \notin L$.

(b)   Let M denote the relation "is a multiple of" for the universe $\mathbf{N}$. Then $4M2$ but $2\bar{M}4$. More generally, xMy if and only if $x = ky$ for some $k \in \mathbf{N}$. Thus for all x, $0Mx$ and $xM1$. If $p > 1$, then p is prime if xMp implies that either $x = 1$ or $x = p$. A number x is odd if $x\bar{M}2$.

(c)   When a compiler translates a computer program it constructs a *symbol table* which contains the symbolic names which occur in the program, the attributes associated with each name, and the program statements in which each name occurs. Thus if S is the set of symbols, A is the set of possible attributes and P is the set of program statements, then the symbol table includes information which represents binary relations from S to A and S to P.

(d)   Let A be a set of documents in a library, and B be a set of *descriptors* used to describe the documents. Let R be the relation from A to B such that aRb if and only if the descriptor b applies to document a. For example, if X is an article on automatic word recognition, then $\langle X$, "pattern recognition"$\rangle$ and $\langle X$, "speech processing"$\rangle$ might be elements of R. Such relations form a basis for automatic document retrieval systems. The user of such a system describes his interests by choosing a set of appropriate descriptors; the document retrieval system uses the relation R to determine what documents in the library are likely to be relevant to the user's needs.

(e)   Binary relations on the set of real numbers can be represented graphically in the cartesian plane. The following is a graph of the relation $\{\langle x, y \rangle \mid |x| + |y| = 1\}$.

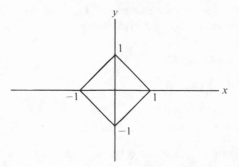

Since relations are sets, some relations can be defined inductively.

Example

The relation "less than" over the natural numbers **N** can be defined inductively as follows (the corresponding "ordered pair" formulation is given on the right for the basis and induction clauses):

1. (Basis) $0 < 1$
2. (Induction)
   If $x < y$, then
   (i) $x < y + 1$
   (ii) $x + 1 < y + 1$
3. (Extremal) For all $x, y \in \mathbf{N}$, $x < y$ only if it is required by clauses 1 and 2.   #

1. $\langle 0, 1 \rangle \in\ <$
2. if $\langle x, y \rangle \in\ <$, then
   (i) $\langle x, y + 1 \rangle \in\ <$
   (ii) $\langle x + 1, y + 1 \rangle \in\ <$

The study of binary relations is closely related to the mathematical field of graph theory. Graphs often provide a convenient way of viewing questions concerning binary relations, and for that reason we will develop the concepts of directed graphs in parallel with our treatment of binary relations.†

Definition 3.1.6: A *directed graph* or *digraph* is an ordered pair $D = \langle A, R \rangle$ where A is a set and R is a binary relation on A. The set A is the set of *nodes* (*points, vertices*) of D and the elements of R are the *arcs* (*edges, lines*) of D. The relation R is called the *incidence relation* of D.

If $D = \langle A, R \rangle$ is a digraph and A is a finite set, then D is called a *finite digraph*. A finite digraph $\langle A, R \rangle$ can be represented graphically by denoting the elements of A by labeled points. An arc xRy is represented by an arrow from x to y.

We will frequently represent digraphs with such diagrams, and in fact we will call such a diagram a digraph, even though it is only a convenient representation.

Examples

(a) Let $D = \langle A, R \rangle$, where $A = \{a, b, c, d\}$ and $R = \{\langle a, c \rangle, \langle b, c \rangle, \langle a, a \rangle\}$. The digraph D is represented by the following diagram.

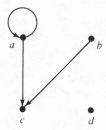

---

†The definitions and terminology used in graph theory vary considerably among different authors. We have chosen the nomenclature most appropriate for our purposes but the reader is advised to be alert for differences in definitions when consulting other works.

(b) Let $D = \langle \mathbf{N}, R \rangle$, where the relation R consists of all integer pairs of the form $\langle x, x + 2 \rangle$. Although $\mathbf{N}$ is infinite, we can represent this digraph by the following (incomplete) diagram:

Digraphs constitute an important class of data structures. They may be represented in a computer memory in a variety of ways, each of which has its particular advantages. If the vertices of the digraph are indexed from 1 to n, the digraph can be represented by an $n \times n$ binary matrix M, called the *incidence matrix*, where the entry in the ith row and jth column of M, denoted $M[i,j]$, is 1 if there is an arc from the ith node to the jth node; otherwise $M[i,j] = 0$.

An alternate representation of a digraph consists of a list of ordered pairs where $\langle i, j \rangle$ is included in the list if and only if there is an arc from node i to node j. Still another representation is a linked list, where each node of the graph is represented by its label and a list of pointers to the other nodes of the graph; each pointer represents an arc. These representations, illustrated in Figure 3.1.1, are only some of many possible ways to represent a digraph.

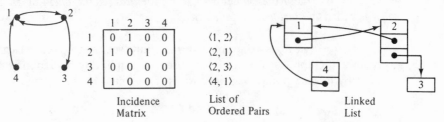

Fig. 3.1.1 Some alternative representations of a directed graph

There is a natural association between digraphs and binary relations. If R is a relation from A to B, the *digraph associated with* R is the digraph $\langle A \cup B, R \rangle$. Conversely, if $D = \langle A, R \rangle$ is a digraph, the *relation associated with* D is the binary relation R from A to A.

Definition 3.1.7: Let $D = \langle A, R \rangle$ be a digraph. If aRb, then the arc $\langle a, b \rangle$ *originates* at a and *terminates* at b. An arc of the form $\langle a, a \rangle$ is called a *loop*. The number of arcs which originate at a node a is called the *outdegree of node a*; the number of arcs which terminate at a is called the *indegree of node a*.

Definition 3.1.8: Let $D = \langle A, R \rangle$ be a digraph with nodes a and b. An *undirected path P from a to b* is a finite sequence of nodes $P = \langle c_0, c_1, \ldots, c_n \rangle$ such that

  (i) $c_0 = a,$

  (ii) $c_n = b,$

  (iii) For all c_i such that $0 \leq i < n$, either $c_i R c_{i+1}$ or $c_{i+1} R c_i$.

If $c_i R c_{i+1}$ for all c_i, $0 \le i < n$, then P is a *directed path from a to b*. The node a is the *initial node* of P and b is the *terminal node* of P. The *length* of the path P is n. If all the nodes of P are distinct except possibly the first and last (i.e., if $c_0, c_1, \ldots, c_{n-1}$ are distinct and $c_1, c_2, \ldots, c_n$ are distinct), then P is a *simple path*. If $c_0 = c_n$, then P is a *cycle*; if P is both a simple path and a cycle, then P is a *simple cycle*.

If there is a path $P = \langle c_0, c_1, \ldots, c_n \rangle$ of nonzero length from node a to node b, then we can construct a simple path P' from a to b by eliminating the cycles from P. This is done by successively replacing subsequences in P of the form $\langle c_i, c_{i+1}, \ldots, c_k \rangle$, where $i \ge 1$ and $c_i = c_k$, by the subsequence $\langle c_i \rangle$ until a simple path results; this is the path P'. If P is directed, then P' will be a simple directed path of nonzero length, and if P is a cycle, then P' will be a simple cycle of nonzero length.

Examples

(a) Let D be the following digraph:

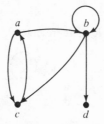

Then $\langle a, c \rangle$, $\langle a, b, c \rangle$, $\langle a, c, a, c \rangle$ and $\langle a, b, b, c \rangle$ are directed paths from a to c; of these, the first two are simple and the last two are not. The sequences $\langle c, b, d \rangle$ and $\langle c, a, b, d \rangle$ are undirected paths from c to d. The sequences $\langle a, c, a \rangle$ and $\langle a, b, c, a \rangle$ are simple cycles; $\langle a, c, a, c, a \rangle$ and $\langle a, b, b, c, a \rangle$ are cycles but not simple. The path $\langle a \rangle$ is a simple cycle of length 0. Node a has indegree 1 and outdegree 2; node d has indegree 1 and outdegree 0.

(b) Algorithms are often represented by flowcharts; a flowchart is a directed graph with labeled nodes and arcs. The node labels are represented by boxes of various shapes, together with notations written inside the boxes; the labelled nodes represent starting points, exits, operations and tests. If a node has only one outgoing arc, the arc is commonly left unlabeled; in the case of a test node, outgoing arcs are labeled to indicate the results of the test, e.g., *true* and *false*, $\le$ and $>$, etc. A careful characterization of the class of flowcharts would include other constraints on the form of a flowchart graph; for example, it would be reasonable to require that each flowchart have exactly one *start* node and at least one *stop* node.

A computation consisting of the execution of an algorithm represented by a flowchart corresponds to a path which begins at the *start* node of the flowchart. The computation halts if the path terminates at a *stop* node. A proof of correctness of the algorithm must treat every directed path from the *start* node to a *stop* node; for this reason, proofs of correctness often take the form of proofs by cases.   #

We often wish to refer to parts of a digraph. For this purpose, we define subdigraphs and partial subdigraphs. A subdigraph is obtained from a digraph by taking a subset of nodes and all arcs between nodes of the subset. A partial subdigraph also contains a subset of nodes but need only contain some of the arcs between nodes of the subset.

Definition 3.1.9:   Let $D = \langle A, R \rangle$ be a digraph.
(a)   A digraph $D' = \langle A', R' \rangle$ is a *subdigraph of* D if
   (i) $A' \subset A$,
   (ii) $R' = R \cap (A' \times A')$.
   If $D' \neq D$, then D' is a *proper subdigraph* of D.
(b)   A digraph $D' = \langle A', R' \rangle$ is a *partial subdigraph of* D if
   (i) $A' \subset A$,
   (ii) $R' \subset R \cap (A' \times A')$.

Examples

If $D = \langle A, R \rangle$ is represented by

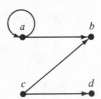

then the following represents a subdigraph of D with nodes $\{a, b, c\}$.

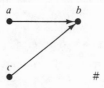

#

The following is a partial subdigraph but not a subdigraph of D, since the loop $\langle a, a \rangle$ is not included.

Definition 3.1.10:   A digraph $D = \langle A, R \rangle$ is *strongly connected* if for every two elements $a, b \in A$, there is a directed path from a to b and from b to a. If for

every two nodes $a, b \in A$, there is an undirected path from a to b, then D is *connected*; otherwise, D is *disconnected*.

Example

Consider the following digraphs:

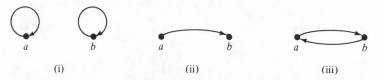

(i)   (ii)   (iii)

The digraph represented by (i) is disconnected, (ii) is connected but not strongly connected, and (iii) is strongly connected.   #

The components of a digraph D are the largest connected "pieces" of D; there are no arcs between nodes of distinct components of a digraph.

Definition 3.1.11:   A *component* of a digraph D is a connected subdigraph of D which is not a proper subdigraph of any connected subdigraph of D.

Example

The following digraph has four components.

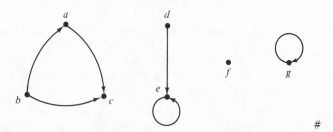

#

Definition 3.1.12:   Let A be a set with n elements. The *complete digraph over* A is the digraph $\langle A, A \times A \rangle$, that is, A together with the universal binary relation on A.

Example

The following digrams are complete digraphs over sets with 1, 2, and 3 elements.

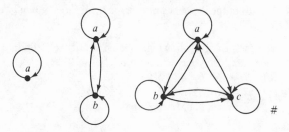

#

Problems: Section 3.1

1. Let $A = \{0, 1, 2, 3, 4\}$. For each of the predicates given below, specify the set of n-tuples in the n-ary relation over A which corresponds to the predicate. For parts (d)-(f), draw the digraph which represents the relation.
   (a) $P(x) \Leftrightarrow x \leq 1$
   (b) $P(x) \Leftrightarrow 3 > 2$
   (c) $P(x) \Leftrightarrow 2 > 3$
   (d) $P(x, y) \Leftrightarrow x < y$
   (e) $P(x, y) \Leftrightarrow \exists k[x = ky \land k < 2]$
   (f) $P(x, y) \Leftrightarrow [x = 0 \lor 2x < 3]$
   (g) $P(x, y, z) \Leftrightarrow x^2 + y = z$

2. For the following digraphs A and B,

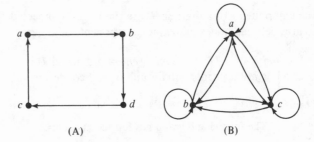

(A)   (B)

   (a) Find all simple paths from node a to node c. Give the path lengths.
   (b) Find the indegree and outdegree of each node.
   (c) Find all simple cycles with initial and terminal node a.
   (d) Find the subdigraph containing the nodes a and c.
   (e) Determine how many partial subdigraphs exist which contain only nodes a and c.

3. For each of the following, sketch a digraph of the given binary relation on A. State whether the digraph is disconnected, connected or strongly connected, and state how many components the digraph has.
   (a) $\{\langle 1, 2 \rangle, \langle 1, 3 \rangle, \langle 2, 4 \rangle\}$, where $A = \{1, 2, 3, 4\}$
   (b) $\{\langle 1, 2 \rangle, \langle 3, 1 \rangle, \langle 3, 3 \rangle\}$, where $A = \{1, 2, 3, 4\}$
   (c) $\{\langle x, y \rangle \mid 0 \leq x < y \leq 3\}$, where $A = \{0, 1, 2, 3, 4\}$
   (d) $\{\langle x, y \rangle \mid 2 \leq x, y \leq 7 \land x$ divides $y\}$ where $A = \{n \mid n \in \mathbf{N} \land n \leq 10\}$
   (e) $\{\langle x, y \rangle \mid 0 \leq x - y < 3\}$, where $A = \{0, 1, 2, 3, 4\}$
   (f) $\{\langle x, y \rangle \mid x$ and y are relatively prime$\}$, where $A = \{2, 3, 4, 5, 6\}$.

4. Construct the incidence matrix for the following binary relation on $\{0, 1, 2, 3, 4, 5, 6\}$:
   $\{\langle x, y \rangle \mid x < y \lor x$ is prime$\}$.

5. For each of the following, give an inductive definition for the relation R on $\mathbf{N}$. In each case, use your definition to show $x \in R$.
   (a) $R = \{\langle a, b \rangle \mid a \geq b\}$; $x = \langle 3, 1 \rangle$
   (b) $R = \{\langle a, b \rangle \mid a = 2b\}$; $x = \langle 6, 3 \rangle$
   (c) $R = \{\langle a, b, c \rangle \mid a + b = c\}$; $x = \langle 1, 1, 2 \rangle$

6. Let $A = \{1, 2, 3\}$.
   (a)   List the unary relations on A.
   (b)   How many binary relations are there on A?

7. Let A be a set with n elements.
   (a)   Prove that there are 2^n unary relations on A.
   (b)   Prove that there are 2^{n^2} binary relations on A.
   (c)   How many ternary relations are there on A?

8. We have taken the notion of an ordered n-tuple to be primitive in the sense that we did not define it in terms of either primitive or previously defined terms. An ordered pair can be defined using set theoretic concepts as follows:

> An *ordered pair* $\langle a, b \rangle$ *with first element a and second element b is* the set $\{\{a\}, \{a, b\}\}$.

Note that according to this definition, $\langle a, a \rangle = \{\{a\}\}$.

   (a)   Prove, using this definition, the following property of ordered pairs:

$$\langle a, b \rangle = \langle c, d \rangle \text{ if and only if } a = c \text{ and } b = d.$$

   (b)   Defining ordered triples is not completely straightforward. Show that the following definition of ordered triples does *not* have the property for equality specified in Definition 3.1.1.

> An *ordered triple* $\langle a, b, c \rangle$ *with first element a, second element b, and third element c* is the set $\{\{a\}, \{a, b\}, \{a, b, c\}\}$.

3.2 TREES

The set of digraphs known as trees represent an important class of binary relations. Trees provide a way to represent hierarchical structures, such as a family genealogy, the administrative structure of a corporation, or a categorization of a collection of objects into classes. We will consider a few of the many applications of trees in computer science, including data structures and the design and analysis of algorithms.

Trees denote a particular kind of binary relation. Because the graphical representation is such a natural one, definitions and theorems are usually couched in the terminology of the digraphs rather than that of the binary relations.

> *Definition 3.2.1:*   A *tree* is a digraph with a nonempty set of nodes such that
>   (i)   there is exactly one node, called the *root* of the tree, which has indegree 0;
>   (ii) every node other than the root has indegree 1;
>   (iii) for every node a of the tree, there is a directed path from the root to a.

We will represent trees with the root node at the top and all arcs directed downward, leaving the arrowheads of the arcs implicit.

Examples

(a)   The following digraphs are trees. The root of each tree is node *a*.

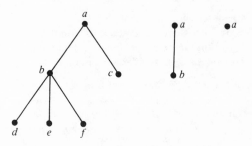

(b)   The following digraphs are not trees.

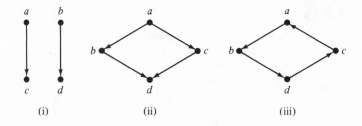

       (i)   (ii)   (iii)

The digraph (i) has two nodes with indegree 0.
The digraph (ii) has a node with indegree 2.
The digraph (iii) has no node with indegree 0.   #

Because trees are such an important class of digraphs, there is a rich terminology associated with them. Different authors, however, do not use the terms
consistently. We will use just a few of the most widely accepted terms.

Definition 3.2.2: Let *a* and *b* be nodes of a tree *T*. If there is an arc from *a*
to *b*, then *a* is said to be the *father* of *b* and *b* is a *son* of *a*. (From the restrictions
on the indegree of nodes of a tree, it is clear that the root node has no father and
every node other than the root has exactly one father.) If there is a directed path
from node *a* to node *b*, then node *a* is said to be an *ancestor* of *b* and *b* is a *descendant* of *a*; if $a \neq b$, then *a* is a *proper ancestor* of *b* and *b* is a *proper descendant* of
a. (It follows that the root is an ancestor of every node of a tree and every node is
is a descendant of the root.) The subdigraph consisting of the node *a* and all its
descendants is a *subtree* of *T*, and *a* is called the *root of the subtree*. If *a* is not the
root of *T*, then the subtree is a *proper subtree of T*. A node with outdegree 0 (i.e.,
one with no sons) is called a *leaf* of a tree. A node which is not a leaf is called an
interior node. The *height* of the tree is the length of the longest directed path of *T*.

Example

Consider the following tree.

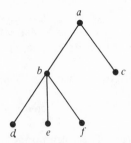

The root of the tree is node a. The root a has two sons, b and c; node b has three sons and d has no sons. The father of d is b. The leaves of the tree are the nodes c, d, e, and f; a and b are the only interior nodes. The height of the tree is 2. The subdigraph with nodes $\{b, d, e, f\}$ is a subtree with root b. The subdigraph consisting only of node d is a subtree of height 0 with root d.   #

The usefulness of trees is due in part to the restrictions on paths which are implied by their definition. These restrictions make it possible to *traverse* a tree algorithmically (visit all its nodes) and perform searches for data more efficiently than is possible with the general class of digraphs. The following theorems establish some of the most important properties of paths in trees.

Theorem 3.2.1:   Let T be a tree with root r and let a be any node of T. Then there is a unique directed path from r to a.

Proof: By the definition of a tree (Definition 3.2.1) there is a directed path from r to a, so we need only show that the path is unique. For each $n \in \mathbf{N}$, we define S_n to be the set of nodes of T such that for each $a \in S_n$, there is a directed path from r to a of length n or less. We will show by induction that the path from r to any node in S_n is unique.

1. Basis: Let $n = 0$. Then $S_n = S_0 = \{r\}$; that is, the only directed path of length 0 which originates at r terminates at r. Since the indegree of r is 0, there can be no other directed path from r to r; it follows that there is a unique directed path in T from r to each node in S_0.

2. Induction: Let $n > 0$. We assume the induction hypothesis that for each node $b \in S_{n-1}$, there is a unique directed path in T from r to b. Suppose $a \in S_n$. We treat two cases, where $a \in S_{n-1}$ and where $a \notin S_{n-1}$. If $a \in S_{n-1}$, then by the induction hypothesis, there is a unique directed path from r to a. If $a \notin S_{n-1}$, then there is a directed path from r to a of length n, but no such path of length $n - 1$. Any directed path of length n must consist of a sequence $\langle r, b_1, b_2, \ldots b_{n-1}, a \rangle$, where $b_{n-1} \in S_{n-1}$. By the

induction hypothesis, the path $\langle r, b_1, b_2, \ldots, b_{n-1} \rangle$ is the only directed path in T from r to b_{n-1}. Since the indegree of a is 1, there is only one directed path of the form $\langle b_{n-1}, a \rangle$; i.e., there is a unique element b_{n-1} such that $\langle r, b_1, b_2, \ldots, b_{n-1}, a \rangle$ is a directed path. Thus the only directed path from r to a consists of the unique path from r to b_{n-1} followed by the unique path from b_{n-1} to a. ∎

The proofs of the following two corollaries are left as exercises.

Corollary 3.2.1a: Every directed path in a tree is a simple path.

Corollary 3.2.1b: There are no loops on nodes of trees.

Theorem 3.2.2: A tree has no directed simple cycles of nonzero length. The only undirected simple cycles of nonzero length are of length 2.

Proof: From Corollary 3.2.1b it follows that no cycles of length 1 can exist. The only simple cycles of length 2 are of the form $\langle a, b, a \rangle$, where either a is the son of b or b is the son of a; such a cycle is always undirected.

Suppose $C = \langle a_0, a_1, a_2, \ldots, a_k, a_0 \rangle$ is a simple cycle of length greater than 2; then $k \geq 2$. If $\langle a_0, a_1 \rangle$ is an arc of the tree and C is not directed, then there must be some a_i such that $\langle a_{i-1}, a_i \rangle$ and $\langle a_{i+1}, a_i \rangle$ are both arcs. Since the path is simple and of length greater than two, $a_{i-1} \neq a_{i+1}$ and hence a_i has indegree 2, violating the definition of a tree. Hence if $\langle a_0, a_1 \rangle$ is an arc, then C is directed. Similarly, if $\langle a_0, a_k \rangle$ is an arc, then the reversal of C, $\langle a_0, a_k, a_{k-1}, \ldots, a_2, a_1 \rangle$ must be directed. Moreover, either $\langle a_0, a_1 \rangle$ or $\langle a_0, a_k \rangle$ must be an arc since otherwise a_0 would have indegree 2. Hence, if C is a cycle of length greater than two, then either C or its reversal must be directed. Without loss of generality, assume C is directed, and let $\langle r, b_1, b_2, \ldots, b_n, a_0 \rangle$ be the directed path from the root r to a_0. Then $\langle r, b_1, b_2, \ldots, b_n, a_0, a_1, \ldots, a_k, a_0 \rangle$ is a different directed path from r to a_0, contradicting Theorem 3.2.1. Thus T contains no cycles of length greater than 2. ∎

Applications of trees often involve restricted classes of trees. A common restriction is to limit the number of sons a node can have; if every node has n or fewer sons, then a tree is called an *n-ary tree*. If every node has either n sons or 0 sons, then the tree is called a *complete n-ary tree*. In many applications it is necessary to impose an order on the arcs emanating from each node, or equivalently, order the sons of each node. A tree in which the outgoing arcs of each node are ordered is called an *ordered tree*, and we refer to the 1st, 2nd, ..., and nth son of a node. The use of ordered trees is so common that it is often not explicitly specified, although it is usually clear from context. We will use the term *binary tree* to denote a 2-ary tree in which every node other than the root is specified to be either the *left son* or the *right son* of its father.

Examples

(a) Consider the following trees.

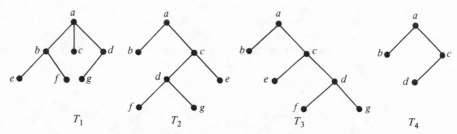

$$T_1 \qquad\qquad T_2 \qquad\qquad T_3 \qquad\qquad T_4$$

The tree T_1 is a ternary tree but not a complete ternary tree; T_2 is a complete 2-ary tree. As unordered trees, T_2 and T_3 are equal; as ordered trees they are not equal because in T_2, d is the first son of c and in T_3, d is the second son of c. The tree T_4 is a 2-ary tree but not a complete 2-ary tree; if T_4 is a binary tree, the node c has a left son but no right son.

(b) The algebraic expression

$$(((6 + 4) * 8) - (4 * 5))$$

can be represented by the following labeled ordered tree.

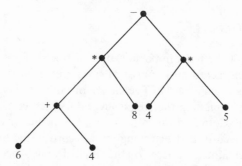

This is an example of the use of labeled ordered trees to represent assertions or expressions in a language. The leaves of the tree are labeled with values or variable names and the interior nodes are labeled with operators or connectives. Such trees must be ordered if the operations and connectives are not commutative, e.g., the trees

represent the expressions $4 - 5$ and $5 - 4$ respectively. Note that the information provided by parentheses in the expression is implicit in the tree representation; each operand of the expression is nested in parentheses to a depth that equals its distance from the root of the tree. Because expressions in innermost parentheses are evaluated first, the tree is evaluated by starting at the bottom and assigning values to each interior node. A node labeled with an operator is assigned the value which results from performing the operation on the values of its sons. The process can be viewed as a collapsing of the tree upward; this is illustrated by the following sequence of trees. Each tree of the sequence is obtained from its predecessor by collapsing a subtree consisting of a node and the two leaves which are its sons.

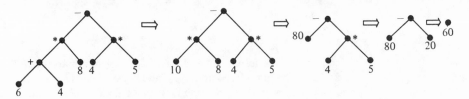

The procedure described above is a "bottom-up" evaluation of the tree representing the expression. Such trees can also be evaluated in a "top-down" fashion by using a recursive procedure to express the value of each node in terms of the values of its sons. We leave it as an exercise to write a recursive procedure for top-down evaluation of trees which represent algebraic expressions.   #

Search Trees

One of the most important uses of trees is for storing collections of records, where each record may consist of several associated data items. Such a collection of records is called a *file*. The choice of how a file is stored is based on a number of factors, including the frequency with which certain operations are performed on the file. Common operations on a file include insertion of a new record, deletion of a record, and searching for a record in the file. The most straightforward search techniques are based on the value of some specific field or item in each record called the *search key*. For example, a file consisting of employee records might use the social security number as a search key; each record would then have the employee's social security number as its search key value. In many search techniques, the value of the search key of the record sought is used to direct the search; if the value of the search key in each record is unique, then the search key can be used for record identification as well.

A file can be organized for fast access using a search key by means of a type of binary tree known as a *binary search tree*. To illustrate search trees and their use, we will assume a file whose key values are all distinct, and a search tree in which a single record of the file is stored at each node of the tree. A binary search tree is constructed so that if node b is the left son of node a, then the key of every descendant of b (including b itself) is less than the key of a. On the other hand, if node b is the right son of node a, then the key of every descendant of b is greater than or equal to the key of a.

Example

> The following is a binary search tree. Each node label is the key of the record stored at the node.

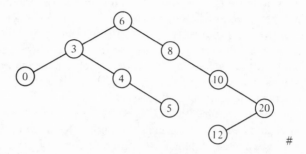

We will illustrate the use of binary search trees by describing two search procedures. To construct these programs, we need a way to refer to the key of the record stored at a node of a tree as well as the left son and right son of the node. If *node* is a program variable whose value is a tree node, then KEY (*node*) will denote the value of the key stored in the record at *node*. LEFTSON (*node*) and RIGHTSON (*node*) will have as values the left son and right son of *node* respectively, if these sons exist; if no left son exists, the value of LEFTSON (*node*) will be the distinguished value *null* and similarly for RIGHTSON (*node*).

> **procedure** TREESEARCH1(*root*, *arg*):
> **comment:**   *arg* is the key of the record sought;
>   *root* is the root of the binary search tree if the file
>   is nonempty; otherwise *root* = *null*.
> **begin**
>   *node* ← *root*;
>   **while** (*node* ≠ *null* **and** *arg* ≠ KEY (*node*)) **do**
>   **if** *arg* < KEY (*node*) **then** *node* ← LEFTSON (*node*)
>   **else** *node* ← RIGHTSON (*node*);
>   **if** *node* = *null* **then return** "record not found"
>   **else return** *node*
> **end**

Fig. 3.2.1   Iterative binary tree search

A search algorithm for records stored in a binary search tree is given in Figure 3.2.1. To find a record in the tree, we call TREESEARCH1 (*root*, *arg*), where the value of *arg* is the key of the record sought and the value of *root* is the root node of the search tree unless the file contains no records, in which case the value of *root* is *null*. After *node* is set equal to *root*, if *node* ≠ *null*, then *arg* is compared with KEY (*node*). If *arg* = KEY (*node*), then the record has been found and is stored at the root node of the search tree. If *arg* < KEY (*node*), then either the record is not in the file, or it is in the subtree whose root is LEFTSON (*node*).

If $arg >$ KEY (*node*), then either the record is not in the file or it is stored in the subtree whose root is RIGHTSON (*node*).

The search proceeds by progressing down into the tree, at each step examining a node which is a son of the node previously examined. If the record is in the file, the procedure will eventually find it by following the (unique) simple directed path from the root of the tree to the correct node. If the record is not in the file, the search will eventually either reach a node whose key value is greater than *arg* and which has no left son, or it will reach a node whose key value is less than *arg* and which has no right son. In these cases, the search procedure will terminate after assigning the value of *null* to *node*.

The procedure TREESEARCH1 given in Fig. 3.2.1 is called an *iterative* procedure because the principal computation is done in a loop; in this case, the loop uses a *while* statement. A search of a binary tree can also be done recursively. The recursive search procedure rests on the following inductive definition of binary trees. (This recursive definition of binary trees is equivalent to the non-recursive characterization given earlier in this section, but we will not prove the equivalence.)

Definition 3.2.3: The following digraphs are binary trees.
1. (Basis) A single node, together with the empty relation, is a binary tree.
2. (Induction) Let T_1 and T_2 be binary trees with disjoint sets of nodes and roots r_1 and r_2 respectively, and let r be a node not in either T_1 or T_2. Then the following digraphs are binary trees with root r:
    (a) The node r together with the tree T_1 and a left arc from r to r_1.
    (b) The node r together with the tree T_2 and a right arc from r to r_2.
    (c) The node r together with the trees T_1 and T_2 and a left arc from r to r_1 and a right arc from r to r_2.
3. (Extremal) No digraph is a binary tree unless it can be constructed in a finite number of steps using clauses 1 and 2.

The iterative strategy of TREESEARCH1 might be described as "plunge down into the tree until the record is found." The recursive strategy implemented by TREESEARCH2, given in Figure 3.2.2, can be described as "search the tree by

```
procedure TREESEARCH2(root, arg):
comment:  arg is the key of the record sought;
              root is the root of the binary search tree if the file is
              nonempty; otherwise root = null.
       if root = null then return "record not found"
       else
              if arg = KEY(root) then return root
              else
                     if arg < KEY(root) then return TREESEARCH2(LEFTSON(root), arg)
                     else return TREESEARCH2(RIGHTSON(root), arg)
```

Fig. 3.2.2   Recursive binary tree search

examining the root and then, if necessary, searching either the left or right subtree of the root." TREESEARCH2 is called in the same way and returns the same value as TREESEARCH1.

The height of a binary search tree is a measure of the maximum number of steps it will take to locate a record in the file. The following theorems relate the size of the file to the height of a binary tree. The proofs are left as exercises.

Theorem 3.2.3: If T is a binary tree of height h and with n nodes, then $h + 1 \leq n \leq 2^{h+1} - 1$. Moreover, there exist binary trees in which these bounds are attained.

Corollary 3.2.3: A binary tree with n nodes, $n > 0$, is of height at least $\lfloor \log n \rfloor$.†

We have described binary search trees with records stored at all nodes of the tree. In some circumstances it is advantageous to store records only at the interior nodes or only at the leaves. If records are stored at interior nodes, each leaf can have an associated action which is to be taken if a search fails at that leaf. If records are stored only at the leaves, each interior node contains a value for comparison rather than an entire record. In this case, each leaf may be a single record, or it may be a "bucket" which contains a subfile. A search for a record in such a tree need not read all records of the file into main storage, since the interior of the tree can be searched and the result used to bring only the appropriate bucket into main storage.

Using only interior nodes or only leaves for record storage significantly increases the number of nodes of the tree, but it has only a small effect on the height of the tree; as a consequence, the number of steps of a search procedure in such a tree is not much larger than that for other search trees. We leave it as an exercise to show that if all leaves of a tree are approximately the same distance from the root, then the height of a search tree with records stored only at the leaves is only slightly greater than the height of one with records stored at all nodes.

If records are stored only at leaves of a search tree, then there must be some value, which we will call a *discriminator*, associated with each internal node of the tree. The discriminator of a node is used to direct the search process in the same way as the key of a record stored at the node.

Example

The following graphs are binary search trees for a file with the key set $\{0, 2, 4, 7, 8, 9\}$. In the tree on the left, records have been stored in all nodes and each node is labelled with the key of its record. In the tree on the right, all records are stored at the leaves, which we have drawn as squares. Labels of the internal nodes of this tree are discriminators and need not be members of the key set.

---

†Unless specified otherwise, all logarithms in this book are to the base 2.

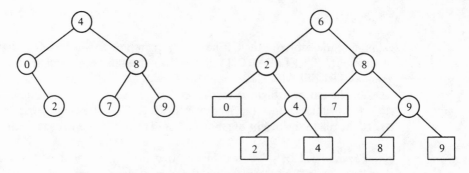

By storing more than one discriminator at each node, it is possible to implement ternary or higher-order searches. For example, for a ternary search, each node has two discriminators d_1 and d_2 and an outdegree of 3 or less. When searching for a record with key k, if $k < d_1$, then the left subtree is searched, if $d_1 \leq k < d_2$, the middle subtree is searched, and if $k \geq d_2$, then the right subtree is searched.

Example

The following graph represents a ternary search tree. The two discriminators of each internal node are given as a node label $x : y$. Records are stored only at the leaves of the tree.

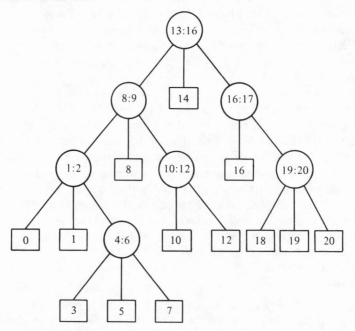

#

Tree Traversal Algorithms

When using trees as data structures, it is often necessary to traverse the tree, that is, to inspect each data item stored in the tree. We will describe three traversal algorithms for binary trees; each traversal scheme will be defined by specifying an order for processing the three components of root, left subtree and right subtree. We consider the following three orders.

> Vist the root, then the left subtree, then the right subtree.
> Visit the left subtree, then the root, then the right subtree.
> Visit the left subtree, then the right subtree, then the root.

Whatever choice is made, it is natural to apply the same strategy to the subtrees as was chosen for the tree, making the traversal algorithm recursive. To describe the three algorithms, we assume a binary tree T with root r, a left subtree T_1 and a right subtree T_2; note that T_1 and T_2 may not exist. The order in which the nodes of T are visited is called *preorder*, *inorder*, or *postorder* depending on whether the root is visited first, second, or third. The following are recursive definitions of the three traversal algorithms.

Preorder: 1. Process the root node r of T.
    2. If T_1 exists, then process T_1 in preorder.
    3. If T_2 exists, then process T_2 in preorder.

Inorder: 1. If T_1 exists, then process T_1 in inorder.
    2. Process the root node r of T.
    3. If T_2 exists, then process T_2 in inorder.

Postorder: 1. If T_1 exists, then process T_1 in postorder.
    2. If T_2 exists, then process T_2 in postorder.
    3. Process the root node r of T.

Example

  The node labels of the following binary trees give the order in which the nodes are visited by each of the traversal algorithms.

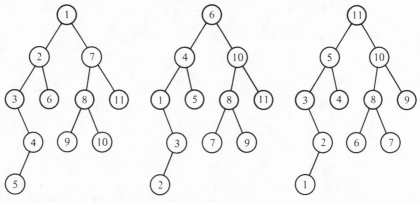

Preorder   Inorder   Postorder   #

Algorithms based on one of these traversal schemes are naturally given as recursive procedures. Figure 3.2.3 gives a recursive procedure which uses an inorder traversal to list all keys stored in a tree.

procedure LIST(*root*):
comment: using inorder traversal, list keys stored in binary tree.
begin
      if LEFTSON(*root*) ≠ *null* **then** LIST(LEFTSON(*root*));
      print KEY(*root*);
      if RIGHTSON(*root*) ≠ *null* **then** LIST(RIGHTSON(*root*))
end

        Fig. 3.2.3 Procedure to list the keys of records stored in a binary tree

If L is the set of possible node labels of a tree, then each traversal order corresponds to a unique word w over the alphabet L for any given tree. In general, it is not possible to reconstruct the tree given only the word w and the traversal order, but this reconstruction can be done in certain important cases. In particular, if a labelled tree represents an algebraic expression, then each internal node is labelled with an operation, such as $+$, $-$, $*$, and $/$, and each leaf is labelled with a variable or a value. For such trees, if the node labels are listed in either preorder or postorder, the result is a word from which the original algebraic expression can be reconstructed. This way of representing algebraic expressions is known as *parenthesis free* or *Polish notation* and is extremely convenient for computer evaluation. Evaluation is usually done using a *pushdown store*; a discussion of this topic is beyond our scope.

Example

      Consider the algebraic expression $(a - (b + c)) * d$ and its associated labelled binary tree:

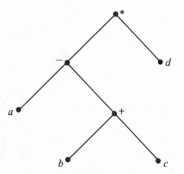

Preorder traversal results in the word $* - a + b\,c\,d$, and postorder traversal produces $a\,b\,c + - d\,*$. Both of these words can be used to reconstruct the original tree, but the inorder expression $a - b + c * d$ is ambiguous.   #

Problems: Section 3.2

1. State which of the following digraphs are trees. For those that are not, state why.

(a)

(b)

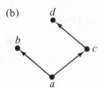

(c)

(d)

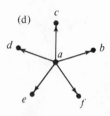

(e)

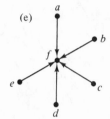

(f)

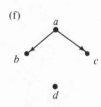

2. For each of the following trees identify the root, the leaves, the height, and all proper subtrees.

(a)

(b)

(c)

(d)

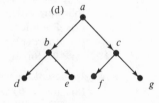

3. Prove Corollary 3.2.1a.

4. Prove Corollary 3.2.1b.

5. Let a and b be distinct nodes of a tree. Prove that there is exactly one simple undirected path from a to b.

6. Prove that if a tree has n nodes, then it has $n - 1$ arcs.

7. (a) Prove that if any arc of a tree is deleted, the resulting digraph is not connected.
    (b) Characterize the digraph which results when a single arc is deleted from a tree.

8. Give a recursive definition of the height of a binary tree.

9. Let S be a finite set of k integers. Describe an algorithm to construct a binary search tree with k nodes, where each node is labelled with a distinct element of the set S. Your algorithm should produce a tree of height $\lfloor \log_2 (k) \rfloor$.

10. Prove Theorem 3.2.3.

11. Prove Corollary 3.2.3.

12. (a) Prove that the number of interior nodes of a binary tree of height $h > 0$ is less than 2^{h-1}.
    (b) Find an upper bound for the number of interior nodes of an n-ary tree of height h.

13. Consider the following labelled binary tree.

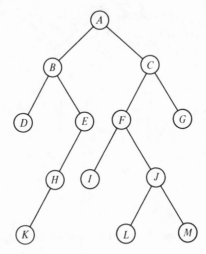

Give the sequence of labels encountered when the tree is traversed in each of the following orders.
    (a) Preorder
    (b) Inorder
    (c) Postorder

14. Represent the following propositional forms as ordered trees.
    (a) $[(A \lor B) \Rightarrow C] \Leftrightarrow (D \lor A)$
    (b) $(A \Rightarrow B) \land [\neg(C \lor B) \Leftrightarrow A]$ (Note that this expression contains a unary operator.)

15. Construct the labelled binary tree corresponding to the following parenthesis-free expressions. These expressions were obtained by traversing the trees in the order given.
    (a) $- - - a\,b\,c\,d$ (preorder)
    (b) $- a - b - c\,d$ (preorder)
    (c) $a\,b\,c*d\,e*/+$ (postorder)

16. Write a recursive procedure to evaluate an algebraic expression represented by a labelled binary tree. Assume that the leaves of the tree are labelled with integers and the only operations used are the binary operations $+$, $-$, $*$, and $/$.

17. Show that inorder traversal of labelled trees representing algebraic expressions may produce an ambiguous expression; in particular, two trees representing different expressions can produce the same word when inorder traversal is used.

18. (a) Show that the number of leaves on a complete binary tree is always one greater than the number of interior nodes of the tree.

(b) Find an expression for the number of leaves on a complete n-ary tree in terms of the number of interior nodes of the tree.

19. Let T_1 be a complete binary search tree of height h_1 with records stored in both interior nodes and leaves such that the length of any path from the root of T_1 to a leaf is either h_1 or $h_1 - 1$. Let T_2 be a complete binary search tree with records stored only at the leaves; T_2 is of height h_2 and the length of any path from the root of T_2 to a leaf is either h_2 or $h_2 - 1$. Suppose both search trees contain n records.
(a) What is the difference in the heights of the trees?
(b) What conclusions can be drawn about the difference in the maximum number of nodes visited in searching for a record in the two trees?

20. An array A can be used to represent a binary tree as follows:
  (i) The root value is stored at $A[1]$.
  (ii) For each i such that a value of a tree node is stored at $A[i]$, the value of the left son of $A[i]$ is stored at $A[2i]$ and the value of the right son of $A[i]$ is stored at $A[2i + 1]$.
A distinguished value can be used to indicate that the corresponding tree node does not exist.
(a) How many entries must the array have if the tree is of height h?
(b) Generalize this technique for n-ary trees.

21. Let T be a complete binary tree with n leaves, $b_1, b_2, \ldots, b_n$, and let d_i be the length of the path from the root to leaf b_i, $1 \leq i \leq n$.
(a) Show that $\sum_{i=1}^{n} 2^{-d_i} = 1$.
(b) (For students with an understanding of elementary probability.) Interpret the equality of part (a) in terms of probabilities, and generalize the equality for complete n-ary trees.
(c) Show $\max\{d_i\} \geq \lceil \log n \rceil$.

Programming Problems

1. Write a recursive program to determine the height of a binary tree.

2. Let T be a binary tree whose nodes are labeled with positive integers, and let A be an array used to represent T as described in problem 20, where the array entry 0 is used to indicate that a node does not exist.
(a) Write a procedure to print out the node labels of T in postorder.
(b) Write a procedure to search for a node label in T.

3.3 SPECIAL PROPERTIES OF RELATIONS

Certain properties of binary relations play particularly important roles in a wide variety of contexts. We will now define these properties and interpret them in terms of digraphs.

Definition 3.3.1: Let R be a binary relation on A. Then
(a) R is *reflexive* if xRx for every x in A.
(b) R is *irreflexive* if $x\bar{R}x$ for every x in A.

(c) R is *symmetric* if xRy implies yRx for every $x, y \in A$.

(d) R is *antisymmetric* if xRy and yRx together imply $x = y$ for every $x, y \in A$.

(e) R is *transitive* if xRy and yRz together imply xRz for every $x, y, z \in A$.

A relation R is reflexive on a set A if xRx for every $x \in A$, i.e., every element is in the relation R to itself. The digraph of a reflexive relation has a loop on every node of the digraph. A relation R is irreflexive on A if no element $x \in A$ is in the relation R to itself. The digraph of an irreflexive relation does not have loops on any nodes. Note that it is possible for a relation R to be neither reflexive nor irreflexive; the graph of such a relation would have loops on some but not all nodes.

Examples

(a)   The relation of equality ($a = b$) is reflexive on any set.

(b)   Consider the set of integers I. The relation $\leq$ is reflexive and not irreflexive, and the relation $<$ is irreflexive and not reflexive.

(c)   Consider the following relations on the set Σ^*, where $\Sigma = \{a, b\}$. The relation "is the same length as" is reflexive and not irreflexive. The relation "is longer than" is irreflexive and not reflexive. Let R be a relation such that xRy if and only if some proper prefix of x is a proper suffix of y. Then R is neither reflexive nor irreflexive, since $aaRaa$ but $ab\cancel{R}ab$.   #

A relation on a set A is symmetric if xRy implies yRx. If D is the digraph of a symmetric relation, then there are either two arcs or no arcs between any two distinct nodes of D. In contrast, if D is the digraph of an antisymmetric relation, then there is either one arc or no arcs between any two distinct nodes of D. Loops may, but need not occur on nodes of digraphs of both symmetric and antisymmetric relations.

Examples

(a)   The relation of equality on any set is both symmetric and antisymmetric.

(b)   For the set of integers I, the relations $<$ and $\leq$ are both antisymmetric; neither is symmetric. The relation "xRy if and only if the absolute values of x and y are equal" is symmetric and not antisymmetric.

(c)   For the set Σ^*, the relation "is a substring of" is antisymmetric and not symmetric. The relation "xRy if and only if x and y have a common nonempty prefix" is symmetric and not antisymmetric.   #

If R is a transitive relation, then whenever xRy and yRz it follows that xRz. If D is the digraph of a transitive relation, and there are arcs from x to y and from y to z, then there is an arc from x to z. It follows that if D is the digraph of a transitive relation R and there is a path of length greater than 0 from x to y, then there is an arc (a path of length 1) from x to y.

Examples

(a)   The equality relation is transitive for all sets.

(b)   For the set of integers **I**, the relations $<$ and $\leq$ are transitive. The relation "xRy if and only if x divides y" is also transitive.

(c)   For the set Σ^*, the relation "is a prefix of," "is a proper prefix of," "is a sub-word of," and "is the same length as" are all transitive relations.   #

We conclude this section with examples which list the properties of some specific relations.

Examples

Consider the set $\{1, 2, 3\}$ and the relations represented by the following digraphs.

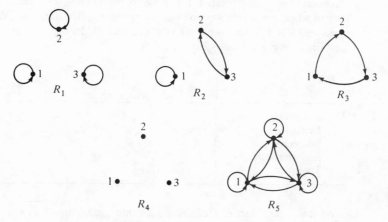

(a) R_1 is the equality relation on the set A. It is reflexive, symmetric, antisymmetric, and transitive. It is not irreflexive.

(b)   The relation R_2 is symmetric but not reflexive, irreflexive, antisymmetric, or transitive.

(c)   The relation R_3 is irreflexive and antisymmetric. It is not reflexive, symmetric, or transitive.

(d)   The relation R_4 is the empty relation on A. It is irreflexive, symmetric, antisymmetric, and transitive, but not reflexive.

(e) R_5 is the universal relation on A. This relation is reflexive, symmetric, and transitive, but not irreflexive or antisymmetric.   #

Problems: Section 3.3

1. List the properties defined in Definition 3.3.1 which hold for the relations represented by the following digraphs.

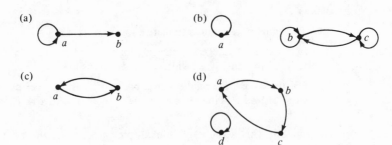

2. Describe the following relations in terms of the properties of Definition 3.3.1.
   (a) For the set of the integers **I**, xRy if and only if x and y are both positive or are both negative.
   (b) For the set of integers **I**, xRy if and only if $|x - y| = 4$ or $|x - y| = 8$ or $x = y$.

3. Consider the set of integers **I**. Fill in the following table with Y(yes) or N(no) according to whether the relation possesses the property. The notation ϕ denotes the empty relation, $\mathbf{I} \times \mathbf{I}$ is the universal relation, and D denotes "divides with an integer quotient" (e.g., $4D8$ but $4\not{D}7$).

	ϕ	$\mathbf{I} \times \mathbf{I}$	$=$	$<$	$\leq$	D
Reflexive						
Irreflexive						
Symmetric						
Antisymmetric						
Transitive						

4. Transcribe each part of Definition 3.3.1 into logical notation. For example, part (a) becomes

$$R \text{ is reflexive} \Leftrightarrow \forall x[x \in A \Rightarrow xRx]$$

5. (a) Find a nonempty set and a relation on it which is neither reflexive nor irreflexive. Choose the set to be as small as possible. What if the set is permitted to be empty?
   (b) Construct a binary relation on a nonempty set which is neither symmetric nor antisymmetric. Choose the set to be as small as possible. What if the set is permitted to be empty?

6. Consider the set of binary relations over an arbitrary set A. We say a property of relations is *preserved* under a particular set operation if applying the operation to the relation(s) results in a relation with the same property. For example, the reflexive property is preserved under the binary operation of set union since the union of two reflexive relations is reflexive. However, the reflexive property is not preserved under the unary operation of set complement, since the absolute complement of a reflexive relation on a nonempty set is not a reflexive relation. Complete the following table

with Y (yes) and N (no) according to whether the given property is preserved under the indicated set operation. For each "no" answer, give a counterexample.

	Union $R_1 \cup R_2$	Intersection $R_1 \cap R_2$	Relative Complement $R_1 - R_2$	Absolute Complement $(A \times A) - R_1$
Reflexive	Y			N
Irreflexive				
Symmetric				
Antisymmetric				
Transitive				

7. Sketch graphs of the following relations on the set of real numbers and determine for each relation which of the properties in Definition 3.3.1 apply.
   (a) $\{\langle x, y \rangle \mid x = y\}$.
   (b) $\{\langle x, y \rangle \mid x^2 - 1 = 0 \wedge y > 0\}$.
   (c) $\{\langle x, y \rangle \mid |x| \leq 1 \wedge |y| \geq 1\}$.

8. (a) State which of the following terms apply to the binary relations represented by trees: reflexive, irreflexive, symmetric, antisymmetric, transitive.
   (b) Does the list of applicable terms completely describe the relations represented by trees, or are there binary relations which possess these characteristics whose digraphs are not trees?

Programming Problem

Write a program which takes as input the ordered pairs of binary relation and determines which of the properties of Definition 3.3.1 apply.

3.4 COMPOSITION OF RELATIONS

It is often easier to describe how to construct a relation than to give a direct characterization. We already have a variety of set operations which can be used to construct new binary relations from old ones. If R_1 and R_2 are binary relations from A to B, then $R_1 \cup R_2$, $R_1 \cap R_2$, $R_1 - R_2$, and $\bar{R}_1$ are all binary relations from A to B, where the complement is taken relative to the universal set $A \times B$.

The operation of composition of relations permits the use of a sequence of relations to define a new relation. Suppose R_1 is a relation from A to B and R_2 is a relation from B to C. The composite relation $R_1 R_2$ is a relation from A to C as shown in Fig. 3.4.1. In terms of this diagram, $\langle a, c \rangle \in R_1 R_2$ if there is a path of length 2 from $a \in A$ to $c \in C$, where the first edge of the path represents an element of R_1 and the second edge of the path represents an element of R_2.

The composite relation $R_1 R_2$ is the result of applying a binary operation of composition to the operands R_1 and R_2. The operation of composition of relations is implicitly defined by the following definition of a composite relation.

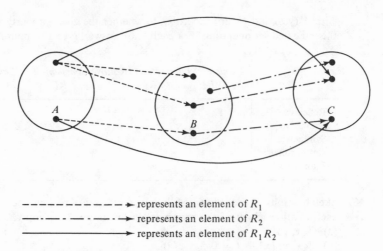

$$\text{--------} \rightarrow \text{ represents an element of } R_1$$
$$\text{--·--·--·} \rightarrow \text{ represents an element of } R_2$$
$$\text{--------} \rightarrow \text{ represents an element of } R_1 R_2$$

Fig. 3.4.1 The composite relation $R_1 R_2$

Definition 3.4.1: Let R_1 be a relation from A to B and R_2 a relation from B to C. The *composite relation from A to C*, denoted $R_1 \cdot R_2$ or $R_1 R_2$, is defined as follows:

$$R_1 R_2 = \{\langle a, c \rangle \mid a \in A \land c \in C \land \exists b[b \in B \land \langle a, b \rangle \in R_1 \land \langle b, c \rangle \in R_2]\}.$$

(Note that if R_1 and R_2 are relations from A to B and from C to D respectively, then $R_1 R_2$ is not defined unless $B = C$.)

Examples

    (a)   If R_1 is the relation "is the brother of" and R_2 is the relation "is the father of," then $R_1 R_2$ is the relation "is the paternal uncle of."

    (b)   If R_1 is the relation "is the father of," then $R_1 R_1$ is the relation "is the paternal grandfather of."

    (c)   In the execution of programs written in a high level language, a sequence of data conversions sometimes occurs. For example, a string of decimal digits in an arithmetic expression may be converted first to a binary integer representation and then to a floating point representation. If $\langle x, y \rangle \in R_1$ implies that digit string x is converted to binary integer y, and $\langle y, z \rangle \in R_2$ implies that binary integer y is converted to floating point number z, then $\langle x, z \rangle \in R_1 R_2$ implies that digit string x is converted to the floating point number z.   #

    Theorem 3.4.1: Let R_1 be a relation from A to B, R_2 and R_3 be relations from B to C, and R_4 be a relation from C to D. Then

    (a) $R_1(R_2 \cup R_3) = R_1 R_2 \cup R_1 R_3$
    (b) $R_1(R_2 \cap R_3) \subset R_1 R_2 \cap R_1 R_3$
    (c) $(R_2 \cup R_3)R_4 = R_2 R_4 \cup R_3 R_4$
    (d) $(R_2 \cap R_3)R_4 \subset R_2 R_4 \cap R_3 R_4$

Proof:

(a) $\langle a, c \rangle \in R_1(R_2 \cup R_3)$ if and only if there exists some $b \in B$ such that $\langle a, b \rangle \in R_1$ and $\langle b, c \rangle \in R_2 \cup R_3$. Furthermore,

$$\exists b[\langle a, b \rangle \in R_1 \wedge \langle b, c \rangle \in R_2 \cup R_3]$$

$$\Leftrightarrow \exists b[\langle a, b \rangle \in R_1 \wedge (\langle b, c \rangle \in R_2 \vee \langle b, c \rangle \in R_3)]$$

$$\Leftrightarrow \exists b[(\langle a, b \rangle \in R_1 \wedge \langle b, c \rangle \in R_2) \vee (\langle a, b \rangle \in R_1 \wedge \langle b, c \rangle \in R_3)]$$

$$\Leftrightarrow \exists b[\langle a, b \rangle \in R_1 \wedge \langle b, c \rangle \in R_2] \vee \exists b[\langle a, b \rangle \in R_1 \wedge \langle b, c \rangle \in R_3]$$

$$\Leftrightarrow \langle a, c \rangle \in R_1 R_2 \vee \langle a, c \rangle \in R_1 R_3$$

$$\Leftrightarrow \langle a, c \rangle \in R_1 R_2 \cup R_1 R_3.$$

We leave the proofs of parts (b)–(d) as exercises. ∎

The operation of composition is clearly not commutative; in fact, $R_2 R_1$ may not be defined even though $R_1 R_2$ is. The next theorem establishes that the operation is associative.

Theorem 3.4.2:   Let R_1, R_2 and R_3 be relations from A to B, B to C and C to D respectively. Then $(R_1 R_2)R_3 = R_1(R_2 R_3)$.

Proof: We first show $(R_1 R_2)R_3 \subset R_1(R_2 R_3)$. Let $\langle a, d \rangle \in (R_1 R_2)R_3$. Then for some $c \in C$, $\langle a, c \rangle \in R_1 R_2$ and $\langle c, d \rangle \in R_3$. Furthermore, since $\langle a, c \rangle \in R_1 R_2$ there exists $b \in B$ such that $\langle a, b \rangle \in R_1$ and $\langle b, c \rangle \in R_2$. Since $\langle b, c \rangle \in R_2$ and $\langle c, d \rangle \in R_3$, it follows that $\langle b, d \rangle \in R_2 R_3$ and therefore $\langle a, d \rangle \in R_1(R_2 R_3)$. The proof that $R_1(R_2 R_3) \subset (R_1 R_2)R_3$ is similar and is left to the reader. ∎

The above proof is in two parts in order to show containment in both directions. The theorem can also be proved using a sequence of equivalences as follows:

Proof:

$$\langle a, d \rangle \in (R_1 R_2)R_3$$

$$\Leftrightarrow \exists c[\langle a, c \rangle \in R_1 R_2 \wedge \langle c, d \rangle \in R_3]$$

$$\Leftrightarrow \exists c[\exists b[\langle a, b \rangle \in R_1 \wedge \langle b, c \rangle \in R_2] \wedge \langle c, d \rangle \in R_3]$$

$$\Leftrightarrow \exists c \exists b[[\langle a, b \rangle \in R_1 \wedge \langle b, c \rangle \in R_2] \wedge \langle c, d \rangle \in R_3]$$

$$\Leftrightarrow \exists c \exists b[\langle a, b \rangle \in R_1 \wedge [\langle b, c \rangle \in R_2 \wedge \langle c, d \rangle \in R_3]]$$

$$\Leftrightarrow \exists b \exists c[\langle a, b \rangle \in R_1 \wedge [\langle b, c \rangle \in R_2 \wedge \langle c, d \rangle \in R_3]]$$

$$\Leftrightarrow \exists b[\langle a, b \rangle \in R_1 \wedge \exists c[\langle b, c \rangle \in R_2 \wedge \langle c, d \rangle \in R_3]]$$

$$\Leftrightarrow \exists b[\langle a, b \rangle \in R_1 \wedge \langle b, d \rangle \in R_2 R_3]$$

$$\Leftrightarrow \langle a, d \rangle \in R_1(R_2 R_3). \blacksquare$$

Since composition is associative, we usually omit parentheses and write

$R_1 R_2 R_3$. As with other associative binary operations, placement of parentheses is unimportant in specifying composite relations.

When R is a relation on a set A, then R can be composed with itself any number of times to form a new relation on the set A. In this case, RR is often denoted by R^2, RRR by R^3, etc. We can define this notation inductively as follows.

Definition 3.4.2:   Let R be a binary relation on a set A and let $n \in \mathbf{N}$. Then, the *nth power* of R, denoted R^n, is defined as follows:
1. R^0 is the relation of equality on the set A; $R^0 = \{\langle x, x \rangle \mid x \in A\}$.
2. $R^{n+1} = R^n R$.

Theorem 3.4.3:   Let R be a binary relation on A, and let m and n be elements of $\mathbf{N}$. Then,
   (a) $R^m R^n = R^{m+n}$
   (b) $(R^m)^n = R^{mn}$

The proofs are by induction and are left as exercises.

If D is the digraph of a binary relation R on a set A, then $\langle x, y \rangle \in R^n$ if and only if there is a path of length n from node x to node y.

Examples

Let $A = \{a, b, c, d\}$ and let R be the relation on A represented by the following digraph:

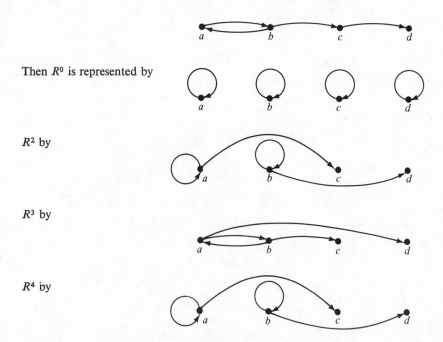

Then R^0 is represented by

R^2 by

R^3 by

R^4 by

We note that $R^4 = R^2$ and hence $R^4R = R^2R$, that is, $R^5 = R^3$. Similarly $R^6 = R^4 = R^2$. It follows (by induction) that $R^{2n+1} = R^3$ and $R^{2n} = R^2$ for $n \geq 1$. This relationship can be represented by the following digraph where each node represents R^k for some k and an arc exists from X to Y if $X \cdot R = Y$.

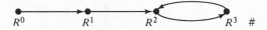

$$R^0 \qquad R^1 \qquad R^2 \qquad R^3 \quad \#$$

In the preceding example, not all powers of the relation R were distinct relations. In fact, if R is a relation on a finite set, this will always be the case, as the following theorem asserts.

Theorem 3.4.4:   If A is a finite set with n elements and R is a relation on A, then there exist s and t such that $R^s = R^t$ and $0 \leq s < t \leq 2^{n^2}$.

Proof: Each binary relation on A is a subset of $A \times A$. Since $A \times A$ has n^2 elements, $\mathcal{P}(A \times A)$ has 2^{n^2} elements. Hence, there are 2^{n^2} distinct relations on A and therefore no more than 2^{n^2} distinct powers of R. But the list $R^0, R^1, \ldots, R^{2^{n^2}}$ has $2^{n^2} + 1$ entries and hence at least two of these powers of R must be equal.   ∎

If R is a relation on an infinite set A, then there may not exist two integers s and t such that $R^s = R^t$. For example, if $A = \mathbf{N}$ and $\langle x, y \rangle \in R \Leftrightarrow y = x + 1$, then $\langle x, z \rangle \in R^s \Leftrightarrow z = x + s$; in this case, all powers of R are distinct relations on A.

Theorem 3.4.5:   Let R be a binary relation on a set A and suppose $R^s = R^t$ for some s and t with $s < t$. Let $p = t - s$. Then
  (a) $R^{s+k} = R^{t+k}$ for all $k \geq 0$.
  (b) $R^{s+kp+i} = R^{s+i}$ for all $k, i \geq 0$.
  (c)   Let $S = \{R^0, R^1, R^2, \ldots, R^{t-1}\}$. Then every power of R is an element of S, i.e., $R^q \in S$ for all $q \in \mathbf{N}$.

Proof: Parts (a) and (b) require proofs by induction and are left as exercises.
  (c)   Let $q \in \mathbf{N}$. If $q < t$, then $R^q \in S$ by definition of S. Suppose $q \geq t$. Then we can express q in the form $s + kp + i$, where $i < p$. By part (b), it follows that $R^q = R^{s+i}$. Since $s + i < t$, this establishes that $R^q \in S$.   ∎

Problems: Section 3.4

1.   Let R_1 and R_2 be relations on a set $A = \{a, b, c, d\}$ where

$$R_1 = \{\langle a, a \rangle, \langle a, b \rangle, \langle b, d \rangle\}$$
$$R_2 = \{\langle a, d \rangle, \langle b, c \rangle, \langle b, d \rangle, \langle c, b \rangle\}.$$

Find R_1R_2, R_2R_1, R_1^2, R_2^3.

2. Let R be represented by the following tree.

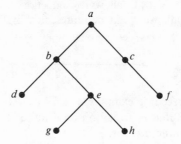

Sketch the digraphs of the relations R^n for $n \in \mathbf{N}$.

3. Let $A = \{a, b, c, d, e, f, g, h\}$ and let R be the binary relation on A as represented by the following two-component digraph.

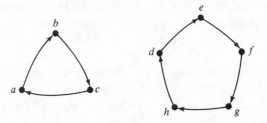

Find the smallest integers m and n such that $m < n$ and $R^m = R^n$.

4. Prove that if R is either the empty relation or the universal relation on a set A, then $R^2 = R$.

5. Prove or disprove:
   (a) If D is the digraph of a relation R and D is connected, then the digraph of R^n is connected for every $n > 0$.
   (b) If D is the digraph of a relation R and D is strongly connected, then the digraph of R^n is strongly connected for every $n > 0$.

6. (a) Prove part (b) of Theorem 3.4.1.
   (b) Give examples to show that the containment of parts (b) and (d) may be proper.

7. Prove Theorem 3.4.3.

8. Prove parts (a) and (b) of Theorem 3.4.5.

9. Let R_1 and R_2 be arbitrary relations on a set A.
   Prove or disprove the following assertions.
   (a) If R_1 and R_2 are reflexive, then $R_1 R_2$ is reflexive.
   (b) If R_1 and R_2 are irreflexive, then $R_1 R_2$ is irreflexive.
   (c) If R_1 and R_2 are symmetric, then $R_1 R_2$ is symmetric.
   (d) If R_1 and R_2 are antisymmetric, then $R_1 R_2$ is antisymmetric.
   (e) If R_1 and R_2 are transitive, then $R_1 R_2$ is transitive.

3.5 CLOSURE OPERATIONS ON RELATIONS

In the previous section we described the use of the operation of composition to generate new relations from old ones. In this section we will show how to construct a new relation R' from a given relation R by requiring that R' contain R and that R' have certain properties. The relation R' will be formed by adding to R only those ordered pairs necessary for the properties to hold. For example, consider a data communications network with data paths between pairs of cities. If we wish to send messages from A to B and there is no direct transmission facility from A to B, then it may be possible to route the message through intermediate cities. The question we address is a global one: For what pairs of cities A, B are there paths from A to B? Most likely, the specification of the communications network is given as a set of local connections, that is, the pairs of cities C and D such that there is a direct transmission route from C to D. Thus, we are given one binary relation R which specifies a local property (the arcs of a graph), but we are interested in another binary relation R' which concerns a global property (the paths of the graph). The relation R' is transitive and can be constructed from R. We will define a class of "closure" operations for binary relations which will enable us to construct R' from R.

Definition 3.5.1: Let R be a binary relation on a set A. The *reflexive (symmetric, transitive) closure* of R is the relation R' such that
   (i) R' is reflexive (symmetric, transitive);
   (ii) $R' \supset R$;
   (iii) For any reflexive (symmetric, transitive) relation R'', if $R'' \supset R$, then $R'' \supset R'$.
We will denote the reflexive closure of R by $r(R)$, the symmetric closure by $s(R)$ and the transitive closure by $t(R)$.

If R is a binary relation on set A, we can form its reflexive (symmetric, transitive) closure by adding to the relation R all the ordered pairs which are needed to make the new relation reflexive (symmetric, transitive). But part (iii) of Definition 3.5.1 stipulates that no pairs shall be added unless necessary. Thus R' is the smallest relation such that R' is reflexive (symmetric, transitive) and $R' \supset R$. If R is already reflexive (or symmetric, or transitive), then the smallest relation which has this property and contains R is R itself. This is implied by the following theorem.

Theorem 3.5.1: Let R be a binary relation on a set A. Then
   (a) R is reflexive if and only if $r(R) = R$.
   (b) R is symmetric if and only if $s(R) = R$.
   (c) R is transitive if and only if $t(R) = R$.

Proof:

(a) If R is reflexive, then R has all the properties given in Definition 3.5.1 for the relation R'. Hence $r(R) = R$. Conversely, if $r(R) = R$, then by property (i) of Definition 3.5.1, R is reflexive.

The proofs of (b) and (c) are similar. ∎

Forming the closure of a binary relation is conveniently viewed in terms of digraphs. For example, a digraph represents a reflexive relation if and only if it has loops on every node. Thus, if D is the digraph of a binary relation R on a set A, we can form the digraph of the reflexive closure of R, $r(R)$, by adding a loop to every node of the digraph D which does not already have one.

The following theorem is another form of this assertion. (In the remainder of this section, E will denote the equality relation on an arbitrary set A; that is, $E = \{\langle x, x \rangle \mid x \in A\}$.)

Theorem 3.5.2: Let R be a binary relation on a set A. Then $r(R) = R \cup E$.

Proof: Let $R' = R \cup E$. We show that R' satisfies Definition 3.5.1. By construction, R' is reflexive and $R' \supset R$. Suppose R'' is a reflexive relation on A and $R'' \supset R$. We must show $R'' \supset R'$. Consider an arbitrary $\langle a, b \rangle \in R'$. Then, since $R' = R \cup E$, either $a = b$ or $\langle a, b \rangle \in R$. If $a = b$, then $\langle a, b \rangle \in R''$ since R'' is reflexive. If $\langle a, b \rangle \in R$, then $\langle a, b \rangle \in R''$ since $R'' \supset R$. Thus, if $\langle a, b \rangle \in R'$, then $\langle a, b \rangle \in R''$. Consequently, the conditions of Definition 3.5.1 are satisfied and $R' = r(R)$. ∎

Examples

(a) The reflexive closure of the relation $<$ on the integers $\mathbf{I}$ is $\leq$.

(b) The reflexive closure of E is E.

(c) The reflexive closure of $\neq$ is the universal relation.

(d) The reflexive closure of the empty relation is the relation of equality, E. #

The concept of the converse of a relation will be useful in discussing symmetric closure.

Definition 3.5.2: Let R be a binary relation from A to B. The *converse* of the relation R, denoted R^c, is the binary relation from B to A defined as follows:

$$R^c = \{\langle y, x \rangle \mid \langle x, y \rangle \in R\}.$$

If D is the digraph of the relation R, the digraph of R^c can be constructed from D by reversing the direction of all the arcs of D.

Examples

(a) The converse of the relation $<$ on I is the relation $>$.

(b) The converse of the relation $\subset$ on a collection of sets is the relation $\supset$. #

The following theorem states some of the properties of converses.

Theorem 3.5.3: Let R, R_1, and R_2 be binary relations from A to B. Then each of the following holds.

(a) $(R^c)^c = R$

(b) $(R_1 \cup R_2)^c = R_1^c \cup R_2^c$

(c) $(R_1 \cap R_2)^c = R_1^c \cap R_2^c$

(d) $(A \times B)^c = B \times A$

(e) $\phi^c = \phi$

(f) $(\bar{R})^c = (\overline{R^c})$, where $\bar{R}$ denotes $(A \times B) - R$.

(g) $(R_1 - R_2)^c = R_1^c - R_2^c$

(h) If $A = B$, then $(R_1 R_2)^c = R_2^c R_1^c$

(i) $R_1 \subset R_2 \Rightarrow R_1^c \subset R_2^c$

Proof:

(a) ($(R^c)^c = R$.) Let $\langle x, y \rangle$ be an arbitrary element of R. Then, $\langle x, y \rangle \in R$
$\Leftrightarrow \langle y, x \rangle \in R^c \Leftrightarrow \langle x, y \rangle \in (R^c)^c$; therefore $(R^c)^c = R$.

(b) ($(R_1 \cup R_2)^c = R_1^c \cup R_2^c$.)
$$\langle x, y \rangle \in (R_1 \cup R_2)^c \Leftrightarrow \langle y, x \rangle \in R_1 \cup R_2$$
$$\Leftrightarrow \langle y, x \rangle \in R_1 \vee \langle y, x \rangle \in R_2$$
$$\Leftrightarrow \langle x, y \rangle \in R_1^c \vee \langle x, y \rangle \in R_2^c$$
$$\Leftrightarrow \langle x, y \rangle \in R_1^c \cup R_2^c.$$

(f) ($(\bar{R})^c = (\overline{R^c})$.) $\langle x, y \rangle \in (\bar{R})^c \Leftrightarrow \langle y, x \rangle \in \bar{R}$
$$\Leftrightarrow \langle y, x \rangle \notin R$$
$$\Leftrightarrow \langle x, y \rangle \notin R^c$$
$$\Leftrightarrow \langle x, y \rangle \in (\overline{R^c}).$$

(g) ($(R_1 - R_2)^c = R_1^c - R_2^c$.) Using the identity $R_1 - R_2 = R_1 \cap \bar{R}_2$, we have $(R_1 - R_2)^c = (R_1 \cap \bar{R}_2)^c = R_1^c \cap (\bar{R}_2)^c$
$$= R_1^c \cap (\overline{R_2^c})$$
$$= R_1^c - R_2^c.$$

The proofs of the remaining parts are left as exercises. ∎

Theorem 3.5.4: Let R be a binary relation on A. Then R is symmetric if and only if $R = R^c$.

We leave the proof as an exercise.

The converse of a relation R is closely related to $s(R)$, the symmetric closure of R. Let R be a binary relation on a set A and let D be the digraph associated with R. The digraph of the symmetric closure of R can be obtained from D by making all the arcs of D into "two-way" edges so that if there is an arc from a to b, then there is also one from b to a. Expressed in terms of R^c, this becomes

Theorem 3.5.5: Let R be a relation on a set A. Then $s(R) = R \cup R^c$.

Proof: We must show that $R \cup R^c$ is the smallest symmetric relation which contains R. We first observe that $R \cup R^c$ contains R. Furthermore, by Theorem 3.5.3, $R \cup R^c$ is symmetric since $(R \cup R^c)^c = R^c \cup (R^c)^c = R^c \cup R$. Now suppose R' is symmetric and $R' \supset R$. We must show $R' \supset R \cup R^c$. Let

$\langle a, b \rangle \in R \cup R^c$. If $\langle a, b \rangle \in R$, then $\langle a, b \rangle \in R'$ by hypothesis. If $\langle a, b \rangle \in R^c$, then $\langle b, a \rangle \in R$ and therefore $\langle b, a \rangle \in R'$. But R' is symmetric and therefore $\langle a, b \rangle \in R'$. It follows that $R \cup R^c \subset R'$. ∎

Examples

    (a) The symmetric closure of the relation $<$ on the integers **I** is the relation $\neq$, or $\bar{E}$.

    (b) The symmetric closure of $\leq$ on the integers **I** is the universal relation.

    (c) The symmetric closure of E is E, and of $\neq$ is $\neq$. #

If D is the digraph associated with a binary relation R on a set A, the transitive closure of R, $t(R)$, corresponds to the digraph D' where D' has an arc from a to b if D has a path of nonzero length from a to b. The next theorem restates this assertion in terms of powers of R.

Theorem 3.5.6: Let R be a binary relation on the set A. Then

$$t(R) = \bigcup_{i=1}^{\infty} R^i = R \cup R^2 \cup R^3 \cup \cdots$$

Proof: The proof is in two parts.

    (i) $\bigcup_{i=1}^{\infty} R^i \subset t(R)$. We first show by induction that $R^n \subset t(R)$ for every $n > 0$.

        1. (Basis) From Definition 3.5.1, part (ii), it is immediate that $R \subset t(R)$.

        2. (Induction) Suppose $R^n \subset t(R)$, $n \geq 1$, and let $\langle a, b \rangle \in R^{n+1}$. Since $R^{n+1} = R^n R$, there exists some $c \in A$ such that $\langle a, c \rangle \in R^n$ and $\langle c, b \rangle \in R$. By the induction hypothesis and the basis step, $\langle a, c \rangle \in t(R)$ and $\langle c, b \rangle \in t(R)$. Because $t(R)$ is transitive it follows that $\langle a, b \rangle \in t(R)$, thus establishing that $R^{n+1} \subset t(R)$.

        Since $R^n \subset t(R)$ for all $n \geq 1$, we conclude that $\bigcup_{i=1}^{\infty} R^i \subset t(R)$.

    (ii) $t(R) \subset \bigcup_{i=1}^{\infty} R^i$. We first show that $\bigcup_{i=1}^{\infty} R^i$ is transitive. Let $\langle a, b \rangle$ and $\langle b, c \rangle$ be arbitrary elements of $\bigcup_{i=1}^{\infty} R^i$. Then for some integers $s \geq 1$ and $t \geq 1$, $\langle a, b \rangle \in R^s$ and $\langle b, c \rangle \in R^t$. Then $\langle a, c \rangle \in R^s R^t$, and by Theorem 3.4.3, $R^s R^t = R^{s+t}$. Thus $\langle a, c \rangle \in \bigcup_{i=1}^{\infty} R^i$ and therefore $\bigcup_{i=1}^{\infty} R^i$ is transitive. Since $t(R)$ is contained in every transitive relation which contains R, it follows that $t(R) \subset \bigcup_{i=1}^{\infty} R^i$. ∎

If R is a binary relation on A, then $\langle a, b \rangle \in t(R)$ if and only if there is a sequence of elements of A, $c_0, c_1, \ldots, c_n$, where $n \geq 1$, $c_0 = a$, $c_n = b$ and for $0 \leq i < n$, $\langle c_i, c_{i+1} \rangle \in R$. If D is the digraph of R, then $\langle a, b \rangle \in t(R)$ if and only if there is a path of nonzero length from node a to node b.

Examples

    (a) Let R be a relation on **I** such that aRb if and only if $b = a + 1$. Then $t(R)$ is the relation $<$.

    (b) Let R be the relation "is the child of." Then $t(R)$ is the relation "is the descendent of."

(c) Let R be the relation $<$ on a set of integers A. Sorting the elements of A according to R requires finding the smallest relation R' on A such that $R = t(R')$.   #

When A is finite with n elements, it follows from Theorems 3.4.4 and 3.4.5 that

$$t(R) = \bigcup_{i=1}^{2^{n^2}} R^i.$$

The following theorem establishes a smaller bound on the number of powers of R required to form $t(R)$.

Theorem 3.5.7:   Let R be a binary relation on a set A where A has n elements. Then

$$t(R) = \bigcup_{i=1}^{n} R^i$$

Proof: It suffices to show that $R^k \subset \bigcup_{i=1}^{n} R^i$ for all $k > 0$. Suppose $\langle x, y \rangle \in R^k$. Then there is a directed path of length k from x to y in the digraph $\langle A, R \rangle$, and by deleting cycles from this path we can construct a simple directed path from x to y. Since the longest possible simple path in a graph with n nodes is of length n, it follows that $\langle x, y \rangle \in R^i$ for some $0 < i \leq n$. Hence $R^k \subset \bigcup_{i=1}^{n} R^i$ for $k > 0$. ∎

Example

Consider the following digraph representing a relation R.

Then, $t(R) = R \cup R^2 \cup R^3 \cup R^3$ is represented by the following digraph.

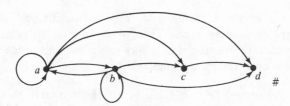

#

The following theorems develop some additional characteristics of the closure operations.

Theorem 3.5.8:
(a) If R is reflexive, then $s(R)$ and $t(R)$ are reflexive.
(b) If R is symmetric, then $r(R)$ and $t(R)$ are symmetric.
(c) If R is transitive, then $r(R)$ is transitive.

The proofs of all parts are straightforward and are left as exercises.

Theorem 3.5.9:   Let R be a binary relation on a set A. Then
(a) $rs(R) = sr(R)$,
(b) $rt(R) = tr(R)$,
(c) $ts(R) \supset st(R)$.

Proof: Let E denote the equality relation on A.
(a) $sr(R) = s(R \cup E) = (R \cup E) \cup (R \cup E)^c$
$\qquad\quad = R \cup E \cup R^c \cup E^c = R \cup R^c \cup E = r(R \cup R^c) = rs(R).$

(b)   We first note that $tr(R) = t(R \cup E)$ and $rt(R) = t(R) \cup E$.

   Using the fact that $ER = RE = R$ and that $E^n = E$ for all $n \in \mathbf{N}$, it follows that $(R \cup E)^n = E \cup \bigcup_{i=1}^n R^i$.

   Therefore,

$$tr(R) = t(R \cup E) = \bigcup_{i=1}^{\infty} (R \cup E)^i$$
$$= (R \cup E) \cup (R \cup E)^2 \cup (R \cup E)^3 \cup \cdots$$
$$= E \cup R \cup R^2 \cup R^3 \cdots$$
$$= E \cup t(R)$$
$$= rt(R).$$

(c)   We use the property that if $R_1 \supset R_2$, then $s(R_1) \supset s(R_2)$ and $t(R_1) \supset t(R_2)$. By definition of the symmetric closure, $s(R) \supset R$. By successively forming the transitive and then symmetric closure of both sides, we find $ts(R) \supset t(R)$ and $sts(R) \supset st(R)$. But $ts(R)$ is symmetric by Theorem 3.5.8, so $sts(R) = ts(R)$. Hence $ts(R) \supset st(R)$.   ■

Example

   The relation $<$ on the set of integers $\mathbf{I}$ can be used to show that in general $st(R) \neq ts(R)$. For $st(<) = s(<) = \neq$ (i.e., $st(<)$ is the inequality relation), while $ts(<) = t(\neq) = \mathbf{I} \times \mathbf{I}$ (i.e., $ts(<)$ is the universal relation).   #

   The transitive closure and reflexive transitive closure operations are used in several application areas. The "plus" and "star" notations are used to denote these closure operations in a way analogous to the use of A^+ and A^* to denote closure operations on a language A.

Definition 3.5.3:   If R is a binary relation on a set A, then R^+ (read "R plus") denotes $t(R)$, the transitive closure of R, and R^* (read "R star") denotes $tr(R)$, the reflexive transitive closure of R.

   The plus and star closure operations are often used in studying formal languages and models of computation as well as application areas such as compiler design.

Example

   Let $P = \{P_1, P_2, \ldots, P_n\}$ be the set of programs and subroutines in a program library. Define the binary relation $\Rightarrow$ over P as follows:

$P_i \Rightarrow P_j$ if and only if P_i calls P_j for some input.

The relation $\Rightarrow^+$ characterizes all programs which might be called during the execution of a program:

$P_i \Rightarrow^+ P_j$ if and only if execution of P_i may cause P_j to be called.

The relation $\Rightarrow^*$ characterizes all programs which might be active at some point during the execution of a program:

$P_i \Rightarrow^* P_j$ if and only if P_j might be active at some time during the execution of P_i.

Note that $P_i \Rightarrow^* P_i$ for all i, but $P_i \Rightarrow^+ P_i$ only if P_i can cause itself to be called, i.e., only if P_i is recursive.   #

Problems: Section 3.5

1. Find the reflexive, symmetric, and transitive closures of each of the following.

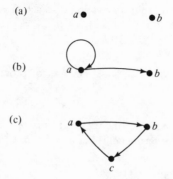

   (a)

   (b)

   (c)

2. Prove the remaining parts of Theorem 3.5.3.

3. Prove Theorem 3.5.4.

4. Let R_1 and R_2 be relations on a set A and suppose $R_1 \supset R_2$. Prove each of the following.
   (a) $r(R_1) \supset r(R_2)$
   (b) $s(R_1) \supset s(R_2)$
   (c) $t(R_1) \supset t(R_2)$

5. Let R_1 and R_2 be relations on A. Prove each of the following.
   (a) $r(R_1 \cup R_2) = r(R_1) \cup r(R_2)$
   (b) $s(R_1 \cup R_2) = s(R_1) \cup s(R_2)$
   (c) $t(R_1 \cup R_2) \supset t(R_1) \cup t(R_2)$.
   Show by counterexample that
   (d) $t(R_1 \cup R_2) \neq t(R_1) \cup t(R_2)$.

6. Find a set A with n elements and a relation R on A such that $R^1, R^2, \ldots, R^n$ are all distinct. This establishes that the bound given in Theorem 3.5.7 is attainable.

7. Prove Theorem 3.5.8.

8. Let $A = \{a, b, c, d, e, f, g, h\}$ and let R be the binary relation on A as represented by the following digraph.

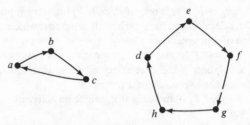

(a)   Construct the digraph $\langle A, t(R)\rangle$.

(b)   Find $tsr(R)$.

9. (a)   Show by counterexample that the statement "If R is transitive, then $s(R)$ is transitive" is false.

(b)   Find an example to show that $st(R)$ and $ts(R)$ may not be equal, even if R is a relation on a finite set.

10. Let R be an arbitrary relation on a set A. Prove each of the following.

(a) $(R^+)^+ = R^+$

(b) $RR^* = R^+ = R^*R$

(c) $(R^*)^* = R^*$

11. Let $S = \{S_1, S_2, \ldots, S_n\}$ be a set of procedures. Define the relation $\Rightarrow$ on S as follows:

$$S_i \Rightarrow S_j \Leftrightarrow S_i \text{ calls } S_j.$$

Some procedure of the set S is recursive if the digraph $\langle S, \Rightarrow^+\rangle$ contains a directed cycle of nonzero length. Let $S = \{A, B, C, D, E\}$ and suppose

A calls B and E,

B calls C,

C calls E,

D calls C, and

E calls B.

Does the set S contain any recursive procedures?

12. Let $A = \{a\}^* = \{a^n \mid n \geq 0\}$, and B be the singleton set $B = \{z\}$ where z is an infinite string of a's: $B = \{aaaa \ldots\}$. Let R be the relation on $A \cup B$ defined as follows:

$$\langle x, y\rangle \in R \Leftrightarrow y = xa.$$

Prove or disprove that $\langle \Lambda, z\rangle \in R^+$.

13. Let $A = \{a_1, a_2, \ldots, a_n\}$ be a set with n elements and let R' and R'' be binary relations A. The *incidence matrix* M' of the relation R' is the $n \times n$ matrix defined as follows:

$$M'[i, j] = 1 \Leftrightarrow a_i R' a_j,$$

$$= 0 \text{ otherwise.}$$

The matrix M'' is defined in the analogous way.

Let the operations of matrix addition and multiplication be defined in the usual way but using the following operations on matrix entries:

$0 = 0 \cdot x = x \cdot 0 = 0 + 0$ and $1 = 1 + x = x + 1 = 1 \cdot 1$, where $x = 0$ or $x = 1$.

(a)   Find the incidence matrix for $R' \cup R''$ in terms of M', M'', and the operations of matrix addition and multiplication.

(b)   Find the incidence matrix for $R'R''$.

Let M be the incidence matrix for R.

(c)   Find the incidence matrix for R^k.

(d)   Find the incidence matrices for R^+ and $R*$.

(e)   Find the smallest relation R on the set $\{a, b, c\}$, for which the incidence matrix for R^+ is

$$\begin{bmatrix} 1 & 1 & 1 \\ 1 & 1 & 1 \\ 1 & 1 & 1 \end{bmatrix}$$

14.   (For students with an understanding of elementary probability.) Consider the following four dice, which we will call A, B, C, and D.

If two dice x and y are chosen and rolled, we say "x beats y" if a higher number shows on x than y.

(a)   For each pair of dice x and y, calculate the probability that x beats y. Present your results as a two-dimensional array whose entries are probabilities.

Let R denote the binary relation "is more likely to win than" on the set $\{A, B, C, D\}$ where R is defined as follows:

$xRy \Leftrightarrow$ the probability that x beats y is greater than $\frac{1}{2}$.

(b)   Give the digraph associated with the relation R.

(c)   Find the transitive closure of R.

(d)   Is the relation R transitive?

(e)   Suppose someone proposes the following game. You may choose whichever die you like from the set $\{A, B, C, D\}$. After your selection, your opponent will select a die from the remaining three dice. You then roll the two dice; the winner is the person whose die beats the other. The loser pays the winner $1. Assuming your moral character is such that this proposal does not make your skin crawl, would you accept, and why?

Programming Problem

Write a program which, when given a set of integers S and a relation R on S (specified as a set of ordered pairs), produces $r(R)$, $s(R)$ and $t(R)$.

3.6 ORDER RELATIONS

An *order relation* is a transitive relation on a set which provides a means to compare elements of the set, although such a relation may not permit a comparison of any two elements of the set. We will consider several types of order relations in this section.

Definition 3.6.1: A binary relation R on a set A is a *partial order* if R is reflexive, antisymmetric, and transitive. The ordered pair $\langle A, R \rangle$ is a *partially ordered set*, or a *poset*. The relation R is said to be a *partial order on A*.

It follows from the preceding definition that a partially ordered set is also a digraph whose relation is a partial order on the set of nodes. We will use the symbol $\leq$ to denote an arbitrary partial order; thus, if R is an unspecified partial order, we will usually write either $a \leq b$ or $b \geq a$ rather than aRb.

Examples

(a) The relation of set containment is a partial order on any collection of subsets of a set A; that is, $\subset$ is a partial order on $\mathcal{P}(A)$ and $\langle \mathcal{P}(A), \subset \rangle$ is a partially ordered set.

(b) The relation $\leq$ is a partial order relation on the set of integers.

(c) Let $B = \{b_1, b_2, \ldots, b_n\}$ be the set of blocks in a program in a block-structured language such as ALGOL or PL/I. For all i and j, define $b_i \leq b_j$ if b_i is contained in b_j. Then $\langle B, \leq \rangle$ is a poset.

(d) The relation $<$ is not a partial order on $\mathbf{I}$ because it is not reflexive. #

The diagrams we have described for digraphs can be used for partially ordered sets as well. However, posets are traditionally represented in a more economial way by *poset* (or *Hasse*) *diagrams*. These diagrams do not explicitly represent all ordered pairs of the partial order. The edges of a poset diagram for the relation R represent the smallest relation R' such that $(R')^* = R$. Thus, on a poset diagram all loops are omitted, eliminating explicit representation of the reflexive property. Furthermore, an arc is not present in a poset diagram if it is implied by the transitivity of the relation. That is, there is an arc from a to b only if there is no other element c such that $a \leq c$ and $c \leq b$. Finally, the antisymmetry of a partial order implies that the only directed cycles in a digraph representation of a poset are the node loops. By convention, poset diagrams are drawn so that all arcs point upward and arrowheads are not used. Poset diagrams are more easily grasped than digraph representations of posets, and we will use them freely.

Examples

(a) The following are alternate diagrammatic representations of a partial order R on a set $S = \{a, b, c, d\}$.

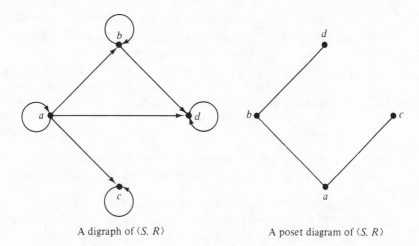

A digraph of ⟨S. R⟩   A poset diagram of ⟨S. R⟩

Note that if the edges of the diagram on the right are directed upward and the reflexive transitive closure is formed, the result is the digraph on the left.

(b)   Consider the binary relation "divides" defined on a set of nonzero integers, where a divides b if and only if b is an integer multiple of a. If we choose the set of positive integers from 1 to 12, the resulting poset is represented by the following diagram.

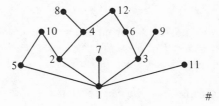

#

The concept of a partial order is closely related to the notion of a quasi order.

Definition 3.6.2:   Let R be a binary relation on A. R is a *quasi order* if R is transitive and irreflexive.

If R is a quasi order, then R is always antisymmetric because the premise of the antisymmetry condition, $xRy \wedge yRx \Rightarrow x = y$, is always false. For suppose xRy and yRx. Since R is transitive, it follows that xRx which violates the irreflexive property of R.

Examples

(a)   The relation $<$ is a quasi order on any set of real numbers.

(b)   The relation "is a proper subset of" is a quasi order on any collection of sets.

(c) The relation "is a prerequisite for" is a quasi order on any set of college courses.

(d) The transitive closure of the relation "calls" is a quasi order on any collection of nonrecursive programs and subroutines.

(e) PERT is a method of scheduling tasks to minimize the total time required for completion of the tasks. Application of the method usually involves the construction of a PERT chart which represents a quasi order on the collection of tasks to be performed; xRy means that task y cannot be started until task x is finished.   #

The only distinction between quasi orders and partial orders is the equality relation E. The proof of the following theorem is left as an exercise.

Theorem 3.6.1: Let R be a binary relation on A.
(a) If R is a quasi order, then $r(R) = R \cup E$ is a partial order.
(b) If R is a partial order, then $R - E$ is a quasi order.

Because of the similarity between quasi orders and partial orders, it is convenient to use the same diagrams to represent both kinds of order relations. Thus, a poset diagram for the partial order $\leq$ over a set of integers can also be used to represent the quasi order $<$ over the same set.

If $\leq$ is a partial order and either $a \leq b$ or $b \leq a$, we say a and b are *comparable*. If $\leq$ is a partial order on A such that every two elements of A are comparable, then $\leq$ is called a linear order.

Definition 3.6.3: A partial order $\leq$ on a set A is a *linear* (or *simple*, or *total*) *order* if either $a \leq b$ or $b \leq a$ for every $a, b \in A$. If $\leq$ is a linear order on A, then the ordered pair $\langle A, \leq \rangle$ is a *linearly ordered set*, or *chain*.

If A is a finite set, we can construct a linear order over the elements of A by listing the elements of A and specifying that $a \leq b$ if and only if a precedes b on the list; thus every finite set can be linearly ordered. The poset diagram of a linearly ordered set is simply a vertical sequence of nodes with an arc connecting each pair of adjacent nodes.

Examples

(a) The linearly ordered set

$$\langle \{1, 2, 3\}, \{\langle 1, 1 \rangle, \langle 2, 2 \rangle, \langle 3, 3 \rangle, \langle 1, 2 \rangle, \langle 1, 3 \rangle, \langle 2, 3 \rangle\} \rangle$$

is represented by

$$
\begin{matrix}
3 \\
2 \\
1
\end{matrix}
$$

(b) The linearly ordered set $\langle \mathbf{I}, \leq \rangle$ can be represented by the following (incomplete) diagram.

$$\begin{array}{c} \cdot \quad \cdot \\ \cdot \quad \cdot \\ 2 \\ 1 \\ 0 \\ -1 \\ -2 \\ \cdot \\ \cdot \quad \cdot \\ \cdot \quad \cdot \end{array}$$

(c)   Consider the universe of real numbers **R**. For every real number a, let $S_a = \{x \mid 0 \le x < a\}$, and let S be the collection $\{S_a \mid a \ge 0\}$. If $a < b$, then $S_a \subset S_b$, and consequently $\langle S, \subset \rangle$ is a linearly ordered set.

(d)   If A is a set with more than one element, then $\langle \mathcal{P}(A), \subset \rangle$ is not a linearly ordered set.   #

Sometimes a subset of a partially ordered set contains distinguished elements which are "greater" or "less" than all other elements of the subset. The following definition characterizes these elements.

Definition 3.6.4:   Let $\langle A, \le \rangle$ be a poset and B a subset of A.
(a)   An element $b \in B$ is a *greatest element* of B if for every element $b' \in B$, $b' \le b$.
(b)   An element $b \in B$ is a *least element* of B if for every element $b' \in B$, $b \le b'$.

Example

Consider the poset $\langle \mathcal{P}(\{a, b\}), \subset \rangle$ represented by the following diagram:

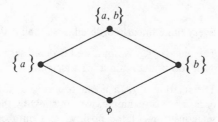

(a)   If $B = \{\{a\}\}$, then $\{a\}$ is a least and greatest element of B.

(b)   If $B = \{\{a\}, \{b\}\}$, then B has no least or greatest element since $\{a\}$ and $\{b\}$ are not comparable.

(c)   If $B = \{\{a\}, \phi\}$, then $\{a\}$ is a greatest element of B and ϕ is a least element.

#

Theorem 3.6.2: Let $\langle A, \leq \rangle$ be a poset and $B \subset A$. If a and b are greatest (least) elements of B, then $a = b$.

Proof: Suppose a and b are both greatest elements of B. Then $a \leq b$ and $b \leq a$. It follows from the antisymmetry of $\leq$ that $a = b$. The proof for the case when a and b are least elements of B is similar. ∎

Definition 3.6.5: A binary relation R on A is a *well order* if R is a linear order and every nonempty subset of A has a least element. The ordered pair $\langle A, R \rangle$ is called a *well ordered set*, and R is a *well ordering of A*.

Theorem 3.6.3: $\langle \mathbf{N}, \leq \rangle$ is well ordered.

Proof: We must show that every nonempty subset of $\mathbf{N}$ has a least element under the relation $\leq$. The proof is by contradiction. We will assume there exists a subset of $\mathbf{N}$, say S, such that S does not have a least element. We will then conclude that $S = \phi$. To show $S = \phi$, we will use induction to prove that every element of S is at least as great as any natural number, i.e.,

$$\forall n \, \forall x[x \in S \Rightarrow n \leq x].$$

Since no natural number is greater than or equal to *every* integer in $\mathbf{N}$, it will follow that $x \in S$ is false; i.e., $S = \phi$.

1. (Basis) $\forall x[x \in S \Rightarrow 0 \leq x]$. This follows immediately from the fact that $S \subset \mathbf{N}$.
2. (Induction) Assume $\forall x[x \in S \Rightarrow n \leq x]$ is true for an arbitrary n. It cannot happen that $n \in S$ since that would violate the assumption that S has no least element. Therefore, it follows that $\forall x[x \in S \Rightarrow n < x]$ is true. We conclude that $\forall x[x \in S \Rightarrow n + 1 \leq x]$ is true. This establishes the inductive step and we conclude that if S has no least element, then $S = \phi$. ∎

Examples

(a) Every finite linearly ordered set is well ordered.

(b) The pair $\langle \mathbf{I}, \leq \rangle$ is not a well ordered set because some subsets of $\mathbf{I}$ (such as $\mathbf{I}$ itself) do not contain a least element.

(c) The relation $\leq$ is a linear ordering of the real numbers $\mathbf{R}$, but not a well ordering. For example, we can show by the following argument that the subset consisting of the positive real numbers does not have a least element. Assume x is a least element of the set of positive real numbers. Since x is positive, $x/2$ is also positive. Yet $x/2 \leq x$ and they are not equal. This contradicts the assumption that x is a least element of the set of positive real numbers under the order relation $\leq$. #

The well ordering of $\mathbf{N}$ by $\leq$ can be used to construct a well ordering R of a set S if we can associate each element of S with a unique element of $\mathbf{N}$. The induced well ordering on S is defined as follows: if $a, b \in S$ and a is paired with n_1 and b with n_2, then $aRb \Leftrightarrow n_1 \leq n_2$.

Example

A well order for the set of integers, **I**, can be constructed by listing the elements of **N** in ascending order and then pairing the elements of **I** with those in **N** as follows:

$$
\begin{array}{ccccccccc}
\textbf{N:} & 0 & 1 & 2 & 3 & 4 & 5 & 6 & \ldots \\
 & \updownarrow & \updownarrow & \updownarrow & \updownarrow & \updownarrow & \updownarrow & \updownarrow & \\
\textbf{I:} & 0 & -1 & 1 & -2 & 2 & -3 & 3 & \ldots
\end{array}
$$

The relation R implied by the above pairing is

$$aRb \Leftrightarrow |a| < |b| \vee (|a| = |b| \wedge a \leq b) \quad \#$$

We are often interested in the set of integer n-tuples $\mathbf{I}^n$ and the set of n-tuples of natural numbers $\mathbf{N}^n$. The linear ordering $\leq$ on **I** or **N** can be used to induce a linear ordering on these sets. For example, if $n = 2$, we can define the ordering on either $\mathbf{I}^2$ or $\mathbf{N}^2$ as follows:

$$\langle a, b \rangle \leq \langle c, d \rangle \Leftrightarrow [a < c \vee (a = c \wedge b \leq d)].$$

The relation of "strictly less than" can be defined as

$$\langle a, b \rangle < \langle c, d \rangle \Leftrightarrow (\langle a, b \rangle \leq \langle c, d \rangle \wedge \langle a, b \rangle \neq \langle c, d \rangle).$$

Note that the set $\langle \mathbf{N}^2, \leq \rangle$ is well ordered, but $\langle \mathbf{I}^2, \leq \rangle$ is not.

If a linear order is imposed on the symbols of a finite alphabet Σ, then this alphabetic ordering can be used to induce two distinct linear orderings of the elements of Σ^*.

Definition 3.6.6: Let Σ be a finite alphabet with an associated alphabetic (linear) order. If $x, y \in \Sigma^*$, then $x \leq y$ in the *lexicographic ordering* of Σ^* if

  (i) x is a prefix of y, or
  (ii) $x = zu$ and $y = zv$, where $z \in \Sigma^*$ is the longest prefix common to x and y, and the first symbol of u precedes the first symbol of v in the alphabetic order.

The lexicographic ordering of Σ^* is the usual "alphabetic" ordering used in dictionaries. Under this ordering, every element of Σ^* has an immediate successor, but if Σ has more than one element, then many elements do not have an immediate predecessor. The lexicographic order of Σ^* is a linear order, but it is not a well order unless Σ consists of a single symbol.

Example

Let $\Sigma = \{a, b\}$, and let a precede b in the alphabetic order. Then if x is any string in Σ^*, the immediate successor of x is xa. The immediate predecessor of xa is x, but there is no immediate predecessor of xb. Moreover, the set $\{b, ab, aab, aaab, \ldots\}$ has no least element, since each string $a^m b$ precedes any string $a^n b$ if $m > n$. It follows that the lexicographic order is not a well order. $\#$

The following definition provides a well ordering of Σ^*.

Definition 3.6.7: Let Σ be a finite alphabet with an associated alphabetic (linear) order, and let $\|x\|$ denote the length of $x \in \Sigma^*$. Then $x \leq y$ in the *standard ordering* of Σ^* if

    (i) $\|x\| < \|y\|$, or
    (ii) $\|x\| = \|y\|$ and x precedes y in the lexicographic ordering of Σ^*.

In the standard order, every element has an immediate successor, and every element other than Λ has an immediate predecessor. The least element of any set is the shortest element of the set which occurs earliest in the lexicographic ordering of Σ^*. Since such an element exists for any subset of Σ^*, it follows that the standard ordering of Σ^* is a well ordering.

Example

    If $\Sigma = \{a, b, c\}$, and $x \in \Sigma^*$, then the immediate successors of xa, xb, and xc under standard order are xb, xc, and xca respectively. The immediate predecessors of xb and xc are xa and xb respectively. If $x \neq \Lambda$, then the immediate predecessor of xa is yc, where y is the immediate predecessor of x. The least element of $\{a^n b \mid n \in \mathbf{N}\}$ is b. #

Universally quantified statements about a well ordered universe are often proved inductively. For example, the standard ordering of Σ^* can be used for inductive proofs about Σ^*. Thus, if $\leq$ represents the standard ordering and we use $S(x)$ to denote the successor of $x \in \Sigma^*$ under this ordering, then the following rule of inference applies:

$$\frac{\begin{array}{c} P(\Lambda) \\ \forall x[P(x) \Rightarrow P(S(x))] \end{array}}{\therefore \quad \forall x P(x).}$$

Thus, if we can prove Λ has property P and whenever x has property P, then $S(x)$ has the same property, then we can conclude that every element of Σ^* has property P.

The rule of inference described above is basically the same as the First Principle of Mathematical Induction; such a rule is applicable only to well ordered sets which "look like" the natural numbers in the sense that every element of the set can be obtained by beginning with the least element of the set and repeatedly taking the successor. (For example, in $\mathbf{N}$, 2 is the successor of the successor of 0.) Some well ordered sets do not have this property; an example is the set $\mathbf{N} \times \mathbf{N}$ under the ordering $\leq$ given above. Under this ordering, every element $\langle a, b \rangle$ has an immediate successor $\langle a, b + 1 \rangle$. But an infinite number of elements do not have immediate predecessors. The element $\langle 0, 0 \rangle$ has no predecessors, while if $a \neq 0$, then $\langle a, 0 \rangle$ has an infinite number of predecessors, none of which are immediate predecessors. The natural generalization of the First Principle of Mathematical Induction is not applicable to this universe of discourse, but the Second Principle (which relies on the well order $\leq$ rather than the successor operation) can be applied, as it can to any well ordered set. Let S be a universe of discourse, let $\leq$ be a well ordering of S, and let $\prec$ denote $\leq - E$ (i.e., $x \prec y$ denotes $x \leq y$ and $x \neq y$). Then the following rule of inference holds:

$$\frac{\forall x[\forall y[y \prec x \Rightarrow P(y)] \Rightarrow P(x)]}{\therefore \ \forall x P(x).}$$

Thus, if we can show that an arbitrary x has property P if every element less than x has property P, then we can conclude that every element of S has property P. To show that the conclusion of the rule of inference is valid, suppose we can prove the premise

$$\forall x[\forall y[y \prec x \Rightarrow P(y)] \Rightarrow P(x)]$$

and suppose T is the subset of S consisting of all the elements of S which do not have the property P. Since S is well ordered, if $T \neq \phi$, then T must have a least element m; it follows that $P(x)$ is true for all elements $x \prec m$. The premise, however, asserts that if $P(x)$ is true for all $x \prec m$, then $P(m)$ is true; we conclude that T must be empty. Hence the conclusion of the Second Principle, $\forall x P(x)$, is true. It follows that the Second Principle of Mathematical Induction is a valid rule of inference for any well ordered set $\langle S, \leq \rangle$.

Finally, we note that the Second Principle of Mathematical Induction is not applicable to sets which are not well ordered.

Example

Let $\Sigma = \{a, b\}$, let a precede b in the alphabetic ordering, and let $\leq$ denote the lexicographic order on Σ^*. Then $\leq$ is a linear ordering but not a well ordering of Σ^*, and the Second Principle using $\leq$ is not a valid rule of inference. For consider the following predicate P on the universe Σ^*:

$$P(x) \Leftrightarrow x \in \{a\}^*.$$

Then assertion

$$\forall y[y \prec x \Rightarrow P(y)]$$

is true if and only if $x \in \{a\}^*$. (Every predecessor of a^m is of the form a^n, where $n \leq m$; hence the assertion is true if $x \in \{a\}^*$. If $x \notin \{a\}^*$, then if n is sufficiently large, $a^n b$ precedes x; hence the assertion is false if $x \notin \{a\}^*$.) Therefore the premise of the Second Principle,

$$\forall x[\forall y[y \prec x \Rightarrow P(y)] \Rightarrow P(x)]$$

is true, since $\forall y[y \prec x \Rightarrow P(y)]$ is true if and only if $P(x)$ is true. However, the conclusion of the Second Principle,

$$\forall x P(x)$$

is false. It follows that the Second Principle cannot be applied to Σ^* using the lexicographic ordering $\leq$.   #

Associating assertions with program statements in the way described in Section 1.6 makes it possible to prove that a program has the correct output if the program halts, but it does not provide a means of establishing that the program halts. Well ordered sets provide a basis for proving that programs terminate. A program will halt if and only if each of its statements is executed only a finite number of times. It follows that a loop-free program always halts because each statement is executed at most once. Programs with loops may not terminate, but in order for this to occur, some program loop must be traversed an infinite number of times. The principal technique for establishing that a loop terminates is to show that some variable quantity v (which is not necessarily a program variable) must assume a value in a subset S of a well ordered set T in order for the loop to be traversed, and that each traversal of the loop causes the value of v to decrease. Then eventually the value of v will no longer be an element of T. For suppose the initial value of the variable v is t_0, and successive executions of the loop cause v to assume the sequence of distinct values $t_0, t_1, t_2, \ldots$, where $t_0 \geq t_1 \geq t_2 \geq \ldots$ Then the sequence $t_0, t_1, t_2, \ldots$ is of finite length, for otherwise the set of values of the sequence form a subset of T without a least element, violating the definition of a well ordered set. Thus the sequence is finite. Since each traversal of the loop causes the value of v to decrease, the value of v will eventually not be a member of T and the loop will not be executed again.

Example

Rather than treat a specific example we will describe the application of termination techniques to the nested loop structure which appears below. Assume that the value of m is a positive integer and is not changed inside either loop, that all statements which affect the values of i and j are shown, and that the loops do not contain other loops or branch statements.

```
for i ← 1 step 1 to m do
    begin
        .
        .
        .
        j ← m
        while j > i do
            begin
                .
                .
                .
                j ← j − 1
            end
        .
        .
        .
    end
```

For the outer (**for**) loop, consider the quantity $(m - i)$. Since we have assumed $m \geq 1$, the initial value of this quantity is in the well ordered set **N**. Incrementing i with each traversal of the loop causes the quantity $(m - i)$ to be decremented. When $i > m$, the quantity $(m - i)$ is no longer an element of **N** and the execution of the loop ceases. Thus, the outer loop will terminate if each execution of the inner loop terminates. The variable j of the inner (**while**) loop is initialized to m and decremented by 1 during each traversal of the loop. Since $i \leq m$ and execution of the loop leaves the value of i unchanged, execution of the loop will cease when j is no longer an element of the well ordered set $\{i + 1, i + 2, \ldots, m\}$. Thus, each execution of the inner loop will terminate and therefore the outer loop will terminate. #

‡Some Additional Concepts for Posets

In Definition 3.6.4, we defined the greatest and least elements of a subset of a partially ordered set. In this section, we introduce other distinguished elements of subsets of posets and explore their properties.

Definition 3.6.8:   Let $\langle A, \leq \rangle$ be a poset and B a subset of A.
(a)   An element $b \in B$ is a *maximal element of B* if $b \in B$ and no element $b' \in B$ exists such that $b \neq b'$ and $b \leq b'$.
(b)   An element $b \in A$ is an *upper bound for B* if, for every $b' \in B$, $b' \leq b$.
(c)   An element $b \in A$ is a *least upper bound* (lub) *for B* if b is an upper bound and for every upper bound b' of B, $b \leq b'$.

The definitions of a *minimal element of B*, a *lower bound for B* and a *greatest lower bound* (glb) *for B* are similar to the definitions above. Note that a greatest element of B and a maximal element of B must be elements of the subset B, while an upper bound for B and a least upper bound may or may not be elements of B. Nothing in the definition assures us that any of these elements exist, and in many cases they do not.

Examples

(a)   Consider the poset $\langle \mathcal{P}(\{a, b\}), \subset \rangle$ represented by the following poset diagram.

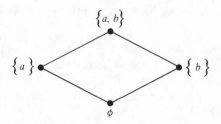

If $B = \{\{a\}\}$, then $\{a\}$ is a least and greatest element of B, as well as a maximal and minimal element of B. The upper bounds of B are $\{a\}$ and $\{a, b\}$, and $\{a\}$ is a least upper bound. The lower bounds of B are ϕ and $\{a\}$, and $\{a\}$ is a greatest lower bound.

(b) Consider the poset $\langle \mathbf{R}, \leq \rangle$, and let $B = [0, 1) = \{x \mid 0 \leq x < 1\}$. Then B has no greatest or maximal elements, but 0 is a least and minimal element. The set of upper bounds of B is the set $\{x \mid x \geq 1\}$, and 1 is a least upper bound. The set of lower bounds of B is $\{x \mid x \leq 0\}$ and 0 is a greatest lower bound.

(c) Consider the set of integers from 1 to 6 under the partial order "divides." The poset diagram is the following.

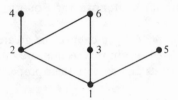

Let B be the entire set $\{1, 2, 3, 4, 5, 6\}$. Then, 4, 5, and 6 are all maximal elements of B, but B has no greatest element. The set B has no upper bounds, and therefore no least upper bounds. The element 1 is a least element, a minimal element, a lower bound, and a greatest lower bound of B.

(d) A *topological sort* is a process of embedding a partial order $\leq$ in a linear order $\leq$. That is, given a partial order $\leq$ we wish to find a linear order $\leq$ such that $a \leq b \Rightarrow a \leq b$. An algorithm for performing a topological sort can be described as follows:
Let $\langle S, \leq \rangle$ be a finite poset. Choose a minimal element of x of S. (Problem 17(a) guarantees that it is always possible to find a minimal element of a nonempty finite poset.) Make this element the first element in a list representation of $\langle S, \leq \rangle$. Now repeat the procedure for the subset $S - \{x\}$. (Problem 8(b) guarantees that $\langle S - \{x\}, \leq \rangle$ is a poset.) Each time a new minimal element is found, it becomes the next element in the list representation of $\langle S, \leq \rangle$. The procedure is repeated until S is exhausted.   #

The following theorem establishes some relationships between the distinguished elements defined in Definitions 3.6.4 and 3.6.8.

Theorem 3.6.4:   Let $\langle A, \leq \rangle$ be a poset and B a subset of A.
(a) If b is a greatest element of B, then b is a maximal element of B.
(b) If b is a greatest element of B, then b is a lub of B.
(c) If b is an upper bound of B and $b \in B$, then b is a greatest element of B.

Proof: (a) We will prove the contrapositive, that is, if b is not a maximal element of B, then b is not a greatest element of B. If b is not maximal, then there exists an element $b' \in B$ such that $b \neq b'$ and $b \leq b'$. Then $b' \leq b$ is false, and hence b is not a greatest element of B.

(b) Since $B \subset A$, it is immediate from the definitions that if b is a greatest element of B, then b is an upper bound for B. If a is an upper bound for B, then $b \leq a$, since $b \in B$. Therefore, b is a least upper bound of B.

(c) If $b \in B$ is an upper bound for B, then $b' \leq b$ for all $b' \in B$. Therefore, b is a greatest element of B. ∎

A theorem similar to Theorem 3.6.4 can be stated using "least" instead of "greatest," "minimal" instead of "maximal" and "glb" instead of "lub."

The examples given previously illustrate that maximal elements and upper bounds may or may not exist, and when they do exist, they may or may not be unique. Similar statements hold for minimal elements and lower bounds. Greatest lower bounds and least upper bounds also may or may not exist, but if they do exist, their more restrictive definitions ensure that they are unique. This is established by the following theorem.

Theorem 3.6.5: Let $\langle A, \leq \rangle$ be a poset and $B \subset A$. If a least upper (greatest lower) bound for B exists, then it is unique.

The proof is left as an exercise.

Problems: Section 3.6

1. Fill in the following table describing the characteristics of the given ordered sets. Use *Y* for *yes* and *N* for *no*.

	Quasi Ordered	Partially Ordered	Linearly Ordered	Well Ordered
$\langle \mathbf{N}, < \rangle$				
$\langle \mathbf{N}, \leq \rangle$				
$\langle \mathbf{I}, \leq \rangle$				
$\langle \mathbf{R}, \leq \rangle$				
$\langle \mathscr{P}(\mathbf{N}), \text{Proper containment} \rangle$				
$\langle \mathscr{P}(\mathbf{N}), \subset \rangle$				
$\langle \mathscr{P}(\{a\}), \subset \rangle$				
$\langle \mathscr{P}(\phi), \subset \rangle$				

2. Prove Theorem 3.6.1.

3. State which of the following digraphs represent a quasi-ordered set; a poset; a linearly ordered set; a well ordered set.

(a)

(b)

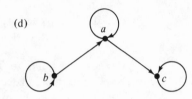

(c)

(d)

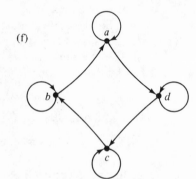

(e)

(f)

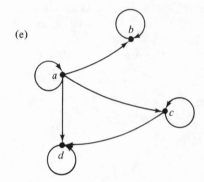

(g)

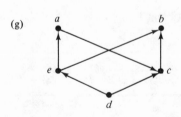

4. Prove or disprove each of the following.
   (a) Let G be a digraph which represents a poset. Then any subdigraph of G represents a poset.
   (b) Any digraph which represents a quasi order has at most one component.
   (c) The digraph of a poset is strongly connected.
   (d) A digraph which represents a linearly ordered set is connected.

5. Let the universe of discourse be **I**. Prove or disprove that $\{\langle a, b\rangle \mid a$ is an integral multiple of $b\}$ is a partial order.

6. (a) Describe a well ordering for the set **I** × **I**.
   (b) Describe a quasi ordering for the set **I** × **I**.

7. Prove the following assertions:
   (a) If R is a quasi order, then so is R^c.
   (b) If R is a partial order, then so is R^c.
   (c) If R is a linear order, then so is R^c.
   (d) There exists a set S and a relation R on S such that $\langle S, R \rangle$ is well ordered but $\langle S, R^c \rangle$ is not.

8. Let R be a relation on a set S, and let S' be a subset of S. Define the relation R' on S' as follows:
   $$R' = R \cap (S' \times S').$$
   Determine the truth or falsity of each of the following assertions:
   (a) If R is transitive on S, then, R' is transitive on S'.
   (b) If R is a partial order on S, then R' is a partial order on S'.
   (c) If R is a quasi order on S, then R' is a quasi order on S'.
   (d) If R is a linear order on S, then R' is a linear order on S'.
   (e) If R is a well order on S, then R' is a well order on S'.

9. (a) Show R is a quasi order if and only if $R \cap R^c = \phi$ and $R = R^+$.
   (b) Show R is a partial order if and only if $R \cap R^c = E$ and $R = R^*$.

10. Let P be a program and S be the set of subroutines which can be called during the execution of P. Define the relation R on $\{P\} \cup S$ by $x_i R x_j$ if x_i calls x_j for some input to program P. Under what conditions is R^* a partial order?

11. Prove that the procedure **PRODUCT** given in Fig. 1.6.1 halts if the initial assertion holds prior to execution.

12. Construct examples of the following sets.
   (a) A non-empty linearly ordered set in which some subsets do not have a least element.
   (b) A non-empty partially ordered set which is not linearly ordered and in which some subsets do not have a greatest element. Construct both finite and infinite examples.
   ‡(c) A partially ordered set with a subset for which there exists a glb but which does not have a least element. Construct both finite and infinite examples.
   ‡(d) A partially ordered set with a subset for which there exists an upper bound but not a least upper bound. Construct both finite and infinite examples.

‡13. Prove Theorem 3.6.5.

14. Let T be a relation on the Cartesian plane $\mathbf{R} \times \mathbf{R}$ defined as follows:
   $$\langle x_1, y_1 \rangle T \langle x_2, y_2 \rangle \text{ if and only if } x_1 \leq x_2 \text{ and } y_1 \leq y_2.$$
   Determine whether each of the following assertions is true or false. Justify your answer if the statement is false.
   (a) T is a partial order.
   (b) T is a linear order.
   (c) T is a well order.
   ‡(d) Every subset of $\mathbf{R} \times \mathbf{R}$ which has a lower bound has a glb.
   (e) If the second condition is eliminated (that is, we only require $x_1 \leq x_2$), then the resulting relation is a partial order.

15. Redefine the relation T of Problem 14 as follows:

$$\langle x_1, y_1 \rangle T \langle x_2, y_2 \rangle \Leftrightarrow [(x_1 < x_2) \vee (x_1 = x_2 \wedge y_1 \le y_2)].$$

Now answer the questions in Problem 14 for the new relation T. (For part (e), the definition of T will only require $x_1 < x_2$.)

16. Let $\Sigma = \{a, b\}$, and let a precede b in the alphabetic order. Use a sketch to characterize each of the following digraphs. All strings of length less than 3 should appear explicitly in your sketch, and the general structure of the complete (infinite) digraph should be apparent. You may use closure operations in your characterization.
    (a) $\langle \Sigma^*, \text{standard order} \rangle$
    (b) $\langle \Sigma^*, \text{lexicographic order} \rangle$

17. Prove each of the following:
    (a) Any finite nonempty subset of a poset has at least one minimal and one maximal element.
    (b) For any linearly ordered set, every minimal element of a subset is a least element and every maximal element is a greatest element.
    (c) Every nonempty finite subset of a linearly ordered set has a least and greatest element.

18. Let S be the set of nonnegative rational numbers, and let $\le$ denote the usual relation of less than or equal. Note that $\langle S, \le \rangle$ is a linearly ordered set but not a well ordered set. Find a predicate P for the universe S which shows that the Second Principle of Mathematical Induction using $\le$ is not a valid rule of inference for this universe.

Programming Problems

1. Write a program which accepts as input a set of ordered pairs and determines if the relation is a quasi order, partial order, or linear order.

2. Write a program which accepts as input a set of ordered pairs denoting adjacent nodes of a poset diagram and produces a minimal element of the poset.

3. Write a program to perform a topological sort of a finite poset. Assume the input is presented as a set of ordered pairs denoting adjacent nodes of a poset diagram. One technique is to select and list a minimal element of a poset, delete the element listed, and repeat the process, continuing until all elements are listed. (Ref. Knuth, [1969], Vol. 1, p. 262.)

3.7 EQUIVALENCE RELATIONS AND PARTITIONS

Often the elements of a set are treated according to their properties rather than as individuals. In such a situation, we can ignore all properties which are not of interest, and treat different elements as "equivalent," or indistinguishable, unless they can be differentiated using only the properties which are of interest. The notion of "equivalence" has three important characteristics:
    (i)   Every element is equivalent to itself (reflexivity).
    (ii) If a is equivalent to b, then b is equivalent to a (symmetry).

(iii) If a is equivalent tŏ b and b is equivalent to c, then a is equivalent to c (transitivity).

These properties form the basis of an important class of binary relations on a set.

Definition 3.7.1: A binary relation R on a set A is an *equivalence relation* if R is reflexive, symmetric, and transitive.

The digraph associated with an equivalence relation R has certain distinguishing characteristics. Since R is reflexive, every node has a loop. The symmetry condition implies that if there is an arc from a to b, there is an arc from b to a. The transitivity condition implies that if there is a path from a to b, there is an arc from a to b. From these considerations, it follows that each component of the digraph of an equivalence relation is a complete digraph.

Examples

(a) The universal relation on any set A is an equivalence relation. If $A = \{1, 2, 3\}$, then the digraph of universal relation on A is a complete digraph with 3 nodes.

(b) The empty relation ϕ is an equivalence relation over the empty set ϕ. However, the empty relation is not an equivalence relation over any nonempty set because it is not reflexive.

(c) Consider the class of propositional forms over some set of propositional variables. The relation R defined by $R = \{\langle P, Q \rangle \mid P \Leftrightarrow Q\}$, where P and Q are propositional forms, is an equivalence relation over this set.

(d) A predicate P with one argument induces a natural equivalence relation $\sim$ over a universe of discourse U. Under this relation, two elements, $a, b \in U$ are equivalent if and only if $P(a)$ and $P(b)$ are logically equivalent:

$$a \sim b \Leftrightarrow [P(a) \Leftrightarrow P(b)].$$

(e) The equality relation, E, on any set is an equivalence relation. #

An important class of equivalence relations over the integers (or any subset of them) consists of the *modular* equivalences.

Definition 3.7.2: Let k be a positive integer and $a, b \in \mathbf{I}$. Then a and b are *equivalent mod k*, written

$$a \equiv b \ (\text{mod } k)$$

if for some integer n, $(a - b) = n \cdot k$. The integer k is called the *modulus* of the equivalence.

Theorem 3.7.1: Equivalence mod k is an equivalence relation over any set $A \subset \mathbf{I}$.

Proof: If $A = \phi$, the assertions that R is reflexive, symmetric, and transitive are vacuously true. If $A \neq \phi$, then the conditions are established as follows:

(i) Reflexivity: For every $a \in A$, since $(a - a) = 0 \cdot k$, it follows that $a \equiv a \ (\text{mod } k)$.

(ii)   Symmetry: If $a \equiv b \pmod{k}$, then there exists some $n \in \mathbf{I}$ such that $(a - b) = n \cdot k$. Then $(b - a) = -n \cdot k$, and hence $b \equiv a \pmod{k}$.

(iii)   Transitivity: Suppose $a \equiv b \pmod{k}$ and $b \equiv c \pmod{k}$. Then there exist $n_1, n_2, \in \mathbf{I}$ such that $(a - b) = n_1 \cdot k$ and $(b - c) = n_2 \cdot k$. Adding both sides of these equations, we find $(a - c) = (n_1 + n_2) \cdot k$ and therefore $a \equiv c \pmod{k}$.   ∎

Examples

(a)   Let the relation R be equivalence mod 3 on the set $A = \{0, 1, 2, 3, 5, 6, 8\}$. The elements 0, 3 and 6 are equivalent, as are 2, 5 and 8. The digraph of the relation R on the set A is the following:

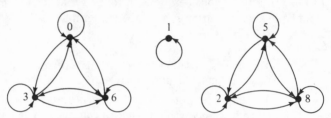

(b)   Odometers of automobiles are devices which count in a modular fashion. If the odometer uses five decimal digits to indicate mileage, then the modulus is 100,000 and driving 123,456 miles registers the same as driving 23,456 miles.

(c)   Many computers use a number representation (such as 1's or 2's complement) where each integer is represented by k binary digits using a form of the usual base 2 positional notation. The result of addition or subtraction of two operands consists of two parts:

(i)   a binary number, obtained using modular arithmetic, and

(ii)   a specification of whether overflow has occurred. If overflow has occurred, the magnitude of the result is too large for the result to be represented using only k digits.   #

Definition 3.7.3:   Let R be an equivalence relation on a set A. For every $a \in A$, the *equivalence class of a with respect to R*, denoted $[a]_R$, is the set $\{x \mid xRa\}$. The *rank* of R is the number of distinct equivalence classes of R if the number of classes is finite; otherwise, the rank is said to be infinite.

The equivalence class $[a]_R$ is nonempty for each $a \in A$ since $a \in [a]_R$. If the equivalence relation R is understood, we will usually write $[a]$ in place of $[a]_R$.

Examples

(a)   Let $A = \{a, b, c, d\}$ and R be the set

$$\{\langle a, a\rangle, \langle a, b\rangle, \langle b, a\rangle, \langle b, b\rangle, \langle c, c\rangle, \langle c, d\rangle, \langle d, c\rangle, \langle d, d\rangle\}.$$

The digraph of $\langle A, R\rangle$ is

The equivalence classes of the elements of A are the following:

$$[a] = [b] = \{a, b\}$$
$$[c] = [d] = \{c, d\}.$$

The relation R has rank 2.

(b) The rank of the equality relation on a set A is equal to the number of elements of A. #

Each equivalence class of an equivalence relation on a nonempty set A is the set of nodes of a component of the digraph of the relation. We will now show that the equivalence classes of an equivalence relation R are pairwise disjoint and that they exhaust the set.

Theorem 3.7.2: Let R be an equivalence relation on a set A.
(a) For all $a, b \in A$, either $[a] = [b]$ or $[a] \cap [b] = \phi$.
(b) $\bigcup_{x \in A} [x] = A$.

Proof:
(a) If $A = \phi$, the assertion is vacuously true. Hence, suppose $A \neq \phi$ and $[a] \cap [b] \neq \phi$, represented by the following sketch.

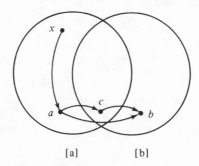

[a]   [b]

Let c be an element of $[a] \cap [b]$. Then $c \in [a]$, so cRa. Similarly, $c \in [b]$, so cRb.

Since R is symmetric, it follows that aRc and since R is transitive, aRb. Now consider an arbitrary element x of $[a]$. Then xRa and by transitivity of R, xRb. Hence $x \in [b]$ which establishes that $[a] \subset [b]$. A similar proof establishes that $[b] \subset [a]$, and we conclude $[b] = [a]$. Therefore, if $[a] \cap [b] \neq \phi$ then $[a] = [b]$. Since $[a]$ and $[b]$ are nonempty, it follows that either $[a] \cap [b] = \phi$ or $[a] = [b]$.

(b) We must show $\bigcup_{x \in A} [x] = A$. We first establish that $\bigcup_{x \in A} [x] \subset A$. Suppose $c \in \bigcup_{x \in A} [x]$. Then $c \in [a]$ for some $a \in A$, and since $[a] \subset A$, $c \in A$. Therefore $\bigcup_{x \in A} [x] \subset A$. We next establish that $A \subset \bigcup_{x \in A} [x]$. Let $c \in A$. Then $c \in [c] \subset \bigcup_{x \in A} [x]$ and therefore $A \subset \bigcup_{x \in A} [x]$. ∎

The proofs of the next two theorems are left as exercises.

Theorem 3.7.3: Let R_1 and R_2 be equivalence relations on a set A. Then $R_1 = R_2$ if and only if R_1 and R_2 have the same set of equivalence classes.

Theorem 3.7.4: Let R_1 and R_2 be equivalence relations on a set A. Then $R_1 \cap R_2$ is an equivalence relation.

Theorem 3.7.4 is most easily proved by showing that the intersection of equivalence relations preserves each of the properties of reflexivity, symmetry, and transitivity. Note, however, that transitivity is not necessarily preserved under union, and consequently the union of two equivalence relations may not be an equivalence relation.

Theorem 3.7.5: Let R be a binary relation on A and let $R' = tsr(R)$, the transitive symmetric reflexive closure of R. Then
  (a) R' is an equivalence relation on A, called the *equivalence relation induced by R*, and
  (b) if R'' is an equivalence relation and $R'' \supset R$, then $R'' \supset R'$. (Thus R' is the smallest equivalence relation which contains R.)

Proof:
  (a) By definition of the closure operations and successive application of Theorem 3.5.8,

      $r(R)$ is reflexive,
      $sr(R)$ is symmetric and reflexive, and
      $tsr(R)$ is transitive, symmetric, and reflexive.

   Hence, $R' = tsr(R)$ is an equivalence relation on A.
  (b) Let R'' be any equivalence relation containing R. Then R'' is reflexive and symmetric so $R'' \supset R \cup R^c \cup E = sr(R)$. Since R'' is transitive and contains $sr(R)$, R'' contains $tsr(R)$. ∎

Example

Let $A = \{a, b, c, d\}$ and let R be represented by the following digraph.

Then, $tsr(R)$ is represented by

The equivalence classes of $tsr(R)$ are $\{a, b\}$ and $\{c, d\}$. Each equivalence class of the induced equivalence relation is the set of nodes of a component of the digraph $\langle A, R \rangle$. #

Partitions

The concept of partition is closely related to that of equivalence relation.

Definition 3.7.4: A *partition* π of a nonempty set A is a collection of nonempty subsets of A such that

   (i)   For all $S \in \pi$ and $T \in \pi$, either $S = T$ or $S \cap T = \phi$.

   (ii) $A = \bigcup_{S \in \pi} S$.

An element of a partition is called a *block*. If π is a finite set, then the *rank* of π is the number of blocks of π. If π is infinite, then the rank is said to be infinite.

A partition of a set A is a collection of nonempty and pairwise disjoint subsets of A which exhaust the set A. One can think of partitions in a variety of ways. Suppose A is a set of objects. We can partition A by placing each element of A in one of a collection of boxes. After all the elements of A have been distributed, each box which is not empty contains a block of the partition (a nonempty subset of A). The elements of the partition are pairwise disjoint subsets of A, since no element of A can be in two boxes at once. The rank of the partition is the number of boxes which are not empty. We can also give a diagrammatic representation of partitions. If the set A is represented by an enclosed area on paper, we can draw lines to divide the area into nonoverlapping regions. Each region of the resulting diagram will correspond to a block of the partition.

Example

   (a)   The following diagram represents a partition of a set.

        The rank of this partition is four. By viewing the diagram alone, there is no way of determining how many elements are in the set or how many elements are in each block of the partition, but by definition, no block is permitted to be empty.

   (b)   Consider the set of positive integers $\mathbf{I}+$. Then the sets

$$S_1 = \{x \,|\, x \in \mathbf{I}+ \,\wedge\, x \text{ is prime}\} \quad \text{and} \quad S_2 = \bar{S}_1$$

        form a partition of $\mathbf{I}+$ of rank 2.

   (c)   Cutting a sheet of paper into pieces results in a partition of the original sheet. (Each piece is a block of the partition.) This notion can be generalized to the physical tearing asunder of any object.

   (d)   The set of tautologies, the set of contingencies, and the set of contradictions form a partition of rank three of the set of all propositional forms.

(e)   A multiprogrammed computer system can interleave the execution of several independent programs; that is, the execution of a program may be interrupted in order to process other programs and then later resumed. The main memory of such a system is partitioned, and each block of the partition contains a separate program. In some multiprogrammed systems, the memory is partitioned in a fixed way; in others, the number and sizes of the blocks can vary according to demand.

(f)   The partition of $\mathbf{I}+$ defined as $\pi = \{\{x\} \mid x \in \mathbf{I}+\}$ has infinite rank.

(g)   Let A be a nonempty set. Then $\mathcal{P}(A) - \phi$ is a collection of nonempty sets whose members exhaust the set A, but this collection is not a partition of A unless A is a singleton set.   #

Except for the fact that equivalence relations are defined for empty sets and partitions are not, equivalence relations and partitions are different descriptions of the same concept. The following theorems establish a natural correspondence between the partitions and equivalence relations over a nonempty set.

Theorem 3.7.6:   Let A be a nonempty set and R an equivalence relation on A. The set $\{[a]_R \mid a \in A\}$ of equivalence classes under R is a partition of A.

The proof is immediate from Theorem 3.7.2 and Definition 3.7.4.

Definition 3.7.5:   Let R be an equivalence relation over a nonempty set A. The *quotient set*, A/R, is the partition $\{[a]_R \mid a \in A\}$. The quotient set is also called *A modulo R* or *the partition of A induced by R*.

Example

Let $\langle A, R \rangle$ be the following digraph:

Then $A/R = \{\{a\}, \{b, c\}\}$. The rank of the relation R is 2; the blocks of A/R are $\{a\}$ and $\{b, c\}$.   #

The following theorem establishes that distinct equivalence relations on a nonempty set A induce distinct partitions of A.

Theorem 3.7.7:   Let R_1 and R_2 be equivalence relations on a nonempty set A. Then $R_1 = R_2$ if and only if $A/R_1 = A/R_2$.

Proof: The theorem follows immediately from Definition 3.7.5 and Theorem 3.7.3 which asserts that two equivalence relations are equal if and only if their sets of equivalence classes are equal.   ▮

Not only do equivalence relations induce partitions in a natural way, but partitions also induce equivalence relations.

Theorem 3.7.8: Let π be a partition of the (nonempty) set A, and define the binary relation $\sim$ on A as follows:

$$a \sim b \Leftrightarrow \exists S[S \in \pi \wedge a \in S \wedge b \in S].$$

Then $\sim$ is an equivalence relation on A, called the *equivalence relation induced on A by the partition π*.

Proof: We must show $\sim$ is reflexive, symmetric, and transitive.
(a) Reflexivity: Since π exhausts A, every element of A is in some element S of π and therefore $a \sim a$ for every $a \in A$.
(b) Symmetry: Suppose $a \sim b$. Then there is some $S \in \pi$ such that $a \in S$ and $b \in S$, and therefore $b \sim a$.
(c) Transitivity: Suppose $a \sim b$ and $b \sim c$. Then there are elements $S_1 \in \pi$, $S_2 \in \pi$ such that $a, b \in S_1$ and $b, c \in S_2$. But since π is a partition, either $S_1 \cap S_2 = \phi$ or $S_1 = S_2$. Since $b \in S_1$ and $b \in S_2$, $S_1 \cap S_2 \neq \phi$. Therefore $S_1 = S_2$, and hence $c \in S_1$. We conclude that $a \sim c$. ∎

Note that each equivalence class of the equivalence relation induced by π is one of the blocks of π.

Example

Let $A = \{a, b, c, d\}$, $\pi = \{\{a, b\}, \{c\}, \{d\}\}$. Then the equivalence relation $\sim$ induced by π is represented by the following digraph.

$\#$

The following theorem summarizes the correspondence between partitions and equivalence relations over nonempty sets. It asserts that each partition corresponds to an equivalence relation and vice versa. The proof is left as an exercise.

Theorem 3.7.9: Let π be a partition of set A and R an equivalence relation over A. Then, π induces R if and only if R induces π.

Since set containment is a partial order over any collection of sets, it is a partial order over any collection of equivalence relations on a set A. A corresponding partial order of "partition refinement" exists over any set of partitions of A.

Definition 3.7.6: Let π and π' be partitions of a nonempty set A. Then π' *refines* π if every block of π' is contained in a block of π. We say π' is a *refinement* of π, or π is *refined by* π'. If π' refines π and $\pi' \neq \pi$, then π' is said to be a *proper refinement* of π.

If π and π' are partitions of a set A and π' refines π, then we can think of the elements of π' as having been obtained by "breaking up" the elements of π into smaller subsets of A.

Examples

(a) Using our diagram representation of partitions, the following illustrates two partitions such that π' refines π;

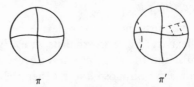

π $\qquad\qquad\qquad$ π'

The rank of π is 4, the rank of π' is 9.

(b) The partition of the natural numbers N induced by "equivalence mod 4" has four elements, which we can denote by $[0]_4$, $[1]_4$, $[2]_4$, and $[3]_4$. Each of these elements of the parition contains an infinite number of integers, e.g., $[0]_4 = \{0, 4, 8, 12, \ldots\}$. The partition of N induced by "equivalence mod 2" has two elements, which we denote by $[0]_2$ and $[1]_2$. The partition induced by equivalence mod 4 refines the partition induced by equivalence mod 2, since both $[0]_4$ and $[2]_4$ are contained in $[0]_2$, and both $[1]_4$ and $[3]_4$ are contained in $[1]_2$.

(c) We noted before that one can form a partition π of a sheet of paper by cutting it into pieces. If one then cuts the resulting pieces again, the result is another partition π' which refines π.

(d) Some search procedures use a strategy of successively reducing the size of the set to be searched (called the *search space*). The search first partitions the search space into two subsets, one which may contain the object of the search and one which does not. The subset which may contain the object of the search becomes the new search space. This procedure corresponds to finding a sequence of partitions $\pi_1, \pi_2, \ldots, \pi_r$ of the original search space, where each partiton π_{i+1} refines π_i by dividing one block of π_i into two blocks of π_{i+1}. #

We will often compare the sizes of different equivalence relations and different partitions of a set. A partition π is larger than π' if π has more blocks than π', and an equivalence relation R is larger than R' if R has more ordered pairs than R'. It is a confusing fact of life that for any set A, the large partitions of A correspond to the small equivalence relations and vice versa. To illustrate the point, consider a set A with n elements. The largest equivalence relation on A is the universal relation $A \times A$; this relation has n^2 elements. This equivalence relation induces the partition $\{A\}$ which has a single block; this is the smallest partition of A. The size of a partition cannot generally be determined on the basis of the size of the associated equivalence relation, but the following theorem shows that if π' refines (and is therefore at least as large as) π then the equivalence relation R' induced by π' is contained in (and is therefore no greater than) the relation R induced by π.

Theorem 3.7.10: Let π and π' be partitions of a nonempty set A, and let R and R' be the equivalence relations induced by π and π' respectively. Then π' refines π if and only if $R' \subset R$.

Proof: We first show that if π' refines π then $R' \subset R$. Suppose $aR'b$. Then there is some block S' of π' such that $a, b \in S'$. Since π' refines π, there is a block S of π such that $S' \subset S$, and therefore, $a, b \in S$. It follows that aRb and hence $R' \subset R$. We next show that if $R' \subset R$ then π' refines π. Let S' be a block of π', and $a \in S'$. Then $S' = [a]_{R'} = \{x \mid xR'a\}$. But for each x, if $xR'a$ then xRa since $R' \subset R$. Therefore, $\{x \mid xR'a\} \subset \{x \mid xRa\}$ and $[a]_{R'} \subset [a]_{R}$. Denote $[a]_{R}$ by S; then S is a block of π and $S' \subset S$, which establishes that π' refines π. ∎

Theorem 3.7.11: Let C be a collection of partitions of a nonempty set A. The relation "refines" is a partial order over the elements of C.

The proof is left as an exercise.

Example

Let $A = \{1, 2, 3\}$ and consider the following equivalence relations on A.

$$A \times A$$
$$E = \{\langle 1, 1 \rangle, \langle 2, 2 \rangle, \langle 3, 3 \rangle\}$$
$$R_1 = \{\langle 1, 1 \rangle, \langle 2, 2 \rangle, \langle 3, 3 \rangle, \langle 2, 3 \rangle, \langle 3, 2 \rangle\}$$
$$R_2 = \{\langle 1, 1 \rangle, \langle 2, 2 \rangle, \langle 3, 3 \rangle, \langle 1, 2 \rangle, \langle 2, 1 \rangle\}$$

The following is a poset diagram of $\langle \{A/(A \times A), A/E, A/R_1, A/R_2\}, \text{refines} \rangle$.

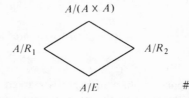

#

‡Sums and Products of Partitions

Let S be the set of partitions of a nonempty set A. We now define two useful binary operations on S, called the "sum" and "product." The sum of two partitions π_1 and π_2 is the largest partition (the one with the most blocks) that is refined by both π_1 and π_2. The product of π_1 and π_2 is the smallest partition (the one with the fewest blocks) that refines both π_1 and π_2.

Definition 3.7.7: Let π_1 and π_2 be partitions of a nonempty set A. The *product* of π_1 and π_2, denoted $\pi_1 \cdot \pi_2$, is a partition π of A such that
(i) π refines both π_1 and π_2.
(ii) If π' refines both π_1 and π_2, then π' refines π.

The following two theorems show that the product of two partitions always exists and is, in fact, unique.

Theorem 3.7.12: Let R_1 and R_2 be the equivalence relations induced by partitions π_1 and π_2 of a nonempty set A. Then the relation $R = R_1 \cap R_2$ induces a product partition π of π_1 and π_2.

    Proof: (i)   Since $R = R_1 \cap R_2$, it follows that $R_1 \supset R$ and $R_2 \supset R$. Therefore, by Theorem 3.7.10, π refines both π_1 and π_2, establishing the first condition of Definition 3.7.7.

        (ii)   Suppose π' refines both π_1 and π_2. If π' induces R', then by Theorem 3.7.10, $R_1 \supset R'$ and $R_2 \supset R'$. Then $R_1 \cap R_2 \supset R'$ and therefore $R \supset R'$ and π' refines π. ∎

Theorem 3.7.13: Let π_1 and π_2 be partitions of a nonempty set A. The product of π_1 and π_2 is unique.

Proof: Suppose π and π' are product partitions of π_1 and π_2. Then from Definition 3.7.7, π and π' refine each other. By Theorem 3.7.11, the relation "refines" is antisymmetric and hence $\pi = \pi'$. ∎

The relationship of π_1 and π_2 to the product partition $\pi_1 \cdot \pi_2$ is illustrated in Figure 3.7.1 The "borders" of $\pi_1 \cdot \pi_2$ consist of all the borders of both π_1 and π_2.

$$\pi_1 \qquad\qquad \pi_2 \qquad\qquad \pi_1 \cdot \pi_2$$

Fig. 3.7.1   The product partition

Example

    Suppose a sheet of paper is marked with red lines and green lines so that cutting the paper on the red lines would result in the partition π_1 and cutting it on the green lines would result in partition π_2. Then cutting it on both the red and green lines would produce the product partition $\pi_1 \cdot \pi_2$.   #

We now discuss the sum of two partitions.

Definition 3.7.8: Let π_1 and π_2 be partitions of a nonempty set A. The *sum* of π_1 and π_2, denoted $\pi_1 + \pi_2$, is a partition π such that

    (i)   both π_1 and π_2 refine π,

    (ii)   if π' is a partition of A such that both π_1 and π_2 refine π', then π refines π'.

Condition (ii) of the preceding definition ensures that the sum of π_1 and π_2 will be the largest partition refined by both π_1 and π_2. The sum of two partitions always exists and is unique, as we show in the two following theorems.

Theorem 3.7.14: Let R_1 and R_2 be equivalence relations on a nonempty set A induced by the partitions π_1 and π_2. Define the relation R to be the transitive closure of $R_1 \cup R_2$:

$$R = (R_1 \cup R_2)^+ = t(R_1 \cup R_2).$$

Then R is an equivalence relation on A, and the partition A/R is a sum of π_1 and π_2.

Proof: $R_1 \cup R_2$ is reflexive and symmetric because the operation of set union preserves these properties. Therefore, by Theorem 3.7.5, $R = t(R_1 \cup R_2) = tsr(R_1 \cup R_2)$ is the smallest equivalence relation which contains R_1 and R_2. Since $R \supset R_1$ and $R \supset R_2$, both π_1 and π_2 refine A/R. Furthermore, any partition which is refined by π_1 and π_2 induces an equivalence relation which contains both R_1 and R_2. Since $t(R_1 \cup R_2)$ is the smallest such equivalence relation, it follows that A/R refines all such partitions. Therefore, A/R is a sum of π_1 and π_2. ∎

Theorem 3.7.15: Let π_1 and π_2 be partitions of a nonempty set A. The sum of π_1 and π_2 is unique.

The proof of this theorem is left as an exercise.

Let π_1 and π_2 be partitions of a nonempty set A, and let R_1 and R_2 be the equivalence relations induced by π_1 and π_2. Two elements $a, b \in A$ are in the same block of the sum partition $\pi_1 + \pi_2$ if and only if there is a path from a to b in the digraph $\langle A, R_1 \cup R_2 \rangle$.

A diagrammatic representation of the sum of two partitions is given in Figure 3.7.2. If π_1 and π_2 are represented by some set of "borders" on a diagram, the borders of $\pi_1 + \pi_2$ are exactly those borders common to both π_1 and π_2.

$$\pi_1 \qquad\qquad \pi_2 \qquad\qquad \pi_1 + \pi_2$$

Fig. 3.7.2 The sum partition

Examples

(a) Suppose a sheet of paper is marked with red lines representing the partition π_1 and green lines representing the partition π_2. Then cutting the paper on those lines which are colored both red and green would produce the sum partition $\pi_1 + \pi_2$.

(b) In an information retrieval system, each "descriptor" induces a partition with two blocks over the set of documents. If one descriptor is "artificial intelligence," then the documents will be categorized according to whether or not this descriptor applies to the document. Suppose ten descriptors are used. If retrieval is done by specifying a single descriptor, any of ten sets of documents can be specified. If retrieval can also be done using the negation of a descriptor (meaning the descriptor is not appropriate), any of twenty sets of documents can be obtained. If a single use of the connective AND is also permitted, then one can obtain a set of documents corresponding to any block of a product partition $\pi_1 \cdot \pi_2$, where π_1 and π_2 are two of the partitions induced by a single descriptor. A single use of the connective OR will not result in a block of the sum partition; instead it will produce the union of some blocks of the product partition.   #

Problems: Section 3.7

1. Prove that the universal relation on any set A is an equivalence relation. What is the rank of this relation?

2. Prove that the empty relation is an equivalence relation on ϕ. What is the rank of the relation?

3. Suppose A is a finite set with n elements.
   (a) How many elements are in the largest equivalence relation on A?
   (b) What is the rank of the largest equivalence relation on A?
   (c) How many elements are in the smallest equivalence relation on A?
   (d) What is the rank of the smallest equivalence relation on A?

4. Suppose $A = \{a, b, c, d\}$ and π_1 is the following partition of A:

   $$\pi_1 = \{\{a, b, c\}, \{d\}\}.$$

   (a) List the ordered pairs of the equivalence relation induced by π_1.
   (b) Do the same for the partitions

   $$\pi_2 = \{\{a\}, \{b\}, \{c\}, \{d\}\}.$$
   $$\pi_3 = \{\{a, b, c, d\}\}.$$

   (c) Draw a poset diagram of the poset $\langle \{\pi_1, \pi_2, \pi_3\}, \text{refines} \rangle$.

5. Let R and R' be equivalence relations on a set A. Show by example that $R \cup R'$ is not necessarily an equivalence relation. What properties of an equivalence relation are violated by your example? Choose the set A to be as small as possible.

6. State whether or not the following binary relations are equivalence relations. If they are not, state which of the properties of an equivalence relation they violate. All relations are on the set $\mathbf{I}$. In each case, find the equivalence relation induced by R.
   (a) $<$
   (b) $\leq$
   (c) $R = \{\langle a, b\rangle | (a > 0 \wedge b > 0) \vee (a < 0 \wedge b < 0)\}$
   (d) $R = \{\langle a, b\rangle | (a \geq 0 \wedge b > 0) \vee (a < 0 \wedge b \leq 0)\}$
   (e) $R = \{\langle a, b\rangle | (a \leq 0 \wedge b \geq 0) \vee (a \leq 0 \wedge b \leq 0)\}$
   (f) $R = \{\langle a, b\rangle | (a \geq 0 \wedge b \geq 0) \vee (a \leq 0 \wedge b \leq 0)\}$
   (g) $R = \{\langle a, b\rangle | (a > 0 \wedge b > 0) \vee (a < 0 \wedge b < 0) \vee (a = b = 0)\}$
   (h) $R = \{\langle a, b\rangle | a \text{ divides } b \text{ with } 0 \text{ remainder}\}$
   (i) $R = \{\langle a, b\rangle | |a - b| \leq 10\}$
   (j) $R = \{\langle a, b\rangle | \exists x [x \in \mathbf{I} \wedge 10x \leq a \leq b \leq 10(x + 1)]\}$
   (k) $R = \{\langle a, b\rangle | \exists x [x \in \mathbf{I} \wedge (10x < a < 10(x + 1)) \wedge (10x \leq b < 10(x + 1))]\}$

(l) $R = \{\langle a, b \rangle \mid \exists x \, \exists y [x \in \mathbf{I} \wedge y \in \mathbf{I} \wedge (10x \leq a \leq 10(x + 1)) \wedge (10y \leq b \leq 10(y + 1))]\}$

7. The following argument purports to prove that every symmetric and transitive relation is an equivalence relation. Let R be a symmetric and transitive relation.
    (i) Because R is symmetric, if $\langle x, y \rangle \in R$, then $\langle y, x \rangle \in R$.
    (ii) Because R is transitive, if $\langle x, y \rangle \in R \wedge \langle y, x \rangle \in R$, then $\langle x, x \rangle \in R$.
         Therefore, R is reflexive and it follows that R is an equivalence relation.
    What is wrong with the argument?

8. Prove Theorem 3.7.3.

9. Prove Theorem 3.7.4.

10. Let $A = \mathbf{I}$. Define aRb if and only if $a \equiv b \bmod (6)$. Describe A/R.

11. Let π_1 and π_2 be partitions of a nonempty set A. State which of the following are always partitions of A, which may be partitions of A, and which are never partitions of A. Justify your answers.
    (a) $\pi_1 \cup \pi_2$
    (b) $\pi_1 \cap \pi_2$
    (c) $\pi_1 - \pi_2$
    (d) $[\pi_1 \cap (\pi_2 - \pi_1)] \cup \pi_1$

12. Let R_1 and R_2 be equivalence relations on a nonempty set A. Determine which of the following are equivalence relations on A. Provide counterexamples for those which are not.
    (a) $(A \times A) - R_1$
    (b) $R_1 - R_2$
    (c) R_1^2
    (d) $r(R_1 - R_2)$ (the reflexive closure of $R_1 - R_2$)
    (e) $R_1 \cdot R_2$

13. Let A be a finite set with n elements and suppose $\pi_1, \pi_2, \pi_3, \ldots, \pi_k$ is a sequence of partitions of A such that π_{i+1} properly refines π_i. Find the maximum possible length of the sequence.

14. Let $A = \mathbf{I}$; define R_1, R_2, R_3 on A as follows:
    $$aR_1b \Leftrightarrow a \equiv b \bmod (3),$$
    $$aR_2b \Leftrightarrow a \equiv b \bmod (5),$$
    $$aR_3b \Leftrightarrow a \equiv b \bmod (6).$$

    (a) Draw a partial order diagram for the poset
         $$\langle \{A/R_1, A/R_2, A/R_3\}, \text{refines} \rangle.$$
    ‡(b) Describe the equivalence relations induced by
         $$(A/R_1) \cdot (A/R_3), (A/R_1) + (A/R_3), (A/R_1) \cdot (A/R_2), (A/R_1) + (A/R_2).$$
         What are the ranks of these relations?

15. Let R_j denote equivalence mod j and R_k denote equivalence mod k over $\mathbf{I}$.
    (a) Prove that $\mathbf{I}/R_k$ refines $\mathbf{I}/R_j$ if and only if k is an integral multiple of j.
    ‡(b) Describe the partition $\mathbf{I}/R_j + \mathbf{I}/R_k$.
    ‡(c) Describe the partition $\mathbf{I}/R_j \cdot \mathbf{I}/R_k$.

16. Prove Theorem 3.7.9.

17. Prove Theorem 3.7.11.

‡18. Prove that if π_1 refines π_2, then $\pi_1 \cdot \pi_2 = \pi_1$ and $\pi_1 + \pi_2 = \pi_2$.

‡19. Prove Theorem 3.7.15.

‡20. Let P denote the set of all partitions of a nonempty set A, and consider the partially ordered set $\langle P, \text{refines} \rangle$. Let π_1 and π_2 be members of P.
    (a) Show that $\pi_1 \cdot \pi_2$ is the greatest lower bound of the set $\{\pi_1, \pi_2\}$.
    (b) Show that $\pi_1 + \pi_2$ is the least upper bound of the set $\{\pi_1, \pi_2\}$.

Programming Problem

Write a program which accepts as input the incidence matrix of a relation and determines if the relation is an equivalence relation.

Suggestions for Further Reading

The text by Deo [1974] is an excellent treatment of graphs with special attention to problems of interest to computer science; the book by Busacker and Saaty [1965] is an earlier work of the same nature which considers applications in a wide variety of areas. Aho, Hopcroft, and Ullman [1974] present and analyze many algorithms associated with sets, graphs, and trees. Knuth [1969] treats the general topic of trees and Knuth [1975] analyzes search trees.

4

FUNCTIONS

4.0 INTRODUCTION

Functions are a special class of binary relations. We commonly think of a function as an input-output relationship; that is, for every input, or argument, a function produces an output, or a value. Functions are the basis of many of our most powerful mathematical tools, and much of our knowledge in computer science is conveniently codified by describing the properties of certain classes of functions. The ability to use and analyze functions is an important skill throughout the field. In this chapter we will define the general class of functions and several special subclasses. The terminology we introduce is widely used in mathematics and computer science.

4.1 BASIC PROPERTIES OF FUNCTIONS

A function from a set A to a set B is a rule which specifies an element of B for each element of A. We will usually denote arbitrary functions by the letters f, g, h.

Definition 4.1.1: Let A and B be sets. A *function* (or *map*, or *transformation*) f from A to B, denoted $f: A \rightarrow B$, is a relation from A to B such that for every $a \in A$, there exists a unique $b \in B$ such that $\langle a, b \rangle \in f$. If $\langle a, b \rangle \in f$, then we write $f(a) = b$.

A function f from A to B is a binary relation from A to B with the special properties that

(a) Every element of A occurs as the first component of an ordered pair of f.
(b) If $f(a) = b$ and $f(a) = c$, then $b = c$.

The terminology associated with functions is consistent with that of relations; if f is a function from A to B, then A is called the *domain* of the function f and B

is called the *codomain* of f. In the expression $f(a) = b$, a is called the *argument* of the function and b is called the *value* of the function for the argument a.

To define a function we must specify the domain, the codomain, and the value $f(x)$ for each possible argument x. The notation $f: A \rightarrow B$ denotes that f is a function with domain A and codomain B. The values of $f(x)$ are specified by a set of rules which cover all possible values of x, e.g.,

$$f: \mathbf{N} \rightarrow \mathbf{N},$$

$$f(x) = 1 \qquad \text{if } x \text{ is odd},$$

$$f(x) = \frac{x}{2} \qquad \text{if } x \text{ is even}.$$

If the domain of the function is finite, the function can be specified explicitly by giving the values for all possible arguments, e.g.,

$$g: \{1, 2, 3\} \rightarrow \{A, B, C\},$$

$$g(1) = A,$$

$$g(2) = C,$$

$$g(3) = C,$$

or by a digraph, e.g.,

Examples

(a) Let $A = \{a, b\}$ and $B = \{1, 2, 3\}$. The following digraphs represent functions from A to B.

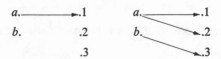

(b) Let A and B be as above. The following digraphs represent relations from A to B which are not functions.

    $a.$————▸$.1$ $a.$————▸$.1$

    $b.$ $.2$ $b.$ ▸$.2$

        $.3$ ▸$.3$

(c) If $A = \phi$ and B is any set, then the empty relation is vacuously a function from A to B. If $A \neq \phi$ and $B = \phi$, then the only relation from A to B is the void relation; but this relation is not a function from A to B. There are no functions which have a nonempty domain and an empty codomain.   #

Suppose $f: A \to B$. We generally think of functions as mapping elements of A to elements of B, but sometimes it is useful to think of f mapping subsets of A to subsets of B. The following definition provides a convenient notation.

Definition 4.1.2: Let f be a function from A to B and let A' be a subset of the domain A. Then $f(A')$ denotes a subset of B, called the *image of A' under f*; $f(A') = \{f(x) \mid x \in A'\}$. The image of the entire domain, $f(A)$, is called the *image of the function f*.

For any function $f: A \to B$, Definition 4.1.2 implicitly specifies another function F, where $F: \mathcal{P}(A) \to \mathcal{P}(B)$; that is, F maps subsets of the domain to subsets of the codomain. For $A' \subset A$, the set $F(A')$ is denoted by $f(A')$. Note that f and F are *not* the same function; the domain and codomain of f are the sets A and B while the domain and codomain of F are the sets $\mathcal{P}(A)$ and $\mathcal{P}(B)$. Thus the function f maps the element of A to elements of B, while the function F maps subsets of A to subsets of B. This is illustrated by the following diagram:

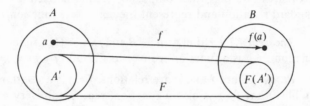

In spite of the distinction between F and f, we will adopt the convention of using f to represent both the original function f and the induced function F. This notation is usually not ambiguous because the argument usually specifies which function is intended.

Examples

(a) Suppose $f: \{0, 1, 2, 3\} \to \{a, b, c\}$ is defined by the following digraph:

Then $f(\{0, 1, 2, 3\}) = \{a, b, c\}$,
$\quad f(\{2, 3\}) = \{b, c\}$,
$\quad f(\{0\}) = \{b\}$,
$\quad f(\{0, 3\}) = \{b\}$, and
$\quad f(\phi) = \phi$.

(b) Let f be a function from $\mathbf{N}$ to $\mathbf{N}$ such that $f(x) = 1$ for every odd integer x and $f(x) = x/2$ for every even integer x. Then

$$f(0) = 0 \qquad f(\{0\}) = \{0\}$$
$$f(1) = 1 \qquad f(\{1\}) = \{1\}$$
$$f(2) = 1 \qquad f(\{0, 2, 4, 6, \ldots\}) = \mathbf{N}$$
$$f(3) = 1 \qquad f(\{4, 6, 8\}) = \{2, 3, 4\}$$
$$f(4) = 2 \qquad f(\{1, 3, 5, 7, \ldots\}) = \{1\}.$$
$$\vdots$$

#

Binary relations are defined to be equal if they have the same domain and codomain and are equal sets of ordered pairs. Because functions are relations, the same definition holds for functions; two functions f and g are equal if and only if their domains and codomains are equal and for every element a of their domain, $f(a) = g(a)$.

Since functions are relations, if g is a function from A to B and f is a function from B to C, a composite relation exists from A to C. Furthermore, the next theorem shows that this composite relation is itself a function. We will use the standard notation and represent the composite function by $f \circ g$ or simply fg.†

Theorem 4.1.1:   Let $g: A \to B$ and $f: B \to C$ be functions. Then the composite function $f \circ g$ is a function from A to C, and $(f \circ g)(x) = f(g(x))$ for all $x \in A$.

Proof: Since f and g are relations, $f \circ g$ is a relation from A to C. We must establish that $f \circ g$ is also a function, that is, for every $a \in A$, there is a unique $c \in C$ such that $\langle a, c \rangle \in f \circ g$.

Since g is a function, for each $a \in A$ there is a $b \in B$ such that $g(a) = b$; since f is a function, for each $b \in B$ there is a $c \in C$ such that $f(b) = c$. Because $\langle a, b \rangle \in g$ and $\langle b, c \rangle \in f$, it follows that $\langle a, c \rangle \in f \circ g$. Furthermore, b was uniquely determined by the argument a for the function g, and c was uniquely determined by the argument b for the function f. It follows that $\langle a, c \rangle$ is the only ordered pair of the composite $f \circ g$ with a as the first element. Thus $f \circ g$ is a function and $(f \circ g)(a) = c = f(b) = f(g(a))$.   ∎

Examples

(a)   Let $g: \{0, 1, 2\} \to \{a, b\}$ and $f: \{a, b\} \to \{A, B, C\}$ be defined by the following digraphs.

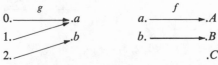

†We adopt the usual convention of representing function composition with a symbol order different from that used for composition of relations. If R_1 and R_2 are relations from A to B and B to C respectively, then the composite relation is denoted by $R_1 R_2$, while if f and g are functions from A to B and B to C respectively, and we are using functional notation, then the composite function is denoted by gf. The inconsistency is due to the convention of putting arguments of functions to the right of the function symbol; if we wrote $f(a)$ as $(a)f$, then we would write $(a)fg = ((a)f)g$ rather than $gf(a)$.

Then $f \circ g: \{0, 1, 2\} \to \{A, B, C\}$, and can be represented as follows.

(b) Let $g : \{0, 1, 2\} \to \mathbf{N}$ be defined by $g(x) = x$ and let $f: \mathbf{N} \to \mathbf{N}$ be defined by $f(x) = x$. The composite $g \circ f$ is not defined because the domain of g is not equal to the codomain of f. However, the composite $f \circ g$ is defined:

$$f \circ g: \{0, 1, 2\} \to \mathbf{N}, \text{ and } f \circ g(x) = x.$$

In this case, $f \circ g = g$.

(c) Let $g: \mathbf{N} \to \mathbf{N}$, where $g(x) = 2x$ for $x \in \mathbf{N}$, and let $f: \mathbf{N} \to \mathbf{N}$, where $f(x) = x/2$ if x is even, $f(x) = 0$ otherwise.
Both $f \circ g$ and $g \circ f$ are defined.

$$fg: \mathbf{N} \to \mathbf{N},$$
$$fg(x) = f(2x) = x.$$

$$gf: \mathbf{N} \to \mathbf{N},$$
$$gf(x) = g(x/2) = x \qquad \text{if } x \text{ is even,}$$
$$gf(x) = g(0) = 0 \qquad \text{if } x \text{ is odd.} \quad \#$$

Relationships between various functions and composite functions are often represented using a *commutative diagram*. A commutative diagram is a diagram in which arcs represent functions and nodes represent domains and codomains; an arc labelled f from a node labelled A to a node labelled B indicates that f is a function from A to B. A directed path from node A to node B represents the sequential application of the functions which appear as labels on the path. For example, the following diagram represents the assertion that $f \circ g(x) = f(g(x))$.

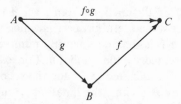

By saying the above diagram *commutes*, we assert that going from A to B by g and then from B to C by f gives the same result as going from A to C by $f \circ g$; this result was established in Theorem 4.1.1.

In general, each path of a commutative diagram can be associated with the composite of functions which appear as labels on the path. If the diagram commutes, then different paths with the same initial and terminal nodes represent different descriptions of the same function. Thus the following commutative diagram asserts that $fg = hk$ for the maps $g: A \to B$, $f: B \to D$, $k: A \to C$, and $h: C \to D$.

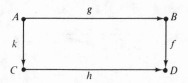

When a composite function appears in a discussion, it is understood that the comments apply only in the case that the composite is defined. Using this convention, the following theorem is a special case of Theorem 3.4.2.

Theorem 4.1.2: Composition of functions is associative: if f, g and h are functions, then $(fg)h = f(gh)$.

The assertion that composition is associative is equivalent to the assertion that the following diagram commutes.

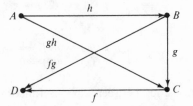

If $f: A \to A$ for some set A, then the function f can be composed with itself any number of times. The notation used to denote the repeated composition of f with itself is defined inductively as follows:

1. $f^0(a) = a$,
2. $f^{n+1}(a) = f(f^n(a))$,   for $n \in \mathbf{N}$.

The set of all functions from a set A to a set B is often denoted by B^A; this notation has some useful properties which will become apparent later. If either of the sets A or B is the first n natural numbers, $\{0, 1, 2, \ldots, n-1\}$, then the set is often represented by the symbol n. For example, the set of all functions from a set A to $\{0, 1\}$ is denoted by 2^A and the set of all functions from $\{0, 1, 2\}$ to a set B is denoted by B^3. Thus, the notation A^n may denote either the set of n-tuples of elements of A or the set of all maps from $\{0, 1, 2, \ldots, n-1\}$ to A†. No difficulties result from this ambiguous use of A^n because there is a natural correspondence between the two possible meanings; defining this correspondence is an exercise in the next section.

The domain of a function is often a cartesian product of sets. A function f

---

†The notation A^n has still a third use in our text. If A is a subset of Σ^* for some alphabet Σ, then A^n is used to denote the set product of A with itself n times (see Definition 2.7.5). The context will determine the intended meaning of A^n.

with domain

$$\overset{n}{\underset{i=1}{X}} A_i$$

is said to be a *function of n variables*. The value of f at $\langle x_1, x_2, \ldots, x_n \rangle$, where $x_i \in A_i$, will be denoted by $f(x_1, x_2, \ldots, x_n)$.

Example

> Arithmetic operations such as addition, subtraction and multiplication are examples of functions of two variables. These functions are commonly represented by an infix notation; thus the function $+ (x, y)$ is denoted by $x + y$.   #

Inductively Defined Functions

When the domain of a function is an inductively defined set, induction often provides a convenient and powerful way of specifying the function. The definition of the function follows the definition of the domain in a natural way.

Examples

> (a) The length of a word $x \in \Sigma^*$ can be inductively defined as a function from Σ^* to $\mathbf{N}$. (The length of x is denoted by $\|x\|$.)
> 1. (Basis) $\|\Lambda\| = 0$.
> 2. (Induction) If $x \in \Sigma^*$ and $a \in \Sigma$, and $\|x\| = n$, then $\|ax\| = n + 1$.
> Note that no extremal clause is necessary here; the function has been defined for the entire domain Σ^* because it follows the inductive definition of Σ^* (Definition 2.5.2).
>
> (b) The *successor function* $S: \mathbf{N} \to \mathbf{N}$ maps each integer $n \in \mathbf{N}$ into its successor, $n + 1$; i.e., $S(n) = n + 1$. Arithmetic operations on $\mathbf{N}$ can be defined inductively using the successor function; we illustrate with a definition of the operation of addition $+ : \mathbf{N}^2 \to \mathbf{N}$.
> 1. (Basis) $+(m, 0) = m$ for $m \in \mathbf{N}$.
> 2. (Induction) $+ (m, S(n)) = S(+(m, n))$ for $m, n \in \mathbf{N}$.
>
> (c) The Fibonacci sequence
>
> $$0, 1, 1, 2, 3, 5, 8, 13, 21, \ldots$$
>
> has the property that each term after the second is the sum of the two preceding terms. This sequence arises in a number of contexts. It can be inductively defined as a function F on $\mathbf{N}$ as follows:
> 1. (Basis) $F(0) = 0$, and $F(1) = 1$.
> 2. (Induction) $F(n + 2) = F(n + 1) + F(n)$ for all $n \in \mathbf{N}$.   #

In each of the above examples, the value of the function in the induction step is specified using values of the function for "earlier" arguments. A specification of $f(n)$ in terms of $f(k)$ for $k \neq n$ is called a *recursion formula*, and f is said to be *recursively defined*. Not all recursively defined functions are defined inductively.

Example

The "91 function" is defined recursively (but not inductively) as follows:

$$f: \mathbf{N} \to \mathbf{N},$$
$$f(x) = x - 10 \qquad \text{if } x > 100,$$
$$f(x) = f(f(x + 11)) \qquad \text{if } x \leq 100.$$

This function has the property that $f(x) = 91$ for all x such that $0 \leq x \leq 100$; otherwise, $f(x) = x - 10$.   #

The mechanism we have described for defining a function on an inductively defined set does not guarantee that the result will be a function. Specifically, the result may not be a function when the inductive definition of the domain allows some elements to be constructed in more than one way. If the object defined satisfies the definition of a function, then we say the function is *well-defined*. When a function is defined recursively, it is often necessary to prove that the function is well-defined.

Example

Consider the set of arithmetic expressions E defined inductively as follows:

1.   Every digit (0 through 9) is an element of E.
2.   If $X \in E$ and $Y \in E$, then $X - Y \in E$.
3.   The set E is the smallest set which satisfied clauses 1 and 2.

The above definition of E allows the construction of some elements, such as $3 - 4 - 5$, in more than one way; in the inductive step one can either let X be 3 and Y be $4 - 5$ and then form $X - Y$, or X can be $3 - 4$ and Y can be 5. A function defined on E following the inductive definition may or may not be well-defined. The following function f is well-defined because the definition does, in fact, characterize a function on the elements of E. The function f sums the digits which appear in an element of E.

$$f: E \to \mathbf{N},$$

1.   If $X \in E$ and X is a digit, then $f(X) = X$.
2.   If $X \in E$ and $Y \in E$, then $f(X - Y) = f(X) + f(Y)$. Thus
      $f(3 - 4 - 5) = 12$.

The following definition of g does not characterize a function.

$$g: E \to \mathbf{N},$$

1.   If $X \in E$ and X is a digit, then $g(X) = X$.
2.   If $X \in E$ and $Y \in E$, then $g(X - Y) = g(X) - g(Y)$.

The difficulty stems from the fact that subtraction is not associative, and consequently there are two possible values of the "function" g for such expressions as $3 - 4 - 5$, namely:

$$g(3 - 4 - 5) = g(3 - 4) - g(5) = (g(3) - g(4)) - g(5) = (3 - 4) - 5$$
$$g(3 - 4 - 5) = g(3) - g(4 - 5) = g(3) - (g(4) - g(5)) = 3 - (4 - 5).$$

Thus, g is a relation but not a function and we conclude g is not well-defined.

Note that by using parentheses in the inductive step of the definition of E, the difficulty can be eliminated. The inductive step would then read

2. If $X \in E$ and $Y \in E$, then $(X - Y) \in E$. #

Inductively defined functions can often be computed either *iteratively* or *recursively*. A program is said to compute a function iteratively if the computation for most arguments is done by the statements in a program loop. A program is said to compute the function recursively if the computation is done by a recursive procedure.

Example

The factorial function can be computed either iteratively or recursively. The following procedure computes $n!$ iteratively for any $n \in N$; the value returned by ITERFACT for the argument n is $n!$.

```
procedure ITERFACT(n):
    begin
        p ← 1;
        for i ← 1 step 1 until n do p ← p * i;
        return p
    end
```

The following subroutine computes $n!$ recursively.

```
procedure RECURFACT(n):
    if n = 0 then return 1 else return n * RECURFACT (n − 1)
```

Two things must be considered in choosing between an iterative and a recursive scheme for computing function values; they are the cost of the computation and the clarity of the algorithm. For something like $n!$, the iterative scheme is quite clear and likely to be somewhat cheaper to compute, but for more complex functions, the clarity of a recursive algorithm often outweighs any incremental cost of computation. #

Partial Functions

It is often convenient to consider a function from a subset A' of A to a set B without exactly specifying the domain A' of the function. Alternatively, we can view such a situation as one where a function has domain A and codomain B, but the value of the function does not exist (is not defined) for some arguments. This is called a partial function.

Definition 4.1.3:   Let A and B be sets. A *partial function f with domain A and codomain B* is any function from A' to B, where $A' \subset A$. For any $x \in A - A'$, the value of $f(x)$ is said to be *undefined*.

Note that if f is a function from A to B, then f is a partial function from A to B. To distinguish partial functions from functions, a function is sometimes called a *total function* for emphasis. We will always use the qualifier "partial" when referring to partial functions; the unqualified term "function" will be reserved to designate total functions.

The notation and theorems we have developed apply to partial functions in straightforward ways. For example, if g and f are partial functions from A to B and B to C respectively, then fg is the partial function from A to C such that $fg(x)$ is defined if and only if $g(x)$ and $f(g(x))$ are both defined, and in that case, $fg(x) = f(g(x))$. We will not develop all the analogous terms and definitions for partial functions, although we will occasionally use them when their meaning is clear.

Examples

(a)   The operation of taking a square root of a real number is a partial function from **R** to **R**; $\sqrt{x}$ is undefined for $x < 0$.

(b)   The partial function $f(x) = 1/x$ from **R** to **R** is undefined for the argument $x = 0$.

(c)   The partial function $f(x) = x$ from **R** to **R** is a total function.

(d)   Computer programs represent partial functions. The input to a program is the argument of the partial function, and the output of the program is the value of the partial function. If the program does not terminate or if it terminates abnormally (e.g., by attempting to execute an illegal operation such as division by 0), then the partial function is undefined for the argument. Using the output of one program as the input of another corresponds to composition of the partial functions implemented by the programs. This view of programs provides a basis (different from the one we described in Section 1.6) for investigating program correctness. The "meaning" of a program can be defined to be the partial function it computes, and a program is correct if it computes the intended partial function. The program will halt for all inputs if the partial function is total.   #

Problems: Section 4.1

1.   Determine which of the relations represented by the following diagrams are functions from $A = \{a, b, c\}$ to $B = \{0, 1, 2\}$. For those that are functions, find the image of the subset $\{a, b\}$. For those that are not, state what properties of a function are not satisfied.

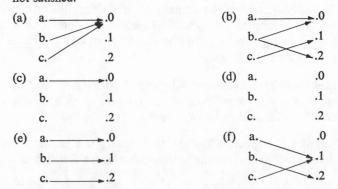

2. Consider the following functions from **R** to **R**

$$f(x) = x + 3$$
$$g(x) = 2x + 1$$
$$h(x) = x/2$$
$$k(x) = x - 2.$$

Construct a commuting diagram relating the functions $f, g, h,$ and k.

3. Let $A = \{0, 1, 2\}$. Find all functions f in A^A for which
    (a) $f^2(x) = f(x)$
    (b) $f^2(x) = x$
    (c) $f^3(x) = x$

4. Let f be a function from A to A. Prove that for all $m, n \in \mathbf{N}, f^m f^n = f^{m+n}$.

5. Let Σ be a finite alphabet.
    (a) Let $x \in \Sigma^*$ and $\|x\|$ denote the length of x. Prove that

    $$\forall x \, \forall y[(x \in \Sigma^* \wedge y \in \Sigma^*) \Rightarrow \|xy\| = \|x\| + \|y\|].$$

    (b) The *reversal* of a string $x \in \Sigma^*$, denoted $\tilde{x}$, is defined inductively as follows:
    1. $\tilde{\Lambda} = \Lambda$
    2. $\widetilde{ax} = \tilde{x}a$ where $a \in \Sigma$ and $x \in \Sigma^*$.
    Prove

    $$\forall x \, \forall y[x \in \Sigma^* \wedge y \in \Sigma^* \Rightarrow \widetilde{xy} = \tilde{y}\tilde{x}].$$

6. Consider the set of functions $f_n: \mathbf{R}^n \to \mathbf{R}$ defined as follows:

    $$f_n(x_1, x_2, \ldots, x_n) = \sum_{i=1}^{n} x_i^2.$$

    Prove by induction on n that $f_n(x_1, x_2, \ldots, x_n) \geq 0$. You may assume $x^2 \geq 0$ for any $x \in \mathbf{R}$ and if $x, y \geq 0$ then $x + y \geq 0$.

7. Define $f: \mathbf{N}^2 \to \mathbf{N}$ as follows.
    1. $f(0, n) = 1$ for all $n \in \mathbf{N}$,
    2. $f(m + 1, n) = f(m, n) \cdot n$.
    Find an algebraic expression for f and prove by induction that it represents f.

8. Using addition, inductively define a function $f: \mathbf{N}^2 \to \mathbf{N}$ such that $f(x, y) = x \cdot y$.

9. Write an iterative algorithm and a recursive algorithm to compute the value of $m + n$ for $m, n \in \mathbf{N}$. Your algorithm should use only the successor function, $S(n) = n + 1$, and the predecessor partial function P, where $P(S(n)) = n$ and $P(0)$ is undefined.

10. Write an iterative algorithm and a recursive algorithm to compute m^n for $m, n \in \mathbf{N}$. Assume only the operations of addition and multiplication together with the predecessor partial function.

11. Let f be the "91 function" defined in this section.
    (a) Show that $f(99) = 91$.
    (b) Prove that $f(x) = 91$ for all x from 0 to 100.

12. Consider the following partial functions from **R** to **R**:

    $$g(x) = \frac{1}{x},$$

$$h(x) = x^2,$$

$$k(x) = \sqrt{x}.$$

For each of the following composite partial functions, characterize the subset of R for which the partial function is defined, give an algebraic expression for the composite partial function, and characterize the image of the partial function.

(a) gg

(b) hk

(c) kh

Programming Problems

1. Write both iterative and recursive procedures which, when passed $n \in N$, will return the nth element of the Fibonacci sequence.

2. Recursion can be used to define functions which grow very fast. Consider the function defined recursively as follows:

$$A: N^2 \to N,$$

$$A(n, 0) = n + 1,$$

$$A(0, m + 1) = A(1, m),$$

$$A(n + 1, m + 1) = A(A(n, m + 1), m).$$

Write a program to evaluate this function for any argument. Investigate the computing time required to calculate $A(0, 0)$, $A(1, 1)$, $A(2, 2)$, ... Warning: The time and storage required to compute $A(i, i)$ grow very fast as i increases.

4.2 SPECIAL CLASSES OF FUNCTIONS

Certain properties of functions are sufficiently important that additional terminology has been developed to describe them.

Definition 4.2.1: Let f be a function $f: A \to B$.

(a) f is *surjective* (onto) if $f(A) = B$,

(b) f is *injective* (one-to-one) if $a \neq a'$ implies $f(a) \neq f(a')$ (i.e., if $f(a) = f(a')$, then $a = a'$),

(c) f is *bijective* (one-to-one and onto) if f is both surjective and injective.

Functions with these properties are called *surjections*, *injections*, and *bijections* respectively.

If $f: A \to B$ is surjective, then every element $b \in B$ is in the image of f. If f is injective, then different elements of the domain are mapped to different elements of the codomain. If f is bijective, then f effectively "pairs off" elements of A and B in what is often called a *one-to-one correspondence*; each element of B is equal to $f(a)$ for exactly one $a \in A$.

Consider the digraph associated with a function $f: A \to B$. Since f is a function, every element of A is the origin of exactly one arc of the digraph. If f is surjective, then at least one arc terminates at each element of B. If f is injective, no more than one arc terminates at each element of B, and if f is bijective, then exactly one arc terminates at each element of B.

Examples

(a) The following digraphs illustrate the concepts of Definition 4.2.1. For each function, the domain and codomain are represented as columns of dots on the left and right sides respectively.

Injective
Not surjective

Surjective
Not injective

Bijective

(b) Let $f: \{1, 2\} \rightarrow \{0\}$.
Since the codomain of f is a singleton set, we need not specify f in detail, because implicitly $f(1) = f(2) = 0$. The function f is surjective but not injective.

(c) Let $f: \{a, b\} \rightarrow \{2, 4, 6\}$, where $f(a) = 2$ and $f(b) = 6$. The function f is injective but not surjective since 4 is not the value of f for any argument.

(d) Let $f: \mathbf{N} \rightarrow \mathbf{N}$, where $f(x) = 2x$.
This function is injective but not surjective; the image of f is the set of even non-negative integers.

(e) Let $f: \mathbf{I} \rightarrow \mathbf{I}$, where $f(x) = x + 1$.
This function is bijective.

(f) Let $[a, b]$ denote the closed interval of real numbers, $[a, b] = \{x \,|\, a \leq x \leq b\}$, where $a < b$, and let $f: [0, 1] \rightarrow [a, b]$, where $f(x) = (b - a)x + a$. This function is a bijection.

(g) The empty relation is an injective function from an empty domain to an arbitrary codomain. If the codomain is also empty, then the function is a bijection.

(h) The properties of being injective, surjective and bijective all can be interpreted in terms of the graphs of functions from $\mathbf{R}$ to $\mathbf{R}$. Consider the following graphs of functions.

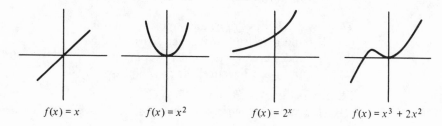

$f(x) = x$ $f(x) = x^2$ $f(x) = 2^x$ $f(x) = x^3 + 2x^2$

Since these are graphs of functions from $\mathbf{R}$ to $\mathbf{R}$, any vertical line will intersect the graph at exactly one point. If every horizontal line intersects the graph at least once, then the graph represents a surjective function. Thus, of the above functions, $f(x) = x$ and $f(x) = x^3 + 2x^2$ are surjective but the others are not. If no horizontal line intersects the graph more than once, then the function is injective. Thus, $f(x) = x$ and $f(x) = 2^x$ are injective but the others are not. If every horizontal line intersects the graph exactly once, then the function is bijective; $f(x) = x$ is bijective and the others are not.

(i)   Sets of data records, called *files*, are often stored in tables or vectors; if T denotes the table, then each record is located at some table address T_i. There are many ways of assigning a table address T_i to each record. In one method, a *hash function* uses a part of each record called the *key* to compute a storage address for the record; hash functions are also *key transformations*. For example, a company might use each employee's social security number as the key to access the employee's record. If the company has 400 employees, their records could be stored in a table with 500 entries by using the first 3 digits of the social security number mod 500 as the table address. Thus, if f is the hash function, then

$$f(136\ 29\ 4516) = 136$$

$$f(729\ 00\ 0345) = 229$$

This hash function would map each social security number into an address T_i where $0 \leq T_i \leq 499$. This particular hash function will probably be unsuitable because it is likely that too many records will be assigned to some table addresses. More suitable hash functions usually involve the entire key. An example of such a function for social security numbers would be

$$f(x_1 x_2 x_3 \ldots x_8 x_9) = y_1 y_1 y_3 \text{ where } y_1 = (x_1 + x_4 + x_7)\ \text{mod } 5,$$

$$y_2 = (x_2 + x_5 + x_8)\ \text{mod } 10, \text{ and}$$

$$y_3 = (x_3 + x_6 + x_9)\ \text{mod } 10,$$

e.g., $f(188\ 26\ 9416) = 253$.

Ideally, a hash function is an injection from the set of key values which occur in the file to the set of possible addresses. When two or more key values have the same hashed address, a *collision* is said to occur; a collision indicates that the function is not injective. It is generally not practical to design hash functions which are injective, and therefore provision must always be made for handling collisions. The number of collisions can usually be reduced by increasing the table size, but this also increases the amount of unused storage. In designing a hashing scheme, one must weigh the cost of handling collisions against the cost of empty storage.   #

Theorem 4.2.1:   Let fg be a composite function.
(a)   If f and g are surjective, then fg is surjective.
(b)   If f and g are injective, then fg is injective.
(c)   If f and g are bijective, the fg is bijective.

Proof: Let $g : A \rightarrow B$ and $f : B \rightarrow C$.
(a)   (If f and g are surjective, then fg is surjective.) Let c be an element of C.

Since f is surjective, there is some element $b \in B$ such that $f(b) = c$. Since g is surjective there is some element $a \in A$ such that $f(a) = b$. Then $fg(a) = f(g(a)) = f(b) = c$, and therefore $c \in fg(A)$. Since c was arbitrary, this establishes part (a).

(b) (If f and g are injective, then fg is injective.) Let a, b be elements of A, and assume $a \neq b$. Since g is injective $g(a) \neq g(b)$. Since f is injective and $g(a) \neq g(b)$, it follows that $f(g(a)) \neq f(g(b))$. Therefore, $a \neq b$ implies $fg(a) \neq fg(b)$, which establishes part (b).

(c) (If f and g are bijective, then fg is bijective.) Since f and g are bijective, they are both surjective and injective. From parts (a) and (b), it follows that fg is both surjective and injective and therefore bijective. ∎

Examples

(a) Let A be the set of negative integers, and define the bijections f and g as follows.

$$g: A \to \mathbf{I+}, \text{ where } g(x) = -x;$$
$$f: \mathbf{I+} \to \mathbf{N}, \text{ where } f(x) = x - 1.$$

Since f and g are bijections, the composite function fg is a bijection and $fg(x) = -x - 1$.

(b) We will construct an injection from $[0, 1]$ to $(0, 1)$. Define $g: [0, 1] \to [0, \frac{1}{2}]$ by $g(x) = x/2$; and $f: [0, \frac{1}{2}] \to (0, 1)$ by $f(x) = x + \frac{1}{4}$. Then $fg: [0, 1] \to (0, 1)$ is the injection $fg(x) = x/2 + \frac{1}{4}$. The image of $[0, 1]$ is the interval $[\frac{1}{4}, \frac{3}{4}]$ which is contained in the open interval $(0, 1)$.   #

The converse of each part of the Theorem 4.2.1 is false, but the following theorem provides a "partial converse" to each of its assertions; its proof is left as an exercise.

Theorem 4.2.2:   Let fg be a composite function.
(a) If fg is surjective, then f is surjective.
(b) If fg is injective, then g is injective.
(c) If fg is bijective, then f is surjective and g is injective.

The following classes of functions are also useful.

Definition 4.2.2:   A function $f: A \to B$ is a *constant function* if there exists some $b \in B$ such that $f(a) = b$ for every $a \in A$, i.e., $f(A) = \{b\}$.

Definition 4.2.3:   The *identity function* on A, denoted $\mathbf{1}_A$, is the function on A such that $\mathbf{1}_A(a) = a$ for all $a \in A$.

Note that every identity function $\mathbf{1}_A$ is a bijection. The next theorem asserts that if $f: A \to B$, then the identity function of A is a "right identity" for f and the identity function on B is a "left identity" for f.

Theorem 4.2.3:   Let $f: A \to B$. Then $f = f \circ \mathbf{1}_A = \mathbf{1}_B \circ f$.

The proof is left as an exercise.

The following commutative diagram represents Theorem 4.2.3.

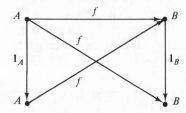

Definition 4.2.4:   A *permutation* on A is a bijective function on A.

Examples
(a)   The identity function on a set A is a permutation on A.
(b)   The function $f: \{0, 1, 2\} \to \{0, 1, 2\}$, where $f(0) = 1$, $f(1) = 0$ and $f(2) = 2$, is a permutation.
(c)   The function $f: \mathbf{I} \to \mathbf{I}$, where $f(x) = x + 3$, is a permutation on the integers.   #

The result of applying a permutation f on A to the entire domain A is a "rearrangement" of A where $a \in A$ is replaced by $f(a)$. A rearrangement of A is often called a *permutation of the set A*. Since every permutation is a bijection and the composite of two bijections is a bijection, it follows that the composite of two permutations is a permutation. This can be expressed by saying that *permutations are closed under (the operation of) composition*.

When the domain and codomain of a function are linearly ordered, the following special terminology is used to describe functions which preserve or reverse the order of elements of the domain. We will state the definitions for functions from **R** to **R**, but the concept generalizes in a straightforward way to other linearly ordered sets.

Definition 4.2.5:   A function $f: \mathbf{R} \to \mathbf{R}$ is *monotone increasing* if $x \leq y$ implies $f(x) \leq f(y)$ and *strictly monotone increasing* if $x < y$ implies $f(x) < f(y)$. The function is *monotone decreasing* if $x \leq y$ implies $f(x) \geq f(y)$ and *strictly monotone decreasing* if $x < y$ implies $f(x) > f(y)$.

If f is strictly monotone increasing, then f is monotone increasing; if f is strictly monotone decreasing, then f is monotone decreasing.

Examples
(a)   Let $f: \mathbf{N} \to \mathbf{N}$ and $f(x) = x + 1$. Then f is strictly monotone increasing.
(b)   Any constant function on **R** is both monotone increasing and monotone decreasing.
(c)   The function $f: \mathbf{R} \to \mathbf{R}$ such that $f(x) = x^2$ is neither monotone increasing nor monotone decreasing.   #

Inverse Functions

If f is a bijection from A to B, then f consists of a set of ordered pairs with the property that every element $a \in A$ appears exactly once as the first element of a pair and every element $b \in B$ appears exactly once as the second element of a pair. The converse relation, formed by reversing the ordered pairs of f, is a relation with the same properties, i.e., the converse of f is a bijection from B to A.

Definition 4.2.6: Let $f: A \to B$ be a bijection from A to B. The *inverse function of f*, denoted f^{-1}, is the converse relation of f.

Note that the inverse function f^{-1} is defined only if f is a bijection.

Theorem 4.2.4: Let f be a bijective function, $f: A \to B$. Then f^{-1} is a bijective function and $f^{-1}: B \to A$.

Proof: Consider the sets of ordered pairs corresponding to f and f^{-1}.

$$f = \{\langle a, b \rangle \mid a \in A \wedge b \in B \wedge f(a) = b\},$$
$$f^{-1} = \{\langle b, a \rangle \mid \langle a, b \rangle \in f\}.$$

Since f is surjective, every $b \in B$ occurs in an ordered pair $\langle a, b \rangle \in f$ and hence appears in an ordered pair $\langle b, a \rangle \in f^{-1}$. Furthermore, since f is injective, for each $b \in B$ there is at most one $a \in A$ such that $\langle a, b \rangle \in f$; hence there is only one $a \in A$ such that $\langle b, a \rangle \in f^{-1}$. These two statements establish that f^{-1} is a function and $f^{-1}: B \to A$.

We leave it as an exercise to show that f^{-1} is bijective. ∎

The inverse function has the property that it can be composed with the function f to form an identity function. For if $f(a) = b$, then $f^{-1}(b) = a$ and it follows that

$$f^{-1}f(a) = f^{-1}(f(a)) = f^{-1}(b) = a;$$

therefore, $f^{-1}f = \mathbf{1}_A$. Similarly,

$$ff^{-1}(b) = f(f^{-1}(b)) = f(a) = b,$$

which establishes that $ff^{-1} = \mathbf{1}_B$. Note that composing f and f^{-1} always results in an identity function but the domain may be either A or B, depending on the order of the composition.

Example

Let $f: \{0, 1, 2\} \to \{a, b, c\}$ be defined by the following digraph:

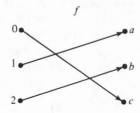

Then f^{-1} is represented as follows:

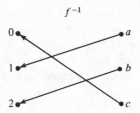

These functions can be composed to form 1_A and 1_B.

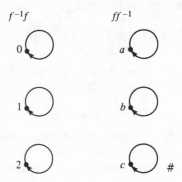

Theorem 4.2.5: If f is bijective, then $(f^{-1})^{-1} = f$.

The proof is left as an exercise.

Definition 4.1.2 established a notation for the image of a subset $A' \subset A$ under a map $f : A \to B$. This notation defined

$$f(A') = \{f(y) \,|\, y \in A'\}.$$

A similar notation is used to denote the set of elements in A which are mapped to a subset $B' \subset B$.

Definition 4.2.7: Let $f : A \to B$, and let $B' \subset B$. Then $f^{-1}(B')$ denotes a subset of A called the *inverse image* or *pre-image of B'* under f:

$$f^{-1}(B') = \{x \,|\, f(x) \in B\}.$$

Just as the symbol f denotes a function from $\mathcal{P}(A)$ to $\mathcal{P}(B)$ when it is written with an argument $A' \subset A$, the symbol f^{-1} denotes a function from $\mathcal{P}(B)$ to $\mathcal{P}(A)$ when it is applied to an argument $B' \subset B$. Thus the notation f^{-1} is used to denote both the inverse function of a bijective function f and the inverse image of a set under an arbitrary function f. The notation f^{-1} is ambiguous only when the argument is both an element of the codomain and a subset of it. In most cases, the argument of f^{-1} specifies whether an inverse function or an inverse image of a set is intended.

Examples

(a) Consider the function represented by the following digraph:

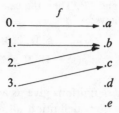

Then $f^{-1}(\{a\}) = \{0\}$, $f^{-1}(\{a, b\}) = \{0, 1, 2\}$, $f^{-1}(\{c, d\}) = \{3\}$, and $f^{-1}(\{d, e\}) = \phi$. Note that f does not have an inverse function.

(b) It is possible for the notation f^{-1} to be ambiguous. Suppose $f: A \to B$, where $A = \{X, Y\}$, $B = \{1, \{1\}\}$ and $f(X) = 1$, $f(Y) = \{1\}$. Then, using the inverse function of the bijection f,

$$f^{-1}(\{1\}) = Y.$$

But, using the induced function from $\mathcal{P}(B)$ to $\mathcal{P}(A)$,

$$f^{-1}(\{1\}) = \{X\}. \quad \#$$

If $A \neq \phi$ and $f: A \to B$, then the collection of sets $\{f^{-1}(\{b\}) \,|\, b \in B\}$ forms a partition of A, and the associated equivalence relation is known as the *equivalence relation induced by f*. Two elements are equivalent under this relation if the function f maps them to the same element of B.

Theorem 4.2.6: Let $f: A \to B$ and define the binary relation $\sim$ on A as follows:

$$a \sim b \Leftrightarrow f(a) = f(b).$$

Then $\sim$ is an equivalence relation on A.

The proof is left as an exercise.

Example

Let $A = \{1, 2, 3, 4\}$, $B = \{a, b, c\}$, and $f: A \to B$.

If $f(1) = a$, $f(2) = b$, $f(3) = c$ and $f(4) = c$, then the equivalence relation on A induced by f has equivalence classes $\{1\}$, $\{2\}$, and $\{3, 4\}$. $\quad \#$

Definiton 4.2.8: Let R be an equivalence relation on a set A. The function

$$g: A \to A/R,$$
$$g(a) = [a]_R,$$

is the *canonical map* from A to the quotient set A/R.

Example

Let $A = \{1, 2, 3\}$ and let $\sim$ be an equivalence relation on A with equivalence classes $\{1, 2\}$ and $\{3\}$. Then the canonical map from A to $A/\sim$ is the function g defined as follows:

$$g: \{1, 2, 3\} \to \{\{1, 2\}, \{3\}\},$$
$$g(1) = \{1, 2\}, g(2) = \{1, 2\}, g(3) = \{3\}. \quad \#$$

The following definitions give us additional facilities for creating and modifying functions. The first definition allows us to form a new function by deleting part of the domain of a given function.

Definition 4.2.9: Let $f: A \to B$, and let A' be a subset of the domain of f. The *restriction of f to A'* is the function denoted $f \mid_{A'}$ and defined as

$$f \mid_{A'} : A' \to B,$$
$$f \mid_{A'} (x) = f(x).$$

The next definition enables us to enlarge the domain of a function.

Definition 4.2.10: Let $f: A' \to B$, $g: A \to B$, and $A \supset A'$. Then g is an *extension of f to the domain A* if $g \mid_{A'} = f$.

Examples

Let f and g be defined by the following diagraphs.

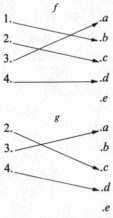

Then $g = f \mid_{\{2, 3, 4\}}$ and f is an extension of g to the domain $\{1, 2, 3, 4\}$. $\quad \#$

The following class of functions provides a way to specify sets using functions.

Definition 4.2.11: Let A be a set. For every set $A' \subset A$, the *characteristic function* (with domain A) *of the set A'*, denoted $\chi_{A'}$, is defined as follows:

$$\chi_{A'}: A \to \{0, 1\},$$
$$\chi_{A'}(a) = 1 \qquad \text{for } a \in A',$$
$$\chi_{A'}(a) = 0 \qquad \text{for } a \notin A'.$$

The domain of a characteristic function is not specified by the notation $\chi_{A'}$, and is usually implicit in the discussion.

Examples

(a) Let $A = \{a, b, c\}$ and let $A' = \{a\}$. Then

$$\chi_{A'}(a) = 1,$$
$$\chi_{A'}(b) = 0,$$
$$\chi_{A'}(c) = 0.$$

(b) Let $A = [0, 1]$ and $A' = [\frac{1}{2}, 1]$. The following is a graph of the function $\chi_{A'}$.

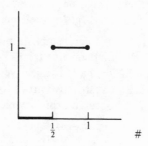

‡One-Sided Inverse Functions

Earlier in this section we established that if $f: A \to B$ is a bijective function, then an inverse function f^{-1} is defined and $f^{-1}f = \mathbf{1}_A$ and $ff^{-1} = \mathbf{1}_B$. In the first case above, we say f^{-1} is acting as a *left inverse* and in the second case as a *right inverse*. Because f^{-1} acts as both a left inverse and a right inverse, it is sometimes called, for emphasis, a *two-sided inverse*. Only bijections have a two-sided inverse, but some other functions possess *one-sided inverses*. The existence of a left or a right inverse is determined by whether the function is injective or surjective.

Definition 4.2.12:   Let $h: A \to B$ and $g: B \to A$. If $gh = \mathbf{1}_A$, then g is a *left inverse* of h and h is a *right inverse* of g.

A function g is a left inverse of h if applying the function g will "undo" the effect of the function h; thus, the composite function gh maps each element of the domain of h to itself. Similarly, a function h is a right inverse for g if applying h before g will nullify the effect of g.

Theorem 4.2.7:   Let $f: A \to B$, with $A \neq \phi$. Then
(a) f has a left inverse if and only if f is injective.
(b) f has a right inverse if and only if f is surjective.

(c) f has a left and right inverse if and only if f is bijective.

(d) If f is bijective, then the left and right inverses of f are equal.

The following illustration is appropriate to part (a) of the theorem.

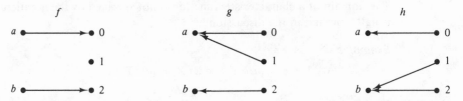

Let $A = \{a, b\}$ and $B = \{0, 1, 2\}$, and let $f: A \to B$. The function f has two distinct left inverses which we have named g and h. If f is injective, a left inverse may always be formed by mapping each element $f(a)$ in the image of f back to a and mapping each element of B which is not in $f(A)$ to some arbitrary element of A. If f were not injective, there would be two elements $a, a' \in A$ such that $a \ne a'$ and $f(a) = f(a')$. Thus f would "merge" two elements of A and no left inverse would exist.

Proof of (a): We first establish that if a left inverse exists for f, then f is injective. Suppose g is a left inverse for f. Then $gf = \mathbf{1}_A$, which is injective. It follows from Theorem 4.2.2b that f is injective.

We next use a constructive proof to show that if f is injective, then there exists a left inverse g. Choose an arbitrary element $c \in A$ and define g as follows:

$$g: B \to A,$$
$$g(b) = a \qquad \text{if } b \in f(A) \text{ and } f(a) = b,$$
$$g(b) = c \qquad \text{if } b \notin f(A).$$

The function g is well-defined, since exactly one value is specified for each argument $b \in B$. Furthermore, g is a left inverse of f since if $f(a) = b$, then $gf(a) = g(f(a)) = g(b) = a$. ∎

The following illustration is appropriate to part (b) of the theorem.

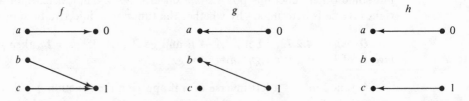

Let $A = \{a, b, c\}$ and $B = \{0, 1\}$. The function f is a surjection from A to B, and f has two distinct right inverses, g and h. Since f is surjective, a right inverse can be formed by mapping each $b \in B$ to some $a \in A$ such that $f(a) = b$. If f is not surjective, then such a construction is not possible and the right inverse does not exist. The proof of (b) is left as an exercise. Part (c) follows immediately from parts (a) and (b). We now prove part (d).

Proof of (d):   Suppose f is bijective with a right inverse h and a left inverse g; then $g \circ f = 1_A$ and $f \circ h = 1_B$. From Theorem 4.2.3,

$$g = g \circ 1_B = g \circ f \circ h = 1_A \circ h = h. \quad \blacksquare$$

If f is surjective, we denote a right inverse of f by f^{-R}; if f is injective, we denote a left inverse by f^{-L}. We will continue to refer to a two-sided inverse of f as the *inverse* of f and denote it by f^{-1}.

Problems: Section 4.2

1. For each of the following functions determine
    (i)   whether the function is injective, surjective, or bijective,
    (ii) the image of the function,
    (iii) the inverse image of the given set S,
    (iv) the equivalence relation induced by the function, and
    (v)   an expression for f^{-1} if f is bijective.

    (a) $f: \mathbf{R} \to \mathbf{R}$,
         $f(x) = x$,
         $S = \{8\}$.

    (b) $f: \mathbf{R} \to \mathbf{R}+$,
         $f(x) = 2^x$,
         $S = \{1\}$.

    (c) $f: \mathbf{N} \to \mathbf{N} \times \mathbf{N}$,
         $f(n) = \langle n, n+1 \rangle$,
         $S = \{\langle 2, 2 \rangle\}$.

    (d) $f: \mathbf{N} \to \mathbf{N}$,
         $f(n) = 2n + 1$,
         $S = \{2, 3\}$.

    (e) $f: \mathbf{I} \to \mathbf{N}$,
         $f(x) = |x|$,
         $S = \{1, 0\}$.

    (f) $f: [0, 1] \to [0, 1]$,
         $f(x) = x/2 + 1/4$,
         $S = [0, 1/2]$.

    (g) $f: \mathbf{R} \to \mathbf{R}$,
         $f(x) = 3$,
         $S = \mathbf{N}$.

    (h) $f: [0, \infty) \to \mathbf{R}$,
         $f(x) = 1/(1 + x)$,
         $S = \{0, 1/2\}$.

    (i) $f: \{a, b\}^* \to \{a, b\}^*$,
         $f(x) = xa$,
         $S = \{\Lambda, b, ba\}$.

    (j) $f: (0, 1) \to (0, \infty)$,
         $f(x) = 1/x$,
         $S = (0, 1)$.

2. Under what conditions is the length function which maps Σ^* to $\mathbf{N}$ a bijection?

3. Let A be an arbitrary set and $n \in \mathbf{N}$. Define S to be the set of all maps from $\{0, 1, 2, \ldots, n-1\}$ to A, and define T to be the set of all n-tuples of elements of A, $T = \{\langle a_0, a_1, a_2, \ldots, a_{n-1} \rangle \mid a_i \in A\}$. Show there exists a "natural" bijection from S to T. Because of this bijection, the notation A^n is used to denote both of the sets S and T.

4. (a) Find a set A and functions $f, g \in A^A$ such that f is injective and g is surjective but neither is bijective. Choose A as small as possible.
   (b) Prove that if $f \in A^A$ and f is injective (surjective; bijective) then f^n is also injective (surjective; bijective) for all $n \in \mathbf{N}$.

5. Let A and B be finite sets. Suppose A has m elements and B has n elements. State the relationship which must hold between m and n for each of the following to be true.
   (a) There exists an injection from A to B.
   (b) There exists a surjection from A to B.
   (c) There exists a bijection from A to B.

6. Prove there exists an injection from A to $\mathcal{P}(A)$ where A is an arbitrary set.

7. For each of the following sets A and B, construct a bijection from A to B.
   (a) $A = \{0, 1, 2\}$, $B = \{a, b, c\}$.
   (b) $A = (0, 1)$, $B = (0, 2)$.
   (c) $A = \mathbf{I}$, $B = \mathbf{N}$.
   (d) $A = \mathbf{N}$, $B = \mathbf{N} \times \mathbf{N}$.
   (e) $A = \mathbf{I} \times \mathbf{I}$, $B = \mathbf{N}$.
   (f) $A = \mathbf{R}$, $B = (0, \infty)$.
   (g) $A = (-1, 1)$, $B = \mathbf{R}$.
   (h) $A = \mathcal{P}(\{a, b, c\})$, $B = 2^{\{a, b, c\}}$
   (i) $A = \mathbf{N}$, $B = \Sigma^*$,   where $\Sigma = \{a, b\}$.
   (j) $A = [0, 1)$, $B = (\frac{1}{4}, \frac{1}{2}]$.

8. Prove Theorem 4.2.2.

9. Prove Theorem 4.2.3.

10. Let f and g be monotone increasing functions on $\mathbf{R}$.
    (a) Show $f + g$ is monotone increasing.
    (b) Show the composite fg is monotone increasing.
    (c) Show that the product of f and g may not be monotone increasing.

11. Let $f: A \to B$ where $C \subset A$ and $D \subset B$.
    (a) Prove $f(A) - f(C) \subset f(A - C)$.
    Under what conditions do the following equalities hold?
    (b) $f^{-1}(B - D) = A - f^{-1}(D)$.
    (c) $f(C \cap f^{-1}(D)) = f(C) \cap D$.

12. Let $f: A \to B$, $B' \subset B$, $A' \subset A$. Show that
    (a) $f(f^{-1}(B')) \subset B'$.
    (b) If f is surjective, then $f(f^{-1}(B')) = B'$.
    (c) $f^{-1}(f(A')) \supset A'$.
    (d) If f is injective, then $f^{-1}(f(A')) = A'$.

13. Complete the proof of Theorem 4.2.4.

14. Prove Theorem 4.2.5.

15. Let f_1, f_2, f_3, f_4 be the following functions from $\mathbf{R}$ to $\mathbf{R}$.
$$f_1(x) = 1 \text{ if } x \geq 0,$$
$$= -1 \text{ if } x < 0.$$
$$f_2(x) = x.$$
$$f_3(x) = -1 \text{ if } x \in \mathbf{I},$$
$$= 1 \text{ if } x \notin \mathbf{I}.$$
$$f_4(x) = 1.$$
Let E_i be the equivalence relation induced by the function f_i.
    (a) Draw a digraph which represents the following poset:
$$\langle \{\mathbf{R}/E_1, \mathbf{R}/E_2, \mathbf{R}/E_3, \mathbf{R}/E_4\}, \text{refines} \rangle$$
    (b) For each i, find the image of 0 under the canonical map from $\mathbf{R}$ to $\mathbf{R}/E_i$.
    (c) Is the digraph of part (a) connected? Strongly connected?

16. Let f be a function from A to B where A has $n \geq 2$ elements. State necessary con-

ditions on B and f for which the rank of the equivalence relation induced by f on A is

(a)   1

(b)   2

(c) n

17.   Let R be an equivalence relation on a set A. Under what conditions is the canonical map $g: A \rightarrow A/R$ a bijection?

18.   Prove Theorem 4.2.6.

19.   (a)   Prove that if $f: A \rightarrow B$ is injective and A' is any subset of A, then $f|_{A'}: A' \rightarrow B$ is an injection.

(b)   Suppose $f: A' \rightarrow B$ is a surjection. Prove that if g is an extension of f to $A \supset A'$, then $g: A \rightarrow B$ is a surjection.

(c)   Prove if $f: A \rightarrow B$ is a surjection, then there exists $A' \subset A$ such that $f|_{A'}: A' \rightarrow B$ is a bijection.

20.   Verify the following for the characteristic functions of subsets A and B of C.

(a) $\chi_{A-B}(x) = \chi_A(x)[1 - \chi_B(x)]$.

(b) $\chi_{A \cup B}(x) = \chi_A(x) + \chi_B(x) - \chi_A(x)\chi_B(x)$.

(c) $\chi_{A \cap B}(x) = \chi_A(x)\chi_B(x)$.

‡21.   Determine left and/or right inverses for the following functions when they exist. Specify the equivalence relation induced on the domain by the function. In each case, construct the canonical map.

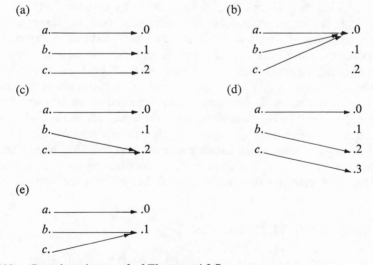

(a)   (b)

(c)   (d)

(e)

‡22.   Complete the proof of Theorem 4.2.7.

Suggestions for Further Reading

The material in this chapter is classical and treated, at least briefly, in a number of books. The first two chapters of the text by MacLane and Birkhoff [1967] will provide a distinct but related development of much of the material of our Chapters 2, 3, and 4, along with some of the material of our Chapter 7.

5

COUNTING AND ALGORITHM ANALYSIS

5.0 INTRODUCTION

In order to compare, evaluate, and predict, we must often count the objects in a finite set. For example, one way to compare the cost of applying two algorithms is to determine, or at least estimate, how many operations each of them executes when solving a problem. This is often done by counting only certain kinds of operations which are executed by the algorithms. Thus, the cost of a direct method for solving sets of simultaneous linear equations can be estimated by counting the number of multiplications and divisions executed by the algorithm. The cost of some sorting algorithms can be estimated by counting the number of comparisons made between data items. The cost of using a particular data structure for a file can be estimated by determining the average and maximum lengths of searches for items stored in the data structure. Problems such as these ultimately involve either counting (exactly or approximately) the elements of a set or enumerating the elements of a set which have a common property. This chapter first introduces some basic techniques for counting and enumerating the elements of finite sets; we then illustrate how these techniques can be applied to the analysis of algorithms.

5.1 BASIC COUNTING TECHNIQUES

In this section, we will introduce some basic techniques of counting. We begin by introducing the concept of the *cardinality* of a finite set. The cardinality of a finite set is simply the number of elements in the set. The definition we give below is chosen so that it can be extended to infinite sets as well.

Definition 5.1.1: A set A is *finite* if there is some natural number $n \in \mathbf{N}$ such that there is a bijection from the set $\{0, 1, 2, \ldots, n-1\}$ to the set A. The integer n is called the *cardinality* of A, and we say "A has n elements," or "n is the *cardinal number* of A." The cardinality of A is denoted by $|A|$.

Example

Let $A = \{a, b, c\}$. Then the cardinal number of A is 3, i.e., $|A| = 3$, since the function

$$f: \{0, 1, 2\} \to A,$$
$$f(0) = a, f(1) = b, f(2) = c,$$

is a bijection from the first three natural numbers to A.   #

The special case of the cardinality of the empty set deserves mention. As we noted in Section 4.2, an "empty" function (consisting of the empty set of ordered pairs) is an injection from the empty set to any set A, and if A is empty, then this function is a bijection. Consequently, our definition states that a set A has cardinality 0 if there is a bijection from the first zero natural numbers to A. But the set consisting of the first zero natural numbers is empty, and a bijection will exist if and only if A is empty. We conclude that $|A| = 0$ if and only if $A = \phi$.

We now introduce a fundamental rule of counting known as the "pigeonhole principle." Informally, the pigeonhole principle asserts that if m objects are placed in n boxes (or pigeonholes) and $m > n$, then some box will contain more than one object. This principle, which we will not prove, can be stated more formally as follows.

Pigeonhole Principle: If A and B are finite sets with $|A| = m$ and $|B| = n$ and $m > n$, then no injection exists from A to B.

When an intuitive notion, such as the size of a set, is characterized by means of a mathematical definition, it is important to verify that the properties of the mathematical characterization agree with our intuitive concept. The next theorem has this purpose; it uses the pigeonhole principle to prove that a finite set has only one cardinal number.

Theorem 5.1.1:   Let A be a finite set. Then the cardinality of A is unique.

Proof: Suppose $|A| = m$ and $|A| = n$; we will show that $m = n$. Assume that $m > n$. Then by the pigeonhole principle, there is no injection from A to A. But $\mathbf{1}_A$ is a bijection from A to A. Thus, the assumption that $m > n$ leads to a contradiction. Similarly, the assumption that $n > m$ will lead to a contradiction. Hence, $m = n$.   ∎

The proof of the following theorem is left as an exercise.

Theorem 5.1.2:   Let A and B be finite sets, and suppose there is a bijection from A to B. Then $|A| = |B|$.

Two additional principles are fundamental for counting sets which have been formed by using the operations of union and cartesian product. We have implicitly used these principles in earlier chapters, but for the sake of completeness, we will state them as theorems about the cardinalities of sets; their proofs are left as exercises. The first principle is called the *Rule of Sum*.

Theorem 5.1.3:   If A and B are finite disjoint sets with cardinalities m and n respectively, then $|A \cup B| = m + n$.

The second fundamental principle of counting is known as the *Rule of Product*.

Theorem 5.1.4:   If A and B are finite sets with cardinalities m and n respectively, then $|A \times B| = mn$.

Examples

(a)   Suppose statement labels in a programming language must be either a single alphabetic symbol or a single decimal digit. The first set, $\{A, B, C, \ldots, Z\}$, has 26 elements, and the second set, $\{0, 1, 2, \ldots, 9\}$ has ten elements. Because the two sets are disjoint, the rule of sum can be applied, and we conclude that there are $26 + 10 = 36$ possible statement labels.

(b)   A variable name in the programming language BASIC must be either an alphabetic symbol or an alphabetic symbol followed by a single decimal digit. If S denotes the set of alphabetic symbols and D denotes the set of digits, there is a one-to-one correspondence between the variable names and the set $S \cup (S \times D)$. By the rule of product, there are $26 \cdot 10$ elements in $S \times D$ and hence by the rule of sum there are 286 possible variable names in BASIC.

(c)   Consider the puzzle sometimes called the "four cubes problem." It involves four cubes such that each face of every cube is painted one of four colors. The problem is to stack the cubes in such a way that each vertical side of the stack contains squares of all four colors.

The order of the cubes in the stack is clearly unimportant, and we do not wish to distinguish between arrangements which are identical except for rotation. We can count the number of significantly different arrangements as follows:

1.   The first cube can be positioned in any of three different ways because there are three pairs of faces which can be made the top and bottom surfaces.

2.   For each remaining cube, one of the six faces must be chosen as the bottom and then one of four possible rotational positions must be chosen. This gives 24 different ways to position each of the last three cubes in the stack.

Thus there are $3 \cdot 24 \cdot 24 \cdot 24 = 41{,}472$ different arrangements, making an exhaustive search costly. For a discussion of how to solve the problem (easily!) by constructing a graph with 4 nodes and 12 edges, the reader is referred to Deo [1974], p. 18, or Busacker and Saaty [1965], p. 153.   #

We will now develop several basic counting results, all of which are based on the rules of sum and product.

Theorem 5.1.5: Let A and B be finite sets with cardinalities m and n respectively. There are n^m functions from A to B, i.e.,

$$|B^A| = |B|^{|A|}.$$

Proof: If $A = \phi$, then the assertion holds since we define $n^0 = 1$ for all $n \in \mathbf{N}$. No functions exist from A to B if B is empty and A is not. If both A and B are nonempty, then index the elements of A in some arbitrary fashion with the first m natural numbers: $a_0, a_1, a_2, \ldots, a_{m-1}$. Each element of A can be mapped to any of n elements of B. Thus, there are n possible values of $f(a_0)$, n possible values of $f(a_1)$, etc. It follows that there are $\underbrace{n \cdot n \cdot n \ldots n \cdot n}_{m \text{ factors}}$ or n^m functions. Hence, $|B^A| = |B|^{|A|}$. ∎

Example

Assume we wish to represent integers using sequences of n digits, where each digit is one of b distinct symbols, $b \geq 2$. Choosing the symbol set to be

$$\{0, 1, 2, \ldots, b - 1\},$$

each n digit sequence of symbols can be associated in a natural way with exactly one function $f: \{0, 1, 2, \ldots, n - 1\} \to \{0, 1, 2, \ldots, b - 1\}$. Thus, there is a bijection from the set of all such sequences to $\{0, 1, 2, \ldots, b - 1\}^{\{0, 1, 2, \ldots, n-1\}}$. By Theorem 5.1.5, there are b^n functions from

$$\{0, 1, 2, \ldots, n - 1\} \text{ to } \{0, 1, 2, \ldots, b - 1\}$$

and therefore we can represent b^n distinct integers. In the case of the standard positional number notation in base b, where the sequence

$$a_{n-1}a_{n-2}a_{n-3} \cdots a_1 a_0$$

represents the number

$$a_{n-1}b^{n-1} + a_{n-2}b^{n-2} + \cdots + a_1 b^1 + a_0 b^0,$$

each sequence of length n represents an integer greater than or equal to 0 and less than b^n. #

We proved the following assertion inductively in Section 2.5. Here the result follows as a special case of the preceding theorem.

Corollary 5.1.5: If A is a finite set, there are $2^{|A|}$ distinct subsets of A.

Proof: For each subset $A' \subset A$, let $\chi_{A'}$ be the characteristic function of A':

$$\chi_{A'}: A \to \{0, 1\},$$

$$\chi_{A'}(x) = 1 \text{ if } x \in A',$$

$$= 0 \text{ otherwise.}$$

For every pair of subsets B, C contained in A, $\chi_B = \chi_C$ if and only if $B = C$. Hence, there are as many subsets of A as there are characteristic functions defined on A, and by Theorem 5.1.5, this number is $2^{|A|}$. ∎

Permutations and Combinations

Recall that a permutation of a set is a bijection from the set to itself and that the set of permutations of a set is closed under function composition, i.e., if f and g are permutations of a set A, then $f \circ g$ and $g \circ f$ are permutations of A.

Theorem 5.1.6:   Let A be a finite set with n elements. The number of distinct permutations of A is $n!$

Proof: If $A = \phi$, then there is one bijection of A to A, namely the empty function. Thus, if $|A| = 0$, there is $0! = 1$ permutation of A. If A is not empty, then let $a_0, a_1, a_2, \ldots, a_{n-1}$ be an arbitrary arrangement of the elements of A. A function $f: A \to A$ can be defined by first choosing $f(a_0)$, then $f(a_1)$, and so on. If f is a bijection on A, then there are n choices for $f(a_0)$, $n - 1$ choices for $f(a_1)$, $n - 2$ choices for $f(a_2)$ and in general $n - i$ choices for $f(a_i)$. Applying the rule of product, it follows that the number of possible bijections is

$$n(n - 1)(n - 2) \ldots 3 \cdot 2 \cdot 1 = n! \quad ∎$$

The permutations of a set can be put in a one-to-one correspondence with ordered arrangements of the elements of the set. Let $a_0, a_1, \ldots, a_{n-1}$ be some arbitrary but fixed arrangement of the elements of a finite set A. Then any arrangement of the elements of A can be associated with a bijection from A to A; the arrangement $a'_0, a'_1, \ldots, a'_{n-1}$ corresponds to the permutation $f: A \to A$ where $f(a_i) = a'_i$.

Examples

(a) Suppose a list is to be formed from n distinct items. If we distinguish between different orderings of the items, then there are $n!$ different lists which can be formed.

(b) Let A and B be finite sets. How many bijections are there from A to B? If $|A| \neq |B|$, then no bijections exist from A to B. If $|A| = |B| = n$, then there are $n!$ bijections.   #

Consider a process which selects r objects sequentially from a set of n objects. If each element of the set is eligible to be chosen repeatedly, then the process is said to be a *selection with replacement*. Thus, if one were drawing items with replacement from a jar, each time an item is drawn from the jar, its identity would be noted and then it would be replaced in the jar, making it a candidate for future draws. If r drawings are made from a jar with n objects and the output of the process is taken to be the resulting sequence of r objects (i.e., an r-tuple of objects from the set), then a selection with replacement has n^r possible values, each of which is an r-tuple, $\langle a_1, a_2, \ldots, a_r \rangle$. (Note that if $r = 0$, then $n^r = 1$; there is only one sequence of 0 length.)

Now suppose the selection process is one in which each item can be selected at most once; in this case, the process is said to be a *selection without replacement*. The sequence which results from a selection without replacement of r objects from n objects where $r \leq n$, is called a *permutation of n objects taken r at a time*. A permutation of n objects taken r at a time is an r-tuple, $\langle a_1, a_2, \ldots, a_r \rangle$ such that each a_i is one of n objects and if $i \neq j$, then $a_i \neq a_j$.

Theorem 5.1.7: The number of permutations of n objects taken r at a time, denoted $\mathbf{P}(n, r)$, is equal to $n(n - 1)(n - 2) \ldots (n - r + 1)$:

$$\mathbf{P}(n, r) = \frac{n!}{(n - r)!}$$

Proof: If $r = 0$, then $\mathbf{P}(n, r) = 1$ because there is only one empty sequence. Suppose $r > 0$. Then there are n possible values for the selection of the first of r objects from n objects. Since selection is without replacement and one object has been chosen, there are only $n - 1$ possible values for the selection of the second object. Similarly, there are $n - i + 1$ possible values for the selection of the ith object for all $i, 1 \leq i \leq r$. By the rule of product, we have

$$\mathbf{P}(n, r) = n(n - 1)(n - 2) \cdots (n - r + 1) = n!/(n - r)! \quad \blacksquare$$

Examples

(a) Let $\Sigma = \{a, b, c, d, e\}$. Find the number of strings in Σ^* of length 3 such that no symbol is used more than once. This is the number of permutations of 5 things taken 3 at a time because selection is without replacement, and $\mathbf{P}(5, 3) = 5 \cdot 4 \cdot 3 = 60$.

(b) Find the number of injections from a finite set A to a finite set B. If $|A| > |B|$, there are no injections from A to B (this follows from the pigeonhole principle). If $|A| \leq |B|$, then the number of injections is $\mathbf{P}(|B|, |A|)$.   #

Consider a process which selects a subset of r objects from a set of n objects, ignoring the order in which the objects are selected. If the selection is without replacement, the result is called a *combination of n objects taken r at a time*. The number of ways in which such a selection can be made is called a *binomial coefficient* and is denoted by either $\binom{n}{r}$ or $\mathbf{C}(n, r)$. The value of $\binom{n}{r}$ is the number of distinct subsets of cardinality r which are contained in a set of size n. Clearly $\binom{n}{0} = 1$, since there is only one empty subset of any collection of n objects, and $\binom{n}{n} = 1$ since there is only one way to choose the entire set of n objects. If $r < 0$ or $r > n$, we define $\binom{n}{r}$ to be 0. The next theorem provides a general expression for $\binom{n}{r}$ when $0 \leq r \leq n$.

Theorem 5.1.8: Let $r, n \in \mathbf{N}$ and $r \leq n$. The number of combinations of n things taken r at a time is $\binom{n}{r} = \dfrac{n!}{r!(n-r)!}$.

Proof: An ordered list of r elements can be formed by first choosing r elements and then ordering them. Consequently, the number of lists of r elements, $\mathbf{P}(n, r)$, is equal to the number of ways of choosing a subset of r elements, $\binom{n}{r}$, times the number of ways of arranging the r elements in a list, $r!$ Thus

$$\mathbf{P}(n, r) = \binom{n}{r} \cdot r!$$

and therefore

$$\binom{n}{r} = \frac{\mathbf{P}(n, r)}{r!} = \frac{n!}{r!(n-r)!} \quad \blacksquare$$

Note that $\binom{n}{r} = \binom{n}{n-r}$. This equality can be understood by considering the ways of choosing a subset B of r elements from a set A of n elements. Each possible choice of r elements to be included in B corresponds to exactly one choice of $(n-r)$ elements to be excluded from B.

Theorem 5.1.9: For every integer $n \geq 0$, $\sum_{r=0}^{n} \binom{n}{r} = 2^n$.

Proof: Let A be a finite set with cardinality n. Then the number of distinct subsets of A with r elements is $\binom{n}{r}$, and the total number of subsets is $\sum_{r=0}^{n} \binom{n}{r}$. By Corollary 5.1.5, the number of subsets of A is 2^n. $\quad \blacksquare$

Counting techniques often enable us to identify algorithmic solutions which are theoretically correct but infeasible because of the magnitude of the computational task. The following problem illustrates this kind of difficulty.

Example: The Traveling Salesman Problem

A salesman wishes to visit each of n cities, beginning and ending in City #1. There is a road between every two cities, and we denote by c_{ij} the distance between the ith and jth cities. The problem is to devise an algorithm which will find the shortest route the salesman can take.

The traveling salesman problem is mathematically equivalent to many problems of considerable practical importance. For example, consider the scheduling problem of a large computer system: In what order should a set of computer programs be run? Each job requires certain resources, such as a compiler in main memory, a segment of main memory, and some set of disk and tape drives. Each combination of resources required by a program corresponds to a city to be visited by the salesman, and City #1 corresponds to the initial configuration of the system. The conversion of the system from one configuration C_i to another, C_j, does not produce useful output; the costs of this conversion, denoted c_{ij}, is part of system overhead. The total system overhead depends on the order in which the jobs are run. For example, if two programs both require an ALGOL compiler, running one program after the other will often eliminate the cost of bringing the compiler into core the second time. This is the reason for "batch processing" programs written in a single language. An algorithm to solve the traveling salesman problem would enable us to specify the sequence of jobs which will minimize the total system overhead for running the programs.

The set of n cities can be thought of as a complete digraph of n nodes; the values c_{ij} represent the distances between the nodes. If the triangle inequality holds, then the shortest route will visit each city other than C_1 only once, and so the only routes of interest are the simple cycles beginning and ending with C_1. It follows that there are $(n - 1)!$ possible routes for the salesman. The most straightforward way of finding the shortest route would be to list all $(n - 1)!$ cycles and then calculate the total distance associated with each cycle. Such a process of "complete enumeration" has the virtue of being easily programmed, but the problems of using such an algorithm become apparent if we consider an example for which the number of nodes is not small.

Finding the total distance for a single route will involve n additions. Since there are $(n - 1)!$ possible routes, the total number of additions is $n!$ Suppose there are 50 nodes. The value of $50!$ is approximately 3×10^{64}. Even assuming a computer which performs 10^9 additions per second, it will take more than 10^{47} years just to perform the additions required by the algorithm.   #

The straightforward algorithms for solving the traveling salesman problem are easily written but impractical for large values of n. This is because the number of operations required to solve the problem by complete enumeration grows very fast as the number of nodes increases. In practice, the number of arithmetic operations can be reduced by eliminating duplications, and the size of the problem can sometimes be reduced by constraining the set of acceptable solutions or by using heuristic methods which consider only some of the cycles. For any but small values of n, one or more of these techniques must be incorporated if an algorithm is to be economically feasible. Depending on the exact techniques chosen, however, the resulting algorithm may not be guaranteed to produce the shortest route, but rather the shortest of all those routes considered by the algorithm.

Decision Trees

Digraphs are often useful for counting and enumeration problems. In modeling system behavior, a *state graph*, or *state diagram*, is a digraph in which each node represents one state of a system, and each edge represents a possible transition from one state to another. Each node of a state graph is labeled with a state name, and the edges are labeled with the input or action which causes the transition.

We often wish to consider systems in which every sequence of transitions causes the system to enter a unique state. If we consider only states which are accessible from some given initial state, then the state graph is a tree whose root represents the initial state; such trees are often called *decision trees*. For some problems, decision trees provide a convenient way of enumerating the set of possible histories of a solution procedure. Each internal node of a decision tree corresponds to a partial solution; each leaf corresponds to a solution. Every internal node is associated with a test to obtain additional knowledge, and each branch outward from a node is labeled with a distinct test outcome. Viewed in terms of its decision tree, execution of a solution procedure corresponds to traversing a path from the root to a leaf. The length of the path traversed is equal to the number of tests made by the solution procedure, and the height of the tree is equal to the maximum number of tests required by any execution of the procedure.

As an illustration of the use of decision trees, suppose we are given eight coins, exactly one of which is known to be counterfeit and heavier than the others. We are asked to find the counterfeit coin using only a pan balance to compare the weights of two sets of coins. Each weighing has three possible outcomes: the left pan can go down (indicating that the coins in the left pan weigh more than those in the right), the pans can remain level, or the right pan can go down. For convenience in describing solution procedures for this problem, we assume the coins are indexed from 1 to 8.

A binary solution procedure is one in which each test has two possible outcomes. Figure 5.1.1 is a decision tree for a binary solution procedure to find the counterfeit coin. In this algorithm, coins 1 through 4 are first weighed against coins 5 through 8 to determine which set of four contains the heavy coin. The set with the heavy coin is then divided in half and the process repeated. This algorithm,

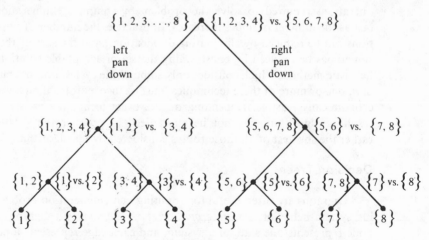

Fig. 5.1.1 Decision tree of a binary solution procedure using a pan balance to find a counterfeit coin known to be heavy. Each node is labeled with the set of coins which is known to contain the counterfeit coin and the two sets of coins which are to be compared in the next step of the algorithm. The left branch corresponds to the left pan going down, and the right branch corresponds to the right pan going down.

which requires three weighings to locate the counterfeit coin, is not very efficient, since the coins are never weighed in a way which permits the pans of the balance to remain level; thus, one of the possible test outcomes can never occur.

A ternary solution procedure involves tests with as many as three possible outcomes. Figure 5.1.2 is a decision tree for a ternary solution procedure to find the counterfeit coin. By exploiting the fact that each weighing can result in any of three outcomes, this procedure reduces the number of weighings to two. A third solution procedure, which requires from one to four weighings, is represented by the decision tree of Fig. 5.1.3.

Efficiency is a prime consideration in algorithm selection but comparisons of algorithms must be made with respect to the particular problem to be solved. For example, if a heavy coin is known to exist and is most likely either coin 1 or coin 2, then the algorithm of Fig. 5.1.3 may be preferred. But in the absence of information to the contrary, we commonly assume that all possible outcomes are equally likely. In this case, we often prefer a procedure in which the maximum number of steps executed by the algorithm is as small as possible. A *minimax* procedure is one which *min*imizes the *max*imum number of steps required to solve the problem. When a solution procedure is represented by a decision tree, the height of the tree is the maximum number of steps that can be executed. It follows that the height of the decision tree of a minimax procedure is no greater than the height of a decision tree for any algorithm which solves the problem. The algorithm represented by Fig. 5.1.2 is minimax for the counterfeit coin problem in which one of eight coins is known to be heavy.

Basic counting techniques can often be used to find bounds on the number of steps of the minimax solution of a task.

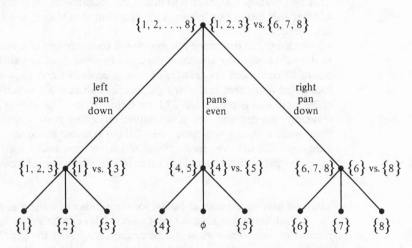

Fig. 5.1.2. Decision tree for a ternary solution procedure using a pan balance to find a counterfeit coin known to be heavy. A node with the label ϕ denotes an outcome which cannot occur.

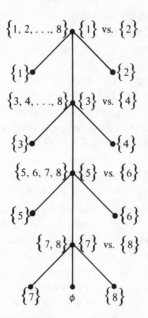

Fig. 5.1.3 Decision tree for using a pan balance to find a counterfeit coin known to be heavy.

Example

Suppose you are given 13 coins where at most one is counterfeit; a counterfeit coin is either heavier or lighter than a genuine one. Consider the problem of devising a minimax algorithm to detect the counterfeit coin if one exists, and state whether it is heavier or lighter. The algorithm should only use a pan balance for comparisons.

Analysis: To determine a lower bound on the height of a decision tree for the problem, we begin by arranging the coins in some fixed but artibrary order. Any one of 27 conditions may exist. For some i between 1 and 13, the ith coin may be counterfeit and either heavy or light; hence, if there is a counterfeit coin, then one of 26 conditions is possible. A 27th condition occurs if no coin is counterfeit. Consequently, the decision tree of a solution procedure must have at least 27 leaves. Since each weighing will have one of three possible outcomes, k weighings can yield any of 3^k different results, from which we must infer which of 27 conditions holds. It follows that a minimum value of k can be obtained from the inequality

$$3^k \geq 27.$$

Thus, we have found a lower bound for the number of weighings necessary; $k \geq 3$.

In fact, three weighings will not suffice. This can be shown by considering the number of cases which must still be distinguished after the initial weighing. If the initial weighing compares coins 1 through 4 with coins 5 through 8 and the weights are equal, then there are still 11 conditions which may hold: any of coins 9 through 13 may be heavy, or light, or all may be equal. But there are only nine possible outcomes for two weighings; thus, two weighings are not sufficient to distinguish among the remaining eleven possible conditions. It follows that any algorithm which uses an initial weighing which compares two sets of four coins will require more than three weighings to distinguish some of the conditions.

Now suppose the initial weighing compares coins 1 through 5 with 6 through 10. If the weights are not equal, then any one of ten conditions may hold since any of the coins on the light side may be light or any of those on the heavy side may be heavy. Again, two additional weighings are not sufficient to determine which of these conditions holds. In a similar way, it can be shown that any other initial weighing will leave too many conditions to be resolved by the last two weighings. This establishes that three weighings are not sufficient and therefore the height of a decision tree for this problem must be at least four.   #

Problems: Section 5.1

1. Let the alphabet Σ be the set $\Sigma = \{a, b, c\}$.
    (a) How many strings of length 4 can be written using the symbols of Σ?
    (b) How many strings of length 4 beginning with the letter "c" can be written using the symbols of Σ?
    (c) How many strings of length 4 beginning with either "a" or "b" and which contain exactly one occurrence of "c" can be written using symbols of Σ?
    (d) How many strings of length 4 beginning with either "a" or "b" and which contain at least one occurrence of "c" can be written using symbols of Σ?

2. Let A and B be finite sets, $|A| = m$ and $|B| = n$. How many binary relations are there from A to B?

3. Let S be the set of kth degree polynomials over a single variable. How many elements of S have integer coefficients such that the magnitude of each coefficient is not greater than some given $n \in \mathbf{N}$ and the coefficient of x^k is not zero?

4. How many distinct ways are there to encode the decimal digits 0–9 as binary sequences of length 4? Consider only codes which represent different digits by different sequences.

5. (a) Find an expression for the number of integers from 0 to 10^{10} whose decimal representations contain no 1's or 2's.
    (b) How many odd 3-digit numbers less than 300 can be formed from the 5 digits 0, 1, 3, 5, 7?

6. Count the number of ways 5 people can be arranged
    (a) in a row of 5 chairs.
    (b) in a circle of 5 chairs. (Rotations of a given arrangement are not considered to be distinct.)

7. A string in $\{0, 1\}^*$ has *even parity* if the symbol 1 occurs in the word an even number of times; otherwise, it has *odd parity*.
    (a) How many words of length n have even parity?
    (b) How many have odd parity?

8. Let Σ be the alphabet $\{a, b, c\}$. Show that the number of words of length n in which the letter a appears an even number of times is $(3^n + 1)/2$.

9. If you flip a coin 5 times, how many different ways can you get exactly 1 head? 2 heads? Find a formula for the number of ways of obtaining r heads with n flips of a coin.

10. Count the number of digraphs with node set $S = \{0, 1, 2, \ldots, n - 1\}$.

11. Prove Theorem 5.1.2.

12. Let A and B be finite sets. Prove each of the following.
    (a) If $B \subset A$, then $|A \cup B| = |A|$.
    (b) $|A| = |A - B| + |A \cap B|$.
    (c) $|A \cup B| = |A| + |B| - |A \cap B|$.

13. Prove Theorem 5.1.5 by induction. Apply the rule of product explicitly.

14. Prove the following combinatoric identities for $n \geq 0$.
    (a) $\mathbf{P}(n, n) = n!$
    (b) $\mathbf{P}(n, n) = \mathbf{P}(n, r)\mathbf{P}(n - r, n - r)$ where $0 \leq r \leq n$.
    (c) $\binom{n + 1}{r} = \binom{n}{r - 1} + \binom{n}{r}$

15. Prove Theorem 5.1.9 by induction. (Hint: Use problem 14(c).)

16. (a) Show by induction on n that for $b \in \mathbf{N}$, $b \geq 2$.

$$(b - 1)\sum_{i=0}^{n} b^i = b^{n+1} - 1$$

   (b) Interpret this identity in the context of number representation in the base b using the standard positional notation. (It may help to expand the identity for $b = 10$ and $n = 4$.)

17. Let S be the set of functions $\{0, 1\}^A$ where A is the set of binary n-tuples, $\{0, 1\}^n$. The set S is called the set of *switching functions* of n variables.
    (a) Specify $|S|$ as a function of n.
    (b) A switching function is *self-dual* if it remains unchanged when all occurrences of 0's and 1's are interchanged in its definition. For example, if $n = 2$ the function

$$f(0, 0) = 0,$$
$$f(0, 1) = 1,$$
$$f(1, 0) = 0,$$
$$f(1, 1) = 1,$$

   is self-dual. Count the number of self-dual switching functions of n variables.

18. Consider a computer in which numbers are represented with p binary digits as follows. For integer arithmetic, a number is represented using one bit to indicate the sign and the remaining $p - 1$ bits represent the magnitude. (This is called a *sign-magnitude* representation.) The floating point representation uses m bits to represent the mantissa of a floating point number and $k = p - m$ bits to represent the exponent, where m, $k \geq 2$. Both the mantissa and the exponent are represented using a single sign bit and the remaining bits as magnitudes. The exponent specifies a power of 2, and the floating point representation is normalized, i.e., the exponent is

adjusted so that the radix point is to the left of the digits of the mantissa and the leading digit of the mantissa is 1 unless the value of the mantissa is 0.

(a) How many distinct integers can be represented in the integer notation? (Note that there are two distinct representations of 0.)

(b) How many distinct real numbers can be represented in the floating point notation?

(c) Estimate the number of distinct integers that can be represented in the floating point notation if $m = 24$ and $k = 8$.

(d) Estimate the ratio of integers representable in integer representation to integers representable in floating point representation if $m = 24$ and $k = 8$.

19. (a) You are given 12 apparently identical coins of which at most one may be counterfeit. A counterfeit coin is always either heavier or lighter than a genuine coin. Find a minimax algorithm using a pan balance to locate the counterfeit coin if it exists and determine whether it is heavy or light. Present your algorithm as a decision tree.

(b) You are given 13 apparently identical coins, exactly one of which is counterfeit and is either heavier or lighter than the others. Find a minimax algorithm to locate the counterfeit coin.

20. Suppose all of $n \geq 2$ coins are of equal weight except for one which is known to be heavier than the others. Find a lower bound for the number of weighings (using a pan balance) needed by a minimax algorithm to locate the heavy coin. (You need not specify an algorithm.)

21. Trees often provide a way of enumerating the set of solutions to problems. For each of the following classical problems, construct a tree of minimal height which contains a path which describes a solution. Each node of the tree should be labeled with a system state and each branch of the tree should correspond to a single action which changes the state of the system. As you construct the tree, do not include any new node which has a label which already appears in the tree; thus, no two nodes of the tree should be labeled with the same system state. The solution with the minimum number of steps may not be unique; for each problem, count the number of minimum step solutions.

(a) *The Towers of Hanoi.* Let A, B, and C denote 3 vertical pegs. Initially, 3 discs of unequal size are arranged on peg A with the largest disc on the bottom and the smallest disc on top. The problem is to move all 3 pegs from peg A to peg C. Each move consists of moving a single disc from one peg to another. No disc may ever be placed on a disc smaller than itself.

(b) *Missionaries and Cannibals.* Three missionaries and three cannibals are initially on the south side of a river and wish to cross to the other side. They have a single boat which holds at most 2 people but can be handled by a single person. However, if at any point the cannibals outnumber the missionaries on either shore, a missionary will be devoured. Find a way to transport all the cannibals and missionaries across the river without losing anyone in the process. You may assume that missionaries do not eat cannibals.

(c) You are given an eight gallon container filled with water and two empty containers of capacity 5 and 3 gallons respectively. The containers are not graduated. Find a way to divide the water into two four gallon quantities.

5.2 ASYMPTOTIC BEHAVIOR OF FUNCTIONS

Programs are representations of algorithms. They can be evaluated and compared either empirically or theoretically. A common way of evaluating a program is to choose a "typical" set of input data and find out how fast the program solves that problem. A more general approach estimates the rate at which a program solves problems; for example, compilers often are evaluated on the basis of the number of source program cards or statements they process per second. But such empirical measures are strongly dependent upon both the program and the machine used to implement the algorithm. Thus, a change in a program may not represent a significant change in the underlying algorithm but may, nevertheless, affect the speed of execution. Furthermore, if two programs are compared first on one machine and then another, the comparisons may lead to different conclusions. Thus, while comparison of actual programs running on real computers is an important source of information, the results are inevitably affected by programming skill and machine characteristics. In this section we will develop a mathematical basis for comparing algorithms which provides a useful alternative to empirical measurements. Judiciously used, this mathematics provides an important means of evaluating the cost of algorithm execution.

We are interested in computer programs which can be applied to a collection of problems of a certain type. Assuming a computer program which eventually halts, solving a problem requires only sufficient time and sufficient storage. In general, the time and storage space required by a program will vary with the particular problem being solved. Consider, for example, the following classes of problems, and note the role of the value of n.

1. Find the largest entry in a sequence of n integers.
2. Let V be a vector of integers with n distinct entries. Sort the entries of V into ascending order.
3. Let g be a digraph with n nodes and a distance associated with each edge. For some specified pair of nodes j and k where $1 \leq j$, $k \leq n$, find the shortest path from node j to node k.
4. Let S be a set with n elements and R a binary relation on S. Find the transitive closure of R.

In each of these problems, the parameter n provides a measure of the "size" or "difficulty" of the problem in the sense that the time required to solve the problem, or the storage space required, or both, will increase as n grows. In order to measure the cost of executing a program, we customarily define a *cost function*, or *complexity function f*, where $f(n)$ is either a measure of the time required to execute an algorithm on a problem of size n or a measure of the memory space required for execution of the algorithm. If $f(n)$ is a measure of the time required to execute an algorithm on a problem of size n, then f is called the *time complexity function* of the algorithm. Similarly, if $f(n)$ measures the storage required for the execution of an algorithm on a problem of size n, then f is called the *space com-*

plexity function of the algorithm. We will refer to either kind of function as simply a complexity or cost function of the algorithm, but our principal concern will be with time complexity functions.

In general the cost of obtaining a solution increases with the problem size n. If the value of n is sufficiently small, then even an inefficient algorithm will not cost much to run; consequently, the choice of an algorithm for small problems is not usually critical. For this reason, our concern is with values of n which are large enough to make some algorithms impractical. In order to compare the performance of algorithms for relatively large values of n, we will consider the behavior of their cost functions as n grows large; this is called the *asymptotic behavior* of the cost functions. The next definition introduces the fundamental concept.†

Definition 5.2.1:   Let f and g be functions from $\mathbf{N}$ to $\mathbf{R}$. Then g *asymptotically dominates f, or f is asymptotically dominated by g,* if there exist $k \geq 0$ and $m \geq 0$ such that $|f(n)| \leq m|g(n)|$ for all $n \geq k$.

If g asymptotically dominates f, and $g(n) \neq 0$, then $|f(n)/g(n)| \leq m$ for all but a finite number of values of n, none of which are greater than k. Thus if f and g are cost functions for algorithms F and G respectively, then for problems of size k or greater, execution of F will never be more than m times as costly as execution of G.

Examples

(a)   Let $f(n) = n$ and $g(n) = -n^3$. Since $|n| \leq |-n^3|$ for all $n \in \mathbf{N}$, Definition 5.2.1 is satisfied by setting $k = 0$ and $m = 1$. Hence, g asymptotically dominates f. Note that f does not asymptotically dominate g, since regardless of the choice of m, $|-n^3| > m|n|$ for all n greater than both 1 and m.

(b)   Let g be an arbitrary function from $\mathbf{N}$ to $\mathbf{R}$, and let $f(n) = cg(n)$, where $c \in \mathbf{R}$ and $c > 0$. Then the functions f and g asymptotically dominate each other since $|f(n)| \leq c|g(n)|$ for all $n \in \mathbf{N}$ and $|g(n)| \leq 1/c|f(n)|$ for all $n \in \mathbf{N}$.

(c)   The functions $f(n) = n$, $g(n) = n + 1/(n + 1)$, and $h(n) = bn + c$, where $b, c \in \mathbf{R}$ and $b > 0$, all asymptotically dominate each other.   #

Definition 5.2.1 implicitly specifies a binary relation over the functions from $\mathbf{N}$ to $\mathbf{R}$. The properties of this relation are summarized in the following theorem.

Theorem 5.2.1:   Let F denote the set of functions from $\mathbf{N}$ to $\mathbf{R}$.
(a)   The binary relation on F defined as

$$\{\langle f, g \rangle | f, g \in F \text{ and } g \text{ asymptotically dominates } f\}$$

is reflexive and transitive.

---

†Our interest is in applying these notions to functions of discrete variables, and we will treat the present topic using functions from $\mathbf{N}$ to $\mathbf{R}$. However, the definitions and theorems of this section extend in a natural and straightforward way to functions from $\mathbf{R}$ to $\mathbf{R}$.

(b)   Let $f, g \in F$. The binary relation

$$f \equiv g \Leftrightarrow f \text{ and } g \text{ asymptotically dominate each other}$$

is an equivalence relation on F.

Proof:

(a)   To show that f asymptotically dominates f, it suffices to choose $k = 0$ and $m = 1$ and apply Definition 5.2.1; thus the relation "asymptotically dominates" is reflexive. We next show that this relation is transitive. Suppose h asymptotically dominates g, and g asymptotically dominates f; then for some $k_1, k_2, m_1, m_2 \geq 0, |f(n)| \leq m_1|g(n)|$ for $n \geq k_1$ and $|g(n)| \leq m_2|h(n)|$ for $n \geq k_2$. By choosing $k = \max\{k_1, k_2\}$ and $m = m_1 m_2$, we have

$$|f(n)| \leq m_1|g(n)| \leq m_1 m_2|h(n)| = m|h(n)|$$

for $n \geq k$. It follows that h asymptotically dominates f.
The proof of part (b) is left as an exercise. ∎

The binary relation of asymptotic domination will provide a basis for comparing complexity functions. If two functions f and g asymptotically dominate each other, then the associated algorithms will be considered equivalent, and any differences in cost of execution will be largely ignored. Suppose, on the other hand, that g asymptotically dominates f but not vice versa, where f and g are the complexity functions of algorithms F and G respectively. Then even if G is speeded up by some arbitrary factor (through clever programming or a faster machine) so that the complexity function of the fast version is cg, where $c < 1$, cg will asymptotically dominate f but not vice versa. Consequently, for any $m \geq 0$, there will exist an infinite number of arguments n such that $cg(n) > mf(n)$.

Definition 5.2.2:   The set of all functions which are asymptotically dominated by a given function g is denoted by $O(g)$ and read "order g," or "big-Oh of g." If $f \in O(g)$, then f is said to be $O(g)$.

Example

(a)   Let $f(n) = n$ and $g(n) = n^3$. Then using an argument similar to that in the previous example, we see that f is $O(g)$ but g is not $O(f)$.

(b)   Let $f(n) = n$ and $h(n) = 3n$. Then f is $O(h)$ and h is $O(f)$.

(c)   Let $f(n) = n$. The following functions from $\mathbf{N}$ to $\mathbf{R}$ are all members of $O(f)$.

$$f_1(n) = k \qquad \text{for } k \in \mathbf{R},$$

$$f_2(n) = kn \qquad \text{for } k \in \mathbf{R},$$

$$f_3(n) = n + k \qquad \text{for } k \in \mathbf{R},$$

$$f_4(n) = n + 1/(n + 1). \qquad \#$$

The next theorem establishes some important relationships between a function f and the set $O(f)$.

Theorem 5.2.2: Consider the class of functions from $\mathbf{N}$ to $\mathbf{R}$. Then
(a) f is $O(f)$.
(b) if f is $O(g)$, then cf is $O(g)$ for any $c \in \mathbf{R}$. (Thus, the set $O(g)$ is closed under multiplication by a constant.)
(c) if f and h are both $O(g)$, then their sum, $(f + h)$, where $(f + h)(n) = f(n) + h(n)$, is $O(g)$. (Thus, the set $O(g)$ is closed under addition of functions.)

Proof:
(a) This follows directly from part (a) of Theorem 5.2.1.
(b) If f is $O(g)$, then for some $m, k \in \mathbf{N}$, $|f(n)| \leq m|g(n)|$ for all $n \geq k$. Then for $c \in \mathbf{R}$, $|cf(n)| = |c| \cdot |f(n)| \leq |cm| \cdot |g(n)|$ for $n \geq k$, and therefore $cf(n)$ is $O(g)$.
(c) If f and h are both $O(g)$, then there exist some m_1, m_2, k_1 and $k_2 \in \mathbf{N}$ such that
$$|f(n)| \leq m_1|g(n)| \qquad \text{if } n \geq k_1, \text{ and}$$
$$|h(n)| \leq m_2|g(n)| \qquad \text{if } n \geq k_2.$$
Let $m = m_1 + m_2$ and $k = \max\{k_1, k_2\}$. Then
$$|f(n) + h(n)| \leq |f(n)| + |h(n)| \leq m_1|g(n)| + m_2|g(n)|$$
$$= (m_1 + m_2)|g(n)| = m|g(n)| \text{ for } n \geq k.$$
Thus $(f + h)$ is $O(g)$. ∎

The following theorem asserts that f is $O(g)$ if and only if every function asymptotically dominated by f is also asymptotically dominated by g.

Theorem 5.2.3: Let f and g be functions from $\mathbf{N}$ to $\mathbf{R}$. Then f is $O(g)$ if and only if $O(f) \subset O(g)$.

Proof:
(a) $(O(f) \subset O(g) \Rightarrow f \in O(g).)$ From Theorem 5.2.2 we know that $f \in O(f)$. Since $O(f) \subset O(g)$ it follows that $f \in O(g)$.
(b) $(f \in O(g) \Rightarrow O(f) \subset O(g).)$ Let h be any element of $O(f)$; then h is asymptotically dominated by f. Since $f \in O(g)$, f is asymptotically dominated by g. Since the relation of asymptotic domination is transitive (by Theorem 5.2.1(a)), it follows that h is asymptotically dominated by g and therefore h is $O(g)$. Since h was chosen to be an arbitrary member of $O(f)$, it follows that $O(f) \subset O(g)$. ∎

The following is an immediate result of the previous theorem; its proof is left as an exercise.

Corollary 5.2.3: Let f and g be functions from $\mathbf{N}$ to $\mathbf{R}$. Then
(a) f is $O(g)$ and g is $O(f)$ if and only if $O(f) = O(g)$.
(b) if f is $O(g)$ and g is $O(h)$, then f is $O(h)$.

If f is a complexity function for an algorithm F, then $O(f)$ is commonly referred to as the *asymptotic behavior* or *asymptotic complexity* of the algorithm F. Because algorithms are often compared on the basis of their asymptotic behavior, it is important to understand that considerable differences may exist between two functions which have the same asymptotic behavior. For example, suppose F and G are two programs which are applicable to the same class of problems, and that execution of F always takes 3 times as long as execution of G. If f and g are defined to be the time complexity functions of F and G respectively, then $f = 3g$. We can show in this case that f and g asymptotically dominate each other, and therefore $O(f) = O(g)$. Thus the asymptotic behavior of these functions does not provide a basis for distinguishing between the cost of the two algorithms. This does not imply that the difference in cost is negligible; a factor of 3 in speed of execution would obviously serve as an important consideration of choosing between the programs F and G. However, since each cost function asymptotically dominates the other, the order of the functions does not provide a basis for choosing between them.

Now suppose $f(n) = cn$ and $g(n) = dn^2$, where c and d are positive constants. We can show, using Definition 5.2.1, that g asymptotically dominates f but not vice versa, and regardless of the values of c and d, if n is sufficiently large, then the execution of program F will require less time than the execution of G. In this case, the order of the functions provides an important consideration for choosing between the algorithms. We will see many important examples of functions f and g where f is asymptotically dominated by g but not vice versa.

Some Important Classes of Asymptotic Behavior

It is often convenient to use order notation with explicit specification of a function rather than the name of a function. Thus, $O(6)$ denotes the set of functions asymptotically dominated by the constant function $f(n) = 6$, $O(n)$ denotes the set of functions asymptotically dominated by the function $f(n) = n$, and $O(n^2)$ denotes the set of functions asymptotically dominated by $f(n) = n^2$.

The asymptotic complexity of an algorithm can often be expressed in a very simple form. For example, the asymptotic behavior of a sum of functions is often equal to the asymptotic behavior of one of the summands. Furthermore, we have already seen that multiplicative constants do not affect asymptotic complexity. As a result, the asymptotic complexity of an algorithm can often be characterized in one of the following ways.

1. f is $O(1)$. For any algorithm of complexity $O(1)$, there exists some $k \in \mathbf{N}$ such that execution of the algorithm will cost $r \leq k$ regardless of the value of n. Thus the cost of applying the algorithm can be bounded independently of the problem size n. Any function which is $O(c)$, where $c \in \mathbf{R}$, is $O(1)$. An algorithm of $O(1)$ complexity is said to have *constant complexity*.

2. f is $O(\log n)$.† An algorithm of $O(\log n)$ complexity is said to have *logarithmic complexity*. For an algorithm of logarithmic complexity, the cost of applying the algorithm to problems of sufficiently large size n can be bounded by a function of the form $k \log n$, where $k \in \mathbf{R}$.

3. f is $O(n)$. An algorithm of $O(n)$ complexity is said to have *linear complexity*. For any such algorithm there will exist some $k \in \mathbf{N}$ such that the cost of executing the algorithm on a problem of sufficiently large size n will be no more than kn.

4. f is $O(n \log n)$. For any algorithm of $O(n \log n)$ complexity, there will exist some $k \in \mathbf{N}$ such that applying the algorithm to a problem of sufficiently large size n will cost no more than $kn \log n$. Such an algorithm is said to have *n log n complexity*.

5. f is $O(n^2)$. An algorithm of complexity $O(n^2)$ is said to have *quadratic complexity*.

6. f is $O(c^n)$, where $c > 1$. An algorithm of complexity $O(c^n)$, $c > 1$, is said to be of *exponential complexity*.

7. f is $O(n!)$.

The following theorem establishes that the classes we have listed are given in order of increasing complexity.

Theorem 5.2.4:   Consider the class F of all functions from $\mathbf{N}$ to $\mathbf{R}$. Then for $c \in \mathbf{R}$ such that $c > 1$,

$$O(1) \subset O(\log n) \subset O(n) \subset O(n \log n) \subset O(n^2) \subset O(c^n) \subset O(n!),$$

and all containments are proper.

Proof: The proofs that containments are proper are left as exercises. We will prove the first, second, and fifth containments and leave the others as exercises. By Theorem 5.2.3, in order to show $O(f) \subset O(g)$ it suffices to show that f is $O(g)$.

(a) ($O(1) \subset O(\log n)$.) Let $f(n) = 1$ and $g(n) = \log n$. For all $n > 2$, $1 \leq \log n$ and therefore f is $O(g)$. By Theorem 5.2.3, it follows that $O(1) \subset O(\log n)$.

(b) ($O(\log n) \subset O(n)$.) For all $n > 0$, $\log n < n$, and therefore $\log n$ is $O(n)$. It follows that $O(\log n) \subset O(n)$.

(c) ($O(n^2) \subset O(c^n)$ for $c > 1$.) We will show that for sufficiently large n,

$$n^2 \leq c^n.$$

†Unless explicit statement is made to the contrary, all logarithms in this book are to the base 2. For ease of exposition, we have defined the concepts of this section only for functions from $\mathbf{N}$ to $\mathbf{R}$. However, because we are concerned with the behavior of functions for large arguments, the definitions can be extended without difficulty to include partial functions from $\mathbf{N}$ to $\mathbf{R}$ which are defined on all but a finite subset of $\mathbf{N}$. Thus, the fact that $f(n) = \log n$ and $g(n) = n \log n$ are not defined for the argument $n = 0$ causes no substantive difficulty, and we will use $O(\log n)$, for example, to denote the set $O(g)$, where

$$g(0) = 0,$$
$$g(n) = \log n, \text{ for } n > 0.$$

Since $c > 1$ it follows that $\log c > 0$, and hence the above inequality will hold if

$$2 \log n \leq n \log c$$

or

$$\frac{2}{\log c} \leq \frac{n}{\log n}.$$

The ratio $n/\log n$ becomes arbitrarily large as n increases, and therefore for any $c > 1$, this inequality can be satisfied by choosing n sufficiently large. Thus n^2 is $O(c^n)$ and hence $O(n^2) \subset O(c^n)$. ∎

Complexity functions which involve various powers of n often occur in the analysis of algorithms. The following theorem and its corollary are important for relating these sets of functions.

Theorem 5.2.5: Let c, $d \in \mathbf{R}$, where $0 < c < d$. Then $O(n^c) \subset O(n^d)$, and the containment is proper.

Proof: For each $n > 1$, if $c < d$, then $n^c < n^d$. It follows that $O(n^c) \subset O(n^d)$.
   To show the containment is proper, we will show that n^d is not $O(n^c)$. If n^d is $O(n^c)$, then for some k such that $k \geq 0$, the inequality $|n^d| \leq k|n^c|$ holds for sufficiently large n. If k is chosen to be 0, the inequality does not hold for $n \geq 1$. If k is positive, then n can be chosen large enough that $\log n > \log k/(d - c)$. But

$$\log n > \frac{\log k}{d - c} \Rightarrow (d - c) \log n > \log k$$

$$\Rightarrow d \log n > \log k + c \log n$$

$$\Rightarrow \log(n^d) > \log(kn^c)$$

$$\Rightarrow n^d > kn^c.$$

Since k was an arbitrary positive number, this shows that n^c does not asymptotically dominate n^d and therefore n^d is not $O(n^c)$. ∎

Corollary 5.2.5: If $P(n)$ is a polynomial in n of degree k, then $P(n)$ is $O(n^k)$.

Examples
   (a)   The function $f(n) = 1/n + 63$ is $O(1)$.
   (b)   The function $f(n) = rn + kn \log n$ is $O(n \log n)$.
   (c)   The function $f(n) = .6n^3 + 28n^2 + 31n + 468$ is $O(n^3)$.   #

The following theorem establishes that the logarithmic base does not affect the asymptotic behavior of functions which are $O(\log n)$.

Theorem 5.2.6: Let b, $c \in \mathbf{R}$ be constants greater than 1. Then $O(\log_b n) = O(\log_c n)$.

Proof: Using the fact that $\log_b (a^x) = x \log_b a$, we observe that

$$\log_b n = \log_b (c^{\log_c n}) = \log_c n \cdot \log_b c = k \log_c n.$$

By application of Theorem 5.2.2 and Corollary 5.2.3 it follows that $O(\log_b n) = O(\log_c n)$. ∎

Theorem 5.2.7:   Let $b, c \in \mathbf{R}$ be constants greater than 1. Then $O(n \log_b n) = O(n \log_c n)$.

The proof is left as an exercise.

The execution time of an algorithm is often equal to the sum of a number of terms, where each term corresponds to the execution time of some part of the algorithm. The following theorem provides some results which characterize the asymptotic behavior of some of these sums.

Theorem 5.2.8:   Let $c \in \mathbf{R}$. Then

(a) $\sum\limits_{i=1}^{n} c$ is $O(n)$

(b) $\sum\limits_{i=1}^{n} i$ is $O(n^2)$

(c) $\sum\limits_{i=1}^{n} i^2$ is $O(n^3)$.

Proof: Part (a) is straightforward; parts (b) and (c) follow from Corollary 5.2.5 and the identities $\sum_{i=1}^{n} i = n(n + 1)/2$ and $\sum_{i=1}^{n} i^2 = n(n + 1)(2n + 1)/6$ respectively. ∎

In practice, any algorithm can be executed on small problems; that is, when n is small enough, but the asymptotic behavior of a complexity function provides important information about whether it will be feasible to execute an algorithm for moderate or large values use of n. This point is illustrated in Tables 5.2.1 and 5.2.2.

Comparing algorithms on the basis of their asymptotic behavior is a powerful and convenient technique, but it must be used with caution. Thus, while we would

Problem Size n	$\log n$	n	$n \log n$	n^2	2^n	$n!$
5	3	5	12	25	32	120
10	4	10	33	10^2	1024	3×10^6
10^2	7	10^2	664	10^4	1.3×10^{30}	*
10^3	10	10^3	9965	10^6	*	*
10^4	14	10^4	1.4×10^5	10^8	*	*

Table 5.2.1   A COMPARISON OF THE GROWTH OF SOME COMMON COMPLEXITY FUNCTIONS. THE TABLE ENTRIES ARE PROPORTIONAL TO THE TIME REQUIRED TO SOLVE A PROBLEM OF SIZE n. AN ASTERISK INDICATES THAT THE NUMBER IS GREATER THAN 10^{100}.

Complexity function	1 sec	1 min.	1 hour
$\log n$	2^{10^6}	$2^{6\cdot10^7}$	$2^{36\cdot10^8}$
n	10^6	6×10^7	3.6×10^9
$n \log n$	62746	2.8×10^6	1.3×10^8
n^2	10^3	7746	$60,000$
2^n	23	26	32
$n!$	9	11	12

Table 5.2.2 A COMPARISON OF THE MAXIMUM SIZES OF PROBLEMS WHICH CAN BE SOLVED USING ALGORITHMS WITH SOME COMMON COMPLEXITY FUNCTIONS. AN AVERAGE EXECUTION TIME OF ONE OPERATION PER MICROSECOND (10^{-6} SEC) IS ASSUMED. PROPORTIONAL VALUES HOLD FOR OTHER SPEEDS.

expect an $O(n)$ algorithm to be "better" than one which is $O(n^2)$, in fact we cannot choose between them without more information. For example, suppose that algorithms F and G have complexity functions $f(n) = cn$ and $g(n) = dn^2$. If the values of the constants are $c = 50$ and $d = 1$, then F is a more attractive algorithm only if n, the problem size, exceeds 50. Since this value of n may be larger than most of the problems of interest, it may be that the $O(n^2)$ algorithm is the best choice. Thus in order to choose between algorithms, it is generally necessary to know the specific complexity functions and the problem size as well as the asymptotic behaviors.

By extending the way in which order notation is used, we can characterize algorithm performance more precisely than is possible with the notation we have developed thus far. In the extended usage, the notation $O(f)$ is used on the right side of an equation to denote a member of the set $O(f)$. For example, the assertion that the algorithm F has asymptotic complexity f, where

$$f(n) = 1.6n^2 + O(n \log n)$$

is interpreted as meaning $f(n) = 1.6n^2 + g(n)$, where $g(n)$ is a member of $O(n \log n)$. This is a stronger assertion than

$$f(n) = O(n^2);$$

the second is implied by the first but not vice versa. Using this extended notation, the complexity function of different algorithms can be compared with one another on the basis of the coefficients of dominating summand functions as well as less important summands. Thus, for sufficiently large n, an algorithm with a complexity function $f(n) = 1.6n^2 + O(n)$ will probably be less costly than one whose complexity function is $g(n) = 2n^2 + O(n)$, which in turn will probably be less costly than one whose complexity function is $h(n) = 2n^2 + O(n \log n)$.

Problems: Section 5.2

1. Let F be the class of functions from $\mathbf{N}$ to $\mathbf{R}$, and let $f, g \in F$. Define the binary relation $\equiv$ as follows:

$f \equiv g$ if and only if f and g asymptotically dominate each other.

(a) Show that $\equiv$ is an equivalence relation. (This is part (b) of Theorem 5.2.1.)

(b) Let $[f]$ denote the equivalence class of f under the relation $\equiv$. Show that the binary relation

$$[f] \leq [g] \text{ if and only if } f \text{ is asymptotically dominated by } g$$

is a partial order on the quotient set $F/\equiv$.

2. Give an example of a function in $O(1)$ which is not a constant function.

3. Find a pair of functions f and g from $\mathbf{N}$ to $\mathbf{R}$ such that $f \notin O(g)$ and $g \notin O(f)$.

4. Define a function $f: \mathbf{N} \to \mathbf{R}$ to be *bounded* if there exists some $r \in \mathbf{R}$ such that for all $n \in \mathbf{N}, |f(n)| < r$. Prove that every bounded function is $O(1)$.

5. For each of the following pairs of functions, $f: \mathbf{N} \to \mathbf{R}$ and $g: \mathbf{N} \to \mathbf{R}$, determine if and how f and g are related in terms of asymptotic domination.

(a) $f(n) = 1 \qquad$ for n even,
     $\qquad = 2 \qquad$ for n odd.
     $g(n) = 2 \qquad$ for n even,
     $\qquad = 1 \qquad$ for n odd.

(b) $f(n) = 0 \qquad$ for n even,
     $\qquad = 1 \qquad$ for n odd.
     $g(n) = 1 \qquad$ for n even,
     $\qquad = 0 \qquad$ for n odd.

(c) $f(n) = n$.
     $g(n) = n/100 \qquad$ if $n \neq 10^k$ for some k,
     $\qquad = 10^{-10}n^2 \qquad$ if $n = 1, 10, 100$, etc.

6. (a) Using logical notation, write out the definition of "f does not asymptotically dominate g."

(b) Using the assertion of part (a), argue that if f does not asymptotically dominate g, then for any m there exists an infinite number of arguments n such that $|g(n)| > m|f(n)|$.

(c) Determine whether the following assertion is true. "If f does not asymptotically dominate g, then for all $m > 0$, if n is sufficiently large, then $|g(n)| > m|f(n)|$."

7. Let f_1 and f_2 be functions such that f_1 is $O(g_1)$ and f_2 is $O(g_2)$.

(a) Prove that if $g_1(n)$ and $g_2(n)$ are nonnegative for all arguments $n \in \mathbf{N}$, then $f_1 + f_2$ is $O(g_1 + g_2)$.

(b) Prove that $f_1 + f_2$ may not be $O(g_1 + g_2)$.

8. Let f and g be functions from $\mathbf{N}$ to $\mathbf{R}$, and denote by $f \cdot g$ the product function:

$$f \cdot g(n) = f(n) \cdot g(n).$$

(a) Prove that if f is $O(h_1)$ and g is $O(h_2)$, then $f \cdot g$ is $O(h_1 \cdot h_2)$.

(b) Find a function $f: \mathbf{N} \to \mathbf{R}$ such that $O(f)$ is not closed under multiplication of functions.

9. Prove Corollary 5.2.3.

10. Show that each of the following containments is proper:

(a) $O(1) \subset O(\log n)$.

(b) $O(\log n) \subset O(n)$.

(c) $O(n^2) \subset O(d^n), \qquad$ for all $d > 1$.

11. Prove the following assertions and show that each of the containments is proper.
     (a) $O(n) \subset O(n \log n)$.
     (b) $O(n \log n) \subset O(n^d)$,   for all $d > 1$.
     (c) $O(c^n) \subset O(n!)$,   for all $c > 1$.

12. Show that for all integer values of k, $n > 0$, $O(\log n) = O(\log(n + k))$.

13. Prove Corollary 5.2.5.

14. Consider the class of functions F, where

$$F = \{f \mid f : \mathbf{N} \to \mathbf{R} \text{ and } f(\mathbf{N}) \subset \mathbf{N}\}$$

     i.e., the image of every member of F is a subset of $\mathbf{N}$. Let f and g be members of F. Prove or disprove the following.
     Conjecture: If f and g are $O(h)$, then fg is $O(h)$ (i.e., the set $O(h)$ is closed under composition of functions).

15. Prove Theorem 5.2.7.

16. Suppose two algorithms F and G have time complexity functions

$$f(n) = n^2 - n + 550$$

     and

$$g(n) = 59n + 50$$

     respectively. Determine those values of $n \in \mathbf{N}$ for which F takes less time to execute than G.

17. Determine which of the following functions asymptotically dominate others. Present your answer as a labelled digraph.

$$f_1(n) = 528$$
$$f_2(n) = 3n^2 \log n + \log n$$
$$f_3(n) = \frac{n}{2} + \frac{1}{n^2}$$
$$f_4(n) = \log \log n$$
$$f_5(n) = (\log n)^2$$
$$f_6(n) = 2^{\log n}$$
$$f_7(n) = \log \left(n + \frac{2}{n}\right)$$
$$f_8(n) = \log (n^2)$$
$$f_9(n) = 3n^4$$

18. From Theorem 5.2.8 we might make the following conjecture for $k \in \mathbf{N}$:

$$\sum_{i=0}^{n} i^k \text{ is } O(n^{k+1}).$$

     Prove or disprove the conjecture.

5.3 RECURRENCE SYSTEMS

The expressions for permutations and combinations developed in Section 5.1 are the most fundamental tools for counting the elements of finite sets. They often prove to be inadequate, however, and many problems of computer science require a different approach. An important alternate approach uses *recurrence equations* (often called *difference equations* or *recurrence relations*) to define the terms of a sequence. A formal definition of recurrence equations is difficult because of the wide variety of forms in which such equations can be written, but the concept is straightforward. We have already seen an example of a recurrence equation in the definition of the Fibonacci sequence, where for $n \geq 2$, the term a_n is defined by the recurrence equation

$$a_n = a_{n-1} + a_{n-2}.$$

The salient characteristic of a recurrence equation is the specification of the term a_n as a function of the terms $a_0, a_1, \ldots, a_{n-1}$. By itself, however, a recurrence equation is not sufficient to define the terms of a sequence; we must also specify the values of some initial terms of the sequence. Thus, in our definition of the Fibonacci sequence, we set $a_0 = 0$ and $a_1 = 1$. These are called the *boundary conditions* or *initial conditions* of the sequence. A recurrence equation together with boundary conditions is a form of recursive definition, although the terminology used is different from that introduced earlier. The topics of recursive definitions and recurrence equations are not coextensive; many classes of recursive definitions do not use recurrence equations and the solution of recurrence equations uses techniques which are not applicable to the broader class of recursive definitions.

A *recurrence system* is a set of boundary conditions and recurrence equations which specify a unique sequence or a function (or sometimes a partial function) from $\mathbf{N}^k$ to $\mathbf{R}$, where $k \in \mathbf{I}+$. Recurrence systems provide a powerful tool for investigating many classes of problems, including counting and enumeration problems. A *solution* to a recurrence system is a function $f: \mathbf{N}^k \to \mathbf{R}$ such that f satisfies both the boundary conditions and the recurrence equations.

Examples

(a) The number of permutations of n objects can be expressed using the following recurrence system:

$$P(0) = 1,$$
$$P(n) = nP(n-1), \quad \text{for } n > 0.$$

The correctness of this system can be established as follows:
1. The objects of an empty set can be arranged in a sequence in exactly one way. Thus, the boundary condition is $P(0) = 1$.
2. Given n objects, $n > 0$, we can choose the first object of a sequence in any of n ways and then arrange the remaining elements in $P(n-1)$ ways. Thus, the recurrence equation is $P(n) = n \cdot P(n-1)$ for $n > 0$.

It can be shown by induction that $n!$ is a solution to this system, where $0! = 1$ and for $n > 0$, $n! = \prod_{i=1}^{n} i$.

(b) Let $f(h, k)$ be the maximum number of leaves of a tree of height h, where each node has outdegree k or less. This function can be expressed as the following recurrence system:

$$f(0, k) = 1,$$
$$f(h, k) = k \cdot f(h - 1, k) \qquad \text{for } h > 0.$$

The system is based on the following arguments.

1. A tree of height 0 has a single node which is a leaf, so $f(0, k) = 1$. This gives the boundary condition.

2. A tree of height $h > 0$ will have the maximum number of leaves if its root has k sons, each of which is the root of a subtree of height $h - 1$ with $f(h - 1, k)$ leaves. A tree of height h can therefore have up to $k \cdot f(h - 1, k)$ leaves.

It can be shown by induction on h that k^h is a solution to this system.

(c) Pascal derived the following recurrence system to evaluate $\binom{n}{k}$, the number of subsets of k objects in a set of n objects.

$$\binom{n}{0} = 1$$

$$\binom{n}{n} = 1$$

$$\binom{n}{k} = \binom{n-1}{k-1} + \binom{n-1}{k} \qquad \text{for } n > k > 0.$$

The argument is as follows:

1. The number of ways of choosing 0 things from n things is 1, and the number of ways of choosing n things from n things is 1. These two assertions provide the boundary conditions.

2. Suppose $n > 0$. We choose some element and delete it from the set, leaving $n - 1$ elements. A subset of $k > 0$ elements can now be chosen from the original n elements in two distinct ways: one can choose $k - 1$ elements from the remaining $n - 1$ elements and then add the deleted element, or one can choose all k elements from the remaining $n - 1$ elements. These possibilities are mutually exclusive and exhaustive. It follows that

$$\binom{n}{k} = \binom{n-1}{k-1} + \binom{n-1}{k}.$$

It can be shown by direct substitution that $n!/[k!(n - k)!]$ is a solution to this system.　#

The number of injections and bijections from a set S to a set T can easily be expressed in terms of permutations involving $|S|$ and $|T|$; these expressions were given in examples in Section 5.1. The number of surjections from one set to another is difficult to characterize using only permutations and combinations, but can be easily expressed using a recurrence system.

Theorem 5.3.1:   Let A and B be finite nonempty sets with $|A| = m$, $|B| = n$, where $m \geq n > 0$. The number of surjections, $S(m, n)$, from A to B is given by the following recurrence system.

$$S(m, 1) = 1,$$

$$S(m, n) = n^m - \sum_{j=1}^{n-1} \binom{n}{j} S(m, j) \qquad \text{for } m \geq n > 1.$$

Proof: If $n = 1$, then there is exactly one surjection from A to B; this establishes the boundary condition $S(m, 1) = 1$.

Suppose $n > 1$. The number of surjections from A to B is equal to the number of functions from A to B minus the number of functions whose images are proper subsets of B. If $B' \subset B$ and $|B'| = j$, then there are $S(m, j)$ functions from A to B whose image is B'. Furthermore, there are $\binom{n}{j}$ different subsets of B of cardinality j. Thus, there are $\binom{n}{j} S(m, j)$ different functions from A to B which have an image of cardinality j, where $j \leq n$. Then the total number of functions from A to B which are not surjections is $\sum_{j=1}^{n-1} \binom{n}{j} S(m, j)$. Since there are a total of n^m functions from A to B,

$$S(m, n) = n^m - \sum_{j=1}^{n-1} \binom{n}{j} S(m, j).$$

This establishes the recurrence system.   ▮

It is obvious that a recurrence system can be used to obtain any term of the associated sequence by iteratively solving the recurrence. Alternatively, it is sometimes possible to find an expression for the solution which can be evaluated directly for any argument n to find the value of the nth term.

Examples

The following are examples of solutions to recurrence systems. In each case the expression can be shown to be a solution by direct substitution. All of these solutions are unique, but we will not prove this.

(a)   The following system describes a function which grows exponentially:

$$a_0 = k,$$

$$a_n = ca_{n-1} \qquad \text{for } n > 0.$$

The solution is $a_n = kc^n$.

(b)   The following function describes the Fibonacci sequence:

$$a_0 = 0,$$

$$a_1 = 1,$$

$$a_n = a_{n-1} + a_{n-2} \qquad \text{for } n > 1.$$

The solution is $a_n = (1/\sqrt{5})[(1 + \sqrt{5})/2]^n - (1/\sqrt{5})[(1 - \sqrt{5})/2]^n$.

(c)   Consider the following recurrence system

$$f(0) = 0,$$
$$f(1) = f(2) = 1,$$
$$f(n) = 2f(n-1) + f(n-2) - 2f(n-3) \qquad \text{for } n > 2.$$

The solution is $f(n) = [(-1)^{n+1} + 2^n]/3.$ #

A treatment of the many techniques for solving recurrence systems is beyond the scope of this text, but we will illustrate one which is both easy and useful. Later in this section we will use this procedure to find solutions for some important classes of recurrence systems.

The technique begins with the specification of a_n and repeatedly applies the recurrence relation to evaluate the terms which appear on the right side. To illustrate, consider a recurrence system of the form

$$a_0 = b_0,$$
$$a_n = c_n a_{n-1} + b_n,$$

where the value of the coefficients b_n and c_n may be functions of n. The value of the general term a_n can be expressed as a sum by adding both sides of the following sequence of equations, where each equation is obtained by using the recurrence relation to express a term in the preceding equation.

$$a_n = c_n a_{n-1} + b_n$$
$$c_n a_{n-1} = c_n c_{n-1} a_{n-2} + c_n b_{n-1}$$
$$c_n c_{n-1} a_{n-2} = c_n c_{n-1} c_{n-2} a_{n-3} + c_n c_{n-1} b_{n-2}$$

$$\cdot$$
$$\cdot$$
$$\cdot$$

$$\prod_{i=0}^{n-2} c_{n-i} a_1 = \prod_{i=0}^{n-1} c_{n-i} a_0 + \prod_{i=0}^{n-2} c_{n-i} b_1$$

$$\prod_{i=0}^{n-1} c_{n-i} a_0 = \prod_{i=0}^{n-1} c_{n-i} b_0$$

Note that the right side of the last equation only involves the coefficients and boundary conditions of the sequence. Forming separate sums of the left and right sides of this set of equations and then cancelling common summands yields

$$a_n = b_n + c_n b_{n-1} + c_n c_{n-1} b_{n-2} + \cdots + \prod_{i=0}^{n-2} c_{n-i} b_1 + \prod_{i=0}^{n-1} c_{n-i} b_0.$$

In many cases, standard summation identities can be applied to derive an expression for the value of a_n.

Example

Consider the recurrence system

$$a_0 = b,$$
$$a_n = c a_{n-1} + b.$$

We form the set of equations

$$a_n = ca_{n-1} + b$$
$$ca_{n-1} = c^2 a_{n-2} + cb$$
$$c^2 a_{n-2} = c^3 a_{n-3} + c^2 b$$
$$\cdot$$
$$\cdot$$
$$\cdot$$
$$c^{n-1} a_1 = c^n a_0 + c^{n-1} b$$
$$c^n a_0 = c^n b$$

Summing the left and right sides and cancelling gives

$$a_n = b + cb + c^2 b + \cdots + c^{n-1} b + c^n b$$
$$= b \sum_{i=0}^{n} c^i.$$

Applying Theorem 2.5.3 gives the solution

$$a_n = (n + 1)b \qquad \text{if } c = 1;$$
$$= \frac{b(1 - c^{n+1})}{(1 - c)} \qquad \text{if } c \neq 1. \quad \#$$

The importance of obtaining an expression for the nth term of a sequence defined by a recurrence system is mitigated by the possibility of obtaining the terms of the sequence iteratively. But a general expression for the nth term often provides additional insights. For example, if the nth term of the sequence describes the cost of applying an algorithm to a problem of size n, then an expression for the nth term will enable us to determine the asymptotic behavior of the complexity function of the algorithm.

Example

The following procedure returns the sum of the first n entries of an array A.

```
procedure SUM(n):
begin
     total ← 0;
     for i ← 1 to n step 1 do
          total ← total + A[i];
     return total
end
```

Suppose we define the complexity function f of SUM to be the number of additions performed by SUM. This function is characterized by the following recurrence system.

$$f(1) = 1,$$
$$f(n) = f(n - 1) + 1 \qquad \text{for } n > 0.$$

By adjusting indices, the expression developed in the preceding example can be applied by setting $b = c = 1$. It follows that the solution is $f(n) = n$ for $n \geq 1$. Hence SUM is an $O(n)$ algorithm and has linear complexity. #

In the remainder of this section we will consider some special classes of recurrence systems which are especially important for characterizing the performance of recursive programs. While we will obtain solutions of some of these recurrence systems, the primary goal will be to determine the asymptotic behavior of a broad class of systems without actually finding solutions for the systems.

Divide and Conquer Algorithms

It is sometimes possible to divide a problem into smaller subproblems, solve the subproblems, and then combine their solutions to obtain the solution to the original problem. This general approach, often referred to as "divide and conquer," is a powerful technique in algorithm design. Since the subproblems are usually of the same type as the original problem, a divide and conquer strategy can often be implemented as a recursive algorithm. In the remainder of this section we will consider some classes of recurrence systems which are useful for describing the complexity functions of recursive algorithms, including many which use a divide and conquer strategy. Our treatment will proceed from the specific to the general. We begin by solving some special classes of recurrence relations explicitly and characterizing their asymptotic behaviors. Then, using the solutions to these systems as bounds, we will show how to determine the asymptotic behavior of the solutions to a larger class of recurrence systems without actually solving the systems.

In general, a divide and conquer algorithm will solve a small problem directly and will solve a larger problem by dividing it into a set of subproblems of approximately the same size. These algorithms are easiest to describe if one assumes the subproblems are equal in size. For example, if an algorithm divides a problem of size $n > 1$ into two subproblems of approximate size $n/2$, then the algorithm can most easily be described if we assume n is a power of 2. This will enable us to divide a problem of size n into two problems of size $n/2$, then divide each of the problems of size $n/2$ into problems of size $n/4$, etc. The recurrence system for such an algorithm will specify the values of the complexity function only for arguments which are powers of the appropriate integer $b > 1$. We will consider the class of divide and conquer algorithms which obey the following constraints:

1. The cost of solving a problem of size $n = 1$ is c, where c is a nonnegative constant.
2. For $k > 0$, problems of size $n = b^k$ are divided into a different subproblems of size n/b.
3. For all problems of size $n > 1$, the cost of breaking the problem into subproblems plus the cost of combining the solutions of the subproblems to obtain a solution to the original problem is $h(n)$, a function of n.

These conditions yield recurrence systems of the following form:

$$f(1) = c,$$
$$f(n) = af(n/b) + h(n) \qquad \text{for } n = b^k, k > 0.$$

Since $f(1) = f(b^0)$, a recurrence system of this form specifies a value of f for all arguments which are (nonnegative) integer powers of b. Because the values of g are not specified for other arguments, the system will not have a unique solution $f: \mathbf{N} \to \mathbf{R}$, but we will see that this does not detract from its usefulness if the cost of solving a problem of size n is monotone increasing with n.

We first treat recurrence systems in which $f(n) = af(n/b) + h(n)$ for the special case where $h(n) = c$. The solutions to these systems for $n = b^k$ will then be used to characterize the asymptotic behavior for all arguments of a large class of recursive algorithms.

Lemma 5.3.2a: Let a, b, and c be integers such that $a \geq 1$, $b > 1$, and $c > 0$, and let $f: \mathbf{N} \to \mathbf{R}$ be any function whose values obey the recurrence system

$$f(1) = c,$$
$$f(n) = af\left(\frac{n}{b}\right) + c \qquad \text{for } n = b^k \text{ where } k > 0.$$

For all arguments which are powers of b,

     (a)   if $a = 1$, then $f(n) = c(\log_b n + 1)$;

     (b)   if $a \neq 1$, then $f(n) = \dfrac{c(an^{\log_b a} - 1)}{a - 1}$.

     Proof: Let $n = b^k$, $k \geq 1$.
Then

$$f(n) = af\left(\frac{n}{b}\right) + c$$

$$af\left(\frac{n}{b}\right) = a^2 f\left(\frac{n}{b^2}\right) + ac$$

$$a^2 f\left(\frac{n}{b^2}\right) = a^3 f\left(\frac{n}{b^3}\right) + a^2 c$$

$$\vdots$$

$$a^{k-1} f\left(\frac{n}{b^{k-1}}\right) = a^k f\left(\frac{n}{b^k}\right) + a^{k-1} c.$$

Summing both sides of the above sequence of equations and cancelling common summands, and noting that $f(n/b^k) = f(1) = c$, we have

$$f(n) = ca^k + c \sum_{i=0}^{k-1} a_i = c \sum_{i=0}^{k} a^i.$$

     (a)   If $a = 1$, then $f(n) = c(k + 1)$. But $k = \log_b n$, so $f(n) = c(\log_b n + 1)$.

(b)   If $a \neq 1$, then from Theorem 2.5.3 we have

$$f(n) = c \left(\frac{a^{k+1} - 1}{a - 1} \right).$$

But $k = \log_b n$, and $a^{\log_b n} = n^{\log_b a}$. Therefore,

$$f(n) = \frac{c(aa^{\log_b n} - 1)}{a - 1} = \frac{c(an^{\log_b a} - 1)}{a - 1}. \quad \blacksquare$$

From Lemma 5.3.2a we can determine the asymptotic behavior of the function f for those arguments which are powers of b. The following definition is a generalization of the concepts introduced in Section 5.2. This generalization permits us to discuss the asymptotic behavior of functions on a subset of the domain **N**.

Definition 5.3.1:   Let f and g be functions from **N** to **R**, and let S be an infinite subset of **N**. Then f is $O(g)$ *on* S if there exists $k \geq 0$ and $m \geq 0$ such that $|f(n)| \leq m|g(n)|$ for all $n \in S$ such that $n \geq k$.

Example

Let $f: \mathbf{N} \to \mathbf{R}$ be defined as follows:

$$f(x) = 1 \quad \text{if } x \text{ is even,}$$
$$f(x) = x \quad \text{if } x \text{ is odd.}$$

Then f is $O(1)$ on the set of even integers, but f is not an $O(1)$ function.   #

It is easy to see that if g is $O(h)$ and $S \subset \mathbf{N}$, then g is $O(h)$ on S. Moreover, the properties of asymptotic behavior we have considered extend in a natural way to asymptotic behavior on S. For example, if c is a constant and f and g are $O(h)$ on S, then cf and $f + g$ are $O(h)$ on S.

The next lemma is an immediate consequence of Lemma 5.3.2a; its proof is left as an exercise.

Lemma 5.3.2b: Let $a, b,$ and c be integers such that $a \geq 1, b > 1,$ and $c > 0$, and let $f: \mathbf{N} \to \mathbf{R}$ be a function such that

$$f(1) = c,$$
$$f(n) = af(n/b) + c \quad \text{for } n = b^k \text{ where } k > 0.$$

Let $S = \{b^k \,|\, k \in \mathbf{N}\}$.

(a)   If $a = 1$, then f is $O(\log n)$ on S.
(b)   If $a \neq 1$, then f is $O(n^{\log_b a})$ on S.

We now use the preceding lemma to characterize the asymptotic behavior for arguments which are powers of b for a large class of recurrence systems.

Theorem 5.3.2:   Let $a, b,$ and c be integers such that $a \geq 1, b > 1,$ and $c > 0$, and let $f: \mathbf{N} \to \mathbf{R}$ be any function such that

$$f(1) \leq c,$$
$$f(n) \leq af(n/b) + c \quad \text{for } n = b^k \text{ where } k > 0.$$

Let $S = \{b^k \mid k \in \mathbf{N}\}$.

(a)   If $a = 1$, then f is $O(\log n)$ on S.

(b)   If $a \neq 1$, then f is $O(n^{\log_b a})$ on S.

Proof: Let g be the solution to the recurrence system where equality holds for both conditions of the recurrence system; that is,

$$g(1) = c,$$

$$g(n) = ag(n/b) + c \qquad \text{for } n = b^k \text{ where } k > 0.$$

By Lemma 5.3.2b, the function g is $O(\log n)$ on S if $a = 1$ and $O(n^{\log_b a})$ on S if $a \neq 1$. It is easy to show by induction that any function f which satisfies the following inequalities

$$f(1) \leq c,$$

$$f(n) \leq af(n/b) + c \qquad \text{for } n = b^k \text{ where } k > 0,$$

is bounded by the function g for all arguments which are powers of b, that is,

$$\text{if } n \in S, \text{ then } f(n) \leq g(n).$$

We conclude that the function f is $O(\log n)$ on S if $a = 1$ and f is $O(n^{\log_b a})$ on S if $a \neq 1$. ∎

Example

The procedure MAXMIN given in Fig. 5.3.1 applies a divide and conquer strategy to return the maximum and minimum values of the entries $A[i], \ldots, A[j]$ of a vector A. MAXMIN first determines if there is a single entry, i.e., if $i = j$; in this case, MAXMIN returns the ordered pair $\langle A[i], A[i]\rangle$. If $i < j$, then MAXMIN divides the entries into two disjoint subproblems of approximately the same size and solves each of the subproblems recursively. The solutions to the subproblems are then used to construct the solution to the original problem. To find the largest and smallest entries of the array $A[1:n]$, we call MAXMIN $(1, n)$. We define the

procedure MAXMIN(i, j):
if $i = j$ **then return** $\langle A[i], A[i]\rangle$
else
    begin
        comment: Divide array into two subarrays of approximately equal size.
        $\langle max1, min1\rangle \leftarrow$ MAXMIN$\left(i, \left\lfloor\dfrac{i+j}{2}\right\rfloor\right)$;
        $\langle max2, min2\rangle \leftarrow$ MAXMIN$\left(\left\lfloor\dfrac{i+j}{2}\right\rfloor + 1, j\right)$;
        comment: Put largest value in *max1* and smallest in *min1*.
        if $max1 < max2$ **then** $max1 \leftarrow max2$;
        if $min1 > min2$ **then** $min1 \leftarrow min2$;
        return $\langle max1, min1\rangle$
    end

Fig. 5.3.1   Procedure to find maximum and minimum entries in an array $A[i:j]$ where $i \leq j$

complexity function f of MAXMIN as follows: $f(n)$ is the number of comparisons between elements of the array when A has n entries. The following recurrence system describes the value of f for each argument which is a power of 2.

$$f(1) = 0,$$
$$f(n) = 2f(n/2) + 2 \quad \text{for } n = 2^k \text{ where } k > 0.$$

The function f obeys the following inequalities:

$$f(1) \leq 2$$
$$f(n) \leq 2f(n/2) + 2 \quad \text{for } n = 2^k \text{ where } k > 0.$$

By Theorem 5.3.2 we can conclude that MAXMIN is an $O(n)$ algorithm if n is a power of 2.   #

The preceding results concerning recurrence relations of the form $f(n) = af(n/b) + h(n)$ can only be applied to arguments which are powers of b. The next theorem states conditions which enable us to characterize the asymptotic behavior of f for all arguments. (The conditions given by the theorem are sufficient but not necessary.) In terms of a complexity function f, the theorem asserts that if a problem does not become easier as the size of the problem increases, and if f is $O(g)$ for all arguments of the form b^k, then we can conclude f is $O(g)$ if g is one of the functions specified in the theorem. An important implication of the theorem is that for most cases of interest, "padding" a problem or an input by adding dummy entries so that the problem appears to be of size b^k will not affect the asymptotic behavior of the complexity function.

Theorem 5.3.3: Let $f: \mathbf{N} \to \mathbf{R}+$ be a monotone increasing function such that f is $O(g)$ for all arguments of the form b^k, where $b, k \in \mathbf{N}$ and $b > 1$.

(a) If g is $O(\log n)$, then f is $O(\log n)$.

(b) If g is $O(n \log n)$, then f is $O(n \log n)$.

(c) If g is $O(n^d)$, then f is $O(n^d)$ for $d \in \mathbf{R}$, $d \geq 0$.

Proof of (a): Let $S = \{n \mid n = b^k\}$; then f is $O(g)$ on S. Since g is $O(\log n)$, it follows that f is $O(\log n)$ on S. Hence there exist numbers $r \in \mathbf{N}$ and $K \in \mathbf{R}+$ such that if $n \geq r$ and $n = b^k$, then $f(n) \leq K \log n$. Consider any $m \in \mathbf{N}$ such that $r < b^k < m \leq b^{k+1}$. Because f is monotone increasing and positive,

$$f(m) \leq f(b^{k+1})$$

and therefore

$$f(m) \leq K \log(b^{k+1}) = K(\log(b^k) + \log b)$$
$$\leq K(1 + \log b) \log(b^k)$$
$$< K(1 + \log b) \log m.$$

Therefore $f(m) \leq K(1 + \log b) \log m$ if m is greater than a power of b which is greater than r. It follows that f is $O(\log n)$.

The proofs of parts (b) and (c) are left as exercises. ∎

Examples

(a) The procedure MAXMIN, given in Fig. 5.3.1 and discussed in the previous example, is $O(n)$ for all $n = 2^k$, and the number of comparisons made by MAXMIN increases with n. Therefore we can conclude from Theorem 5.3.3 that MAXMIN is an $O(n)$ algorithm for all arguments $n \in \mathbb{N}$.

(b) A binary search of a sorted list stored in $A[i:j]$ is given in Fig. 5.3.2. The procedure determines whether an argument *arg* is contained in any of the locations $A[i]$, $A[i + 1]$, ..., $A[j]$. If so, the procedure returns the index of the argument in A; otherwise the procedure reports that the argument was not found. To search array $A[1:n]$ for *arg*, we call BINSEARCH (*arg*, 1, n). The procedure first compares *arg* with an element near the middle of the list. If they match, the search is successful and the index of the element is returned. Otherwise, if *arg* is less than the element, the search is resumed recursively on the initial portion of A, and if *arg* is greater than the element, the search is continued on the second portion of A.

procedure BINSEARCH(*arg*, i, j):
begin

$$m \leftarrow \left\lfloor \frac{i+j}{2} \right\rfloor;$$

　if *arg* $= A[m]$ **then return** m
　else
　　　if *arg* $< A[m]$ **and** $i < m$ **then return** BINSEARCH(*arg*, i, $m - 1$)
　　　else
　　　　　if $m < j$ **then return** BINSEARCH(*arg*, $m + 1$, j)
　　　　　else return "not found"
end

Fig. 5.3.2　Binary search for *arg* in the array $A[i:j]$ where $i \leq j$ and entries are sorted in increasing order

Let f be the complexity function of BINSEARCH, where $f(n)$ is defined to be the *maximum* number of comparisons made between *arg* and the entries of a list with n entries. (Counting the maximum number of comparisons is called a "worst case" analysis.)

If $j = i$, a call to BINSEARCH (*arg*, j, j) will result in no more than two comparisons.
Thus

$$f(1) = 2.$$

If $j - i + 1 = 2^k$ for some $k > 0$, then BINSEARCH makes one comparison to determine whether *arg* $= A[m]$. If not, then BINSEARCH may call itself to search either the initial portion of the array (which has $2^{k-1} - 1$ entries) or the final portion (which has 2^{k-1} entries). Since $f(n)$ is defined to be the maximum number of comparisons made,

$$f(2^k) = f(2^{k-1}) + 2.$$

Applying Theorem 5.3.2 with $a = 1$, $b = 2$, and $c = 2$, it follows that BIN-

SEARCH is an $O(\log n)$ algorithm for $n = 2^k$. Moreover, f is monotone increasing, so by Theorem 5.3.3, binary search has $O(\log n)$ complexity. #

When the recurrence relation of a divide and conquer algorithm is of the form $f(n) = af(n/b) + c$, the constant c represents the cost of splitting the problem into subproblems plus the cost of combining their solutions to solve the original problem. Sometimes the cost of splitting the problem, and more often the cost of combining the solutions of the subproblems, increases with n. We next consider recurrence relations of the form $f(n) = af(n/b) + cn$; these recurrence relations can be applied when the splitting and combining costs grow linearly with n. Using the techniques and results developed previously, we can prove the following result.

Theorem 5.3.4: Let a, b, and c be integers such that $a \geq 1$, $b > 1$, and $c > 0$, and let $f: \mathbf{N} \to \mathbf{R}+$ be a monotone increasing function such that

$$f(1) \leq c,$$
$$f(n) \leq af(n/b) + cn \qquad \text{for } n = b^k \text{ where } k > 0.$$

(a)   If $a < b$, then f is $O(n)$.
(b)   If $a = b$, then f is $O(n \log n)$.
(c)   If $a > b$, then f is $O(n^{\log_b a})$.

Proof: Suppose $n = b^k$, where $k \in \mathbf{N}$ and $k > 0$. Then we can bound $f(n)$ as follows:

$$f(n) \leq af\left(\frac{n}{b}\right) + cn$$

$$af\left(\frac{n}{b}\right) \leq a^2 f\left(\frac{n}{b^2}\right) + \frac{acn}{b}$$

$$a^2 f\left(\frac{n}{b^2}\right) \leq a^3 f\left(\frac{n}{b^3}\right) + a^2 \frac{cn}{b^2}$$

$$\vdots$$

$$a^{k-1} f\left(\frac{n}{b^{k-1}}\right) \leq a^k f\left(\frac{n}{b^k}\right) + a^{k-1} \frac{cn}{b^{k-1}}.$$

Summing both sides of these inequalities and cancelling summands which appear on both sides, we obtain

$$f(n) \leq cn \sum_{i=0}^{k} \left(\frac{a}{b}\right)^i.$$

(i)   If $a = b$, then $\left(\frac{a}{b}\right) = 1$ and

$$f(n) \leq n(k + 1) = cn \log_b(n) + cn \text{ for } n = b^k.$$

But $O(cn \log_b n) = O(n \log n)$ and $O(cn) = O(n)$; furthermore,

$$O(n) \subset O(n \log n).$$

It follows from Theorem 5.3.3 that f is $O(n \log n)$ in the case that $a = b$.

(ii) If $a \neq b$, then we can apply the identity

$$\frac{1 - x^{n+1}}{1 - x} = \sum_{i=0}^{n} x^i$$

to the inequality

$$f(n) \leq cn \sum_{i=0}^{k} \left(\frac{a}{b}\right)^i$$

to obtain

$$f(n) \leq cn \left(\frac{1 - \left(\frac{a}{b}\right)^{k+1}}{1 - \frac{a}{b}}\right)$$

$$\leq \frac{cn}{b^k} \left(\frac{b^{k+1} - a^{k+1}}{b - a}\right) = c \left(\frac{b^{k+1} - a^{k+1}}{b - a}\right).$$

Since $b - a$ is a constant, we can set $d = c/(b - a)$ to obtain

$$f(n) \leq d(b^{k+1} - a^{k+1})$$

$$\leq dbn - ada^{\log_b n}.$$

But $a^{\log_b n} = n^{\log_b a}$, and therefore

$$f(n) \leq dbn - adn^{\log_b a} \quad \text{for } n = b^k.$$

If $a < b$, then $\log_b a < 1$ and by Theorem 5.2.5, $O(n^{\log_b a}) \subset O(n)$. It follows from Theorem 5.3.3 that if $a < b$, then f is $O(n)$.

If $a > b$, then $\log_b (a) > 1$ and therefore $O(n) \subset O(n^{\log_b a})$. It follows that if $a > b$, then f is $O(n^{\log_b a})$. ∎

Example

Suppose S is an arbitrary sequence of n distinct elements and we wish to build a binary search tree of minimum height which contains the elements of S as node values. The following algorithm can be used.

1. Find the median element m of S. (The median is the element of S that would appear in the $\lceil n/2 \rceil$th position if the sequence S were sorted.) The root of the tree is assigned the value m.

2. Form two sequences S_1 and S_2 such that S_1 consists of those elements of S which are less than m and S_2 consists of those elements of S which are greater than m.

3. Apply this procedure recursively to S_1 to construct the left subtree of the root, and to S_2 to construct the right subtree.

An $O(n)$ algorithm† exists for finding the kth largest (and therefore the $\lceil n/2 \rceil$th largest, or median) element of any sequence; it follows that there exists some

---

†A careful description of a linear algorithm to find the median of a sequence of elements is beyond our scope. The reader is referred to Aho, Hopcroft and Ullman [1974], page 97.

integer c such that the median of any set with n elements can be found with no more than cn comparisons. Thus, step 1 can be performed with at most cn comparisons. After the median m has been found, the sequences S_1 and S_2 can be formed by comparing m with every element $a_i \in S - \{m\}$; we add a_i to S_1 if $a_i < m$ and add it to S_2 if $a_i > m$. Thus step 2 can be accomplished with $n - 1$ comparisons. Consequently, we can characterize the number of comparisons necessary to build the binary search tree from S as follows:

$$f(n) \leq 2f\left(\frac{n}{2}\right) + cn + (n - 1).$$

Therefore,

$$f(1) \leq c + 1,$$

$$f(n) \leq 2f\left(\frac{n}{2}\right) + (c + 1)n.$$

Since f is monotone increasing, we can apply Theorem 5.3.4 and conclude that the number of comparisons made in constructing the search tree is $O(n \log n)$.

#

Problems: Section 5.3

1. In each of the following prove that the given expression is a solution for the recurrence system.

    (a) $y_0 = 2$,
         $y_n = 3y_{n-1}$ for $n > 0$.
         $y_n = 2 \cdot 3^n$.

    (b) $y_0 = 1$,
         $y_n = \dfrac{y_{n-1}}{n}$ for $n > 0$.
         $y_n = \dfrac{1}{n!}$.

    (c) $y_0 = 2$,
         $y_n = y_{n-1}^2$ for $n > 0$.
         $y_n = 2^{2^n}$.

2. Find a solution for each of the following recurrence systems and determine the asymptotic complexity of the solution. (The symbols a and b denote arbitrary positive constants.)

    (a) $x_0 = 1$,
         $x_n = x_{n-1} + a$ for $n > 0$.

    (b) $x_0 = a$,
         $x_n = x_{n-1} + b^n$ for $n > 0$.

    (c) $x_1 = 1$,
         $x_n = 2x_{n-1} - 1$ for $n > 1$.

    (d) $x_0 = 1$,
         $x_n = (n + 1)x_{n-1}$ for $n > 0$.

    (e) $x_1 = 1$,
         $x_n = ax_{n-1}$ for $n > 1$.

    (f) $x_0 = 0$,
         $x_n = x_{n-1} + n - 1$ for $n > 0$.

    (g) $x_0 = 3$,
         $x_n = 3x_{n-1} + n$ for $n > 0$.

3. (a) Find a recurrence system to describe the number of moves that must be made in a Tower of Hanoi problem with n discs, where $n > 0$. (See problem 5.1.21(a).)

    (b) Solve the recurrence system of part (a).

4. (a) Consider n coplanar straight lines, no two of which are parallel and no three of which pass through a common point. Find a recurrence system to describe the

number of disjoint areas into which the lines divide the plane. Show that $(n^2 + n + 2)/2$ is a solution.

(b) Suppose that $n \geq 3$ and exactly three of the lines pass through a common point. Find a recurrence system for the number of regions into which the lines divide the plane.

5. A *derangement* of n objects is permutation which leaves none of the objects fixed. Thus, if f is a derangement function defined on the first n natural numbers, then $f(k) \neq k$ for all $k < n$. Let g be the number of derangements of n objects. Argue the correctness of the following recursive characterization of g.

$$g(1) = 0,$$
$$g(2) = 1,$$
$$g(n) = (n-1)g(n-1) + (n-1)g(n-2) \qquad \text{for } n > 2.$$

(Hint: A derangement either interchanges the first element with another, or it does not.)

6. (a) The *total path length* of a tree is the sum of the lengths of all simple directed paths from the root of the tree to a node. Find a recurrence system for the minimum total path length of a complete n-ary tree of height h.

(b) Find the solution to the recurrence system of part (a).

(c) The *external path length* of a tree is the sum of the lengths of all simple directed paths from the root of the tree to a leaf. Find a recurrence system for the minimum external path length of a complete n-ary tree of height h.

(d) Find the solution to the recurrence system of part (c).

7. Prove Lemma 5.3.2b.

8. Let $f: \mathbf{N} \to \mathbf{R}$ be a function which satisfies the following relations where $b, c > 0$:

$$f(0) \leq c,$$
$$f(n) \leq af(n-1) + b \qquad \text{for } n > 0.$$

If a is a nonnegative real number, describe how the asymptotic behavior of f is affected by the value of a.

9. Prove parts (b) and (c) of Theorem 5.3.3.

10. It has been shown (Pohl [1972]) that if a vector A has n entries, then $\lceil \frac{3}{2}n - 2 \rceil$ comparisons suffice to find the largest and smallest entries of A. Modify the procedure MAXMIN so that it never requires more than $\lceil \frac{3}{2}n - 2 \rceil$ comparisons of elements of A for all $n \geq 1$. (Hint: Handle $n = 1$ and $n = 2$ as special cases, and make sure your algorithm does not divide an array with an even number of entries into two arrays both of which have an odd number of entries.)

11. (a) Construct a recursive procedure MAX2 to implement a divide and conquer strategy for finding the largest element in the entries $A(i), \ldots, A(j)$ of an array A. Your procedure should divide the array into two approximately equal subarrays.

(b) State the recurrence system which characterizes the complexity function f for MAX2 if $f(n)$ is defined to be the number of comparisons made between entries of an n element array A, where n is a power of 2.

(c) Find the solution of the recurrence system of part (b).

    (d)   Determine the asymptotic behavior of the complexity function.

    (e)   Design a procedure MAX3 to find the largest element in an array by dividing the array into 3 approximately equal subproblems.

    (f)   Describe how you could generalize this procedure to one which creates k subproblems. Discuss the asymptotic complexity of this class of algorithms.

12. (a)   Design a recursive procedure TWOMAX which finds the largest two elements of an array A.

    (b)   State the recurrence system for the complexity function f of TWOMAX where $f(n)$ is defined as in problem 11(b).

    (c)   Solve the recurrence system of part (b) and determine the asymptotic complexity of f.

13. (a)   A binary search such as that given in Fig. 5.3.2 can be viewed as an implementation of a tree search algorithm such as that given in Fig. 3.2.2. Describe how the entries of the array correspond to node values of the tree and how to find the values of the left son and right son of the root.

    (b)   The tree search algorithm given in a recursive form in Fig. 3.2.2 can also be given in an iterative form, as in Fig. 3.2.1. Write an iterative form of BINSEARCH (Fig. 5.3.2).

5.4 ANALYSIS OF ALGORITHMS

The evaluation and comparison of algorithms is a central concern of computer science. Two kinds of questions predominate:

    (a)   What is the cost of using a given algorithm to solve a problem of a specified class?

    (b)   What is the least costly algorithm which will solve the problems of a specified class?

By choosing an appropriate measure of cost, we can often answer such questions. If the same measure of cost is applied to different algorithms for the same task, we can compare algorithms and choose from among them. In some cases, we can establish a lower bound on the cost of solving the problems of a specified class; such a bound provides a measure of the inherent difficulty of solving those problems. Furthermore, if the cost of applying an algorithm is equal to the lower bound, then we can conclude that the algorithm is optimal for this measure, that is, no algorithm exists which will solve the problems of the class with a lower cost. The topics of algorithm analysis and computational complexity are concerned with the construction, evaluation, and comparison of algorithms.

    The cost of applying an algorithm can be measured in a variety of ways. It is often inappropriate to measure the cost of operations using real programs run on real machines because of the difficulty of generalizing such results. We usually prefer to measure the cost using a mathematical model based on an idealized programming language or computing machine. However, in any such analysis, the set of operations which can be performed must be specified and the cost associated with performing each operation must be given. For example, we may assume that all arithmetic operations cost the same or we may assume (more accurately, for most computers) that multiplication is more costly than addition. Alternatively, we may choose to ignore the cost of some operations. For example, the cost of applying some sorting algorithms is essentially proportional to the number of comparisons made between elements of the set being sorted. In the analysis of such sorting algorithms, it is common to ignore operations such as assignments, arithmetic operations, and comparisons of loop indices.

In this section we will consider some algorithms and discuss their cost of execution. In some cases we will also comment on the optimality of these algorithms. Optimality can be discussed in a variety of ways, of which two will be important to us here. First, we can investigate the *absolute optimality* of an algorithm with respect to a specified set of operations. If an algorithm is optimal in the absolute sense, then if the primitive operations are restricted appropriately, no algorithm can perform the task using fewer operations than the optimal algorithm. Second, there is the weaker concept of *asymptotic optimality*. Suppose f is the complexity function of an algorithm A which solves a specified problem. Then A is *asymptotically optimal* if for every other algorithm B that solves the problem, if the complexity function of B is g, then f is $O(g)$. Thus for sufficiently large arguments, the value of f is bounded by a multiple of the value of g. Informally, we say $O(f)$ is a lower bound on the asymptotic complexity of the class of algorithms. Note that two algorithms with distinct complexity functions can both be asymptotically optimal. In contrast, if f and g are complexity functions of algorithms for some problem class, and if f is optimal in the absolute sense, then $f(n) \leq g(n)$ for every argument $n \in \mathbf{N}$.

Table 5.2.1 describes how the growth of the cost of an algorithm is determined by its asymptotic behavior. As a rule of thumb, we can say that it is usually feasible to execute algorithms of $O(n)$ and $O(n \log n)$ complexity for fairly large values of n. Time or space limitations often make it difficult or impossible to execute $O(n^2)$ and $O(n^3)$ algorithms for even moderate values of n. Exponential algorithms (those of $O(a^n)$ where $a > 1$) cannot generally be executed except for small values of n.

We will now analyze several algorithms, characterize their complexity functions, and consider their optimality. We will describe algorithms for finding the maximum element of a set, algorithms for searching for a specified element in a set, and algorithms for sorting the elements of a set. All of the algorithms we describe are based on comparisons; that is, the result of applying the algorithm is determined by a sequence of comparisons between elements of a set. We will treat the question of optimality only for the class of algorithms based on comparisons where the number of outcomes of any comparison is bounded. (Most algorithms of interest have either two or three possible outcomes for each comparison, e.g., $<$ and $\geq$, or $<$, $=$ and $>$.) Thus, our claims that certain algorithms are asymptotically optimal depend on our considering only a restricted class of algorithms; the claims may not hold if we consider algorithms which are not based on comparisons or algorithms in which the number of outcomes of a comparison is not bounded.

Finding the largest element of an array: an $O(n)$ algorithm

Let $A[1:n]$ be a vector with $n \geq 1$ entries. We are to find the largest entry in A and set the variable *max* equal to its value. Let f be the complexity function such that $f(n)$ is the number of comparisons made between entries of A if A has n entries.

```
procedure MAX:
begin
    max ← A[1];
    for i = 2 until n do
        if max < A[i] then max ← A[i]
end
```

Fig. 5.4.1 An algorithm to find the maximum entry in an array
$A[1:n]$ where $n \geq 1$

We consider the algorithm MAX of Fig. 5.4.1. Each comparison in MAX occurs within a loop which is traversed for loop index values of $i = 2, 3, \ldots, n$. Hence the procedure MAX makes $n - 1$ comparisons of entries of A, and its complexity function is the following:

$$f: \mathbf{N} \to \mathbf{R},$$
$$f(1) = 0,$$
$$f(n) = n - 1 \qquad \text{for } n > 1.$$

Clearly f is $O(n)$, and therefore the algorithm is linear. We now show that MAX is, in fact, optimal in the absolute sense and therefore in the asymptotic sense as well.

Theorem 5.4.1: Any algorithm to find the maximum element of a set with n members, $n > 0$, must make at least $n - 1$ comparisons.

Proof: Each comparison establishes that one element is not larger than another. In order to find the maximum element, each of $n - 1$ elements must be shown (by means of a comparison) to be no larger than some other element. Hence $n - 1$ comparisons are necessary to find the maximum of n elements. ∎

It follows immediately from Theorem 5.4.1 that if the number of comparisons between elements of an array is used to measure the cost of applying an algorithm, then MAX is optimal in the absolute sense.

The procedure MAX uses more comparisons than just those between elements of A, since each execution of the loop will be preceded by a comparison of the value of the loop index i with n. If the algorithm were implemented as a decision tree for a particular n, or if the data items were read sequentially, then the comparisons associated with the loop index would be eliminated. Thus these additional comparisons are a consequence of the algorithm implementation. Since we are interested in the operations performed by the algorithms rather than their implementations, these comparisons are usually ignored.

   Alternative optimal methods exist for finding the maximum of a sequence of
n elements. In a sports tournament, players are often paired off for each round
of contests, with the winners of round i competing against each other in round
$i + 1$. The following graph represents this method for finding the best of eight
players; it uses seven comparisons. This approach generalizes easily to values of
n which are not powers of two.

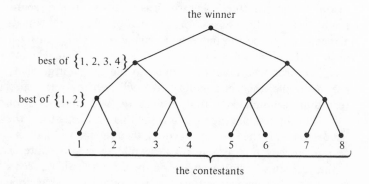

   After the winner has been found, the resulting labeled tree provides some help in
finding the second best player, since he must have been one of the three players who
lost to the winner. Thus, only two more matches need be played to find the second
place winner.

   The algorithms we have described for finding the largest element of a sequence
have the property that the cost is uniform over all problems of size n. In general,
however, the cost of applying an algorithm to a problem of size n may depend on
the particular problem solved. Consider, for example, sorting a list of n entries.
If all the entries are distinct, then there are $n!$ different permutations of the n
entries and consequently $n!$ different lists with the same set of entries. The cost of
applying a particular sorting algorithm to a list with these n entries will usually
depend on the order in which the entries appear; for example, if the list is nearly
sorted, then the algorithm may have to do very little work. The cost of applying
an algorithm to a problem of size n is usually based on either a *worst case* or an
average case analysis. A worst case analysis defines the cost of applying an algorithm to a problem of size n as the maximum cost over all problems of size n. Thus,
if f is a complexity function based on a worst case analysis, then for every problem
of size n, the cost of applying the algorithm is no greater than $f(n)$. In an average
case analysis, a probability distribution is assumed over the set of problems of size
n and the average cost is calculated based on this probability distribution. Such
an analysis often assumes all problems of size n are equally likely; in this case,
the value of $f(n)$ is equal to the sum of the costs of applying the algorithm to all
problems of size n divided by the number of problems of that size. Of the two
kinds of analysis, worst case is usually simpler because it only requires that we
determine how bad things can be and then analyze that single case, whereas an

average case analysis must account for all possible cases and then weight them appropriately.

Searching Algorithms

Sequential searching: an O(n) algorithm.

Consider the problem of accessing the records of a file. We assume that each record includes a *search key* which is used to retrieve records from the file. For example, if the file consists of information about individuals, the search key of a record might be the individual's name or social security number. In order to locate a record in a file, a *search argument* is specified. The result of a search is the set of records whose keys are equal to the search argument; if no such records are in the file, this set is empty. We will treat only the special case where each record has a unique key; thus, each search will return at most one record.

The simplest file organization for this problem stores the records in a linear list or vector. If the file has n records, then the list will have n entries. The simplest search procedure is a "sequential search"; this procedure examines the records in the order in which they appear on the list until either a record whose key is equal to the search argument is found or it is established that no such record is in the file. We define the cost of a search to be the number of records examined, i.e., the number of times the search argument is compared with the search key of a record. In the worst case, either the record sought will be the last record of the file or the record will not be in the file; all n records for the file must be examined to establish either of these possibilities. Thus, for a worst case analysis, the complexity function of a linear search is $f(n) = n$, and hence the search is of $O(n)$ complexity.

We now analyze the average case performance of a sequential search with the assumptions that each record of the list is equally likely to be the object of a search, and every search results in a record being found; thus, there are no unsuccessful searches. A search for the ith record will occur approximately one out of every n times and will require i records be examined. Since the complexity function f is defined to be the average number of records examined,

$$f(n) = \frac{1}{n}(1 + 2 + 3 + \cdots + n) = \frac{1}{n}\sum_{i=1}^{n} i = \frac{n(n+1)}{2n} = \frac{n+1}{2}.$$

Thus, an average case analysis (with the assumptions stated above) leads us to conclude that "on the average," each search of the file will examine about half the records. Note that the value of $f(n)$ for a worst case analysis is about twice that for an average case analysis, but both analyses yield complexity functions which are $O(n)$.

Searching with a binary search tree: an O(log n) algorithm

In Section 3.2 we described the use of binary search trees for storing and accessing the records of a file. If the height of a binary search tree is h, it was shown that searching for a record using the tree would require examining no more than $h + 1$ records in the file. If a file contains n records, $n \geq 1$, then the height h of the binary search tree satisfies the inequality

$$\lfloor \log n \rfloor \leq h \leq n - 1.$$

If $h = n - 1$, the tree is "degenerate" and each node of the tree has at most one son. In this case the tree has only one leaf and the records are accessed just as they would be if they were stored as successive entries in a linear list. If the height of the tree is $\lfloor \log n \rfloor$, then the tree is said to be "balanced." Generally, a balanced tree is one which is not too lopsided or skewed, i.e., one whose height is not very much greater than necessary in order to contain a specified number of nodes. We will use the following characterization of a balanced binary tree.

Definition 5.4.1:   A binary tree T of height h is *balanced* if T is complete and every path from the root of T to a leaf is of length h or $h - 1$.

The following theorem relates the number of nodes of a balanced binary tree to its height.

Theorem 5.4.2:   The height of a balanced binary tree with n nodes is $\lfloor \log n \rfloor$.

To measure the cost of searching with a binary search tree, we take the number of records in the file to be the problem size and define the cost of a search as the number of records examined during the search. By Theorem 5.4.2, a balanced binary search tree with n nodes is of height $h = \lfloor \log n \rfloor$. Since as many as $h + 1$ records may be examined in the course of a search, a worst case analysis of a search in a balanced binary tree yields the complexity function $f(n) = \lfloor \log n \rfloor + 1$. The search is therefore an $O(\log n)$ algorithm if the search tree is balanced. In fact, a balanced tree may not be possible if too many records in the file have the same key, but if all keys are distinct, then a balanced tree can be always constructed. (A recursive algorithm for constructing a balanced binary search tree was given in the last example of Section 5.3.)

Many ways of organizing files and searching for records have been developed, and whether a particular search algorithm is optimal depends on what operations are permitted and are consistent with the file organization. For search algorithms which locate records by comparing a search argument with record keys, a search which uses a balanced tree is asymptotically optimal. This result is established by the following theorem.

Theorem 5.4.3:   Let A be an algorithm to search for a value *arg* in a sequence S such that the output of A is either the index of *arg* in the sequence S or a report that the search was not successful. If f is a worst case complexity function (that is, $f(n)$ is the maximum number of comparisons made when S has n elements), then $\log n$ is $O(f)$.

Proof: We will treat the case where each comparison has no more than three possible outcomes, such as $<$, $=$, and $>$. The generalization to the case of k outcomes, $k > 1$, is straightforward.

Consider the decision tree representation of a search based on comparisons. Each internal node of the decision tree represents a comparison and has no more than three outgoing branches. Since the sequence S has n elements, the decision tree must have at least $n + 1$ leaves, where n of the leaves denote outcomes of the form "*arg* is the *i*th element of S" and one leaf denotes "*arg* is not an element of S." Since no node can have more than three sons, if h is the height of the decision tree, then $3^h \geq n + 1$, than is, $h \geq \log_3 (n + 1)$. Therefore some paths from the root to a leaf contain at least $\log_3 (n + 1)$ internal nodes, each of which represents a comparison made in the course of a search for some value of *arg*. It follows that if f is the worst case complexity function of a search based on comparisons, then for all n, $f(n) \geq \log_3 (n + 1)$, and hence $O(\log_3 (n + 1)) \subset O(f)$. Since $O(\log_3 (n + 1)) = O(\log_3 n) = O(\log n)$, it follows that $O(\log n) \subset O(f)$ and hence $\log n$ is $O(f)$. ▮

Corollary 5.4.3: The worst case performance of a search in a balanced binary search tree is asymptotically optimal.

Now consider the average case performance of searches using a binary search tree. For the purpose of this analysis, we assume that all records are equally likely to be the object of a search, and that every search is successful. Furthermore, we assume the binary search tree is balanced. Note that approximately half the nodes of a balanced binary search tree are leaves, approximately $\frac{3}{4}$ of the nodes are either leaves or one step removed, approximately $\frac{7}{8}$ of them are within two steps of a leaf, etc. Thus, unless n is small, most of the nodes of a binary search tree are nearly as far from the root as the leaves.

Let C_i be the number of comparisons required to find the ith record stored in the binary search tree T. The average cost C of a search in T is then

$$C = \frac{1}{n} \sum_{i=1}^{n} C_i$$

We can calculate C_i easily if we can determine the length of the path from the root of the search tree to the ith node; C_i is one greater than the length of this path, and therefore C is equal to n plus the sum of the lengths of all such paths.

Definition 5.4.2: Let T be a tree with n nodes, $a_1, a_2, \ldots, a_n$, and let d_i be the length of the unique directed path from the root of T to node a_i. Then the *total path length* of T, L_T, is defined as

$$L_T = \sum_{i=1}^{n} d_i.$$

Theorem 5.4.4: If T is a binary tree of height $h \geq 0$, then

$$L_T \leq (h - 1)2^{h+1} + 2.$$

Proof: The total path length L_T of a binary tree T of height h is greatest when all leaves are distance h from the root and T is complete, that is, each node of T

has either no sons or two sons. Such a tree has one node a distance 0 from the root, 2 nodes a distance 1 from the root, and in general 2^k nodes a distance k from the root for all $k \leq h$. The total path length of a complete binary tree is therefore no greater than $\sum_{i=0}^{h} i2^i$. From Theorem 2.5.3, it follows that

$$L_T \leq \sum_{i=0}^{h} i2^i = (h-1)2^{h+1} + 2. \quad \blacksquare$$

We now use the bound on L_T found in Theorem 5.4.4 to investigate the average case performance of a search in a balanced binary search tree for the special case where all leaves are distance h from the root. A complete binary tree of height h with all leaves a distance h from the root contains $2^{h+1} - 1$ nodes. Recall that the number of comparisons made in locating any record is 1 plus the length of the path from the root to the node where the record is stored. Hence, the number of comparisons necessary to locate each of the $n = 2^{h+1} - 1$ records exactly once is

$$L_T + n = (h-1)\,2^{h+1} + 2 + 2^{h+1} - 1 = h2^{h+1} + 1.$$

If we assume that all searches are successful, and all records are sought with equal probability, then the average cost of a search is

$$C = \frac{1}{n}(L_T + n) = \frac{h2^{h+1} + 1}{2^{h+1} - 1}.$$

But $2^{h+1} \geq h + 2$ for all $h \geq 0$. Hence,

$$C \leq \frac{h2^{h+1} + 1}{2^{h+1} - 1} + 2^{h+1} - (h+2) = h + 1,$$

Moreover,

$$C > \frac{h2^{h+1} + 1 - (h+1)}{2^{h+1} - 1} = \frac{h2^{h+1} - h}{2^{h+1} - 1} = h.$$

Thus, for this class of binary search trees, the average cost of a search lies between h and $h + 1$. Since both h and $h + 1$ are $O(\log n)$, it follows that the average search cost is $O(\log n)$. Note that worst case and average case performances of searches in a balanced binary search tree have the same asymptotic complexity.

Sorting Algorithms

Consider the problem of sorting a sequence of elements drawn from a linearly ordered set. We define the complexity function of a sorting algorithm which sorts by comparisons to be the function f such that $f(n)$ is either the maximum number of comparisons or the average number of comparisons required to sort a sequence of n elements. For this measure of complexity, we can use decision trees to show that $O(n \log n)$ is a lower bound for the worst case asymptotic complexity.

Theorem 5.4.5: Let A be an algorithm for sorting a finite sequence. If f is the worst case complexity function such that $f(n)$ is the maximum number of comparisons necessary to sort a sequence of n elements, then $O(n \log n) \subset O(f)$.

Proof: A decision tree can be used to represent any sorting algorithm based on comparisons. Each internal node of the decision tree will be associated with the comparison of some element x_i with another element x_j. Each possible outcome of a comparison is represented by an arc from the corresponding internal node. If the result of comparing x_i with x_j is either $x_i \leq x_j$ or $x_i > x_j$, then the decision tree is binary.† Each leaf of the decision tree must specify a rearrangement of the sequence which places the elements in sorted order. Since it may be necessary to apply any one of $n!$ permutations to arrange correctly the n elements of a sequence S, the decision tree must have at least $n!$ leaves.

The number of comparisons made by an algorithm to specify a particular permutation is the length of the path from the root to the leaf representing that permutation. A minimax algorithm to sort n elements is therefore represented by a tree with at least $n!$ nodes and of height as small as possible. Since a binary tree of height h has no more than 2^h leaves, the height of the decision tree must be large enough to satisfy the inequality $n! \leq 2^h$. Thus, $\log(n!) \leq h$. But for $n > 0$,

$$n! = n\cdot(n-1)\cdot(n-2)\cdot\ldots\cdot 2\cdot 1 \geq n\cdot(n-1)\cdot(n-2)\cdot\ldots\cdot \left\lceil \frac{n}{2} \right\rceil > \left(\frac{n}{2}\right)^{n/2}$$

and therefore

$$\log(n!) > \frac{n}{2}\log\left(\frac{n}{2}\right) = \frac{n}{2}(\log n - \log 2)$$

$$= \frac{n}{2}(\log n - 1)$$

$$= \frac{1}{2}n\log n - \frac{n}{2}.$$

Since $h \geq \log(n!)$, it follows that $h > \frac{1}{2}n\log n - \frac{1}{2}n$. But h is the largest number of comparisons required to sort n elements with a decision tree of height h; hence $f(n) = h$. Therefore $f(n) > 1/2\, n\log n - n/2$ and hence $O(f) \supset O(n\log n)$. ∎

The preceding theorem establishes that any $O(n\log n)$ sorting algorithm is asymptotically optimal. Several $O(n\log n)$ sorting algorithms are known and we will present one later in this section, but the most straightforward sorting algorithms are $O(n^2)$, and we begin by analyzing one of these.

Bubble sort: an $O(n^2)$ algorithm

The n entries of the vector A are to be sorted into nondecreasing order; thus, the smallest entry is to be placed in $A[1]$ and the largest is to be placed in $A[n]$. The procedure BUBBLE given in Fig. 5.4.2 makes $n - 1$ passes over the vector A, where a pass always starts at $A[n]$ and proceeds upward through the unsorted portion of the vector. Each pass consists of a sequence of steps, each of which compares some $A[i]$ with $A[i + 1]$ and interchanges their values if they are in the

---

†We leave it as an exercise to show that if the decision tree is ternary with branches labelled $<$, $>$, or $=$, then $O(n\log n)$ is still a lower bound on the worst case asymptotic complexity.

procedure BUBBLE(n):

  for $j \leftarrow 1$ **step** 1 **until** $n - 1$ **do**

    for $i \leftarrow n - 1$ **step** -1 **until** j **do**

      if $A[i] > A[i + 1]$ **then** interchange $A[i]$ and $A[j + 1]$

Fig. 5.4.2   Bubble sort of $A[1:n]$

wrong relative order, i.e., if $A[i] > A[i + 1]$, then the entries are interchanged. The initial pass starts with $i = n - 1$ and continues until $i = 1$. At the end of the first pass, the smallest entry of A has been "bubbled up" into the position $A[1]$ and need not be considered further. In the second pass, the value of i ranges from $n - 1$ to 2; this pass bubbles the smallest entry of $A[2] \ldots A[n]$ into $A[2]$. In general, in the jth pass the index i ranges from $n - 1$ to j and the jth smallest element of A is bubbled into $A[j]$. After the $(n - 1)$th pass, the values of $A[1], A[2], \ldots, A[n - 1]$ are all in place, and consequently the largest entry of A has been moved to $A[n]$.

To analyze the bubble sort, we first observe that there are $n - 1$ passes, and the jth pass makes $n - j$ comparisons. The total number of comparisons is therefore $\sum_{j=1}^{n-1} (n - j) = n(n - 1)/2 = n^2/2 - n/2$. It follows from Theorem 5.2.5 that the bubble sort is an $O(n^2)$ algorithm.

Alternatively, the complexity function of a bubble sort can be characterized with a recurrence system. The boundary condition is obtained by noting that no comparisons are necessary for a list with one entry. For the recurrence relation, we observe that if a list has n entries, where $n > 1$, then $(n - 1)$ comparisons are used to move the smallest entry into place and this process leaves a list of $n - 1$ entries to be sorted. Thus, the recurrence system is

$$T(1) = 0,$$
$$T(n) = T(n - 1) + n - 1 \qquad \text{for } n > 1,$$

which has the solution $n(n - 1)/2$.

We have remarked that $O(n \log n)$ sorting algorithms exist. Since the bubble sort is an $O(n^2)$ algorithm and $O(n \log n)$ is properly contained in $O(n^2)$, it follows that the bubble sort is not asymptotically optimal. Nevertheless, this sorting algorithm is commonly used where the value of n is not too large and programming effort is to be kept to a minimum. A modified version is also useful if only the first k entries of the sorted list are to be found; in this case only k passes need be made. The bubble sort has the additional virtue that it requires almost no space in addition to that used to contain the input vector.

The bubble sort operates by successively reducing the problem; each pass reduces the size of the unsorted portion of the vector by 1. Sequential search of a list of length n is similar; each comparison either finds the record sought or reduces the problem size by 1. If the record sought is not found at step i of a sequential search, then a problem of size $n - i$ must be solved. Compare this with a binary search: if the ith comparison of a binary search does not locate the record, the problem is reduced to one of approximate size $n/2^i$. Two subproblems are defined at each step of a binary search, but each subproblem is only about half as big as the original problem, and only one of them needs to be solved. Because the subproblems are approximately equal in size, the algorithm is said to be "balanced."

An algorithm is *balanced* if for some k, $0 < k < 1$, the algorithm breaks a problem of size n (where n is sufficiently large) into a collection of subproblems, none of which is greater than size kn. In contrast, an algorithm may reduce a problem of size n to one of size $n - p$ where p is a fixed integer; such an algorithm is not balanced. Thus, bubble sort and sequential search are not balanced algorithms because they reduce a problem of size n to one of size $n - 1$. Binary search, on the other hand, is balanced because it changes a problem of size n into one of size $n/2$. Moreover, the binary search of Fig. 5.3.2 would remain balanced even if m were assigned the value of $\lfloor (i + j)/r \rfloor$ for some $r > 2$ rather than $\lfloor (i + j)/2 \rfloor$. Such a "skewed" binary search would still have $O(\log n)$ complexity, but it would not be as efficient as the usual binary search. In general, the most efficient algorithms are those which are balanced, and among the balanced algorithms the most efficient are those which break a problem into subproblems of approximately equal size.

We will now describe a sorting algorithm which implements a balanced divide and conquer strategy; then we will show the algorithm is asymptotically optimal by proving that the complexity function of the algorithm is $O(n \log n)$.

Mergesort: an $O(n \log n)$ sorting algorithm

Mergesort exploits the ease with which two sorted lists can be merged into a single sorted list. The input to mergesort is an unsorted list. If the list has more than one entry, the algorithm splits the list into two sublists, sorts them recursively, and then merges the resulting lists into a single sorted list which is the output. The divide and conquer characteristic is manifested by the strategy of breaking the original unsorted list into smaller lists, each of which is then processed and the results combined by merging the smaller lists. If the original list is broken into sublists of approximately equal size, the algorithm is balanced.

As before, we will define the cost of sorting a list of length n to be the number of comparisons made between elements of the list. In mergesort, all such comparisons are made in the process of merging sorted sublists. In order to determine the worst case asymptotic complexity of mergesort, we need the following result.

Theorem 5.4.6: Two sorted lists of lengths m and n respectively can be merged into a single sorted list using no more than $m + n - 1$ comparisons.

Proof: Let LIST1 and LIST2 be two lists of length m and n respectively, both sorted in ascending order. We will describe an algorithm to merge LIST1 and LIST2. At each step, the entries at the heads of the lists LIST1 and LIST2 are compared and the smaller of the two is removed and added to the tail of LIST, which is initially empty. This process is repeated until one of the two input lists is empty, at which time the remainder of the nonempty list is concatenated to the tail of LIST. Since each comparison of an element of LIST1 with an element of LIST2 results in an element being removed from one of these lists and added to LIST, there can be no more than $m + n$ comparisons. Moreover, since no comparison can be made when either of the lists is empty, there can be at most $m + n - 1$ comparisons. Thus, the algorithm will merge two sorted lists into a single sorted list while making no more than $m + n - 1$ comparisons between elements of the two lists. ▮

The procedure MERGE given in Fig. 5.4.3 is an implementation of the algorithm described in the preceding proof.

```
procedure MERGE(LIST1, LIST2):
begin
        m ← LENGTH(LIST1); n ← LENGTH(LIST2);
        i ← 1; j ← 1;
        make LIST empty;
        comment:   move entries from LIST1 and LIST2 to LIST until one list is
                       exhausted.
        while i ≤ m and j ≤ n do
            begin
                if LIST1[i] ≤ LIST2[j] then
                    begin
                        concatenate LIST1[i] to end of LIST;
                        i ← i + 1
                    end
                else
                    begin
                        concatenate LIST2[j] to end of LIST;
                        j ← j + 1
                    end
            end;
        comment:   add remainder of nonempty input list to LIST.
        if i ≤ m then concatenate LIST1[i] . . . LIST1[m] to LIST
        else concatenate LIST2[j] . . . LIST2[n] to LIST;
        return LIST
    end
```

Fig. 5.4.3   Procedure to merge two sorted lists

The next theorem shows that any algorithm to merge two lists of lengths m and n requires $m + n - 1$ comparisons for some pairs of lists.

Theorem 5.4.7:   Let A be an algorithm which merges two sorted lists on the basis of comparisons between list entries. There exist an infinite number of values of m, $n \in N$ and lists of lengths m and n respectively such that the algorithm A requires at least $m + n - 1$ comparisons to merge the lists.

Proof: It suffices to treat the case $m = n$. Let LIST1 and LIST2 be lists of length m such that for all i, $\text{LIST1}[i] < \text{LIST2}[i] < \text{LIST1}[i + 1]$. Then the merged output LIST must be constructed by selecting elements from the lists alternately. If we represent the original lists by the following pair of digraphs,

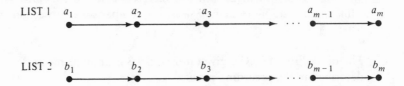

then the output LIST can be represented by the following digraph:

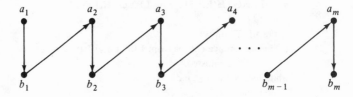

Each edge of the digraph of LIST represents the result of a single comparison. If any comparison is not made, the resulting partial subdigraph is consistent with more than one ordering. Since a merging algorithm must be able to produce any of the orderings consistent with such a partial subdigraph, all the comparisons must be made. Because the digraph has $2m - 1$ edges, it follows that $m + n - 1$ comparisons are necessary. ∎

There exist values of m and n such that fewer than $m + n - 1$ comparisons will suffice to merge two sorted lists. For example, if $n = 1$, then merging can be done by inserting the single element of LIST2 in the sorted list LIST1; this requires only $\lceil \log(m + 1) \rceil$ comparisons using binary search. But the preceding theorem shows that for some values of m and n, $m + n - 1$ comparisons are necessary.

The procedure MERGESORT, which uses the procedure MERGE as a subroutine, is given in Fig. 5.4.4. The next theorem establishes that the worst case behavior of MERGESORT is asymptotically optimal.

procedure MERGESORT(LIST):
if LENGTH(LIST) ≤ 1 **then return** LIST
else
    begin
        $k \leftarrow$ LENGTH(LIST);
        set LIST1 to LIST[1] ... LIST[$\lfloor k/2 \rfloor$];
        set LIST2 to LIST[$\lfloor k/2 \rfloor + 1$] ... LIST[k];
        return MERGE(MERGESORT(LIST1), MERGESORT(LIST2))
    end

Fig. 5.4.4 Mergesort

Theorem 5.4.8:   If LIST is a list of n items and MERGESORT is used to sort LIST, then the number of comparisons made between elements of LIST is $O(n \log n)$.

Proof: We will apply Theorem 5.3.4, which requires that we characterize the number of comparisons by a recurrence system in the form

$$f(1) \leq c,$$
$$f(n) \leq af(n/b) + cn \qquad \text{for } n = b^k \text{ where } k > 0.$$

Procedure MERGESORT divides a problem of size $n = 2^k$ into two problems of size $n/2$, and therefore $a = b = 2$. The term cn must bound the number of comparisons made in merging the two resulting sorted sublists. Since the sublists are both of length $n/2$, by Theorem 5.4.6, this will require no more than $n - 1$ comparisons. We therefore choose $c = 1$. This value obviously suffices for the boundary condition as well, since no comparisons are made by the procedure MERGESORT for the case $n = 1$. Since $a = b$, and $f(n)$ is monotone increasing, it follows from Theorem 5.3.4 that f is $O(n \log n)$.   ∎

The preceding theorem together with Theorem 5.4.5 shows that the worst case behavior of MERGESORT is asymptotically optimal. A number of other $O(n \log n)$ sorting algorithms are known, including *heapsort*, which has a worst case behavior of $O(n \log n)$ and *quicksort*, which has an average case behavior of $O(n \log n)$ but a worst case behavior of $O(n^2)$. A careful treatment of these algorithms is beyond our scope; the reader is referred to Aho, Hopcroft and Ullman [1974].

Problems: Section 5.4

1. Construct a binary decision tree of minimum height for finding the maximum of four elements. Prove that your tree is of minimum height.

2. It can be shown that using comparisons to find the largest and second largest elements of a sequence of length n requires $n + \lceil \log n \rceil - 2$ comparisons, where the outcome of each comparison is $<$, $=$, or $>$. Describe an algorithm which accomplishes the task with this number of comparisons.

3. Prove Theorem 5.4.2.

4. (a) Find an expression for the minimum total path length of a balanced binary tree of height h.
    (b) Estimate the cost of an average search in a balanced binary search tree of height h which has minimum total path length. Assume all searches are successful.
    (c) Use Theorem 5.4.3 to find the average case asymptotic complexity of a search in a balanced binary search tree.

5. In this section we used decision trees to investigate the performance of searches in binary search trees. The distinction between these classes of trees is an important one; a decision tree is a representation of an algorithm, while a binary search tree is a data structure. Construct the decision tree corresponding to a search in the following binary search tree. The search is to return the node index if the record sought is found; otherwise it is to return "not found." Each node of the search tree is labelled $i\!:\!j$, where i is the node index and j is the key value of the record stored at the node.

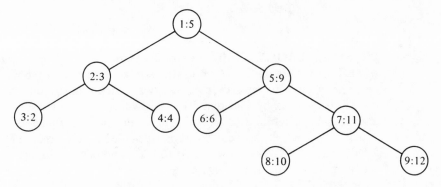

6. In this section it was shown that the worst case asymptotic complexity of a search in a balanced binary search tree is $O(\log n)$. Characterize the asymptotic behavior of the worst case performance for the set of all binary search trees with n nodes; i.e., what happens if we drop the restriction that the tree is balanced?

7. Find the worst case asymptotic complexity of a ternary tree search as described in Section 3.2. Assume the ternary search tree is balanced.

8. Theorem 5.4.5 was proved using the assumption that a comparison of two elements resulted in one of two possible outcomes: either $x_i < x_j$ or $x_i \geq x_j$. Show that if three outcomes are permitted (i.e., $x_i < x_j$, $x_i > x_j$, or $x_i = x_j$) the result still holds.

9. Consider the algorithm for sorting by interchange given in Fig. 5.4.5. The input is

```
procedure SORT(n):
for i ← 1 until n − 1 do
    begin
        comment:  find minimum entry in A[i: n].
        min ← A[i];
        position ← i;
        for j ← i + 1 until n do
            if A[j] < min then
                begin
                    min ← A[j];
                    position ← j
                end;
        comment:  interchange minimum entry with A[i].
        A[position] ← A[i];
        A[i] ← min
    end
```

Fig. 5.4.5 Sorting the array $A[1:n]$ by interchange

the number of entries in the vector A; when the algorithm terminates, the entries of A are sorted in nondecreasing order. The algorithm makes a sequence of $n - 1$ passes with the ith pass finding the smallest entry in $A[i : n]$ and interchanging it with $A[i]$. Prior to the ith pass, the first $i - 1$ entries are in place. Let $f(n)$ be the number of comparisons made in sorting a vector with n entries. Find the asymptotic behavior of f.

10. The final example of Section 5.3 described how a binary search tree can be constructed from an unsorted sequence of length n using $O(n \log n)$ comparisons. Prove that it is not possible to accomplish this task with $O(n)$ comparisons. (Hint: Show that if this task could be accomplished with $O(n)$ comparisons, then we could devise an $O(n)$ algorithm to sort by comparisons.)

11. Let $A[0 : n]$ be a vector of coefficients and consider the problem of evaluating the polynomial

$$P_n(z) = \sum_{i=0}^{n} A[i]\, z^i$$

for an arbitrary real argument z. Define the time complexity function f of an algorithm to evaluate $P_n(z)$ as the function such that $f(n)$ is the maximum number of multiplications required to evaluate $P_n(z)$ for any vector $A[0 : n]$.

(a) Find the asymptotic complexity of the following algorithms for evaluating $P_n(z)$.

 (i) (This algorithm is known as *Horner's method* and is known to use a minimal number of multiplications.)

    procedure HORNER:
    begin
        value ← $A[n]$;
        for i ← $n - 1$ **step** -1 **until** 0 **do**
            value ← (*value* $*$ z) $+$ $A[i]$
    end

 (ii) **procedure** TWO:
    begin
        power ← 1;
        value ← $A[0]$;
        for i ← 1 **until** n **do**
            begin
                power ← *power* $*$ z;
                value ← *value* $+$ ($A[i]$ $*$ *power*)
            end
    end

 (iii) **procedure** THREE:
    begin
        value ← 0;
        for i ← 0 **until** n **do**
            begin
                summand ← $A[i]$;
                for j ← 1 **until** i **do** *summand* ← *summand* $*$ z;
                value ← *value* $+$ *summand*
            end
    end

(b) Suppose it is known that $A[i] = 0$ for all odd i. Construct an algorithm to take advantage of this restriction and analyze its asymptotic complexity.

12. (a) Using the programming language of this text, write a recursive procedure to perform a sequential search on an array $A[i:j]$, where $i < j$.

(b) Write a recursive procedure to implement the interchange sort of Figure 5.4.5. (*Note:* It would be poor practice to implement either of these algorithms recursively. The exercise will illustrate, however, that they can be viewed as examples of unbalanced divide and conquer algorithms.)

Suggestions for Further Reading

The counting techniques described in this chapter are a part of *combinatorial mathematics*. Liu [1968] is an excellent introduction to this area. A somewhat more concise treatment of some of the same topics is given by Even [1973]; this work emphasizes algorithmic techniques and is particularly appropriate for computer science. The book by Bellman, Cooke and Lockett [1970] is a readable and informal introduction to some combinatorial techniques.

The analysis of algorithms is the subject of the book by Aho, Hopcroft and Ullman [1974]. Knuth, in his series *The Art of Computer Programming*, presents and analyzes many algorithms.

6

INFINITE SETS

6.0 INTRODUCTION

Many interesting and important sets are not finite; two obvious examples are the set of natural numbers and the set of all ALGOL programs. But even with these sets, we will never have to treat more than a finite number of the individual elements. For example, it should suffice to be able to answer questions about all ALGOL programs with less than, say, $10^{10^{10}}$ symbols; there is no need to find a way to answer the same questions for all ALGOL programs. It can therefore be argued that we are only interested in a finite number of ALGOL programs. Then why should the computer scientist be interested in infinite sets? In fact, treating infinite sets is often easier and more useful than dealing with the finite subset in which we are interested. Many infinite sets of interest are inductively defined; investigations of such sets tend to produce results about the entire infinite set and often provide insight into the structure of the set and its elements.

As with finite sets, we are often interested in the size, or cardinality, of an infinite set. *Cardinality arguments*, based on principles similar to the pigeonhole principle, can be used to establish important results. For example, we will use cardinality arguments to show that there exist tasks which cannot be performed by any computer. This is demonstrated by showing that there are more tasks than there are programs; it follows immediately that some tasks cannot be performed by any of the programs. This technique will be used to show that there exist real numbers which cannot be computed by any computer program, even if a computer of unlimited storage and speed is assumed to exist.

6.1 FINITE AND INFINITE SETS

Finite sets can be distinguished from infinite sets using either of two definitions. We will present both definitions and illustrate their use.

Definition 6.1.1a: A set A is *finite* with cardinality $n \in \mathbf{N}$ if there is a bijection from the set $\{0, 1, \ldots, n - 1\}$ to A. A set is *infinite* if it is not finite.

Theorem 6.1.1:   The set $\mathbf{N}$ of natural number is infinite.

Proof: To prove $\mathbf{N}$ is not finite, we must show that there is no $n \in \mathbf{N}$ such that a bijection exists from $\{0, 1, \ldots, n - 1\}$ to $\mathbf{N}$. Let n be any element of $\mathbf{N}$ and f an arbitrary function from $\{0, 1, 2, \ldots, n - 1\}$ to $\mathbf{N}$. Let

$$k = 1 + \max \{f(0), f(1), \ldots, f(n - 1)\}.$$

Then $k \in \mathbf{N}$, but for every $x \in \{0, 1, \ldots, n - 1\}$, $f(x) \neq k$. Hence, f cannot be a surjection, and therefore f is not a bijection. Since n and f were chosen arbitrarily, we conclude that $\mathbf{N}$ is infinite.   ∎

To prove a set A is infinite by using definition 6.1.1a, one must establish that no bijection exists from $\{0, 1, \ldots, n - 1\}$ to A for any n. Because it is necessary to rule out an infinite number of possibilities, such a proof can be quite difficult. For this reason, it is often useful to use the following alternate definitions of finite and infinite sets.

Definition 6.1.1b: A set A is *infinite* if there exists an injection $f : A \to A$ such that $f(A)$ is a proper subset of A. A set is *finite* if it is not infinite.

Definition 6.1.1a states explicitly how to recognize a finite set and then says that everything else is infinite; Definition 6.1.1b does just the reverse. It is usually most convenient to use the first definition to show that a set is finite, and the second to show that a set is infinite. Definitions 6.6.1a and 6.6.1b can be shown to be equivalent by using the Axiom of Choice.† In our discussions we will use whichever definition is most convenient.

Using Definition 6.1.1a, we can give a shorter proof for Theorem 6.1.1 than the one given previously.

Theorem 6.1.1:   The set $\mathbf{N}$ of natural numbers is an infinite set.

Proof: The map $f : \mathbf{N} \to \mathbf{N}$ defined by $f(x) = 2x$ is an injection whose image is the proper subset of even integers.   ∎

†The Axiom of Choice is a principle of mathematical reasoning of considerable power when treating infinite sets. It can be stated in a bewildering variety of forms; one of the more easily understood statements of the axiom is the following:

Axiom of Choice: If C is a collection of nonempty sets, then there exists a set T such that T has as elements exactly one x from each set $S \in C$.

Conceptually this principle allows us to choose an arbitrary element from any nonempty set, and in fact make an infinity of such choices. This seemingly reasonable assertion has some discomforting implications. The interested reader is referred to Wilder [1965] for a discussion of the Axiom of Choice and a proof of the equivalence of Definitions 6.1.1a and 6.1.1b.

Examples

(a) The set of real numbers, **R**, is infinite. We use Definition 6.1.1b and the following map:

$$f: \mathbf{R} \to \mathbf{R},$$
$$f(x) = x + 1 \quad \text{if } x \geq 0,$$
$$f(x) = x \quad \text{if } x < 0.$$

Then f is an injection and $f(\mathbf{R}) = \{x \mid x \in \mathbf{R} \land x \notin [0, 1)\}$.

(b) Let $\Sigma = \{a, b\}$. Then Σ^* is infinite. Let $f: \Sigma^* \to \Sigma^*$ be defined by $f(x) = ax$. Then f is an injection and the image of f is the proper subset of Σ^* which contains all strings beginning with the letter a.

(c) The closed interval, $[0, 1]$, is infinite. The function $f: [0, 1] \to [0, 1]$ defined by $f(x) = x/2$ is an injection whose image is the proper subset $[0, 1/2]$.   #

The following theorems establish some of the important properties of finite and infinite sets.

Theorem 6.1.2:   Let A' be a subset of A. If A' is infinite, then A is infinite.

Proof: If A' is infinite, then there must be a proper subset A'' of A' and an injection $f: A' \to A'$ such that $f(A') = A''$. To show that A is infinite, we will extend the domain of f to all of A by mapping each element of $A - A'$ to itself. In particular, we define $g: A \to A$ as follows:

$$g(x) = f(x) \quad \text{if } x \in A',$$
$$g(x) = x \quad \text{if } x \in A - A'.$$

Then g is injective, and the image of g does not include the nonempty set $A' - A''$; this establishes that A is infinite. (Figure 6.1.1 illustrates the construction used in the proof: the shaded portion is not in the image of g.) ▌

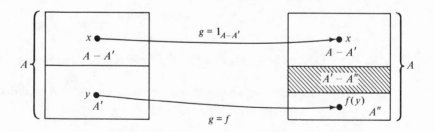

Fig. 6.1.1 Construction for Theorem 6.1.2

Example

Let A denote the set of ALGOL programs which never halt. We will show the set A is infinite by constructing an infinite subset $A' \subset A$ of programs which never halt.

begin
    label: **go to** *label*
end

This program, which we denote by P_0, is an element of A. By inserting the statement

go to *label*;

immediately after **begin**, we have a different program P_1 which is also in A. Consider the program P_n obtained from P_0 by inserting n copies of the statement "**go to** *label*;" after **begin**. Then $A' = \{P_0, P_1, P_2, \ldots\}$ is an infinite subset of A. Hence, by Theorem 6.1.2, A is infinite. We can use a similar construction to show that the set of ALGOL programs which always halt is infinite.   #

Corollary 6.1.2:   Every subset of a finite set is finite.

Proof: The result follows from the contrapositive of Theorem 6.1.2.   ∎

Theorem 6.1.3:   Let $f : A \to B$ be an injection and suppose that A is infinite. Then B is infinite.

The proof is left as an exercise.

The next theorem shows that the property of a set being infinite is preserved under certain set operations.

Theorem 6.1.4:   Let A and B be sets where A is infinite. Then
(a) $\mathcal{P}(A)$ is infinite,
(b) $A \cup B$ is infinite,
(c)   if $B \neq \phi$, then $A \times B$ is infinite,
(d)   if $B \neq \phi$, then A^B is infinite.

Proof: We will prove parts (a) and (c) and leave the others as exercises.
(a)   Define the map f as follows:

$$f : A \to \mathcal{P}(A),$$

$$f(x) = \{x\}.$$

Then f is an injection and it follows from Theorem 6.1.3 that $\mathcal{P}(A)$ is infinite.

(c)   Since $B \neq \phi$, we can choose some element $b \in B$, and define the map

$$f : A \to A \times B,$$

$$f(x) = \langle x, b \rangle.$$

Since A is infinite and f is injective, it follows from Theorem 6.1.3 that $A \times B$ is infinite.   ∎

This section has introduced the notion of infinite set and the use of injections to show that sets are not finite. We are accustomed to dealing with finite sets, where any injection from a set to itself is also a surjection. In contrast, infinite sets do not have this property and we have used this fact to distinguish between the classes of finite and infinite sets. In a later section, injections will play a crucial role; we will use them to determine when two infinite sets are the same size, as well as to establish when one infinite set is "larger" than another.

Problems: Section 6.1

1. Prove that the set [0, 1] is infinite using Definition 6.1.1a.

2. For some general purpose programming language, prove that the set of all programs which halt and have no input statements is infinite.

3. (a) Prove that the intersection of two infinite sets is not necessarily infinite, i.e., the class of infinite sets is not closed under intersection.
    (b) Let A and B be infinite sets such that $B \subset A$. Is the set $A - B$ necessarily finite? Is it necessarily infinite? Give examples to support your assertions.

4. Prove Theorem 6.1.3.

5. Prove parts (b) and (d) of Theorem 6.1.4.

6. Determine which of the following sets are finite and which are infinite. If the set is finite, find an expression for its cardinal number.
    (a) The set of all strings in $\{a, b\}^*$ of prime length.
    (b) The set of all strings in $\{a, b, c\}^*$ of length no greater than k.
    (c) The positive rational numbers, $\mathbf{Q}+ = \{x \mid x \in \mathbf{Q} \land x > 0\}$.
    (d) The set of all $m \times n$ matrices with entries from $\{0, 1, \ldots, k\}$, where k, m, and n are given positive integers.
    (e) The set of all ALGOL programs with four statements.
    (f) The set of all propositional forms over the propositional variables P, Q, R, and S.
    (g) The set of all functions from $\{0, 1\}$ to $\mathbf{I}$.
    (h) The set of all points in $\mathbf{R} \times \mathbf{R}$ with positive integer coordinates where the points lie properly between the axes and the hyperbola $y = 3/x$.
    (i) $\mathbf{N}^\phi$

6.2 COUNTABLE AND UNCOUNTABLE SETS

When dealing with sets, fundamental questions often occur concerning how "big" a set is, and whether one set is larger than another. For the case of finite sets, the natural numbers provide the basis for answering such questions; we characterize the size of a finite set A by saying that A has cardinality n if A has n elements. In his work on set theory, Cantor developed a technique for measuring the size or cardinality of infinite as well as finite sets. The numbers which are used to measure the size of a set are called *cardinal numbers*. In the following sections, we will introduce some of the infinite cardinal numbers and explore their properties.

A formal definition of the cardinal numbers requires considerable care; for example, the concept of "the set of all cardinal numbers" leads to a set-theoretic paradox. We can avoid paradoxes by introducing new cardinal numbers one at a time, and since we are interested in only a few of them, this presents no difficulties. The technique used for establishing the size of an infinite set is essentially the same as that used for finite sets. For the finite sets, each set of the form

$$\{0, 1, 2, \ldots, n - 1\}$$

is used as a "standard set" with which other sets are compared by means of bijections. Thus, a finite set A has cardinality n if and only if there is a bijection from $\{0, 1, \ldots, n - 1\}$ to A. Each time we introduce a new infinite cardinal number α we will choose an appropriate standard set S and assert "the set A has cardinality α (or, the cardinal number of A is α) if there is a bijection from the set S to A."

In the last section, we proved that the set of natural numbers $\mathbf{N}$ is infinite. Since no natural number can be the cardinality of $\mathbf{N}$, we must introduce a standard set for $|\mathbf{N}|$. We choose $\mathbf{N}$ itself to be the standard set and denote $|\mathbf{N}|$ by $\aleph_0$, called *aleph null*†. This results in the following definition.

Definition 6.2.1:   A set A is of cardinality $\aleph_0$, denoted $|A| = \aleph_0$, if there is a bijection from $\mathbf{N}$ to A.

Examples

    (a) $|\mathbf{I}+| = \aleph_0$.
The function $f \colon \mathbf{N} \to \mathbf{I}+$ defined by $f(x) = x + 1$ is a bijection.
    (b) $|\mathbf{I}| = \aleph_0$.
The function $f \colon \mathbf{N} \to \mathbf{I}$ defined by $f(x) = x/2$ if x is even, $f(x) = -(x + 1)/2$ if x is odd, is a bijection.   #

The existence of a bijection from either $\mathbf{N}$ or some set $\{0, 1, 2, \ldots, n - 1\}$ to a set A suggests that one can "count" the elements of A, even though the counting process might not terminate. This leads to the following terminology.

Definition 6.2.2:   A set A is *countably infinite* if $|A| = \aleph_0$. The set A is *countable*, or *denumerable*, if it is either finite or countably infinite. The set A is *uncountable*, or *uncountably infinite*, if it is not countable.

We say a set can be *enumerated* if its elements can be listed. The list may be finite or infinite, and repetitions may occur, that is, not all entries of the list need be distinct. If a list enumerates the set A, then every entry in the list is an element of A and every element of A appears as an entry of the list. These concepts can be formalized as follows.

Definition 6.2.3:   An *initial segment of* $\mathbf{N}$ is either the set $\mathbf{N}$ or else a set of the first n natural numbers, $\{0, 1, 2, \ldots, n - 1\}$.

---

†$\aleph$ is the first letter of the Hebrew alphabet. This notation was introduced by Cantor.

Definition 6.2.4:   Let A be a set. An *enumeration of A* is a surjective function f from an initial segment of N to A. If f is injective as well (and therefore bijective), then f is an *enumeration without repetitions*; if f is not injective, then f is an *enumeration with repetitions*.

When an enumeration f is presented, the function is usually specified implicitly by giving the sequence $\langle f(0), f(1), f(2), \ldots \rangle$. We will refer to f as an *enumeration function*.

Examples

(a)   If $A = \phi$, there is only one enumeration of A; it is the empty function.
(b)   If $A = \{a, b, c\}$, then $\langle a, b, a, c \rangle$ and $\langle b, c, a \rangle$ are both finite enumerations of A, the first with repetitions and the second without.
(c)   Let A be the set of even natural numbers. Then

$$\langle 0, 2, 4, \ldots \rangle \text{ and}$$

$$\langle 2, 0, 6, 4, 10, 8, \ldots \rangle$$

are both enumerations of A. (The second enumeration function is $f(n) = 2(n + 1)$ if n is even and $f(n) = 2(n - 1)$ if n is odd.)   #

Theorem 6.2.1:   A set A is countable if and only if there exists an enumeration of A.

Proof:
(a)   (only if) If A is countable, then A is finite or A is countably infinite. Then, by definition, there exists a bijection from an initial segment of N to the set A. This establishes that if A is countable, then there exists an enumeration of A.
(b)   (if) We assume that f is an enumeration of a set A. We consider two cases.

Case 1:   If A is finite, then by the definition of a countable set, A is countable.

Case 2:   Suppose A is not finite and f is an enumeration of A. The enumeration f must necessarily have the entire set N as its domain. If f is a bijection, then by the definition of a countably infinite set, the cardinality of A is $\aleph_0$ and A is countable. Suppose f is an enumeration but not a bijection. In order to show that A is countable, we will describe how to construct a bijection g by eliminating the repetitions from the enumeration f. We first set $g(0) = f(0)$. Now step through the elements of A in the order of $f(1), f(2), f(3), \ldots$, and each time a new value occurs, assign the new value to the next available argument for the function g. Since we are eliminating repetitions, g is injective by construction. Furthermore, because every element of A is the value $f(m)$ for some integer m, it follows that each element of A is the value of the function g for some argument n where $n \leq m$; hence g is surjective. Since A is infinite, the domain of g will be the entire set $\mathbf{N}$. Therefore, g is a bijection from $\mathbf{N}$ to A which establishes that $|A| = \aleph_0$ and A is countable. ∎

Examples

(a) The set Σ^* is countably infinite for any finite alphabet Σ. This can be shown by exhibiting the elements of Σ^* in standard order (Definition 3.6.7). If $\Sigma = \{a, b\}$ and a precedes b in the alphabetic order of Σ, then the enumeration of Σ^* in standard order is

$$\langle \Lambda, a, b, aa, ab, ba, bb, aaa, aab, \ldots \rangle$$

Note that if $|\Sigma| > 1$, then Σ^* cannot be enumerated in lexicographic order.

(b) The set of positive rational numbers $\mathbf{Q}+$ is countably infinite. Clearly $\mathbf{Q}+$ is not finite, since the natural numbers $\mathbf{N}$ can be mapped injectively to a proper subset of $\mathbf{Q}+$. We will show $\mathbf{Q}+$ is countable by exhibiting an enumeration with repetitions. The order of the enumeration is specified by the directed path of the following array.

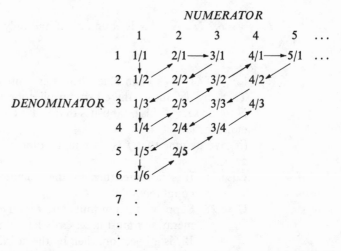

Since this enumeration will include every integer ratio m/n, it is an enumeration of $\mathbf{Q}+$, and therefore $\mathbf{Q}+$ is countably infinite. The enumeration is with repetitions, e.g., $\frac{1}{2}$ and $\frac{2}{4}$ denote the same element of $\mathbf{Q}+$. From Theorem 6.2.1, it follows that there is a bijection from $\mathbf{N}$ to $\mathbf{Q}+$. #

The following theorem establishes an important property of the cardinal number $\aleph_0$. This result will be used later to show that $\aleph_0$ is the "smallest" infinite cardinal number.

Theorem 6.2.2: Every infinite set contains a countably infinite subset.

Proof: Let A be an infinite set. Applying the Axiom of Choice to a sequence of subsets of A, we construct an infinite sequence $\langle a_0, a_1, a_2, \ldots \rangle$ as follows:

> Choose a_0 from A
>
> Choose a_1 from $A - \{a_0\}$
>
> Choose a_2 from $A - \{a_0, a_1\}$
>
> Choose a_3 from $A - \{a_0, a_1, a_2\}$
>
> $\cdot$
>
> $\cdot$
>
> $\cdot$

Each of the sets $A - \{a_0, a_1, a_2, \ldots, a_n\}$ is infinite. If this were not so, then A would be equal to the union of the two finite sets $A - \{a_0, a_1, \ldots, a_n\}$ and $\{a_0, a_1, \ldots, a_n\}$. But the union of two finite sets is a finite set and A is infinite. Therefore each set $A - \{a_0, a_1, a_2, \ldots, a_n\}$ is infinite and we can select a new element a_{n+1}. Thus we can construct an infinite sequence $\langle a_0, a_1, a_2, \ldots \rangle$ without repetitions; the elements of this sequence comprise a countably infinite subset of A. ∎

Like the finite sets, countable sets are closed under certain set operations. The following theorems list the principal results.

Theorem 6.2.3: The union of a countable collection of countable sets is countable.

Proof: Let S be an initial segment of $\mathbf{N}$, and set $A = \bigcup_{i \in S} A_i$ where each A_i is a countable set. If $S = \phi$ or if $A_i = \phi$ for each $i \in S$, then $A = \phi$ and the result holds. Suppose that $S \neq \phi$ and that there is at least one nonempty set A_i; without loss of generality, we assume $A_0 \neq \phi$. We construct an infinite array using enumerations of the nonempty sets. If $A_i \neq \phi$, then the ith row of the array is an enumeration of A_i; we use an infinite enumeration with repetitions if A_i is finite. If $A_i = \phi$, we set the ith row equal to the $(i-1)$th. Thus, the array contains all the elements of A and no others. An enumeration of the elements of A is specified by the directed path in the diagram below.

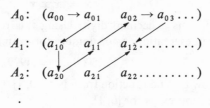

Since this is an enumeration of A, it follows from Theorem 6.2.1 that A is countable. ∎

Examples

The preceding theorem can be used to show that each of the following sets is countably infinite.

(a) $I^n = \{\langle x_1, x_2, \ldots, x_n \rangle \mid x_i \in I\}$ (the set of n-tuples with integer components).
(b) $Q^n = \{\langle x_1, x_2, \ldots, x_n \rangle \mid x_i \in Q\}$.
(c) The set of all nth degree polynomials with rational coefficients.
(d) The set of all polynomials with rational coefficients.
(e) The set of all $n \times m$ matrices with rational components.
(f) The set of all matrices of arbitrary finite dimension with rational components. #

Theorem 6.2.4: Let A and B be countable sets. Then

(a) $A \times B$ is countable,
(b) if A is finite, then B^A is countable.

Proof: The proof of part (a) is left as an exercise.

(b) If A or B is empty, then $|B^A| = 0$ or $|B^A| = 1$. Now assume both A and B are nonempty, where B is countable and $|A| = n$. Each element of B^A is a function $f: A \to B$. Let $g: N \to B$ be an enumeration of B, and for each positive $k \in N$ define the set F_k as follows:

$$F_k = \{f \mid f \in B^A \text{ and } f(A) \subset g(\{0, 1, 2, \ldots, k - 1\})\}.$$

Then F_k includes every function whose image is contained in the set consisting of the first k elements of the enumeration of B; $|F_k| = k^n$. Since A is finite, for each function $f: A \to B$ there exists some $m \in N$ such that if $k > m$, then $f \in F_k$; therefore $B^A = \bigcup_{k \in N} F_k$. But each set F_k is finite and therefore countable. Hence, by Theorem 6.2.3, we conclude $\bigcup_{k \in N} F_k$ is countable. ∎

As our definitions have suggested, not all infinite sets are countably infinite. The next theorem establishes that we need another infinite cardinal number.

Theorem 6.2.5: The subset of real numbers, $[0, 1]$, is not countably infinite.

Proof: Recall that $[0, 1]$ denotes the set $\{x \mid x \in R \land 0 \leq x \leq 1\}$. Each $x \in [0, 1]$ can be represented by an infinite decimal expansion:

$$x = .x_0 x_1 x_2 x_3 \ldots$$

where each x_i is a decimal digit. Using this representation requires some care, since the representation is not unique; for example:

$$.5000\ldots = .4999\ldots\dagger$$

We will show that no function from N to $[0, 1]$ is surjective. This will establish that no enumeration exists for $[0, 1]$.

---

†To show that $.4999\ldots$ is an alternative representation of $.5$, let x denote $.4999\ldots$ Then
$$10x = 4.999\ldots,$$
$$100x = 49.999\ldots,$$
and $100x - 10x = 45$. It follows that $x = .5$.

Let $f : \mathbf{N} \rightarrow [0, 1]$ be an arbitrary function from the natural numbers to the set $[0, 1]$. Arrange the elements $f(0), f(1), \ldots,$ in a vertical array, using a decimal representation for each value $f(x)$. The resulting array appears as follows:

$$f(0): \quad .x_{00}x_{01}x_{02}\ldots$$
$$f(1): \quad .x_{10}x_{11}x_{12}\ldots$$
$$\cdot$$
$$\cdot$$
$$\cdot$$
$$f(n): \quad .x_{n0}x_{n1}x_{n2}\ldots$$
$$\cdot$$
$$\cdot$$
$$\cdot$$

where x_{ni} is the ith digit in the decimal expansion of $f(n)$. We now specify a real number $y \in [0, 1]$ as follows: $y = .y_0y_1y_2 \ldots,$ where

$$y_i = 1 \text{ if } x_{ii} \neq 1,$$
$$= 2 \text{ if } x_{ii} = 1.$$

The number y is determined by the digits on the diagonal of the array. Clearly, $y \in [0, 1]$. However, y differs from each $f(n)$ in at least one digit of the expansion (namely, the nth digit). Hence, $y \neq f(n)$ for any n, and we conclude that the map $f : \mathbf{N} \rightarrow [0, 1]$ is not a surjection. Therefore, f is not an enumeration of $[0, 1]$. Since the map f was arbitrary, this establishes that $|[0, 1]| \neq \aleph_0$. ∎

The preceding theorem and proof are due to Cantor. The proof technique is sometimes called the "Cantor diagonal technique" or simply "diagonalization." Essentially, this technique begins with an infinite list such that each element on the list has an infinite description. It then produces an object distinct from each element of the list. This technique has many variations and is applied extensively in the theory of computability.

Theorem 6.2.6: If Σ is a finite nonempty alphabet, then $\mathcal{P}(\Sigma^*)$ is uncountably infinite.

Proof: Let $\langle w_0, w_1, w_2, \ldots \rangle$ be an enumeration of Σ^* and let

$$\langle A_0, A_1, A_2, \ldots \rangle$$

be an enumeration of any nonempty collection of subsets of Σ^*. We will show that there is a subset of Σ^* which is not in the enumeration. Construct a (possibly infinite) binary matrix

	w_0	w_1	w_2	
A_0	a_{00}	a_{01}	a_{02}	...
A_1	a_{10}	a_{11}	a_{12}	...
A_2	a_{20}	a_{21}	a_{22}	...
.	.	.	.	
.	.	.	.	
.	.	.	.	

by letting the ith row represent the characteristic function of A_i. Then $a_{ij} = \chi_{A_i}(w_j)$; that is, $a_{ij} = 1$ if $w_j \in A_i$, otherwise $a_{ij} = 0$. Now define a language L by traversing the diagonal elements of the array and including in L exactly those elements which are not in their respective subsets:

$$L = \{w_i \mid a_{ii} = 0, i \in \mathbf{N}\} = \{w_i \mid w_i \notin A_i, i \in \mathbf{N}\}.$$

By construction, $L \neq A_i$ for any $i \in \mathbf{N}$; that is, L does not appear in the enumeration. But $L \in \mathcal{P}(\Sigma^*)$. Therefore, $\langle A_0, A_1, A_2, \ldots \rangle$ is not an enumeration of $\mathcal{P}(\Sigma^*)$. Since the enumeration was an arbitrary enumeration of any nonempty subset of $\mathcal{P}(\Sigma^*)$, it follows that no enumeration of the entire set $\mathcal{P}(\Sigma^*)$ exists. ∎

The sets $[0, 1]$ and $\mathcal{P}(\Sigma^*)$ are examples of sets which are infinite but not countably infinite. In the next section we will develop tools for showing that $[0, 1]$ and $\mathcal{P}(\Sigma^*)$ have the same cardinality. We choose $[0, 1]$ to be the "standard set" for this cardinality and make the following definition.

Definition 6.2.5:   A set A is of cardinality $\mathbf{c}$ if there is a bijection from $[0, 1]$ to A.

The choice of $\mathbf{c}$ is based on the fact that the set $[0, 1]$ is often called a *continuum*.

Examples

(a) $|[a, b]| = \mathbf{c}$ where $[a, b]$ is any closed interval in $\mathbf{R}$ with $a < b$. This is established by noting that $f(x) = (b - a)x + a$ is a bijection from $[0, 1]$ to $[a, b]$.

(b) $|(0, 1)| = |[0, 1]|$. These two sets differ only in their containment of the end points of the interval; in order to construct a bijection from $[0, 1]$ to $(0, 1)$ we must find an image for 0 and 1 in the interval $(0, 1)$ while keeping the map surjective. Define the set A to be $\{0, 1, 1/2, 1/3, \ldots, 1/n, \ldots\}$. Define the map f as follows:

$$f : [0, 1] \to (0, 1),$$

$$f(0) = \frac{1}{2},$$

$$f\left(\frac{1}{n}\right) = \frac{1}{n + 2} \text{ for } n \geq 1,$$

$$f(x) = x \text{ for } x \in [0, 1] - A.$$

Then f is bijective and therefore $|(0, 1)| = \mathbf{c}$. The following diagram is a representation of the function f.

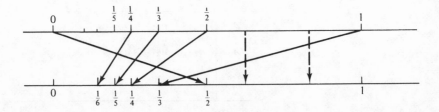

(c) $|\mathbf{R}| = \mathbf{c}$. We define a bijection g from $(0, 1)$ to $\mathbf{R}$ as follows:

$$g: (0, 1) \rightarrow \mathbf{R},$$

$$g(x) = \frac{(1/2 - x)}{x(1 - x)}.$$

The function g has the following graph.

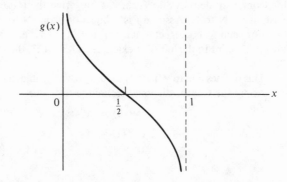

Since f of the preceding example is a bijection from $[0, 1]$ to $(0, 1)$, and g is a bijection from $(0, 1)$ to $\mathbf{R}$, the composite function gf is a bijection from $[0, 1]$ to $\mathbf{R}$. Hence, $|\mathbf{R}| = \mathbf{c}$. #

Problems: Section 6.2

1. Show that each of the following sets is countably infinite.
   (a) Σ^*, where $\Sigma = \{a\}$.
   (b) $\{\langle x_1, x_2, x_3 \rangle | x_i \in \mathbf{I}\}$.
   (c) The set of all finite subsets of $\{a, b\}^*$.
   (d) The set of all first-degree polynomials with integer coefficients.
   (e) The set of all finite digraphs with nodes in $\mathbf{N}$.

2. Show that each of the following sets has cardinality $\mathbf{c}$ by constructing a bijection from $[0, 1]$ to the set.
   (a) (a, b), where $a < b$ and $a, b \in \mathbf{R}$.
   (b) $\{x | x \in \mathbf{R} \wedge x \geq 0\}$.
   (c) $\{\langle x, y \rangle | x, y \in \mathbf{R} \wedge x^2 + y^2 = 1\}$.

3. Let $|A| = \mathbf{c}$, $|B| = \mathbf{c}$, $|D| = \aleph_0$, $|E| = n > 0$, where $A, B, D,$ and E are disjoint. Prove each of the following.
   (a) $|A \cup B| = \mathbf{c}$.
   (b) $|A \cup D| = \mathbf{c}$.
   (c) $|D \times E| = \aleph_0$.

4. Try to find a set S such that $|\mathcal{P}(S)| = \aleph_0$. If you do not succeed, describe the difficulties encountered.

5. Prove part (a) of Theorem 6.2.4.

6. (a) In Theorem 6.2.5, suppose we use a binary expansion for $f(i)$ and define the digits of y in the obvious way:

$$y_i = 0 \text{ if } x_{ii} = 1, \ y_i = 1 \text{ if } x_{ii} = 0.$$

Show that y may be equal to $f(j)$ for some $j \in \mathbf{N}$.

(b) Explain what difficulties might arise because of the nonuniqueness of the decimal representation of some numbers in $[0, 1]$. How does this influence the selection of the values for y_i in the real number y in the proof of Theorem 6.2.5?

7. Joe Cool, a student at Silo Tech, has suggested the following proof that no bijection exists from $\mathbf{N}$ to $\mathbf{N}$. Assume f is a bijection from $\mathbf{N}$ to $\mathbf{N}$, with $f(k) = i_k$.

For each i_k, construct a number in $[0, 1]$ by reversing the digits of i_k and putting a decimal point to the left. For example, if $i_k = 123$, the number constructed becomes $.321000\ldots$

This defines a map g from $\mathbf{N}$ to $[0, 1]$ which is injective, e.g., $g(123) = .321000\ldots$ Apply the Cantor diagonal technique to the array

$$g \circ f(0) = .x_{00}x_{01}\ldots$$
$$g \circ f(1) = .x_{10}x_{11}x_{12}\ldots$$
$$\vdots$$

to construct the number $y \in [0, 1]$. Now reverse the digits of y and put the decimal point to the right. The result is a number which does not appear in the list $f(0), f(1), \ldots$, which contradicts the assertion that f is surjective. Hence, no bijection can exist from $\mathbf{N}$ to $\mathbf{N}$.

Should we promote Joe to full professor or suggest he find a job as a COBOL programmer (assuming the two are mutually exclusive)?

6.3 COMPARISON OF CARDINAL NUMBERS

The preceding sections introduced the finite cardinal numbers, the cardinal number $\aleph_0$ for a countable infinity, and the cardinal number $\mathbf{c}$ for some sets of an uncountable infinity. In each case, the cardinality of a set A was established by constructing a bijection from a standard set to A. This allows us to show that two sets have the same cardinality, but so far, we have not defined an order relation which will enable us to assert that one set is larger than another. In this section, we develop the order relations $\leq$ and $<$ on cardinal numbers and show that they have properties similar to the usual order relations over the real numbers. The following definition formalizes the concept of two sets having the same cardinality even when a standard set has not been specified.

Definition 6.3.1: Let A and B be sets. Then, A and B are *equipotent* or *have the same cardinality*, denoted by $|A| = |B|$, if there is a bijection from A to B.

Example

Let E be the set of positive even integers. Then, $|\mathbf{I}+| = |E|$ because the function

$$f: \mathbf{I}+ \ \to E,$$

$$f(x) = 2x$$

is a bijection from $\mathbf{I}+$ to E.   #

Because bijections are closed under composition, and inverses of bijections are bijections, the relation of equipotence has the following property.

Theorem 6.3.1:   Equipotence is an equivalence relation over any collection of sets.

The proof is straightforward and left as an exercise.

It follows from the preceding theorem that to show a set S has cardinality α, it suffices to choose *any* set S' which we know has cardinality α and establish the existence of a bijection from S to S' or from S' to S. In general, we choose the set S' to make the proof as easy as possible.

We now consider order relations on sets of cardinal numbers. Our goal is to be able to compare the sizes of sets. For example, our intuition tells us that sets with cardinality $\mathbf{c}$ are "larger" than countable sets. Before we formally define the order relation for arbitrary collections of sets, we make the following observations concerning finite sets and their cardinal numbers.

Let A and B be finite sets with $|A| = n$, $|B| = m$.

(a)   If there exists an injection from A to B, then $n \leq m$.

(b)   If there exists a bijection from A to B, then $n = m$.

(c)   If there exists an injection from A to B, but no bijection exists, then $n < m$.

These relationships between functions and cardinalities can be extended in a natural way to apply to arbitrary sets.

Definition 6.3.2:   The *cardinality of A is no greater than* (or *is less than or equal to*) *the cardinality of B*, denoted $|A| \leq |B|$, if there is an injection from A to B. The *cardinality of A is less than the cardinality of B*, written $|A| < |B|$, if there exists an injection but no bijection from A to B.

We have chosen to use the notation $<$ and $\leq$ because the order relations we have just defined have the properties which we usually associate with these symbols. However, the proofs that the properties hold are, in some cases, lengthy and intricate. The following two theorems establish some of these properties, but their proofs are too involved to be presented here. The first theorem, called the *Law of Trichotomy*, asserts that any two sets can be compared using either the relation $<$ or $=$.

Theorem 6.3.2 (Zermelo):   Let A and B be sets. Then exactly one of the three following conditions holds:

(a) $|A| < |B|$,
(b) $|B| < |A|$, or
(c) $|A| = |B|$.

The second theorem asserts that the relation $\leq$ is antisymmetric.

Theorem 6.3.3 (Cantor-Schröder-Bernstein): Let A and B be sets. If $|A| \leq |B|$ and $|B| \leq |A|$, then $|A| = |B|$.

The preceding theorem often provides a powerful mechanism for showing that two sets have the same cardinality. If we can construct an injection $f: A \to B$, thus establishing that $|A| \leq |B|$, and another injection $g: B \to A$ to establish that $|B| \leq |A|$, then we can conclude that $|A| = |B|$. Note that f and g need not be surjective. Thus Theorem 6.3.3 allows us to conclude that a bijection exists from A to B on the basis of injections from A to B and B to A. It is often easier to construct two such injections than a single bijection.

Theorem 6.3.4: Let S be a set of cardinal numbers. The order relation $\leq$ on S is a linear order. The order relation $<$ on S is a quasi order.

The proof is left as an exercise.

Examples

(a) We show $|(0, 1)| = |[0, 1]|$ by exhibiting an injection from each set to the other as follows:
   (i) $f: (0, 1) \to [0, 1]$,
   $f(x) = x$.
   (ii) $g: [0, 1] \to (0, 1)$,
   $g(x) = \dfrac{x}{2} + \dfrac{1}{4}$.

(b) $|\mathcal{P}(\mathbf{N})| = \mathbf{c}$.
   (i) We show that $|\mathcal{P}(\mathbf{N})| \leq \mathbf{c}$ by constructing an injection as follows:
   $$g: \mathcal{P}(\mathbf{N}) \to [0, 1]$$
   For every subset $S \subset \mathbf{N}$, g maps S to a real fraction,
   $$g(S) = .x_0 x_1 x_2 \ldots,$$
   where the fraction is expressed in binary representation and
   $$x_{2j} = 0 \quad \text{for } j = 0, 1, 2, \ldots,$$
   $$x_{2j+1} = 1 \quad \text{for } j \in S, \text{ and}$$
   $$= 0 \quad \text{for } j \notin S;$$
   e.g., $g(\phi) = 0$,
   $$g(\mathbf{N}) = .01010101 \ldots,$$
   $$g(\{1, 3, 5\}) = .00\ 01\ 00\ 01\ 00\ 01 \ldots$$
   (Note that we cannot use (in place of g) the function g' such that $g'(S)$ is the binary fraction $.x_0 x_1 x_2 \ldots$, where $x_j = 1$ if $j \in S$ and $x_j = 0$ if

$j \notin S$. Since the value of $g'(S)$ is expressed as a binary fraction, the function g' is not an injection from $\mathcal{P}(\mathbf{N})$ to the $[0, 1]$: for example, the sets $\{0\}$ and $\{n \mid n \in \mathbf{N} \wedge n > 0\}$ would be mapped to $.1000\ldots$ and $.0111\ldots$ respectively; in the binary number system, these are different representations of the same fraction. However, if $g'(S)$ is specified to be a ternary (base 3) fraction, then the same characterization of g' will specify an injective function.)

(ii) We show $\mathbf{c} \leq |\mathcal{P}(\mathbf{N})|$ by constructing an injection from $[0, 1]$ to $\mathcal{P}(\mathbf{N})$. Let $x = .x_0 x_1 x_2 \ldots$ be a binary representation of $x \in [0, 1]$. (If x does not have a unique representation, choose one arbitrarily.) Define $f(x)$ to be the set such that $j \in f(x)$ if and only if $x_j = 1$;

$$\text{e.g., } f(0) = \phi,$$
$$f(1) = f(.1111\ldots) = \mathbf{N},$$
$$f(.101010000\ldots) = \{0, 2, 4\}.$$

Then f is an injection. (Note that f is not a surjection. For example, if $.1000\ldots$ is chosen as the representation of $1/2$ rather than $.0111\ldots$, then the set $\{0\}$ will be in the image of f but the set $\{n \mid n \in \mathbf{N} \wedge n > 0\}$ will not.)

It follows from the Cantor-Schröder-Bernstein theorem that $|\mathcal{P}(\mathbf{N})| = \mathbf{c}$.

(c) $|\mathbf{N}^{\mathbf{N}}| = \mathbf{c}$.

(i) $|\mathbf{N}^{\mathbf{N}}| \leq \mathbf{c}$. We first construct an injection from $\mathbf{N}^{\mathbf{N}}$ to $(0, 1)$. Let f be an element of $\mathbf{N}^{\mathbf{N}}$ and let x_i be the binary representation of $f(i)$ for each argument $i \in \mathbf{N}$. Using the digit "2" in a ternary base as a separator for the values of the function, we define $g(f) = (.x_0 2 x_1 2 x_2 \ldots)$ and interpret $g(f)$ as a ternary fraction constructed from the values of f. For example, consider $h: \mathbf{N} \to \mathbf{N}$, $h(x) = 2x$. Then $h \in \mathbf{N}^{\mathbf{N}}$ and $g(h) = .021021002\ldots$ It is easy to show that g is an injection but not a bijection from $\mathbf{N}^{\mathbf{N}}$ to $(0, 1)$.

(ii) $\mathbf{c} \leq |\mathbf{N}^{\mathbf{N}}|$. We construct an injection h from $(0, 1)$ to $\mathbf{N}^{\mathbf{N}}$. Let x be an element of $(0, 1)$ and let $x = .x_0 x_1 x_2 x_3 \ldots$ be a decimal expansion of x. Define $h(x)$ to be that function $f \in \mathbf{N}^{\mathbf{N}}$ for which $f(0) = x_0$, $f(1) = x_1$, $\ldots$ etc. Then, h is an injection from $(0, 1)$ to $\mathbf{N}^{\mathbf{N}}$.

It follows that $|\mathbf{N}^{\mathbf{N}}| = \mathbf{c}$.　#

The relationship between the finite cardinal numbers, $\aleph_0$, and $\mathbf{c}$ is established by the following theorem.

Theorem 6.3.5: Let A be a finite set. Then $|A| < \aleph_0 < \mathbf{c}$.

Proof: Suppose $|A| = n$. We use the standard set $\{0, 1, 2, \ldots, n - 1\}$ and prove that $\{0, 1, 2, \ldots, n - 1\} < |\mathbf{N}| < |[0, 1]|$ for every $n \in \mathbf{N}$. We first define the function f as follows:

$$f: \{0, 1, 2, \ldots, n - 1\} \to \mathbf{N},$$
$$f(x) = x;$$

Since f is an injection, it follows that $|A| \leq |\mathbf{N}|$. In Theorem 6.1.1, we showed that there was no bijection from N to A, so $|A| \neq |N|$. It follows that $|A| < |N|$, i.e., $|A| < \aleph_0$.

We next observe that the map

$$f: N \to [0, 1],$$

$$f(n) = \frac{1}{n + 1},$$

is an injection from N to $[0, 1]$; hence $|N| \leq |[0, 1]|$. In Theorem 6.2.5, we showed that $|N| \neq |[0, 1]|$. It follows that $|N| < |[0, 1]|$, i.e., $\aleph_0 < c$. ∎

Example

Define a number $x \in (0, 1)$ to be *computable* if and only if there is an ALGOL (or PL/I, or FORTRAN, etc.) program P which, when given any nonnegative integer i as an input, will halt after producing, as its only output, the ith digit of the decimal expansion of x. The time required for the computation can be arbitrarily large but must be finite. Thus, the number $x = .x_0 x_1 x_2 \ldots$ is computable in the sense that the program P can be used to determine x to an arbitrary precision, or to produce any digit of the expansion of x. A number $x \in (0, 1)$ is *noncomputable* if it is not computable. The following procedure computes the digits of the repeating decimal $.514141414 \ldots$

```
procedure COMP(i):
if i = 1 then return 5
else
    if i mod 2 = 0 then return 1
    else return 4
```

We now show that there exist noncomputable numbers in the open interval $(0, 1)$. The proof uses a cardinality argument and is nonconstructive. The following sets will be used:

Σ, the ALGOL character set,

A, the set of all ALGOL programs,

C, the set of ALGOL programs which compute some number in $(0, 1)$,

S, the numbers in $(0, 1)$ which are computed by some ALGOL program.

Since Σ is a finite set, the set of nonempty strings over the alphabet Σ has cardinality $\aleph_0$, i.e., $|\Sigma^+| = \aleph_0$. Since any ALGOL program is a finite string over Σ,

$$|A| \leq |\Sigma^+|.$$

Since C is a proper subset of A, $|C| \leq |A|$. Any program P can compute the digits of at most one element of S, but different programs might compute the digits of the same number. It follows that $|S| \leq |C|$. Thus, we have

$$|S| \leq |C| \leq |A| \leq \aleph_0.$$

But in Section 6.2, we showed that $|(0, 1)| = c$, and in Theorem 6.3.5 we showed $\aleph_0 < c$. Hence $|S| < |(0, 1)|$, i.e., some of the numbers in $(0, 1)$ are not computable.   #

We have established that the cardinality of the continuum is greater than countably infinite and that countably infinite is greater than finite. Might there be other cardinal numbers that lie between those that we have considered? For example, is it possible that there is an infinite set which has cardinality less than $\aleph_0$? The next theorem gives a negative answer; it establishes that $\aleph_0$ is the smallest infinite cardinal number.

Theorem 6.3.6: If A is an infinite set, then $\aleph_0 \leq |A|$.

Proof: By Theorem 6.2.2, if A is infinite, then A contains a countably infinite subset A'. Since the map

$$f: A' \to A,$$
$$f(x) = x \qquad \text{for } x \in A',$$

is an injection of A' into A, it follows that $|A'| \leq |A|$, and since $|A'| = \aleph_0$, we conclude $\aleph_0 \leq |A|$. ∎

Is it possible that there is an infinite set whose cardinality is strictly greater than $\aleph_0$ and strictly less than $\mathbf{c}$? The assertion that no such cardinal number exists is known as the *continuum hypothesis*. It has been known for some time that the continuum hypothesis is consistent with the axioms of set theory. In 1963, Paul Cohen showed that the negation of the continuum hypothesis is *also* consistent with the axioms of set theory. As a consequence, one can (at least abstractly) deal with a mathematical universe in which the hypothesis does or does not hold. For our purposes, we are only interested in the fact that acceptance or rejection of the hypothesis has implications for proof techniques. For example, suppose we wish to prove that a given set A has cardinality $\mathbf{c}$. If we accept the continuum hypothesis, then it suffices to show that

(i) $|A| \leq \mathbf{c}$, and
(ii) $|A| > \aleph_0$.

However, if we reject the hypothesis, then the above approach does not yield the conclusion we seek since it might happen that $\aleph_0 < |A| < \mathbf{c}$. We will avoid using the hypothesis.

From the next theorem, it follows that there is at least a countably infinite set of infinite cardinal numbers, and hence, there is no largest cardinal number and no largest set.

Theorem 6.3.7 (Cantor): Let A be a set. Then $|A| < |\mathcal{P}(A)|$.

Proof: We first show that $|A| \leq |\mathcal{P}(A)|$ by noting that the following function is injective.

$$f: A \to \mathcal{P}(A),$$
$$f(a) = \{a\}.$$

Next we show that $|A| \neq |\mathcal{P}(A)|$. Let g be an arbitrary function,

$$g: A \to \mathcal{P}(A).$$

We will show that g is not surjective and hence not bijective. The function g maps each element of A to a subset of A; an element x may or may not be in the subset $g(x)$. The set $S \subset A$ is defined as follows:

$$S = \{x \mid x \notin g(x)\}.$$

Now S is a subset of A, but $g(a) \neq S$ for any $a \in A$. For if $g(a) = S$, then

$$a \in S \Leftrightarrow a \in \{x \mid x \notin g(x)\} \qquad \text{by definition of } S,$$

$$\Leftrightarrow a \notin g(a) \qquad \qquad \text{by application of the predicate which defines } S,$$

$$\Leftrightarrow a \notin S \qquad \qquad \text{by the assumption that } g(a) = S.$$

Since this is a contradiction, the assumption that $g(a) = S$ is false. Since a was arbitrary, it follows that g is not surjective; and hence, not bijective. Since g was an arbitrary function, this establishes that no bijection exists and therefore $|A| \neq |\mathcal{P}(A)|$. ∎

Using the previous theorem, we can construct a countably infinite set of infinite cardinal numbers, each of which is smaller than the one which follows:

$$|\mathbf{N}| < |\mathcal{P}(\mathbf{N})| < |\mathcal{P}(\mathcal{P}(\mathbf{N}))| < \cdots$$

Problems: Section 6.3

1. Prove that if $A' \subset A$, then $|A'| \leq |A|$.

2. Prove that if $|A| \leq |B|$ and $|C| = |A|$, then $|C| \leq |B|$.

3. Prove that if there exists a surjection from A to B, then $|B| \leq |A|$.

4. If $A \in B$, does it follow that $|A| \leq |B|$? Prove your assertion.

5. Prove that if A is finite and B is infinite, then $|A| < |B|$.

6. Prove that if A is infinite and $|A| \leq |B|$, then B is infinite.

7. Show that every infinite subset of a countable set is countable.

8. Prove Theorem 6.3.1.

9. Prove Theorem 6.3.4.

10. Find the cardinality of each of the following sets. Prove your assertion.
    (a) $\mathbf{Q}$, the set of rational numbers
    (b) $[0, 1] \times [0, 1]$ (Hint: Interleave the representations of x and y in the pair $\langle x, y \rangle$.)
    (c) $\mathbf{Q}^{\mathbf{N}}$
    (d) $\mathcal{P}(\mathbf{Q})$
    (e) $\mathbf{R} - \mathbf{Q}$
    (f) $\mathbf{R} \times \mathbf{R}$

11. Let π_1 and π_2 be partitions of A such that π_1 refines π_2. Prove that $|\pi_2| \leq |\pi_1|$.

12. Denote $|\mathcal{P}([0, 1])|$ by 2^c. Find examples of other sets which have cardinality 2^c.

13. Prove or disprove each of the following:
   (a) $|A| = |B| \Rightarrow |\mathscr{P}(A)| = |\mathscr{P}(B)|$
   (b) $(|A| \leq |B| \land |C| \leq |D|) \Rightarrow |A^C| \leq |B^D|$
   (c) $(|A| \leq |B| \land |C| = |D|) \Rightarrow |A \times C| \leq |B \times D|$
   (d) $(|A| \leq |B| \land |C| \leq |D|) \Rightarrow |A \cup C| \leq |B \cup D|$

14. (a) Prove that there exists a noncomputable number between any two rational numbers in [0, 1].
   (b) Show that all rational numbers in [0, 1] are computable.

‡6.4 CARDINAL ARITHMETIC

Previous sections have described the cardinal numbers as well as the order relations $<$ and $\leq$. We can now define an arithmetic for cardinal numbers. The arithmetic is a generalization of the familiar finite arithmetic and includes the operations of addition, multiplication, and exponentiation.

We will present some of the fundamental properties of cardinal arithmetic but will prove only a few of our assertions. In some cases, proofs are most naturally given using *ordinal numbers*, which we have not developed but which include the cardinal numbers as a proper subset. Consequently, although we quote a set of theorems intended to illustrate the characteristics of the arithmetic, in many cases the proofs are beyond the scope of this text and will be omitted.

Definition 6.4.1:   Let a and b be cardinal numbers and let A and B be disjoint sets such that $|A| = a$ and $|B| = b$. The *sum* of a and b is defined to be

$$a + b = |A \cup B|.$$

The following is easily proven using the preceding definition and the properties of set union.

Theorem 6.4.1:   Addition of cardinal numbers is commutative and associative.

The following theorem asserts that the order relations $\leq$ and $<$ are preserved by the operation of addition.

Theorem 6.4.2:   Let a, b, d, and e be cardinal numbers. Then
(a) if $a \leq b$ and $d \leq e$, then $a + d \leq b + e$.
(b) if $a < b$ and $d < e$, then $a + d < b + e$.

Proof:
(a) Let A, B, D, and E be sets such that $|A| = a$, $|B| = b$, $|D| = d$, $|E| = e$, and $(A \cup B) \cap (D \cup E) = \phi$. Since $a \leq b$, there is an injection $f: A \to B$, and since $d \leq e$, there is an injection $g: D \to E$. Define the map h as follows:

$$h: A \cup D \to B \cup E,$$
$$h|_A = f,$$
$$h|_D = g.$$

Since $A \cap D = \phi$, the map is well-defined. Since $B \cap E = \phi$ and both f and g are injective, it follows that h is injective. Hence, $|A \cup D| \leq |B \cup E|$ and therefore $a + d \leq b + e$.

The proof of (b) is beyond our scope and will not be given. ∎

The following theorem illustrates one way in which arithmetic involving infinite cardinal numbers differs from the familiar arithmetic.

Theorem 6.4.3: Let a and b be cardinal numbers such that a is an infinite cardinal number and $b \leq a$. Then $a + b = a$.

We will not prove the theorem; however, the special cases of $a = \aleph_0$ and $a = \mathbf{c}$ follow from our previous work.

Example

      We show that $\mathbf{c} + \aleph_0 = \mathbf{c}$. Let $A = \{x \,|\, x \in \mathbf{R} \text{ and } x \geq 1\}$, and let $B = \{1/(n + 2) \,|\, n \in \mathbf{N}\}$. Then $|A| = \mathbf{c}$, $|B| = \aleph_0$ and $A \cap B = \phi$. Furthermore, $A \cup B \subset \mathbf{R}$; hence, $|A \cup B| \leq \mathbf{c}$. But $|A| = \mathbf{c}$, so $|A \cup B| \geq \mathbf{c}$. Hence $|A \cup B| = \mathbf{c} + \aleph_0 = \mathbf{c}$. #

We now consider multiplication of cardinal numbers, which is defined using the cartesian product.

Definition 6.4.2: Let a and b be cardinal numbers, and let A and B be sets such that $|A| = b$ and $|B| = b$. Then the *product* of a and b, denoted $a \cdot b$ or simply ab, is defined as follows:

$$a \cdot b = |A \times B|.$$

The proof of the following theorem is left as an exercise.

Theorem 6.4.4: Multiplication of cardinal numbers is commutative and associative, and it distributes over addition, i.e., $a(b + d) = ab + ad$.

Theorem 6.4.5: The operation of multiplication preserves the order relations $\leq$ and $<$; i.e., for all cardinal numbers a, b, d, and e,

(a)   if $a \leq b$ and $d \leq e$, then $ad \leq be$;
(b)   if $a < b$ and $d < e$, then $ad < be$.

The proof of (a) is an exercise; the proof of (b) is beyond our scope.

Theorem 6.4.6: Let a and b be cardinal numbers such that a is an infinite cardinal number, $b \neq 0$, and $a \geq b$. Then $ab = a$.

We will not prove the general statement of the theorem, but the special cases where $a = \mathbf{c}$ and $b = \aleph_0$ can be shown on the basis of our earlier work.

Example

We show that $\aleph_0 \cdot \mathbf{c} = \mathbf{c}$. Let $A = \mathbf{N}$ and $B = (0, 1)$; then $|A| = \aleph_0$ and $|B| = \mathbf{c}$. We must show $|A \times B| = \mathbf{c}$. Define a function f from $A \times B$ to the positive real numbers:

$$f: A \times B \to \{x \mid x \in \mathbf{R}+\},$$

$$f(n, x) = n + x.$$

Then f is injective, and since $|\mathbf{R}+| = \mathbf{c}$, it follows that $|A \times B| \le \mathbf{c}$. Furthermore, the map

$$g: (0, 1) \to A \times B,$$

$$g(x) = \langle 0, x \rangle,$$

is injective and establishes that $\mathbf{c} \le |A \times B|$. Hence $|A \times B| = \mathbf{c}$. #

The last operation we will discuss is exponentiation.

Definition 6.4.3: Let a and b be cardinal numbers, and let A and B be sets such that $|A| = a$ and $|B| = b$. Then *a to the power b*, denoted a^b, is defined as $a^b = |A^B|$.

It is an immediate consequence of this definition that $|A^B| = |A|^{|B|}$.

The most important properties of exponentiation are known as *laws of exponents*; these properties are characterized by the next theorem.

Theorem 6.4.7: Let a, b, and d be cardinal numbers. Then

(a) $a^{b+d} = a^b a^d$

(b) $(ab)^d = a^d b^d$

(c) $(a^b)^d = a^{bd}$

Proof of (a): The proof consists of showing that a bijection exists between sets of functions.

Let A, B, and D be sets such that $|A| = a$, $|B| = b$, and $|D| = d$, where $B \cap D = \phi$. Let $g: B \to A$ and $h: D \to A$. Because B and D are disjoint, there exists a map $f: B \cup D \to A$ such that f is an extension of both g and h. Thus we can define a function α as follows:

$$\alpha: A^B \times A^D \to A^{B \cup D},$$

$$\alpha(\langle g, h \rangle) = f \quad \text{where } f\mid_B = g \text{ and } f\mid_D = h.$$

The function α is an injection and hence $|A^B \times A^D| \le |A^{B \cup D}|$. Furthermore, we can define a function β

$$\beta: A^{B \cup D} \to A^B \times A^D,$$

$$\beta(f) = \langle f\mid_B, f\mid_D \rangle$$

which is also an injection. (It is easy to show that $\beta = \alpha^{-1}$.) Thus

$$|A^{B \cup D}| \le |A^B \times A^D|,$$

and we conclude that $|A^{B \cup D}| = |A^B \times A^D|$. ∎

Exponentiation preserves the order relations $<$ and $\leq$ in the expected fashion.

Theorem 6.4.8: Let a, b, d, and e be cardinal numbers. Then

(a) if $a \leq b$ and $d \leq e$, then $a^d \leq b^e$.
(b) if $a < b$ and $d < e$, then $a^d < b^e$.

Once again, the proof of part (b) is beyond our scope. We leave the proof of part (a) as an exercise.

Problems: Section 6.4

1. Determine the values of the following expressions. The letter n denotes an arbitrary member of $\mathbf{N}$.

    (a) $n + \aleph_0$ (b) $n + c$ (c) $\aleph_0 + \aleph_0$
    (d) $c + c$ (e) $n \cdot \aleph_0$ (f) $n \cdot c$
    (g) $\aleph_0 \cdot \aleph_0$ (h) $c \cdot c$ (i) $0^{\aleph_0}$
    (j) 1^c (k) $2^{\aleph_0}$ (l) $\aleph_0^1$
    (m) $\aleph_0^3$ (n) $\aleph_0^{\aleph_0}$ (o) c^0
    (p) c^3 (q) $c + (\aleph_0 \cdot c + 3^{\aleph_0})$

2. Find the cardinality of each of the following sets.

    (a) $\mathbf{R} \cup \mathbf{R}^2$
    (b) $S \times \Sigma^*$ where $|S| = n$ for $n \in \mathbf{N}$.
    (c) The set of all $m \times n$ matrices with components in $\mathbf{R}$.
    (d) The set of all n component vectors with integer components.
    (e) The set of all functions from Σ^* to $\mathbf{N}$.
    (f) The set of all functions from $\mathbf{I} \times \mathbf{I}$ to $\mathbf{I}$.
    (g) The set of $n \times n$ matrices with rational components.

3. Prove Theorem 6.4.1.

4. We have not defined an operation of subtraction for cardinal numbers. Show that the following definition is unsatisfactory because the operation is not well defined. "Definition": Let A and B be sets such that $|A| = a$, $|B| = b$, and $B \subset A$. Then $a - b = |A - B|$.

5. Let a, b, and d be cardinal numbers.

    (a) Prove that if $a \leq b$, then $a + d \leq b + d$.
    (b) Show by counterexample that $a < b$ does not imply that $a + d < b + d$.
    (c) Prove that if $a \leq b$, then $ad \leq bd$.
    (d) Show that $a < b$ does not imply $ad < bd$.

6. Prove Theorem 6.4.4.

7. Prove part (a) of Theorem 6.4.5.

8. Show that for any integer $n \geq 2$, $n^{\aleph_0} = c$.

9. Prove part (a) of Theorem 6.4.8.

Suggestions for Further Reading

Halmos [1960] develops the ordinal and cardinal numbers, along with their arithmetics. More extensive treatments of these topics are given in the books by Stoll [1963] and Suppes [1960]. Cohen [1966] discusses the role of the continuum hypothesis in set theory. Vilenkin [1968] presents many of the concepts of this chapter in an informal and entertaining way.

7

ALGEBRAS

7.0 INTRODUCTION

In Chapter 0, mathematical models were described as consisting of three components: a phenomenon or process of the real world which we wish to investigate, a mathematical structure, and a description of the way in which the mathematical structure represents the real world process. To be useful, a mathematical model must have a structure whose operations and relations reflect the real world in a satisfactory way. Choosing a mathematical structure therefore requires understanding how properties can be characterized mathematically and how some properties imply others. A familiarity with the concepts of mathematical structures will facilitate the understanding of abstract characterizations of new models and provide a basis for the construction of new models.

The mathematical structure of a model is often presented implicitly; in this case there is no precise specification of the mathematical structure being used. This usually causes no difficulty, because in most cases the structure is a familiar one and an obvious choice. In this chapter, however, it will be useful to specify in detail each mathematical structure we consider. In addition, we will develop a few basic properties of some of these structures, emphasizing those properties which are useful for the models which interest us.

The mathematical structures we will investigate are *algebras*, sometimes called *algebraic systems* or *algebraic structures*, and their study is often referred to as "modern algebra." These structures have been used in computer science for such purposes as to describe the functions computable by classes of machines, to investigate the complexity of arithmetic computations, to characterize abstract data structures, and as a basis for programming language semantics. Unfortunately, the formalisms used in various applications are often quite different from one another, although the fundamental concepts and techniques are the same. We will develop only some of the most basic topics of this area, but at the end of the chapter we will describe ways in which they can be augmented to treat various applications.

7.1 THE STRUCTURE OF ALGEBRAS

It is possible to give a general definition of an algebra, but such a definition would take us too deep into mathematical formalism. Instead, we will describe the concept informally and then illustrate it with a number of examples.

An algebra is characterized by specifying the following three components:

1. a set, called the *carrier* of the algebra,
2. *operations* defined on the carrier, and
3. distinguished elements of the carrier, called the *constants* of the algebra.

The *carrier* is the set of mathematical objects we wish to manipulate, such as integers, real numbers or a set of character strings; we will represent the carrier of an algebra by S. An *operation* defined on the carrier is a map from S^m to S. The value of m is called the "arity" of the operation. If an operation is from $S = S^1$ to S, such as the operation which takes an integer x to $-x$ or a real number y to its absolute value $|y|$, the operation is called a *unary* operation. Operations from S^2 to S, such as addition or multiplication of numbers, are called *binary* operations. *Ternary* operations are functions from S^3 to S; for example, if the carrier is a set of numbers, the construct **if** $x \neq 0$ **then** y **else** z can be defined as a ternary operation with operands x, y, and z. The *constants* of an algebra are distinguished elements of the carrier; these elements usually have properties of special importance.

Algebras are often formally presented as n-tuples, where the entries of the n-tuple specify the carrier, the operations, and the constants, in that order.†

Examples

(a) The integers with the binary operation of addition and the constant 0 can be described as an algebra in the following way.
1. The carrier is the set $\mathbf{I} = \{\ldots -3, -2, -1, 0, 1, 2, \ldots\}$.
2. There is a single operation, addition (denoted "+"), from $\mathbf{I}^2$ to $\mathbf{I}$.
3. The element 0 is a constant.
Alternatively, this algebra can be presented as the triple $\langle \mathbf{I}, +, 0 \rangle$.

(b) The real numbers $\mathbf{R}$ with addition, multiplication and unary minus can be described as an algebra as follows:
1. The carrier is $\mathbf{R}$, the set of real numbers.
2. There are two operations ("+" and "·") from $\mathbf{R}^2$ to $\mathbf{R}$ and one ("−") from $\mathbf{R}$ to $\mathbf{R}$.
3. The elements 0 and 1 are constants.
This algebra can be denoted by $\langle \mathbf{R}, +, \cdot, -, 0, 1 \rangle$.   #

The two examples above are of specific and familiar structures. To specify them precisely, we would present them as n-tuples by stating, for example, "Let

---

†Note that the carrier of an algebra may be empty and the operations and constants may not all be distinct. Our examples, however, will have nonempty carriers, and the operations and constants will generally be distinct.

$A = \langle \mathbf{I}, +, 0 \rangle$ be the integers under addition." It is also common to denote an algebra by its carrier; thus the statement "Let $\mathbf{I}$ be the integers under addition" would refer to the structure $\langle \mathbf{I}, + \rangle$, or perhaps $\langle \mathbf{I}, +, 0 \rangle$.

Frequently we do not wish to specify a single algebra but instead a class of algebras such that each member of the class has certain characteristics. To provide a mechanism for this, we first introduce the concept of the *signature*, or *species* of an algebra. Two algebras have the same *signature* (or are of the same *species*) if they have corresponding operations of each arity and corresponding constants. In other words, two algebras have the same signature if their *n*-tuples (consisting of carrier, operations, and constants) include the same number of operations and constants and the arities of corresponding operations are the same.

Examples

(a) The algebras $\langle \mathbf{N}, \cdot, 0 \rangle$ and $\langle \mathbf{I}, -, 0 \rangle$ have the same signature, since each has a single binary operation and a single constant.

(b) The structures $\langle \mathbf{R}, +, \cdot, 1, 0 \rangle$ and $\langle \mathcal{P}(S), \cup, \cap, S, \phi \rangle$ have the same signature.

(c) The algebras $\langle \mathbf{I}, +, 0 \rangle$ and $\langle \mathbf{I}, + \rangle$ do not have the same signature because the number of constants is not the same. #

Two algebras can have the same signature but not be related in any substantive way. In order to prove useful theorems about classes of algebras, we generally need to consider properties in addition to those implied by signature. We will treat only properties specified by *axioms*, where each axiom is an equation written in terms of the elements of the carrier and the operations of the algebra. A set of axioms, together with a signature, specifies a class of algebras called a *variety*; algebras which have the same signature and which obey the same set of axioms are said to be of the same variety. Investigations of algebras are generally concerned with particular varieties; the theorems that are proved are based on the axioms of the variety, and the results hold for all algebras in the given variety.

Examples

(a) Consider the variety of algebras with the same signature as $\langle \mathbf{I}, +, 0 \rangle$ and the following axioms:
  (i) $x + y = y + x$,
  (ii) $(x + y) + z = x + (y + z)$,
  (iii) $x + 0 = x$.
  Then $\langle \mathbf{R}, +, 0 \rangle$, $\langle \Sigma^*, \text{concatenation}, \Lambda \rangle$, $\langle \mathcal{P}(S), \cup, \phi \rangle$, $\langle \mathcal{P}(S), \cap, S \rangle$, and $\langle \mathbf{I}, \cdot, 1 \rangle$ are all members of this variety, and theorems proved about this variety will hold for these specific algebras.

(b) Consider the variety of algebras with the same signature as $\langle \mathbf{R}, +, \cdot, -, 0, 1 \rangle$ (where "$-$" is a unary operation) and the following axioms:

(i) $x + y = y + x$,

(ii) $x \cdot y = y \cdot x$,

(iii) $(x + y) + z = x + (y + z)$,

(iv) $(x \cdot y) \cdot z = x \cdot (y \cdot z)$,

(v) $x \cdot (y + z) = (x \cdot y) + (x \cdot z)$,

(vi) $x + (-x) = 0$,

(vii) $x + 0 = x$,

(viii) $x \cdot 1 = x$.

Then $\langle I, +, \cdot, -, 0, 1 \rangle$ and $\langle Q, +, \cdot, -, 0, 1 \rangle$ are algebras of the same variety, but $\langle \mathcal{P}(S), \cup, \cap, \bar{V}, \phi, S \rangle$, where $^-$ denotes set complementation, is not because axiom (vi) does not hold for this algebra.

(c) Consider the variety of algebras with the signature $\langle S, \circ, c \rangle$, (where $\circ$ is a binary operation and c is a constant) and the following axioms:

$$a \circ c = a,$$

$$c \circ a = a.$$

Any theorems we prove for this variety will hold for the algebras $\langle I, +, 0 \rangle$, $\langle R, \cdot, 1 \rangle$ and $\langle \Sigma^*, \text{concatenation}, \Lambda \rangle$. Not all these theorems will hold for the algebra $\langle I, -, 0 \rangle$ (where "$-$" denotes subtraction), because $0 - 1 \neq 1$, thus violating the second axiom.   #

For the remainder of this chapter, rather than deal with algebras with arbitrary signatures, we will usually treat an arbitrary algebra such as $A = \langle S, \circ, \Delta, k \rangle$, where $\circ$ is a binary operation, Δ is a unary operation, and k denotes a constant. This will simplify the presentation by eliminating the need to treat arbitrary numbers of operations and constants and arbitrary arities of operations, but the definitions and concepts can be extended to include algebras with other signatures as well.

Before we introduce the concept of a subalgebra, we must first define the notion of a set of elements being closed under an operation.

Definition 7.1.1: Let $\circ$ and Δ be binary and unary operations on a set T, and let T' be a subset of T. Then T' is *closed with respect to* $\circ$ if $a, b \in T'$ implies $a \circ b \in T'$. The subset T' is *closed with respect to* Δ if $a \in T'$ implies $\Delta a \in T'$.

Examples

(a) Consider the set of natural number N, and let $T' = \{x \mid 0 \leq x \leq 10\}$. The set T' is not closed with respect to the operation $+$, since $7 + 7 = 14$ and $14 \notin T'$. However, T' is closed with respect to the operation *max*, where the operation is defined as $max(x, y) = x$ if $x \geq y$, otherwise $max(x, y) = y$.

(b) Since each operation of an algebra with carrier S is defined as a function from S^m to S, it follows that the carrier of an algebra is closed under all its operations.   #

If A is an algebra, a subalgebra of A is an algebra with the same signature which is "contained" in A.

Definition 7.1.2:   Let $A = \langle S, \circ, \Delta, k \rangle$ and $A' = \langle S', \circ', \Delta', k' \rangle$ be algebras. Then A' is a *subalgebra* of A if

(i) $S' \subset S$;
(ii) $a \circ' b = a \circ b$ for all $a, b \in S'$;
(iii) $\Delta'a = \Delta a$ for all $a \in S'$;
(iv) $k' = k$.

If A' is a subalgebra of A, then A' has the same signature as A and obeys the same axioms. Furthermore, the carrier of A' is a subset of the carrier of A which is closed under all the operations of A and contains all the constants of A. The largest possible subalgebra of A is A itself; this subalgebra always exists. If the set of constants of A is closed under the operations of A, then this is the carrier of the smallest subalgebra of A.

Examples

(a)   Let E denote the set of even integers. Then $\langle E, +, 0 \rangle$ is a subalgebra of $\langle \mathbf{I}, +, 0 \rangle$.

(b)   Let $\cdot$ denote multiplication. Then $\langle [0, 1], \cdot \rangle$ is a subalgebra of $\langle \mathbf{R}, \cdot \rangle$.

(c)   If M denotes the set of odd integers, then $\langle M, \cdot, 1 \rangle$ is a subalgebra of $\langle \mathbf{I}, \cdot, 1 \rangle$. But $\langle M, + \rangle$ is not a subalgebra of $\langle \mathbf{I}, + \rangle$ because the odd integers are not closed under addition; e.g., $1 + 1 = 2$.   #

The constants of an algebra are usually distinguished because of their special properties relative to one or more of the operations of the algebra. The following two definitions describe the most important of these properties for binary operations.

Definition 7.1.3:   Let $\circ$ be a binary operation on S. An element $1 \in S$ is an *identity* (or *unit*) *for the operation* $\circ$ if for every $x \in S$,

$$1 \circ x = x \circ 1 = x.$$

An element $0 \in S$ is a *zero for the operation* $\circ$ if for every $x \in S$,

$$0 \circ x = x \circ 0 = 0.$$

When no confusion can result, the operation may not be specified, and we will speak of an *identity*, or an *identity element*, and a *zero*, or a *zero element*.

Examples

(a)   The algebra $\langle \mathbf{I}, \cdot, 1, 0 \rangle$, where $\cdot$ denotes multiplication, has an identity 1 and a zero 0.

(b)   The algebra $\langle \mathbf{I}, + \rangle$ has an identity 0 but no zero element.

(c)   The algebra $\langle \mathbf{N}, max \rangle$ has an identity 0 but no zero element.

(d)   The algebra $\langle \mathbf{N}, min \rangle$ has a zero element 0 but no identity element.

(e)   Let T be the set of integers between m and n, where $m < n$ and both m and n are included in T. Then $\langle T, max \rangle$ is an algebra with an identity m and a zero n.

(f)   Consider the algebra $\langle \mathbf{R}, +, \cdot \rangle$. The element 0 is an identity for $+$, but there are no zeroes for this operation. The element 1 is an identity and 0 is a zero for the operation $\cdot$.   #

Identities and zeros are sometimes called *two-sided identities* and *two-sided zeroes* since they have the same effect when used on either the right or left. In contrast, the following definitions characterize *one-sided identities* and *one-sided zeroes*.

Definition 7.1.4:   Let $\circ$ be a binary operation on S. An element 1_l is a *left identity for the operation* $\circ$ if for every $x \in S$,

$$1_l \circ x = x.$$

An element 0_l is a *left zero for the operation* $\circ$ if for every $x \in S$,

$$0_l \circ x = 0_l.$$

A right identity 1_r and a right zero 0_r can be defined in an analogous manner.

Example

Let $A = \langle S, \circ \rangle$ where $S = \{a, b, c\}$ and $\circ$ is a binary operation defined by the following operation table. (The entry in the row labeled x and the column labeled y is the value of $x \circ y$.)

$\circ$	a	b	c
a	a	b	b
b	a	b	c
c	a	b	a

Then both a and b are right zeroes but neither is a left zero. The operation $\circ$ is neither associative nor commutative.   #

The following theorems establish the most useful properties of identities and zeroes.

Theorem 7.1.1:   Let $\circ$ be a binary operation on S with left identity 1_l and right identity 1_r. Then $1_l = 1_r$, and this element is a two-sided identity.

Proof: Since 1_l and 1_r are left and right identities,

$$1_r = 1_l \circ 1_r = 1_l. \quad \blacksquare$$

Theorem 7.1.2:   Let $\circ$ be a binary operation on S with left zero 0_l and right zero 0_r. Then $0_l = 0_r$, and this element is a two-sided zero.

The proof is similar to that of Theorem 7.1.1. The above theorems have the following immediate consequence:

Corollary 7.1.2: A two-sided identity (or zero) for a binary operation is unique.

If an identity exists in an algebra, then inverses may also exist.

Definition 7.1.5: Let ∘ be a binary operation on S and 1 an identity for the operation ∘. If $x \circ y = 1$, then x is a *left inverse* of y and y is a *right inverse* of x with respect to the operation ∘. If both $x \circ y = 1$ and $y \circ x = 1$, then x is an *inverse* of y (or a *two-sided inverse* of y) with respect to the operation ∘.

Note that if x is an inverse of y, then y is an inverse of x.

Examples

(a) The algebra $\langle \mathbf{I}, + \rangle$ has an identity 0 and every element $x \in \mathbf{I}$ has an inverse with respect to the operation $+$; the inverse of x is denoted $-x$:

$$x + (-x) = 0.$$

(b) The algebra $\langle \mathbf{N}, + \rangle$ has an identity 0 which is the only element that has an inverse.

(c) In the algebra $\langle \mathbf{I}, \cdot \rangle$, only the identity 1 has an inverse, but in $\langle \mathbf{R}, \cdot \rangle$ all elements except the zero element 0 have an inverse.

(d) Let T be the set of integers between m and n, where $m < n$ and m and n are included in T. Then $\langle T, max \rangle$ has an identity m, but only m has an inverse.

(e) Consider the set $\mathbf{F}$ of all functions on a set A under the operation of function composition. Then $\mathbf{1}_A$ is an identity. By Theorem 4.2.8, every surjection has a right inverse, every injection has a left inverse, and every bijection has a two-sided inverse. Note that one-sided inverses may not be unique.

(f) Let $\mathbf{N}_k$ be the first k natural numbers, where $k > 0$:

$$\mathbf{N}_k = \{0, 1, 2, \ldots, k - 1\}.$$

Define $+_k$ to be an addition mod k; for every $x, y \in \mathbf{N}_k$,

$$x +_k y = x + y \qquad \text{if } x + y < k,$$
$$= x + y - k \qquad \text{if } x + y \geq k.$$

Then $+_k$ is an associative binary operation with an identity 0. Every element of $\mathbf{N}_k$ has an inverse; the inverse of 0 is 0 and the inverse of every nonzero element x is $k - x$.

(g) Let $\mathbf{N}_k$ be the first k natural numbers, where $k \geq 2$, and define multiplication mod k as follows:

$$x \cdot_k y = z, \text{ where } z \in \mathbf{N}_k \text{ and } xy - z = nk \text{ for some } n \in \mathbf{N}.$$

Then 1 is an identity for the operation. An element $x \in \mathbf{N}_k$ has an inverse in

N_k only if x and k have no nontrivial divisors in common, i.e., only if x and k are relatively prime.   #

Theorem 7.1.3:   If an element has both a left and a right inverse with respect to an associative operation, then the left and right inverse elements are equal.

Proof: Let 1 be an identity for the operation $\circ$, and let x be an element with a left inverse w and a right inverse y. Then

$$w \circ x = x \circ y = 1.$$

By associativity of the operation $\circ$, it follows that

$$w = w \circ 1 = w \circ (x \circ y) = (w \circ x) \circ y = 1 \circ y = y. \quad \blacksquare$$

Problems: Section 7.1

1. Show that if $\circ$ is a commutative operation defined on a set S, then every one-sided identity is a two-sided identity.

2. Let the universe be the integers **I**. Fill in the following table with Y (yes) or N (no) according to whether the set listed in the left column is closed under the operation listed in the top row. Interpret the operations *max* and *min* as binary operations. Note that the last two columns specify unary operations.

	sum $+$	*product* $\cdot$	*difference* $-$	*abs* $\|x-y\|$	*max*	*min*	*unary minus* $-$	*absval* $\|x\|$
(a) **I**								
(b) **N**								
(c) $\{x\,\|\,0 \le x \le 10\}$								
(d) $\{x\,\|\,-5 \le x \le 5\}$								
(e) $\{x\,\|\,-10 \le x \le 0\}$								
(f) $\{2x\,\|\,x \in \mathbf{I}\}$								

3. Let the universe be the real numbers **R**. Fill in the following table with Y (yes) or N (no) according to whether the binary operations listed in the top row have the properties listed in the leftmost column.

	sum $+$	*difference* $-$	*product* $\cdot$	*max*	*min*	*abs* $\|x-y\|$
(a) associative						
(b) commutative						
(c) identity exists						
(d) zero exists						

4. Prove Theorem 7.1.2.

5. Prove Corollary 7.1.2.

6. Consider the algebras $\langle\{a, b, c, d\} \circ\rangle$ and $\langle\{a, b, c\}, \circ\rangle$, where in each case $\circ$ is defined by one of the following operation tables:

(a)

$\circ$	a	b	c	d
a	a	b	c	d
b	b	c	d	a
c	c	d	a	b
d	d	a	b	c

(b)

$\circ$	a	b	c
a	a	b	c
b	b	b	c
c	c	c	b

For each algebra,
 (i)   Is the operation commutative?
 (ii) Is the operation associative?
 (iii) Determine if there exists an identity with respect to the operation. If one exists, which element is it?
 (iv) If an identity element exists, determine which elements have inverses.
 (v)   Determine if there exists a zero with respect to the operation. If one exists, which element is it?

7. Find examples of algebras with a single binary operation which have the properties listed below. In each case, choose your algebra to have a nonempty carrier as small as possible if such an algebra exists. Your answer can be given as an operation table.
 (a) An identity element exists.
 (b) A zero element exists.
 (c) An identity element and a zero element exist.
 (d) The carrier has more than one element. Both an identity element and a zero element exist.
 (e) An identity exists but not a zero.
 (f) A zero exists but not an identity.
 (g) The operation is not commutative.
 (h) The operation is not associative.
 (i) A left zero exists which is not a right zero.
 (j) A right identity exists which is not a left identity.
 (k) An identity exists and every element has an inverse.
 (l) The carrier has more than one element. An identity exists, and every element has a left inverse, but no element other than the identity has a right inverse.

8. Describe a variety with the signature $\langle S, \circ\rangle$, where $\circ$ is a binary operation, such that for every algebra $\langle T, \cdot\rangle$ of this variety, if $V \subset T$, then $\langle V, \cdot\rangle$ is a subalgebra of $\langle T, \cdot\rangle$.

Programming Problem

Write a program to determine if a binary operation on a finite set of elements is associative. The program should accept the operation table as input.

7.2 SOME VARIETIES OF ALGEBRAS

Many algebraic varieties are useful in various areas of computer science. We will consider only four of the most important varieties: semigroups, monoids, groups, and Boolean algebras. Semigroups and monoids find application in formal languages and automata theory, groups are used in automata and coding theory, and Boolean algebras for many aspects of information processing as well as in switching theory. The utility of the structures is not limited to these areas, however; all of them are used in many other areas of investigation. In this section we will develop some of the properties of these varieties.

Semigroups

The following deceptively simple structure has been extensively studied, and a rich theory has emerged.

Definition 7.2.1: A *semigroup* is an algebra with signature $\langle S, \circ \rangle$, where $\circ$ is a binary associative operation.

The preceding definition establishes that the variety of semigroups consists of all algebras with a single binary operation which satisfies the axiom of associativity:

$$a \circ (b \circ c) = (a \circ b) \circ c.$$

From Definition 7.1.2, it follows that if $\langle S, \circ \rangle$ is a semigroup and T is a subset of S such that T is closed with respect to $\circ$, then $\langle T, \circ \rangle$ is a subalgebra of $\langle S, \circ \rangle$; we call $\langle T, \circ \rangle$ a *subsemigroup* of $\langle S, \circ \rangle$. The use of the term "subsemigroup" to denote a subalgebra of a semigroup is justified by the following theorem.

Theorem 7.2.1: If $\langle S, \circ \rangle$ is a semigroup and $\langle T, \circ \rangle$ is a subalgebra of $\langle S, \circ \rangle$, then $\langle T, \circ \rangle$ is a semigroup.

Proof: Since $\langle T, \circ \rangle$ is a subalgebra of $\langle S, \circ \rangle$, the set T is closed under the operation $\circ$. Since $\circ$ is an associative operation on S, it is also associative when restricted to T. Therefore $\langle T, \circ \rangle$ is an algebra with a binary operation which is associative and hence $\langle T, \circ \rangle$ is a semigroup. ∎

Examples

(a) Let $k \geq 0$ and S_k be the set of integers greater than or equal to k; $S_k = \{x \,|\, x \in \mathbf{I} \wedge x \geq k\}$. Then $\langle S_k, + \rangle$ is a semigroup, where $+$ denotes ordinary addition, since the operation is associative and S_k is closed with respect to $+$. Note that if $k < 0$, the set S_k is not closed under the operation of addition and $\langle S_k, + \rangle$ is not an algebra.

(b) The algebras $\langle \mathbf{I}, - \rangle$ and $\langle \mathbf{R}+, / \rangle$ are not semigroups because the operations of subtraction and division are not associative.

(c) If $\cdot$ denotes the operation of multiplication, the algebras $\langle [0, 1], \cdot \rangle, \langle [0, 1), \cdot \rangle,$

and $\langle N, \cdot \rangle$ are all semigroups. Moreover, they are all subsemigroups of $\langle R, \cdot \rangle$.

(d)   Let Σ denote a finite nonempty alphabet. Then $\langle \Sigma^*, \text{concatenation} \rangle$ and $\langle \Sigma^+, \text{concatenation} \rangle$ are semigroups.

(e)   Let $S = \{a, b\}$ and define the operation $\circ$ so that both a and b are right zeroes:

$$a \circ a = b \circ a = a$$
$$a \circ b = b \circ b = b.$$

The operation $\circ$ on S is associative, since for any $x, y, z \in S$,

$$x \circ (y \circ z) = x \circ z = z = y \circ z = (x \circ y) \circ z.$$

The algebra $\langle S, \circ \rangle$ is a semigroup, called the *right zero semigroup* of two elements.

(f)   The algebras $\langle S, max \rangle$ and $\langle S, min \rangle$ are semigroups for any set S of real numbers.

(g)   Let R be a binary relation on a set S. Then $\langle \{R^n \mid n \in N\}, \text{composition} \rangle$ is a semigroup.   #

Monoids

We next consider the variety of monoids. A monoid is essentially a semigroup which has a two-sided identity element.

Definition 7.2.2:   A *monoid* is an algebra with signature $\langle S, \circ, 1 \rangle$, where $\circ$ is a binary associative operation on S and 1 is a two-sided identity for the operation $\circ$, i.e., the following axioms hold for all elements $a, b, c \in S$:

$$a \circ (b \circ c) = (a \circ b) \circ c,$$
$$a \circ 1 = a,$$
$$1 \circ a = a.$$

If $\langle S, \circ, 1 \rangle$ is a monoid and $T \subset S$, $1 \in T$, and $T \circ T \subset T$, then by Definition 7.1.3, $\langle T, \circ, 1 \rangle$ is a subalgebra of $\langle S, \circ, 1 \rangle$; a subalgebra of a monoid is called a *submonoid*. We leave it as an exercise to show that a submonoid is a monoid.

Examples

(a)   The algebra $\langle R, +, 0 \rangle$ is a monoid because $+$ is associative and 0 is an identity element for $+$. Both $\langle I, +, 0 \rangle$ and $\langle N, +, 0 \rangle$ are submonoids of $\langle R, +, 0 \rangle$.

(b)   The algebras $\langle I, \cdot, 1 \rangle$, $\langle N, \cdot, 1 \rangle$, $\langle I+, \cdot, 1 \rangle$ and $\langle R, \cdot, 1 \rangle$ are all monoids.

(c)   The algebras $\langle I, \cdot, 0 \rangle$ and $\langle I, +, 1 \rangle$ are not monoids because in each case the constant is not an identity for the specified operation.

(d)   If Σ is a finite nonempty alphabet, then $\langle \Sigma^*, \text{concatenation}, \Lambda \rangle$ is a monoid. If $X \subset \Sigma^*$ then $\langle X^*, \text{concatenation}, \Lambda \rangle$ is a submonoid of

$$\langle \Sigma^*, \text{concatenation}, \Lambda \rangle.$$

(e) Let S be any subset of the real numbers which contains a lower bound, i.e., there is some $m \in S$ such that $m \leq x$ for all $x \in S$. Then $\langle S, max, m \rangle$ is a monoid. Similarly, if S contains an upper bound n, then $x \in S \Rightarrow x \leq n$ and $\langle S, min, n \rangle$ is a monoid.

(f) The systems $\langle \mathbf{N}_k, +_k, 0 \rangle$ and $\langle \mathbf{N}_k, \cdot_k, 1 \rangle$ are monoids, where

$$\mathbf{N}_k = \{0, 1, 2, \ldots, k - 1\}$$

and the operations $+_k$ and $\cdot_k$ are addition and multiplication mod k.   #

If $\langle S, \circ, a \rangle$ is a monoid, then $\langle S, \circ \rangle$ is a semigroup; this is sometimes expressed by the assertion that "every monoid is a semigroup." On the other hand, some semigroups, such as $\langle \mathbf{N}, + \rangle$, have an identity, and some, such as $\langle \mathbf{I}+, + \rangle$, do not. A semigroup $\langle S, \circ \rangle$ can always be converted into a monoid by "adjoining" (i.e., adding) a new element whose behavior is defined to be that of an identity for the operation $\circ$. Suppose 1 is an element not in S. (If necessary we can relabel the elements of S so that $1 \notin S$.) We can extend the operation $\circ$ to $S \cup \{1\}$ so that for all $x \in S \cup \{1\}$, $x \circ 1 = 1 \circ x = x$. Then $\langle S \cup \{1\}, \circ, 1 \rangle$ is a monoid. This process is called "adjoining an identity" to the semigroup $\langle S, \circ \rangle$. Note that even if c was an identity of $\langle S, \circ \rangle$, it will *not* be one for the monoid $\langle S \cup \{1\}, \circ, 1 \rangle$, since

$$c \circ 1 = 1 \circ c = c \neq 1.$$

Groups

We next consider the variety of groups. Informally, a group is a monoid in in which every element has an inverse with respect to the binary operation of the monoid. More specifically a group is an algebra consisting of a set, a binary associative operation, a unary operation and a distinguished element which is a two-sided identity for the binary operation. The unary operation maps each element of the group to its inverse with respect to the binary operation. If we denote the identity of the operation $\circ$ by 1 and the inverse of x by $\bar{x}$, then for every element x, there exists an element $\bar{x}$ such that $x \circ \bar{x} = \bar{x} \circ x = 1$.

Definition 7.2.3: A *group* is an algebra with signature $\langle S, \circ, ^-, 1 \rangle$ such that $\circ$ is an associative binary operation on S, the constant 1 is a two-sided identity for the operation $\circ$, and $^-$ is a unary operation defined over the carrier such that for all $x \in S$, $\bar{x}$ is an inverse for x with respect to $\circ$.

If $A = \langle S, \circ, ^-, 1 \rangle$ is a group and $A' = \langle T, \circ, ^-, 1 \rangle$ is a subalgebra of A, then A' is called a *subgroup* of A. A subalgebra of a group is a group.

The requirement that an inverse exist for every element of a group places strong restrictions on the binary operation. In particular, both right and left cancellation laws hold; that is, if $a \circ c = b \circ c$, then $a = b$, since

$$a \circ c = b \circ c \Rightarrow (a \circ c) \circ \bar{c} = (b \circ c) \circ \bar{c}$$

$$\Rightarrow a \circ (c \circ \bar{c}) = b \circ (c \circ \bar{c})$$

$$\Rightarrow a \circ 1 = b \circ 1$$

$$\Rightarrow a = b.$$

Similarly, if $c \circ a = c \circ b$, then $a = b$. Cancellation laws do not generally hold for the operations of either semigroups or monoids; for example, if c is a zero element, then $a \circ c = b \circ c$ for all elements a and b of the carrier.

Another property of the binary operation of a group is that all equations of the form

$$a \circ x = b$$

have a unique solution for the value of x:

$$x = \bar{a} \circ b;$$

an analogous assertion holds for equations of the form $x \circ a = b$. The operation of a group is injective in the sense that if $x \neq y$, then $a \circ x \neq a \circ y$ and $x \circ a \neq y \circ a$; thus "multiplication" by an element on either the right or left induces an injection from the carrier to itself. Moreover, the operation of a group is surjective in the sense that $a \circ S = S = S \circ a$, where we use $a \circ S$ to denote the set

$$\{a \circ x \mid x \in S\}.$$

We leave the proofs of these assertions as exercises.

Examples

(a) The algebra $\langle \mathbf{I}, +, -, 0 \rangle$ is a group, where $+$ denotes addition and $-$ denotes unary minus. If K denotes the set of all multiples of a given $k \in \mathbf{N}$, then $\langle K, +, -, 0 \rangle$ is a subgroup of $\langle \mathbf{I}, +, -, 0 \rangle$.

(b) The algebra $\langle \mathbf{Q}+, \cdot, {}^{-1}, 1 \rangle$ is a group, where $\cdot$ denotes multiplication, and $^{-1}$ denotes the unary operation of taking the reciprocal of a rational number.

(c) Let A be any set and let $\mathbf{P}$ denote the set of permutations on A. Then $\mathbf{P}$ is the set of bijective functions from A to A. The structure $\langle \mathbf{P}, \circ, {}^{-1}, 1_A \rangle$ is a group, where $\circ$ denotes composition of functions, and f^{-1} is the inverse function of f.

(d) The operations *max* and *min* cannot generally be used as the binary operation of a group because an inverse operation cannot be defined if the carrier has more than one element.

(e) The algebras $\langle \mathbf{N}_k, +_k, {}^-, 0 \rangle$ are groups, if we define $\bar{x} = k - x$.

(f) The algebras $\langle \mathbf{N}_k, \cdot_k, {}^-, 1 \rangle$ are not groups because the element $0 \in \mathbf{N}_k$ has no inverse.   #

Boolean Algebras

The last variety we will consider is that of Boolean algebras.

Definition 7.2.4:   A *Boolean algebra* is an algebra with signature

$$\langle S, +, \cdot, {}^-, 0, 1 \rangle$$

(where $+$ and $\cdot$ are binary operations and ${}^-$ is a unary operation called *complementation*) and the following axioms hold. (We write ab for $a \cdot b$.)

(i)	$a + b = b + a$	commutative laws
(ii)	$ab = ba$	
(iii)	$(a + b) + c = a + (b + c)$	associative laws
(iv)	$(ab)c = a(bc)$	
(v)	$a(b + c) = ab + ac$	distributive laws
(vi)	$a + (bc) = (a + b)(a + c)$	
(vii)	$a + 0 = a$	0 is an identity for $+$
(viii)	$a1 = a$	1 is an identity for $\cdot$
(ix)	$a + \bar{a} = 1$	properties of the complement
(x)	$a\bar{a} = 0$	

Less formally, we can say that a Boolean algebra has two commutative, associative binary operations $+$ and $\cdot$ which distribute over each other, together with a single unary operation ${}^-$. The constants 0 and 1 are identities for $+$ and $\cdot$ respectively, and for every element a, $a + \bar{a} = 0$ and $a \cdot \bar{a} = 1$.

If $\langle S, +, \cdot, {}^-, 0, 1 \rangle$ is a Boolean algebra and T is a subset of S which is closed under the operations $+$, $\cdot$, and ${}^-$, and $0, 1 \in T$, then $\langle T, +, \cdot, {}^-, 0, 1 \rangle$ is a subalgebra of $\langle S, +, \cdot, {}^-, 0, 1 \rangle$ called a *Boolean subalgebra*. A Boolean subalgebra is a Boolean algebra.

Examples

(a) It can be shown that if the carrier of a Boolean algebra is finite and has more than one element, then the cardinality of the carrier is an even integer. The following operation tables describe the operations of a Boolean algebra with carrier $\{0, 1\}$.

$+$	0	1		$\cdot$	0	1		${}^-$	
0	0	1		0	0	0		0	1
1	1	0		1	0	1		1	0

Note that these operations are similar to the operations $\vee$, $\wedge$ and $\neg$ defined for truth values in Chapter 1.

(b) Let A be any set and let ${}^-$ denote the operation of set complementation relative to A. Then $\langle \mathcal{P}(A), \cup, \cap, {}^-, \phi, A \rangle$ is a Boolean algebra. This is an example of a Boolean *set algebra*. The carrier of a Boolean set algebra need not be a power set; it can be any collection of sets which is closed under union, intersection and complement relative to some universal set.

(c) Let S be the set of positive divisors of 30; $S = \{1, 2, 3, 5, 6, 10, 15, 30\}$. Let $x_1 + x_2$ denote the least common multiple of x_1 and x_2; let $\cdot$ denote the greatest common divisor and $\bar{x}$ denote the number $30/x$. Then $\langle S, +, \cdot, \bar{\ }, 1, 30\rangle$ is a Boolean algebra.   #

Problems: Section 7.2

1. Construct a semigroup using the operation *max* which has a zero but no identity.

2. Let $S_k = \{x \mid x \in \mathbf{I} \wedge x \geq k\}$ where $k \geq 0$. Show that $\langle S_k, +\rangle$ is a subsemigroup of $\langle \mathbf{I}, +\rangle$.

3. Construct a monoid using the operation *max* which has no zero and an infinite carrier.

4. Let E denote the even natural numbers; $E = \{0, 2, 4, \ldots\}$. Show that $\langle E, +, 0\rangle$ is a submonoid of $\langle \mathbf{N}, +, 0\rangle$.

5. Show that every subalgebra of a monoid is a monoid.

6. Construct a group using *max* as the binary operation.

7. Let E denote the even integers; $E = \{0, -2, 2, -4, 4, \ldots\}$. Show that $\langle E, +, -, 0\rangle$ is a subgroup of $\langle \mathbf{I}, +, -, 0\rangle$, where the symbol $-$ denotes unary minus.

8. Construct tables for the operations of addition and inverse for the group

$$\langle \mathbf{N}_k, +_k, -, 0\rangle$$

   where $k = 5$.

9. Show that if $\circ$ is a binary operation on T and 0 is a zero element with respect to the binary operation $\circ$, then T cannot be made the carrier of a group unless $T = \{0\}$.

10. Prove that if $\langle S, \circ, \bar{\ }, 1\rangle$ is a group, then for every $a \in S$,
    (a) if $x \neq y$, then $a \circ x \neq a \circ y$. Similarly, if $x \neq y$, then $x \circ a \neq y \circ a$.
    (b) $1 \circ S = S = S \circ a$.
    (c) $\bar{\bar{a}} = a$ (the inverse of the inverse of a is a).

11. Show that if $\langle S, \circ, \bar{\ }, 1\rangle$ is a group and T is a nonempty subset of S such that

$$\forall x\, \forall y[x, y \in T \Rightarrow x \circ \bar{y} \in T],$$

    then $\langle T, \circ, \bar{\ }, 1\rangle$ is a subgroup of $\langle S, \circ, \bar{\ }, 1\rangle$.

12. For each of the following digraphs, let R be the binary relation represented by the digraph, and let $S = \{R^n \mid n \in \mathbf{I}+\}$ be the carrier of an algebra in which composition of relations is the binary operation. In each case, determine whether the algebra can be presented as a semigroup, monoid, or group, and state the cardinality of the carrier.

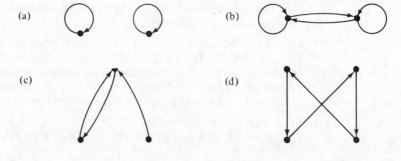

(e)

13. (a) State necessary and sufficient conditions on a binary relation R so that the set $\{R^n \mid n \in \mathbf{N}\}$ can be made the carrier of a monoid with the operation of composition.

   (b) State necessary and sufficient conditions on a binary relation R so that the set $\{R^n \mid n \in \mathbf{I+}\}$ can be made the carrier of a monoid using the operation of composition.

   (c) State necessary and sufficient conditions on a binary relation R on a finite set so that the set $\{R^n \mid n \in \mathbf{I+}\}$ can be made the carrier of a group with the binary operation of composition.

14. Let S be a set. Show that $\langle \{S, \phi\}, \cup, \cap, {}^-, \phi, S \rangle$ is a Boolean subalgebra of $\langle \mathcal{P}(S), \cup, \cap, {}^-, \phi, S \rangle$.

15. Consider the following questions to determine when a Boolean algebra can be constructed from the set of integers between and including m and n where $m < n$, using the operations of *max* (for $+$) and *min* (for $\cdot$).

   (a) Do the operations *max* and *min* satisfy Axioms 1–4 of Definition 7.2.4?

   (b) Do the operations *max* and *min* satisfy Axioms 5 and 6?

   (c) What would be the constants if Axioms 7 and 8 are to be satisfied?

   (d) Can an inverse operation be defined which satisfies Axioms 9 and 10? (Hint: Your answer should be expressed as a function of the size of the carrier, i.e., of $n - m + 1$.)

16. Consider a computer which uses words of k bits to represent nonnegative integers in binary notation. The only operation is addition. When overflow occurs, the high order bits are lost.

   (a) What algebraic variety would be most appropriate to model addition in the machine? How big is the carrier?

   (b) Suppose overflow causes the result to be set to the largest representable number. What algebraic variety would best model addition in this case?

7.3 HOMOMORPHISMS

We wish to find ways of characterizing the structural similarities of two algebras A and A'. Clearly one possibility is for A' to "look just like" A, that is, for A' to be simply a relabeled version of A. Then A and A' must have the same signature, the carriers of A and A' must have the same cardinality, and the operations and constants of the two algebras must have the same properties. If two algebras are similar in the sense we have described, then the similarity can be established by exhibiting a bijection from the carrier of A to that of A' such that the function describes how A' can be viewed simply as a a a relabelling of A. The concept is made precise in the following definition. For ease of exposition, we restrict ourselves to the algebras $A = \langle S, \circ, \Delta, k \rangle$ and $A' = \langle S', \circ', \Delta', k' \rangle$ where $\circ$ and $\circ'$ are binary operations, Δ and Δ' are unary operations, and k and k' are constants.

Definition 7.3.1: The algebras $A = \langle S, \circ, \Delta, k \rangle$ and $A' = \langle S', \circ', \Delta', k' \rangle$ are *isomorphic* if there exists a bijection h such that

(i) $h: S \to S'$;
(ii) $h(a \circ b) = h(a) \circ' h(b)$;
(iii) $h(\Delta(a)) = \Delta'(h(a))$;
(iv) $h(k) = k'$.

The map h is called an *isomorphism* from A to A', and A' is said to be an *isomorphic image* of A under the map h.

The preceding definition is phrased in terms of a specific signature, but an analogous definition can be formulated for any signature. In each case, if h is an isomorphism from an algebra A to an algebra A', then

1. A and A' must have the same signature,
2. the function h maps each constant of A to the corresponding constant of A', and
3. each operation of A is preserved by the function h.

If A and A' are isomorphic algebras, they are essentially the same structure with different names; the algebra A' can be obtained from A by a simple change of notation.

Examples

(a) Let E denote the set of even integers; $E = \{\ldots -4, -2, 0, 2, 4, \ldots\}$. Then the algebras $\langle I, +, 0 \rangle$ and $\langle E, +, 0 \rangle$ are isomorphic. This is established by showing the map

$$f: I \to E,$$

$$f(x) = 2x,$$

is an isomorphism, that is, by showing the conditions of Definition 7.3.1 are satisfied:

1. The function f is clearly bijective.
2. For any integers x and y, $f(x + y) = 2(x + y)$
$$= 2x + 2y$$
$$= f(x) + f(y).$$
3. $f(0) = 2 \cdot 0 = 0$.

(b) Let $\mathbf{R}+$ denote the set of positive real numbers. Then $\langle \mathbf{R}+, \cdot, 1 \rangle$ is isomorphic to $\langle \mathbf{R}, +, 0 \rangle$ and the map

$$h: \mathbf{R}+ \to \mathbf{R},$$

$$h(x) = \log x,$$

is an isomorphism. To show this, we first establish that h is a bijection from

$\mathbf{R}+$ to $\mathbf{R}$. The function h is surjective because for $x > 0$, the equation $\log x = y$ always has a solution of $x = 2^y$. Because the log function is monotone increasing, h is injective. Hence, h is bijective and condition (i) of Definition 7.3.1 is satisfied. Furthermore,

$$h(a \cdot b) = \log(a \cdot b) = \log(a) + \log(b) = h(a) + h(b),$$

thus satisfying condition (ii). Since $h(1) = \log(1) = 0$, condition (iv) is also satisfied.

The isomorphism h is the mathematical basis for the slide rule.

(c) The semigroups $\langle \mathbf{N}, + \rangle$ and $\langle \mathbf{I}+, \cdot \rangle$ are not isomorphic. We establish this using a proof by contradiction. Suppose h is an isomorphism from $\langle \mathbf{N}, + \rangle$ to $\langle \mathbf{I}+, \cdot \rangle$. There are infinitely many prime numbers in $\mathbf{I}+$. Since h is a surjection from $\mathbf{N}$ to $\mathbf{I}+$, there must be some $x \in \mathbf{N}$ where $x \geq 2$ and some prime number p, where $p \geq 3$, such that $h(x) = p$. If h is an isomorphism from $\langle \mathbf{N}, + \rangle$ to $\langle \mathbf{I}+, \cdot \rangle$, then
   (i) $p = h(x) = h(x + 0) = h(x) \cdot h(0)$, and
   (ii) $p = h(x) = h((x - 1) + 1) = h(x - 1) \cdot h(1)$.
But since p is a prime number, the only factors of p are p and 1. Therefore, by (i), either $h(x) = 1$ or $h(0) = 1$, and by (ii), either $h(1) = 1$ or $h(x - 1) = 1$. Since $0 < 1 \leq x - 1 < x$, it follows that 1 is the image of at least two elements under the function h. We conclude that h is not a bijection and therefore not an isomorphism.   #

Theorem 7.3.1:   Let C be a collection of algebras, and let $\sim$ be the relation defined by $A \sim A'$ if and only if A is isomorphic to A'. Then $\sim$ is an equivalence relation on C.

The proof is left as an exercise.

In order for A to be isomorphic to A', the map $h: S \to S'$ must be bijective. If h is not necessarily bijective, but the other conditions are still satisfied, then h is called a homomorphism from A to A'.

Definition 7.3.2:   Let $A = \langle S, \circ, \Delta, k \rangle$ and $A' = \langle S', \circ', \Delta', k' \rangle$ be algebras with the same signature, and let h be a function such that

   (i) $h: S \to S'$;
   (ii) $h(a \circ b) = h(a) \circ' h(b)$;
   (iii) $h(\Delta(a)) = \Delta'(h(a))$;
   (iv) $h(k) = k'$;

then h is a *homomorphism* from A to A'.†

Figure 7.3.1 depicts how two algebras can be related by a homomorphism.

---

†There is a rich terminology associated with homomorphisms. Let h be a homomorphism from A to A'. If h is injective, then h is a *monomorphism* and if h is surjective, then h is an *epimorphism*. If $A = A'$, then h is an *endomorphism*; if $A = A'$ and h is an isomorphism, then h is an *automorphism*. We will not use this terminology.

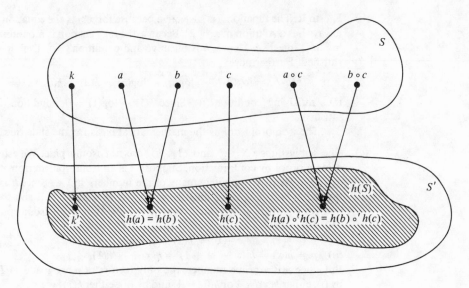

Fig. 7.3.1   Representation of a homomorphism h from

$$A = \langle S, \circ, k \rangle \text{ to } A' = \langle S', \circ'. k' \rangle.$$

The shaded portion of S' represents $h(S)$, the homomorphic image
of S under h.

Alternatively, we can characterize a homomorphism from $A = \langle S, \circ, k \rangle$ to $A' = \langle S', \circ', k' \rangle$ as a map h such that $h(k) = k'$ and the following diagram commutes.

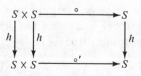

Figure 7.3.2

From Definitions 7.3.1 and 7.3.2 it is immediate that an isomorphism is a homomorphism which is also a bijection.

Examples

(a) For $k \in \mathbf{I}$, the map $f_k: \mathbf{I} \to \mathbf{I}$ defined by $f_k(x) = kx$ is a homomorphism from $\langle \mathbf{I}, +, 0 \rangle$ to $\langle \mathbf{I}, +, 0 \rangle$. If $k \neq 0$, then f is injective. If $k = 1$ or $k = -1$, then f is bijective and therefore an isomorphism.

(b) Let $f: \mathbf{R} \to \mathbf{R}$ where $f(x) = 2^x$. Then f is an injective homomorphism (but not an isomorphism) from $\langle \mathbf{R}, +, 0 \rangle$ to $\langle \mathbf{R}, \cdot, 1 \rangle$.

(c) Let $f: \mathbf{N} \to \mathbf{N}_k$ where $f(x) = x \bmod k$. Then f is a surjective homomorphism from $\langle \mathbf{N}, +, 0 \rangle$ to $\langle \mathbf{N}_k, +_k, 0 \rangle$.

(d) Let Σ be a finite nonempty alphabet, and let $\|x\|$ denote the length of a string $x \in \Sigma^*$. Then the function h defined by

$$h: \Sigma^* \rightarrow \mathbf{N},$$

$$h(x) = \|x\|,$$

is a homomorphism from $\langle \Sigma^*, \text{concatenation}, \Lambda \rangle$ to $\langle \mathbf{N}, +, 0 \rangle$. If Σ is a singleton set, then h is an isomorphism.   #

Theorem 7.3.2:   Let h be a homomorphism from $A = \langle S, \circ, \Delta, k \rangle$ to $A' = \langle S', \circ', \Delta', k' \rangle$. Then $\langle h(S), \circ', \Delta', k' \rangle$ is a subalgebra of A', called the *homomorphic image of A under h.*

Proof: To show that $\langle h(S), \circ', \Delta', k' \rangle$ is a subalgebra of A', the following conditions must be established.

1. $h(S) \subset S'$. This follows from the fact that $h: S \rightarrow S'$.
2. The constant k' is an element of $h(S)$. By definition of a homomorphism, $h(k) = k'$, and since $k \in S$, it follows that $k' = h(k) \in h(S)$.
3. The set $h(S)$ is closed under the operation $\circ'$, i.e., if $a, b \in h(S)$, then $a \circ b \in h(S)$. But if $a, b \in h(S)$, then there exist elements $x, y \in S$ such that $h(x) = a$ and $h(y) = b$. Furthermore, $x \circ y = z$ for some $z \in S$, and therefore

    $$a \circ' b = h(x) \circ' h(y) = h(x \circ y) = h(z) \in h(S).$$

4. The set $h(S)$ is closed under the operation Δ', i.e., if $a \in h(S)$, then $\Delta'a \in h(S)$. If $a \in h(S)$, then $a = h(x)$ for some $x \in S$. Therefore $\Delta x \in S$, and $h(\Delta x) = \Delta'h(x) = \Delta'a$; hence $\Delta'a \in h(S)$. ∎

The homomorphic image of an algebra A is of the same variety as A. The following theorem establishes this result for the varieties we have defined.

Theorem 7.3.3:   Let h be a homomorphism from the algebra A to the algebra A'.

(a) If A is a semigroup, then the homomorphic image of A under h is a semigroup.
(b) If A is a monoid, then the homomorphic image of A under h is a monoid.
(c) If A is a group, then the homomorphic image of A under h is a group.
(d) If A is a Boolean algebra, then the homomorphic image of A under h is a Boolean algebra.

Proof: Let $A = \langle S, \circ \rangle$ be a semigroup, and let $A' = \langle S', \circ' \rangle$. By Theorem 7.3.2, $\langle h(S), \circ' \rangle$ is a subalgebra of A'. Furthermore, the operation $\circ'$ must be associative on $h(S)$, since by the associativity of $\circ$ and the properties of h,

$$h(a) \circ' (h(b) \circ' h(c)) = h(a) \circ' h(b \circ c) = h(a \circ (b \circ c))$$

$$= h((a \circ b) \circ c) = h(a \circ b) \circ' h(c) = (h(a) \circ' h(b)) \circ' h(c).$$

It follows that $\langle h(S), \circ' \rangle$ is a semigroup.

The proofs of parts (b), (c), and (d) are left as exercises. ∎

Examples

(a) Let h be a homomorphism from the monoid $\langle I, +, 0 \rangle$ to $\langle I, +, 0 \rangle$ defined by

$$h: I \to I,$$

$$h(x) = 3x.$$

The homomorphic image of $\langle I, +, 0 \rangle$ under h is the monoid $\langle \{3n \mid n \in I\}, +, 0 \rangle$, which is a submonoid of $\langle I, +, 0 \rangle$.

(b) Define the map $h: R \to R$ as $h(x) = 2^x$. Then h is a homomorphism from the monoid $A = \langle R, +, 0 \rangle$ to the monoid $A' = \langle R, \cdot, 1 \rangle$. The image of A under h is the submonoid $\langle R+, \cdot, 1 \rangle$.

(c) Let $S_k = \{x \mid x \in I \wedge x \geq k\}$, where $k \in N$. Let $k, m,$ and n be elements of N such that $kn \geq m$, and define h as follows:

$$h: S_k \to S_m,$$

$$h(x) = nx.$$

Then h is a homomorphism from the semigroup $\langle S_k, + \rangle$ to a subsemigroup of $\langle S_m, + \rangle$.

(d) Let S be a nonempty set, and consider the Boolean algebras

$$A = \langle \mathcal{P}(S), \cup, \cap, {}^-, \phi, S \rangle$$

$$B = \langle \{0, 1\}, +, \cdot, {}^-, 0, 1 \rangle$$

Then the following function h is a homomorphism from A to B.

$$h: \mathcal{P}(S) \to \{0, 1\},$$

$$h(\phi) = 0,$$

$$h(A) = 1 \quad \text{for } A \subset S \text{ and } A \neq \phi.$$

Note that $h(\phi) = 0$ and $h(S) = 1$, thus satisfying the condition that a homomorphism maps the constants of one structure to the corresponding constants of the other.

(e) Let $N_k = \{0, 1, 2, \ldots, k - 1\}$, where $k \geq 1$, and let $p \in N$. The map

$$h: N \to N_k,$$

$$h(x) = y \quad \text{where } y = px \bmod k,$$

is a homomorphism to a submonoid of $\langle N_k, +_k, 0 \rangle$.

(f) For the universe of integers I and some $k \in N$, define $x \sim y$ if and only if $x \equiv y \bmod k$. Let $I/\sim$ be the quotient set; then $[x] = \{y \mid y = x \bmod k\}$. Define the operation $+$ on $I/\sim$ as $[x] + [y] = [x + y]$, and unary minus as $-[x] = [-x]$. Then $\langle I/\sim, +, -, [0] \rangle$ is a group and

$$h: I \to I/\sim,$$

$$h(x) = [x],$$

is a homomorphism from $\langle I, +, -, 0 \rangle$ to $\langle I/\sim, +, -, [0] \rangle$.   #

Problems: Section 7.3

1. (a) Show that two algebras cannot be isomorphic if their carriers have different cardinalities.
   (b) Give an example to show that two algebras with the same signature may not be isomorphic even though their carriers have the same cardinality.

2. Prove Theorem 7.3.1 for algebras with signature $\langle S, \circ, k \rangle$, where $\circ$ is a binary operation and $k \in S$.

3. Suppose h is a homomorphism from $\langle S, \circ \rangle$ to $\langle S', \circ' \rangle$, where $\circ$ and $\circ'$ are binary operations.
   (a) Show that if $1 \in S$ is an identity with respect to the operation $\circ$, then some element $1' \in S'$ is an identity with respect to $\circ'$ for the subalgebra $\langle h(S), \circ' \rangle$.
   (b) Show that an identity for $\langle h(S), \circ' \rangle$ may not be an identity for $\langle S', \circ' \rangle$.
   (c) Show that if $0 \in S$ is a zero with respect to $\circ$, then some element $0' \in S'$ is a zero for the subalgebra $\langle h(S), \circ' \rangle$ and $h(0) = 0'$.
   (d) Show that a zero for $\langle h(S), \circ' \rangle$ may not be a zero for $\langle S', \circ' \rangle$.

4. (a) Show that there are exactly i homomorphisms from $\langle \mathbf{N}_i, +_i, 0 \rangle$ to itself.
   (b) Describe the set of all homomorphisms from $\langle \mathbf{N}, +, 0 \rangle$ to $\langle \mathbf{N}_i, +_i, 0 \rangle$.
   (c) Describe the set of all homomorphisms from $\langle \mathbf{N}_2, +_2, 0 \rangle$ to $\langle \mathbf{N}_3, +_3, 0 \rangle$.

5. Prove parts (b), (c), and (d) of Theorem 7.3.3.

6. Most computers represent numbers with binary sequences of a fixed length. Only a finite set of numbers can be represented exactly, and "arithmetic overflow" occurs when the result of a computation is larger than any of the numbers which can be represented. Consider the following strategies for treating arithmetic overflow. For simplicity, we will treat only the natural numbers and the operation of addition. For each of the following functions f, determine whether f is a homomorphism from $\langle \mathbf{N}, +, 0 \rangle$ to the specified algebra $\langle S, \oplus, 0 \rangle$, where S is the set of binary sequences of length k. In each case, the operation $\oplus$ is based on binary addition and is described by means of examples. In the illustrative examples given below, we use $k = 3$.
   (a) The k bits represent the least significant digits of the k digit binary representation of each natural number. The operation $\oplus$ is the usual binary addition except that if overflow occurs, the leading digits are lost. Thus, $f(3) = 011$, $f(6) = 110$, and $f(9) = f(3 + 6) = 011 \oplus 110 = 001 = f(8n + 1)$ for all $n \in \mathbf{N}$.
   (b) If $n < 2^k$, then $f(n)$ is the k digit binary representation of n. If $n \geq 2^k$, then $f(n)$ is represented by the k digit binary representation of $2^k - 1$. Thus $f(3) = 011$, $f(6) = 110$, and $f(9) = f(3 + 6) = 011 \oplus 110 = 111 = f(x)$ for all $x \geq 7$.
   (c) One bit is reserved for an indication that overflow has occurred. (We will use 0 for no overflow, 1 for overflow, and use the leftmost bit as the overflow indicator.) For all numbers less than $2^{(k-1)}$, the numbers are represented in their $k - 1$ digit binary representation and the overflow bit is set to 0. If $n \geq 2^{(k-1)}$, then $f(n)$ consists of the digit 1 followed by the $k - 1$ least significant digits of the binary representation of n; e.g., if $k = 3$, then $f(12) = 100$. Thus $f(3) = 011$, $f(2) = 010$, and $f(3 + 2) = 011 \oplus 010 = 101 = f(4n + 1)$ for all $n \in \mathbf{N}$.

7. Let $A = \langle S, \circ, k \rangle$ and $A' = \langle S', \circ', k' \rangle$ and let h be a homomorphism from A to A'. Show that if $\langle T, \circ', k' \rangle$ is a subalgebra of A', then $\langle h^{-1}(T), \circ, k \rangle$ is a subalgebra of A.

8. Let Σ be a finite alphabet, and consider the monoid $\langle \Sigma^*, \text{concatenation}, \Lambda \rangle$. This is sometimes called the *free monoid generated by* Σ. The free monoid has the following important property:

Let $\langle S, \circ, 1 \rangle$ be an arbitrary monoid. For any map $h: \Sigma \to S$, there is a unique extension of h to a homomorphism $h^*: \Sigma^* \to S$.

Prove this property.

7.4 CONGRUENCE RELATIONS

A congruence relation is an equivalence relation defined on the carrier of an algebra such that the equivalence classes of the relation are "preserved" by the operations of the algebra. The notion of congruence is a generalization of the notion of equality.

The most familiar example of a congruence relation is one used to associate ordered pairs of integers with rational numbers. We define a *fraction* as an ordered pair of integers $\langle p, q \rangle$ (written p/q where $q \neq 0$, and let $\mathbf{F}$ be the set of all fractions. The binary operations of $+$, $-$, and $\cdot$ and unary $-$ can be defined on $\mathbf{F}$ using the corresponding operations on integers as follows:

$$(p/q) + (r/s) = (ps + rq)/(qs),$$
$$(p/q) - (r/s) = (ps - rq)/(qs),$$
$$(p/q) \cdot (r/s) = (pr)/(qs),$$
$$- (p/q) = (-p)/q.$$

Note that the fractions $1/2$ and $2/4$ are not equal; they are distinct by virtue of their being different ordered pairs. However, we usually want to treat $1/2$ as indistinguishable from $2/4$ and $2/2$ the same as $1/1$. This is done by establishing an equivalence relation $\sim$ over $\mathbf{F}$ as follows:

$$p/q \sim r/s \Leftrightarrow ps = rq.$$

The set of rational numbers $\mathbf{Q}$ is defined to be the quotient set $\mathbf{F}/\sim$. Thus, the rational number commonly denoted by "$1/2$" actually represents the set

$$\{\ldots, (-3/-6), (-2/-4), (-1/-2), (1/2), (2/4), (3/6), \ldots\}$$

and we write, for example, $1/2 = 2/4$ because these fractions represent the same equivalence class. The equivalence relation $\sim$ over $\mathbf{F}$ is particularly useful because of a "substitution property" which makes this relation analogous to equality with respect to arithmetic operations; substituting one operand for another of the same equivalence class will not change the equivalence class of the result. For example, just as the relation of equality of two integers a and b is preserved when both integers are multiplied by an integer c, i.e.,

$$\text{if } a = b, \text{ then } ac = bc,$$

the relation $\sim$ is preserved when two equivalent fractions are multiplied by another:

$$p/q \sim r/s \Rightarrow ps = rq$$
$$\Rightarrow (ps)(tu) = (rq)(tu)$$
$$\Rightarrow (pt)(su) = (rt)(qu)$$
$$\Rightarrow \left(\frac{pt}{qu}\right) \sim \left(\frac{rt}{su}\right)$$
$$\Rightarrow \left(\frac{p}{q}\right)\left(\frac{t}{u}\right) \sim \left(\frac{r}{s}\right)\left(\frac{t}{u}\right).$$

This establishes that for any fractions a, b, and c,

$$\text{if } a \sim b, \text{ then } ac \sim bc.$$

In fact, equivalence of fractions is preserved under the other operations as well; if a, b, and c are fractions and $a \sim b$, then the following assertions hold:

$$c + a \sim c + b \qquad a + c \sim b + c$$
$$c - a \sim c - b \qquad a - c \sim b - c$$
$$c \cdot a \sim c \cdot b \qquad a \cdot c \sim b \cdot c$$
$$-a \sim -b$$

Because $\sim$ is an equivalence relation which is preserved under these operations, we say $\sim$ is a *congruence relation* with respect to the binary operations of $+$, $-$, $\cdot$, and the unary operation $-$.

Rather than define congruence relations for operations of arbitrary arities, we will restrict our formal definition to the algebra $A = \langle S, \circ, \Delta \rangle$, where $\circ$ is a binary operation and Δ is a unary operation. We will usually write ab for $a \circ b$.

Definition 7.4.1: Let $A = \langle S, \circ, \Delta \rangle$ be an algebra with a binary operation $\circ$ and a unary operation Δ and let $\sim$ be an equivalence relation on S. Then $\sim$ is a *congruence relation on A* if and only if for all elements $a, b, c \in S$,
   (i)   if $a \sim b$, then $ac \sim bc$ and $ca \sim cb$
   (ii) if $a \sim b$, then $\Delta a \sim \Delta b$.
The equivalence classes of $\sim$ are called the *congruence classes* of the relation $\sim$.

Informally, we will speak of a relation $\sim$ on a set S as a congruence relation with respect to the operation $\circ$ if $\sim$ is a congruence relation on the algebra $\langle S, \circ \rangle$. A relation $\sim$ is a congruence relation on an algebra A with carrier S if and only if $\sim$ is a congruence on S with respect to each of the operations of A.

Examples

   (a)   Equality is a congruence relation on any algebra.

   (b)   Consider the integers **I** together with the operation of addition. The equivalence relation $\sim$ of "equivalence mod k" for some given $k \in \mathbf{N}$ is a congruence relation on the algebra $\langle \mathbf{I}, + \rangle$, where

$$x \sim y \text{ if and only if } x \equiv y \text{ mod } k.$$

To show $\sim$ is a congruence relation with respect to the operation $+$, we must first show that it is an equivalence relation; this was established by Theorem 3.7.1. Then we must show that if $a \sim b$, then $a + c \sim b + c$ and $c + a \sim c + b$. Suppose $a \sim b$. Then $a - b = kn$ for some $n \in \mathbf{I}$. Then $(a + c) - (b + c) = a - b = kn$; hence $a + c \sim b + c$. Moreover, by the commutativity of addition, $c + a \sim c + b$. Thus $\sim$ is a congruence relation over $\langle \mathbf{I}, + \rangle$.

The relation $\sim$ can also be shown to be a congruence relation on $\mathbf{I}$ with respect to the operations of multiplication, subtraction, and unary minus. Note that if $k = 0$, then equivalence mod k on $\mathbf{I}$ is the equality relation and there are $\aleph_0$ congruence classes in $\mathbf{I}/\sim$. If $k \neq 0$, then there are k congruence classes in $\mathbf{I}/\sim$:

$$\mathbf{I}/\sim \ = \{[0], [1], [2], \ldots, [k - 1]\}.$$

(c)   Consider the algebra $A = \langle \mathbf{N}, \cdot, 0 \rangle$ and the equivalence relation

$$x \sim y \Leftrightarrow [(x \text{ is even and } y \text{ is even}) \lor (x = y)].$$

We will show that $\sim$ is a congruence relation on A.

Since multiplication is commutative, it will suffice to show that if $x \sim y$ then $kx \sim ky$. Suppose $x \sim y$. Then either $x = 2m$ and $y = 2n$ for some $m, n \in \mathbf{N}$, or $x = y$.

Case 1:   If $x = 2m$ and $y = 2n$, then for any $k \in \mathbf{N}$, $kx = 2km$ and $ky = 2kn$. Since both kx and ky are even, $kx \sim ky$.

Case 2:   If $x = y$, then $kx = ky$ and therefore $kx \sim ky$.

It follows that $\sim$ is a congruence relation on A.

(d)   Consider the unary operation Δ defined on the set of fractions $\mathbf{F}$ as

$$\Delta\left(\frac{p}{q}\right) = \frac{p}{q^2},$$

and define $p/q \sim r/s \Leftrightarrow ps = rq$ as before. Clearly if $a = b$ then $\Delta(a) = \Delta(b)$; but $a \sim b$ does not imply $\Delta(a) \sim \Delta(b)$, e.g., $\Delta(1/2) \not\sim \Delta(2/4)$. Thus, $\sim$ is not preserved by the operation Δ, and consequently $\sim$ is not a congruence relation on $\langle \mathbf{F}, \Delta \rangle$.   #

The following theorem gives another characterization of a congruence relation with respect to a binary operation.

Theorem 7.4.1:   The equivalence relation $\sim$ is a congruence relation with respect to the binary operation $\circ$ if and only if whenever $a \sim b$ and $c \sim d$, then $ac \sim bd$.

Proof:

(a)   (only if) Let $\sim$ be a congruence relation with respect to the binary operation $\circ$, and suppose $a \sim b$ and $c \sim d$. But $a \sim b$ implies $ac \sim bc$, and $c \sim d$ implies $bc \sim bd$. By transitivity of $\sim$, we conclude $ac \sim bd$.

(b)   (if) Suppose $\sim$ is an equivalence relation such that if $a \sim b$ and $c \sim d$, then $ac \sim bd$. Since $c \sim c$, it follows that if $a \sim b$, then $ac \sim bc$. Similarly, if $a \sim b$, then $ca \sim cb$. It follows that $\sim$ is a congruence relation with respect to the operation $\circ$. ∎

A homomorphism h from an algebra A with carrier S to an algebra A' with carrier S' is a map from S to S' which preserves the operations of A. As with any map, a homomorphism induces a natural equivalence relation over its domain; under this relation, $a \sim b$ if and only if $h(a) = h(b)$. The next theorem shows that if h is a homomorphism, then the induced equivalence relation is, in fact, a congruence relation on A.

Theorem 7.4.2: Let $A = \{S, \circ \; \Delta\}$, be an algebra with a binary operation $\circ$ and a unary operation Δ, and let h be a homomorphism from A to $A' = \langle S', \circ', \Delta' \rangle$. Then the equivalence relation over S induced by h is a congruence relation on the algebra A.

Proof: Two elements $a, b \in S$ are equivalent under the relation induced by h if and only if $h(a) = h(b)$. To show this is a congruence relation on A we must show

 (i) if $a \sim b$, then $\Delta a \sim \Delta b$, and
 (ii) if $a \sim b$ and $c \sim d$, then $a \circ c \sim b \circ d$.

(i) If $a \sim b$, then $h(a) = h(b)$, and therefore $\Delta' h(a) = \Delta' h(b)$. But since h is a homomorphism, $h(\Delta a) = \Delta' h(a)$ and $h(\Delta b) = \Delta' h(b)$. Therefore $h(\Delta a) = h(\Delta b)$, and hence $\Delta a \sim \Delta b$. This establishes that $\sim$ is a congruence relation with respect to the unary operation Δ.

(ii) If $a \sim b$ and $c \sim d$, then $h(a) = h(b)$ and $h(c) = h(d)$. Therefore

$$h(a) \circ' h(c) = h(b) \circ' h(d).$$

Since h is a homomorphism, $h(a \circ c) = h(a) \circ' h(c)$ and $h(b \circ d) = h(b) \circ' h(d)$; hence $h(a \circ c) = h(b \circ d)$. It follows that $a \circ c \sim b \circ d$, thus establishing that $\sim$ is a congruence relation with respect to the binary operation $\circ$.

Thus $\sim$ is a congruence relation on the algebra A. ∎

Example

Consider the homomorphism h from the algebra $\langle \Sigma^*, \text{concatenation}, \Lambda \rangle$ to $\langle \mathbf{N}, +, 0 \rangle$ defined by $h(x) = \|x\|$. The equivalence relation $\sim$ induced by h is the following:

$$w \sim v \Leftrightarrow h(w) = h(v) \Leftrightarrow \|w\| = \|v\|.$$

Since h is a homomorphism, the equivalence relation $w \sim v \Leftrightarrow \|w\| = \|v\|$ is a congruence relation on Σ^* with respect to concatenation. It follows that if $\|w\| = \|x\|$ and $\|y\| = \|z\|$, then $\|wy\| = \|xz\|$. #

Problems: Section 7.4

1. Let $\mathbf{F}$ denote the set of fractions as defined in this section. Show that the relation $p/q \sim r/s \Leftrightarrow ps = rq$ is a congruence relation on $\langle \mathbf{F}, +, -, - \rangle$ where the first occurrence of "$-$" represents the binary operation of subtraction and the second

occurrence of "−" represents the unary minus. (Note that you must show that ~ is an equivalence relation.)

2. For an arbitrary monoid $A = \langle S, \circ, 1 \rangle$, show that equality and the universal relation $S \times S$ are both congruence relations on A.

3. Consider the algebra $A = \langle \mathbf{I}, + \rangle$. For each of the following binary relations on $\mathbf{I}$, prove or disprove that the relation is a congruence relation on A.
   (a) $x \sim y \Leftrightarrow (x < 0 \wedge y < 0) \vee (x \geq 0 \wedge y \geq 0)$
   (b) $x \sim y \Leftrightarrow |x - y| < 10$
   (c) $x \sim y \Leftrightarrow (x = y = 0) \vee (x \neq 0 \wedge y \neq 0)$
   (d) $x \sim y \Leftrightarrow x \geq y$.

4. Let k be a natural number. Describe the class of all congruence relations on an algebra of the form $\langle \{0, 1, 2, \ldots, k\}, \max \rangle$.

5. An *ideal* of a semigroup $A = \langle S, \circ \rangle$ is a subset K of the carrier S such that if $x \in K$ and $y \in S$, then $x \circ y \in K$ and $y \circ x \in K$. For an arbitrary ideal K, define the equivalence relation ~ over the carrier S as follows:

$$x \sim y \Leftrightarrow [x, y \in K \vee (x = y)].$$

   (a) Show that if A has a zero element 0, then $0 \in K$.
   (b) Show that if A has an identity element 1 and $S \neq K$, then $1 \notin K$.
   (c) Show that ~ is a congruence relation on A.

6. Find an infinite ideal of the semigroup $\langle \mathbf{I}, \cdot \rangle$. (The definition of an ideal is given in the preceding problem.)

7. Let $A = \langle S, \circ, \Delta \rangle$ be an algebra, where $\circ$ is a binary operation and Δ is a unary operation. Show that if ~ and $\approx$ are both congruence relations on A, then the intersection of ~ and $\approx$ is also a congruence relation on A.

8. State the conditions for ~ to be a congruence relation on $\langle S, \square \rangle$, where $\square$ is a ternary operation on S. Denote the result of the operation $\square$ on the operands a, b, c by $\square(a, b, c)$.

9. Let Σ be the alphabet of a programming language, where Σ contains the two symbols **end** and **continue** (note that the keywords of a language are often treated simply as special symbols). Using $\cdot$ to denote concatenation, we define the relation ~ on $\langle \Sigma^*, \text{concatenation} \rangle$ to be the smallest congruence relation such that for any $x \in \Sigma^*$,

$$x \cdot \textbf{continue} \sim \textbf{continue} \cdot x \sim x$$

$$\textbf{end} \cdot x \sim \textbf{end}$$

Thus, ~ is reflexive, symmetric, and transitive, and if $w \sim x$ and $y \sim z$, then $wy \sim xz$. Let $[x]$ denote the equivalence class of $x \in \Sigma^*$ under the relation ~.
   (a) Describe the members of the congruence class $[\Lambda]$.
   (b) For a given $x \in \Sigma^*$, describe the shortest string in $[x]$.
      Consider the operation $\cdot$ on the quotient algebra $\Sigma^*/\sim$:

$$[x] \cdot [y] = [x \cdot y].$$

Show that with respect to this operation,
   (c) **[continue]** is an identity on $\Sigma^*/\sim$, and
   (d) **[end]** is a left zero, but not a right zero.

For $U, V \subset \Sigma^*/\sim$, let $U \cdot V$ denote the set $\{[xy] \,|\, [x] \in U$ and $[y] \in V\}$. We define a matrix product on these sets in the usual way, but using union for $+$ and set product for multiplication; thus

$$\begin{bmatrix} U_{11} & U_{12} \\ U_{21} & U_{22} \end{bmatrix} \cdot \begin{bmatrix} V_{11} & V_{12} \\ V_{21} & V_{22} \end{bmatrix} = \begin{bmatrix} (U_{11} \cdot V_{11}) \cup (U_{12} \cdot V_{21}) & (U_{11} \cdot V_{12}) \cup (U_{12} \cdot V_{22}) \\ (U_{21} \cdot V_{11}) \cup (U_{22} \cdot V_{21}) & (U_{21} \cdot V_{12}) \cup (U_{22} \cdot V_{22}) \end{bmatrix}$$

(e) Find an $n \times n$ matrix which is a left identity for this matrix operation (each entry of the matrix will be either [end] or [continue]).

(f) Is this left identity also a right identity?

7.5 NEW ALGEBRAS FROM OLD

There are several ways of combining algebras to build new ones. We will discuss two methods in this section.

Quotient Algebras

We first treat the topic of *quotient algebras*. Recall that if $\sim$ is an equivalence relation over a set S, then $[x]$ denotes the equivalence class of $x \in S$.

Definition 7.5.1: Let $A = \langle S, \circ, \Delta, k \rangle$ be an algebra with a binary operation $\circ$, a unary operation Δ, and a constant k, and let $\sim$ be a congruence relation on A. *The quotient algebra of A with respect to the relation* $\sim$, denoted by $A/\sim$, is the algebra $\langle S/\sim, \circ', \Delta', [k] \rangle$, where

(i) $S/\sim$ is the quotient set of S under the relation $\sim$ (the elements of $S/\sim$ are the equivalence classes of the relation $\sim$),

(ii) For all $[a], [b] \in S/\sim$, $[a] \circ' [b] = [a \circ b]$; and $\Delta'[a] = [\Delta a]$,

(iii) $[k]$ is the equivalence class of k under $\sim$.

To show the system defined above is indeed an algebra, we must prove that the operations $\circ'$ and Δ' are well-defined. This requires showing that the result of applying $\circ'$ or Δ' does not depend on which elements of the equivalence classes are used to compute the result. This can be shown as follows:

(a) To show that Δ' is well-defined, we must show that if $[a] = [b]$, then $\Delta'[a] = \Delta'[b]$. If $[a] = [b]$, then $a \sim b$. Since $\sim$ is a congruence relation, $\Delta a \sim \Delta b$; therefore $[\Delta a] = [\Delta b]$. Since $\Delta'[a] = [\Delta a]$ and $\Delta'[b] = [\Delta b]$, it follows that $\Delta'[a] = \Delta'[b]$. Thus, the operation Δ' is well-defined.

(b) To show that the operation $\circ'$ is well-defined, we must show that if $[a] = [b]$ and $[c] = [d]$, then $[a] \circ' [c] = [b] \circ' [d]$. If $[a] = [b]$, and $[c] = [d]$, then $a \sim b$ and $c \sim d$. Since $\sim$ is a congruence relation, $a \circ c \sim b \circ d$, and therefore $[a \circ c] = [b \circ d]$. Since $[a] \circ' [c] = [a \circ c]$ and $[b] \circ' [d] = [b \circ d]$, it follows that $[a] \circ' [c] = [b] \circ' [d]$. Therefore, $\circ'$ is well-defined.

Since Δ' and $\circ'$ are well-defined operations on $S/\sim$, it follows that $A/\sim$ is an algebra with the same signature as A.

The operations and constants of a quotient algebra retain many of the properties of the original algebra. For example, if the operation $\circ$ is commutative, then $\circ'$ is as well, since

$$[a] \circ' [b] = [a \circ b] = [b \circ a] = [b] \circ' [a].$$

Similarly, if $\circ$ is associative, so is $\circ'$. If k is an identity for $\circ$, then $[k] \circ' [a] = [k \circ a] = [a]$ and therefore $[k]$ is an identity for $\circ'$. Similarly, if k is a zero for $\circ$, then $[k]$ is a zero for $\circ'$. It follows that if $\sim$ is a congruence relation on a semigroup A, then $A/\sim$ is a semigroup. Corresponding statements hold for monoids, groups and Boolean algebras, since all the axiomatic properties of the structures are preserved in the quotient algebras.

Example

Let **F** be the set of fractions as defined in Section 7.4 and consider the algebra $A = \langle \mathbf{F}, +, -, - \rangle$. If $\sim$ is the relation $p/q \sim r/s \Leftrightarrow ps = rq$, then $\sim$ is a congruence relation on the algebra A. The carrier $\mathbf{F}/\sim$ of the quotient algebra $A/\sim$ is the set of rational numbers **Q**.   #

Recall that if $\sim$ is an equivalence relation on a set S, then the canonical map from S to $S/\sim$ is defined as follows:

$$f : S \to S/\sim,$$

$f(a) = [a]$, where $[a]$ is the equivalence class of $a \in S$.

If S is the carrier of an algebra and $\sim$ is a congruence relation, then the canonical map is a homomorphism. This is established by the following theorem.

Theorem 7.5.1:   Let A be an algebra, and let $\sim$ be a congruence relation on A. Then the canonical map $h : S \to S/\sim$ defined by $h(a) = [a]$ is a homomorphism from the algebra A to the quotient algebra $A/\sim$.

Proof: We will prove the theorem for the special case $A = \langle S, \circ, \Delta, k \rangle$, where $\circ$ and Δ are binary and unary operations respectively. Let $\sim$ be a congruence relation on A, and $A/\sim = \langle S/\sim, \circ', \Delta', [k] \rangle$ be the quotient algebra. Let h be the canonical map from S to $S/\sim$. Then, by definition of the quotient algebra,

   (i) $[a] \circ' [b] = [a \circ b]$, and
   (ii) $\Delta'[a] = [\Delta a]$.

To show that h is a homomorphism, we first show that h preserves the operations of A:

   (i) $h(a \circ b) = [a \circ b] = [a] \circ' [b] = h(a) \circ' h(b)$, and
   (ii) $h(\Delta a) = [\Delta a] = \Delta'[a] = \Delta' h(a)$.

Finally, we observe that $h(k) = [k]$, so the constant of A is mapped to that of $A/\sim$. Hence h is a homomorphism.   ∎

The preceding theorem establishes that if $\sim$ is a congruence relation on the algebra $A = \langle S, \circ, \Delta \rangle$, where $\circ$ and Δ are unary and binary operations respectively, then the following diagrams commute (where $h \times h$ is the map on $S \times S$ such that $h \times h(\langle a, b \rangle) = \langle h(a), h(b) \rangle$):

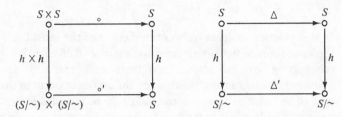

Product Algebras

Another way of constructing new algebras from old ones is by taking a "direct product" of two algebras with the same signature. Recall that two sets S' and S'' can be combined by the operation of cartesian product to form $S' \times S''$. The operation of cartesian product can be extended so that two algebras A' and A'' can be combined to form the product algebra $A' \times A''$. The carrier of the product algebra is the cartesian product of the carriers, and each operation of the product algebra corresponds to the operations of the original algebras acting in a "pairwise" fashion on the elements of the carrier. Note that definitions similar to the following one apply only if the algebras A' and A'' have the same signature.

Definition 7.5.2: Let $A' = \langle S', \circ', \Delta', k' \rangle$, and $A'' = \langle S'', \circ'', \Delta'', k'' \rangle$ be algebras, where $\circ'$ and $\circ''$ are binary operations and Δ' and Δ'' are unary operations. The *direct product of A' with A''*, is the algebra

$$A' \times A'' = \langle S' \times S'', \circ, \Delta, \langle k', k'' \rangle \rangle,$$

where $\langle a, c \rangle \circ \langle b, d \rangle = \langle a \circ' b, c \circ'' d \rangle$ and $\Delta \langle a, c \rangle = \langle \Delta' a, \Delta'' c \rangle$ for all $\langle a, c \rangle$, $\langle b, d \rangle$ in $S' \times S''$. The algebra $A' \times A''$ is also called the *product algebra*.

If the direct product of two algebras is defined, then the product algebra has the same signature as the operands. If both operand algebras are of the same variety, then the variety of the product algebra will be the same as that of the operands; for example, the direct product of two semigroups is a semigroup.

Examples

(a) Let $A = \langle N, +, 0 \rangle$ and $A' = \langle N, +, 0 \rangle$. Then $A \times A' = \langle N^2, +, \langle 0, 0 \rangle \rangle$; the operation $+$ of the product algebra is defined by the equation

$$\langle a, c \rangle + \langle b, d \rangle = \langle a + b, c + d \rangle.$$

(b) Let $A = \langle N_2, +_2, 0 \rangle$ and $A' = \langle N_3, +_3, 0 \rangle$, where $N_2 = \{0, 1\}$, $N_3 = \{0, 1, 2\}$, and $+_2$ and $+_3$ denote the operations of addition mod 2 and mod 3 respectively. The product algebra $A \times A'$ is $\langle N_2 \times N_3, +, \langle 0, 0 \rangle \rangle$. The carrier of $A \times A'$ is the set $\{\langle 0, 0 \rangle, \langle 0, 1 \rangle, \langle 0, 2 \rangle, \langle 1, 0 \rangle, \langle 1, 1 \rangle, \langle 1, 2 \rangle\}$. The operation $+$ of the product algebra is pairwise modular addition; thus $\langle 1, 1 \rangle + \langle 1, 1 \rangle = \langle 0, 2 \rangle$. The constant of the product algebra is the ordered pair $\langle 0, 0 \rangle$. We leave it as an exercise to show that $A \times A'$ is isomorphic to $\langle \mathbf{N}_6, +_6, 0 \rangle$.   #

In this chapter we have only covered some of the most basic and well-understood topics of the field usually referred to as *universal algebra*. It is possible to extend the concepts we have described in many interesting and important ways. For example, *relational algebras* permit relations on the carrier to occur in the signature of the algebra; in our treatment, relations could only be included indirectly, e.g., by choosing a partially ordered set as the carrier. Another extension would be to relax the requirement that the operations of an algebra be defined for all possible operands. For example, in the formulation we have presented, $\langle \mathbf{R}, / \rangle$ is not an algebra because the operation of division is not defined if the divisor is 0. Permitting operations to be defined only for some of the possible operands gives another kind of mathematical structure called a *partial algebra*. We can also extend the concept of algebra to that of a *many-sorted algebra*; this is a mathematical system in which elements from various sets (rather than a single carrier) can occur as operands, and not all operations need be defined for all operands. Thus, we could use one set to represent the integers, another set to represent the floating point numbers, and a third set to represent truth values. In such an algebra, arithmetic operations are defined on the sets of numbers, and Boolean operations are defined on truth values. The ceiling and floor functions are unary operations which map the real numbers to the integers. A relation such as "$\leq$" can be represented as an operation which has numbers as operands and whose result is a truth value. Extensions such as these are currently being applied to a number of problem areas of computer science, the most notable of which is the semantics of programming languages.

Problems: Section 7.5

1. Let $S_k = \{x \mid x \in \mathbf{I} \wedge x \geq k\}$, where $k \in \mathbf{N}$. Let m and n be elements of $\mathbf{N}$ such that $nk \geq m$, and let h be the following homomorphism from $A = \langle S_k, + \rangle$ to $A' = \langle S_m, + \rangle$:

$$h: S_k \to S_m,$$
$$h(x) = nx.$$

   Let $\sim$ be the congruence relation on A induced by h. Describe the quotient algebra $A/\sim$.

2. Let h be a homomorphism from $A = \langle S, \circ, \Delta, k \rangle$ to $A' = \langle S', \circ', \Delta', k' \rangle$, and let $\sim$ be the equivalence relation induced on S by h:

$$x \sim y \Leftrightarrow h(x) = h(y)$$

   Show that $A/\sim$ is isomorphic to the subalgebra $\langle h(S), \circ', \Delta', k \rangle$ of A'.

3. Let $A = \langle S, \circ, 1 \rangle$ and $A' = \langle S', \circ', 1' \rangle$ be monoids. Show that the product algebra $A \times A'$ is a monoid.

4. Let $A = \langle\{1, 2, 3\}, \max, 1\rangle$ and $A' = \langle\{5, 6\}, \min, 6\rangle$. Specify the product algebra $A \times A'$ by constructing an operation table and identifying the constants.

5. Let $A' = \langle S', \circ', \Delta', 1'\rangle$ and $A'' = \langle S'', \circ'', \Delta'', 1''\rangle$ where $\circ'$ and $\circ''$ are binary operations and Δ' and Δ'' unary operations, and consider the product algebra $A' \times A'' = \langle S' \times S'', \circ, \Delta, \langle 1', 1''\rangle\rangle$.
   (a) Show that if the binary operations of A and A' are commutative, then the binary operation of the product algebra is commutative.
   (b) Show that if the binary operations of A' and A'' are associative, then the binary operation of the product algebra is associative.
   (c) Show that if the constants of A' and A'' are identity elements with respect to their binary operations, then the constant of the product algebra is an identity with respect to its binary operation.
   (d) Show that if the constants of the algebras A' and A'' are zeroes with respect to their binary operations, then the constant of the product algebra is a zero with respect to its binary operation.
   (e) Show that if A and A' are groups, then the product algebra is a group.

6. Let A and A' be algebras with nonempty carriers and define the relation $\sim$ over a product algebra $A \times A'$ as follows:
$$\langle w, x\rangle \sim \langle y, z\rangle \Leftrightarrow w = y.$$
   (a) Determine when $\sim$ is a congruence relation on $A \times A'$.
   (b) Show that if the relation $\sim$ defined above is a congruence relation, then $(A \times A')/\sim$ is isomorphic to A.

7. Let $A_j = \langle \mathbf{N}_j, +_j, 0\rangle$ where $\mathbf{N}_j = \{0, 1, 2, \ldots, j - 1\}$ and $+_j$ denotes addition mod j.
   (a) Show that $A_2 \times A_3$ is isomorphic to A_6.
   (b) Describe the set of congruence relations on $A_2 \times A_3$.
   (c) Describe the set of congruence relations on A_m, where $m \in \mathbf{I}+$.

Suggestions for Further Reading

A number of excellent books treat a range of topics in algebra; these include Fraleigh [1969] and Herstein [1964]. More advanced treatments which are closer to the spirit of what was presented in this chapter include MacLane and Birkhoff [1967], Cohn [1965], and Gratzer [1968]. Gill [1976] and Stone [1973] treat a variety of structures with an emphasis on applications relevant to computer science.

THE PROGRAMMING LANGUAGE

The programs of this text have been written in an informal programming language based on ALGOL 60. Because our principal concern is the clear and unambiguous description of algorithms, we have used the ALGOL 60 framework whenever it has been convenient, but abandoned it when doing so resulted in a more easily understood algorithm description. This has resulted in a language with the following properties:

1. Simple data types include integers, real numbers, and character strings. Complex data types include whatever is convenient for treating the problem, including arrays, lists, graphs, edges and nodes. The data type of a program variable will be evident from the context; we will not include formal declarations in the programs. Similarly, the scopes of variables will be clear from the context.
2. The operations used in the language include the arithmetic operations, the floor and ceiling functions, and concatenation of character strings. When convenient we will also use other operations, requiring only that they be clear and unambiguous.
3. The conditions of the language (used in conditional and iteration statements) include all propositions whose truth values can be established at the appropriate time during program execution.

A program is a (single) statement. Each statement of the language is of one of the types specified in the following table. The clauses in brackets [ ] are optional and may be omitted under some specified conditions.

Because the language is informally specified and the data types and statement types are not completely characterized, a careful specification of the syntax and semantics of the language is not possible. Nevertheless, the informal description following the table of each of the statement types and how they are used will enable the reader to understand the programs of the text with a minimum of effort.

1.	variable ← expression	the *assignment* statement
2.	**if** condition **then** statement1 [**else** statement2]	the **if** statement
3.	**begin**	
	statement1;	
	statement2;	
	.	the **begin** statement
	.	
	statement$k$	
	end	
4.	**while** condition **do** statement	the **while** statement
5.	**for** variable ← initial-value [**step** step-size] **until** final-value **do** statement	the **for** statement
6.	**procedure** procedure-name [(list of parameters)]: statement	the *procedure definition* statement
7.	**return** [expression]	the **return** statement
8.	procedure-name (list of arguments)	the *procedure call* statement
9.	**comment:** character string	the **comment** statement
10.	other statements	

---

1.   An *assignment* statement is of the form

$$\text{variable} \leftarrow \text{expression}$$

Execution of an assignment statement causes the expression on the right of the assignment arrow "←" to be evaluated, and the resulting value to be assigned to the variable on the left side of the assignment arrow. For example, execution of

$$x \leftarrow y + z$$

causes the variable x to be assigned the value of the sum of y and z. Execution of

$$i \leftarrow i + 1$$

causes the value of i to be incremented by 1.

2.   An **if** statement (or *conditional* statement) is of the form

$$\textbf{if } \text{condition } \textbf{then } \text{statementl [}\textbf{else}\text{ statement2]}$$

where condition is a proposition and statement1 and statement2 are statements. Execution of an **if** statement causes condition to be evaluated. If its truth value is *true*, then statement1 is executed. If the optional **else** clause is present and condition has the truth value *false*, then statement2 is executed. For example, after execution of

$$\textbf{if } x < 0 \textbf{ then } x \leftarrow -x$$

the value of x will be nonnegative. After execution of

$$\textbf{if } x = 0 \textbf{ then } y \leftarrow 1 \textbf{ else } y \leftarrow 2$$

the value of y will be 1 if x is equal to zero; otherwise the value of y will be 2.

3. A **begin** statement is of the form:

begin
    statement1;
    statement2;
    .
    .
    .
    statement$k$
end

and consists of a sequence of statements separated by semicolons and enclosed between **begin** and **end**. A **begin** statement is called a *block*; it can be used any way a statement can be used in the language. Execution of a **begin** statement consists of execution of the sequence of statements enclosed in the **begin-end** pair. A block causes the enclosed sequence of statements to be treated as an entity. For example, to interchange the values of x and y if x is less than y, we could execute the following (single) statement:

if $x < y$ **then**
    begin
        temp ← *x*;
        x ← *y*;
        y ← *temp*
    end

4. The **while** statement is used to control the repeated execution of a statement. It has the following form:

while condition do statement

Execution of a **while** statement causes condition to be evaluated. If the truth value of condition is *true*, then the statement after **do** is executed. This process is repeated until condition becomes false. Note that if condition is false at the time of execution of a **while** statement, then the statement following the **do** will not be executed. On the other hand, if the truth value of condition is *true* and this value is not changed by repeated executions of the statement following **do**, then execution of the statement will not terminate.

The following statement causes the variable *nfact* to be assigned the value $n!$, when n is a nonnegative integer. The value of $n!$ is defined to be 1 if $n = 0$; otherwise, $n! = n(n-1)(n-2)\ldots2\cdot1$.

begin
    nfact ← 1;
    while $n > 1$ **do**
        begin
            nfact ← *nfact* ∗ *n*;
            n ← *n* − 1
        end
end

5. A **for** statement is an alternative way to control repeated execution of a statement. It has the following form:

    for variable ← initial-value [**step** step-size] **until** final-value
        do statement

where variable is a variable name (called the *index* of the loop) and initial-value, step-size, and final-value are expressions. If the optional **step** clause is omitted, then the value of step-size is assigned the default value of 1. If the value of step-size is positive, then the effect of executing the **for** statement is defined to be the same as executing the following statement:

begin
    variable ← initial-value;
    while variable ≤ final-value **do**
        begin
            statement;
            variable ← variable + step-size
        end
end

If the value of step-size is nonpositive, then the effect of executing the **for** statement is defined to be equivalent to the following:

begin
    variable ← initial-value;
    while variable ≥ final-value **do**
        begin
            statement;
            variable ← variable + step-size
        end
end

The following statement assigns the value 0 to all array entries $A[i]$ for $0 \leq i \leq n$ and i an even number:

    for i ← 0 **step** 2 **until** n **do** $A[i]$ ← 0

6, 7, 8.   A procedure in our language is an algorithm which can be invoked, or called, by another algorithm. Three kinds of variables occur in a procedure. A *global variable* is one which can be accessed and changed by either the procedure or the program which invokes it; the same name is used in both the calling program and a procedure when referring to a global variable. A *local variable* is one whose value is accessible only to the procedure; these variables are used in the execution of the algorithm of the procedure but are not used to communicate information between the program and the procedure called. A *parameter* is a data item which is specified explicitly at the time a procedure is invoked. Global variables and parameters provide two ways of passing information between a program and the procedures it invokes.

A procedure is defined by specifying the algorithm to be executed when the procedure is invoked and the information to be passed by parameters. A *procedure definition* statement has the form

procedure procedure-name [(parameter list)]: statement

where procedure-name is the name used to invoke the procedure and parameter list is a finite sequence of dummy variables called *formal parameters*; the elements of the parameter list are separated by commas. When the procedure is invoked, the statement following the colon is executed. Note that a procedure definition statement merely defines an algorithm; the algorithm is not executed until the procedure is invoked.

Procedures are either *function procedures* or *subroutine procedures*. A function procedure is invoked by using the procedure name in an expression, just as a variable name would be used; the procedure name is followed by a (possibly empty) list of arguments called the *actual parameters*. A value for the procedure name will be computed according to the algorithm specified in the procedure definition statement. The value to be substituted for the procedure name is specified in the procedure definition by a statement of the form

return expression

For example, the following is a definition of a procedure to compute the absolute value of a real number.

procedure ABS(x):
if $x \geq 0$ **then return** x **else return** $-x$

Execution of the following program segment will set the variable y equal to the absolute value of z:

$$y \leftarrow \text{ABS}(z)$$

and execution of the program segment

$$y \leftarrow 2 + \text{ABS}(z + 1)$$

will assign the value 6 to y if $z = 3$ and the value 4 to y if $z = -3$.

A subroutine procedure is called by executing a statement of the form

procedure-name (argument list)

A subroutine procedure definition may or may not have a **return** statement; execution of the subroutine algorithm terminates either by executing the statement

return

or by completion of the execution of the statement which defines the algorithm. The following subroutine procedure interchanges the values of two entries of an array A:

procedure SWITCH(i, j):
begin
    $temp \leftarrow A[i]$;
    $A[i] \leftarrow A[j]$;
    $A[j] \leftarrow temp$
end

In this procedure, $temp$ is a local variable, A is a global variable, and i and j are formal parameters. (There is no unambiguous specification in the above that $temp$ is local; it could, in fact, be global. For the programs of this text, the context will suffice to determine which variables are intended to be local.) If $n = 4$, then execution of the statement

SWITCH $(2, n + 3)$

will cause the values of $A[2]$ and $A[7]$ to be interchanged.

Most of the algorithms described in this text are presented as procedures rather than programs. These procedures would be executed as the result of being invoked by another procedure or program.

9. A **comment** statement is of the form

comment: character string

where character string is any string of characters. A **comment** statement does not affect the algorithm execution; its function is to help the reader understand the program. We have not avoided the use of semicolons in comments, but the extent of the comment statement will be clear in all cases.

10. We also permit the use of other unambiguous instructions so long as they can be implemented in a high-level programming language. Examples include the following:

    interchange $A[i]$ and $A[j]$
    set max to the largest element in the array A
    make LIST empty
    concatenate LIST1 to the end of LIST

ANSWERS TO SELECTED PROBLEMS

Section 1.1

3. Tautologies: $a, c, d, e, f, h, i, k, l, n$.
   Contingencies: g, j, m.
   Contradictions: b.

4. (a) (i) $(\neg P \wedge R) \Rightarrow Q$
   (iii) $\neg P$
   (b) (i) I will go to town if and only if I have time and it is not snowing.
   (iii) If I will go to town then I have time and if I have time, I will go to town.

5. (a) Converse: If I don't go, then it rains.
   Contrapositive: If I go, then it doesn't rain.
   (c) Converse: If you can bake the cake, you get 4 pounds.
   Contrapositive: If you cannot bake the cake, you don't get 4 pounds.

6. (a) $P \vee Q \vee \neg R \Leftrightarrow \neg(\neg P \wedge \neg Q) \vee \neg R$
   $$\Leftrightarrow \neg((\neg P \wedge \neg Q) \wedge R)$$
   $$\Leftrightarrow \neg(\neg P \wedge \neg Q \wedge R)$$
   (c) $P \Rightarrow (Q \Rightarrow P) \Leftrightarrow \neg P \vee (\neg Q \vee P)$
   $$\Leftrightarrow \neg P \vee P \vee \neg Q$$
   $$\Leftrightarrow 1 \vee \neg Q$$
   $$\Leftrightarrow 1$$
   (e) $[P \Rightarrow (Q \vee \neg R)] \wedge \neg P \wedge Q \Leftrightarrow [\neg P \vee Q \vee \neg R] \wedge [\neg P \wedge Q]$
   $$\Leftrightarrow [\neg P \wedge \neg P \wedge Q] \vee [Q \wedge \neg P \wedge Q]$$
   $$\vee [\neg R \wedge \neg P \wedge Q]$$
   $$\Leftrightarrow [\neg P \wedge Q] \vee [\neg P \wedge Q] \vee [\neg P \wedge Q \wedge \neg R]$$
   $$\Leftrightarrow [\neg P \wedge Q]$$
   $$\Leftrightarrow \neg[P \vee \neg Q]$$

8. Suppose P is false. Then $P \Rightarrow Q$ is true for any proposition Q. If we know $P \Rightarrow Q$ is true and accept the false hypothesis P as true, then we can infer the truth of Q from the truth table of $\Rightarrow$. Since Q is arbitrary, Q may or may not be true.

9. The only noncommutative operator is $\Rightarrow$.

10. The only nonassociative operator is $\Rightarrow$.

11. (b) No.

12. (a) $(P \oplus Q) \Leftrightarrow (\neg P \wedge Q) \vee (P \wedge \neg Q)$

13. (a) (i) $P|P \Leftrightarrow \neg(P \wedge P) \Leftrightarrow \neg P$

      (ii) $(P|P)|(Q|Q) \Leftrightarrow \neg((P|P) \wedge (Q|Q))$

$$\Leftrightarrow \neg(\neg P) \vee \neg(\neg Q)$$

$$\Leftrightarrow P \vee Q$$

      (iii) $(P|Q)|(P|Q) \Leftrightarrow \neg((P|Q) \wedge (P|Q))$

$$\Leftrightarrow \neg(\neg(P \wedge Q) \wedge \neg(P \wedge Q))$$

$$\Leftrightarrow P \wedge Q$$

Section 1.2

1. (a) $\forall x \, \forall y \, \exists z \, S(x, y, z)$
    (b) $\forall x[\neg L(x, 0)]$ or $\neg \exists x[L(x, 0)]$

3. (a) True
    (b) False

4. (a) $P(x, y)$ denotes $x + y = 0$

5. (a) All integers greater than 10.
    (b) The universe contains only 3.

6. (a) $P(0, 0) \wedge P(0, 1)$
    (c) $[P(0, 0) \vee P(0, 1)] \wedge [P(1, 0) \vee P(1, 1)]$

7. (a) $P(x)$ denotes $x = x + 1$.

8. No.

9. (a) $\forall x \, \forall y \, \exists z \, P(x, y, z)$
    (d) $\forall x \, P(x, 0, x)$

Section 1.3

1. (a) $\forall y[E(y, 1) \Rightarrow \forall x P(x, y, x)]$
    (d) $\forall x[P(3, x, 6) \Leftrightarrow E(x, 2)]$
    (g) $\forall x \, \forall y[[\neg G(x, y) \wedge \neg G(y, x)] \Rightarrow E(x, y)]$
    (h) $\forall x \, \forall y \, \forall z[[G(y, x) \wedge G(0, z)] \Rightarrow \forall u \, \forall v[[P(x, z, u) \wedge P(y, z, v)] \Rightarrow G(u, v)]]$

2. (a) Every arithmetic assertion which is provable is true.
    (d) If $z = x \vee y$ and z is provable, then x is provable or y is provable.

3. (a) If $P(x)$ denotes "x is prime" and $E(x)$ denotes "x is even", then $\exists\,!x[P(x) \land E(x)]$.

(c) $T(x)$: x is a train

$C(x)$: x is a car

$F(x, y)$: x is faster than y

$\forall x[T(x) \Rightarrow \exists y[C(y) \land F(x, y)]]$

(e) Let R denote "it rains tomorrow" and $W(x)$ denote "x will get wet."

$$R \Rightarrow \exists x[W(x)]$$

4. $\forall(x)P(x) \Leftrightarrow \neg\exists x \neg P(x)$

$\exists x P(x) \Leftrightarrow \neg\forall x \neg P(x)$

5. $\exists\,!P(x) \Leftrightarrow \exists x[P(x) \land \forall y[P(y) \Rightarrow y = x]]$

7. (a) True.

(b) False. Consider the universe consisting of 0 and 1, and let $P(x)$ denote "$x = 0$" and $Q(x)$ denote "$x = 1$."

8. (Refer to Tables 1.1.1 and 1.1.2.)

(a) $\exists x[P(x) \land Q(x)] \Leftrightarrow [P(0) \land Q(0)] \lor [P(1) \land Q(1)]$ (expansion)

$\Leftrightarrow [[P(0) \land Q(0)] \lor P(1)] \land [[P(0) \land Q(0)] \lor Q(1)]$

                (distributivity)

$\Leftrightarrow [[P(0) \lor P(1)] \land [Q(0) \lor P(1)]] \land [[P(0) \lor Q(1)]$

$\land [Q(0) \lor Q(1)]]$ (distributivity)

$\Rightarrow [P(0) \lor P(1)] \land [Q(0) \lor Q(1)]$ (simplification)

Moreover, for this universe,

$$[P(0) \lor P(1)] \land [Q(0) \lor Q(1)] \Leftrightarrow \exists x P(x) \land \exists x Q(x).$$

(b) Let $P(x)$ denote "$x = 0$" and $Q(x)$ denote "$x = 1$".

9. (b) $\exists x \exists y[P(x) \land Q(y)] \Leftrightarrow \exists x[P(x) \land \exists y Q(y)]$

$\Leftrightarrow \exists x P(x) \land \exists y Q(y)$

$\Rightarrow \exists x P(x)$

(d) $\exists x \exists y[P(x) \Rightarrow P(y)] \Leftrightarrow \exists x \exists y[\neg P(x) \lor P(y)]$

$\Leftrightarrow \exists x[\neg P(x) \lor \exists y P(y)]$

$\Leftrightarrow \exists x \neg P(x) \lor \exists y P(y)$

$\Leftrightarrow \neg\forall x P(x) \lor \exists y P(y)$

$\Leftrightarrow \forall x P(x) \Rightarrow \exists y P(y)$

11. (a) $\forall i_{1 \le i \le 20} \, \forall j_{1 \le j \le 30}[A[i, j] \ge 0]$

(c) $\exists i_{1 \le i \le 20} \, \exists j_{1 \le j \le 30}[A[i, j] = 0]$

Section 1.4

1. (a) F: I'm fat.

T: I'm thin.

$F \lor T$

$\underline{\neg T}$

$\therefore F$ Disjunctive syllogism

Conclusion: I'm fat.

(b) R: I run.
    B: I get out of breath.

$$R \Rightarrow B$$
$$\frac{\neg B}{\therefore \neg R} \quad \textit{Modus tollens}$$

Conclusion: I didn't run.

(c) B: The butler did it.
    H: His hands are dirty

$$B \Rightarrow H$$
$$\frac{H}{\rule{2cm}{0pt}}$$

The only conclusions are the hypotheses.

(e) I am not happy and my program does not run. (By *modus tollens* and conjunction.)

(f) All trigonometric functions are continuous functions. (Universal instantiation, hypothetical syllogism and universal generalization.)

(i) Let $A(x)$ denote "x is good for the auto industry."
Let $C(x)$ denote "x is good for the country."
Let $Y(x)$ denote "x is good for you."
Let b denote the constant of "you buying an expensive car."
The given hypotheses are:

$$\forall x[A(x) \Rightarrow C(x)]$$
$$\forall x[C(x) \Rightarrow Y(x)]$$
$$A(b)$$

Then by universal instantiation

$$A(b) \Rightarrow C(b)$$
$$C(b) \Rightarrow Y(b)$$

By *modus ponens*

$$C(b).$$

And again by *modus ponens*

$$Y(b)$$

and by conjunction

$$C(b) \wedge Y(b)$$

Conclusion: It is good for you and the country for you to buy an expensive car.

3. (a) I: IBM will take over the copier market.
    X: Xerox will take over the copier market.
    R: RCA returns to the computer market.
We wish to show

$$\neg(I \vee X)$$
$$\frac{R \Rightarrow I}{\therefore \neg R}$$

$$
\begin{array}{llll}
\textit{Proof:} & 1. & \neg(I \lor X) & \text{Hypothesis} \\
& 2. & R \Rightarrow I & \text{Hypothesis} \\
& 3. & \neg I \land \neg X & \text{1, DeMorgan} \\
& 4. & \neg I & \text{3, Simplification} \\
& 5. & \neg R & \text{2, 4, } \textit{modus tollens}
\end{array}
$$

5. (b) Valid. The proof is as follows:

$$
\begin{array}{lll}
1. & A \lor B & \text{hypothesis} \\
2. & A \Rightarrow C & \text{hypothesis} \\
3. & \neg B \Rightarrow A & \text{1, implication} \\
4. & \neg B \Rightarrow C & \text{2, 3, hypothetical syllogism} \\
5. & C \lor B & \text{4, implication.}
\end{array}
$$

6. (a) T: Today is Tuesday.
C: I have a test in Computer Science.
E: I have a test in Economics.
P: The Economics professor is sick.

$$
\begin{array}{llll}
\textit{Proof:} & 1. & T \Rightarrow (C \lor E) & \text{hypothesis} \\
& 2. & P \Rightarrow \neg E & \text{hypothesis} \\
& 3. & T \land P & \text{hypothesis} \\
& 4. & T & \text{3, simplification} \\
& 5. & C \lor E & \text{1, 4, } \textit{modus ponens} \\
& 6. & P & \text{3, simplification} \\
& 7. & \neg E & \text{2, 6, } \textit{modus ponens} \\
& 8. & C & \text{5, 7, disjunctive syllogism.}
\end{array}
$$

(c) $T(x)$: x is a trigonometric function.
$P(x)$: x is a periodic function.
$C(x)$: x is a continuous function.

$$
\frac{\begin{array}{l} \neg \exists x[T(x) \land \neg P(x)] \\ \exists x[P(x) \land C(x)] \end{array}}{\therefore \neg \forall x[T(x) \Rightarrow \neg C(x)]}
$$

The argument is invalid. For a different interpretation consider a universe consisting of a (round, glass) marble and a (round, rubber) ball. Define the predicates as follows:

$T(x)$ denotes "x is a marble."
$P(x)$ denotes "x is a round object."
$C(x)$ denotes "x is made of rubber."

7. (b) The third step, which asserts

$$
\neg \exists x[\neg P(x) \land \neg Q(x)] \Rightarrow \neg[\exists x \, \neg P(x) \land \exists x \, \neg Q(x)]
$$

is fallacious, although

$$
\exists x[A(x) \land B(x)] \Rightarrow [\exists x \, A(x) \land \exists x \, B(x)]
$$

is true. Thus, if $R \Rightarrow S$, we cannot conclude that $\neg R \Rightarrow \neg S$. The faulty step corresponds to the fallacy of denying the antecedent.

8. The error is in applying universal generalization to d. Although d was arbitrary when it was chosen, the value of c was constrained by that of d, and choosing a new value for d may violate these constraints.

Section 1.5

1. (a) $\forall x[x^2$ is odd $\Rightarrow x$ is odd$]$.

    Proof: (Indirect) Let x be an arbitrary integer and assume x is not odd. Then x is even. In an example in the text, we showed

    $$x \text{ is even} \Leftrightarrow x^2 \text{ is even.}$$

    Negating both sides, it follows that

    $$x \text{ is odd} \Leftrightarrow x^2 \text{ is odd}$$

    and therefore

    $$x^2 \text{ is odd} \Rightarrow x \text{ is odd.}$$

    By universal generalization

    $$\forall x[x^2 \text{ is odd} \Rightarrow x \text{ is odd}]. \quad \blacksquare$$

    (b) $\forall x\, \forall y[(x$ is even $\wedge$ y is even$) \Rightarrow x + y$ is even$]$.

    Proof: (Direct) Assume x and y are arbitrary even integers. Then $x = 2m$ and $y = 2n$ for some integers m and n. Therefore, $x + y = 2m + 2n = 2(m + n)$. It follows that $x + y = 2k$ where $k = m + n$. Hence, $x + y$ is even. $\quad \blacksquare$

    (d) $\exists x\, \exists y[x$ is odd $\wedge$ y is odd $\wedge$ $x + y$ is odd$]$.
    The assertion is false. To show this it suffices to prove that the negation

    $$\forall x\, \forall y[(x \text{ is odd} \wedge y \text{ is odd}) \Rightarrow x + y \text{ is even}]$$

    is true.

    Proof: (Direct) Let x and y be arbitrary odd integers. Then $x = 2m + 1$ and $y = 2n + 1$ for some integers m and n. Therefore,

    $$x + y = (2m + 1) + (2n + 1) = 2(m + n + 1).$$

    Hence, $x + y$ is even. $\quad \blacksquare$

    (f) $\exists x[x$ is prime $\wedge$ x^2 is even$]$.

    Proof: (Constructive existence proof) Observe that 2 is prime and 2^2 is even. Then

    $$2 \text{ is prime} \wedge 2^2 \text{ is even.}$$

    By existential generalization,

    $$\exists x[x \text{ is prime} \wedge x^2 \text{ is even}]. \quad \blacksquare$$

    (g) $\neg\exists x[x^2 + 1 < 0]$.

    Proof: (Contradiction) Assume $\exists x[x^2 + 1 < 0]$ is true. Then for some c, $c^2 + 1 < 0$ or $c^2 < -1$. But $-1 < 0$, hence $c^2 < 0$. By property (iii), $c^2 > 0$. This contradicts property (iv) (with $x = c^2$ and $y = 0$). Hence $\neg\exists x[x^2 + 1 < 0]$ is true. $\quad \blacksquare$

    (h) $\forall x\, \forall y[x - y \geq 0 \vee y - x \geq 0]$.

    Proof: (By cases) By property (iv), one of the following holds: $x > y$, $x = y$, or $x < y$. If $x > y$, then (by property (v)), $x - y$ is positive and therefore nonnegative. If $x = y$, then $x - y = 0$ and is therefore nonnegative. If $x < y$, then $y - x$ is positive and therefore nonnegative. Thus, in each of the three cases, either $x - y$ or $y - x$ is nonnegative. ∎

(i) $1 = 3 \Rightarrow \forall x[x^2 < 0]$.

   Proof: (Vacuous) The assertion $1 = 3$ is false. Hence, the implication is true. ∎

(m) $\exists x[x^2 < 0] \Rightarrow 1 = 1$.

   Proof: (Trivial) The assertion $1 = 1$ is true. Hence, the assertion is true. ∎

3.   (a)   The proposition

$$[(H_1 \wedge H_2 \wedge \neg Q) \Rightarrow 0] \Leftrightarrow [(H_1 \wedge H_2) \Rightarrow Q]$$

is a tautology.

(b)   To prove by contradiction that $(H_1 \wedge H_2 \wedge \cdots \wedge H_n) \Rightarrow Q$, we would assume the negation of the assertion, i.e.,

$$\neg[\neg(H_1 \wedge H_2 \wedge \cdots \wedge H_n) \vee Q]$$

or

$$H_1 \wedge H_2 \wedge \cdots \wedge H_n \wedge \neg Q.$$

Then (by applying rules of inference), we would derive a contradiction. The proof technique described in the problem is a straightforward variation. A proof by contradiction assumes an assertion A and proves that the contradiction B follows by rules of inference; the proof technique described simply establishes $A \Rightarrow B$.

Section 1.6

2.   Any program which does not halt is a solution (see Definition 1.6.1). The following program is correct, because if it halts (it won't), the final assertion *false* will be true.

*A*1: *true*
while *true* **do** $x \leftarrow 1$
*A*2: *false*

3.   (a)   (i)   using forward construction:

AI: *true*
$x \leftarrow 1$
*A*1: $\exists y[true \wedge x = 1]$

But *A*1 is equivalent to the assertion "$x = 1$", hence

AI: *true*
$x \leftarrow 1$
*A*1: $x = 1$

is correct.
Similarly

*A*1: $x = 1$
$y \leftarrow 2$
*A*2: $\exists z[x = 1 \wedge y = 2]$

is correct and equivalent to

*A*1: $x = 1$
$y \leftarrow 2$
AF: $x = 1 \wedge y = 2$

By the rule of composition, the program is correct with respect to AI and AF.

(ii) Using the Alternate Axiom of Assignment to construct assertions in the backward direction from AF, we have

$$(x = 1 \wedge 2 = 2)\{y \leftarrow 2\}(x = 1 \wedge y = 2).$$

But $x = 1 \wedge 2 = 2$ is equivalent to the intermediate assertion

$$A1: x = 1.$$

Again using the Alternate Axiom of Assignment we have

$$(1 = 1)\{x \leftarrow 1\}(x = 1).$$

But $1 = 1 \Leftrightarrow true$, which is precisely the initial assertion AI. Hence, the program is correct with respect to AI and AF.

4. (a) In order to apply the *if-then* rule, we must establish the following two assertions:
   (i) $[x = x' \wedge \neg(x < 0)] \Rightarrow [(x' < 0 \Rightarrow x = -x') \wedge (x' \geq 0 \Rightarrow x = x')]$
   and
   (ii) $(x = x' \wedge x < 0)\{x \leftarrow -x\}[(x' < 0 \Rightarrow x = -x') \wedge (x' \geq 0 \Rightarrow x = x')]$.
   To establish the implication (i), we note that

$$[x = x' \wedge \neg(x < 0)] \Rightarrow \neg(x' < 0), \text{ and}$$

$$\neg(x' < 0) \Rightarrow [x' < 0 \Rightarrow x = -x'].$$

By hypothetical syllogism (Table 1.1.2), it follows that

$$[x = x' \wedge \neg(x < 0)] \Rightarrow [x' < 0 \Rightarrow x = -x']. \tag{1}$$

Moreover,

$$[x = x' \wedge \neg(x < 0)] \Rightarrow x = x', \text{ and}$$

$$(x = x') \Rightarrow [x' \geq 0 \Rightarrow x = x']. \text{ Hence,}$$

$$[x = x' \wedge \neg(x < 0)] \Rightarrow [x' \geq 0 \Rightarrow x = x']. \tag{2}$$

It follows from (1) and (2) that (i) holds:

$$[x = x' \wedge \neg(x < 0)] \Rightarrow [(x' < 0 \Rightarrow x = -x') \wedge (x' \geq 0 \Rightarrow x = x')].$$

To establish (ii), we first use the Alternate Axiom of Assignment to conclude

$$[(x' < 0 \Rightarrow x = x') \wedge (x' \geq 0 \Rightarrow x = -x')]\{x \leftarrow -x\}[(x' < 0 \Rightarrow x = -x')$$
$$\wedge (x' \geq 0 \Rightarrow x = x')].$$

We then show

$$[x = x' \wedge x < 0] \Rightarrow [(x' < 0 \Rightarrow x = x') \wedge (x' \geq 0 \Rightarrow x = -x')].$$

(This can be done either with truth tables or by using the identities of Tables 1.1.1 and 1.1.2.) Applying a rule of consequence, it follows that (ii) is true. Thus, the *if-then* rule can be applied and we conclude that the program segment is correct.

6. **procedure** ZERO
   $AI: n > 0$
   begin
   $\quad i \leftarrow 1;$
   $\quad A1: n > 0 \wedge i = 1$
   $\quad A2: i \leq n + 1 \wedge \forall j[1 \leq j < i \Rightarrow V[j] = 0]$

while $i \leq n$ **do**
$\quad A3: i \leq n \land \forall j[1 \leq j < i \Rightarrow V[j] = 0]$
$\quad$ **begin**
$\quad\quad V[i] \leftarrow 0;$
$\quad\quad A4: i \leq n \land \forall j[1 \leq j \leq i \Rightarrow V[j] = 0]$
$\quad\quad i \leftarrow i + 1$
$\quad\quad A2: i \leq n + 1 \land \forall j[1 \leq j < i \Rightarrow V[j] = 0]$
$\quad$ **end**
$\quad AF: \forall j[1 \leq j \leq n \Rightarrow V[j] = 0]$
end

Either axiom of assignment can be used to show

$\quad AI\{i \leftarrow 1\}A1$. We note that $A1 \Rightarrow A2$ since $n > 0 \land i = 1 \Rightarrow i \leq n + 1$,

and the assertion $1 \leq j < i$ is false for all j.

By a rule of consequence, this establishes that $AI\{i \leftarrow 1\}A2$.

We next establish that the hypothesis of the rule of iteration holds, that is,

$$(A2 \land i \leq n)\{V[i] \leftarrow 0; i \leftarrow i + 1\}A2.$$

We note that $A2 \land i \leq n \Leftrightarrow A3$. Hence, it suffices to show

$$A3\{V[i] \leftarrow 0; i \leftarrow i + 1\}A2.$$

We will first prove $A3\{V[i] \leftarrow 0\}A4$ and then $A4\{i \leftarrow i + 1\}A2$. The assertion $A3\{V[i] \leftarrow 0\}A4$ follows immediately from an application of the Alternative Axiom of Assignment. Applying the same Axiom, we find

$$i + 1 \leq n + 1 \land \forall j[1 \leq j < i + 1 \Rightarrow V[j] = 0]\{i \leftarrow i + 1\}A2.$$

Since the assertion on the left is equivalent to $A4$, it follows that $A4\{i \leftarrow i + 1\}A2$. This establishes that the rule of iteration holds, and we conclude that

$$A2\{\text{while } i \leq n \text{ do begin } V[i] \leftarrow 0; i \leftarrow i + 1 \text{ end}\}[A2 \land \neg(i \leq n)].$$

But

$$[A2 \land \neg(i \leq n)] \Rightarrow \{i = n + 1 \land \forall j[1 \leq j < i \Rightarrow V[j] = 0]\} \Rightarrow AF.$$

It follows by the rule of composition that the procedure ZERO is correct with respect to AI and AF.

7. The procedure SNEAKY illustrates one of the problems associated with constructing initial and final assertions for a procedure. For example, suppose a procedure is intended to sort the entries of a list, but the final assertion of the procedure specifies merely that the entries are in nondecreasing order. Then a procedure which assigns the same value to each entry of the list will be correct with respect to the final assertion. Thus it is necessary to specify not only that the entries are in order, but that the final list can be obtained by rearranging the entries of the original list.

In practice, however, there is often some sacrifice of precision in order to make the proof of correctness more manageable; thus, the initial and final assertions we gave for PRODUCT would be considered acceptable by some, with the understanding that SNEAKY would not be constructed by virtue of our understanding of the problem.

If desired, the initial and final assertions for PRODUCT can be changed so that SNEAKY is no longer formally correct. This is done with auxilliary variables as follows:

$AI: a \geq 0 \wedge a = a' \wedge b = b'$
$AF: y = a' \cdot b'$.

Since the values of a' and b' are not affected by program execution, the appropriate value of y will be guaranteed.

9. (a) $AI: n \geq 1 \wedge \exists i[V[i] = arg]$

    begin
        $index \leftarrow 1;$
        $A1: n \geq 1 \wedge index = 1 \wedge \exists i[V[i] = arg]$
        $A2: \forall j[1 \leq j < index \Rightarrow V[j] \neq arg] \wedge \exists i[V[i] = arg]$
        while $V[index] \neq arg$ **do**
            $A3: \forall j[1 \leq j \leq index \Rightarrow V[j] \neq arg] \wedge \exists i[V[i] = arg]$
            $index \leftarrow index + 1$
            $A2: \forall j[1 \leq j < index \Rightarrow V[j] \neq arg] \wedge \exists i[V[i] = arg]$
        $AF: (V[index] = arg) \wedge \forall j[1 \leq j < index \Rightarrow V[j] \neq arg]$
    end

    The loop invariant relation is $A2$.

   (b) The Alternate Axiom of Assignment can be used to show

$$AI\{index \leftarrow 1\}A1.$$

   Since $A1 \Rightarrow A2$, it follows by a rule of consequence that

$$AI\{index \leftarrow 1\}A2.$$

   To show the rule of iteration applies, we must show

$$A2 \wedge V[index] \neq arg\{index \leftarrow index + 1\}A2.$$

   We note that the assertion $A2 \wedge V[index] \neq arg$ is equivalent to $A3$. By the Alternate Axiom of Assignment,

$$\forall j[1 \leq j < index + 1 \Rightarrow V[j] \neq arg] \wedge \exists i[V[i] = arg]\{index \rightarrow index + 1\}A2.$$

   Since the assertion on the left is equivalent to $A3$, the rule of iteration applies and we conclude

$$A2\{\textbf{while } V[index] \neq arg \textbf{ do } index \leftarrow index + 1\}A2 \wedge V[index] = arg.$$

   But $A2 \wedge V[index] = arg \Rightarrow AF$. Hence we can apply the rule of composition to conclude that SEARCH is correct with respect to AI and AF. ∎

Section 2.1

1. (a) $\{0, 1, 2, 3, 4\}$
   (c) $\{$George Washington$\}$

2. (a) If the universe of discourse is $\mathbf{I}$, then the set is

$$\{x \mid 0 < x \wedge x < 100\}.$$

   (b) If the universe is $\mathbf{I}$, then the set is

$$\{x \mid \exists y[x = 2y + 1]\}.$$

4. $A = G = \phi$, $B = E = \{x \mid x \text{ is even}\}$, and $C = F = \{1, 2, 3\}$.

Section 2.2

1. If he shaves himself, he will break his vow not to shave anyone who shaves himself. Therefore he must find someone else to shave him. Since only a barber can shave someone else and he is the town's only barber, he must leave town to be shaved.

3. (a) If the assertion "heterological is heterological" is true, then heterological applies to itself, and is therefore homological; thus the assertion is false and we have a contradiction. On the other hand, if the assertion is false, then heterological is not heterological, i.e., heterological does not apply to itself. It follows that heterological is heterological, and therefore the assertion is true. This is another contradiction. Therefore the assertion is neither true nor false.

Section 2.3

1. (b) $\phi, \{1\}, \{\{2, 3\}\}, \{1, \{2, 3\}\}$
   (d) $\phi, \{\phi\}$
   (f) $\phi, \{\{1, 2\}\}$

2. $A \subset A$: Let A be an arbitrary set and x an arbitrary element of A. Then
   $$\neg(x \in A) \lor (x \in A) \text{ is a tautology for any } x.$$
   Hence, by universal generalization
   $$\forall x[x \in A \Rightarrow x \in A]$$
   is true; therefore, by definition, $A \subset A$. ∎

3. It is possible but not always true.

4. (a) False. Let $A = \phi$, $B = \{a\}$, and $C = \{\phi\}$.

5. They are both singleton sets, but one is an element of the other.
   The single element of $\{2\}$ is 2. The subsets of $\{2\}$ are ϕ and $\{2\}$.
   The single element of $\{\{2\}\}$ is $\{2\}$. The subsets of $\{\{2\}\}$ are ϕ and $\{\{2\}\}$.

Section 2.4

2. $A \cup B \cup C = (A - (B \cup C)) \cup (B - C) \cup C$

3. A proof of part (b) of Theorem 2.4.1 can be obtained by replacing all occurrences of $\cup$ with $\cap$, and $\lor$ with $\land$ in the proof of part (a). A proof of part (d) can be obtained from that of part (c) in the same way.

4. (a) Assume $C \subset A$ and $C \subset B$. Then
   $$\forall x[x \in C \Rightarrow x \in A] \land \forall x[x \in C \Rightarrow x \in B]$$
   is true. Since $\forall$ distributes over $\land$, this is equivalent to
   $$\forall x[(x \in C \Rightarrow x \in A) \land (x \in C \Rightarrow x \in B)]$$
   which is equivalent to
   $$\forall x[x \in C \Rightarrow [x \in A \land x \in B]].$$
   Hence
   $$\forall x[x \in C \Rightarrow x \in A \cap B],$$
   and therefore
   $$C \subset A \cap B. \quad ∎$$

8. (b) Let x be an arbitrary element. Then

$$x \in A \cap A \Leftrightarrow x \in A \wedge x \in A$$
$$\Leftrightarrow x \in A.$$

Hence, $\forall x[x \in A \cap A \Leftrightarrow x \in A]$, so $A \cap A = A$. ∎

(h) We know that $A \subset A$ and $\phi \subset B$ for any sets A and B. Hence, by part (f),

$$A \cup \phi \subset A \cup B.$$

By part (c), $A \cup \phi = A$. Therefore $A \subset A \cup B$. ∎

(k) Assume $A \subset B$. Then by part (g), and since $A \subset A$,

$$A \cap A \subset A \cap B.$$

But by part (b), $A \cap A = A$. Hence, $A \subset A \cap B$. From part (i), $A \cap B \subset A$. It follows that if $A \subset B$, then $A \cap B = A$. ∎

(n) Let x be arbitrary. Then

$$x \in A \cup (B - A) \Leftrightarrow x \in A \vee x \in (B - A)$$
$$\Leftrightarrow x \in A \vee (x \in B \wedge \neg(x \in A))$$
$$\Leftrightarrow (x \in A \vee x \in B) \wedge (x \in A \vee \neg(x \in A))$$
$$\Leftrightarrow (x \in A \vee x \in B) \wedge 1$$
$$\Leftrightarrow x \in A \vee x \in B$$
$$\Leftrightarrow x \in A \cup B.$$

Hence, $A \cup (B - A) = A \cup B$. ∎

9. (a) ($A \cup \bar{A} = U$.) We first note that $\bar{A} = U - A$. Then applying Theorem 2.4.3n,

$$A \cup \bar{A} = A \cup (U - A) = A \cup U = U. \quad ∎$$

10. (a) From Theorem 2.4.3i, we know that $A \cap B \subset A$. Hence, by Theorem 2.4.3j,

$$A \cup (A \cap B) = A. \quad ∎$$

(c) $A - B = \{x \mid x \in A \wedge x \notin B\}$
$$= \{x \mid x \in A \wedge 1 \wedge x \notin B\}$$
$$= \{x \mid x \in A \wedge x \in U \wedge x \notin B\}$$
$$= \{x \mid x \in A \wedge x \in U - B\}$$
$$= \{x \mid x \in A \wedge x \in \bar{B}\}$$
$$= A \cap B. \quad ∎$$

11. (a) $\bigcup\limits_{S \in C} S = \phi$; $\bigcap\limits_{S \in C} S = \phi$.

(c) $\bigcup\limits_{S \in C} S = \{a, b\}$; $\bigcap\limits_{S \in C} S = \phi$.

12. (b) $(\bar{A} \cap \bar{B} \cap \bar{C}) \cap (\bar{A} \cap \bar{B} \cap C) = \bar{A} \cap \bar{B} \cap (\bar{C} \cap C)$
$$= (\bar{A} \cap \bar{B}) \cap \phi$$
$$= \phi.$$

D is a disjoint collection of sets.

13. (a) $\displaystyle\bigcup_{S \in C} S = U - \{x \mid \exists S[S \in C \wedge x \in S]\}$.

$\displaystyle\bigcap_{S \in C} \bar{S} = \{x \mid \forall S[S \in C \Rightarrow x \in \bar{S}]\}$.

Therefore,

$$\bigcap_{S \in C} \bar{S} = \{x \mid \forall S[\neg(S \in C) \vee \neg(x \in S)]\}$$
$$= \{x \mid \forall S \ \neg[S \in C \wedge x \in S]\}$$
$$= \{x \mid \neg \exists S[S \in C \wedge x \in S]\}$$
$$= \overline{\{x \mid \exists S[S \in C \wedge x \in S]\}}$$
$$= \overline{\bigcup_{S \in C} S} \quad \blacksquare$$

14. (b) $\{\phi, \{\{a, b\}\}, \{\{c\}\}, \{\{a, b\}, \{c\}\}\}$.

15. $\mathcal{P}(S_{n+1}) = \mathcal{P}(S_n) \cup \{A \cup \{a_{n+1}\} \mid A \subset S_n\}$.

Note that each subset A of S_n corresponds to two subsets of S_{n+1}: A and $A \cup \{a_{n+1}\}$. It follows that S_{n+1} has twice as many subsets as S_n. (In the next section, we will use this analysis to show that if S has n elements, then $\mathcal{P}(S)$ has 2^n elements.)

Section 2.5

1. (a) *Basis:* The digits 0, 1, 2, 3, 4, 5, 6, 7, 8 and 9 (i.e., all decimal digits) are in the set.

Induction: If x is in the set and d is a decimal digit then xd is in the set.

Extremal: An object is in the set if and only if it can be constructed from a finite number of applications of clauses 1 and 2.

(c) *Basis:* 0 is in S.

Induction:

(i) If $x \in S$, then $1x \in S$.

(ii) If $(x \in S \wedge x \neq 0)$, then $x0 \in S$.

(iii) If $(x \in S \wedge y \in S \wedge x \neq 0)$, then $xy \in S$.

Extremal: as in part (a).

2. (a) **procedure** MULT(a, b):

if $b = 0$ **then return** 0 **else return** MULT$(a, b - 1) + a$

4. *Basis:* We must show

$$\left(\sum_{i=1}^{1} i\right)^2 = \sum_{i=1}^{1} i^3.$$

But

$$\left(\sum_{i=1}^{1} i\right)^2 = 1^2 = 1$$

and

$$\sum_{i=1}^{1} i^3 = 1^3 = 1.$$

Hence, the assertion holds for $n = 1$.

Induction: Assume the assertion holds for arbitrary $n \geq 1$, i.e.,

$$\left(\sum_{i=1}^{n} i\right)^2 = \sum_{i=1}^{n} i^3.$$

Then

$$\left(\sum_{i=1}^{n+1} i\right)^2 = \left(\sum_{i=1}^{n} i + (n+1)\right)^2$$

$$= \left(\sum_{i=1}^{n} i\right)^2 + \left(2(n+1)\sum_{i=1}^{n} i\right) + (n+1)^2$$

$$= \sum_{i=1}^{n} i^3 + \left(2(n+1)\cdot\frac{n(n+1)}{2}\right) + (n+1)^2$$

$$= \sum_{i=1}^{n} i^3 + (n+1)^3$$

$$= \sum_{i=1}^{n+1} i^3. \quad\blacksquare$$

5. Let m be an arbitrary integer in N. We prove $\forall n[(a^m)^n = a^{mn}]$ by induction.
Basis: Suppose $n = 0$. Then by Definition 2.5.4, $(a^m)^0 = 1$ and $a^{m\cdot 0} = a^0 = 1$. This establishes the basis step.
Induction: The induction hypothesis is "Assume the assertion holds for arbitrary n", i.e., $(a^m)^n = a^{mn}$. Then

$$(a^m)^{n+1} = (a^m)^n\cdot a^m \qquad \text{by Definition 2.5.4}$$

$$= a^{mn}\cdot a^m \qquad \text{Induction hypothesis}$$

$$= a^{mn+m} \qquad \text{Theorem 2.5.5}$$

$$= a^{m(n+1)} \qquad \text{distributivity of multiplication.} \quad\blacksquare$$

6. (b) $\sum_{i=0}^{n} (2i+1) = (n+1)^2$.

Using the properties of summation and Theorem 2.5.3 we have

$$\sum_{i=0}^{n} (2i+1) = 2\sum_{i=0}^{n} i + \sum_{i=0}^{n} 1 = \frac{2n(n+1)}{2} + (n+1)$$

$$= n^2 + 2n + 1 = (n+1)^2. \quad\blacksquare$$

Note that a proof by induction is not required.

(d) *Basis:* For $n = 0$, we have $1 + 2n = 1$ and $3^n = 1$. Therefore, $1 + 2^n \le 3^n$ for $n = 0$.
Induction: Assume $1 + 2n \le 3^n$ for arbitrary n. The inequality $1 \le 3^n$ holds for all n; hence

$$2 \le 2\cdot 3^n,$$

and therefore,

$$3^n + 2 \le 3^n + 2\cdot 3^n = 3\cdot 3^n = 3^{n+1}.$$

By the induction hypothesis, $1 + 2n \le 3^n$,
so

$$1 + 2n + 2 \le 3^{n+1}$$

and

$$1 + 2(n+1) \le 3^{n+1}. \quad\blacksquare$$

7. (a) *Case 1:* If $r = 1$, then $r^i = 1$ for all $i \in N$, and hence $\sum_{i=0}^{n} r^i = (n+1)$.
Case 2: Suppose $r \ne 1$. We prove the assertion by induction.

Basis: For $n = 0$ we have

$$\sum_{i=0}^{0} r^i = r^0 = 1, \text{ and}$$

$$\frac{r^{(0+1)} - 1}{r - 1} = \frac{r - 1}{r - 1} = 1.$$

Therefore, the assertion is true for $n = 0$.

Induction: Assume the assertion is true for arbitrary n. Then

$$\sum_{i=0}^{n+1} r^i = \sum_{i=0}^{n} r^i + r^{(n+1)}$$

$$= \frac{r^{(n+1)} - 1}{r - 1} + r^{(n+1)}$$

$$= \frac{r^{(n+1)} - 1}{r - 1} + \frac{r^{n+2} - r^{n+1}}{r - 1}$$

$$= \frac{r^{n+2} - 1}{r - 1}. \quad \blacksquare$$

8.   *Basis:*   The sum of the interior angles of a triangle is $180° = (3 - 2)180°$. Hence, the assertion is true for $n = 3$.

Induction: Assume the assertion holds for an arbitrary convex polygon with $n \geq 3$ sides, and consider a convex polygon C with $n + 1$ sides. The polygon C can be divided into a triangle T and a polygon P of n sides by connecting two non-adjacent vertices. The sum of the interior angles of C is equal to the sum of the interior angles of P and T. Since P has n sides, we can apply the induction hypothesis to conclude that the sum of the interior angles of P is $(n - 2)180°$. By the basis step, the sum of the interior angles of T is $180°$. Therefore, the sum of the interior angles of C is

$$(n - 2)180° + 180° = ((n + 1) - 2)180°.$$

This establishes the assertion for all $n \geq 3$. $\blacksquare$

10.   The induction step of the proof is fallacious. In particular, if $n = 1$ or $n = 2$, it is not true that the set S contains two nonequal subsets of n people which must overlap.

Section 2.6

1.   (a)   The empty set is a model of axioms (b) through (e). (This postulate plays the same role as the basis step in an inductive definition.)

   (b)   The "infinite rooted binary tree" example of this section suffices as an example which satisfies all postulates but (b).

   (c)   The set $\{0\}$ where $0' = 0$ satisfies all the postulates but (c).

   (d)   Let $S = \{0, 1, 2\}$ where $0' = 1, 1' = 2$, and $2' = 1$. Then S satisfies all postulates but (d).

   (e)   Let $S = \{0, x_1, x_2, \ldots, y_1, y_2, \ldots\}$,
   where $0' = x_1$ and $x_i' = x_{i+1}$ for $i \in \mathbf{I}+$,

$$y_i' = y_{i+1} \quad \text{for } i \in \mathbf{I}+.$$

   Then S satisfies all postulates but (e).

2. (a) We show
$$\forall p \,\forall q \,\forall r[(p + q) + r = p + (q + r)].$$
Let p and q be arbitrary natural numbers. We establish
$$\forall r[(p + q) + r = p + (q + r)]$$
by induction.

Basis: Let $r = 0$. Then by the basis step of the definition with $m = p + q$ we have
$$(p + q) + 0 = p + q.$$
Also by the basis step with $m = q$ we have
$$p + (q + 0) = p + q.$$
Hence
$$(p + q) + r = p + (q + r)$$
if $r = 0$.

Induction: By the inductive step of the definition of addition,
$$
\begin{aligned}
p + (q + r') &= p + (q + r)' \\
&= (p + (q + r))' \\
&= ((p + q) + r)' \qquad \text{(Induction Hypothesis)} \\
&= (p + q) + r'.
\end{aligned}
$$
Thus the assertion holds for all $r \in \mathbf{N}$. ∎

Section 2.7

1. (a) $A^2 = \{\Lambda, a, aa\}$.
    (e) $B^* = \{(ab)^n \,|\, n \geq 0\} = \{\Lambda, ab, abab, \ldots\}$.

2. (b) $A^m A^n = A^{m+n}$ for all $m, n \geq 0$.

    Proof: Let m be an arbitrary integer. We show $\forall n[A^m A^n = A^{m+n}]$ by induction on n.

    Basis: $n = 0$.
    $$
    \begin{aligned}
    A^m A^0 &= A^m\{\Lambda\} \\
    &= A^m \\
    &= A^{m+0}
    \end{aligned}
    $$

    Induction: Assume the assertion is true for arbitrary $n \in \mathbf{N}$. Then,
    $$
    \begin{aligned}
    A^m A^{n+1} &= A^m (A^n \cdot A) & \text{(definition of } A^n) \\
    &= (A^m A^n)A & \text{(Theorem 2.7.1c)} \\
    &= A^{m+n} \cdot A & \text{(induction hypothesis)} \\
    &= A^{(m+n)+1} & \text{(definition of } A^n) \\
    &= A^{m+(n+1)} & \text{(associativity of } +)
    \end{aligned}
    $$
    Hence the assertion is true for $n + 1$, and we conclude
    $$\forall n[A^m A^n = A^{m+n}].$$
    Since m was arbitrary, it follows by universal generalization that
    $$\forall m \,\forall n[A^m A^n = A^{m+n}]. \quad \blacksquare$$

3. Let $A = \{a^i | i \in \mathbf{N}\} = A^*$ and $B = \{a^i | i \in \mathbf{N} \wedge i \neq 2\} = A^* - \{aa\}$. Then $A^2 = B^2$ but $A \neq B$.

5. (a) $x \in A(\bigcup_{i \in N} B_i) \Leftrightarrow x = yz$ for some $y \in A$ and $z \in \bigcup_{i \in N} B_i$,

$\Leftrightarrow x = yz$ for some $y \in A$ and $z \in B_k$ for some $k \in \mathbf{N}$,

$\Leftrightarrow x \in AB_k$ for some $k \in \mathbf{N}$,

$\Leftrightarrow x \in \bigcup_{i \in N} (AB_i)$.

6. (b) By Theorem 2.7.3a, $A^* = \{\Lambda\} \cup A^+$. Hence $A^* = A^+$ if and only if $\{\Lambda\} \subset A^+$; i.e., $\Lambda \in A^n$ for some $n \in \mathbf{I}+$. If $\Lambda \in A$, then $\Lambda \in A^1$ and therefore $A^* = A^+$. Conversely, if $A^* = A^+$, then $\Lambda \in A^n$ for $n \in \mathbf{I}+$. But if $\Lambda \in A^n$ it follows that $\Lambda \in A$. ∎

(c) We apply parts (a) and (b) of this problem. Since $\Lambda \in A^*$,

$$(A^*)^+ = (A^*)^* = A^*. \qquad ∎$$

8. (a) Counterexample: Let $A = \{a\}$ and $n = 2$.

(e) True. By Theorem 2.7.3m, $(A^*B^*)^* = (A \cup B)^* = (B \cup A)^* = (B^*A^*)^*$.

9. The assertion is always true. We prove containment in both directions.

(i) $(E_1 \cup E_2 \cup \cdots \cup E_n)^* \subset (E_1^* E_2^* \cdots E_n^*)^*$

1. $E_i \subset E_1^* E_2^* \cdots E_n^*$ for all i (by induction on i, using Theorems 2.7.3d and e)

2. $(E_1 \cup E_2 \cup \cdots \cup E_n) \subset E_1^* E_2^* \cdots E_n^*$

3. $(E_1 \cup E_2 \cup \cdots \cup E_n)^* \subset (E_1^* E_2^* \cdots E_n^*)^*$ (2, Theorem 2.7.3f)

(ii) $(E_1^* E_2^* \cdots E_n^*)^* \subset (E_1 \cup E_2 \cup \cdots \cup E_n)^*$

1. $E_i \subset (E_1 \cup E_2 \cup \cdots \cup E_n)$ for all i

2. $E_i^* \subset (E_1 \cup E_2 \cup \cdots \cup E_n)^*$ (1, Theorem 2.7.3f)

3. $E_1^* E_2^* \cdots E_n^* \subset (E_1 \cup E_2 \cup \cdots \cup E_n)^*$ (2, Theorems 2.7.1d and 2.7.3j)

4. $(E_1^* E_2^* \cdots E_n^*)^* \subset (E_1 \cup E_2 \cup \cdots \cup E_n)^*$ (3, Theorem 2.7.3j). ∎

10. We establish that A^*B is a solution by substituting A^*B for X on the right and showing that the remaining occurrence of X is equal to A^*B.

$$X = A(A^*B) \cup B \qquad \text{Substitution}$$
$$= (AA^*)B \cup B \qquad \text{Associativity}$$
$$= A^+B \cup \{\Lambda\}B \qquad \text{2.7.3h and 2.7.1b}$$
$$= (A^+ \cup \{\Lambda\})B \qquad \text{2.7.1f}$$
$$= A^*B$$

11. If $X = XA \cup B$ and $\Lambda \notin A$, then $X = BA^*$ is the unique solution. The proof is essentially the same as that of Theorem 2.7.4.

13. (a) (1) $X_1 = AX_1 \cup BX_2$

(2) $X_2 = (A \cup B)X_1 \cup BX_2 \cup \{\Lambda\}$

Since $\Lambda \notin A$, solving equation 1, for X_1 using Theorem 2.7.4 yields

$$X_1 = A^*BX_2.$$

Substituting this into equation 2,

$$X_2 = (A \cup B)A^*BX_2 \cup BX_2 \cup \{\Lambda\}$$
$$= ((A \cup B)A^*B \cup B)X_2 \cup \{\Lambda\}$$

Now $\Lambda \notin (A \cup B)A^*B \cup B$, so again applying Theorem 2.7.4,

$$X_2 = ((A \cup B)A^*B \cup B)^*\{\Lambda\}$$
$$= ((A \cup B)A^*B \cup B)^*$$

and therefore,

$$X_1 = A^*B((A \cup B)A^*B \cup B)^*.$$

14. (a) $\{aa, ab, ba, bb\}^*\{a, b\}$.
    (b) $\{b\}^*\{a\}\{b\}^*$
    (c) $\{a\}\{a, b\}^* \cup \{a, b\}^*\{bb\}$.
    (d) $\{a, b\}^*\{aaa\}\{a, b\}^*$
    (e) $\{a, b\}^*\{bbab\}\{a, b\}^*$

Section 3.1

1. (a) $\{\langle 0 \rangle, \langle 1 \rangle\}$
   (e) $\{\langle 0, 0 \rangle, \langle 0, 1 \rangle, \langle 0, 2 \rangle, \langle 0, 3 \rangle, \langle 0, 4 \rangle, \langle 1, 1 \rangle, \langle 2, 2 \rangle, \langle 3, 3 \rangle, \langle 4, 4 \rangle\}$

2. (a) $A: \langle a, b, d, c \rangle$, length $= 3$
      $B: \langle a, c \rangle$, length $= 1$
      $\langle a, b, c \rangle$, length $= 2$.
   (b) All nodes of A have indegree and outdegree of 1. All nodes of B have indegree and outdegree of 3.
   (c) $A: \langle a \rangle, \langle a, b, d, c, a \rangle$
      $B: \langle a \rangle, \langle a, a \rangle, \langle a, c, a \rangle,$
      $\langle a, b, a \rangle, \langle a, b, c, a \rangle, \langle a, c, b, a \rangle.$

3. (a) The graph is connected and consequently has one component.
   (c) The graph is disconnected and has two components.
   (f) The graph is strongly connected and consequently has one component.

5. (a) *Basis:* $0 \geq 0$
      Induction: if $y \geq x$ then
      $$y + 1 \geq x \text{ and}$$
      $$y + 1 \geq x + 1$$
      Extremal: $x \geq y$ only if it can be shown by a finite number of applications of clauses 1 and 2.
      By the basis clause, $0 \geq 0$. By successive applications of the induction clause,
      $0 \geq 0 \Rightarrow 1 \geq 1 \Rightarrow 2 \geq 1 \Rightarrow 3 \geq 1$.

6. (a) $\phi, \{\langle 1 \rangle\}, \{\langle 2 \rangle\}, \{\langle 3 \rangle\}, \{\langle 1 \rangle, \langle 2 \rangle\}, \{\langle 1 \rangle, \langle 3 \rangle\}, \{\langle 2 \rangle, \langle 3 \rangle\}, \{\langle 1 \rangle, \langle 2 \rangle, \langle 3 \rangle\}$
   (b) $2^{(3^2)} = 2^9$

8. (a) We wish to show
      $$\langle a, b \rangle = \langle c, d \rangle \Leftrightarrow a = c \wedge b = d$$
      i.e., $\{\{a\}, \{a, b\}\} = \{\{c\}, \{c, d\}\} \Leftrightarrow a = c \wedge b = d$.
      Proof by cases:
      Case 1. If $a = b$, then $\langle a, b \rangle = \langle a, a \rangle = \{\{a\}\}$. Then $\langle a, b \rangle = \langle c, d \rangle$ if and only if $\langle c, d \rangle = \{\{a\}\}$, in which case it follows that $\{c\} = \{a\}$ and $\{c, d\} = \{a\}$; i.e., $a = c = d$.

Case 2. If $a \neq b$, then $\langle a, b \rangle = \{\{a\}, \{a, b\}\}$. Then $\langle a, b \rangle = \langle c, d \rangle$ only if $\{c\} = \{a\}$ and $\{c, d\} = \{a, b\}$. But if $\{c\} = \{a\}$, then $c = a$, and therefore, since $a \neq b$, $\{c, d\} = \{a, d\} = \{a, b\}$; hence $d = b$. ∎

(b)   Under the given definition the ordered triples $\langle 1, 2, 1 \rangle$ and $\langle 1, 1, 2 \rangle$ are equal, but they are not equal according to Definition 3.1.1.

Section 3.2

1. (a)   No; no node has indegree 0, and there exists a cycle.
   (b)   Yes; node a is the root.

2. (a)   The root is a; the leaves are b, d and e; the height is 2. There are four proper subtrees.

3. Suppose there is a directed path which is not simple from a node a to a node b in the tree. Because the path is not simple, it contains a cycle of length ≥ 1. Since there is a directed path from the root r to a there must be at least two distinct directed paths from r to b, one of which contains a cycle and one of which does not. But this contradicts Theorem 3.2.1. Hence, every directed path is a simple path. ∎

5. From Theorem 3.2.1, there is a directed path from the root r to a and from r to b. It follows that there is at least one undirected path from a to b. Now suppose $\langle c_0, c_1, \ldots, c_m \rangle$ and $\langle d_0, d_1, \ldots, d_n \rangle$ are distinct simple undirected paths from a to b. Then $a = c_0 = d_0$ and $b = c_m = d_n$. Let i be the least integer such that $c_k = d_k$ for all $k \leq i$, but $c_{i+1} \neq d_{i+1}$. Note that since the paths are distinct, i exists and $0 \leq i \leq m - 2$. Let j be the least index such that $j > i$ and $c_j = d_r$ for some $r > i$. Since $c_m = d_n$, j exists, $j \leq m$, and either $j \neq i + 1$ or $r \neq i + 1$. By the choice of j, there is no c_s, $i < s < j$ which is equal to any d_t, $i < t < r$. Hence the path $\langle c_i, c_{i+1}, \ldots, c_j, d_{r-1}, d_{r-2}, \ldots, d_i \rangle$ is an undirected simple cycle of length greater than 2, contradicting Theorem 3.2.2. Hence, if $a \neq b$, then there is at most one simple path from a to b. ∎

6. *Basis:* If $n = 1$, then the only node is the root. Since there are no loops on nodes there are $0 = n - 1$ arcs. Hence the assertion holds for trees with 1 node. *Induction:* Suppose the assertion is true for all trees with n nodes; $n \geq 1$. Let T be a tree with $n + 1$ nodes. Then T has at least one node a with outdegree 0 and indegree 1; a is a leaf. Consider the tree T' formed by deleting the node a and its incident arc from the tree T. Then T' has n nodes and by the induction hypothesis, T' has $n - 1$ arcs. But T has one more node and one more arc than T'; hence T has $n + 1$ nodes and n arcs. This establishes the induction step and completes the proof. ∎

9. The recursive procedure given below uses a procedure MEDIAN which returns the median value of a finite set of integers. The median of a finite set of integers S is the element $x \in S$ such that either the number of elements of S less than x is equal to the number of elements of S greater than x (if S has an odd number of elements), or the number of elements less than x is one more than the number of elements greater than x (if S has an even number of elements).

procedure CONSTRUCT_TREE(S):
comment: Construct a binary search tree whose node values are the elements of the set S.

if $S = \phi$ **then return** ϕ
else
    begin
        $m \leftarrow \text{MEDIAN}(S)$;
        $S_1 \leftarrow \{x \mid x \in S \wedge x < m\}$;
        $S_2 \leftarrow \{x \mid x \in S \wedge x > m\}$;
        construct the tree T such that
            (a) the root r of T is labelled m
            (b) the left subtree of r is CONSTRUCT_TREE(S_1)
            (c) the right subtree of r is CONSTRUCT_TREE(S_2);
        return T
    end

10. We first show that the bounds are attainable. Consider a tree in which each interior node has a single descendant. Then the tree has a single leaf, and for each integer d such that $0 \leq d \leq h$, there is a single node a distance d from the root. In such a tree, $n = h + 1$, so the lower bound is attainable.

    Now consider a tree in which each internal node has two descendants, and all leaves are a distance h from the root. Then the number of nodes in the tree is

$$1 + 2 + 4 + \cdots + 2^h = \sum_{i=0}^{h} 2^i = 2^{h+1} - 1,$$

so the upper bound is also attainable.

    We now show that $h + 1 \leq n \leq 2^{h+1} - 1$. Let T be a binary tree of height h, and let k_d be the number of nodes of T which are a distance d from the root of T. Then $1 \leq k_d \leq 2^d$, and $n = \sum_{d=0}^{h} k_d$. Therefore

$$h + 1 \leq \sum_{d=0}^{h} 1 \leq n \leq \sum_{d=0}^{h} 2^d = 2^{h+1} - 1. \quad \blacksquare$$

13. (a) Preorder: $A\,B\,D\,E\,H\,K\,C\,F\,I\,J\,L\,M\,G$
    (b) Inorder: $D\,B\,K\,H\,E\,A\,I\,F\,L\,J\,M\,C\,G$
    (c) Postorder: $D\,K\,H\,E\,B\,I\,L\,M\,J\,F\,G\,C\,A$

19. (a) The height of T_2 is one greater than the height of T_1.
    (b) No more than h_1 records are examined in a search in T_1, and no more than $h_1 + 1$ records are examined in a search in T_2.

21. (a) Since T is complete, every node has either no sons or two sons. If the root has no sons then $n = 1$ and $d_1 = 0$. Hence

$$\sum_{i=1}^{n} 2^{-d_i} = 2^0 = 1.$$

Now assume the assertion is true for all complete binary trees with n leaves, $n \in \mathbf{I}+$, and let T' be a complete binary tree with $n + 1$ leaves. Then T' can be constructed from some complete binary tree T with n leaves $b_1, b_2, \ldots, b_n$ by adding two sons to a leaf b_k of T, $1 \leq k \leq n$. Let these leaves be b'_k and b'_{k+1}, and associate the remaining leaves of T with those of T' in the natural way: if $1 \leq m < k$, then b_m corresponds to b'_m, and if $k + 1 < m \leq n$, then b_m corresponds to b'_{m+1}. Then for $1 \leq m < k$, $d'_m = d_m$, and for $k + 1 < m \leq n$,

$d'_{m+1} = d_m$. Moreover, by construction, $d'_k = d'_{k+1} = d_k + 1$. Hence

$$\sum_{i=1}^{n+1} 2^{-d_{i'}} = \sum_{i=1}^{k-1} 2^{-d_i} + 2 \cdot 2^{-(d_k+1)} + \sum_{i=k+1}^{n} 2^{-d_i}$$

$$= \sum_{i=1}^{k-1} 2^{-d_i} + 2^{-d_k} + \sum_{i=k+1}^{n} 2^{-d_i}$$

$$= \sum_{i=1}^{h} 2^{-d_i}$$

$$= 1 \text{ by the induction hypothesis. } \blacksquare$$

(b) Suppose we begin at the root of a tree T and follow a path from the root to a leaf. If at each node in the path it is equally likely that we turn left or right, then the probability of travelling any particular path of length m is 2^{-m}, and consequently the probability of reaching node b_k is 2^{-d_k}. The sum of these probabilities must be 1.

If T is a complete k-ary tree with n leaves, $b_1, b_2, \ldots, b_n$ and d_i is the length of the path from the root to leaf b_i, $1 \le i \le n$. Then

$$\sum_{i=1}^{n} k^{-d_i} = 1.$$

(c) The height h of the tree is the maximum path length of the d_i; that is, $h = \max \{d_i\}$. The maximum number of leaves n of a binary tree of height h is 2^h. Hence,

$$n \le 2^{\max \{d_i\}}$$

and therefore

$$\log n \le \max \{d_i\}.$$

Since $\max \{d_i\}$ is an integer,

$$\lceil \log n \rceil \le \max \{d_i\}. \quad \blacksquare$$

Section 3.3

1.

	Reflexive	Irreflexive	Symmetric	Antisymmetric	Transitive
(a)	NO	NO	NO	YES	YES
(b)	YES	NO	YES	NO	YES
(c)	NO	YES	YES	NO	NO
(d)	NO	NO	NO	YES	NO

3.

	ϕ	$I \times I$	$=$	$<$	$\le$	D
Reflexive	N	Y	Y	N	Y	N
Irreflexive	Y	N	N	Y	N	N
Symmetric	Y	Y	Y	N	N	N
Antisymmetric	Y	N	Y	Y	Y	N
Transitive	Y	Y	Y	Y	Y	Y

(Note: D is not reflexive because $0/0$ is not defined. D is not antisymmetric because $1D(-1)$ and $(-1)D1$.)

6.

	Union	Intersection	*Relative* *Complement*	*Absolute* *Complement*
Reflexive	Y	Y	N	N
Irreflexive	Y	Y	Y	N
Symmetric	Y	Y	Y	Y
Antisymmetric	N	Y	Y	N
Transitive	N	Y	N	N

7. (a) The relation is not irreflexive; all other properties hold.

8. (a) irreflexive, antisymmetric

(b) The relation $\{\langle a, b \rangle, \langle b, c \rangle, \langle c, a \rangle\}$ is irreflexive and antisymmetric but is not a tree.

Section 3.4

1. $R_1 R_2 = \{\langle a, c \rangle, \langle a, d \rangle\}$ $R_2 R_1 = \{\langle c, d \rangle\}$

$R_1^2 = \{\langle a, a \rangle, \langle a, b \rangle, \langle a, d \rangle\}$ $R_2^3 = \{\langle b, c \rangle, \langle c, b \rangle, \langle b, d \rangle\}$

3. $m = 0, n = 15$.

5. Both (a) and (b) are false assertions.

6. (a) $(R_1(R_2 \cap R_3) \subset R_1 R_2 \cap R_1 R_3)$

Proof: $\langle x, y \rangle \in R_1(R_2 \cap R_3)$

$\Leftrightarrow \exists z[\langle x, z \rangle \in R_1 \wedge \langle z, y \rangle \in R_2 \cap R_3]$

$\Leftrightarrow \exists z[\langle x, z \rangle \in R_1 \wedge \langle z, y \rangle \in R_2 \wedge \langle z, y \rangle \in R_3]$

$\Leftrightarrow \exists z[\langle x, z \rangle \in R_1 \wedge \langle z, y \rangle \in R_2 \wedge \langle x, z \rangle \in R_1 \wedge \langle z, y \rangle \in R_3]$

$\Rightarrow \langle x, y \rangle \in R_1 R_2 \wedge \langle x, y \rangle \in R_1 R_3$

$\Rightarrow \langle x, y \rangle \in R_1 R_2 \cap R_1 R_3.$ ∎

(b) Let $A = \{a\}, B = \{1, 2\}$ and $C = \{c\}$, and define

$$R_1 = \{\langle a, 1 \rangle, \langle a, 2 \rangle\},$$
$$R_2 = \{\langle 1, c \rangle\},$$
$$R_3 = \{\langle 2, c \rangle\}.$$

Then $R_1(R_2 \cap R_3) = \phi$, but $R_1 R_2 \cap R_1 R_3 = \{\langle a, c \rangle\}$.
A similar example can be constructed for part (d) of the theorem.

9. (a) True. Since R_1 and R_2 are reflexive, $\langle x, x \rangle \in R_1$ and $\langle x, x \rangle \in R_2$ for all $x \in A$. Therefore $\langle x, x \rangle \in R_1 R_2$ for all $x \in A$. Hence $R_1 R_2$ is reflexive.

(b) False. Let $A = \{a, b\}$. $R_1 = \{\langle a, b \rangle\}$ and $R_2 = \{\langle b, a \rangle\}$. Then $R_1 R_2 = \{\langle a, a \rangle\}$ which is not an irreflexive relation on A.

Section 3.5

1. (b) $r(R)$ is $\{\langle a, a \rangle, \langle a, b \rangle, \langle b, b \rangle\}$.

$s(R)$ is $\{\langle a, a \rangle, \langle a, b \rangle, \langle b, a \rangle\}$.

$t(R) = R$.

2. Theorem 3.5.3(c): $(R_1 \cap R_2)^c = R_1^c \cap R_2^c$.

Proof: Let x and y be arbitrary elements of A and B respectively.

Then
$$\langle x, y \rangle \in (R_1 \cap R_2)^c \Leftrightarrow \langle y, x \rangle \in R_1 \cap R_2$$
$$\Leftrightarrow \langle y, x \rangle \in R_1 \wedge \langle y, x \rangle \in R_2$$
$$\Leftrightarrow \langle x, y \rangle \in R_1^c \wedge \langle x, y \rangle \in R_2^c$$
$$\Leftrightarrow \langle x, y \rangle \in R_1^c \cap R_2^c. \quad \blacksquare$$

Theorem 3.5.3(e): $\phi^c = \phi$.

Proof: $\phi^c = \{\langle x, y \rangle \mid \langle y, x \rangle \in \phi\}$.
But the predicate $\langle y, x \rangle \in \phi$ is false for all $\langle y, x \rangle$. Hence, $\phi^c = \phi$. $\quad\blacksquare$

Theorem 3.5.3(i): $R_1 \subset R_2 \Rightarrow R_1^c \subset R_2^c$.

Proof: Let x and y be arbitrary elements of A and B respectively and assume $R_1 \subset R_2$. Then
$$\langle y, x \rangle \in R_1^c \Leftrightarrow \langle x, y \rangle \in R_1 \Rightarrow \langle x, y \rangle \in R_2 \Leftrightarrow \langle y, x \rangle \in R_2^c.$$

Hence $R_1^c \subset R_2^c$. $\quad\blacksquare$

4. (a) If $R_1 \supset R_2$, then $R_1 \cup E \supset R_2 \cup E$. By Theorem 3.5.2, $R \cup E = r(R)$; hence $r(R_1) \supset r(R_2)$. $\quad\blacksquare$

   (c) By Definition 3.5.1, $t(R_1) \supset R_1$ and $t(R_1)$ is transitive. Since $R_1 \supset R_2$, if follows that $t(R_1) \supset R_2$. By property (iii) of Definition 3.5.1, $t(R_1) \supset t(R_2)$. $\quad\blacksquare$
   (With minor modification, this proof can be used to establish 4a and 4b.)

5. (c) Since $R_1 \cup R_2 \supset R_1$, it follows from part (ii) of Definition 3.5.1 that $t(R_1 \cup R_2) \supset R_1$. Since $t(R_1 \cup R_2)$ is transitive, by part (iii) of Definition 3.5.1, $t(R_1 \cup R_2) \supset t(R_1)$. Similarly, $t(R_1 \cup R_2) \supset t(R_2)$, and hence $t(R_1 \cup R_2) \supset t(R_1) \cup t(R_2)$. $\quad\blacksquare$

7. (a) By hypothesis, R is reflexive and therefore $R \supset E$. By definition, $s(R) \supset R$, and hence $s(R) \supset E$. Therefore $s(R) = s(R) \cup E$, which establishes that $s(R)$ is reflexive. A similar proof establishes that $t(R)$ is reflexive. $\quad\blacksquare$

   (c) Since R is transitive, $R = t(R)$. To show $r(R)$ is transitive, it suffices to show that $tr(R) = r(R)$ as follows:
$$tr(R) = t(R \cup E)$$
$$= \bigcup_{i=1}^{\infty} (R \cup E)^i$$

It is easy to show by induction that
$$(R \cup E)^i = \bigcup_{j=0}^{i} R^j;$$
we leave this to the reader. Thus
$$tr(R) = \bigcup_{i=1}^{\infty} \bigcup_{j=0}^{i} R^j$$
$$= \bigcup_{i=0}^{\infty} R^i$$
$$= E \cup \bigcup_{i=1}^{\infty} R^i$$
$$= E \cup t(R)$$
$$= E \cup R$$
$$= r(R) \quad\blacksquare$$

8. (a) The digraph of $t(R)$ has two components, one the complete digraph on $\{a, b, c\}$ and the other the complete digraph on $\{d, e, f, g, h\}$.

10. (a) $(R^+)^+ = t(t(R))$. But $t(R)$ is transitive and hence by Theorem 3.5.1, $t(t(R)) = t(R)$.

11. Yes. The procedures B, C and E are all recursive.

13. (a) $M' + M''$
(c) If $k = 0$, then the incidence matrix for R^k is the identity matrix I. If $k > 0$, then the incidence matrix for R^k is M^k.

14. (a) In the following array, the entry in row i and column j is the probability that the ith die beats the jth die.

	A	B	C	D
A	2/9	2/3	4/9	1/3
B	1/3	0	2/3	1/2
C	5/9	1/3	2/9	2/3
D	2/3	1/2	1/3	1/4

(b) $R = \{\langle A, B \rangle, \langle B, C \rangle, \langle C, A \rangle, \langle C, D \rangle, \langle D, A \rangle\}$.
(c) The transitive closure is the universal relation on the set $\{A, B, C, D\}$.
(d) In most games of this sort, the relation "is more likely to win than" is transitive. But in this game, $R \neq t(R)$; it follows that the relation is not transitive. If the relation were transitive, there would be a *best* die.
(e) If you wanted to make money, the proposed game would be a poor vehicle because no matter which die you pick, your opponent can choose one which will beat yours 2/3 of the time. Note that this would not be possible if the relation of part (b) were transitive.

Section 3.6

1.

	Quasi ordered	Partially ordered	Linearly ordered	Well ordered
$\langle N, < \rangle$	Y	N	N	N
$\langle N, \leq \rangle$	N	Y	Y	Y
$\langle I, \leq \rangle$	N	Y	Y	N
$\langle R, \leq \rangle$	N	Y	Y	N
$\langle \mathcal{P}(N)$, proper containment$\rangle$	Y	N	N	N
$\langle \mathcal{P}(N), \subset \rangle$	N	Y	N	N
$\langle \mathcal{P}(\{a\}), \subset \rangle$	N	Y	Y	Y
$\langle \mathcal{P}(\phi), \subset \rangle$	N	Y	Y	Y

2. (a) Since R is a quasi order, R is transitive and irreflexive (and hence, antisymmetric). By Theorem 3.5.8(c), $r(R)$ is transitive and by definition of reflexive closure, $r(R)$ is reflexive. It remains to show that $r(R)$ is antisymmetric. We first note that the antisymmetry condition on a relation T

$$(\langle x, y \rangle \in T \wedge \langle y, x \rangle \in T) \Rightarrow x = y$$

is logically equivalent to the condition

$$(x \neq y \wedge \langle x, y \rangle \in T) \Rightarrow \langle y, x \rangle \notin T).$$

Now suppose $x \neq y$ and $\langle x, y \rangle \in r(R)$. Then $\langle x, y \rangle \in R$. But since R is antisymmetric, $\langle y, x \rangle \notin R$ and since $x \neq y$, $\langle y, x \rangle \notin E$. Hence $\langle y, x \rangle \notin r(R)$, which establishes that $r(R)$ is antisymmetric. Thus, if R is a quasi order, then $r(R)$ is a partial order. ∎

5. False. The antisymmetry condition fails for any pair of integers $\langle x, -x \rangle$, where $x \neq 0$.

7. (a) Suppose R is a quasi order. Then R is irreflexive and transitive. Since $\langle x, x \rangle \notin R$ for any x, it follows that $\langle x, x \rangle \notin R^c$ for any x. Hence R^c is irreflexive. To show R^c is transitive, consider any $\langle x, y \rangle \in R^c$ and $\langle y, z \rangle \in R^c$. Then $\langle y, x \rangle \in R$ and $\langle z, y \rangle \in R$, and by the transitivity of R, $\langle z, x \rangle \in R$. Hence $\langle x, z \rangle \in R^c$, which establishes that R^c is transitive and therefore a quasi order. ∎

8. All of the assertions are true.

9. (a) (only if) If R is a quasi order, then R is irreflexive and transitive. Since R is transitive, by Theorem 3.5.1, $R = t(R) = R^+$. Now suppose $\langle x, y \rangle \in R$. If $\langle x, y \rangle \in R^c$, then $\langle y, x \rangle \in R$, and since R is transitive, it follows that $\langle x, x \rangle \in R$, violating the irreflexivity of R. Thus, if $\langle x, y \rangle \in R$, then $\langle x, y \rangle \notin R^c$ and hence $R \cap R^c = \phi$.
(if) We must show that if $R \cap R^c = \phi$ and $R = R^+$, then R is irreflexive and transitive. Clearly R must be irreflexive, since if $\langle x, x \rangle \in R$, then $\langle x, x \rangle \in R^c$ and $R \cap R^c \neq \phi$. Moreover, if $R = R^+$, then $R = t(R)$ and it follows that R is transitive. ∎

11. The procedure PRODUCT has a single loop and will terminate if this loop is traversed only a finite number of times. The loop will be traversed so long as $i < a$, that is, so long as $a - i > 0$. Since both a and i are integer variables, this means that the loop will be traversed if $a - i$ is a member of the well-ordered set $I+$. By the initial assumption, $a \geq 0$, and the first assignment statement initializes i to 0. If $a = 0$, then $a - i \notin I+$ and the loop is not traversed at all. If $a > 0$, then the loop is traversed causing i to be incremented and $a - i$ to be decreased in value. Since $I+$ is well-ordered, the value of $a - i$ will not be a member of $I+$ after a finite number of executions of the loop, causing the *while* loop to terminate. ∎

13. *Proof:* Suppose a and b are least upper bounds of B. Then by definition of lub, $a \leq b$ and $b \leq a$. Since $\leq$ is antisymmetric it follows that $a = b$. A similar proof holds if a and b are glbs. ∎

14. (a) True.
(b) False.   (Consider $\langle 1, -1 \rangle$ and $\langle -1, 1 \rangle$.)
(c) False.   (Because T is not a linear order.)
(d) True.
(e) False.   (T is not antisymmetric.)

17. (a) Let $\langle S, \leq \rangle$ be a poset, and let B be a finite subset of S. If B does not have a minimal element, then for each $x_i \in B$ we can find some $x_{i+1} \in B$ such that $x_i > x_{i+1}$, that is, $x_i \geq x_{i+1}$ and $x_i \neq x_{i+1}$. It follows that we can construct an infinite sequence of strictly decreasing values of B:

$$x_i > x_{i+1} > x_{i+2} > \cdots$$

But B is finite, so in any infinite sequence of values of B, some value must be repeated. By antisymmetry, it follows that all intervening values in the sequence must be equal, contradicting the condition that $x_i \neq x_{i+1}$. Thus any strictly decreasing sequence of elements of B must terminate, and it follows that B must have a minimal element. The proof that B has a maximal element is similar. ∎

Section 3.7

1. The conditions for R to be an equivalence relation on A can be expressed as follows:
   (i) $\forall x[x \in A \Rightarrow \langle x, x \rangle \in R]$
   (ii) $\forall x \, \forall y[(x, y \in A \wedge \langle x, y \rangle \in R) \Rightarrow \langle y, x \rangle \in R]$
   (iii) $\forall x \, \forall y \, \forall z[(x, y, z \in A \wedge \langle x, y \rangle \in R \wedge \langle y, z \rangle \in R) \Rightarrow \langle x, z \rangle \in R]$
   For each of these implications, the conclusion is true if $R = A \times A$; hence, $A \times A$ is an equivalence relation. The rank of $A \times A$ is 1.

3. (a) n^2. (The relation is $A \times A$).
   (b) 1.

5. The union of two reflexive (symmetric) relations will be reflexive (symmetric), but the union of two transitive relations is not necessarily transitive.

6. (a) Not reflexive or symmetric;
   $$tsr(R) = \mathbf{I} \times \mathbf{I}.$$
   (b) Not symmetric;
   $$tsr(R) = \mathbf{I} \times \mathbf{I}.$$
   (c) Not reflexive;
   $$tsr(R) = R \cup \{\langle 0, 0 \rangle\}.$$

7. The fallacy in the argument is the assumption that every element is related to some other element by R. If this is not true, then the hypothesis of the symmetry condition is always false, and therefore the conclusion is false. Thus, the void relation on a nonempty set is vacuously symmetric and transitive but not reflexive, and the relation $\{\langle a, a \rangle, \langle a, b \rangle, \langle b, a \rangle, \langle b, b \rangle\}$ is symmetric and transitive but not reflexive on the set $\{a, b, c\}$.

8. (only if) Suppose $R_1 = R_2$, and let a be an arbitrary element of A. Then
   $$[a]_{R_1} = \{x \mid xR_1a\} = \{x \mid xR_2a\} = [a]_{R_2}.$$
   It follows that
   $$\{[a]_{R_1} \mid a \in A\} = \{[a]_{R_2} \mid a \in A\}.$$
   (if) Suppose $\{[a]_{R_1} \mid a \in A\} = \{[a]_{R_2} \mid a \in A\}$.
   Then for each $a, b \in A$,
   $$\langle a, b \rangle \in R_1 \Leftrightarrow a \in [b]_{R_1} \Leftrightarrow a \in [b]_{R_2} \Leftrightarrow \langle a, b \rangle \in R_2.$$
   Hence $R_1 = R_2$. ∎

10. $A/R = \{[0], [1], [2], [3], [4], [5]\}$, where $[k] = \{y \,|\, y = 6i + k$ for some $i \in \mathbf{I}\}$.

11. (a) Maybe. (Yes, if $\pi_1 = \pi_2$; otherwise, no.)
  (c) Maybe. (Yes, if $\pi_1 \cap \pi_2 = \phi$; otherwise, no.)

12. (a) No. (Let $A = \{a\}$ and $R_1 = \{\langle a, a \rangle\}$.)
  (c) Yes.

13. n.

15. By definition
$$\langle x, y \rangle \in R_j \Leftrightarrow x - y = cj \qquad \text{for some } c \in \mathbf{I}.$$
$$\langle x, y \rangle \in R_k \Leftrightarrow x - y = dk \qquad \text{for some } d \in \mathbf{I}.$$

  (a) (only if) Suppose $\mathbf{I}/R_k$ refines $\mathbf{I}/R_j$; then $R_k \subset R_j$. The pair $\langle k, 0 \rangle \in R_k$ and hence $\langle k, 0 \rangle \in R_j$; therefore
$$k - 0 = 1 \cdot k = cj \qquad \text{for some } c \in \mathbf{I}.$$
It follows that k is an integral multiple of j.
  (if) If $k = rj$ for some $r \in \mathbf{I}$, then
$$\langle x, y \rangle \in R_k \Leftrightarrow (x - y) = ck \qquad \text{for some } c \in \mathbf{I}$$
$$\Rightarrow (x - y) = crj \qquad \text{for some } c, r \in \mathbf{I}$$
$$\Rightarrow \langle x, y \rangle \in R_j;$$
hence $R_k \subset R_j$ and therefore $\mathbf{I}/R_k$ refines $\mathbf{I}/R_j$. ∎
  (b) Let d be the greatest common divisor of j and k, and let R_d denote equivalence mod d. Then
$$\mathbf{I}/R_d = \mathbf{I}/R_j + \mathbf{I}/R_k.$$
  (c) Let m be the least common multiple of j and k, and let R_m denote equivalence mod m. Then
$$\mathbf{I}/R_m = \mathbf{I}/R_j \cdot \mathbf{I}/R_k.$$

16. (only if) Suppose π induces R and R induces a (possibly different) partition π'. Let a be an arbitrary element of A, and let B and B' be blocks of π and π' respectively such that $a \in B$ and $a \in B'$.
Then for any b,
$$b \in B \Leftrightarrow aRb$$
$$\Leftrightarrow [a]_R = [b]_R$$
$$\Leftrightarrow b \in B'.$$
Hence, $B = B'$. Since the blocks of π and π' exhaust A, it follows that $\pi = \pi'$.
  (if) Suppose R induces π and π induces a (possibly different) equivalence relation R'. Then for any $a, b \in A$,
$$aRb \Leftrightarrow [a]_R = [b]_R$$
$$\Leftrightarrow a, b \in [a]_R$$
$$\Leftrightarrow \exists B[B \in \pi' \wedge a \in B \wedge b \in B]$$
$$\Leftrightarrow aR'b.$$
Hence, $R = R'$. ∎

19. Suppose π and π' are sum partitions of π_1 and π_2. Then by Definition 3.7.8, π and π' refine each other. By Theorem 3.7.11, the relation "refines" is antisymmetric and hence $\pi = \pi'$. ∎

20. (a) Part (i) of Definition 3.7.7 establishes that $\pi_1 \cdot \pi_2$ is a lower bound of the set $\{\pi_1, \pi_2\}$ under the relation "refines." Part (ii) of the same definition asserts that $\pi_1 \cdot \pi_2$ is the greatest lower bound. ∎

Section 4.1

1. (a) Function; $f(\{a, b\}) = \{0\}$.
   (b) Not a function; b has two images.

2. $fk(x) = gh(x) = x + 1$.

3. (a) There are ten such functions, consisting of the following disjoint classes.
   (i) The constant functions $f(x) = 0$, $f(x) = 1$ and $f(x) = 2$.
   (ii) The identity function $f(x) = x$.
   (iii) The functions which map two elements to themselves and the remaining element to one of those two. (For example, $f(0) = 0$, $f(1) = 1$ and $f(2) = 1$.)

5. (a) Let y be an arbitrary string in Σ^*. We prove

$$\forall x[\| xy \| = \| x \| + \| y \|]$$

by induction based on the inductive definition of Σ^*.
Basis: If $x = \Lambda$, then

$$\| xy \| = \| \Lambda y \| = \| y \| = 0 + \| y \| = \| x \| + \| y \|.$$

Induction: Assume the assertion holds for an arbitrary $x \in \Sigma^*$. Then, for $a \in \Sigma$, consider the string ax:

$$
\begin{aligned}
\| axy \| &= 1 + \| xy \| && \text{Definition of length} \\
&= 1 + (\| x \| + \| y \|) && \text{Induction Hypothesis} \\
&= (1 + \| x \|) + \| y \| && \text{Associativity of } + \\
&= \| ax \| + \| y \| && \text{Definition of length.}
\end{aligned}
$$

Hence, it follows that

$$\forall x[\| xy \| = \| x \| + \| y \|].$$

Since y was arbitrary, the result follows by Universal Generalization. ∎

7. $f(m, n) = n^m$. (We define $0^0 = 1$.)

Proof: Let n be an arbitrary element of $\mathbf{N}$.
Basis: If $m = 0$, then
$$f(0, n) = 1 = n^0.$$

Hence, the assertion holds for $m = 0$.
Induction: Assume that $f(m, n) = n^m$ for an arbitrary $m \in \mathbf{N}$.
Then

$$
\begin{aligned}
f(m + 1, n) &= f(m, n) \cdot n && \text{Definition of } f \\
&= n^m \cdot n && \text{Induction hypothesis} \\
&= n^{m+1} && \text{property of exponents.}
\end{aligned}
$$

Hence, the assertion is true for all $m \in \mathbf{N}$. Since n was arbitrary the result follows by Universal Generalization. ▮

9. The procedure SUM1 is a recursive algorithm:

procedure SUM1(m, n)
if $n = 0$ **then return** m
    else return $S(\text{SUM1}(m, P(n)))$

The procedure SUM2 is an iterative algorithm;

procedure SUM2(m, n):
begin
    $sum \leftarrow m$;
    $count \leftarrow n$;
    while $count > 0$ **do**
        begin
            $sum \leftarrow S(sum)$;
            $count \leftarrow P(count)$
        end;
    return sum
end

11. (a)
$$f(99) = f(f(99 + 11))$$
$$= f(f(110))$$
$$= f(110 - 10)$$
$$= f(100)$$
$$= f(f(100 + 11))$$
$$= f(f(111))$$
$$= f(111 - 10)$$
$$= f(101)$$
$$= 101 - 10 = 91$$

(b) The proof is in two parts.
    (i) We first show $f(x) = 91$ for all $90 \le x \le 100$.
$$f(90) = f(f(101))$$
$$= f(91)$$
$$= f(f(102))$$
$$= f(92)$$
$$= f(f(103))$$
$$= f(93)$$
$$\vdots$$
$$= f(99)$$
$$= 91 \text{ by part (a)}.$$

(ii)   Now let $x < 90$ and let k be the smallest integer such that
$$90 \leq x + 11k \leq 100.$$
Then $f(x) = f(f(x + 11))$
$$= f(f(f(x + 2 \cdot 11)))$$
.
.
.
$$= f^{(k+1)}(x + 11k)$$
where $90 \leq x + 11k \leq 100$ and $k \geq 1$. By part (i), it follows that $f(x + 11k) = 91$; hence
$$f(x) = f^k f(x + 11k)$$
$$= f^k(91) \qquad \text{by part (i).}$$
But by part (i), $f(91) = 91$; hence $f^k(91) = 91$ for all $k \geq 0$. It follows that
$$f(x) = f^k(91) = 91 \qquad \text{for all } x < 90. \quad \blacksquare$$
The argument 91 is called a *fixed point* of f because application of f to this argument leaves it unchanged.

12.   (a)   The function $g \circ g$ is defined on $\mathbf{R} - \{0\}$ and $g \circ g(x) = x$. The image of $g \circ g$ is $\mathbf{R} - \{0\}$.

Section 4.2

1.   (a)   (i) f is bijective.
(ii) $f(\mathbf{R}) = \mathbf{R}$.
(iii) $f^{-1}(\{8\}) = \{8\}$.
(iv)   The equality relation on $\mathbf{R}$.
(v) $f^{-1}(x) = x$.
(c)   (i) f is injective.
(ii) $f(\mathbf{N}) = \{\langle x, y \rangle \mid y = x + 1\}$.
(iii) $f^{-1}(\{\langle 2, 2 \rangle\}) = \phi$.
(iv)   The equality relation.
(e)   (i) f is surjective.
(ii) $f(\mathbf{I}) = \mathbf{N}$.
(iii) $f^{-1}(\{1, 0\}) = \{-1, 1, 0\}$.
(iv) $xRy \Leftrightarrow |x| = |y|$.

3. $S = A^{\{0, 1, 2, \ldots, n-1\}}$, and $T = A^n = \{\langle a_0, a_1, \ldots, a_{n-1} \rangle \mid a_i \in A\}$. Define the map $g: S \to T$ as follows:
$$g(f) = \langle f(0), f(1), \ldots, f(n-1) \rangle.$$
We show that g is injective. Suppose $f_1 \neq f_2$, where $f_1, f_2 \in S$. Then for some k, $0 \leq k < n$, $f_1(k) \neq f_2(k)$. Then $g(f_1) \neq g(f_2)$; hence g is injective. Now consider an n-tuple $\langle a_0, a_1, \ldots, a_{n-1} \rangle \in A^n$. Let f be the function
$$f: \{0, 1, 2, \ldots, n-1\} \to A,$$
$$f(i) = a_i \qquad \text{for } 0 \leq i < n;$$

then $\langle a_0, a_1, \ldots, a_{n-1} \rangle$ is the image of the function f under g. Hence g is surjective. It follows that g is bijective. ∎

5. (a) $m \leq n$

6. Define f as follows:
$$f: A \to \mathcal{P}(A),$$
$$f(a) = \{a\} \qquad \text{for all } a \in A.$$
Then f is injective, since if
$$f(a) = f(b), \text{ then } \{a\} = \{b\}, \text{ which implies } a = b. \quad ∎$$

7. (a) $f(0) = a, f(1) = b, f(2) = c$.
   (b) $f(x) = 2x, x \in (0, 1)$.
   (c) $f(n) = 2n$ for $n \geq 0$
       $= -(2n + 1)$ for $n < 0$.

8. (a) Suppose $g: A \to B$ and $f: B \to C$, and let c be an arbitrary element of C. Since fg is surjective, there is some element $a \in A$ such that $fg(a) = c$. But by Theorem 4.1.1, $fg(a) = f(g(a))$, where $g(a) \in B$. Thus c is the image of an element of B under f. Since c was arbitrary, it follows that f is surjective. ∎

10. (a) Since f and g are monotone increasing, if $x \leq y$, then $f(x) \leq f(y)$, and $g(x) \leq g(y)$. Hence, if $x \leq y$ then
$$(f + g)(x) = f(x) + g(x) \leq f(y) + g(y) = (f + g)(y),$$
and it follows that $f + g$ is monotone increasing. ∎
   (c) Let $f(x) = g(x) = x$. Then f and g are monotone increasing, but the product function $f \cdot g(x) = f(x) \cdot g(x) = x^2$ is not a monotone increasing function on **R**. ∎

11. (a) Let y be an arbitrary element such that $y \in f(A) - f(C)$. Then $f(x) = y$ for some $x \in A$, but for every $z \in C$, $y \neq f(z)$. Hence $x \in A - C$, and since $y = f(x)$, this implies that $y \in f(A - C)$. Since y was arbitrary, this establishes that $f(A) - f(C) \subset f(A - C)$. ∎

12. (a) Suppose $y \in f(f^{-1}(B'))$. Then there is an x in $f^{-1}(B')$ such that $f(x) = y$. Since $x \in f^{-1}(B')$, it follows that $f(x) \in B'$. Hence $y \in B'$; therefore $f(f^{-1}(B')) \subset B'$.
   (b) By part (a), $f(f^{-1}(B')) \subset B'$. Suppose $y \in B'$. Since f is surjective, there is an $x \in f^{-1}(B')$ such that $f(x) = y$. Since $x \in f^{-1}(B')$, it follows that $f(x)$ is in $f(f^{-1}(B'))$. Hence, $y \in f(f^{-1}(B'))$; therefore $B' \subset f(f^{-1}(B'))$. ∎

14. By Theorem 4.2.4, since f is bijective, f^{-1} is bijective. Hence $(f^{-1})^{-1}$ is defined and equal to the converse relation of f^{-1}. But f^{-1} is the converse of f, so by Theorem 3.5.3a, $(f^{-1})^{-1} = f$. ∎

17. The relation R is the equality relation E on A.

19. (a) Let $x_1, x_2 \in A'$ and suppose $x_1 \neq x_2$. Since f is injective, $f(x_1) \neq f(x_2)$. But $f|_{A'}(x_1) = f(x_1)$ and $f|_{A'}(x_2) = f(x_2)$. Hence, $f|_{A'}(x_1) \neq f|_{A'}(x_2)$. It follows that $f|_{A'}$ is injective. ∎

20. (a) Suppose $x \in A - B$. Then $x \in A$ and $x \notin B$. Hence $\chi_A(x) = 1$ and $\chi_B(x) = 0$. In this case $\chi_A(x)[1 - \chi_B(x)] = 1 = \chi_{A-B}(x)$. Now suppose $x \notin A - B$; then $x \in \overline{A - B} = \overline{A} \cup B$. It follows that $\chi_A(x) = 0$ or $\chi_B(x) = 1$, and therefore either $\chi_A(x) = 0$ or $1 - \chi_B(x) = 0$. Hence $\chi_A(x)[1 - \chi_B(x)] = 0 = \chi_{A-B}(x)$.

21. (a) The function has one left and one right inverse and they are both equal to the inverse function. The equivalence relation induced by the function is the equality relation. The canonical map g is defined by $g(x) = \{x\}$.

(b) Since the function is neither injective nor surjective, it has no left or right inverses. The equivalence relation induced by the function is the universal relation. The canonical map g is defined by

$$g(x) = \{a, b, c\} \qquad \text{for } x \in \{a, b, c\}.$$

Section 5.1

1. (a) $3^4 = 81$.

(c) The c can occur in any of the last three positions in the string. Once the position of c is specified, either of two letters can occur in each of the other three positions. Thus there are $3 \cdot 2^3 = 24$ such strings.

2. A binary relation from A to B is a subset of $A \times B$. There are $2^{|A \times B|} = 2^{|A| \cdot |B|} = 2^{mn}$ such subsets.

4. There are 16 binary sequences of length 4. Representation for the sequence of digits $0, 1, 2, \ldots, 9$ can be chosen in $P(16, 10)$ ways.

7. (a) $(\frac{1}{2}) \cdot 2^n = 2^{n-1}$. This can be proved by induction.

(b) 2^{n-1}.

9. Exactly 1 head: $\binom{5}{1} = 5$.

Exactly 2 heads: $\binom{5}{2} = 10$.

Exactly r heads in n flips: $\binom{n}{r}$.

11. Let $|A| = m, |B| = n$, and let $f: A \to B$ be a bijection. Note that f is an injection from A to B. Then by the pigeonhole principle, $m \leq n$, for if $m > n$, no injection from A to B exists. Since f is a bijection, the inverse function f^{-1} exists and is an injection from B to A; this implies, by the pigeonhole principle, that $n \leq m$. Hence $m = n$, i.e., $|A| = |B|$. ∎

12. (a) If $B \subset A$, then $A \cup B = A$; hence $|A \cup B| = |A|$. ∎

(b) It is easy to show that $A = (A - B) \cup (A \cap B)$ and that $A - B$ and $A \cap B$ are disjoint. It follows from Theorem 5.1.3 that $|A| = |A - B| + |A \cap B|$. ∎

15. *Basis:* If $n = 0$, then $\sum_{r=0}^{n} \binom{n}{r} = \binom{0}{0} = 1 = 2^0$.

Induction: Suppose the assertion holds for some arbitrary $n \geq 0$; we now show this implies that the assertion holds for $n + 1$.

$$\sum_{r=0}^{n+1} \binom{n+1}{r} = \sum_{r=0}^{n+1} \left[\binom{n}{r-1} + \binom{n}{r} \right] \qquad \text{by Problem 14(c).}$$

$$= \sum_{r=0}^{n+1} \binom{n}{r-1} + \sum_{r=0}^{n+1} \binom{n}{r}.$$

Next we change variables by letting $k = r - 1$ in the first sum. Since $\binom{n}{-1} = 0$, we can change the lower limit of the resulting sum from $k = -1$ to $k = 0$. Moreover, since $\binom{n}{n+1} = 0$, we can change the upper limit of the second sum from

$n + 1$ to n without affecting the value of the sum. Hence,

$$\sum_{r=0}^{n+1} \binom{n+1}{r} = \sum_{k=0}^{n} \binom{n}{k} + \sum_{r=0}^{n} \binom{n}{r}$$

$$= 2^n + 2^n \quad \text{by the induction hypothesis}$$

$$= 2^{n+1}. \quad \blacksquare$$

16. (a) The equality follows directly from Theorem 2.5.3(a).

(b) For any base b, positional notation represents b by 10 and b^n by $10^n = \underbrace{100 \ldots 0}_{n \text{ zeros}}$.

Therefore, in base b notation, $(b-1)[1 + 10 + 10^2 + \cdots + 10^n] = 10^{n+1} - 1$.
If $b = 6$ and $n = 3$, then (in base 6 positional notation),

$$5[1 + 10 + 10^2 + 10^3] = 5555 = 10000 - 1.$$

18. (a) There are 2^p distinct bit patterns. Since $+0$ and -0 are distinct representations of the integer 0, only $2^p - 1$ distinct integers can be represented.

(b) We first count the number of nonzero real numbers that can be represented. The leading digit of the mantissa on a nonzero number must be a 1. The other $m - 1$ bits of the mantissa (including its sign bit) can each be chosen in one of two ways; hence there are 2^{m-1} choices for the mantissa of a nonzero number. By part (a), the exponent can represent any of $2^k - 1$ distinct values. Since distinct pairs of mantissas and exponents denote distinct real numbers, the rule of product applies. Thus there are $(2^k - 1)(2^{m-1})$ distinct nonzero representable real numbers, and therefore one can represent $(2^k - 1)(2^{m-1}) + 1$ distinct real numbers.

(c) We first restrict ourselves to the nonnegative integers. Every integer n, where $0 \le n \le 2^{23}$, can be represented by choosing an appropriate mantissa and exponent. Above this range, not every integer can be represented (e.g. $2^{23} + 1$ is not representable). But all such integers greater than 2^{23} require an exponent with a value greater than or equal to 24, and every configuration with an exponent this large represents an integer. Hence there are about $2^{23}(2^7 - 24)$ integers greater than 2^{23} which are representable, making a total of

$$2^{23} + 2^{30} - 24 \cdot 2^{23}$$

or

$$2^{30} - 23 \cdot 2^{23}$$

positive integers. Taking negative integers into account gives a total of about

$$2(2^{30} - 23 \cdot 2^{23}) \approx 1.76 \cdot 10^9$$

distinct representable integers.

(d) About 2^{24} integers can be represented in integer notation. Using the results of part (c), the ratio is about 1 to 100.

Section 5.2

1. (a) The proof of part (a) of Theorem 5.2.1, given in the text, establishes that the relation "g asymptotically dominates f" is reflexive and transitive. It follows that the relation $\equiv$ is reflexive and transitive. Moreover, by the symmetry of the roles of f and g in the definition of $\equiv$, it follows that $\equiv$ is symmetric and therefore an equivalence relation. $\quad \blacksquare$

3. Let $f(n) = n$ if n is even,

         $= 0$ otherwise;

    $g(n) = 0$ if n is even,

         $= n$ otherwise.

5. (a) $f(n) \leq 2g(n)$ for all n, and $g(n) \leq 2f(n)$ for all n. Hence f and g asymptotically dominate each other, i.e., $O(f) = O(g)$.

  (b) Neither function asymptotically dominates the other.

  (c) The function f is asymptotically dominated by g but g is not asymptotically dominated by f; i.e.,

$$O(f) \subset O(g) \text{ but } O(f) \neq O(g).$$

6. (a) $\forall k_{k \geq 0} \ \forall m_{m \geq 0} \ \exists n_{n \in \mathbb{N}}[n \geq k \ \wedge \ |g(n)| > m|f(n)|]$ or

$$\forall k[k \geq 0 \Rightarrow \forall m[m \geq 0 \Rightarrow \exists n[n \in \mathbb{N} \ \wedge \ [n \geq k \ \wedge \ |g(n)| > m|f(n)|]]]]$$

  (b) The universal quantifiers in the first expression of (a) can be interchanged. Therefore, for any fixed nonnegative value of m, the following assertion holds:

$$\forall k_{k \geq 0} \ \exists n_{n \in \mathbb{N}}[n \geq k \ \wedge \ |g(n)| > m|f(n)|].$$

Choose an arbitrary $k_1 \in \mathbb{N}$. It follows by the above assertion that there exists $n_1 \geq k_1$ such that $|g(n_1)| > m|f(n_1)|$. Let $k_2 = n_1 + 1$. Again applying the above assertion there is an $n_2 \geq k_2$ such that $|g(n_2)| > m|f(n_2)|$. Let $k_3 = n_2 + 1$. Then there is an $n_3 \geq k_3$ such that $|g(n_3)| > m|f(n_3)|$. Continuing in this manner, we can construct an infinite set $S = \{n_1, n_2, n_3, \ldots\}$ such that $|g(n_i)| > m|f(n_i)|$ for all $n_i \in S$. ∎

  (c) The assertion is not true in general. Suppose $f(n) = n$ for all n and

$$g(n) = n^2 \quad \text{for } n \text{ even,}$$

$$= 0 \quad \text{for } n \text{ odd.}$$

Then f does not asymptotically dominate g but $f(n) \leq g(n)$ for all n which are even.

9. *Corollary 5.2.3, part (a)*

  (i) (only if) Suppose f is $O(g)$ and g is $O(f)$. Then by Theorem 5.2.3, $O(f) \subset O(g)$ and $O(g) \subset O(f)$; hence $O(f) = O(g)$.

  (ii) (if) Suppose $O(f) = O(g)$. Then $O(f) \subset O(g)$ and $O(g) \subset O(f)$. Thus, by Theorem 5.2.3, f is $O(g)$ and g is $O(f)$. ∎

Corollary 5.2.3, part (b)

Suppose f is $O(g)$ and g is $O(h)$. Then by Theorem 5.2.3, $O(f) \subset O(g)$ and $O(g) \subset O(h)$. Thus $O(f) \subset O(h)$. Hence by Theorem 5.2.3, f is $O(h)$. ∎

10. (a) We show that $\log n \notin O(1)$. Suppose to the contrary that $\log n \in O(1)$; then there must be some $k, m \geq 0$ such that if $n \geq k$, then $\log n \leq m \cdot 1 = m$. But if $n > 2^m$, then $\log n > m$; thus $\log n$ is not asymptotically dominated by $g(n) = 1$ and hence $\log n$ is not $O(1)$. By Theorem 5.2.4, $O(1) \subset O(\log n)$ and it follows from the above argument that the containment is proper. ∎

  (c) We show that if $d > 1$, then $d^n \notin O(n^2)$. Suppose d^n is $O(n^2)$. Then there exists $k, m \geq 0$ such that if $n \geq k$, then $d^n \leq mn^2$. Then for these values of n, $n \log d \leq \log m + 2 \log n$, and for $n > 1$,

$$\frac{n}{\log n} \le \frac{2}{\log d} + \frac{\log m}{(\log n)(\log d)}.$$

But the ratio on the left grows arbitrarily large as n increases, whereas the first summand on the right is a constant, and the second term decreases as n increases. Thus the inequality can be violated by choosing n sufficiently large. We conclude that $d^n \notin O(n^2)$. From this result and Theorem 5.2.4, we conclude that the containment is proper. ∎

11. (c) Let K and n be arbitrary positive integers such that $K \ge \lceil c \rceil$ and $n > \max (c^K, K)$. Then

$$n! = n(n-1)(n-2) \dots (K+1)K(K-1) \dots 2 \cdot 1.$$

Since $K \ge \lceil c \rceil$,

$$(n-1)(n-2) \dots (K+1)K \ge c^{n-K}.$$

Since $n > c^K$,

$$n! > c^K c^{n-K} = c^n.$$

Hence $n! > c^n$ if n is sufficiently large, and therefore $O(c^n) \subset O(n!)$.

To show the containment is proper, it suffices to show that for any $m \ge 0$, the value of n can be chosen large enough that $n! > mc^n$. Without loss of generality, we can assume $m > 1$. We showed above that if n is chosen large enough, $n! > (mc)^n$. But for $n \ge 2$, $(mc)^n > mc^n$; hence $n! > mc^n$ for n sufficiently large. It follows that $n!$ is not $O(c^n)$. ∎

13. If P is a polynomial of degree k, then $P(n) = a_0 + a_1 n + a_2 n^2 + \dots + a_k n^k$, where $a_k \ne 0$. By Theorems 5.2.5, 5.2.2(b), and 5.2.3, $a_i n^i \in O(n^k)$ for each i, $0 \le i \le k$. It follows from Theorem 5.2.2(c) that P is $O(n^k)$. ∎

16. Algorithm F takes less time than G to execute if and only if $10 < n < 50$.

17. $f_9 \to f_2 \to f_3 \leftrightarrow f_6 \to f_5 \to f_8 \leftrightarrow f_7 \to f_4 \to f_1$

18. The conjecture is true and can be proved by induction on k.

Basis: If $k = 0$, then $\sum_{i=0}^{n} i^k = \sum_{i=0}^{n} 1 = n + 1 \in O(n)$.

Induction: We assume $\sum_{i=0}^{n} i^k \in O(n^{k+1})$ for some arbitrary k. Then there exist values $M, K \ge 0$ such that if $n \ge K$, then

$$\sum_{i=0}^{n} i^k \le M(n^{k+1}).$$

It follows that

$$\sum_{i=0}^{n} i^{k+1} = \sum_{i=0}^{n} i^k \cdot i$$

$$\le \sum_{i=0}^{n} i^k \cdot n$$

$$\le n \sum_{i=0}^{n} i^k$$

$$\le nMn^{k+1} \qquad \text{if } n \ge K$$

$$\le Mn^{k+2} \qquad \text{if } n \ge K.$$

Hence $\sum_{i=0}^{n} i^{k+1}$ is $O(n^{k+2})$. ∎

Section 5.3

1. (a) The proof is by induction on **N**.

   By substitution, $y_0 = 2 \cdot 3^0 = 2 \cdot 1 = 2$. We now assume (as our induction hypothesis) that

   $$y_n = 2 \cdot 3^n.$$

   Then $y_{n+1} = 3 \cdot y_n = 3 \cdot 2 \cdot 3^n = 2 \cdot 3^{n+1}$.

2. (a) The solution is $x_n = 1 + na$, which is $O(n)$.

   (b) The value of x_n is $a + \sum_{i=1}^{n} b^i$. If $0 < b < 1$, then x_n is $O(1)$. If $b = 1$, then

   $x_n = a + n$ and therefore x_n is $O(n)$. If $b > 1$, then $x_n = a + \dfrac{b(1 - b^n)}{1 - b}$ and

   therefore x_n is $O(b^n)$.

4. (a) Clearly $x_0 = 1$. Each line after the first one intersects each preceding line exactly once, and so the nth line intersects $(n - 1)$ preceding lines and hence passes through n old regions. It divides each of these old regions into two new regions. Thus,

   $$x_n = x_{n-1} + n.$$

   It is easy to show by induction on n that $(n^2 + n + 2)/2$ is a solution to this recurrence system.

6. (a) Let x_h denote the minimum total path length of a complete n-ary tree of height h. Each internal node of such a tree has n sons. The total path length for a tree of height 0 is 0; thus,

   $$x_0 = 0.$$

   Suppose T' is a complete n-ary tree of height h with minimum total path length. Then a complete n-ary tree of height $h + 1$ of minimal total path length is constructed by adding n sons to some node a of T' where a is distance h from the root of T'. Then the path length from the root to each son of a is $h + 1$; thus

   $$x_{h+1} = x_h + n(h + 1), \text{ where } h \geq 0.$$

   (b) $x_h = \dfrac{nh(h + 1)}{2}$.

7. By Lemma 5.3.2a, if $a = 1$, then $f(n) = c(\log_b n + 1)$ for $n \in S$. By results analogous to those of Section 5.2,

   $$O(c \log_b n) \text{ on } S = O(\log n) \text{ on } S \text{ and } O(c) \text{ on } S = O(1) \text{ on } S.$$

   It follows that f is $O(\log n)$ on S. Similarly, if $a \neq 1$, then $f(n) = \dfrac{c(an^{\log_b a} - 1)}{a - 1}$

   for $n \in S$; hence

   $$f(n) = \frac{ca}{a - 1}(n^{\log_b a}) - \frac{c}{a - 1}.$$

   Since c and a are constants, f is $O(n^{\log_b a})$ on S. ∎

9. (a) (Proof of part (b) of Theorem 5.3.3.)

   Let $S = \{n \mid n = b^k\}$. Since f is $O(g)$ on S and g is $O(n^d)$, it follows that f is $O(n^d)$ on S. Hence there exist numbers $r \in \mathbf{N}$ and $K \in \mathbf{R}+$, such that if $n \geq r$ and $n = b^k$, then $f(n) \leq Kn^d$. Consider any $m \in \mathbf{N}$ sufficiently large that for some $k \in \mathbf{N}$,

$$r \leq b^k < m \leq b^{k+1}$$

Because f is monotone increasing,

$$f(m) \leq f(b^{k+1})$$

and therefore

$$f(m) \leq K(b^{k+1})^d$$
$$= Kb^{dk+d}$$
$$= Kb^d(b^k)^d$$
$$< Kb^d(m)^d.$$

Therefore, $f(m) \leq Kb^d(m)^d$ if m is greater than a power of b which is at least as great as r. It follows that f is $O(n^d)$. ∎

11. (a) **procedure** MAX2(i,j):
    if $i = j$ **then return** $A[i]$
    else
        begin
            comment: Divide A into two subarrays of approximately equal size.
            $m \leftarrow \left\lfloor \dfrac{i+j}{2} \right\rfloor$;
            $maxa \leftarrow$ MAX2(i, m);
            $maxb \leftarrow$ MAX2$(m + 1, j)$;
            if $maxa \geq maxb$ **then return** $maxa$
            else return $maxb$
        end

(b) $f(1) = 0$

$$f(n) = 2f\left(\frac{n}{2}\right) + 1 \qquad \text{for } n = 2^k \text{ where } k > 1.$$

(c) Suppose $n = 2^k$. Then by a proof similar to that for Lemma 5.3.2a it follows that

$$f(n) = 2^k f\left(\frac{n}{2^k}\right) + \sum_{i=0}^{k-1} 2^i.$$

But $n/2^k = 1$ and $f(1) = 0$. Hence

$$f(n) = \sum_{i=0}^{k-1} 2^i = 2^k - 1 = n - 1.$$

(d) By part (c) the complexity function is $O(n)$.

13. (a) The entries of the array are the node values of the search tree. If the array is $A[i:j]$, where $i \leq j$, then the root of the tree corresponds to $A[m]$, where $m = \left\lfloor \dfrac{i+j}{2} \right\rfloor$. The node values of the left subtree of the root are contained in $A[i:m-1]$, and those of the right subtree of the root are in $A[m+1:j]$. If $i < m$, then the node value of the left son of the root is stored in $A\left[\left\lfloor \dfrac{m+i-1}{2} \right\rfloor\right]$. If $i = m$, then the root has no left son. If $m < j$, then the node value of the right son of the root is stored in $A\left[\left\lfloor \dfrac{m+j+1}{2} \right\rfloor\right]$. If $m = j$, no right son exists.

(b)   **procedure** ITBINSEARCH(arg, i, j):
  begin
    $lo \leftarrow i$;
    $hi \leftarrow j$;
    while $lo \leq hi$ **do**
      begin
        $m \leftarrow \left\lfloor \dfrac{lo + hi}{2} \right\rfloor$;
        if $A[m] = arg$ **then return** m
        else
            if $A[m] < arg$ **then** $lo \leftarrow m + 1$
            else $hi \leftarrow m - 1$
      end;
    return "not found"
  end

Section 5.4

1. By Theorem 5.4.1, at least 3 comparisons must be made to find the maximum of 4 elements. Thus the height of a binary decision tree for finding the maximum of 4 elements must be at least 3.

2. The algorithm is the same as the method described in this section for finding the top two players in a sports tournament. We first index the objects of the set from 1 to n. The first round of comparisons compares x_i with x_{i+1} for all odd i. The next round compares the winners of the first round comparisons in a similar way. The competition can be represented as a binary tree even if n is not a power of 2.

   Let $max1$ denote the largest and $max2$ denote the second largest values in a collection of n objects; note that $max1$ may be equal to $max2$. The competition tree to find $max1$ will involve a total of $n - 1$ comparisons and will be of height $\lceil \log n \rceil$; therefore, in the course of the competition, $max1$ will be compared with no more than $\lceil \log n \rceil$ elements. If one of these comparisons is a tie, then $max2 = max1$. Otherwise, $max2$ must be one of the elements compared with $max1$, since $max2$ could not lose to any other element of the set. Hence, to find $max2$ we need only find the largest element of the $\lceil \log n \rceil$ elements which competed with $max1$; this will require $\lceil \log n \rceil - 1$ comparisons. The total number of comparisons is therefore

   $$n - 1 + (\lceil \log n \rceil - 1) = n + \lceil \log n \rceil - 2.$$

3. Let T be a balanced binary tree with n nodes. If $n = 1$, then $h = 0$ and the assertion holds. Now suppose $n > 1$. Since T is balanced, T is complete by definition. Hence there must be at least two and no more than 2^h leaves a distance h from the root. Furthermore, there are exactly $2^h - 1$ nodes which are no farther than distance $h - 1$ from the root. It follows that

   $$2^h - 1 + 2 \leq n \leq 2^{h+1} - 1$$
   $$2^h + 1 \leq n \leq 2^{h+1} - 1$$
   $$2^h < n < 2^{h+1}$$
   $$h < \log n < h + 1$$

Since h is an integer and $\log n$ lies properly between h and $h + 1$, it follows that
$$h = \lfloor \log n \rfloor. \quad \blacksquare$$

7. Let T be a balanced ternary search tree with n nodes and height h. Then T is complete and

$$\sum_{i=0}^{h-1} 3^i + 3 \le n \le \sum_{i=0}^{h} 3^i$$

$$\frac{3^h - 1}{2} + 3 \le n \le \frac{3^{h+1} - 1}{2}$$

$$3^h + 5 \le 2n \le 3^{h+1} - 1$$

$$3^h < 2n < 3^{h+1}$$

$$h < \log_3 (2n) < h + 1$$

Hence, $h = \lfloor \log_3 (2n) \rfloor$, and it follows that the worst case complexity of a search in a ternary search tree is $O(\log n)$.

10. Suppose an $O(n)$ algorithm exists for constructing a binary search tree T from an unsorted list of n elements. Then traversing the tree T in inorder (using the LIST procedure of Fig. 3.2.3) produces the list in sorted order. Since the traversal algorithm requires no comparisons between elements of the list, the entire sorting procedure would require $O(n)$ comparisons. But by Theorem 5.4.5, if f is the worst case complexity function of an algorithm for sorting by comparisons, then $O(n \log n) \subset O(f)$. Since $O(n \log n) \not\subset O(n)$, the supposition that a binary search tree can be constructed in $O(n)$ time leads to a contradiction of Theorem 5.4.5.

12. (a) **procedure** SEQSEARCH(arg, i, j):
       if $arg = A[i]$ **then return** i
       else
           if $i = j$ **then return** "not found"
           else return SEQSEARCH($arg, i+1, j$)

    (b) **procedure** RECSORT(i, j):
       if $i = j$ **then return**
       else
           begin
               comment: find minimum entry in list.
               $min \leftarrow A[i]$;
               $position \leftarrow i$;
               for $k \leftarrow i + 1$ **until** j **do**
                   if $A[k] < min$ **then**
                       begin
                           $min \leftarrow A[k]$;
                           $position \leftarrow k$
                       end;
               comment: interchange minimum with $A[k]$.
               $A[position] \leftarrow A[i]$;
               $A[i] \leftarrow min$;
               comment: sort remainder of the list.
               call RECSORT($i + 1, j$)
           end

Section 6.1

1. Assume $[0, 1]$ is finite with cardinality n. Then for some $n \in \mathbf{N}$, there is a bijection $f \colon \{0, 1, \ldots, n - 1\}$ to $[0, 1]$. We show there is a real number $z \in [0, 1]$, such that $f(m) \neq z$ for any $m \in \{0, 1, \ldots, n - 1\}$.

   Suppose $f(0) = x_0$,
   $$f(1) = x_1,$$
   $$\vdots$$
   $$f(n - 1) = x_{n-1}.$$
   Since f is an injection, all x_i's must be distinct. Order them by increasing value,
   $$x_{j_0} < x_{j_1} < \cdots < x_{j_{n-1}},$$
   and choose $z = (x_{j_0} + x_{j_1})/2$. Then z is not the image of any element in $\{0, 1, \ldots, n - 1\}$. Hence f is not a surjection and therefore not a bijection. Thus, $[0, 1]$ is not finite and therefore it must be infinite. ∎

4. Suppose $f \colon A \to B$ is an injection and A is infinite. To show B is infinite we construct an injection $g \colon B \to B$ such that $g(B)$ is a proper subset of B.

   Since f is injective from A to B, f is bijective from A to $f(A)$; thus an inverse function f^{-1} exists which is a bijection from $f(A)$ to A. (Note that we are using f^{-1} to denote a function from $f(A)$ to A rather than from B to A.) Moreover, since A is infinite, there is an injection $h \colon A \to A$ such that $h(A)$ is a proper subset of A. We define the function $g \colon B \to B$ as follows:
   $$g(x) = x \text{ if } x \in B - f(A).$$
   $$g(x) = f \circ h \circ f^{-1}(x) \text{ if } x \in f(A).$$
   Then fhf^{-1} is an injection from B to itself and $fhf^{-1}(B) = fh(A)$. Since $h(A)$ is properly contained in A and f is an injection, $fh(A)$ is properly contained in $f(A)$. It follows that $f^{-1}hf(B) \neq B$ and hence B is infinite. ∎

5. *Proof of Theorem 6.1.4(d):* It suffices to construct an injection from A to A^B. Define $f \colon A \to A^B$ as follows:
   $$f(x) = g \qquad \text{where } g(b) = x \text{ for all } b \text{ in } B;$$
   that is, $f(x)$ is the constant function $g \colon B \to A$ such that $g(b) = x$. Clearly, f is an injection. Since A is infinite, it follows that A^B is infinite by Theorem 6.1.3. ∎

6. (a) Infinite (there is no largest prime).
   (b) Finite, $(3^{k+1} - 1)/2$.
   (c) Infinite.
   (d) Finite, $(k + 1)^{mn}$.
   (e) Infinite (there is no bound on the length of a statement).

Section 6.2

1. (a) Define the function f as follows:
   $$f \colon \mathbf{N} \to \Sigma^*,$$
   $$f(n) = a^n.$$
   Then f is a bijection from $\mathbf{N}$ to Σ^*; hence $|\Sigma^*| = \aleph_0$.

(c)   For each $n \in \mathbf{N}$, let $\tilde{n}$ denote the sequence of digits of the binary representation of n in reverse order. Let $\langle w_0, w_1, w_2, \ldots \rangle$ be an enumeration without repetitions of Σ^*. Then define $f: \mathbf{N} \to \mathcal{P}(\{a, b\}^*)$ as follows

$$f(n) = \{w_i \mid \text{the } (i + 1)\text{th digit of } \tilde{n} \text{ is } 1, \text{ where } i \geq 0\}.$$

For example, if the enumeration of Σ^* is in standard order,

$$\langle \Lambda, a, b, aa, ab, ba, bb, aaa, aab, \ldots \rangle$$

then

$$f(0) = \phi,$$
$$f(1) = \{\Lambda\},$$
$$f(2) = \{a\},$$
$$f(3) = \{\Lambda, a\},$$
$$f(4) = \{b\},$$

etc.

The function f is a bijection from $\mathbf{N}$ to the set of finite subsets of Σ^*.

2.   (b)   Define $f: [0, 1] \to [0, 1)$ by

$$f(1) = \tfrac{1}{2},$$
$$f(\tfrac{1}{2}) = \tfrac{1}{3},$$
$$\vdots$$
$$f\left(\frac{1}{n}\right) = \frac{1}{n + 1}, \quad n \in \mathbf{I}+,$$
$$f(x) = x \text{ for } x \neq \frac{1}{n}.$$

Then f is a bijection from $[0, 1]$ to $[0, 1)$. Now let $g: [0, 1) \to [0, \infty)$ be defined by $g(x) = x/(1 - x)$. Then $gf: [0, 1] \to [0, \infty)$ is a bijection.

3.   Let f_A be a bijection from $[0, 1]$ to A, f_B be a bijection of $[0, 1]$ to B, f_D be a bijection from N to D, and f_E be a bijection from $\{0, 1, 2, \ldots, n - 1\}$ to E.
(a)   Let $g_1: [0, \tfrac{1}{2}) \to [0, 1]$,

$$g_1(x) = 1/(n - 2) \quad \text{if } x = 1/n \text{ for } n > 2 \text{ where } n \in \mathbf{N},$$
$$g_1(x) = 2x \text{ otherwise};$$
$$g_2: [\tfrac{1}{2}, 1] \to [0, 1],$$
$$g_2(x) = 2x - 1.$$

Then g_1 and g_2 are bijections. Using these functions we can define the following bijection from $[0, 1]$ to $A \cup B$;

$$h: [0, 1] \to A \cup B,$$
$$h(x) = f_A g_1(x) \quad \text{if } x \in [0, \tfrac{1}{2}),$$
$$h(x) = f_B g_2(x) \quad \text{if } x \in [\tfrac{1}{2}, 1].$$

Since A and B are disjoint and h is a bijection from $[0, 1]$ to $A \cup B$, $|A \cup B| = \mathbf{c}$.

(c) Let $\langle d_0, d_1, d_2, \ldots \rangle$ and $\langle e_0, e_1, \ldots, e_{n-1} \rangle$ be enumerations without repetitions of D and E respectively. Define a function f as follows:

$$f : \mathbf{N} \to D \times E,$$

$$f(k) = \langle d_{\lfloor k/n \rfloor}, e_{k \bmod n} \rangle.$$

Then f is a bijection and therefore $|D \times E| = \aleph_0$.

4. No such set exists, although we have not yet developed the tools necessary to show this. Later we will show that the cardinal numbers can be ordered and that no cardinal number is greater than every finite cardinal number and yet less than $\aleph_0$. Moreover, we will show $|S| < |\mathcal{P}(S)|$ for every set S. It will follow that if S is finite, then $\mathcal{P}(S)$ is finite, and if S is infinite, then $|\mathcal{P}(S)| > \aleph_0$.

6. (a) Some numbers have two distinct representations in the conventional binary representation; for example, $.10000 \ldots = .01111 \ldots$. We must make sure that the nonunique representation does not invalidate the conclusion of the diagonalization. Using the procedure described in the problem statement on the matrix

$$.10000 \ldots$$

$$.10000$$

$$.10000$$

$$.10000$$

$$\cdot$$

$$\cdot$$

$$\cdot$$

would produce the number $.011111 \ldots$, which is different from every representation in the list but denotes a number equal to the first item on the list.

7. The digits of y form an infinite string which has a left end but no right end. Reversing the digits results in a string which has a right end but no left end, i.e., this string is not a member of Σ^*, where Σ is the set of decimal digits. Since only strings in Σ^* represent elements of $\mathbf{N}$, the result of the diagonalization is not an element of $\mathbf{N}$.

Section 6.3

1. The map $f : A' \to A$ defined by

$$f(x) = x$$

is an injection. Therefore, by Definition 6.3.2, $|A'| \leq |A|$. ∎

3. It suffices to show that an injection exists from B to A. Let $g : A \to B$ be a surjection. Define $f : B \to A$ as follows. Let $b \in B$. Then $f(b) = a$ where a is an arbitrary but fixed element of $g^{-1}(\{b\})$. Then f is an injection from B to A. Hence, $|B| \leq |A|$. ∎

6. This assertion follows directly from the definition of $|A| \leq |B|$ and Theorem 6.1.3.

9. (a) We first show that the order relation $\leq$ on S is a partial order.
    (i) Let a be a cardinal number in S and let A be a set such that $|A| = a$. The identity function on A, $\mathbf{1}_A$, is a bijection from A to A. It follows that an injection exists from A to A and therefore $|A| \leq |A|$. Hence, $a \leq a$ for any $a \in S$ which establishes that the order relation $\leq$ is reflexive.

(ii) Let a and b be elements of S suppose $a \leq b$ and $b \leq a$. It follows from Theorem 6.3.3 that $a = b$, and hence $\leq$ is antisymmetric.

(iii) Let a, b and c be elements of S and assume $a \leq b$ and $b \leq c$. Let A, B and C be sets with cardinalities a, b and c respectively. Since $a \leq b$, an injection f exists from A to B. Since $b \leq c$, an injection g exists from B to C. Let h be the composite function $h = gf$, where $gf: A \rightarrow C$. Then, by Theorem 4.2.1(b), h is injective and therefore $a \leq c$. It follows that $\leq$ is transitive.

To show that $\leq$ is a linear order, we need to show that any two elements of S are comparable, i.e., either $a \leq b$ or $b \leq a$. By Theorem 6.3.2, for any $a, b \in S$, $a < b$, $a = b$, or $b < a$. By Definition 6.3.2, if $a < b$, then $a \leq b$; if $a = b$, then $a \leq b$, and if $b < a$, then $b \leq a$. Hence a and b are comparable and therefore $\leq$ is a linear order. ∎

10. (a) $|\mathbf{Q}| = \aleph_0$. We show this by noting that

$$\mathbf{Q} = \{0\} \cup \mathbf{Q}+ \cup \mathbf{Q}-$$

where $\mathbf{Q}+$ is the set of positive rationals and $\mathbf{Q}-$ is the set of negative rationals. Clearly $|\mathbf{Q}+| = |\mathbf{Q}-|$ and therefore $\mathbf{Q}$ is the union of three countable sets. Hence, by Theorem 6.2.3, $\mathbf{Q}$ is countable, i.e., $|\mathbf{Q}| \leq \aleph_0$. Since there is an injection from $\mathbf{Q}+$ to $\mathbf{Q}$ and $|\mathbf{Q}+| = \aleph_0$, it follows that $\aleph_0 \leq |\mathbf{Q}|$. Therefore, by Theorem 6.3.3, $|\mathbf{Q}| = \aleph_0$.

(b) $|[0, 1] \times [0, 1]| = \mathbf{c}$.

(i) The function $f: [0, 1] \rightarrow [0, 1] \times [0, 1]$ defined by $f(x) = \langle x, 0 \rangle$ is an injection. Therefore, $\mathbf{c} = |[0, 1]| \leq |[0, 1] \times [0, 1]|$.

(ii) Let $x = .x_0 x_1 x_2 \ldots$ and $y = .y_0 y_1 y_2 \ldots$ be the decimal expansions of $x, y \in [0, 1]$, where we choose a representation which does not terminate in an infinite sequence of 9's. (Thus, $.50000\ldots$ is acceptable, but $.4999\ldots$ is not. This ensures that each $x \in [0, 1]$ will have a unique representation.) Define g as follows:

$$g: [0, 1] \times [0, 1] \rightarrow [0, 1],$$

$$g(\langle x, y \rangle) = z,$$

where $z = .x_0 y_0 x_1 y_1 x_2 y_2 \ldots$. Then g is an injection which shows that $|[0, 1] \times [0, 1]| \leq |[0, 1]| = \mathbf{c}$.

Hence, by Theorem 6.3.3, $|[0, 1] \times [0, 1]| = \mathbf{c}$. ∎

13. (a) The assertion is true. Let f be a bijection from A to B, and define

$$g: \mathcal{P}(A) \rightarrow \mathcal{P}(B),$$

$$g(S) = f(S) \qquad \text{for all } S \subset A.$$

Then g is a bijection and the result follows. ∎

(b) The assertion is true. Let f be an injection from A to B, and g be an injection from C to D. We construct an injection

$$h: A^C \rightarrow B^D.$$

Let $r \in A^C$. Define $h(r) \in B^D$ to be that function $s: D \rightarrow B$ such that if $r(c) = a$, then $s(g(c)) = f(a)$. The function s can be defined arbitrarily on $D - g(C)$. Then h is an injection, and the assertion follows. ∎

Section 6.4

1. (a) $\aleph_0$
   (e) 0 if $n = 0$; $\aleph_0$ if $n \geq 1$.
   (i) 0

2. (a) $\mathbf{c}$
   (b) $\aleph_0$

3. Let α, β, and δ be cardinal numbers of the sets A, B and C respectively and assume A, B and C are pairwise disjoint. Then

$$\alpha + \beta = |A \cup B|$$
$$= |B \cup A| \quad \text{by commutativity of set union}$$
$$= \beta + \alpha,$$

so addition of cardinal numbers is commutative. Moreover,

$$\alpha + (\beta + \delta) = |A| + |B \cup C|$$
$$= |A \cup (B \cup C)|$$
$$= |(A \cup B) \cup C| \quad \text{by associativity of set union}$$
$$= |A \cup B| + |C|$$
$$= (\alpha + \beta) + \delta;$$

hence addition of cardinal numbers is associative. ∎

4. Although we have not proved it, the result of the operations of addition, multiplication and exponentiation of cardinal numbers is independent of the sets chosen as representatives for the cardinal numbers, i.e., if $|A| = |B|$, $|C| = |D|$ and $A \cap C = B \cap D = \phi$, then

$$|A| + |C| = |B| + |D|.$$

This is not the case with the operation of subtraction proposed in the problem. For example, let $A = B = C = \mathbf{N}$ and let D be the set of even integers. Then $|A| = |B|$ and $|C| = |D|$, but $|A - C| = 0 \neq \aleph_0 = |B| - |D|$.

5. (a) Let A, B, and D be sets such that $|A| = a$, $|B| = b$, $|D| = d$, and

$$A \cap D = B \cap D = \phi.$$

Since $a \leq b$, there exists an injection $f: A \to B$. Define g as follows:

$$g: A \cup D \to B \cup D,$$
$$g(x) = f(x) \quad \text{if } x \in A,$$
$$= x \quad \text{if } x \in D.$$

Then g is an injection from $A \cup D$ to $B \cup D$; hence $|A \cup D| \leq |B \cup D|$. Since $A \cap D = B \cap D = \phi$, it follows that $a + d \leq b + d$. ∎

   (b) Let $a = n$, $b = n + 1$, and $d = \aleph_0$. Then $a < b$ but $a + d = \aleph_0 = b + d$.

8. The set $\{0, 1\}^{\mathbf{N}}$ has cardinality $2^{\aleph_0}$. Since this is the set of characteristic functions of subsets of $\mathbf{N}$, it follows that $|\mathcal{P}(\mathbf{N})| = 2^{\aleph_0}$. In (b) of the examples immediately preceding Theorem 6.3.5, we showed $|\mathcal{P}(\mathbf{N})| = \mathbf{c}$; hence $2^{\aleph_0} = \mathbf{c}$. In (c) of the same examples,

we showed $|\mathbf{N}^\mathbf{N}| = \mathbf{c}$. But $|\mathbf{N}^\mathbf{N}| = \aleph_0^{\aleph_0}$. Since for every $n \geq 2$, $2 \leq n \leq \aleph_0$, it follows from Theorem 6.4.8 that

$$\mathbf{c} = 2^{\aleph_0} \leq n^{\aleph_0} \leq \aleph_0^{\aleph_0} = \mathbf{c};$$

hence $n^{\aleph_0} = \mathbf{c}$ if $n \geq 2$. ∎

Section 7.1

1. Let 1 be a left identity; then for all x,

$$1 \circ x = x.$$

By commutativity it follows that

$$1 \circ x = x \circ 1.$$

Combining these assertions we conclude

$$1 \circ x = x \circ 1 = x.$$

2.

	$+$	$\cdot$	$-$	$\lvert x-y \rvert$	max	min	unary $-$	$\lvert x \rvert$
(a)	Y	Y	Y	Y	Y	Y	Y	Y
(b)	Y	Y	N	Y	Y	Y	N	Y
(c)	N	N	N	Y	Y	Y	N	Y
(d)	N	N	N	N	Y	Y	Y	Y
(e)	N	N	N	N	Y	Y	N	N
(f)	Y	Y	Y	Y	Y	Y	Y	Y

4. Suppose 0_l is a left zero and 0_r is a right zero. Then

$$0_r = 0_l \circ 0_r = 0_l. \quad ∎$$

6. (a) This algebra is just a presentation of the integers $\{0, 1, 2, 3\}$ under addition mod 4. The operation is commutative and associative. The element a is an identity. All elements have inverses (because the element a appears in every row of the operation table.) No zero element exists (because no row (column) has entries which are all equal to the row (column) label).

7. (a)

	a
a	a

(d)

	a	b
a	a	b
b	b	b

(f)

	a	b
a	a	a
b	a	a

(h)

	a	b
a	a	b
b	a	a

In this algebra, $(ba)b \neq b(ab)$.

Section 7.2

1. Let $T_k = \{x \mid x \in \mathbf{R}$ and $x \leq k\}$. Then k is a zero element of $\langle T_k, max \rangle$, but no identity element exists.

2. We must show that $\langle S_k, + \rangle$ is a subalgebra of $\langle \mathbf{I}, + \rangle$. By definition of S_k it follows that $S_k \subset \mathbf{I}$. Furthermore, since $k \geq 0$, the set S_k is closed under addition, i.e.

$$\text{if } x \geq k \text{ and } y \geq k, \text{ then } x + y \geq k;$$

therefore $\langle S_k, + \rangle$ is an algebra. It follows that $\langle S_k, + \rangle$ is a subalgebra of $\langle \mathbf{I}, + \rangle$ and hence a subsemigroup of $\langle \mathbf{I}, + \rangle$. ∎

5. Let $\langle T, \circ', 1' \rangle$ be a subalgebra of a monoid $\langle S, \circ, 1 \rangle$. Then $T \subset S$, $1' = 1$, and $a \circ' b = a \circ b$ for all $a, b \in T$. The operation $\circ$ is associative on S; hence the operation $\circ'$ is associative on T since

$$(a \circ' b) \circ' c = (a \circ b) \circ c = a \circ (b \circ c) = a \circ' (b \circ' c).$$

Moreover, $1'$ is an identity with respect to $\circ'$, since

$$1' \circ' x = 1 \circ x = x.$$

Therefore $\langle T, \circ', 1' \rangle$ is a monoid. ∎

8.

$+_k$	0	1	2	3	4
0	0	1	2	3	4
1	1	2	3	4	0
2	2	3	4	0	1
3	3	4	0	1	2
4	4	0	1	2	3

x	$\bar{x}$
0	0
1	4
2	3
3	2
4	1

9. Suppose $A = \langle T, \circ, {}^-, 1 \rangle$ is a group, and for some $0 \in T$, $0 \circ x = 0$ for every $x \in T$. Since A is a group, there is an element $\bar{0}$ such that

$$0 \circ \bar{0} = 1.$$

But $0 \circ \bar{0} = 0$, hence $0 = 1$; i.e., the identity of A is the element 0. Then for every $x \in T$,

$$x = x \circ 1 = x \circ 0 = 0$$

and therefore $T = \{0\}$. ∎

10. Let $A = \langle S, \circ, {}^-, 1 \rangle$ be a group.
   (a) We prove the contrapositive of the implication $[x \neq y] \Rightarrow [a \circ x \neq a \circ y]$.

$$a \circ x = a \circ y \Rightarrow \bar{a} \circ (a \circ x) = \bar{a} \circ (a \circ y)$$
$$\Rightarrow (\bar{a} \circ a) \circ x = (\bar{a} \circ a) \circ y$$
$$\Rightarrow 1 \circ x = 1 \circ y$$
$$\Rightarrow x = y.$$

In the same way, we can show that if $x \circ a = y \circ a$, then $x = y$. ■

(b) By definition, $a \circ S = \{a \circ x \mid x \in S\}$. Since S is closed under $\circ$, $a \circ S \subset S$. Now suppose y is an arbitrary element of S. Then for some $x \in S$, namely $x = \bar{a} \circ y$,

$$a \circ x = a \circ (\bar{a} \circ y) = (a \circ \bar{a}) \circ y = 1 \circ y = y;$$

hence $a \circ S \supset S$. Therefore $a \circ S = S$. Similarly, one can show that $S = S \circ a$. ■

(c) Let x be the inverse of $\bar{a}$; then

$$\bar{a} \circ x = x \circ \bar{a} = 1,$$

and

$$x = 1 \circ x = (a \circ \bar{a}) \circ x = a \circ (\bar{a} \circ x) = a \circ 1 = a. \quad ■$$

12.

	Variety	Cardinality
a	group	1
b	semigroup	1
c	semigroup	2
d	group	4
e	semigroup	3

13. (b) The algebra $\langle \{R^n \mid n \in \mathbf{I}+\}$, composition, $R^k \rangle$ is a monoid if and only if $R^k = R^0$; thus, the necessary and sufficient condition is that $R^k = R^0$ for some positive integer k.

16. (a) Since k binary digits are used to represent each representable integer, the carrier has 2^k elements. The variety is a group, because 0 is an additive identity and if $2^k - x$ is added to any representable integer x, the result will be 0.

(b) The carrier still has 2^k elements, but the variety is a monoid with identity element 0. For every representable x and y, the operation $\oplus$ of the monoid is defined by

$$x \oplus y = \min (x + y, 2^k - 1).$$

Section 7.3

1. (a) An isomorphism is a bijective map from one carrier to another; if the carriers of two algebras have different cardinalities, then no bijections exist from one to the other.

(b) Let $A_1 = \langle \{a, b\}, \circ \rangle$ and $A_2 = \langle \{c, d\}, \square \rangle$, where $\circ$ and $\square$ have the operation tables

$\circ$	a	b
a	a	b
b	b	a

$\square$	c	d
c	c	c
d	c	c

2. Let $A_1 = \langle S_1, \circ, k_1 \rangle$, $A_2 = \langle S_2, \square, k_2 \rangle$ and $A_3 = \langle S_3, \triangle, k_3 \rangle$.

   (i) The relation $\sim$ is reflexive since 1_S is an isomorphism from any algebra $\langle S, \circ, k \rangle$ to itself.

   (ii) Suppose $A_1 \sim A_2$; then there is some isomorphism h from A_1 to A_2. We will show h^{-1} is an isomorphism from A_2 to A_1. The inverse h^{-1} exists, since h is a bijection from S_1 to S_2. Choose elements c, d in S_2, and suppose $h(a) = c$ and $h(b) = d$. Then, since h is a homomorphism,

   $$h(a \circ b) = h(a) \square h(b) = c \square d,$$

   and

   $$h(k_1) = k_2.$$

   It follows that

   $$\begin{aligned} h^{-1}(c \square d) &= h^{-1}(h(a) \square h(b)) \\ &= h^{-1}(h(a \circ b)) \\ &= h^{-1}h(a \circ b) \\ &= a \circ b \\ &= h^{-1}(c) \circ h^{-1}(d), \end{aligned}$$

   and

   $$h^{-1}(k_2) = h^{-1}(h(k_1)) = h^{-1}h(k_1) = k_1.$$

   Thus h^{-1} is an isomorphism from A_2 to A_1, which establishes that $A_2 \sim A_1$ and that $\sim$ is symmetric.

   (iii) Suppose $A_1 \sim A_2$ and $A_2 \sim A_3$; and let h be an isomorphism from A_1 to A_2 and g be an isomorphism from A_2 to A_3. We show that gh is an isomorphism from A_1 to A_3:

   $$\begin{aligned} gh(a \circ b) &= g(h(a \circ b)) \\ &= g(h(a)) \square g(h(b)). \\ &= gh(a) \triangle gh(b). \end{aligned}$$

   Moreover,

   $$gh(k_1) = g(k_2) = k_3.$$

   It follows that $A_1 \sim A_3$ and that $\sim$ is transitive. ∎

5. (Proof of Theorem 7.3.3b) Let $A = \langle S, \circ, 1 \rangle$ be a monoid and $A' = \langle S', \circ', 1' \rangle$ (note that A' need not be a monoid). The same proof given in the text for part (a) of the Theorem establishes that the operation $\circ'$ is closed and associative over the set $h(S)$. To show that $1'$ is an identity with respect to $\circ'$ for the set $h(S)$, we note that $h(1) = 1'$ since h is a homomorphism from A to A'. Then for any $x \in h(S)$, there is some $a \in S$ such that $h(a) = x$, and

   $$1' \circ' x = h(1) \circ' h(a) = h(1 \circ a) = h(a) = x.$$

   Thus $1'$ is an identity for the set $h(S)$ and hence $\langle h(S), \circ', 1' \rangle$ is a monoid. ∎

6. (a) The function $f: \mathbf{N} \to S$ is defined by

   $$f(n) = n \bmod 2^k$$

   and is a homomorphism since

   $$\begin{aligned} f(a + b) &= (a + b) \bmod 2^k = (a \bmod 2^k + b \bmod 2^k) \bmod 2^k \\ &= a \bmod 2^k \oplus b \bmod 2^k \\ &= f(a) \oplus f(b). \end{aligned}$$

(c) If we use $\frown$ to denote concatenation, the function f can be represented as

$$f(n) = 0 \frown (n \bmod 2^{k-1}) = 0 \frown n \quad \text{for } n < 2^{k-1},$$
$$= 1 \frown (n \bmod 2^{k-1}) \quad \text{for } n \geq 2^{k-1}.$$

If $a + b < 2^{k-1}$, then both a and b are less than 2^{k-1}, and

$$f(a + b) = 0 \frown (a + b)$$
$$= 0 \frown a \oplus 0 \frown b$$
$$= f(a) \oplus f(b).$$

If $a + b \geq 2^{k-1}$, then

$$f(a + b) = 1 \frown (a + b) \bmod 2^{k-1}$$
$$= x \frown (a \bmod 2^{k-1}) \oplus y \frown (b \bmod 2^{k-1})$$

where $x = 0$ or $x = 1$ and $y = 0$ or $y = 1$. In any case,

$$f(a + b) = f(a) \oplus f(b),$$

which establishes that f is a homomorphism.

Section 7.4

1. We first show that $\sim$ is an equivalence relation.
   (i) Reflexivity: $p/q \sim p/q$, since $pq = pq$.
   (ii) Symmetry: $p/q \sim r/s \Rightarrow ps = rq \Rightarrow rq = ps \Rightarrow r/s \sim p/q$
   (iii) Transitivity:

$$p/q \sim r/s \wedge r/s \sim t/u$$
$$\Rightarrow ps = rq \wedge ru = ts \qquad \text{by definition of } \sim$$
$$\Rightarrow ps \cdot ut = rq \cdot ut \wedge ru = ts \qquad \text{multiplication by } ut$$
$$\Rightarrow pu \cdot ts = tq \cdot ru \wedge ru = ts \qquad \text{by commutativity of } \cdot$$

We must now proceed by cases.

Case 1: If ru and ts are nonzero, then $pu = tq$ by cancellation, and we conclude that $p/q \sim t/u$.

Case 2: If ru and ts are equal to 0, then $r = t = 0$, because u and s cannot be 0. Since $ps = rq$ and q cannot be 0, it follows that $p = 0$. Then $pu = tq$, and we conclude that $p/q \sim t/u$. It follows that $\sim$ is transitive.

We next show that for arbitrary fractions a, b and c, if $a \sim b$ then $a + c \sim b + c$. Let $a = p/q$, $b = r/s$, and $c = t/u$.

$$a \sim b \Rightarrow p/q \sim r/s \Rightarrow ps = rq.$$

Then
$$a + c \sim b + c \Leftrightarrow p/q + t/u \sim r/s + t/u$$
$$\Leftrightarrow (pu + tq)/qu \sim (ru + ts)/su$$
$$\Leftrightarrow (pu + tq)su = (ru + ts)qu.$$

But since $ps = rq$, $(pu + tq)su = psuu + tqsu = rquu + tqsu = (ru + ts)qu$. Hence, $a + c \sim b + c$. Moreover, since $+$ is commutative, $a \sim b \Rightarrow c + a \sim c + b$. To show that $a \sim b$ implies $a - c \sim b - c$, the preceding proof can be altered by replacing each occurrence of $+$ by $-$. To prove that $a \sim b$ implies that $c - a \sim c - b$, however, we cannot appeal to commutativity because $-$ is not commutative. But the proof is essentially the same; we need only show

$$(tq - pu)us = (ts - ru)uq.$$

To show that $\sim$ is a congruence relation for unary minus, we observe that

$$p/q \sim r/s \Rightarrow ps = rq \Rightarrow -ps = -rq \Rightarrow (-p)/q \sim (-r)/s \Rightarrow -(p/q) \sim -(r/s).$$

3. (a) This is not a congruence relation, since

$$-1 \sim -2 \text{ but } -1 + 1 \not\sim -2 + 1.$$

   (b) This is not a congruence relation because it is not an equivalence relation; it is reflexive and symmetric, but not transitive.

4. Let $\sim$ be any equivalence relation over $\{0, 1, 2, \ldots, k\}$ such that every equivalence class of $\sim$ is a sequence of successive integers:

$$a \sim b \Rightarrow \forall x[a < x < b \Rightarrow a \sim x].$$

   Then $\sim$ is a congruence relation on the algebra $\langle\{0, 1, 2, \ldots, k\}, \max\rangle$.

5. (a) Since K is an ideal, $K \circ 0 \subset K$. But by the properties of a zero element, $K \circ 0 = \{0\}$. Therefore, $\{0\} \subset K$; i.e., $0 \in K$.

6. The set of multiples of any integer k is an ideal of $\langle \mathbf{I}, \cdot \rangle$.

8. The relation $\sim$ is a congruence relation on $\langle S, \square \rangle$ if $\sim$ is an equivalence relation and for all $a, b, c, d \in S$, if $a \sim b$, then
   (i) $\square(a, c, d) \sim \square(b, c, d)$
   (ii) $\square(c, a, d) \sim \square(c, b, d)$
   (iii) $\square(c, d, a) \sim \square(c, d, b)$.
   From these conditions we can show that the following (which can be used as an alternative definition):
   An equivalence relation $\sim$ is a congruence relation over $\langle S, \square \rangle$ if and only if for all elements $a, a', b, b', c, c' \in S$,

$$a \sim d' \wedge b \sim b' \wedge c \sim c' \Rightarrow \square(a, b, c) \sim \square(a', b', c').$$

9. (a) $[\Lambda]$ consists of the set $\{\mathbf{continue}\}^*$, where * denotes the star closure.
   (b) For any string x, we can obtain the shortest string in $[x]$ by the following procedure.
      (i) Delete all occurrences of **continue** from x, giving x'.
      (ii) Delete all symbols to the right of the leftmost occurrence of **end** in x'.
   (c) Since $x \cdot \mathbf{continue} \sim \mathbf{continue} \cdot x \sim x$,

$$[x] \cdot [\mathbf{continue}] = [x \cdot \mathbf{continue}] = [x], \text{ and}$$

$$[\mathbf{continue}] \cdot [x] = [\mathbf{continue} \cdot x] = [x].$$

Section 7.5

1. If $n = 0$, then $m = 0$ and the congruence relation on A is the universal relation $\mathbf{N} \times \mathbf{N}$. In this case, the quotient algebra is isomorphic to $\langle\{0\}, +\rangle$, where $0 + 0 = 0$. If $n \neq 0$, then the function h is injective and the congruence relation induced on A is equality. In this case, the quotient algebra is isomorphic to A.

2. Define the map f from $A/\sim$ to $\langle h(S), \circ', \triangle', k' \rangle$ as follows:

$$f: S/\sim \;\rightarrow h(S);$$

$$f([x]) = h(x).$$

(i) We first show that f is well-defined by showing that if $[x] = [y]$, then $f([x]) = f([y])$. If $[x] = [y]$, then $x \sim y$ and therefore $h(x) = h(y)$. Since $f([x]) = h(x)$ and $f([y]) = h(y)$, it follows that $f([x]) = f([y])$. Therefore f is well-defined.

(ii) We next show that f is a bijection.

To show that f is injective, we note that

$$[x] \neq [y] \Rightarrow x \nsim y$$

$$\Rightarrow h(x) \neq h(y)$$

$$\Rightarrow f([x]) \neq f([y]).$$

To show f is surjective, we observe that for any $a \in S'$,

$$a \in h(S) \Rightarrow \exists x[h(x) = a]$$

$$\Rightarrow \exists x[f[x]) = a].$$

(iii) We now show that f preserves the operations. We use $\circ$ and $\triangle$ to denote the operations of $A/\sim$ as well as those of A; $\circ'$ and $\triangle'$ are the operations of A'.

$$f([x] \circ [y]) = f([x \circ y])$$

$$= h(x \circ y)$$

$$= h(x) \circ' h(y)$$

$$= f([x]) \circ' f([y])$$

$$f(\triangle[x]) = f([\triangle x])$$

$$= h(\triangle x)$$

$$= \triangle' h(x)$$

$$= \triangle' f([x])$$

Thus the map f preserves the operations. Moreover, $f([k]) = h(k) = k'$, so the constant of $A/\sim$ is mapped to that of $\langle h(S), \circ', \triangle', k' \rangle$. Thus f is an isomorphism.

3. The product monoid is $\langle S \times S', \square, \langle 1, 1' \rangle \rangle$, where

$$\langle a, b \rangle \square \langle c, d \rangle = \langle a \circ b, c \circ' d \rangle.$$

The operation is associative, since

$$(\langle a, b \rangle \square \langle c, d \rangle) \square \langle e, f \rangle = \langle a \circ c, b \circ' d \rangle \square \langle e, f \rangle$$

$$= \langle (a \circ c) \circ e, (b \circ' d) \circ' f \rangle$$

$$= \langle a \circ (c \circ e), b \circ' (d \circ' f) \rangle$$

$$= \langle a, b \rangle \square \langle c \circ e, d \circ' f \rangle$$

$$= \langle a, b \rangle \square (\langle c, d \rangle \square \langle e, f \rangle).$$

Furthermore, $\langle 1, 1' \rangle$ is a left identity, since

$$\langle 1, 1' \rangle \square \langle a, b \rangle = \langle 1 \circ a, 1 \circ' b \rangle = \langle a, b \rangle;$$

an analogous proof can be used to show that $\langle 1, 1' \rangle$ is a right identity. It follows that the product algebra of two monoids is a monoid. ∎

6. (a) Always.
    (b) This is easily shown by establishing that the function
    $$h : A \rightarrow (A \times A')/\sim ,$$
    $$h(x) = [x] = \{\langle x, y \rangle\},$$
    is an isomorphism.

7. (a) This can be shown by constructing the operation tables of the two algebras and showing that they are identical except for notation. In particular, the map f such that $f(\langle 0, 0 \rangle) = 0$, $f(\langle 1, 1 \rangle) = 1$, $f(\langle 0, 2 \rangle) = 2$, $f(\langle 1, 0 \rangle) = 3$, $f(\langle 0, 1 \rangle) = 4$ and $f(\langle 1, 2 \rangle) = 5$ is an isomorphism from $A_2 \times A_3$ to A_6.

BIBLIOGRAPHY

AHO, ALFRED V., JOHN E. HOPCROFT, AND JEFFREY D. ULLMAN, *The Design and Analysis of Computer Algorithms*. Reading, Mass.: Addison-Wesley, 1974.

AHO, ALFRED V., AND JEFFREY D. ULLMAN, *The Theory of Parsing, Translation, and Compiling*. Englewood Cliffs, N.J.: Prentice-Hall, Inc., 1972.

BELLMAN, RICHARD, KENNETH L. COOKE, AND JO ANN LOCKETT, *Algorithms, Graphs and Computers*. New York: Academic Press, 1970.

BUSACKER, ROBERT G., AND THOMAS L. SAATY, *Finite Graphs and Networks; An Introduction with Applications*. New York: McGraw-Hill, 1965.

COHEN, PAUL J., *Set Theory and the Continuum Hypothesis*. New York: W. A. Benjamin, 1966.

COHN, P. M., *Universal Algebra*. New York: Harper & Row, 1965.

DELONG, HOWARD, *A Profile of Mathematical Logic*. Reading, Mass.: Addison-Wesley, 1970.

DEO, NARSINGH, *Graph Theory with Applications to Engineering and Computer Science*. Englewood Cliffs, N.J.: Prentice-Hall, Inc., 1974.

ELSPAS, B., ET AL., "An Assessment of Techniques for Proving Program Correctness," *ACM Computing Surveys*, Volume 4, Number 2, June 1972.

EVEN, SHIMON, *Algorithmic Combinatorics*. New York: The Macmillan Co., 1973.

FLOYD, R. W., "Assigning Meanings to Programs," in *Mathematical Aspects of Computer Science, Proc. Symp. Appl. Math.*, Volume 19, ed. J. T. Schwartz., Providence, R. I.: American Mathematical Society, 1967.

FRALEIGH, J. B., *A First Course in Abstract Algebra*. Reading, Mass.: Addison-Wesley, 1969.

GILL, ARTHUR, *Applied Algebra for the Computer Sciences*. Englewood Cliffs, N.J.: Prentice-Hall, Inc., 1976.

GRATZER, G., *Universal Algebra*. New York: Van Nostrand, 1968.

HALMOS, PAUL R., *Naive Set Theory*. New York: Van Nostrand, 1960.

HERSTEIN, I. N., *Topics in Algebra*. Waltham, Mass.: Blaisdell, 1964.

HOARE, C. A. R., "An axiomatic basis for computer programming," *Communications of the ACM*, Volume 12, Number 10, October, 1969.

KNUTH, D. E., *The Art of Computer Programming; Vol. 1/ Fundamental Algorithms* (2nd Ed.). Reading, Mass.: Addison-Wesley, 1973.

KNUTH, D. E., *The Art of Computer Programming; Vol. 3/ Sorting and Searching*, Reading, Mass.: Addison-Wesley, 1973.

KNUTH, D. E., *Surreal Numbers*, Reading, Mass.: Addison-Wesley, 1974.

KRIVINE, JEAN-LOUIS, *Introduction to Axiomatic Set Theory*. Dordrecht, Holland: D. Reidl Publishing Co., 1971.

LANDAU, EDMUND, *Foundations of Analysis*. New York: Chelsea Publishing Co., 1951.

LIU, C. L., *Introduction to Combinatorial Mathematics*. New York: McGraw-Hill, 1968.

MACLANE, SAUNDERS, AND GARRETT BIRKHOFF, *Algebra*. New York: The Macmillan Co., 1967.

MAKI, D. P., and M. THOMPSON, *Mathematical Models with Applications*. Englewood Cliffs, N.J.: Prentice-Hall, Inc., 1973.

MANNA, ZOHAR, *Mathematical Theory of Computation*. New York: McGraw-Hill, 1974.

MINSKY, MARVIN, *Computation: Finite and Infinite Machines*. Englewood Cliffs, N.J.: Prentice-Hall, 1967.

MONK, J. DONALD, *Introduction to Set Theory*. New York: McGraw-Hill, 1969.

NIVEN, IVAN, *Mathematics of Choice, or How to Count Without Counting*. New York: Random House, 1965.

RESCHER, NICHOLAS, *Many-valued Logic*. New York: McGraw-Hill, 1969.

ROBERTS, FRED S., *Discrete Mathematical Models*. Englewood Cliffs, N.J.: Prentice-Hall, Inc., 1976.

ROSEN, SAUL, ED., *Programming Systems and Languages*. New York: McGraw-Hill, 1967.

SHOENFIELD, JOSEPH R., *Mathematical Logic*. Reading, Mass.: Addison-Wesley, 1967.

STEINHAUS, H., *Mathematical Snapshots* (3rd American ed.). New York: Oxford University Press, 1969.

STOLL, ROBERT R., *Set Theory and Logic*. San Fransisco: W. H. Freeman and Co., 1963.

STONE, HAROLD S., *Discrete Mathematical Structures*. Chicago: Science Research Associates, 1973.

SUPPES, PATRICK C., *Axiomatic Set Theory*. New York: Van Nostrand, 1960.

VILENKIN, N. YA., *Stories About Sets*. New York: Academic Press, 1968.

WILDER, RAYMOND L., *Introduction to the Foundations of Mathematics* (2nd ed.). New York: John Wiley, 1965.

INDEX